ENGINEERING A NATION

ADVANCE PRAISE FOR THE BOOK

'*Engineering a Nation* is an exemplary work of scholarship that reconstructs the long life of India's legendary engineer Mokshagundam Visvesvaraya. Few technocrats are the subject of as much oral lore as Mysore's legendary engineer, who contributed as much to civil construction as to nation-building. Taking up the challenge of covering an illustrious and achievement-filled life of a workaholic that covered the better part of two momentous centuries, Aparajith Ramnath's writing narrates the story with skill. Sympathetic but not uncritical'—A.R. Venkatachalapathy, author of *Swadeshi Steam: V.O. Chidambaram Pillai and the Battle against the British Maritime Empire*

'This brilliant biography of the engineer-statesman Visvesvaraya is surely one of the richest biographies of an engineer we have, and a vitally necessary historical treatment of the role of the engineer in modern politics. It is built on a deep understanding of the history of professional engineers and of Indian history'—David Edgerton, Hans Rausing Professor of the History of Science and Technology and Professor of Modern British History, King's College London; author of *The Shock of the Old: Technology and Global History since 1900*

'Aparajith Ramnath excavates the life and work of the understudied iconic engineer, Sir M. Visvesvaraya, with elegance and care. The first critical biography of the legendary figure from Mysore, *Engineering the Nation* also vividly illuminates the passions and ironies of the vision of modernizing the Indian economy—and indeed Indian society—that took shape in colonial times'—Chandan Gowda, author of *Another India* and Ramakrishna Hegde Chair Professor of Decentralization and Development, Institute for Social and Economic Change, Bengaluru.

'M. Visvesvaraya has finally found the biographer his life warrants. Aparajith Ramnath has done a remarkable job of bringing together a rich trove of documents to present us with a full picture of the most important Indian engineer of the colonial period. For too long, historians have neglected the achievements of Indian engineers of the colonial period. As India's place on the global technological stage continues to grow, we would do well to consider the role that Visvesvaraya played in bringing India to this point, as well as the limits of his technocratic vision'—Ross Bassett, North Carolina State University, author of *The Technological Indian*

ENGINEERING A NATION

The Life and Career *of*
M. VISVESVARAYA
(1861–1962)

Aparajith Ramnath

PENGUIN
VIKING
An imprint of Penguin Random House

VIKING

Viking is an imprint of the Penguin Random House group of companies
whose addresses can be found at global.penguinrandomhouse.com

Published by Penguin Random House India Pvt. Ltd
4th Floor, Capital Tower 1, MG Road,
Gurugram 122 002, Haryana, India

Penguin
Random House
India

First published in Viking by Penguin Random House India 2024

10 9 8 7 6 5 4 3 2

ISBN 9780670090501

Typeset in Adobe Caslon Pro by Manipal Technologies Limited, Manipal
Printed at Replika Press Pvt. Ltd, India

www.penguin.co.in

For Amma and Appa

Contents

Author's Note

As is standard in historical narratives, I refer to key places by the name that was current at the time of the events being described. Thus, I use Mysore, Bangalore, Poona, Madras, Simla when the narrative covers Visvesvaraya's lifetime; and Bengaluru, Mysuru, Pune, and so on when writing about the present day.

I refer to members of the dynasty that ruled the princely state of Mysore (1881–1947) as 'Wadiyar' rather than 'Wodeyar'. While both spellings are widely used, I follow the official spelling used by Krishnaraja IV, the monarch who appears most frequently in this narrative.

In quotations, I have retained the spelling and punctuation used in the original (the exception being terminal full stops and commas, which follow house style).

List of Abbreviations

The following abbreviations are used in the endnote citations:

APAC	Asia, Pacific and Africa Collections, British Library, London.
CENT-VOL	*'M. V.': Dr. M. Visvesvaraya: Birth Centenary Commemoration Volume* (Bangalore: Visvesvaraya Centenary Celebration Committee, 1960).
CWMG	*Collected Works of Mahatma Gandhi*. Multi-volume collection brought out by the Publications Division, Government of India. (Accessed via https://www.gandhiserve.net/about-mahatma-gandhi/collected-works-of-mahatma-gandhi/.)
GAZETTEER-VOL3	C. Hayavadana Rao (ed.), *Mysore Gazetteer: Compiled for Government, Volume III: Economic*, New Edition (Bangalore: Government Press, 1929).
GAZETTEER-VOL4	C. Hayavadana Rao (ed.), *Mysore Gazetteer*, New Edition, vol. IV (Bangalore: Government Press, 1929).
GAZETTEER-VOL5	C. Hayavadana Rao (ed.), *Mysore Gazetteer*, New Edition, vol. V (Bangalore: Government Press, 1930).
IBD 1915	C. Hayavadana Rao (ed.), *The Indian Biographical Dictionary 1915* (Madras: Pillar & Co., 1915).

IOL	*India Office List.* An annual publication with details of government departments and officials in India, brought out in London in the pre-Independence era.
KSA-DIGITIZED	Karnataka State Archives, Bengaluru, digitized collections, accessed via https://archives.karnataka.gov.in/.
KSA-MV-VOL	*Mysore Administrative Papers: Karnataka Letters,* Vol. IV: *Dewan M. Visvesvaraya* (Bangalore: Department of Karnataka State Archives, 1994).
KSA-MIRZA-VOL	*Mysore Administrative Papers: Karnataka Letters, Vol. V: Dewan Mirza M Ismail* (Bangalore: Department of Karnataka State Archives, 1997).
MAR	*Report on the Administration of Mysore* (Bangalore: Government Press). Annual report brought out by the princely state of Mysore before Indian Independence.
MSA	Maharashtra State Archives, Mumbai.
MV-PAPERS-IEI	Photocopies of Visvesvaraya's papers, running to several bound volumes, held at the Institution of Engineers (India), Mysore Local Centre, Mysuru.
MV-SPEECHES-VOL	*Speeches by Sir M. Visvesvaraya, K.C.I.E. Dewan of Mysore. 1910–11 to 1916–17* (Bangalore: Government Press, 1917).
NAI-DIGITIZED	National Archives of India, New Delhi, digitized records, accessed via https://www.abhilekh-patal.in.
NMML	Nehru Memorial Museum and Library, New Delhi (renamed Prime Ministers' Museum and Library in 2023). Houses Visvesvaraya's papers (on microfilm) and a number of letters to and from Visvesvaraya.
TOI	*Times of India.* Accessed via ProQuest Historical Newspapers (digitized database).

Introduction

In September 1935, the *Mirror* of Perth, Australia, ran a short profile of a 'tiny, birdlike' Indian engineer in his seventies, whom it described as 'one of India's most eloquent examples of the perfect "go-getter"'. At one point in his interaction with the paper's correspondent, the engineer piped up: 'At Mysore there stands the second largest reservoir in the world. I designed it . . .' He bit his lip, realizing the indelicacy of praising himself. But the paper had no such compunctions, anointing him 'India's GREATEST BUILDER OF DAMS'. At the time, the engineer was on a visit to London, seeking technical assistance that might enable his associates to establish the first automobile manufacturing plant in India. 'In the near future,' the *Mirror* continued, 'it may come to pass that this engineering genius will become the Henry Ford of India.'

The report had a whiff of the exotic: it appeared in a section of the paper devoted to 'Queer Happenings in Many Places . . . Strange Stories of the Week'. Complimentary as it was, there was a sense of wonder that a 'native' of tradition-bound India should have the audacity to contemplate something as technologically advanced as the production of motor cars.[1] Nevertheless, it illustrates vividly the international renown achieved by its subject, Sir Mokshagundam Visvesvaraya (1861–1962),[2] as a representative of Indian engineering. Indians of his generation had won worldwide fame as mystics, poets, and political leaders—think of Vivekananda, Tagore, Gandhi—but rarely as technologists or engineers. Even within India, the profession of engineering was riddled with racial stereotypes, and few 'natives' received the kind of regard Visvesvaraya commanded from the colonial establishment. Not to put too fine a point on it, Visvesvaraya was the most famous Indian engineer of the twentieth century.

And yet he was also much more. Six decades after his death, there is scarcely a walk of life in India that does not bear in some form the imprint of Visvesvaraya's work, not only as civil engineer, but also as public administrator, constitutional analyst, and economic thinker. If you have picnicked in the Brindavan Gardens alongside the Krishnarajasagara dam near Mysuru, if you have studied in Bengaluru's Indian Institute of Science or Mumbai's Institute of Chemical Technology, if you lived through the heyday of the Planning Commission, if you are a cultivator in the vicinity of Pune, if you are a Hyderabadi whose drinking water is supplied by the lakes Himayat Sagar and Osman Sagar, or if you swear by Mysore Sandal Soap, you have experienced directly a part of Visvesvaraya's legacy.

Born in a village near Bangalore around the time the administration of India passed from the East India Company to the British Crown, Visvesvaraya began his career as a public works engineer in the Bombay Presidency, where he spent a quarter of a century. As a government engineer and later as a consultant, he contributed to the design, building, and maintenance of large irrigation works, dams, and urban water supply and drainage schemes across the length and breadth of the Indian subcontinent. Eager for a larger role as he approached the age of fifty, he accepted the position of chief engineer and then dewan (prime minister) of the princely state of Mysore, where he pursued ambitious public works projects as part of a programme to industrialize the state and rationalize its administration. He was instrumental in the inauguration of a gigantic multipurpose dam project on the river Cauvery, the institution of the first university in princely India, the establishment of several industries in Mysore (including a factory for the production of charcoal iron), and the founding of a bank and a chamber of commerce in the state.

In retirement, Visvesvaraya placed himself on the all-India stage. He developed a distinctive vision for national development, becoming one of the pioneering proponents of economic planning and a tireless campaigner for Indian industrialization, as exemplified in his tracts *Reconstructing India* (1920), *Planned Economy for India* (1934) and *Nation Building* (1937). As scholars have argued, Visvesvaraya's vision, with its emphasis on large-scale industry, technical education, and planning, was a precursor to Jawaharlal Nehru's nation-building programme after Independence.[3] In fact, both men received the republic's highest civilian honour, the Bharat Ratna, in the same year (1955).

Indeed, it would be no exaggeration to say that Visvesvaraya's life mirrored the emergence of the modern Indian nation. He belonged to the first generation of Indians born after the cataclysmic events of 1857, which had resulted in the British Crown replacing the East India Company as suzerain of the Indian subcontinent. A centenarian, he outlived most of his contemporaries. He was in his twenties when the Indian National Congress was established; in his forties when the Swadeshi movement reached its peak; in his fifties when the First World War shook the foundations of colonial rule; and nearly seventy when Mahatma Gandhi led his epochal Salt March to Dandi. By the time he was done with the business of life, Visvesvaraya had witnessed not just the coming of Independence, but also the first two general elections and the first two Five-Year Plans of the Indian republic.

Today, Visvesvaraya is enjoying a resurgence as a national icon. His memory is invoked frequently in the context of nation-building. His birthday is celebrated every year as Engineers' Day. Metro rail stations have been named after him in Delhi and Bengaluru. Educational institutions across the land bear his name. So does an ambitious doctoral scholarship programme run by the Indian government's Ministry of Electronics and Information Technology, which seeks to sponsor 3000 PhD scholars in nine years.[4] In Karnataka, Visvesvaraya has long been deified. Statues, busts, and portraits of the former dewan are to be found in public parks, residential localities, street corners, shops, factories, and institutions of various kinds.

Part of Visvesvaraya's appeal lies in his image as an apolitical, technocratic champion of development. Speaking at Bombay's Sydenham College in 1930, Visvesvaraya called for a greater emphasis on engineering and management education. 'In an age in which the capacity for management and direction is most prized everywhere,' he declared, 'our Universities, instead of training efficient leaders and experts to direct the country's industrial and business affairs, continue to send out unwanted Arts graduates.'[5] Nowadays lakhs of engineers graduate in India each year, and management degrees have never enjoyed greater prestige. We live in the age of 'Make in India' and an emphasis on 'skilling'. Technological solutions to challenges of governance enjoy wide popularity. At the same time, there is increasing public debate on the limits of such visions, not least from the viewpoint of sustainability and the environment. Are large, multipurpose dams the best way to serve the aims of electricity generation and irrigation? Is large-scale industrialization the only route to poverty alleviation, and to what extent is economic autarky necessary or useful for a nation? In this context, there is an urgent need for a deeper understanding of Visvesvaraya's life and a nuanced appreciation of his legacy.

There are other reasons, too, why it's time for a reappraisal of Visvesvaraya's career. Despite his renewed ubiquity as an icon, he remains a cipher to most Indians (at least outside Karnataka), who may be familiar with his frail, unsmiling, turbaned visage, but know little of his career and contributions. When he is highlighted, he is seen in narrow terms, as an ingenious engineer and an uncompromising administrator.

Yet, as this book will show, Visvesvaraya was also an important figure in India's *political* history, one who deserves to be studied as seriously as Nehru, Gandhi, Ambedkar, Tilak or Bose. Technocrat he certainly was, but he was far from apolitical. He developed a well-articulated critique of the political economy of colonial rule and was deeply involved in the vital constitutional debates of his day, even though he appears in few standard accounts of the nationalist movement. He parleyed with viceroys and maharajas. He played an important role in the fortunes and outlook of the princely states, even though he is not spoken of in the same breath as Sardar Patel or V.P. Menon, the conventional heroes in the story of the integration of the princely states into the Indian republic. In many ways an honorary member of the Indian Liberals—the intellectual descendants of Dadabhai Naoroji and M.G. Ranade—he was a close associate of Moderate Congress leaders such as Gopal Krishna Gokhale, Madan Mohan Malaviya, and M.R. Jayakar, working closely with the last two to push for a Round Table Conference in the interwar years.

The engineering side of Visvesvaraya's career, too, requires deeper analysis. He is popularly thought of as the *greatest*, or even the *first*, modern Indian engineer, but in fact there were several other accomplished Indians in the profession both before and during his time. How, then, do we understand and account for his larger-than-life image as an engineer? Further, in what specific ways did Visvesvaraya's career as an engineer shape his ideas on industrialization, economic development, and social reform? Were these beliefs already developing while he was a public works engineer or can they be attributed mainly to his study tours of

Japan, Europe, and America? How did Visvesvaraya—consultant to princely and provincial governments, member of official commissions on economic matters, venerated figure in his home state of Mysore—construct his claim to authority and expertise in diverse fields?

Finally, we know little about the man, his strengths, his foibles, and the conflicts and negotiations in his career. Icons are always in danger of becoming caricatures, and so it has been in Visvesvaraya's case. The public's understanding of his historical role is shaped largely by reverential and even hagiographic accounts, anecdotal history, and, indirectly, by Visvesvaraya's own (rather reticent) autobiographical writings. Placed in the pantheon of national heroes, he has ceased to be a person.

If we are to do justice to Visvesvaraya's life and career, we must peel back the layers of the public persona. What made this idealistic and fastidious personality tick, who seldom appeared in public without a suit, leather shoes and Mysore *peta* (turban), who was almost never photographed smiling, who refused to meet visitors without an appointment, who apparently shirked publicity as a person while publicizing his ideas throughout his life? What gave him his unshakeable belief in the possibility of turning India, with its bewildering diversity of peoples, into a melting pot?

*

I first encountered Mokshagundam Visvesvaraya in a lesson in our Hindi textbook in middle school. (I was then in Pune—a city that Visvesvaraya had called home a century previously.) I have a vague, possibly inaccurate, memory of a monochrome illustration of a dam alongside the engineer's face, and of the contortions the Devanagari script had to put itself through to render his name phonetically. Visvesvaraya next entered my consciousness when I was in engineering college. A reluctant engineer myself, I knew of the annual Engineers' Day celebrations on campus, but never attended them.

It was only later, when I found my métier as a budding historian of science and technology, that I developed a keener perspective on what it meant to be an engineer in India. For it was the history of that profession that I chose to research for my doctoral work. There was certainly an element of the autobiographical in my choice of topic. As a school-leaving student in the early twenty-first century, I had experienced first-hand the craze for engineering as a career path. Now I wanted to understand how it had all begun. As the project developed, I found myself mapping the engineering bureaucracies of the early twentieth century, and how their evolution was bound up with the politics of late-colonial India. I followed the profession as it moved from a near-exclusive focus on civil engineering to one that increasingly catered to emerging large-scale industries, even as Indians began to replace British engineers, who had long held sway in the subcontinent. Throughout my research, Visvesvaraya's name kept popping up. But as I was interested in larger sociological shifts, my project did not have room for detailed individual stories. So the iconic Mysorean was relegated to a couple of stray mentions in my thesis and in the book that grew out of it. Yet I knew I would return to him someday.

When, several years later, I finally embarked on this biographical study, I began by trying to collect everything that had been written about him. Starting from the 1940s, when Visvesvaraya's secretary Y.G. Krishnamurti composed a lyrical profile,[6] many books have been published in English and Kannada. V. Sitaramiah, a Kannada litterateur, and V.S. Narayana Rao (a journalist who knew Visvesvaraya and apparently received access to some of his papers) published biographies in English in the 1970s.[7] In Kannada, Tirumale Tatacharya Sharma's book appeared in 1960; around the same time, the writer Masti Venkatesa Iyengar edited a volume of reminiscences and articles on Visvesvaraya by various authors.[8]

I benefited immensely from reading some of these accounts, which provided a useful sense of the chronology of Visvesvaraya's life, and of the reactions he evoked in his contemporaries. Without them I would not have known where to start (and in a handful of instances, as my citations will show, I have relied on them directly). But in the end, I was left with as many questions as when I'd started out, for most of these works adopt a reverential and unquestioning approach to the subject's actions, and barely explore contrasting viewpoints or explicate the historical context. As I proceeded, I found many other short volumes in various languages that rely largely on Visvesvaraya's own (rather terse) memoirs. These are often didactic in tone, written with the aim of providing moral instruction to younger generations, and hence allow for little nuance in characterization or in the discussion of Visvesvaraya's legacy.

On the other hand, I did come across some short but stimulating essays by historians and sociologists on various aspects of Visvesvaraya's life, in the form of papers, articles, or passages within monographs on more general themes. These included thought-provoking analyses by historians Dhruv Raina and Benjamin Zachariah, both of which are concerned primarily with Visvesvaraya's thinking on economic and social development.[9] Sunil Khilnani's miniature portrait in his *Incarnations* exemplified what an empathetic yet sceptical lens might reveal, while a bracing newspaper article by Chandan Gowda backed up my belief that serious historical work remained to be done on Visvesvaraya.[10] I also found invaluable insights on the history of Mysore, Bombay, and other topics in the work of other academics such as Janaki Nair, Bjørn Hettne, Manu Bhagavan, Gyan Prakash, and Sunil

Amrith.[11] The book in your hands owes something to all of them, and to others besides.

*

My goal, then, was to carry out a detailed examination of Visvesvaraya's entire oeuvre, one that tied together a reconstruction of the minutiae of his life with a more critical assessment of his role in Indian history. I also wanted to explore the interconnections between the wide variety of activities he engaged in over the course of his long life. This goal dictated the kind of book I would try to write.

First, I decided I would pay close attention to the engineering side of Visvesvaraya's life. Most popular accounts confine his twenty-five-year career in the Bombay Public Works Department to a single chapter, serving as a prelude to his Mysore years. The few academic historians who have studied Visvesvaraya have likewise been most interested in his career as a public intellectual and advocate of planning.[12] I resolved to look in detail at Visvesvaraya's training as an engineer, his possible influences, and his philosophy of irrigation. Crucially, I wanted to understand how his experiences in this phase influenced his thinking on developmental and economic issues later on.

Second, the book would stress the historical context in which Visvesvaraya worked. Existing works on Visvesvaraya tend to see him as a timeless genius, focusing exclusively on his accomplishments without attempting to evaluate them against prevailing trends. What, for instance, did the average public works engineer do in his working life? We need to know this in order to assess whether, and to what degree, Visvesvaraya's initiatives were exceptional. As a historian of the engineering profession in interwar India, I was in a position to describe the social and professional context in which Visvesvaraya worked. For instance, his views on irrigation emerged in the particular context of late-nineteenth-century expansion in large-scale canal systems by the colonial government, which was increasingly concerned about famine in the subcontinent. His views on industrialization had a discernible lineage in the thinking of his Liberal friends and mentors. This was acknowledged in the literature, but the extent and nature of this intellectual influence had not been explored.

Third, I knew I must give the supporting cast of the story ample stage time, for nobody exists in a vacuum. At least two accomplished biographers with whom I had the privilege of being acquainted had emphasized the importance of this.[13] Maharaja Krishnaraja Wadiyar IV of Mysore, the later dewan Mirza Ismail, and the engineer Alfred Chatterton are among the more prominent of these players in Visvesvaraya's case, and yet even they appear as flickering shadows in standard accounts of his life. I decided I would spend more time illuminating these actors, as also Visvesvaraya's industrialist friends, his bureaucratic colleagues and subordinates, the teachers of his youth, and the dewans of Mysore who preceded him.

Finally, the book's narrative would be firmly anchored in primary sources. As Chandan Gowda has noted, myths and unverifiable stories about Visvesvaraya abound,[14] many of them designed to place him in the realm of unexplainable genius or divine virtue. Even the basic facts of his life have become fuzzy over many retellings, each one referring to the last. I resolved early on, therefore, to prioritize contemporary sources such as newspaper reports, official documents, letters, and memos, while triangulating between them.

At first the pickings were slim, and there were times when I despaired of finding enough material. Visvesvaraya had few intimate friends, and no family life to speak of. I was told he had destroyed most of his letters and diaries. There was no collection of candid personal papers of the kind most prominent figures of his vintage left behind. He was a fascinating subject, but an elusive one. What the journalist George Creel once said of the thirty-first President of the United States might well apply to Visvesvaraya. 'Writing about Herbert Hoover,' Creel declared, 'is like trying to describe the interior of a citadel where every drawbridge is up and every portcullis down.'[15] Like the Iowa-born President, the Mysorean was taciturn and starchily formal. He did not write unguarded letters to friends—at least none that have survived. He never let his hair down. He had the unremitting earnestness of an evangelist.

Over time, however, the breakthroughs started to come. The single most important source was Visvesvaraya's papers, such as they were: a carefully curated collection of newspaper cuttings, government reports, and official correspondence related to his career. This I consulted partly in its microfilm version at the erstwhile Nehru Memorial Museum and Library (NMML), but mostly in the photocopied version, running to some thirty volumes, housed in the Mysuru branch of the Institution of Engineers (India). These documents have survived, of course, because Visvesvaraya decided to preserve them, and hence they have the potential to present a one-sided picture. But by immersing oneself in them, reading between the lines and against the grain, one can get a good, rounded sense of their compiler. I also visited government archives in Mumbai, Hyderabad, and Bengaluru in search of official documents connected to Visvesvaraya's time as public works engineer, consultant, and dewan. Some of these, Mumbai in particular, yielded crucial nuggets. Through a research assistant, I found several useful files related to Visvesvaraya's Mysore years in the India Office Records in London's British Library, supplementing the notes I had taken there in earlier years. I also looked at out-of-print books and reports in the libraries of the Gokhale Institute of Public Affairs and the Mythic Society in Bengaluru, the Indian Institute of Management Ahmedabad, and Mysore University.

As archives and publications around the world embark on digitization projects, one is tempted to scavenge for morsels in every available bin. This I duly did, through extensive keyword searches. (The possible permutations were many, given the many ways in which Visvesvaraya's name has been spelt over the years.) Digitized archives of newspapers including the *Times of India*, the *Bombay Chronicle*, and the *Pioneer*, and a handful of British and Australian dailies, proved extremely useful for context. They often reproduced long extracts of official reports that were otherwise difficult to trace, and made it possible to establish detailed chronologies. I was able to access many official publications, memoirs, reports, and journals from the early twentieth century via repositories such as the Internet Archive (archive.org), South Asia Commons, Granth Sanjeevani (hosted by the Asiatic Society of Mumbai), and the online database of the library at Pune's Gokhale Institute of Politics and Economics. At an advanced stage of my research, I found some very useful digitized files via the website of the Karnataka State Archives.

Very few individuals alive today knew or worked with Visvesvaraya closely—after all, he was born more than 160 years ago at the time of writing, eight years before Gandhi and twenty-eight years before Nehru. Nevertheless, his relatives in Bengaluru, some of whom he stayed with towards the end of his life, were kind enough to invite me home, answer my questions, and make introductions. I had lived briefly in that city before, but now I made field trips, including a blissful summer with my family in Bengaluru and Mysuru the year before a global pandemic put paid to such wanderings for a long time. There and in Pune, I traced Visvesvaraya's footsteps, visiting locations and institutions that were of significance in his life. Everywhere, I met scholars and professionals who had thought carefully about aspects of Visvesvaraya's legacy and generously engaged in helpful discussions.

Most of the sources I found, I must note, are in English. But I have made a conscious effort also to collect sources in Kannada, which I can read laboriously and understand only partially. I have had some of the important ones read aloud and explained to me; in some cases, there were pre-existing English translations. But these are mostly of secondary importance: newspaper articles, formal and laudatory tributes by Visvesvaraya's contemporaries, and the like. Visvesvaraya himself did not write anything of note in Kannada. He spoke Telugu at home, and his thinking seems to have been done entirely in English, which was the language of his professional and administrative worlds. So, while my understanding of certain aspects of his milieu must necessarily be less deep than someone who is fluent in Kannada, I flatter myself that it does not detract substantially from the larger analysis presented here.

*

It is hard to imagine a world in which Mokshagundam Visvesvaraya had not lived. Counterfactuals are never easy, but this one would be particularly challenging. Scholars in recent decades have rightly questioned the Great Man approach to history, stressing the importance of wider social and political forces. But it is still possible to argue that the particular texture of our world bears the imprint of some individuals more than others—if only because of the positions they found themselves in. Moreover, as great literature reminds us, it is through the particular that we can best understand the universal. So it is with Visvesvaraya's life. His story is also the story of irrigation in the subcontinent; of princely

India in a time of great flux; of technology and industrialization in an incipient nation; of the conundrum of what it meant to be a scientific Indian.

Here is that story.

PART I

Becoming an Engineer

1

From Halli[1] to Nagara

As a stickler for punctuality and a devotee of data, Sir M. Visvesvaraya would have been annoyed by the confusion surrounding the timing of his entry into this world. Chroniclers have been unable to agree on a date. Was he born on 27 August or 15 September? Was it 1860 or 1861? He himself was quite definite on the point, consistently giving the date on official forms as 15 September 1861.[2]

Whatever the exact date, it was a moment when countries across the world stood at the brink of new epochs. In India, the British had recently quelled the fiercest and most widespread uprising to have taken place since the East India Company gained political control of the subcontinent; Company rule had been replaced by Crown rule. In America, the northern and southern states were entering a conflict that was to turn into a long and bloody civil war. Imperial Russia, emerging from the Crimean War, had decided to free its serfs and reform its economy. In Japan, the isolationist Tokugawa shogunate, under pressure from Western powers and internal dissidents, was about to give way to a new, modernizing regime.[3]

The scene of Visvesvaraya's arrival, however, was far removed from these grand historical events. He was born in the small, idyllic village of Muddenahalli, thirty-six miles from Bangalore—a long way in those days of horse-drawn *jutkas* and bullock carts. The village lay in the Chikkaballapur taluka in the princely state of Mysore, which was at this time ruled directly by the British through a commissioner stationed in Bangalore. It was a growing household—Visvesvaraya's parents, Venkatalakshmamma and Mokshagundam Srinivasa Sastri, already had one child when he was born, and would have four more after him—but the setting was decidedly bucolic. Visvesvaraya's natal home still exists, a single-storeyed building with sloping tiled roof and mustard-hued walls, at the end of a quiet lane. Nearby, monkeys frolic in the branches of a banyan tree; beyond lie open fields. In the background loom the Nandi Hills, at the foot of which Muddenahalli nestles.[4]

Visvesvaraya (pronounced Vish-vesh-varayyaa) is believed to have been named after Lord Visvesvara (one of the names of Shiva) of Kashi, where his father had gone on a pilgrimage before his birth.[5] The family were Mulakanadu Brahmins,[6] Telugu speakers whose ancestors had arrived in Mysorean territory some generations previously. The Mulakanadu Brahmins traced their origins to the Mulaka country in south-central India. Since the start of the Christian era, it is said, they migrated southwards from their capital at Pratishthana on the banks of the Godavari (modern-day Paithan near Aurangabad), settling predominantly around Kadapa and Nellore in today's Andhra Pradesh.[7]

One of the places they settled in was Mokshagundam, a village around eighty-five miles north of Kadapa. (This is what the initial 'M' in Visvesvaraya's name stood for.) Mokshagundam was situated next to the locally prominent Muktesvara temple, a hilltop shrine dedicated to Lord Shiva. The village got its name from the fact that it was home to a pond (*gundam* in Telugu) in which, legend had it, one could take a dip to attain salvation (*moksha*). A nineteenth-century handbook described the village as being 'the seat of native astrologers who calculate the native panchangams (calendars) in this part of the country'.[8] From here, Visvesvaraya's ancestors had drifted further south by the late seventeenth century, settling in various parts of the Kannada-speaking Kolar region.[9]

As in most parts of the subcontinent, Brahmins in Mysore made up a minuscule proportion of the population—less than 4 per cent in this case—but dominated the learned professions, even prior to the spread of English education.[10] Visvesvaraya's father, Srinivasa Sastri, was a Sanskrit scholar and a practitioner of Ayurvedic medicine: very much a product of his lineage. As a learned Brahmin, he would have enjoyed a modest lifestyle but high social status in Muddenahalli.[11] Indeed, a palm leaf inscription in the possession of the family indicates that a direct ancestor, Lakshmipatibhatta, had been gifted the entire villages of Muddenahalli and nearby Bandahalli by a local chieftain in 1692.[12]

When Visvesvaraya was still a child, the family moved to the nearest taluka town, Chikkaballapur.[13] Here he was enrolled in the local High School, where he would have taken his lessons mainly in Kannada.[14] Had he been born a generation earlier, he would have been educated at home or in a traditional *pyol* school, chanting Sanskrit verses and studying Ayurvedic texts as his ancestors had done before him. But in the 1850s, the ruling British had finally made education a matter of state policy, defining it as the bestowal of western knowledge on the natives through the limpid medium of English and other modern languages rather than the ossified pathways of Sanskrit or Arabic. To this end, they sponsored a network of vernacular-medium primary schools; vernacular or 'Anglo-vernacular' secondary schools; and English-medium colleges affiliated to the emerging universities in the large cities of the Raj. Visvesvaraya's school was among them. His subsequent educational career was also spent largely in institutions established by the colonial government.[15]

Little is known about Visvesvaraya the boy. Apart from what seem to be fanciful stories of his floating paper boats in puddles (somehow prefiguring his association with dams and waterworks), we have only family lore and second-hand reports of the testimony of his peers, who remembered him as reserved and hard-working.[16] With a number of siblings, he would not have lacked company at home, but no tales of fun and frolic have been handed down to us. Nor do we know if he had any close friends. Yet we can say with confidence that Chikkaballapur, although it was but a middling mofussil town with a few thousand residents, became Visvesvaraya's first window on the wider world. In later life, he waxed nostalgic when he looked back upon his time there. He remembered in particular his headmaster, Venkatapathiengar, and one of his teachers, Nadamuni Naidu, who 'took a personal interest in me as a student and used to give me lessons outside the school hours'.[17]

Visvesvaraya was in his mid-teens when he lost his father. Popular accounts of his childhood stress the family's subsequent poverty, but he undoubtedly possessed what Pierre Bourdieu, a century later, would call social capital. As an early biographical piece on Visvesvaraya has it, Srinivasa Sastri was 'rich in scholarship and piety' while being 'poor in material goods'.[18] After his passing, the family was in the sole care of Venkatalakshmamma—known to her kin as Venkachamma—until her brother in Bangalore, H. Ramaiah, lent his support. Ramaiah, who appears to have been an official in the government secretariat, brought Visvesvaraya to Bangalore, where he was enrolled in the Wesleyan Mission High School in 1875.[19]

*

The Wesleyan Mission was one of several Protestant missionary societies that began functioning in India in the eighteenth and nineteenth centuries. Named after John Wesley (1703–1791), an Oxford don and Anglican priest, the Wesleyan Church recognized the Bible as its only holy text. By the middle of the nineteenth century, it had sent out missions across the world, to places as far apart as Australia, New Zealand, southern and western Africa, India, and the Caribbean. In Bangalore, the administrative capital of Mysore state and home to a cantonment and British settlement, the Wesleyan Mission had a presence from 1822. By 1875, it had succeeded in creating a congregation of 560 Christians in the state of Mysore, 300 of them in Bangalore itself.[20]

The Mission's efforts in education were an important part of its work. Within decades of its arrival in Mysore, it established a network of English, vernacular, and Anglo-vernacular schools. These schools, some of which were reserved for girls, served both the Kannada- and the Tamil-speaking sections of the populace.[21] The most prominent of them, dating from the 1830s, was the Mission's English-medium high school in Bangalore, the school that Visvesvaraya joined in 1875.[22]

By the latter decades of the nineteenth century, the Wesleyan Mission High School was well entrenched, its pillared Greco-Roman building set in a wide, tree-studded lawn.[23] In this school Visvesvaraya had his first extended acquaintance with the English language. Here he would have been exposed not only to British teachers, but also to the outlook on life that Weber would later call the 'Protestant ethic'. Another prominent alumnus, a couple of decades junior to Visvesvaraya, would in later years describe the atmosphere at the school. It had a strong sporting culture, he noted, and the teachers, while showing 'sympathy with the pupils in every kind of need', did not 'tenderly [condone] slackness or laziness'. 'There is,' he remarked,

> nothing soft about these Mission Schools. Law presides over sentiment. They seek to teach the life of order and control. . . . There is a certain firmness and stability in their moral construction.[24]

It was in his Wesleyan school years that Visvesvaraya also had his first experience of spending time in the midst of a European settlement. The school itself was located near the Bangalore *pete*—the township around the fort said to have been built by the sixteenth-century Vijayanagar chieftain Kempe Gowda—which now housed the predominantly Kannada-speaking local population. But it was only a mile or two west of the Civil and Military Station, the heart of European Bangalore since the arrival of the British.[25]

A couple of years later, Visvesvaraya moved up the road to the Central College, another recently established institution. It had begun life in 1858 in the form of a high school, its first principal being the Rev. John Garrett, who was, coincidentally, a Wesleyan. It soon evolved into an integrated school-cum-college whose students could study up to the BA degree exam of the Madras University (Mysore did not then have its own university). In 1875, a couple of years before Visvesvaraya joined it, the institution was renamed the Central College.[26] As of 1879—two years after Visvesvaraya had entered the BA programme—there were around sixty students in the university-level classes, and a further 400 in the school.[27]

Despite its Wesleyan connections, the Central College was run by the government and not by missionaries.[28] Although it would go on to nurture prominent professionals and public figures,[29] it was not yet a very distinguished college in Visvesvaraya's time. It had a meagre teaching staff—four professors and a couple of 'munshis' to teach Kannada and Tamil. Its students were not, on the whole, very successful in the BA examinations of Madras University.[30] Yet the college seemed marked out for eventual distinction, if only by its wooded campus with brick-red buildings in the Indo-Saracenic style, complete with clocktower and portico decorated with arches.[31] It also had a distinct asset in the shape of its inspirational principal, Charles Waters.

Waters, a Cambridge-educated Englishman with a walrus moustache and a kindly glint in his eye,[32] had presided over the institution's transformation into the Central College. A pillar of the local British settlement, he was married to Alice Pope, daughter of another prominent Bangalore educationist, the principal of Bishop Cotton's School.[33] Waters was also an active member of Bangalore's Boat Club (established on the Ulsoor Lake in the 1870s), serving as its honorary secretary in 1881.[34] A local correspondent wrote in 1874 that a 'four' was likely to represent the club at the following year's regatta in Poona, and that 'if Charley Waters has time to coach the crew, . . . Poona will have to look sharp lest their laurels be dimmed'.[35]

Waters had a deep impact on the young Visvesvaraya, who in turn impressed him with his industriousness. His mentorship of Visvesvaraya has passed into legend, especially his description of his protégé as a 'capital mathematician and a very good English scholar', and the fact that he presented the young man with a giant Webster's Dictionary (still on display in Muddenahalli, where an annexe to Visvesvaraya's ancestral home now serves as a museum) and, years later, a pair of gold cuff links.[36] Visvesvaraya himself described Waters in glowing terms. Returning to his alma mater three decades after he left it, Visvesvaraya recalled his days there, when 'the College, the High School and the Middle School were all accommodated in [a single] building and under one Principal'. He continued: 'One of the pleasantest memories of my College days is my association with the first Principal of this College, Mr.

Charles Waters . . . By his sympathy and earnestness, Mr. Waters exercised much influence on the students of my time.' Waters left India in 1882, but Visvesvaraya had occasion to meet him more than a quarter of a century later. The two wrote to each other 'almost to the day of [Waters's] death' in 1911. His old teacher's missives, Visvesvaraya said, 'have acted as an inspiration in my work all through my life'.[37]

Although its students were enrolled for a BA, the Central College was primarily a science college, arts courses being the specialty of the Maharaja's College in Mysore city. Madras University did not offer a separate Bachelor of Science degree in those days.[38] To qualify for the BA, a student had to take subjects under five heads: English Language, Optional Language, History, Mental Philosophy, and Optional Subjects. For English, the set texts were eclectic in terms of form and vintage. For the batch immediately before Visvesvaraya's, they included Shakespeare's historical play *Cymbeline*, Tennyson's poem 'Guinevere', George Eliot's novel *Silas Marner*, and John Locke's philosophical treatise, *Conduct of the Understanding*. The second language could be a classical language like Sanskrit, Greek, or Latin, or a modern ('vernacular') language like Tamil, Telugu, Kannada, or Urdu. (Visvesvaraya chose Kannada—or Kanarese, as it was then called.) As of 1879–80, History and Mental Philosophy each consisted of a single paper: the former focused mostly on English and European themes, while the latter dealt, inter alia, with Alexander Bain's *Mental and Moral Science* and David Masson's *Recent British Philosophy*.

There were three categories under Optional Subjects: Mathematics and Natural Philosophy; Physical Science; and Logic and Moral Philosophy. Visvesvaraya chose the first. When he took the exams for the BA degree in February 1881, his papers, shoehorned into six gruelling days in Madras city, would have looked like this:

English Poetry
English Prose
General English
English Composition
Kannada: Text-books and Grammar
Kannada: Translation
Kannada: Composition
Pure Mathematics (Algebra, Geometry, Plane Trigonometry)
Statics and Dynamics
Hydrostatics and Pneumatics
Astronomy and Optics
Mental Philosophy
History.[39]

*

Bangalore, known for its pleasant climate and green environs, was a preferred destination for retiring British and Anglo-Indian government servants. It boasted a population of over 1,40,000 in 1870.[40] True to its name, the Central College was located in the heart of the city. It was part of an area a few miles in radius that included the Parade Grounds (where the British-Indian troops marched), the commercial section on South Parade (today's M.G. Road), a number of churches, the Residency (where the British Resident of the state of Mysore lived), the vast and wooded Cubbon Park, and the government secretariat, known as the *Attara Kacheri*. The European settlement's social life revolved around the military, the clergy, and British officialdom.[41]

Visvesvaraya's family would have hoped that the young man, coming of age in these surroundings, would grow into a gentleman and a pillar of society. In a photo that survives from his teenage years, he is wearing a turban, a long coat buttoned at the neck, creased trousers, and leather shoes, his legs crossed casually as he sits confidently on a chair upholstered in velvet. He is yet to shed entirely the chubbiness of adolescence and inhabit the thin, wiry physique he will maintain for the rest of his life. His eyes have a faraway, pensive look.[42]

His aristocratic air notwithstanding, family lore suggests that Visvesvaraya's life as a student in Bangalore was no bed of roses. He is reported to have walked all the way to Chikkaballapur on some of his periodic visits home to spend time with his mother.[43] During his days at the Central College, he earned money by giving tuitions to the children of a Mysore minister at his home in the *pete*. He would sleep at his employer's home, wake up at the crack of dawn to guide the children through their lessons, stop off at his uncle's for breakfast, then walk to his college for the day's lectures. His wards remembered him as a strict tutor, not averse to handing out that classic Indian punishment: 'Stand up on the bench!'[44] With a packed schedule and a shoestring budget, Visvesvaraya could scarcely have sampled such entertainments as the city had to offer, though he probably played some sports at his college, which, in addition to a library and a debating club, boasted a cricket ground and a gym, and hosted an annual athletics meet.[45]

Circumstances aside, Visvesvaraya appears to have been a serious young man by temperament. In what was to become a lifelong habit,[46] he immersed himself in books on self-improvement. A key influence was the oeuvre of Samuel Smiles, the Victorian author of earnest tomes such as *Self-Help*, *Character*, and *Thrift*. He also studied *The Student's Manual* by John Todd, a Philadelphia-based preacher who issued detailed advice on how to study effectively, develop good habits, manage one's time, and husband one's health by eating healthily and taking exercise.[47]

In 1881, Visvesvaraya was placed sixth among 113 students who passed the BA exams of Madras University. He graduated in the second class; firsts were rarely awarded.[48] As his time at the

Central College drew to a close, he had to decide on a future course of action. As a prospective Bachelor of Arts in a state without its own university, Visvesvaraya was already among the most highly credentialled Indians in Mysore. The usual career option for a young man in his position was to seek a post in the lower rungs of the government bureaucracy, and Visvesvaraya appears to have considered this avenue.[49] As it turned out, he took a different option, seeking the opportunity to pursue a professional degree.

He was in luck, for this was the precise juncture when the British were turning the administration of Mysore back to its hereditary monarchs after fifty years of direct rule.[50] The new maharaja's dewan, or prime minister, C.V. Rangacharlu, was an ardent modernizer. Rangacharlu decided to groom local talent for responsible positions, setting up scholarships to enable young Mysoreans to undertake studies outside the state in fields—engineering, medicine, agriculture—that had not yet been institutionalized in Mysore. Scholarship holders usually went on to join professional colleges in the Madras or Bombay Presidency.[51]

Visvesvaraya applied for one of the engineering scholarships, and was selected.[52] Sadly, his application is not traceable, although those of some of his contemporaries are available to view. The scholarships, it would appear from these papers, were not particularly competitive: after all, the pool of students who had reached the stage of matriculation was not large. In most cases, the applicants were not driven by any particular interest or aptitude in the field they sought to enter; they knew, however, that qualifying as an engineer or doctor would enable them to earn a living.[53] Nor was the government particular about detecting such an interest: there were instances in which officials suggested that since the agricultural scholarships for the year were taken, students who had applied for one of them should be considered for an engineering scholarship instead.[54]

Be that as it may, it is quite probable that Visvesvaraya had already discovered a genuine interest in engineering. His aptitude for mathematics was noted at the time, and he had studied science subjects. He must have been conscious of the rapid changes occurring in the Indian subcontinent in the 1870s, as the colonial establishment began to enmesh the land in a network of railroads, telegraphs, canals, and irrigation works.[55] He would have heard stories of larger-than-life engineers like Sir Arthur Cotton, builder of dams and irrigation works on the great rivers of southern India.[56] He had surely read about Isambard Brunel, the Stephensons Robert and George, and other larger-than-life engineers who symbolized post-Industrial Revolution Britain. (Samuel Smiles, for instance, idolized George Stephenson, and wrote admiringly of many other engineers.)[57]

Possibly it was the influence of Visvesvaraya's mentors like his uncle Ramaiah and his professor Charles Waters that clinched the issue. He would go, scholarship in hand, to the Bombay Presidency, and study to become a civil engineer.

2

Becoming an Engineer[1]

In 1881, Visvesvaraya enrolled in the civil engineering programme at the government-run College of Science in Poona, in the heart of the Bombay Presidency. It was the first time he had left his home state of Mysore for any length of time.[2]

Picture the nineteen-year-old on his first day as he stands before the central building, an imposing structure of grey stone. A carved frog, flanked by two other gargoyles, casts an appraising glance at him from atop the portico. He is surrounded by the chirping of birds among large banyans and leaf-strewn paths; in the distance he hears the thrum and clang of the workshops. A few hundred yards away, the rivers Mula and Mutha flow sluggishly towards their meeting point.[3]

These were the grounds of a young institution, dedicated to a profession the colonial state had only recently begun to institutionalize.

*

To be an engineer in nineteenth-century India meant being employed in public works or in the railways. Mechanized industry was mostly confined to a few centres—the cotton and jute mills of Bombay, Ahmedabad and Calcutta—and employed few engineers. The bridges, buildings, and waterworks undertaken by the British in India until then had been carried out largely by military men belonging to the Royal Engineer Corps. Trained in the academies of Chatham, Addiscombe and Woolwich in England, they were Britons to a man.

It was only from the middle of the nineteenth century that the colonial state, which had recently ramped up expenditure on public infrastructure and created an Indian Public Works Department (PWD), considered seriously the possibility of recruiting civilians as officers in charge of building these works. Initially, the PWD officers were recruited by open competition in Britain from among engineers trained by apprenticeship. That was the dominant mode of engineering education in Britain: you paid a practising engineer a premium for the privilege of serving for some years as his pupil and assistant.

But the British soon decided they wanted more polished, college-educated men to represent them in India. Thus, in 1871, a college was set up at Cooper's Hill near London specifically to train engineers for the Indian PWD. Its costs were borne by the Indian taxpayer. The Royal Indian Engineering College, as it was called, became the premier source of PWD recruits in London, supplemented later by graduates of engineering degree programmes that were emerging in various British universities like London, Glasgow, Edinburgh, and Sheffield. These graduates, recruited by the Secretary of State for India, sailed to India and spread out to their postings across the subcontinent. In each province they were joined by a handful of engineers (and a large number of subordinates) recruited locally. Most of those recruited in England were Britons; most of the others were Indian by ancestry. Needless to say, there was a clear racial hierarchy. The London-recruited members of the PWD received substantially better pay and perquisites than their Indian counterparts, enjoyed greater prestige, and dominated the upper ranks.

The engineers recruited in India were typically graduates of one of the four engineering colleges that had been set up by the colonial government. The first of them was the Thomason College (1847) at Roorkee, which grew out of the need to train engineers and overseers for the Ganges Canal project. It was succeeded in the following decades by similar institutions at Guindy (near Madras), Sibpur (near Calcutta), and Poona (in the Bombay Presidency).[4]

The college in Poona had its origins in a school set up in 1854 to train subordinates for the PWD, and was initially known as the Poona Engineering Class and Mechanical School. Soon after, the Government of Bombay made plans to establish a college to train officers at multiple levels of the PWD hierarchy. In 1865, the Engineering Class of the existing school was converted into a college to fulfil this purpose. The Poona Civil Engineering College (as it was now known) was affiliated the following year to the University of Bombay and empowered to award the LCE degree (Licentiate in Civil Engineering). Around 1880, it was rechristened the College of Science, Poona, after programmes of study in agriculture and forestry were instituted.[5]

In 1863, when plans were being made for the new college, the aptly named businessman-philanthropist Cowasjee Jehangir Readymoney offered to donate the staggering sum of Rs 50,000 for a new building, if the Bombay government would match the amount and make available the required land. A design for the building was then drawn up by an architect named Trubshawe. In 1865, Bartle Frere, the Governor of Bombay, laid the foundation stone in the presence of the presidency's director of public instruction. Although an indisposed Readymoney could not be present that Saturday evening, '[a] very numerous assembly of the fashionable world responded to [his] invitation'. Tents were put up at the chosen site, and a large crowd of ladies and gentlemen, including some in military uniform, gathered. In the speeches that followed, handsome tributes were paid to C.J. Readymoney, and Bartle Frere predicted grandly that the new college would contribute to the 'creation of a new profession of native educated engineers and architects', leading to an improvement in 'the moral and intellectual feature of this part of India'.[6]

*

Even before Visvesvaraya arrived at the college, he would have heard about a towering personality who was already synonymous with the institution—its square-jawed, bearded principal, Theodore Cooke.[7]

An Irishman who championed the cause of Indian engineers and played a key role in their training, Cooke was born in County Waterford in 1836. He studied at Trinity College, Dublin, where he took what would today be called a double major in the arts and engineering faculties. He then joined the Bombay, Baroda and Central India Railway, and led the building of an iron bridge at Bassein (now Vasai, a Mumbai suburb). Just a few years into his career as a railway engineer, he was snapped up by the Bombay government's Educational Service, becoming principal at Poona in 1864, when he was only in his late twenties. He would continue in that position until his retirement in 1893.

As a scholar and teacher, Cooke was a polymath who straddled the worlds of theory and practice, of classical and scientific learning. As an undergraduate at Dublin, he had been 'Hebrew prizeman, first honoursman, and senior moderator and gold medallist in science' in the arts faculty; he had also won 'special certificates in mechanics, chemistry, mineralogy, mining, and geology' in the engineering faculty. His scientific specialization was geology and his vocation civil engineering, but in his spare time he studied the plants of the Bombay Presidency, eventually heading the work of the Botanical Survey of India for western India in 1891. After his retirement, he set to work producing what would become a seven-volume *Flora of the Presidency of Bombay* from his base at Kew (the London suburb that was home to the Royal Botanical Gardens). He had other, less academic hobbies too, such as photography and music (he even trained the college band at Poona).[8]

Cooke was a gifted lecturer. In the manner made popular by scientists like Humphry Davy at London's Royal Institution, he delivered public lectures with the aid of elaborately prepared, often spectacular live experiments. On one such occasion in 1878 at Bombay's Sassoon Mechanics' Institute, Cooke spoke on the practical uses of electricity. The *Times of India* reported that he used a galvanic battery to melt iron and copper, showed a magnet being deflected by the passage of electric current in its vicinity (Oersted's experiment), explained the working of the telegraph, and demonstrated 'the luminous effects of electricity' when he 'produced a very brilliant light by passing the current through gas carbon obtained from the retorts of the Bombay Gas Works'.[9]

Among Cooke's pedagogical contributions at Poona was the compilation of a handbook of geology, which had been commissioned by the Bombay government as 'a small and cheap elementary textbook, which should present to native youths some of the leading facts of the science of Geology, without entering too much into detail'. He also brought a refreshing approach to the teaching of geology, insisting on the importance of field trips. 'I cannot too strongly recommend an occasional geological excursion,' he wrote in the preface to his textbook, 'as I believe that nothing tends more to make Geology popular to youths, as a study, than freeing it from the trammels of a school-room, and associating it with pleasant rambles in the open air.'[10] If he was not quite a Renaissance man, he was a good approximation of one.

The college that Cooke helmed was a well-equipped one. In addition to the grand hall that Readymoney had endowed, it boasted a laboratory, a room for teaching engineering drawing, a museum, and a library believed to have 'the most complete assortment of books on the physical sciences of any of the College libraries'. The centrepiece was a state-of-the-art workshop with a foundry and a forge, where 'a great deal of work [was] turned out by the College for the general public'.[11] Speaking of Principal Cooke's emphasis on learning by doing, the Governor of Bombay said at a public event in 1878: 'Not only does he teach the theory of engineering, but he insists upon making his pupils go through the workshop and handle things with their own hands, so that they have a practical knowledge of the manner in which they are to earn their living.'[12]

Like its older counterpart at Roorkee, the Poona College had separate classes for students with differing aspirations. In Visvesvaraya's time, it had four departments. One was for those aspiring to become engineer or subordinate officers in the PWD; they were enrolled in a three-year programme leading to Bombay University's Licentiate in Civil Engineering. A separate department, catering to those aiming for other subordinate positions in the PWD, provided a course of instruction in the college and its workshops to create 'educated Maistries'. There were also separate departments for those studying 'Scientific Agriculture' and forestry respectively.[13]

A range of fellowships and scholarships were available to the students of the college. In 1882, Visvesvaraya was awarded the competitive Bartle Frere Scholarship, worth Rs 25 per month. The following year he received a fellowship worth an equal amount.[14]

By 1885, the Poona College had produced 143 successful LCE graduates. This means an average of around eight students received the degree each year since 1868, when the first one had been awarded.[15] In Visvesvaraya's year (he was examined in 1883), there were eleven graduates in the LCE class. If one included the other departments, however, the student body was much larger. In 1877, for instance, there were around 120 students in total, which works out to an intake of around forty to fifty students each year in all departments combined. The student body was dominated by Hindu Brahmins. Christians and Parsis formed notable minorities, while Jewish and Muslim students were rare. A majority were sons of government officials or landowners.[16] They were all men, as were all professional engineers in India for several decades to come.

*

For all the advantages the college boasted, Visvesvaraya and his fellow Indian students in Poona could not take it for granted that they would go on to gain employment as fully fledged professional engineers. Although the raison d'être of the college was to supply personnel for the PWD, this was confined largely to the subordinate ranks. Only the top-ranking graduate of the LCE class in each year was guaranteed a job as assistant engineer in the Bombay PWD.[17] Given the size of the class and the difficulty of obtaining engineering jobs outside government, this meant the odds of parlaying the LCE qualification into gainful employment were slim.

Even this one appointment had at one time been under threat, as parts of the colonial bureaucracy were apparently not enthused about the prospect of recruiting Indian engineers. In 1871, for instance, the Government of Bombay had declared that it would only offer an appointment to the top student if he obtained a first class.

Principal Cooke, who had only been in harness a few years at this point, wrote an eloquent missive of protest to the Bombay government's director of public instruction. He argued that this new requirement (insisting on a first class), if applied suddenly, would amount to 'a breach of faith on the part of Government'. He extolled the abilities of the Indian students he had observed, and argued against the prejudice they faced. 'As a refutation of the idea too frequently entertained as to the unfitness of the natives of this country for the Engineering profession,' he wrote, 'it will be sufficient for me to point to the many monuments of ancient Engineering and Architectural skill which are everywhere to be found throughout India, and which in beauty, fitness of design, and stability have never been equalled here by any of our European Engineers.' The graduates of the LCE course, he said, were in no way inferior to the engineers being imported each year from Britain, where they were recruited by open competition.

Cooke provided a vivid sense of the curriculum at the college. He submitted that the LCE programme at Poona was so wide-ranging and rigorous that even to pass was a creditable achievement, let alone secure a first class. The programme, he wrote, 'demands from each candidate a high knowledge of pure and mixed Mathematics, Chemistry (General and Analytical), Physical Science (including Heat, Electricity, and Magnetism), Geology, Architecture, Engineering, and Surveying. In addition, the candidate must be a good Draftsman', and would not pass unless he scored a certain minimum in all these branches of study. 'Intellects which have the power of grasping in a tolerably equal degree subjects so various and distinct', he opined, were 'not commonly met with'. A first class was naturally even harder to earn; it required an aggregate score of 66.67 per cent, in those days a very tall order, and was intended to be a 'distinction . . . but seldom gained'. If the government insisted on a first class, therefore, the prospect of a PWD appointment would virtually vanish, and few students would want to join the college in the future.[18]

The matter went up to the Educational Department, which, in February 1872, issued a resolution recommending that the PWD, as a one-time concession, exempt the top LCE graduate from 1871, Gungadhur Kirane (who had not received a first class), from the new rule.[19] But the question was not settled yet, and the ensuing discussion indicated another obstacle faced by the college in its early years. Cooke's focus on the workshop notwithstanding, the LCE programme stressed the scientific and theoretical basis of engineering, which some of the old guard in the Bombay PWD did not set much store by. A government official argued in a handwritten note that the rules could not be relaxed 'without injuring the Public Works Departt. service for the men they get are generally young Brahmins with a smattering of theory and little aptitude for practical Engineering'. Military engineers in the PWD, on the other hand, had been through the programme at Chatham 'which is far better and more practical and useful'. These British engineers, continued the official,

> are also older men of a race that takes more kindly to such practical work as Engineering, and though they may not be able to solve an equation, it is of little consequence, if they can lay out and superintend a building for except in the higher branches of Engineering equations are never needed.[20]

It is not clear whether the rule was ultimately overturned. As it turned out, however, first classes were awarded regularly in the years that followed, and the college flourished.[21] And yet, those graduates who successfully made it to the PWD would face similar prejudices all over again once they began their careers.[22]

*

The Bombay University Calendar for 1883–84 gives a list of the faculty members at the Poona College as of 1882. These professors, most of whom would have taught Visvesvaraya, included Principal Theodore Cooke; his brother Samuel Cooke (professor of chemistry and geology); James Scorgie (professor of mechanism and applied science); Daji Nilkanth Nagarkar (acting professor of chemistry and geology); Bamanji Sorabji (acting professor of mathematics and civil engineering); F.M. Dastur (assistant professor of mathematics); and G.M. Woodrow (lecturer in botany). Visvesvaraya and his peers would also have been guided by Raghunath Vinayak Dhairyavan, the drawing master, and Robert Royal, superintendent of the college's workshops.[23]

Whether Theodore Cooke ever became a Charles Waters-like mentor to Visvesvaraya we do not know, but his influence must have been palpable. More than a decade later, after Cooke retired and left to take up an appointment at the Imperial Institute in London, Visvesvaraya became one of the secretaries of a committee formed to collect contributions towards a memorial fund in the former principal's name.[24]

The picture that emerges of the college in Visvesvaraya's time is that of a small, close-knit group of students in the LCE class, accompanied by a larger subordinate trainee class, and a sprinkling of students in agriculture and forestry. The LCE students were at the heart of the college's mission, and probably considered themselves the social superiors of their fellow students in the workshops. The professors were a mix of Irishmen, Britons, and Indians.[25] The main buildings were as stately as anything the University of Bombay could boast, and the Licentiate engineers were being prepared to enter not just a mechanical occupation but a venerable, locally trained profession that would be even more influential than law or medicine.[26] They were visited by governors and viceroys, a clear indication that the programme and the college had symbolic as well as utilitarian value for the colonial state.[27] The students in the LCE class were mostly upper-caste Hindus or Parsis—unsurprisingly so, given the fees, the fact that it was conducted entirely in English, and the emerging views of some colonial officials on the need to find genteel practitioners for the engineering profession.

As Cooke had observed, the syllabus was heavy. Students took a 'First Examination' in civil engineering, usually at the end of two years, and their final Licentiate exam after a third year. Subjects for the Licentiate exam were categorized under four heads: Mathematics and Natural Philosophy; Experimental and Natural Science; Civil Engineering; and an additional area of the student's choice (options included combinations such as Optics and Astronomy; Mining and Metallurgy; and Botany and Meteorology). Under each of these heads were several papers. Most of them were written, but some took the form of oral or practical exams. The textbooks prescribed for some of these subjects were enormous, though the students probably took more concise notes based on their professors' lectures. For Civil Engineering, for instance, the syllabus included the *Roorkee Treatise on Civil Engineering*, a compendium whose first volume ran to 592 pages plus appendices in its 1873 edition, and most of Glasgow professor William Rankine's *A Manual of Civil Engineering*, a 783-page doorstopper.[28]

In November 1883, Visvesvaraya spent a hectic fortnight in Bombay city taking his Licentiate exams. On the first Monday (12 November) he had Inorganic Chemistry in the morning and Heat, Voltaic Electricity and Magnetism in the afternoon. The next day he tackled Conic Sections and Analytical Geometry (and possibly Differential and Integral Calculus, an optional paper, in the afternoon). On day three, it was Statics and Dynamics followed by Hydrostatics. The Thursday was reserved for optional papers. On Friday (16 November) came Mensuration of Surfaces and Solids, and then Geology. A few days later came the exams in his core subjects. On 22 November he was examined in Engineering Field and Office Work followed by Strength of Materials. The next day it was Bridges, followed by Irrigation and Harbour. On 24 November he answered the paper on Specification and Estimating, and then the one on Railways.[29]

The question papers for these exams are still available—they were printed in the Bombay University Calendar for 1884–85—and give a sense of the kind of knowledge and analytical abilities Visvesvaraya and his cohort were expected to display. Many of the questions tested theoretical and abstract knowledge, and were formulated entirely as word problems requiring mathematical proofs or brief essays. Others required candidates to have facts at their fingertips. There were also numerical problems. Some examples:

> How do you suppose the Sahyadri Hills or Western Ghats have been formed? To what causes do you attribute the peculiar flatness of their tops and the stair-like appearance of their slopes? Let your answer be as detailed as possible.
> [Geology; 16 marks]

> Explain carefully the formula $F = Mf$.
> A weight of 16 lbs. is placed on a plane which is made to ascend vertically with an acceleration of 12 ft. per second; find the pressure on the plane, g being taken = 32.
> [Statics and Dynamics; 8 marks]

> Name and state the composition of the several metallic salts used as white, yellow, red, and green pigments.
> [Inorganic Chemistry; 12 marks]

Explain the method of integration by substitution.
Find the value of

$$\int_0^1 \tan^{-1} \frac{1}{1 - x\,(1 - x)}\, dx.$$

[Differential and Integral Calculus; 10 marks]

In a Ghat road or railway on a steep hill-side, why is it necessary to have frequent accurate cross sections?
[Engineering Field and Office Work; 10 marks]

In an open river channel what is the ratio between the mean and greatest velocity?
[Irrigation and Harbour; 10 marks]

A brick wall 25 feet high and 5 feet thick has to sustain the pressure of water. Find the highest point the depth of water could reach without overturning the wall. (C. ft. brickwork = 112 lbs.)
[Strength of Materials; 10 marks]

Take out the quantities of a rectangular domed store-room measuring 24 feet by 15 feet interior measurement, having walls 4 feet thick and 12 feet high to the springing of the arch, which is a semicircle of 15 feet diameter 18 inches thick at the crown and backed at the haunches. There is one door 6 feet wide by 8 feet high and two windows each 5 feet by 4 feet.
[Specification and Estimating; 30 marks].[30]

We have no definite information on Visvesvaraya's friendships, routine, hobbies, or leisure activities during his days at the Poona college. He did have a slight advantage in his studies, since at least a few of his subjects in his BA programme in Bangalore overlapped with the syllabus at Poona (especially the mathematics and theoretical physics courses).[31] Still, he could not afford to relax. To throw together a dozen or more students from the traditional middle classes of a subject population, all of them aiming for a solitary government job, was to create a high-pressure cauldron. In the midst of it was the young man from Mysore, one of only a handful in his programme hailing from outside the Bombay Presidency, living far from home and family, hearing the unfamiliar sounds of Hindustani, Marathi, and Gujarati, yearning perhaps for the comforting rhythms of Telugu and Kannada.[32]

And now, nearly three years later, it had all come down to this: two intense weeks of examinations. The result would determine his future.

3

Becoming an Officer

1884: the third Tuesday of January. At 5.15 p.m., the procession for the twenty-third convocation of the University of Bombay made its way into the Cowasjee Jehangir Hall in Bombay's Esplanade—a narrow stretch of flat land near the southern end of the island, the Arabian Sea lapping at both flanks. Stepping first into the long, neo-Gothic chamber as the evening light streamed in through stained-glass windows was Sir James Fergusson, Governor of Bombay and Chancellor of the University. He was followed by the vice-chancellor, deans, syndics, registrar, and members of the Board of Accounts; the chief justice and the Bishop of Bombay; judges of the high court and members of the Legislative Council; and a large group of fellows of the university. The assistant registrar, holding the ceremonial mace, brought up the rear.

When everyone was seated, Major-General Merriman of the Royal Engineers, Dean for Civil Engineering in the University, rose. 'Mr. Chancellor,—On behalf of Mokshagundam Visvesvaraiya, B.A.; Vaman Narayan Dev; Mangesh Rao Katre; Bhailal Purshottumdas Shah; Sitaram Sambasiv Varneshiyar;

Nasarvanji Mancherji Dalal; Vithal Balkrishna Date; Narayan Dattatraya Garde; Moro Govind Joshi; Kavasji Bejanji Sethna; and Gavrishankar Harjivandas Vyas, of the Poona College of Science, I submit the Certificates required by this University and move that the Senate do pass a Grace for their admission to the Degree of Licentiate of Civil Engineering.'

Visvesvaraya had topped the list.[1]

That January evening, the Chancellor of the University of Bombay conferred on Visvesvaraya not only his degree but also the James Berkley prize for standing first in the LCE class at Poona in the exams held in November 1883. The prize was named for the first Chief Resident Engineer of the Great Indian Peninsula Railway, the company that built and operated the most important railway network connecting Bombay to other parts of the subcontinent.[2] The boy from Mysore had also won a first class, but he had missed out on the gold medal that went with the Berkley prize (the medal was only awarded if the top student had won a special mention from the examiners in the subjects of Engineering and Engineering Drawing).[3] Nevertheless, his prize was more than the set of books that he accepted in the Jehangir Hall. For he had also, by virtue of bagging the top rank in the examinations, obtained a coveted government job in the Bombay Public Works Department.

Two months after the convocation ceremony, Visvesvaraya reported to work at Nasik, a town around 100 miles north-east of Bombay city. This posting was fleeting; he was transferred almost immediately to Dhulia (now Dhule), headquarters of the nearby Khandesh District, and it was here that he was initiated into the rituals of life in the PWD.[4]

*

Visvesvaraya was the proverbial big fish from a small pond who had now been cast into the ocean. Mysoreans saw him as their representative and the bearer of their hopes. When he joined the Bombay PWD, a Bangalore newspaper, the *Daily Post*, published a brief profile of Visvesvaraya. He was, the piece noted, 'the first that ever went out [from Mysore] to fill a graded appointment in another presidency'. He was held up as an example 'that Mysore can boast of having as highly educated and intelligent men as any other part of India'. There were serious expectations of him: 'Mr Visvesvaraya is generally known in Mysore to be a very intelligent man. . . . looking at his abilities and intelligence, we should not be surprised if he were made a Superintending Engineer in a few years.'[5]

The *Post* was being a touch sanguine. As an assistant engineer, Visvesvaraya was at the bottom of the departmental hierarchy. He would be expected to spend several years assisting his immediate superior, sometimes by assuming responsibility for a small administrative unit called a *subdivision*. The superior bore the rank of executive engineer and was in charge of a larger unit called a *division*. Several divisions in turn made up a *circle*, each of them overseen by a superintending engineer. At the very top of the hierarchy, in charge of the entire presidency, were one or two chief engineers. It was not uncommon for engineers to retire without ever making it to the rank of superintending engineer, let alone getting there 'in a few years'. For an Indian, the chances were even slimmer.[6]

Visvesvaraya, then, was only a junior officer. But he was an officer nevertheless: already the social and bureaucratic superior of the overseers, draughtsmen and surveyors who made up the subordinate establishment of the department.[7] And he was all of twenty-two.

*

The engineering profession at this time was a long way from the specialization that was to mark it in the twentieth century. Civil engineering, as its name implied, claimed to subsume all facets of engineering that supported civilian (as opposed to military) life. Electrical and chemical engineering were still in their infancy, and mechanical engineering was a Johnny-come-lately. In Britain, this was mirrored by the sequence in which the great professional institutions were founded: the Institution of Civil Engineers in 1818, the Institution of Mechanical Engineers in 1847, and the forerunner of the Institution of the Electrical Engineers in 1871.[8]

In India, too, the PWD required its civil engineers to be generalists. They could, over the course of their careers, be asked to tackle anything within the entire gamut of engineering works—from barracks to prisons, roads to bridges, canals to dams. The PWD bureaucracy was divided into three branches (Irrigation; Roads and Buildings; and Railways—the last of these becoming a separate department in 1905), and engineers were frequently shunted from one branch to another. They were also expected to be competent managers with a good grasp of accounts and a flair for report-writing and official correspondence.[9]

Visvesvaraya was gradually socialized into the role of a generalist working on different kinds of project. In the Khandesh District, he began with some humdrum office work, then spent his initial months supervising routine maintenance and repair work on check dams and canals around the river Panjra. Over the next few years, he was assigned to sundry projects involving the design, implementation, or supervision of works, and some administrative or clerical duties. Among other projects, he designed a water-supply reservoir for the town of Dhulia, and oversaw the early phase of its building. He also conducted a survey for a proposed reservoir near the Satpura Hills.[10]

One particular assignment, though, left a strong impression on the young engineer. A few months into his posting in Dhulia,

H.G. Palliser, the executive engineer he reported to, presented him with his first substantial challenge. The fields of Datarti, a village in the district, were served by a channel carrying water from the Panjra. However, the channel was blocked by a stream flowing in its path. An older (possibly pre-colonial) aqueduct built of masonry, which had carried the channel's water across the stream in earlier times, had given way. Palliser now entrusted Visvesvaraya with the laying of a syphon to replace it. The timing was not propitious: it was the start of the south-west monsoon season.

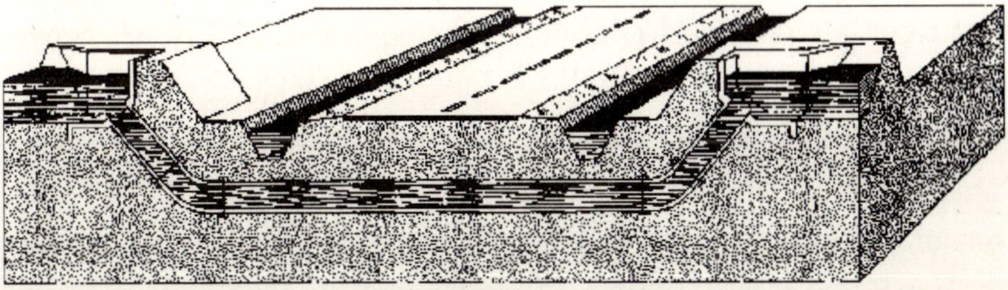

Fig. 3.1. A diagram of an inverted syphon

Source: C. Brouwer, A. Goffeau and M. Heibloem, *Irrigation Water Management: Training Manual No. 1 – Introduction to Irrigation* (n.p.: Food and Agriculture Organization, 1985), Chapter 5, fig. 86, accessed online at http://www.fao.org/3/r4082e/r4082e06.htm on 22 April 2023.

Visvesvaraya and his staff set to work just as the monsoon arrived, his task being to cut a groove into rocky terrain and dig the sand out of the bed of the intervening stream, so that the syphon pipes could be laid. But the rains kept washing sand into the trench, and he feared that funds would be wasted if they continued work in the teeth of the monsoon. With encouragement from a local civil servant, Visvesvaraya asked Palliser for permission to put off the work until after the rains. To his surprise, he received a reprimand, his superior chiding him in a memo for disobeying orders and lacking initiative.

Stung, Visvesvaraya went back to work despite the rains (but not before suggesting that he was not to be blamed if the work overshot its budget). He forded the river Panjra on his horse each day to reach the construction site, where artisans and labourers from the neighbourhood helped dig a trench and put the pipes in place. On one occasion the river was in spate, and Visvesvaraya was unable to get back to his bungalow. Stranded, he spent one night in Nandwan, a village near the site of the syphon, and another in Datarti (the village it was to serve), where the villagers treated him as an honoured guest. He then swam across the Panjra to get back to his camp, helped by his local workers, who put together rafts and fetched his horse for him. The work was eventually finished, and Palliser sent him a letter 'cancelling the adverse remark he had passed in his [earlier] memorandum'.[11]

His grand-nephew recorded that in his later years, Visvesvaraya recounted this story with delight—calling it, in Erle Stanley Gardner fashion, 'The case of the ass, the horse and the tent'.[12] At the time, though, the thought that his superior should think him less than diligent caused him genuine horror. Indeed, it is telling that he included a detailed description of the episode in his memoirs nearly seven decades later. There are few other accounts of adventure or daredevilry in Visvesvaraya's reminiscences, quite unlike the machismo running through the memoirs of many expatriate engineers who worked in colonial India.[13] It would appear that the significance of the syphon incident for him was to establish that he would leave no stone unturned to demonstrate his bureaucratic loyalty and maintain an unblemished record of service, the cancellation of a critical remark becoming the grand culmination of the project. While this says something about him as an organization man, it also shines a light on the times. For it was not easy being a 'native' engineer in the PWD in the heyday of colonial rule.

*

The public works officer, as we have seen, was expected to be something of an all-rounder. Perhaps more importantly, he had to display the gentlemanly bearing of the sahib, the civil servant who was responsible, in a paternalistic way, for the welfare of the ordinary folk within his jurisdiction. The majority of these engineer officers were British, and their training at institutions like the Royal Indian Engineering College at Cooper's Hill—where they encountered languages and the classics alongside their theodolites and chain-measures—was designed expressly to fit them for the company of Oxbridge-educated bureaucrats, not to speak of governors and viceroys plucked from the aristocracy.

Throughout the colonial period, Indian engineers laboured to demonstrate that they were at home in this organizational culture, dominated as it was by old-boy networks from Cooper's Hill (and earlier the Royal Engineer Corps). Like the official who saw the students of the Poona College of Science as bookish Brahmins (see Chapter 2), colonial authorities often betrayed scepticism of the Indian engineers in the PWD, not on account of their technical knowledge, but because of a supposed lack of 'character', reliability, and practical acumen.[14]

In 1878, a few years before Visvesvaraya's time in the department, the Bombay government, at the behest of the Government of India, had asked British engineers in the PWD to report on the performance of 'native' engineers working under them. In their responses, these British officers were sometimes generous in their estimate of Indian *subordinates* who eventually worked their way up to officer rank, but they found it difficult to adjust to the idea of college-trained Indians entering the service as fellow engineer officers: they generally saw these graduate engineers as feckless and lacking the stomach for tough outdoor work. Some of the British respondents were appalled by the prospect of Indians rising to positions of authority—especially over other British engineers. One superintending engineer went so far as to suggest that the real value of hiring Indian engineers was that they could function as 'the eyes of the Department': being more in tune with the thinking of their fellow Indian subordinates, contractors, and labourers, they could help root out corrupt practices. 'Evils which the European believes to be latent, the Native knows to exist, and if his heart is in his work he can lay his hand on them, and by this means alone afford a proof of his fitness for the public service, far more valuable than if he exhibited signs of genius in Engineering skill.'[15]

Into such an organization Visvesvaraya stepped. When he joined the Bombay PWD, almost all his superiors would have been British officers, and he would not have met his Indian colleagues too often, scattered as they were in districts across the presidency. Little wonder, then, that he was so deeply affected by Palliser's throwaway remark.

*

In the vaults of the Maharashtra State Archives, in the grand old building it shares with the Elphinstone College in Mumbai, lie a few fragile pages in which engineers of the Bombay PWD filled out evaluations of their junior colleagues in the 1880s. They were given a pro forma with several headings. Was the person under evaluation a civil or a military engineer by training? What were his language qualifications? Did he possess any noteworthy talents?

Among the forms is a surviving leaf with Visvesvaraya's name on it—his first official evaluation. Filled out when he was in his first posting as an assistant engineer in the Khandesh District, it pertains to the year 1887. The superior evaluating him (the signature is not easily decipherable) deemed Visvesvaraya's language skills 'very good' and his English 'unexceptionable'. His 'Energy' and 'Industry' were both 'good', and he was 'careful and painstaking' in keeping accounts. As for his 'General fitness for duty', the gaunt young Mysorean was 'not very strong but willing'. Asked to comment if he had a 'Special aptitude for particular duties', the superior listed 'Canal administn.' On the whole, he judged Visvesvaraya 'a very valuable assistant'.[16]

That Palliser revised his early opinion is apparent from the fact that he encouraged Visvesvaraya to take his departmental exam barely a year into his service. This was an exam that new recruits typically took a couple of years after joining the PWD. The subjects included some practical ones and a local language. The latter would have been less of a challenge for Visvesvaraya than for his British counterparts, for he had already been exposed to Marathi since his student days in Poona. He passed, was made permanent, and received his first promotion, moving into the second grade as assistant engineer. Ten months later he was promoted again, becoming assistant engineer (first grade) with a monthly salary of Rs 500.[17] In 1887, it was Palliser once more who acted as proposer when Visvesvaraya applied for membership to the premier professional society for those in his line of work, London's Institution of Civil Engineers. That May, the Council of the ICE confirmed him as an associate member of the Institution.[18]

Meanwhile, Visvesvaraya's benefactors in Mysore kept track of his progress. When Chamaraja Wadiyar X, the Maharaja of Mysore, visited Bombay city in December 1887, he invited Visvesvaraya to call on him at his official residence there. Their conversation, which Visvesvaraya recorded in a scrapbook, reveals the engineer's curiosity and engagement with problems beyond his immediate job description, and his emerging belief in technocratic ideas of development. The maharaja, who was of a similar age to Visvesvaraya, began by asking him what he thought of Bombay city. They discussed the narrowness and the insanitary state of the lanes of the metropolis; the mode of construction of the buildings in the lanes, several stories high; and the prospect of reclamation from the sea as a solution for the city's shortage of space. Visvesvaraya also described to the visiting royal the climate of various parts of the Bombay Presidency.[19] Less than four years into his career, Visvesvaraya was finding his feet in the public works bureaucracy of British India.

*

Around 1890, Visvesvaraya felt confident enough to request a transfer: malaria was prevalent in the Khandesh District, and it was taking a toll on his health. Whereas he had cut his teeth on irrigation projects in Dhulia and the country surrounding it, he was now placed under the executive engineer for Roads and Buildings in Poona, thus returning to the city of his college days. In Poona, he began to build social contacts even as he discharged his official duties looking after government buildings and roads in and around the city.[20]

The details of Visvesvaraya's personal life in these years—which he barely ever spoke about—are hazy, and must be reconstructed from accounts handed down over the years. When he was eighteen, his family had arranged a match with Savithri (neeé Saraswathi), the daughter of a Chikkaballapur schoolteacher named Ramachandra Sastry. They were married a couple of years later, during his days at the Poona engineering college. Savithri came to live with Visvesvaraya and his mother Venkachamma in Poona around 1884—probably arriving just before he took up his first posting in the PWD. Venkachamma did not find life in the Bombay Presidency to her liking, and returned home shortly thereafter. But Savithri got along well with her husband, and stories handed down in the family suggest that the couple's early days were characterized by domestic bliss, Visvesvaraya even (unusually for those times) teaching his wife to play tennis. But their happiness was short-lived: in 1888, Savithri died while giving birth. The child did not survive either.

Visvesvaraya was to be desperately unlucky in his conjugal life. His family prevailed upon him to remarry, and he did, in March 1889. His second wife also perished in childbirth. He married a third time, but his wife parted ways with him. Thus, by the age of thirty, he was twice widowed, once separated, and childless.[21] There is no indication of his having had a conjugal or romantic relationship ever again in the seventy years that remained to him.

How Visvesvaraya dealt with the duties of office in the midst of such turbulent events we do not know. He made absolutely no mention of them in his memoirs. All we have is a scrap of an official form that indicates that he was on 'Leave on urgent private affairs' from 17 September 1890 to 19 January 1891.[22] More than twenty years later, he gave a small indication of his feelings in a letter to a friend who had recently been widowed. 'I [have] gone through the same trials,' Visvesvaraya wrote, 'and I know how terrible it is to suffer such a shipwreck in mid-life.'[23]

*

Back at work, Visvesvaraya pulled himself together well enough to make a favourable impression on his boss in Poona, E.K. Reinold. In 1893, Reinold was asked by the government if he knew 'a really good Assistant Engineer' whose services could be spared for a project in Sind that had been stalled following the unexpected death of the engineer in charge of it.[24] The task was to create a water-supply system and reservoir for the town of Sukkur (now in Pakistan). Reinold asked Visvesvaraya if he would like the job. In return for braving the trying climate of Sind, Visvesvaraya was offered a hardship allowance of Rs 200 per month over and above his regular salary, and a further sum to pay for his accommodation while on the project.

Visvesvaraya pondered the offer for some time.[25] If he accepted it, he would have to acclimatize quickly to a new area and carry out the project rapidly while working with an unfamiliar bureaucracy. On the other hand, it was an opportunity to handle on his own a project with visibility, and thus to make a name for himself. He would also be able to save some money. Perhaps it would enable him to get away for a while from the scene of his personal tragedies. He accepted the assignment.

Sukkur, a town with around 30,000 inhabitants, lay on the banks of the river Indus. Considered 'of military importance due to its location at a strategic crossing point of the river', it had been taken over by the British in the early 1840s.[26] Visvesvaraya arrived there in February 1894. His task—as he recalled in his memoirs several decades later—was to carry water from the river up to the summit of a neighbouring hill, purify it, and route it from there to the town. But the municipality could not afford the filter beds that would be needed, and Visvesvaraya had to devise another way to collect potable water. He had a well dug at the bottom of the river 'to obtain spring water by percolation'. This water was then directed through an underground tunnel to a pumping station on the riverbank, from where it was pumped up to a reservoir constructed at the top of the hill. The clear spring water obviated the need for filtration, which would have been necessary had water been taken from the flowing river, which carried mud and impurities. Visvesvaraya left Sukkur in August 1895, having implemented the water supply project and drawn up plans for a drainage system for the town.[27]

Later accounts, relying solely on the terse report in Visvesvaraya's memoirs, have stressed the ingenuity of his solution.[28] But contemporary sources suggest a more nuanced narrative. Giving a resumé of the project on the day of its inauguration, the president of the Sukkur municipality, Khan Saheb Pirbaksh, said it had been under discussion for several years. Plans had been prepared and revised by at least three British engineers since the late 1880s. The latest proposals, as of Visvesvaraya's arrival in Sukkur, had come from the engineer to whom he was to report. This was the fabulously named Scrope Berdmore Doig, Superintending Engineer of the Indus Right Bank Division. Doig had suggested

> that a well should be sunk in the rock in the riverbed . . . and that a collecting gallery, if necessary, might be driven from it under the riverbed until a sufficient supply was obtained. . . . It was also suggested and arranged that the whole town should have a constant service, and that this could be obtained by the addition of a small high level reservoir erected over the low level one and by enlarging some of the principal mains. The analysis of the water from a trial well on the Sukkur side proving satisfactory, Mr. Doig's valuable suggestion was adopted, and the project was revised accordingly by Mr. Visvesvaraya.

In the finished works, Pirbaksh continued,

> [t]he supply of water obtained is from two sources. One is by percolation from the Indus through the rocky sides of the supply well and gallery, and the other from a spring which it was our good luck to strike while driving the gallery under the bed of the river. The works were entirely constructed by Mr. Visvesvaraya, Executive Engineer, under the supervision of Mr. S.B. Doig, . . . to both of whom the warmest thanks of the Municipality are due, for their untiring zeal and exertions in bringing the work so quickly to a satisfactory termination.[29]

In other words, Visvesvaraya had successfully executed plans which he had inherited from Doig and other engineers, after making necessary modifications based on the conditions he encountered. This, of course, is exactly how projects were routinely carried out in the PWD. If we accept Pirbaksh's account, the main innovative element, the use of spring water, appears to have been the result of an accident.

Making this point does not detract from the fact that the completion of the works was a significant achievement for the young engineer. Visvesvaraya worked under great scrutiny, for he was in Sukkur around the time the British were marking fifty years of their presence in Sind. In late 1894, the town received visits from the Viceroy of India as well as the Governor of Bombay. Amidst itineraries filled with pomp and ceremony, both were shown the water works then in progress.[30] By all accounts, Visvesvaraya was swift and efficient in his execution of the works, which were eventually inaugurated in December 1895 by a new Bombay governor, Lord Sandhurst. Visvesvaraya had left Sukkur, but Doig was present at the function. Standing on a dais festooned with decorations, covered in Persian rugs, and flanked by shamianas for the invitees, Sandhurst complimented the Sukkur municipality for '[taking] great care to obtain the services of the most able engineer that you could provide yourself with'.[31] It is not entirely clear from the context if he was referring to Visvesvaraya, though that may well have been the case. But the municipality was unambiguous in congratulating the Mysorean, thanking him for realizing the project 'with care, ability and zeal, and no small self-sacrifice, in the trying climate of Sukkur, . . . in a comparatively short time'.[32]

*

After Sukkur, Visvesvaraya spent the best part of a year in the much larger town of Surat, where, once again, he was placed in charge of building the waterworks according to an existing design.[33] By the mid-1890s, then, he had accumulated substantial experience in a particular kind of work, namely waterworks and irrigation. Although he was still an assistant engineer by rank, he had officiated as executive engineer on at least two projects (Sukkur and Surat), which meant he had worked on them independently and been directly responsible for their progress. He had also come to the notice, however briefly, of officials in the highest echelons of the colonial bureaucracy. At the age of thirty-five, he had made a solid start to his career as a public works engineer.

4

Poona Circles

Among the many epithets used to describe Visvesvaraya after he was placed in the pantheon of Indian greats, one is particularly common: karmayogi. A man who sought salvation through work; an ascetic who sublimated his desires in the pursuit of duty. What else was a man to do after fate had so cruelly cut down his every foray into family life?

The biographer is indeed tempted to play amateur psychologist and declare a turning point in the subject's life at the moment when he re-entered bachelorhood. Having performed the last rites for two wives and been separated from a third, did Visvesvaraya decide to insulate himself from the emotional vicissitudes of family life and pour his energies into work? Certainly, as a single man for the rest of his life, he had the financial freedom and leisure to follow his professional interests with a doggedness that few of his colleagues could afford.

But even karmayogis need companionship. Visvesvaraya found it among the Liberal reformist intellectuals of Poona, who came closest to fulfilling the role of friends in this stage of his life. Years earlier he had received a formal introduction to M.G. Ranade, the veteran judge and social reformer. Now he began spending time with the indigenous elite of Poona, which included Ranade and his protégé Gopal Krishna Gokhale, along with an assortment of traditional chiefs and lawyers. Visvesvaraya participated in sports 'on local play-grounds and in associations' where these acquaintances were present. He seems to have found some solace in their society, for he thought it would be a good idea to set up a club as a permanent forum for such interactions. Or as he put it—rather more stiffly—'I was struck with the idea that a club on the English pattern was a desideratum in Poona.'[1]

*

So, in July 1891, Visvesvaraya and a Poona-based judge named C.R. Bhat wrote to the elite of the city, announcing a proposal to found a club. The endeavour received a blow when Bhat died unexpectedly, but some prominent Parsi citizens of Poona stepped into the breach. Among them were Major Dinshah Khambatta, a distinguished army officer, who was to become a joint secretary of the new club; and Dorabjee Pudumjee, considered 'the head of the Parsee community in Poona', who became its first chairman. Pudumjee was also a former member of the Bombay Legislative Council, a long-time President of the Poona City Municipality, and a participant in the governance of several other organizations in the city. With Ranade and Gokhale also lending their support, the club had powerful backers.[2]

It was Ranade who helped the Deccan Club (as the new institution was christened) find a venue. He got the local authorities to share with the club a historic building named Hirabaug, which had housed the Town Hall since the 1870s.[3] Built at the behest of one of the Peshwas—the Brahmin rulers of the Deccan before the British conquest—for his queen in 1768, Hirabaug was a pretty country house set in picturesque grounds. An early nineteenth-century visitor had described 'with pleasure . . . the beauty of the extensive garden with noble trees, fountains, and vine pergolas'. The gardens led up to an artificial lake adjoining the hill known as Parvati, on which was perched a complex of temples also dating back to the reign of an eighteenth-century Peshwa. (The lake was drained around 1900; in its place today is a public garden, Saras Baug.)[4]

The choice of Hirabaug was of symbolic significance. The Town Hall represented a small island of Indian influence in a British-governed presidency. It was where exhibitions were held to showcase indigenous crafts and manufactured goods. It was where crowds gathered to choose the local delegates for the sessions of the Indian National Congress, which had been established some years previously. (The very first session of the Congress itself would have been held there had a cholera scare in Poona not caused the organizers to move it to Bombay.) Hirabaug was also where, some years later, local eminences would meet to discuss how to raise funds to repair the tomb of the seventeenth-century Maratha emperor Chhatrapati Shivaji at Raigad.[5]

Visvesvaraya and his colleagues ensured that Hirabaug was renovated and comfortably appointed. The interiors received a fresh coat of paint. The central hall was set up as a reading room, complete with the latest journals and newspapers; upstairs were rooms for billiards and cards. The adjoining land was graced by a pair of tennis courts.[6]

The club's formal opening was scheduled for 17 November 1891. To the organizers' dismay, very few people were in the hall at the appointed time. But more began to trickle in, fashionably late. Eventually there were a few dozen important attendees, a veritable who's who of 'native' Poona society.[7]

Speeches were made. Khan Bahadur Kazi Shahabuddin, one of the members of the managing committee, spoke first. The Deccan Club, he said, 'supplied a great want, for hitherto they [the denizens of Poona] were as sand, loose and without any binding'. Visvesvaraya spoke next: as was his wont, factual and to the point, a report of progress made and future aims. Then Ranade rose. He recalled earlier efforts to set up similar bodies, which had met with hostility from the city's orthodox Brahmins, who saw in them an assault on the institution of caste. Around 1889, an Indian style 'City Club' had been established, 'a place without chairs or carpets', the emphasis being on indoor games. Now they were going a step further, and he welcomed it. He thought the Deccan Club would act as a civilizing influence, and encouraged each member to make sure he spent an hour a day there during its initial months.

The club, the *Times of India* reported, was to be 'strictly non-political and non-sectarian, its main object being to promote social intercourse, good feeling and fellowship among the members, and to provide healthy, intellectual and physical recreation and amusement'. It was progressive, being open to all irrespective of 'creed or nationality'. Yet this progressiveness had its limits. Women members were conspicuous by their absence, as was anyone without the benefit of a high social standing. No alcohol was served, and the eating rooms were segregated according to caste.[8]

*

Nearly 130 years after it was founded, I visited the Deccan Club—still housed in Hirabaug. A narrow passageway leads from the entrance to a large hall, which opens out on the left to what is now the Jawaharlal Nehru cricket stadium. The grounds are greatly truncated (several other buildings and a busy road now separate them from Saras Baug and the Parvati Hill), but still contain tennis courts and leafy trees. Wooden beams hold up the ceiling of the central hall, fans whirring gently as elderly members sit around cards tables and carom boards. On the walls are fading portraits of

Ranade, Gokhale, Visvesvaraya, Pudumjee, Khambatta, and other Poona notables. In one corner stands the bust of an unidentified Englishman—much to the chagrin of an old-timer from the area, with whom I chatted about the club's history that day. At one point, it emerged that he had mixed feelings about the founders of the club. They were greats, no doubt, but at some level, were they not merely card-playing, English-speaking panderers to the colonial bosses?

The gentleman's views reflected, across the chasm of an intervening century, some of the criticisms the Deccan Club faced at its inception. As Ranade had indicated on the opening day, the club was always suspect in the eyes of the city's orthodox community leaders. In 1890, the year before the club's establishment, he had been part of a group of Poona Brahmins who had ventured to partake of tea and biscuits at a gathering organized by Christian missionaries, kicking up a furore among their caste brethren.[9] A club where Indians and Britons were to mingle, where a Brahmin and a Parsi might share a game—even if not a meal—with a Muslim or a Hindu of another caste, was, in this context, a bold venture. But the criticisms also reflected a growing political divide among Poona's leaders. Ranade and his associates, in addition to being oriented towards social reform, were what would come to be known as 'Moderates' in their political views. Unlike their colleague, the firebrand Bal Gangadhar Tilak, who later took the path of a more muscular and religious nationalism, they believed in working with the British, appealing to the rulers' sense of fair play in order to secure a better deal for Indians.[10]

Not that the British were eager to mingle with Indians of an evening. Across the length and breadth of the subcontinent, the civil servants who ran the Raj set up racially exclusive clubs that they could retire to at the end of a day's work and, so to speak, be themselves.[11] The Deccan Club, then, was a rare instance of a club where they became members alongside Indians. Located a stone's throw from the traditional Brahmin neighbourhoods of the Peshwas' city[12] but several miles from the European cantonment, the club was admittedly not the most natural destination for colonial officials. Yet some of them did play an active part in its functioning.

The Deccan Club clearly prized its achievement in bringing together—after a fashion—British and Indian residents of Poona. Among its British members were a General Burnett, Master of a Freemason Lodge, and a Mr Sheppard. At a reception in 1901, Dorabjee Pudumjee, the club's president, thanked Burnett and Sheppard and others like them, 'by the good offices of [whom] . . . they were able to call theirs a cosmopolitan club'. Burnett, for his part, 'spoke of the necessity for a good understanding among all the races of the empire' and 'of the kindly sympathy he had received, in trying to aid those around him, from every class and sect of Poona society'.[13] In 1904, the Bombay governor, Lord Lamington, paid a visit to the Deccan Club. Visvesvaraya, Gokhale, and Dr Bhandarkar, the club's president, were among the prominent citizens on hand to welcome him. The club was adorned for the occasion with 'flags and coloured bunting'. There was food, music, and speeches, and the governor accepted a garland. 'He was very pleased, he said, with all he had seen, and hoped the club would flourish and be a potent source of good, social and friendly intercourse among its members.'[14] Observers outside Poona took note of the club, too. In a 1910 profile of founding member Dinshah Khambatta, the Allahabad-based *Pioneer* noted that '[i]n bringing together the [diverse] conflicting elements in a cosmopolitan city like Poona, where the rulers and the ruled could meet on a footing of social equality, and where personal contact removed misunderstandings, this institution has during its life of twenty years done much useful work'.[15]

It is clear that the club, from the beginning, was meant to be more than a place for socializing and recreation. Whether it amounted to anything as an intellectual organization is doubtful. It did not bring out a journal. It did not raise petitions or organize debates. But in its intention to create a secular space in the public life of Poona it achieved considerable success. By bringing Poona residents of different backgrounds together socially, it may have helped oil the wheels of other organizations which *were* at the heart of Poona's intellectual life—such as the Sarvajanik Sabha, the Deccan Education Society, and the Servants of India Society—and helped them negotiate with the government. In that sense, it was a microcosm of the city's Liberal circles, which, taken as a whole, were to have a strong impact on Visvesvaraya's thinking.

*

Late nineteenth-century Poona still retained the aura it had gained as capital of the Peshwas' kingdom. It continued to be seen as a cultural and intellectual centre in the Deccan, attracting the educated and the ambitious from the surrounding regions. Prominent among these groups were the Chitpavan Brahmins, hailing from the districts near Ratnagiri along the Konkan coast south of Bombay. Ranade, Gokhale, Tilak, and many other dominant figures of the time belonged to this community.[16] Visvesvaraya's Brahmin background and upbringing probably meant he was socially at ease among the Poona Liberals, although—as his later career attests—he had no time for religious orthodoxy of any kind. As a result, he was much more closely associated with Ranade, Gokhale, and their ilk than with Tilak.[17]

The pre-eminent figure among the Liberals was Mahadev Govind Ranade (1842–1901). Born in Niphad (near Nasik), he was educated at Kolhapur's English School and Bombay's Elphinstone College. He became one of the first BA graduates of Bombay University in 1862, before going on to study law while working as a professor and translator. In 1871, he joined the government's judicial service, arriving that November in Poona to take up the position of subordinate judge—an influential position for a twenty-nine-year-old. He was to spend the best part of the next two decades in Poona.[18]

While he had a distinguished career as a judge in the British Indian courts, Ranade's lasting contribution was in social service and reform. During his student days he had edited the English section of the reformist journal *Indu Prakash* and joined the Widow-Marriage Association. Ranade also joined the Prarthana Samaj, a revivalist-reformist movement within Hinduism that was partly inspired by Bengal's Brahmo Samaj and bore similarities to the later Arya Samaj, although it was less radical than either.[19] His stance towards religion and reform was characteristic of the early generations of Indians who came through the newly anglicized education system. While rooted in Sanskrit and Marathi literature,[20] he had been reared on a diet of British authors such as David Hume, Thomas Macaulay, and Thomas Malthus.[21] Ranade declared that the advent of the English language, and with it the keys to Western Enlightenment thought, was a blessing for India.[22]

The most influential Poona institution Ranade belonged to was the Poona Sarvajanik Sabha. The Sabha was founded by G.V. Joshi in 1870, but once Ranade joined it the following year, he became its real engine.[23] Its aim was to function as a 'mediating body (between the government and the people) which may afford to the latter facilities for knowing the real intention and objects of Government as well as adequate means for securing their rights, by making a true representation of the real circumstances in which they are placed'.[24] The Sabha concerned itself with various matters including government legislation and the administration of religious grants. Its activities were based in a traditional house, the Nagarkar Wada, in the Vishrambagh area of the old city. In 1878, a *Quarterly Journal* was established. There was also an accompanying monthly compendium in Marathi, the *Poona Sarvajanik Sabheche Masik Pustak*, from 1880 onwards.

Ranade wrote the majority of the contents of the *Quarterly Journal*, often anonymously. He wrote on economics, religion, philosophy, education, and history. According to the scholar Manorama Barnabas, the *Journal* dealt with quintessentially Liberal issues. It campaigned for the freedom of the press; stressed the importance of the scientific method; emphasized the need to overturn scriptural exhortations ('go forth and multiply') when they had consequences (overpopulation) for the ability of humans to live a life of dignity; and drew attention to the responsibility of the intelligentsia to drive social change, if necessary through legislation.[25]

Ranade's influence spread to the national stage when the Poona Sarvajanik Sabha played a leading role in the founding of the Indian National Congress (1885). Although Ranade, owing to his position as a judge, could not initially take on a direct role in the proceedings of the Congress, he helped establish, and was a key figure in, a Social Conference, which was held in conjunction with the annual sessions of the Congress from 1887.[26]

If Ranade was 'the uncrowned King of Poona',[27] his chosen prince was Gopal Krishna Gokhale, the son of a classmate from Kolhapur. Gokhale (1866–1915) also graduated from Bombay University via Elphinstone College, after which he studied law while teaching at the New English School in Poona. This school had been set up by a group of private individuals in 1880 with the aim of bringing Western education to a wide range of Indian students.[28] A few years later, its promoters decided to extend their work to collegiate education. This cause was taken up by Bal Gangadhar Tilak and Gopal Ganesh Agarkar (who had also assisted with the founding of the school), resulting in the establishment of the Deccan Education Society in 1884. The Society in turn established an undergraduate arts college in

Poona in January 1885, and named it after James Fergusson, the outgoing Governor of Bombay.[29] Coming under the influence of Agarkar, Gokhale abandoned his dreams of a legal career and committed to serve the Deccan Education Society for twenty years at the nominal salary of Rs 75 per month.[30] He taught English; Mathematics; and History and Economics at the Fergusson College over the next twenty years, gradually rising to the forefront of public life in Poona and, indeed, India.[31]

Gokhale began working closely with Ranade around 1887.[32] They were kindred spirits. A generation apart, they came nevertheless from almost identical milieus. If Ranade's girth, gentle ways and lumbering gait earned him the sobriquet of 'Baby Elephant',[33] Gokhale was described as sincere, hardworking, simple-minded and 'very sensitive'.[34] Both men were steeped in the works of English and European authors and had developed gargantuan memories and an eye for detail. Both believed in reform, but through constitutional methods. Gokhale was no radical, showing an affinity for the works of Edmund Burke, which he knew by heart, as he did the poetry of Walter Scott. At Elphinstone College he had been taught by Dr William Wordsworth, grandson of the celebrated poet who shared his name.[35]

Ranade now began to train the younger man to study problems related to '[l]and-revenue, finance, and the general administration of the country', putting forth the Indian point of view to the colonial government. Gokhale was taught to 'study all these questions at their very fountain,—namely, the Government Blue Books, Green Books and Red Books issued from time to time. Cumbrous statistics, masses of evidence, voluminous correspondence, various statements and comments proceeding from diverse sources had to be grasped, and for a faithful comparison or contrast of the situation, a close study of foreign conditions was equally indispensable.'[36] In two years' time, the protégé had proved himself sufficiently to be appointed Secretary of the Sarvajanik Sabha and editor of its *Quarterly Journal*.[37]

But the intellectual leadership of Poona was soon riven by 'angry dissensions'.[38] Differences cropped up first between Agarkar and Tilak. Agarkar was more interested in social and educational reform than political activism, and less enamoured of orthodoxy and Hindu tradition than Tilak. Their partnership foundered on the rock of these differences, and was sunk by disagreements on the running of the institutions they were involved in. In the late 1880s, Agarkar parted ways with the *Mahratta* and *Kesari*—reformist newspapers in English and Marathi, respectively, which he had set up and run with Tilak and others since 1881—and started his own journal, the *Sudharak*. Gokhale, who had earlier contributed to the *Mahratta*, also broke links with the paper and threw in his lot with Agarkar. For his part, Tilak quit the Deccan Education Society in 1890.[39]

Tilak and his supporters also began to break away from the Ranade-Gokhale group in other Poona organizations. They wrested control of the Sarvajanik Sabha in 1895. They saw to it that the Social Conference, beloved of Ranade but bugbear of conservative thinkers, did not take place alongside the Congress session of that year, which was held in Poona. They spoke in a populist idiom, transforming the annual Ganpati festival and celebrations of the Maratha ruler Shivaji into large-scale public events.[40]

Gokhale commented privately that he '[had] grown absolutely sick of the public life in Poona',[41] but in 1896 he, Ranade and their associates established an alternative body, the Deccan Sabha, its manifesto declaring that 'Liberalism and Moderation will be the watchwords of this Association'.[42] Unsurprisingly, the Deccan Sabha became the colonial government's preferred interlocutor.[43] By the time of Ranade's death in 1901, Gokhale had inherited the mantle of spokesperson of the Liberal middle classes. In

1896 he was invited to England to depose before a commission inquiring into the Government of India's expenditures; in 1899 he was elected to the Bombay Legislative Council; and in 1901 he became a member of the Imperial Legislative Council.[44]

In 1905, Gokhale and his friends founded the (possibly Jesuit-inspired) Servants of India Society to render public service on an all-India scale. The Society would recruit university graduates, who were to take a series of vows, subsist on a minimal allowance, and dedicate themselves full-time to its work. Members would spend their first five years apprenticed to Gokhale, 'studying and travelling and working under trusted leaders, but never making themselves responsible either for a speech or for a newspaper article or for any public action' in that time. (Gokhale would famously suggest a similar one-year moratorium to M.K. Gandhi when the latter returned from South Africa the following decade.) The Servants of India Society, as it developed, had both political and social goals, and stressed the need to transcend caste distinctions, to foster industrialization, and to work for the uplift of the historically disadvantaged.[45]

*

Despite their differences, the competing sections of Poona's intelligentsia were agreed on one theme: the necessity for Indians to acquire mastery of technology and drive the industrial growth of their country. An 1893 article in the Sarvajanik Sabha's journal, likely written by Ranade, declared that a country's claim to being civilized must be assessed

> by the practical pursuits of its people, the number and magnitudes of their callings, their industries, their enterprises, their skill, their ambition and their performances and by the extent to which they employ natural forces as aids to production.[46]

The crux of Ranade's thinking, as described by his contemporary and biographer G.A. Mankar, was as follows. British rule, with its insistence on free trade, had contributed to—or caused—the destruction of India's traditional industries. Unable to compete (in the absence of state aid) with the onslaught of mass-produced, machine-made goods from Britain, Indian artisans and manufacturers had been driven to agriculture. An urban society had been made increasingly rural. But agriculture could only contribute so much to prosperity, as there were limits to the amount of crop one could grow. Ranade was thus part of the tradition of 'drain' theorists identified with Dadabhai Naoroji. He also developed a sophisticated critique of the government's laissez-faire stance. It would be all very well, he argued, to apply the teachings of James Mill, David Ricardo, and Richard Cobden to the Indian economy if political economy were an exact science; but since it involved the vagaries of people and societies, this was questionable. Indeed, a variety of continental thinkers like Jean-Charles-Léonard de Sismondi, Charles Dunoyer, and Adam Müller had begun to stress the need for the state to intervene in matters of the economy.[47]

Ranade complemented his theorizing on economics with advocacy of industrial enterprises. He encouraged and supported several ventures in Poona (though we do not know in what way exactly, as he almost certainly did not have any capital to invest), such as Dorabjee Pudumjee's Reay Paper Mill, the Silk and Cotton Spinning and Weaving Company, the Metal and Manufacturing Factory, and the Poona Rangshalla (Dyeing Company).[48] The Sarvajanik Sabha, over which he held sway, attempted in the 1870s and 1880s to send individuals outside India to obtain a technical education, but could not find the necessary funds.[49] Ranade also tried to get the Indian National Congress to hold an industrial conference alongside its annual gatherings, but its leaders had other priorities. So he took it upon himself, with the help of some associates, to start an Industrial Association in Poona in 1890. This became an annual event during the monsoon, hosting both scholarly discussions of economic questions and displays of local manufactures.[50] At its opening, Ranade laid out his expectations from the colonial government:

> to lend the assistance of the State in regulating our co-operative efforts by helping us to form Deposit and Finance Banks, and facilitating recoveries of advances made by them, by encouraging new industries with guarantees and subsidies, or loans at low interest, by pioneering the way to new enterprises and affording facilities for emigration and immigration, and establishing technical institutes, and buying more largely the stores they require here, and in many cases by producing their own stores.[51]

As the historian Ross Bassett has demonstrated in vivid detail, the Tilak-controlled *Mahratta* and *Kesari* were equally keen on such themes, enthusiastically covering sundry developments in industry and technological education across the world. The *Mahratta* described and praised the Massachusetts Institute of Technology (MIT, established in 1861), suggesting that the United States was far ahead of India's colonial masters in the race for technological progress. Tilak's newspapers saw in the US and Germany more relevant exemplars for India than Britain, and averred that India could indeed dream of an industrial future. For this, Indians must develop a global mindset, set up industries, and establish technical institutes. To foster this process, the *Mahratta* brought to its readers reprints, extracts, or summaries of articles from foreign journals like *Nature, Engineering, North American Review*, and *Scientific American*. It profiled inventors and scientists like Alexander Graham Bell, Thomas Edison, and Louis Pasteur, presenting them as universal exemplars.

Bassett's account suggests that the crux of the *Mahratta's* analysis was very similar to that of Ranade (although its phraseology may have been more combative and less grounded in economic theory). The industrial revolution in Britain and the iniquitous economic policies under colonial rule had wiped out India's traditional manufacturing industries while leaving the country unequipped for the emerging era of science-based industry. This made India a potential dumping ground for manufactured goods from across the globe. A new technological era was dawning across the world, but 'India was being left out of [this] fundamental global transformation.'[52]

Even as Tilak turned to a more orthodox cultural politics—a move some have argued was more strategic than ideological—his belief in the importance of industrialization remained undimmed.[53] The *Mahratta* campaigned for technical education through the 1880s and appreciated the eventual establishment of the Victoria Jubilee Technical Institute (1889) in Bombay. When the colonial government decided to use the Indian taxpayer's money to build a memorial to Queen Victoria after her death in 1901, the paper fought a losing campaign to ensure the memorial took the form of a technical institute. (What the public got instead was a majestic monument in marble, in Calcutta.) The *Mahratta* lauded the annual conferences of the Industrial Association, despite its association with Ranade. It reported favourably on the efforts of Keshav Bhat, an entrepreneurial Poona resident who sailed twice for MIT in the 1880s and 1890s to obtain training in technical subjects, returning to set up a dyeing company and other ventures with little apparent success. Tilak even organized a public event in 1896 where Bhat was presented as a man ahead of his time.[54]

*

For much of his adult life, Visvesvaraya kept meticulous scrapbooks of cuttings from newspapers and journals. These were primarily articles that concerned his own public life in some way, but they did contain other items of interest.[55] It is very likely that he followed closely the articles appearing in the *Mahratta* and the *Quarterly Journal* of the Sarvajanik Sabha. On at least one occasion, he himself contributed to the *Quarterly Journal*, writing an article 'on national uplift' around 1893.[56] If the literati of Poona were so enamoured of Edison and Bell, one can only imagine what the technically-minded Visvesvaraya's reaction must have been. The interest in MIT clearly registered in Visvesvaraya's mind, for he was to cite it as a model decades later, when he chaired a committee on technical education for the Bombay Presidency.[57] More generally, the admiration for American technological progress and the country's perceived can-do attitude became a cornerstone of Visvesvaraya's thinking in later years.

We also know that Visvesvaraya 'attended most of the industrial conferences and exhibitions held in Poona between the years 1891 and 1893', before his residence in the city was interrupted by his Sukkur assignment.[58] However, while the young engineer was deeply interested in the discussions on industrialization and technical education, he was cautious about appearing to criticize publicly the colonial government that employed him, for he had a strong sense of bureaucratic loyalty.[59]

This sense of bureaucratic propriety may also have ensured that he did not directly join organizations such as the Sarvajanik Sabha. Joining the Servants of India Society was out of the question, unless he was prepared to give up his professional work and devote himself full-time to it. Nevertheless, he was a friend of these organizations. As an integral part of Poona's intellectual circles, he was in regular contact with their members. He was frequently to be found at the Deccan Club, although—being a public works officer—he lived some distance away in Queen's Gardens, in the predominantly European part of Poona.[60]

*

In the late 1890s, Visvesvaraya found a way to satisfy his thirst for information about industrialization and technical education: he would spend some time in Japan. This was a time when Japan had begun to loom large in the Indian imagination: that nation, once pummelled into submission by American gunboats, had rapidly modernized and become a dominant Asian power, emerging victorious in the First Sino-Japanese War of 1894–95. By the following year, the *Mahratta* was '[suggesting] that Indians could now use Japan as a training school instead of looking to Europe or the United States'. Very soon, there was a noticeable trend of Indians making their way to Japanese shores to study technical subjects.[61]

Having accumulated enough leave, Visvesvaraya took three months off in 1898 and sailed for Japan. Little detailed information survives about this trip. Although Visvesvaraya wrote down and collected his observations in 'a small book', he did not make it public, held back once more by his cautiousness as a government officer. He did not want his appreciation of Japan to be read as a critique of British India (which, of course, it was in a sense).

But we can be certain that like many foreign visitors to Japan in those years, Visvesvaraya saw an ancient nation hurtling towards modernity. Visiting Japan in the late 1890s, a globe-trotting British Conservative MP, Ernest Hatch, commented that the country was moving forward 'at . . . lightning speed', its people imbued with a sense of 'national confidence' after the Sino-Japanese War. 'The modern and the old jostle at every turn,' he observed. 'In one quarter you will find electric tramways, electric lighting, and all the latest adjuncts of civilisation; in another you will see men carrying through the streets by means of poles and ropes a huge stone, the entire weight of which is imposed upon the shoulders of the perspiring bearers'. While Japan drew liberally on Western examples in modernising its economy, Hatch felt that the many expats who were in the country to provide training in educational, commercial or military matters '[had] been tolerated rather than sanctioned', and 'it is morally certain that the Western element will not be favoured a day longer than is absolutely necessary'.[62] Another Western observer, George Rittner, was likewise struck by the transformation, but it left him ambivalent. 'Civilisation and modern trains of thought have brought the country to the fore, have increased its trade, and found a market for its merchandise and manufactures; but they have also killed . . . its most priceless possession, its artistic taste.' But not entirely: the Japanese 'are also clever enough not to destroy all their originality or artistic taste . . . and therefore Japan is one of the few nations that has been able to conform to the demands of civilisation and still retain a certain amount of its individuality'.[63]

That 'certain amount of . . . individuality' was more than enough in the eyes of Visvesvaraya, who had also internalized the easy equation of 'civilization' with Western society. In the tantalizingly short remarks he recorded much later, he said of the Japanese academics he had seen in 1898 that '[t]heir working dress out of doors was modern and European, and in everything else in home life except business they were Japanese'. He was particularly interested in understanding the Japanese education system and its connection with industries. He was impressed by their Code of Education, which aimed for near-universal instruction at the lower levels, focused on economically useful learning, and endeavoured to promote national pride. He was particularly struck by the progress in female education, noting that the proportion of girls enrolled in school was much larger than was the case in India. He met professors in the universities in Tokyo and Kyoto, remarking on their 'high thinking and plain living'. Despite Japan's growing quasi-imperialist ambitions, he saw with uncritical eyes the prevalence of '[m]ilitary drill . . . in the various schools', noting only that '[c]hildren were kept most cheerful and instructed in loyalty, patriotism, behaviour, morals and human relations'.[64] For Visvesvaraya, it was the start of a lifelong love affair with Japan—or, more precisely, his idea of it.

*

After his tour, Visvesvaraya slipped back into his routine in Poona, which remained his base for many more years. His long association with Ranade and Gokhale, in particular, moulded him in many ways, starting from the mundane: in later life he would say that it was Gokhale who showed him the correct way to wear a tie.[65] Gokhale, in turn, complimented Visvesvaraya on his appearance, remarking to a visitor: 'You see, how correctly he is dressed; he is equally precise in his work and in his engagements.' The visitor was V.S. Srinivasa Sastri, Headmaster of the Hindu High School in Madras, who was in Poona in 1906 to be interviewed for admission to Gokhale's Servants of India Society. Gokhale subsequently took Sastri to the Deccan Club, where Visvesvaraya played host and introduced him to the other members. Sastri, not generally given to sanctimoniousness in his reminiscences, felt that Visvesvaraya 'bore a deep similarity [to Gokhale] in scrupulous observance of the courtesies of social life, in strict regard for duty, in catholic outlook and in passion for work'.[66]

There was clearly a temperamental affinity. Like Ranade and Gokhale, Visvesvaraya was highly anglicized in his sensibilities. If anything, he was more westernized in sartorial matters, and less rooted (than Ranade, certainly) in the literary culture of his ancestors.[67] As an employee of the colonial state, he clearly found their constitutional approach to reform appealing. Years later, in commenting on the excellence of Gokhale's debating skills in the Bombay and Imperial legislatures, he noted approvingly that the Maharashtrian 'had a balanced intellect and studied both sides of a subject too well to take extreme views'.[68] Visvesvaraya learnt from Ranade and Gokhale, but was no acolyte. Indeed, he had to deal with them professionally as well as personally (for instance, he worked on designing a drainage system for the city of Poona while Gokhale was president of the municipality).[69]

Most of all, Visvesvaraya shared with his Poona friends a quintessentially nineteenth-century belief in the idea of *progress*. This is well captured by an oft-repeated anecdote. One day in the late 1890s, Visvesvaraya called at Ranade's house in Bombay. (As Visvesvaraya remembered it, this was soon after his travels in the land of the rising sun, and the pair 'talked chiefly about progress in Japan'.) As he was leaving, his host pointed to a room in the house. 'Do you know,' asked Ranade, 'that there is a friend of mine in that room who is suffering from a disease from which all India suffers?' The friend was Waman Abaji Modak, a social reformer and retired school headmaster. His ailment was paralysis.

The story is recounted by Visvesvaraya in his memoirs, published in 1951.[70] But it was also told nearly fifty years before that, in G.A. Mankar's biography of Ranade.[71] This lends it credence. More importantly, it underlines what both men, and their acquaintances, wished to highlight about their opinions. For the nation, standing still was not an option.

Manorama Barnabas's analysis of an 1893 article in the *Quarterly Journal* of the Sarvajanik Sabha shows clearly the position of the Sabha's ideologues on these matters. The unsigned essay, probably written by Ranade, was titled 'The Exigencies of Progress', and pondered what it meant to be modern.[72] 'Modern civilization', it began,

> is a condition of existence in which every person is ceaselessly striving to improve his station in life, to develop his powers, to raise the standard of his comforts, and as far as he can, with reasonable sacrifices on his part, of the country or nation, with which his personal interests and the welfare of his kindred are in some measure bound up . . .[73]

To be modern meant to be pragmatic, and to challenge

> the inquisitorial power of religion, and the overpowering influence of tradition and custom, which have associated the highest ideal of happiness in our minds with in-activity [sic] and ease . . . we have stood before the world with folded hands, a picture of helplessness and despair, lost in dutiful veneration of everything pertaining to the past . . . [74]

The emphasis on practicality, on overcoming fatalism and sloth, on industrial production as an aid to material wellbeing, and the paternalistic assumption that intellectuals knew best what was good for the masses, neatly pre-figure Visvesvaraya's thoughts as he was to formulate them in the second half of his career. But it was only later, when he went to Mysore and began to express himself more on issues of policy and administration at the top levels, that the lessons absorbed at the feet of the Poona Liberals would be deployed more directly.

For the moment, there was another strand of Ranade's thought that had a more direct bearing on Visvesvaraya's career. This was their shared interest in the modernization of agriculture. Ranade's worldview was deeply influenced by the experience of famines in western India in the last quarter of the nineteenth century.[75] As Visvesvaraya's work took him across the agrarian districts of the Deccan and Gujarat, he began to think carefully about the role of irrigation in making agriculture more productive and insulating the peasant from the vagaries of climate. From the late 1890s, Visvesvaraya's professional work in Poona would be centred on these questions.

5

Transforming Irrigation in the Deccan

In 1896–7, the Bombay Presidency was dealt a triple blow. Plague broke out in the cities of Bombay and Poona, spreading gradually to the hinterlands. Cholera was an ever-present danger. To cap it all, the monsoon failed. Harvests everywhere suffered, leading to famine. The Deccan, in particular, was severely affected.[1]

Famines in colonial India were accompanied by the collapse of local economies; farm labourers and village artisans were the worst hit. The usual response of provincial governments was to commission relief works—public construction projects undertaken primarily to provide paying work for those who had lost their sources of subsistence. These were organized in line with the Famine Codes, put in place by the influential Famine Commission of 1880. Underlying the codes was '[t]he idea of preventing famines by generating purchasing power in affected areas and letting private trade supply the food'. The government, wedded as it was to laissez faire economics, would not participate in the procurement of crop or the regulation of prices.[2]

In some districts of the Deccan, labourers broke rocks to produce metalling for roads; in others, they helped lay railway lines. But officials increasingly veered around to the view that the best relief works were large-scale projects in which workers, living on site in labour camps, helped build reservoirs for irrigation. These projects would help save crops in future drought years; they were also considered a more efficient way to provide paying work to those who really needed it. (Other kinds of relief work could be undertaken by walking a few miles from one's village each day, and officials did not want to encourage those with other means of survival to join these works to supplement their income.)

As of 1897, thirteen irrigation works were in progress in Bombay's Central Division, with dozens more under consideration. Labourers on the larger works lived in huts in grid-like settlements. Often, entire families laboured on these projects, including children as young as seven years old. Dependants were sometimes paid an allowance, and in other cases, given food. The works were managed mostly by the engineers and subordinates of the Public Works Department.[3]

Visvesvaraya would have been well acquainted with such sites: between 1897 and 1899, he worked near the summit of the bureaucracy in charge of relief irrigation works in the Deccan, the most severely affected region in the Bombay Presidency. As a special assistant to three different superintending engineers and one chief engineer of the Central Division (an administrative unit within the presidency), he scrutinized and helped to further develop proposals submitted for irrigation projects throughout the division.[4]

The experience of famine work no doubt left an impression on Visvesvaraya. More generally, discussions on famine and its prevention were a part of the organizational culture he was steeped in, for the Deccan—an arid region with unpredictable rainfall—frequently faced the prospect of drought.[5] When, a couple of years later, Visvesvaraya was placed in charge of irrigation in the Poona district, these issues were at the centre of the official discourse on irrigation.

*

The events of 1896–97 were not an aberration: famine shadowed British India throughout the nineteenth century. In the second half of the century alone, there were no fewer than twenty-four severe famines along the length and breadth of the country. Among the regions afflicted were Orissa (1866–67); Rajputana (1868–70); Bihar and Bengal (1873–74); and—in what became known as 'The Great Famine'—Bombay and much of southern India (1876–78).[6]

On the face of it, famines were caused by failures of the monsoon, on which Indian agriculture was heavily dependent. But an equally important cause was the dereliction of traditional systems of irrigation in the period after the East India Company took over vast swathes of the subcontinent. As the authority of indigenous elites dwindled, they were unable to perform their traditional functions of maintaining and protecting the decentralized networks of canals and embankments that served local cultivators.[7]

Faced with famines, the colonial government doubled down on its efforts to modernize. Where it had earlier tried to cut out traditional elites, historian Jon Wilson argues, the state now sought to bypass the people entirely, and 'impose [its] power directly over the region's natural resources'. This it would do by turning to technology, using large-scale centralized irrigation works to subdue and harness the waters of the subcontinent. The process began with the ambitious work of the military engineer Arthur Cotton, who built a barrage (1852) on the river Godavari and a network of canals in its delta, and was lionized for converting the basin into a prosperous agricultural region. After the war of 1857, when the British Crown took over from the East India Company, these efforts were intensified.[8] In the decades that followed, the state wrought a dramatic change in the hydraulic landscape of the subcontinent. Across the country, new canal networks were built. In some cases, they replaced older methods of irrigation in existing agricultural areas. In other regions, such as the Punjab, barren, pastoral lands were transformed into 'canal colonies', while the control of water resources grew more and more centralized, handled largely by the emerging bureaucracy of the Public Works Department, which was established in the 1850s.[9]

Clearly, the spectre of famine loomed large in the minds of colonial policymakers. In a bravura passage, the economist Jean Drèze lists some of the reasons for this:

> The desire to preserve political stability or the revenue base, a feeling of obligation to the people arising from the more obviously deleterious aspects of colonial expansion (such as the ruin of the weaving industry), the so-called 'weight of irresponsible public opinion in England', concern with the administration's image in the eyes of the British public, and genuine humanitarian concern, may all have played a more or less important role.[10]

In essence, colonial officials began to view irrigation through a dual lens. On the one hand, it was a means to avert famine; on the other, a means to improve agricultural productivity (and with it the revenue accruing to the state). This distinction was codified into government policy in the aftermath of the Famine Commission Report of 1880, when the Government of India classified irrigation works as 'productive' and 'protective'.

Productive works were new dam-and-canal projects designed to bring large areas under the cultivation of crops with a high market value. These included wheat, sugarcane, rice, and cotton, and were referred to as *perennial crops*, as they needed water throughout the year.

Protective works, on the other hand, were only meant 'to be supplementary [to rainfall], enough to save the traditional food crop during a drought', and hence 'were not required to pay back interest on capital expenditure'. These crops included grains like millets, bajra, and jowar, and were also known as *dry crops* (as they were traditionally rain-fed and did not use artificial irrigation). Protective works included not only the thousands of tanks that dotted the peninsula—some of them pre-dating colonial rule by centuries—but also new reservoir-cum-canal projects undertaken specifically to provide an insurance against famine.[11]

In practice, though, the colonial-era protective works faced many challenges. In the basin of the river Krishna, stretching across large parts of the Indian peninsula, the long canal systems were designed to spread small amounts of water across thousands of square kilometres, so that they could safeguard as many lands as possible in the event of drought. But they proved largely ineffective. In years of regular rainfall, the majority of the cultivators, who grew dry crops like sorghum, had no need for the canal water; so the water was taken mostly by cultivators closer to the headworks, who used them for wet crops. Unfortunately, when drought did occur, canal managers, facing pressure from these wealthy farmers, were unable or unwilling to divert water to growers of dry crops, whose fields were situated at the lower ends of the canals.[12] The result was that these irrigation works were neither very remunerative for the state, nor very effective in relieving the effects of drought. In the Deccan, the Nira Left Bank Canal, a protective work built in the 1870s and '80s, was able to serve only 'between 16 and 46 per cent of the total irrigable area' in the following decade, achieving a maximum return of 1.4 per cent on the capital invested.[13]

*

Around the turn of the twentieth century, then, the question of protective works was being discussed actively in the Bombay PWD.[14] At this time, Visvesvaraya received his first promotion to a higher rank. In 1899, he was appointed executive engineer and made responsible for the Poona Irrigation District, 'the principal irrigation district then in the Bombay Presidency excluding Sind'. This meant he oversaw, among other things, the functioning of the Nira and Mutha Canals; he also managed the water supply to the cantonments in Poona and nearby Kirkee, and to parts of the city of Poona.[15]

1899 was also the year Lord Curzon took over as Viceroy of India. Struck by the still visible effects of famine across India, he appointed, in 1901, a high-powered 'special Commission to report on the Irrigation of India as a protection against famine'. The Indian Irrigation Commission, as it was known, was to conduct an exhaustive assessment of the different kinds of irrigation works built by the government across India, and the feasibility of establishing more such works.[16] The commission was presided over by Colonel Sir Colin Scott-Moncrieff, a sixty-five-year-old ex-military engineer who had served long years on irrigation works in India and Egypt. Among its other members were Sir Thomas Higham, Inspector-General of Irrigation for India; Denzil Ibbetson, a highly regarded ICS officer serving as Chief Commissioner of the Central Provinces; and Dewan Bahadur P. Rajaratna Mudaliar, a member of the Madras Legislative Council.[17]

In the Bombay Presidency, the Irrigation Commission chose to visit the Poona Irrigation District. As the officer responsible for the district, Visvesvaraya was required to provide the commission with background information. He took the opportunity to produce a detailed 'Memorandum on Irrigation Works in the Bombay Presidency, Excluding Sind'. This was a revised version of a note he had first written a few years earlier, partly under the tutelage of R. Joyner, one of the superintending engineers he had worked with during the famine.[18]

The memo gave a comprehensive picture of irrigation in the Gujarat and Deccan regions. Visvesvaraya was particularly concerned that the Government of India considered Bombay Presidency's irrigation works inefficient—as they generated a lower rate of revenue than those in other provinces—and was sensitive about the light in which this cast the public works engineers of the presidency. His purpose, then, was to highlight the challenges faced by the PWD's engineers, to explain why Bombay's irrigation works were less remunerative than those in other provinces, and to suggest improvements based on his experience. The memo was simultaneously a defence of the province, an indictment of what he saw as mistaken measures in the past, and a meditation on irrigation policy at the pan-Indian level. It was lawyer-like in its marshalling of facts and figures to make these points.[19]

Visvesvaraya began by giving an exhaustive list of reasons why Bombay's irrigation returns were low. Some of these were related to the special topographical and climatic conditions in the Deccan. The rocky terrain made the building of canals a costly exercise. Black soil, which was native to the region, was not particularly amenable to irrigation as it tended to trap too much moisture. Unlike the sub-Himalayan provinces with their snow-fed rivers, the Bombay Presidency did not have mighty perennial rivers, which meant storage tanks had to be built to capture water in the rainy season.[20] Considerations such as these had not been kept in mind while constructing protective works in Bombay, most of which had been undertaken hurriedly as famine-relief projects.[21]

Visvesvaraya also saw the mindset of the cultivators—often stemming from financial compulsions—as a stumbling block in the rational use of irrigation works. They opted for canal water only at the eleventh hour, when they were convinced that rain was not going to arrive (and then usually overwatered their fields). The terrain was irregular, and farmers usually didn't want to go the trouble and expense of preparing the soil and digging ditches to convey the canal water to their fields. Further, the indebted peasants of the Deccan couldn't afford to buy manure, which had to be added to black soil for perennial crops.[22]

Finally, he described in great detail, with the aid of comparative statistics, how the vagaries of 'the system of administration, accounts and assessments' contributed to Bombay's returns appearing in a poor light.[23]

Crucially, Visvesvaraya argued that protective works were being evaluated on the returns they provided, whereas 'both during construction and maintenance [these] works subserve . . . a wide variety of purposes of public policy and civil administration' (such as serving as famine-relief works and providing water to save food crops in times of drought).[24] As he explained later, water had to be kept in storage every year on the off-chance that the monsoon might fail and food crops would need the water; but in a year of regular rainfall, this only meant that the perennial crops like sugarcane (which were charged more for irrigation water and were also more commercially valuable) were deprived of water. As we shall see below, he favoured the reverse approach: determine in advance the area under sugarcane to be given water, and divert some of that water for dry crops in the event of famine.[25]

In other words, while Visvesvaraya acknowledged that there was a need for more protective works to safeguard the Deccan from famine, he leaned towards a productive philosophy. This gave rise to the two-pronged approach he proposed. First, the government should build new works to extend irrigation in the region. He recommended '[a]n annual outlay of from 6 to ten lakhs, or about 2 [per cent] on the land revenue of the Presidency' and that the government 'lay down a definite policy in this respect for, say, ten years at a time'.[26] Second, while these works would provide insurance in famine years, they ought to be used productively in years of regular rainfall. Indeed, he argued,

> A 'Productive Work' is also largely 'Protective.' If a work is managed so as to get the best return from it every year, not merely as a reserve for the protection of ordinary crops in seasons of drought, the wealth produced in normal seasons will help to mitigate distress in times of scarcity.[27]

Or, as he put it later in his personal testimony to the Irrigation Commission, the optimum strategy to prevent famine was to manage the works

> . . . on 'productive' lines; we should not lock up water on the chance of a famine; we should every year make an estimate of the water available for high class crops, and in famine years make some concession in favour of dry crops[.][28]

This was easier said than done. How should one make the same work serve both protective and productive functions? This question led to the most important portion of Visvesvaraya's memo. Here he articulated the first version of what would later develop into his 'block system' of irrigation.

Under this system, which Visvesvaraya drew up based on his observation of traditional practices on pre-colonial irrigation works in the Nasik and Khandesh regions, one-third of the available canal water in each year would be guaranteed for perennial crops. These would be grown in areas marked off in each village for a period of six years at a time, known as the 'fixed' areas. The remaining two-thirds of water would be kept for the rest of the lands, which would be divided into 'permissible' and 'dry-crop' areas. Cultivators could use the 'permissible' areas to grow sugarcane, and could buy canal water in non-drought years. In a drought year, they would be obliged to water this area from wells in their fields, which would leave two-thirds of the total canal water available to safeguard the food crops in the 'dry-crop' areas.[29]

*

Visvesvaraya's memorandum was ambitious, far-reaching, and based on serious study. Recognizing this, the Indian Irrigation Commission spent a significant amount of time examining him in person when their investigations brought them to Poona. The interview, which took place on 20 December 1901, ran to no less than 358 numbered exchanges.[30]

Visvesvaraya was firm and extraordinarily confident. He was a relatively junior officer, having spent less than three years as executive engineer, but he parleyed on terms of professional parity with the distinguished commissioners, who had been appointed personally by the viceroy.[31] He did not hesitate to contradict the views of his bureaucratic superiors where necessary. At one point he even turned interrogator, asking Chairman Scott-Moncrieff to clarify his assumptions, and walking him through the implications.[32]

Visvesvaraya was questioned closely on the details of his memorandum, but he also spoke freely on matters that were, strictly speaking, outside his purview. Stressing his philosophy of irrigation, he went so far as to tell his interviewers that in his experience,

> each work is judged by its direct productive value, and if this [is] unsatisfactory the Government of India will hesitate to grant funds, no matter how strong the recommendations of the [Irrigation] Commission may be. Sound finance is the test of success in irrigation as in every other public department and our first concern should be to show a good return . . . Financial considerations are everything.

To which Scott-Moncrieff, whose commission had been instructed to place the avoidance of famine above matters of revenue, replied: 'We would not be here if financial considerations were everything.' Visvesvaraya was unfazed by the rebuff. Speaking of the main protective work under his direct supervision, he said: 'I guarantee that if I am given a chance to work the Nira Canal on our own lines, we will make it pay the full interest on the capital outlay; but there are two things necessary: we must be given more money and allowed to work on our own lines.'[33]

The publication of these exchanges caused great excitement among the Indian intelligentsia. One chronicler writes that Visvesvaraya's views were 'emblazoned in the press', and argues that 'Visvesvaraya was, so to say, speaking as a technical tribune of the Indian people before the Commission which had to shape the future destinies of the irrigation works in India'.[34]

In fact, it was not just Visvesvaraya's testimony that was reported in the mainstream press; other engineers were quoted too, including Indians.[35] However, it is clear that few had thought through the problems of irrigation as painstakingly as he had, or articulated their opinions with the same frankness as he did in what was 'the longest and perhaps the most searching interrogation by the Commission in India'. What is more, the symbolic importance of the event was unmistakable. Here was a young Indian, at a time when Indians were hardly credited as competent engineers, exhibiting an uncommon degree of confidence and self-worth.[36]

But not all Visvesvaraya's professional colleagues were impressed, especially some of his British superiors in the PWD. In 1902, a number of engineers from the Bombay PWD submitted to the secretary of the department their responses to Visvesvaraya's memorandum. One of them, the superintending engineer on the Indus Left Bank Division in Sind, declared that the memo was 'of a fragmentary character and loosely put together'. He considered Visvesvaraya's recommendations for fresh irrigation works grandiose. Ironically, he used Visvesvaraya's own language of financial soundness to criticize them. 'By all means prospect for likely schemes,' this official wrote, 'but some regard must be had for cost, working expenses and possible return. Such visionary ideas as very large canals from the ghauts out into the famine zone costing fabulous sums and requiring large annual expenditure which would probably not nearly be covered by the return in ordinary years are quite useless for practical purposes.'

As for the system of 'fixed' blocks, the Sind-based superintending engineer argued that the government could not just mark out blocks and distribute the land among farmers. 'In former days these things were done by an executive order—what would now be termed "Zoolum" [tyranny] . . . Mr: Visvesvaraya has utopian ideas if he imagines that any owner of land at the head of a canal will willingly give it up so that all the people of the village may share in the benefit of the water, and it is easy to imagine the outcry of the "people's representatives" [most likely a reference to Indian politicians] if any attempt were made to enforce this by legislative action or otherwise.' The concluding remarks were damning: 'Mr: Visvesvaraya writes rather as an Irrigation fanatic and particularly as an apologist for the Deccan works, and except as showing that he takes a keen interest in his duty his memorandum has I think but little practical value.'[37]

Other British engineers were more temperate in their comments, expressing broad agreement, making additional points, or countering the odd contention in the memo.[38] Among those who furnished their opinions was H.G. Palliser—Visvesvaraya's first boss in the PWD and now chief engineer in the Indus Right Bank Division—who remarked that 'the subject' had been 'ably and thoughtfully dealt with by my old pupil, Mr. M. Visvesvaraya'.[39] It is unlikely that Visvesvaraya got to see this remark, but it was a poignant one in the light of his run-in with Palliser nearly two decades previously.

Enthusiastic support came from Visvesvaraya's contemporary from the Poona College of Science, Parshuram Krishna Chitale,[40] who was now serving as executive engineer on the Jamrao Canal in Sind.[41] Chitale seemed particularly taken by Visvesvaraya's proposed block system, modelled on the *thal* system. He painted an idyllic picture of the traditional irrigation systems of the Deccan while developing a scathing critique of British irrigation policies in the region. When the British first took over parts of the subcontinent, he noted, they built works on the Godavari and Krishna in the south, and on the Ganges in the north. They then extended 'the same system . . . in the designing and the management of the irrigation works in this [Bombay] Presidency. Sufficient attention was not paid to the varying conditions of the climate and the soil and the old irrigation works existing in the country were not properly studied. It is therefore no wonder,' he declared, 'if the forecasts made proved wrong and the works have come to be looked on with disfavour by the Government of India.'

In the traditional system of irrigation, Chitale wrote, 'the supply is concentrated for irrigating the best paying crops such as sugarcane and rice'; now, however, 'it is spread over a very large area, not more than a third of which can be irrigated from it annually and that too mostly under light crops which could bear only moderate assessment'. Visvesvaraya's suggested system, modelled as it was on the older philosophy, was 'eminently suitable'. Chitale did, however, have reservations (like others) over the feasibility of winning the cooperation of the cultivators, especially those whose lands were situated near the head of a canal. Such landowners might 'try to rack-rent [their lands] to their neighbours or to the highest bidders'. This would endanger the entire system, as those who rented the lands would have little money left over to spend on manure, without which the crops would fail. Chitale thought the solution might be to legislate to get 'the lands so selected for continuous irrigation and redistribute them amongst the villagers as they did in olden times'.[42]

*

Encouraged by the Irrigation Commission (and undaunted by his colleagues' critiques, if indeed he was informed of them), Visvesvaraya sat down to work out the details of his proposed block system. He did so for three irrigation projects in Poona District, the most important of which was the Nira Canal, a large protective work. In April 1903, he had the resulting scheme printed and circulated.[43]

To his earlier system of fixed, permissible and dry-crop areas, he now made some modifications and added further features. A number of *blocks*, similar to the fixed areas he had earlier proposed, would be marked off in each village, and canal water could be supplied only to land within these blocks. One-third of each block would be dedicated to perennial crops like sugarcane. This area would get canal water throughout the year. Fields in the other two-thirds of the block would grow food crops and vegetables, and would only get canal water for eight months a year, i.e., from July through February. The area under sugarcane would be rotated from year to year within the block, helping keep the soil fresh.[44] This can be explained based on the following diagram:

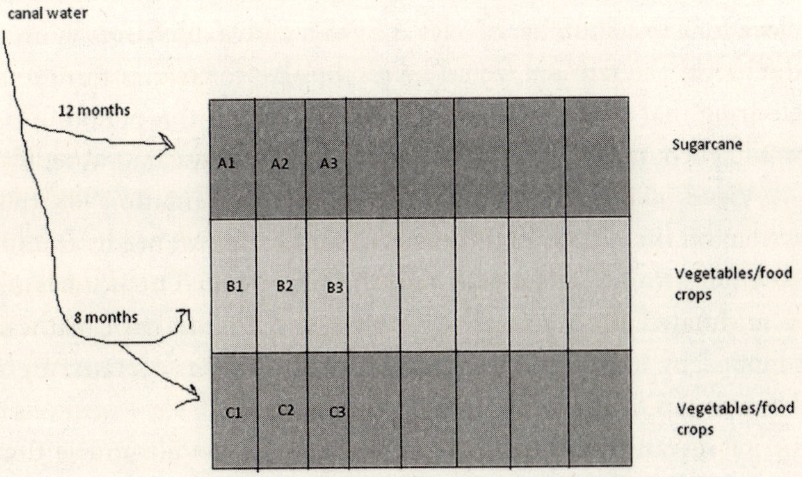

Fig. 5.1. Visvesvaraya's Block System of irrigation

Figure represents author's understanding.

In this figure, the entire rectangle represents a single block. Individual farmers' fields are designated A1 to An, B1 to Bn, C1 to Cn. In the first year under the block system, the region A is earmarked for sugarcane and the regions B and C for vegetables or food crops. Sugarcane is grown in region B in the second year and region C in the third year before reverting to region A in the fourth year. In this way, Visvesvaraya argued, '[t]here will . . . be a sort of triennial crop rotation in each block'.

All those with farms leased within the block would be required to pay 'a fixed rate per acre irrespective of the crop grown'.[45] This differed from the old system whereby each farmer would have a revenue official assess how many acres of land he had used for which crop, and then be charged a crop-specific rate per acre.

Blocks would be assigned for a period of six years at a time, and the farmers within each block would commit to buying canal water for that duration. This would reduce enormously the number of applications and the resulting paperwork for the PWD.[46]

The amount of water being released to each block would be measured—or, more precisely, the water would be given to each block for a fixed number of days at a given rate of discharge. Within the block, the farmers would be responsible for taking turns and ensuring that all their fields were watered within this period. This would encourage them to be watchful and avoid wasting water.[47]

Visvesvaraya next turned to the implementation of this system on the Nira Canal. This canal ran for a distance of around 100 miles from its headworks on the river Nira. The headworks were situated at a place called Virwadi near Poona; the canal was supplied by a storage tank named Lake Whiting, created by a dam around fifteen miles from Virwadi.[48]

Visvesvaraya proposed to apply the block system to the first sixty-five miles served by the Nira Canal. Thirty villages in this stretch would account for a total of 18,000 acres under blocks, which meant the total area of sugarcane cultivation in the blocks would be 6,000 acres. On average, each village would have 600 acres under blocks.

Of the 5,313 million cubic feet of water that could be stored in Lake Whiting, 2,900 million cubic feet (around 55 per cent by volume) would be allotted to the blocks. The villages left out of the block system—those at the lower end of the canal—would have first right over 'the surplus monsoon and rabi supply'. These villages would also be assured of canal water in the monsoon and rabi seasons.[49]

A two-member committee would be set up to mark out the blocks and assign them to cultivators. One member should be a PWD officer (possibly an assistant engineer), and the other an officer of the Revenue Department (called a *mamlatdar*). They would receive additional help in each village from a five-member council 'consisting of three persons from the village and two private gentlemen of standing, and interested in agriculture, within the taluka'.[50]

The sensitive question that remained to be discussed was how the lands *within* each block should be divided among individual cultivators. The cultivators whose existing lands fell within the blocks would have the opportunity to grow sugarcane, but what of those whose fields fell outside the blocks? After consulting revenue and irrigation officers as well as prominent farmers, Visvesvaraya came up with a solution. Farmers who did not own land within the blocks, he said, should be allowed to lease it from the official owners for a fixed period of time, or swap their lands with them temporarily. Each village would have to come to an internal agreement in this regard.[51]

*

Having concluded its investigations across the subcontinent, the Irrigation Commission published a compendious report in 1903.

The sections dealing with the Deccan clearly echoed Visvesvaraya's thinking in many respects, and on some points gave him a direct and ringing endorsement. The commission recommended the building of new storage tanks in the ghat regions, as Visvesvaraya had suggested in his memo of 1901.[52] They also concluded, as he had, that protective works needed to be run on a more commercial basis. It was now possible, they noted, to transport food to famine-struck regions; so the people were better off maximizing their cultivation of revenue-generating crops like sugarcane or cotton, which they could sell in times of distress and buy food grain from other areas. '[I]n the long run the cultivators may be trusted to know their interests better than the authorities.'[53]

The commission also backed Visvesvaraya's proposed block system. Through this system, 'no individual owner would be able to appropriate permanently or continuously more than his fair share of the supply; and apart from the more equal distribution of water, a substantial reduction might be effected in the cost of revenue management, as the disposal of applications, and the subsequent inspection and measurement of irrigated areas, would be greatly facilitated'.[54] They suggested that the Bombay government should 'give the system . . . an early and thorough trial'.[55]

While cultivators under the block system would be charged a fixed rate for canal water supplied to each block, this did not mean an indefinite amount of water would be given. The existing device that was used to divert water from the canals towards irrigated lands was called a 'gated pipe outlet'. Operated manually, the flow depended on the 'head' or difference in water level on either side of the gate, and could not be controlled or measured easily. Instead, Visvesvaraya had suggested the use of a contraption called a 'module'. This was to be designed in such a way that it would work independently of the head, and could be used to measure and standardize the amount of water supplied to the blocks. (As we shall see in the next chapter, Visvesvaraya tried to design just such a module.) Over time, the farmers would get a sense of how much water they had a right to. This was part of a long-term plan espoused by the Irrigation Commission—to shift to a system of charging for water by volume.[56]

In a resolution dated 17 December 1903, the Bombay PWD approved a trial of Visvesvaraya's block system in up to ten villages on the Nira Canal and in the land under a couple of tanks in the Deccan. The resolution recorded that the Governor of Bombay 'desire[d] . . . to express to [Visvesvaraya] his appreciation of the great care with which the proposed scheme has been worked out and of the zeal displayed in its inception and preparation'.[57]

In 1904, a committee was appointed to help Visvesvaraya demarcate the blocks. It consisted of W.G. Rale, a *mamlatdar*, and N.V. Barve, an engineering subordinate from the PWD.[58] In June, Visvesvaraya issued a comprehensive set of directions for the committee.[59] He also engaged personally with the issue of legalizing the new system, writing on the subject to the Superintending Engineer of the Central Division.[60] The Remembrancer of Legal Affairs worked with Visvesvaraya in drafting the necessary new rules.[61]

By October 1904, the committee had completed their work of allocating blocks in four villages, and made progress in some others. Visvesvaraya reported that the officers had 'found . . . that there was no occasion to appoint a *Panch* [five-member council] as no difficulty was experienced in making the cultivators agree among themselves'. He urged that orders be passed to inaugurate the system by January 1905 (when the sugarcane crop would next be sown). He even had the self-confidence to push for extending the scheme from the ten villages originally sanctioned to all thirty villages along the Nira Canal, enabling 'the system [to] have the thorough trial which the Irrigation Commission recommended in . . . their report'.[62]

*

By early 1907, blocks had been allocated in all thirty villages. Although Visvesvaraya resigned from the Bombay PWD in 1909 (more on this in the next chapter), the system became entrenched in the administrative practices of the irrigation bureaucracy. Over the next decade and a half, it resulted in the spectacular growth of sugarcane cultivation. It was also a huge financial success. The Nira Canal, which had yielded a 1.5 per cent return on investment in 1899–1900, gave an 8.28 per cent return in 1922–23. In the words of anthropologist Donald Attwood, 'few administrative reforms can have been so timely and effective, both in stimulating increased production and repaying public investment'.[63]

According to Attwood, who spent decades studying the agrarian landscape of Maharashtra, the block system also helped stave off famines in some of the ways Visvesvaraya and the Irrigation Commission had envisioned. Food production increased, as the manuring and soil preparation undertaken for sugarcane cultivation in the blocks indirectly helped the food crops grown there as part of the stipulated crop rotation. The expanding sugarcane production also required the use of more bullocks; this in turn boosted the production of sorghum, which could be used as cattle fodder. Meanwhile, year-round cultivation under canal irrigation created tens of thousands of jobs in the form of hired agricultural labour. Moreover, increased efficiency in the use of water under the block system allowed the government to invest in further irrigation projects. The result, Attwood observed, was that 'though the Deccan Canals were no longer regarded as purely protective works, they helped famine-proof the region to an extent which had been impossible under the older, extensive irrigation policy'.[64]

Behind these successes, however, lay several complications. From the outset, the block system did not work exactly as Visvesvaraya had envisaged it. Researchers Alex Bolding, Peter Mollinga, and Kees van Straaten have detailed the ways in which it departed from the ideal. For one thing, the blocks were not in reality as consolidated as Visvesvaraya had hoped, since officials had to accommodate most lands that previously grew sugarcane, even if they were not adjacent to each other. As a consequence, it became difficult to restrict sugarcane cultivation to one-third of the block areas. It also became more challenging to regulate the distribution of water. Furthermore, Visvesvaraya and his fellow irrigation engineers failed to create a satisfactory module that could discharge fixed amounts of water. This meant other methods of regulating the water distribution had to be tried. These included the appointment of officials called *patkari*s, who would manually let the water into individual fields. The result was that the Irrigation Commission's aim of moving to a system of charging for water by volume was not realized.[65]

By 1910, when the first six-year lease for blocks ended, other problems were noted. The new system resulted in—or at any rate failed to prevent—salinity and waterlogging in the fields within the blocks. Farmers whose lands were in the blocks became disproportionately powerful; some were even able to coerce or influence the *patkaris* to supply their blocks with extra water. Later observers noted that those with lands in the blocks were very reluctant to swap them with others in the village (as Visvesvaraya had suggested they do from time to time), 'partly because the cultivators had a natural ingrained attachment to their ancestral acres, and partly because it was realised that land in a block was potentially far more valuable than land outside a block'.[66] In a sharp critique of the system, historian Raj Sekhar Basu also notes that the involvement of a village *panch* in the assigning of blocks was likely to favour the local elites. Furthermore, Visvesvaraya had declared imperiously that recalcitrant landowners should be excluded from the blocks. The result, Basu writes, was that the block system became 'essentially an arrangement for safeguarding the interests of the rich farming lobby, wholly engaged with the production of commercial crops'.[67]

Despite these challenges, however, it was soon apparent that the system was going to boost revenues to the state. As early as 1906–07, the Nira Canal gave a return of 3.5 per cent on capital expenditure, more than ever before.[68] Over time, the block system also reduced overheads in the distribution of water, and introduced a sense of stability. Farmers, knowing they were guaranteed water for a period of years, invested in preparing their fields.[69] Loath to give up a system that was so profitable, the government made several adjustments to the block system in an attempt to address the various issues it threw up. In an effort to address the problems of drainage, the PWD undertook soil studies, which enabled them to understand what methods of drainage would work on which lands, and informed the selection of block areas for sugarcane in subsequent iterations.[70] Although farmers in some places resisted or subverted the block system, it was not only continued on the Nira Canal but also extended, by the 1920s, to other parts of the Deccan such as the Pravara Canal and other canals in the Godavari basin.[71] By the late 1930s, it was in vogue on 'four of the six major irrigation schemes' in the Deccan.[72]

Over the decades, several commissions and studies in colonial and post-Independence India—when these areas came under the state of Bombay and later Maharashtra—looked into the system of irrigation in the Deccan. (One of these was chaired by Visvesvaraya himself, now a venerable septuagenarian, in 1938; see Chapter 20 below.) While some suggested alternate forms of irrigation that would prioritize food crops, others proposed minor modifications in the block system. In the 1990s, when Alex Bolding and Kees van Straaten visited the Nira Canal, the block system was still in operation.[73]

*

Although the block system never took on the exact character Visvesvaraya had had in mind, it did, in the long run, alter the agricultural landscape of the Bombay Deccan. There are differing views on whether it exacerbated social inequality—in contrast to Basu, Attwood insists that it did not disenfranchise the peasantry—but it is clear that it paved the way for the creation of a sugar belt in the Deccan and brought prosperity to the region as a whole.[74]

The block system is mentioned in every resumé of Visvesvaraya's career, but few accounts give a sense of its scope and significance. The specialist literature on irrigation, on the other hand, recognizes the importance of this intervention. It was by no means a de novo invention. As was noted at the time, the system itself was based on Visvesvaraya's observation of a traditional system in use on pre-colonial irrigation works. Moreover, some features of the block system were similar to a system used on certain canals in Bengal.[75] Visvesvaraya's thinking was conditioned by his professional environment, and others in the Bombay Presidency, notably his superior H.F. Beale, had had similar thoughts about the need to run the protective works on a more commercial basis.[76]

Nevertheless, Visvesvaraya was the one who came up with a way of translating these ideas into practice. Few of his colleagues matched the persistence of his advocacy or the vigour with which he worked to see the new system implemented. Add to this the context in which he worked, where independence of thought from an Indian subordinate was not often taken kindly to, and it becomes clear why Visvesvaraya's reputation was already on the rise by the time he was forty.

Visvesvaraya's approach to irrigation also set the tone for his later engagements with public policy. While his language did not quite drip with empathy for the impoverished and famine-prone peasants of his district, he was nevertheless concerned with improving their material circumstances. The means he advocated, however, were market-based. In the process, he devised a system which—although it theoretically democratized access to irrigation water and sugarcane cultivation—evolved to support a capitalist mode of agriculture. And this would not have concerned him unduly, for he believed in what we would now call the 'trickle-down effect': if the overall prosperity of the province increased, the lives of the poorest would also improve.

6

Poona's All-Rounder

The public works engineers of colonial India were trained to be generalists. Their work covered a gamut of tasks. They constructed and maintained roads, official buildings, and irrigation works. They also had to be adept at bureaucratic and managerial tasks—maintaining accounts, dealing with subordinates and contractors, and liaising with private engineering firms.[1]

In the decade after he took over as executive engineer in Poona, Visvesvaraya's resumé was very much in line with this ideal. The block system may have been his most enduring contribution to public works in the Deccan, but it was by no means the only project he worked on while he was there. Visvesvaraya also designed or improved—albeit with varying levels of success—mechanical devices meant to automate portions of the irrigation infrastructure. In addition, he established himself as an authority in the related but parallel field of sanitary engineering, contributing to the design of water supply and drainage works for several cities. As a result, he rose in the hierarchy of the Public Works Department, enjoyed good relations with his British superiors, was given special assignments, won honours, and became, if not a pillar of the Poona establishment, at least a recognizable component of it. And yet—as we shall see—he ended the decade yearning for something more.

*

In his extensive memorandum submitted to the Irrigation Commission in 1901, one of the points Visvesvaraya had stressed was the need to improve the storage capacity of the irrigation works in the Bombay Presidency.[2] The construction of new storage tanks would depend on the government's ability and willingness to sanction substantial funds. Meanwhile, Visvesvaraya concentrated on trying to optimize the functioning of existing reservoirs.

Chief among these reservoirs were Lake Fife and Lake Whiting, built by the Bombay government in the late nineteenth century. They were named after J.G. Fife and J.E. Whiting, the British military engineers who had spearheaded the respective projects.

Lake Fife was the reservoir of a dam built at Khadakwasla, some ten miles to the south-west of Poona. Traversing the river Mutha, the masonry dam rose ninety-nine feet above the river bed and was 5136 feet long. Its reservoir was the starting point of the Mutha Canals, which were used not only for irrigation but also to supply water to Poona city and the cantonment at Kirkee.

Lake Whiting, on the other hand, was the reservoir formed by the 127-foot-high, 4067-foot-long dam (also of masonry) constructed on the river Yelwandi—a tributary of the river Nira—at Bhatghar, around thirty miles to the south of Poona. It fed the Nira Canal system. As of the early twentieth century, Lake Whiting was the second-largest reservoir in India.[3]

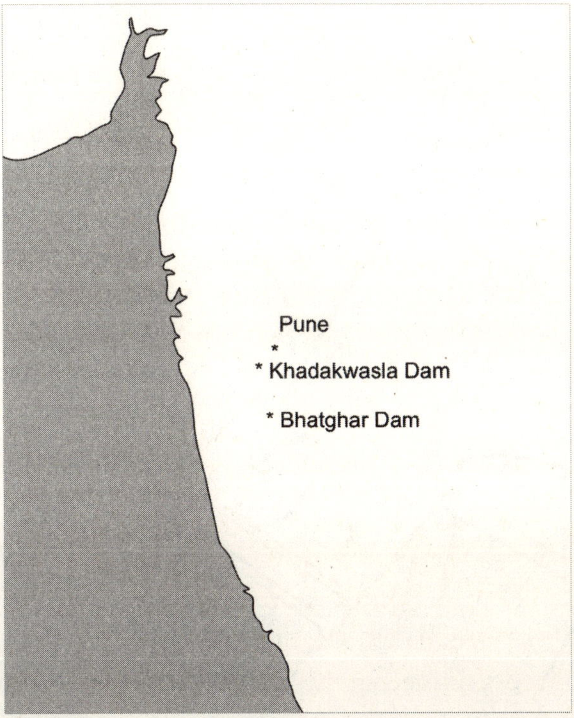

Fig. 6.1. Location of Bhatghar and Khadakwasla dams in relation to Poona (now Pune)

Figure 6.2 shows a schematic diagram of a generic dam. The dam wall serves to impound water, which can then be diverted for irrigation, hydroelectric power generation, or other uses. Dams also include one or more structures called spillways, which function as safety valves. When, as in the rainy season, the water upstream rises beyond a safe level, the spillway allows the excess water to flow downstream. Usually, it takes the form of a weir, which, in its basic form, is a wall built perpendicular to the direction of the flow of water. As can be seen in the figure, this weir (referred to as a surplus weir or waste weir) rises to a lower height than the wall of the dam.

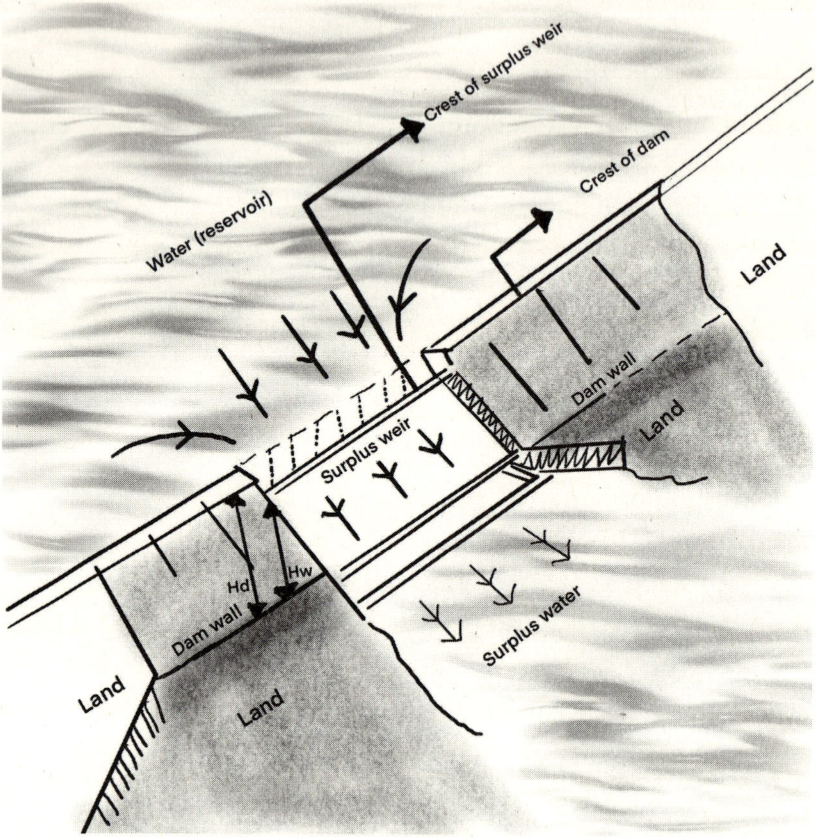

Fig. 6.2. Schematic diagram showing surplus weir of a dam. Gates are shown with dotted lines

Source: Figure adapted from illustration on p. 2 of 'Term Definitions', at the website of the Wisconsin Department of Natural Resources (https://dnr.wi.gov/topic/Dams/documents/TermDefinitions.pdf, accessed 5 March 2021).

The dams at Bhatghar and Khadakwasla had such waste weirs, which prevented flooding during storms or periods of high rainfall. The problem was that in other seasons, their presence reduced the storage capacity of the lake. For although the wall of a dam (whose height is marked as H_d in Figure 6.2) may be several metres higher than its waste weir (with height H_w), it is the latter that determines the maximum water level that can be held in the lake. Thus, at times when the water is not in danger of overtopping the dam wall, the surplus weir can effectively reduce the capacity of the reservoir by several thousand million cubic feet.

Bombay's hydraulic engineers tried various methods to overcome this disadvantage. One of these was to place planks atop the waste weir in the months after the monsoon. At this time no floods were expected, but water still flowed downstream, and the planks enabled the reservoir to hold water up to the height of the dam wall. This system, however, was risky: in the event of unforeseen or unseasonal flooding, the water would gush over the dam wall before operators had enough time to dismantle the planks.

Eventually, a consensus emerged that the best way to maximize the storage capacity of the reservoir was to place atop the crest of the waste weir a series of sluices or gates that would open and close automatically depending on the water level.[4] Such gates would be positioned as shown by the dotted lines in Figure 6.2. The height of each gate (say H_g) would be the difference between the height of the dam and that of the waste weir ($H_d - H_w$).

One of the earliest attempts at designing such gates was made by Whiting himself, who used a system of counterweights and water chambers. However, the effectiveness of his 'self-acting waste weir gate' was limited. Although it opened as required when the water rose above the height of the dam (H_d), it was slow to close, shutting only by the time the water level went down to a height of H_w + 2 feet. This meant a significant reduction in the amount of water impounded.

The next intervention came from E.K. Reinold, who had been Visvesvaraya's immediate superior during the latter's stint in the Roads and Buildings branch of the PWD (see Chapter 3 above). Although he was not part of the irrigation bureaucracy himself, Reinold devised a more sophisticated form of gate, receiving a patent in 1889. This design, which drew upon some of the principles of Whiting's earlier effort, formed the basis for the gates that were eventually installed at the Bhatghar dam in 1895.[5] Figure 6.3 shows one of the waste weirs at Bhatghar with these gates open.

Fig. 6.3. Waste weir with Reinold's gates (open) at the top, Bhatghar dam/Lake Whiting

Source: R.B. Buckley, *The Irrigation Works of India*, 2nd edition (London: E. & F. N. Spon, 1905), illustration facing p. 198.

Reinold's gates were made of iron. Each covered a sluice of dimensions 10' x 8', and weighed close to three tonnes. Each gate hung from chains attached to pulleys, balanced on the other side by a wrought iron counterweight inside a chamber. Each chamber had an inlet (facing upstream) and an outlet (facing downstream) for water to flow through. Depending on the level of water in the chamber, the counterweight sank and rose, causing the gate to open and close. The result was that the gates opened when water rose above the height of the dam, and closed when it went below that level.[6] The gates moved vertically on rollers placed on their sides, as opposed to regular sluice gates, which slid up and down an iron frame. This meant they '[had] . . . to overcome only rolling friction instead of sliding friction', resulting in an 'enormous saving in the power required to open or close the shutters'.[7]

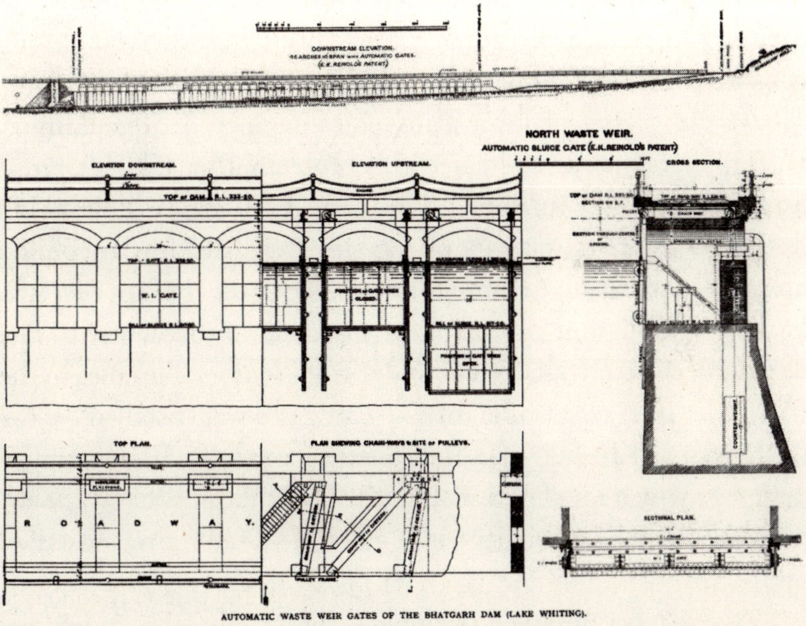

Fig. 6.4. Reinold gates at Bhatghar dam

Source: R.B. Buckley, *The Irrigation Works of India*, 2nd edition (London: E. & F. N. Spon, 1905), p. 197.

By 1895, Reinold's gates had been installed on the two waste weirs of the Bhatghar dam: forty-five automatic gates on one weir, and a further thirty-six, operated manually, on the other. The result was a 36 per cent increase in the volume of water that could be stored in Lake Whiting.[8]

Successful as they were at Bhatghar, Reinold's gates could not be used in the same form at Khadakwasla. Here, the drop just downstream of the waste weir was not steep enough to accommodate a counterweight for each gate. In addition, the creation of chambers for the counterweights would require the weir itself to be rebuilt or supplemented by an additional weir further downstream. Both were expensive propositions, as they would reduce the storage capacity of the reservoir during construction. An alternative solution had to be found.[9]

At the urging of John Tate, chief engineer in the Bombay PWD, Visvesvaraya addressed this problem after taking over as executive engineer in Poona. He worked on adapting Reinold's design to the requirements of the site at Khadakwasla, coming up with an alternative system of gates. Towards the end of 1900, he had a miniature prototype of his gates manufactured. The design received favourable comment from senior colleagues in the PWD. In 1901, a set of eight full-size gates was installed on the waste weir at Khadakwasla and tested successfully. Visvesvaraya's design provided for eleven such sets to cover the entire waste weir, bringing the total to eighty-eight gates. The full set was installed by 1903.[10]

Visvesvaraya retained Reinold's design for the individual gates: each gate was again set in a 10' x 8' sluice, and moved up and down its frames on rollers.[11] The key difference from the Bhatghar arrangement was that instead of providing a counterweight for each gate, Visvesvaraya made a single counterweight operate an entire set of eight gates. Moreover, as explained below, the gates did not all descend; instead four of them were made heavier (upwards of 100 cwts, or around five tonnes, each) and moved down, while the other four were made lighter (44 cwts, or 2.2 tonnes, each) and moved up.

Figure 6.5 shows the design of one set of eight gates. At the top of the diagram is the front view of the weir (as viewed from the upstream side). The left side of the sketch shows the gates in open position, and the right side shows them in closed position (in reality they would all be open or closed at the same time). On the downstream side of the weir, and at the centre of the set of eight gates, is a cylindrical chamber containing the counterweight. The figure also shows the aerial view of this chamber, followed by a cross-section showing the counterweight inside it.

An inlet pipe allows water from the reservoir (in this case, Lake Fife) into the chamber, and an outlet pipe allows it to flow out of the chamber on the downstream side. On either side of the chamber are two heavy gates and two light gates. Chains and pulleys are used to link the counterweight to the heavy gates, and the latter to the light gates.

The gates worked as follows. In closed position, all eight gates sat on the crest of the waste weir. When the water in Lake Fife rose to the height of the inlet valve (approximately the height of the main dam), it would enter the cylindrical chamber. When this inflow exceeded the outflow from the exit pipe on the other side, the chamber started to fill. Buoyed by the water, the counterweight began to rise. As it rose, the heavy gates, attached to it by chains, began to sink; the light gates, attached to the heavy ones, were pulled up by the chains. The result was that all eight gates were open, four going above the sluices and four below them. Water from the reservoir was now free to flow out of the sluices. Conversely, when the river fell below the highest level in the lake, water stopped entering the cylindrical chamber, and the water already inside flowed out through the outlet pipe. The counterweight now sank. By the action of the chains and pulleys, the heavy gates were pulled back upwards and the lighter gates descended, so that all of them were shut once more.

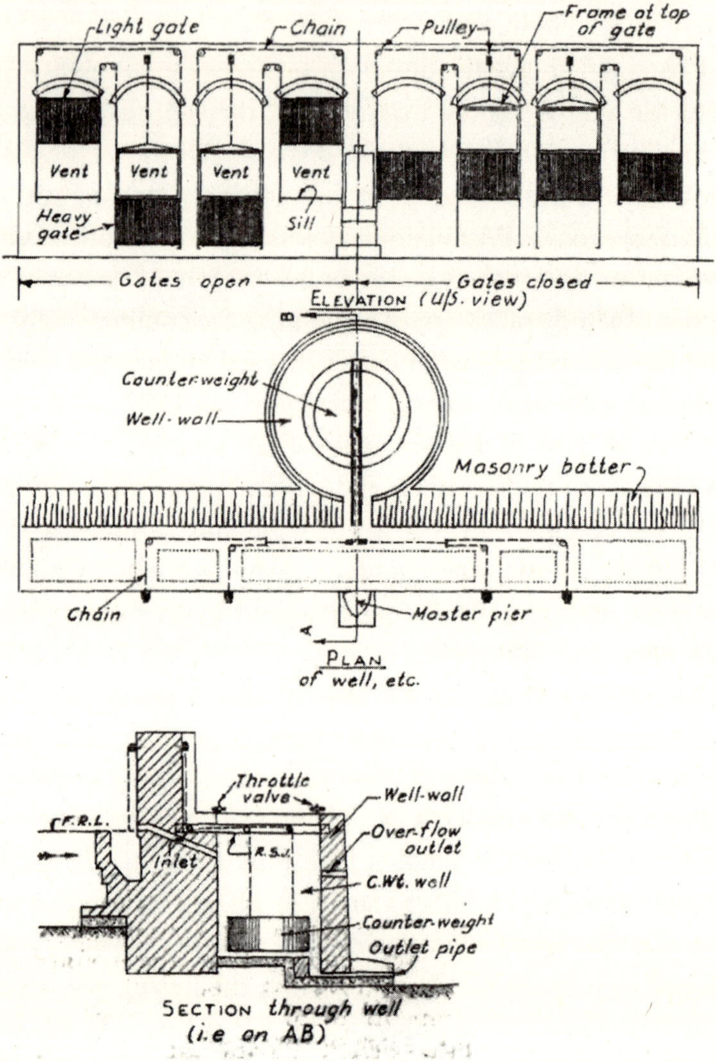

Fig. 6.5. Operation of Visvesvaraya's gates at Khadakwasla

Source: Reproduced from V.B. Priyani, *The Fundamental Principles of Irrigation Engineering [A Basic Text Book for Engineering Students]*, 3rd edition (Anand: Charotar Book Stall, 1957), p. 90.

A photograph from the early 1900s (Figure 6.6) shows a section of the waste weir at Khadakwasala while the river Mutha is in flood and the gates are in open position (the lighter ones have risen). The view is from the downstream side, and shows the cylindrical counterweight chambers at the centre of each set of eight gates.

In addition to its suitability to the terrain at Khadakwasla, Visvesvaraya's design had a number of other advantages. By setting off pairs of gates against each other, it allowed the use of fewer and lighter counterweights as compared to the Bhatghar setup.[12] It worked in such a way that the majority of the gates and counterweights stayed out of the water and were therefore easy to maintain. Finally, it could be customized, with small modifications, for other sites having different characteristics.[13] This last was implemented at Khadakwasla itself, where two of the eleven sets of gates were modified to suit the terrain.[14] In these sets, 'an intermediate balance weight' was added, and all eight gates rose in flood conditions.[15]

Visvesvaraya patented the design, and had the gates manufactured by George Gahagan & Co., an expat-run engineering firm in Bombay.[16] However, he waived his claim to royalties: since he was the engineer officiating at Khadakwasla, it would amount to him as an individual receiving payment from a government undertaking of which he himself was in charge.[17]

Fig. 6.6. Visvesvaraya's gates on the waste weir of the Khadakwasla dam

Source: R.B. Buckley, *The Irrigation Works of India*, 2nd edition (London: E. & F. N. Spon, 1905), illustration facing p. 198.

*

In July 1904, an essayist described 'A Visit to Lake Fife' for the *Deccan Herald.* After romantic descriptions of the road from Poona, of the lake, and the birds in the vicinity of the irrigation officers' bungalow at Khadakwasla, the author described a visit to the dam in the company of 'a genial official who is a perfect *vade mecum* of all that relates to the machinery and all that appertains to the dam' (this was most likely Visvesvaraya himself). They saw the famed waste weir, with 'eleven cisterns which look like large buttresses, and eighty eight arches or gates'. There was no flood that day, but the writer's host demonstrated the working of the gates by filling the cisterns with water.

> [A]t once a marvellous scene arose. It could easily be described as a 'Grand Water Transformation Scene' and at first produced a lovely rainbow—and as it developed all along the line a murmur rose from the spectators on the bank, like that which greet the Grandes Eaux des Versailles on a summer Sunday afternoon. Half the doors came up, and half the doors went down, and the flood burst forth—the former a mass of white foam, the latter of brown. The waters grew and multiplied exceedingly, till at last huge foaming rapids were formed, and the river horses splashed and jumped over the rocks in their new-found freedom, sweeping their ivory foam over the black boulders, away to the river Mutha below, with 'the noise of the voice of many waters.'[18]

This writer, moved by the sight of the gates to lyrical descriptions and Biblical quotations, gives us a vivid sense of how the lay public must have perceived them. No wonder, then, that Visvesvaraya's automatic gates have become a part of his legend. They are unfailingly mentioned in most popular accounts of his life. In these narratives, the gates appear fully formed and without precedent of any kind, the intervention of a lone mechanical genius in an archaic system; the invention then spreads across the world, being used everywhere from Gwalior's Tigra Dam to the Panama Canal.[19]

To assess an invention or innovation, however, one must examine the state of the art at the time and the institutional environment in which the inventor worked. As the preceding account indicates, the context was all-important.[20] Visvesvaraya himself never overstated his contribution. His patent was for 'a certain invention of *an improved system* of Automatic Sluice

Gates'[21] (emphasis mine), his work being a further development of the system devised by Reinold (who, in turn, had built upon the contributions of Whiting). Further, Visvesvaraya acknowledged the guidance of Chief Engineer John Tate[22] and the support of his Superintending Engineer, C.N. Clifton, who was 'closely associated with the design in all its stages'.[23] Clifton had chaired a committee of engineers that inspected the working of the pilot set of eight gates in 1901, and continued to work with Visvesvaraya until the final installation. Another colleague, A. Hill, had been called upon to give an independent opinion. These interactions had a significant impact on the final shape of Visvesvaraya's gates. For instance, he had initially provided for sets of sixteen gates per counterweight, but this was reduced later to eight, partly on Hill's advice.[24]

Moreover, Visvesvaraya was not the only person trying to design automatic gates. Record exists of his PWD colleague E.O. Mawson having devised 'Improvements in Automatic Weirs', while a certain Lt. Walker had come up with his own version of 'an automatic flood gate'. It is not clear whether these were in competition with Visvesvaraya's design, but it is noteworthy that he was working in an environment in which several engineers were trying to address this particular problem.[25]

Nor was interest in the problem restricted to engineers within the Bombay PWD. In April 1904, Ardeshir T. Mirza, a municipal officer in Jamnagar (part of a princely state in the vicinity of Bombay Presidency) wrote to the Bombay PWD saying he had designed an improved version of Mawson's gates. He even met a joint secretary in the Bombay government to discuss, it and was asked to consult Visvesvaraya.

Mirza sent Visvesvaraya details of his design. In August 1904, Visvesvaraya forwarded these to his boss, C.N. Clifton, requesting urgent sanction for a trial of the gate, so that it could be built and tested while the monsoon was still on and water levels were high enough to observe its action. In October the same year, Visvesvaraya and Clifton went to Lake Fife to oversee a trial of Mirza's gate in prototype. Clifton declared: 'Personally I think well of the gate and I believe Mr. Visvesvaraya does also.'

Clifton also remarked that as Mirza's gates were designed to work independently of each other, 'there can be no chance of any failure as might occur when the gates are connected and dependent on one common channel for the waste discharge from the counter weight chambers'.[26] From this we may infer that Mirza's gates were seen as a possible improvement on, or an alternative to, Visvesvaraya's gates. Considering this, and the fact that Mirza was an outsider to the Bombay PWD, Visvesvaraya seemed to have received his innovation with remarkable fairness and maturity. He gave it every chance of succeeding. However, it is not clear what finally became of Mirza's gates, and they do not appear to have superseded the existing ones.

As for the spread of Visvesvaraya's innovation: his gates were subsequently used in other dams with which he was associated,[27] but they did not become the standard even in the Bombay Presidency. When a later dam came up at Chanakpur, Clifton noted that he preferred to use Reinold's gates: while Visvesvaraya's gates were 'admirably suited' to the specific requirements at Khadakwasla, Reinold's were 'simple' and '[had] been found to work very satisfactorily at Bhatghar'.[28]

But bringing the legend down to realistic proportions need not obscure the fact that Visvesvaraya's gates represented an important achievement. His intervention showed initiative and confidence, for on it hinged not only the supply of drinking and irrigation water to Poona and its environs, but also the safety of the city—a failure of the gates at Khadakwasla could easily have led to floods in Poona.[29] The gates were discussed in an article in the well-known journal *Indian Engineering*,[30] and described in a standard reference work on irrigation in India.[31] All this bolstered Visvesvaraya's reputation as a hydraulic expert (which is why, for instance, he was requested to evaluate Mirza's subsequent designs). Moreover, the Bombay PWD was clearly proud of Visvesvaraya's gates, which were demonstrated before visiting dignitaries such as Sidney Preston, the Inspector-General of Irrigation in India; Lord Lamington, the Governor of Bombay; and Lord Kitchener, who came to India as commander-in-chief after stamping out Boer opposition in the South African War.[32]

*

Another technical innovation that Visvesvaraya worked on at this time was directly related to his philosophy of irrigation. When he proposed the block system on the canal systems of the Deccan, he stressed the need to channel fixed amounts of water to each block of fields, preferably without the need for human intervention. In this way he aimed to rationalize the use of water by moving towards a system where irrigation water could be charged on a volumetric basis (see Chapter 5 above). This required an instrument called a module.

While modules of various kinds had been used in different parts of the world in centuries past, none had been used with success in India. Visvesvaraya took it upon himself to design one that would serve the particular requirements of his block system.[33] It was in this context that he drew up plans for a 'Self Acting Module', using which water could be discharged 'at a uniform rate, notwithstanding variations of level in the canal or basin of supply'. In order to do this, the device had to maintain 'a constant head of pressure'.

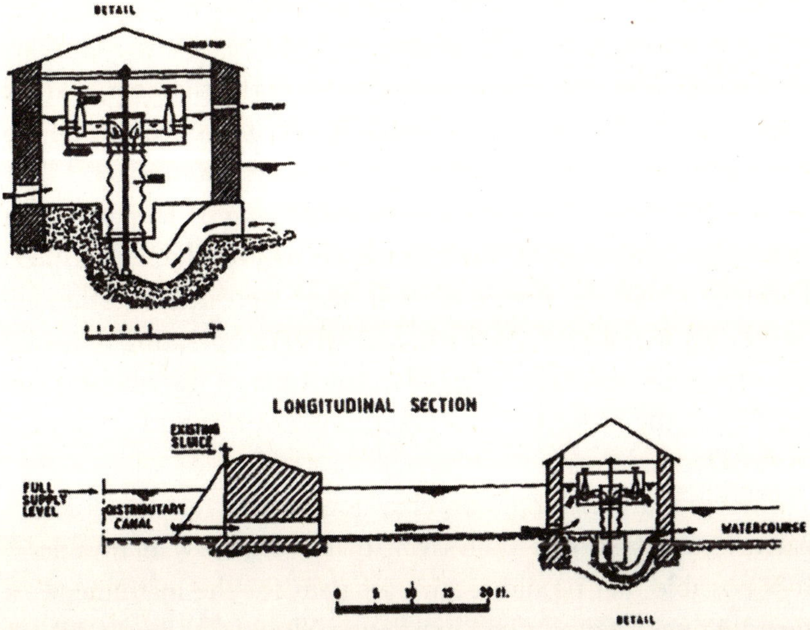

Fig. 6.7. Visvesvaraya's design for a module to channel canal water to blocks

Source: Reprinted in Alex Bolding, Peter P. Mollinga, and Kees Van Straaten, 'Modules for Modernisation: Colonial Irrigation in India and the Technological Dimension of Agrarian Change', *Journal of Development Studies* 31, no. 6 (August 1995): 805–44, here p. 822, from a government volume on the Irrigation Conference held in Simla in 1904.

Figure 6.7 shows Visvesvaraya's design. In the figure, the module is the structure on the right. In Visvesvaraya's design, it is placed just after the sluice gate that directs water from the main canal into a distributary channel. The module contains 'a hollow watertight iron tank floating in the water' inside a chamber, and a 'flexible tube' or hose made of canvas or leather, which is connected to the lower end of this tank. (The latter, Visvesvaraya said, was 'the principal novelty' in his design.) Water enters the module from the left, filling the chamber and, through valves, the iron tank floating in it. The hose carries water out into the watercourse that will go into the fields. Depending on the rate of water entering the module, the tank moves up and down in the chamber, and the hose 'elongates or contracts as in a bellows or a concertina'. Thus the rate of water emerging out of the hose remains steady.[34]

Visvesvaraya thought his module would help practice 'scientific regulation' of water on canals while reducing wastage. Farmers would be reassured that they were getting the full quota of water allotted to them, and officials operating the canal system would now have 'a standard measure of distributing and regulating the water with an exactitude not hitherto attempted in the Deccan'.[35]

Visvesvaraya asked the Bombay government for permission to patent his module, once again saying that he did not want royalties.[36] It is possible that he did receive a patent for the instrument—a superior once referred it as 'your Patent Module'[37]—but it did not fare well under scrutiny from his peers. At an all-India conference of irrigation engineers in 1904, colleagues objected to the device's high cost, the intricacy of its design, and the difficulty of keeping it in working order. They pointed out that cultivators could tamper with the module by placing a weight on the iron tank, thereby getting more water to flow into their fields. The module was never commissioned on the canal systems of Bombay. Other designs, especially one called 'the Gibb Module', were tried and later abandoned, so that the volumetric pricing of water remained, as it were, a pipe dream.[38]

Nevertheless, Visvesvaraya's module is interesting for a number of reasons. First, it demonstrates that Visvesvaraya had his share of failures: not all that he touched turned to gold. Second, the module was, like his gates, designed to function with minimal human intervention. In this it embodied Visvesvaraya's penchant for a rational system of distribution that would be unclouded by human bias—the kind that might come to the fore if canal officials were left in charge of diverting water manually to individual blocks. In later years, Visvesvaraya envisioned an even more ambitious system, in which modules along the canal could be operated remotely using electricity. Needless to say, it was never implemented.[39]

*

At the beginning of the twentieth century, then, Visvesvaraya was at the centre of efforts to modernize the irrigation systems of the Deccan, both administratively and technologically.[40] As if this was not enough, he was given an additional portfolio. When the Sanitary Engineer to the Bombay government went on leave in November 1901, Visvesvaraya was asked to officiate in his place. He served as acting sanitary engineer again the following April. In 1904 he became full-time sanitary engineer, and remained four years in that position while simultaneously discharging his duties as an irrigation engineer.[41] In 1905, the government declared that he would hold the higher rank of superintending engineer for as long as he occupied the post of sanitary engineer.[42]

The post of sanitary engineer was a relatively new one. It was only in 1887 that the colonial government had begun to constitute 'sanitary boards' at the provincial level to maintain public hygiene, and a few years later that sanitary engineers were appointed as part of these boards. Around this time, the germ theory of disease was gaining acceptance (Robert Koch had found the bacilli responsible for tuberculosis and cholera in 1882 and 1883 respectively), and new techniques of water filtration became de rigueur. This led to municipalities building new water supply and drainage works. 'After 1890,' writes historian of medicine Mark Harrison, 'it seems that sanitary engineering became a priority for most of the larger Indian towns'.[43]

In Britain, on the other hand, sanitary engineering works predated the germ theory. Historian John Broich has shown how, beginning in the 1840s, British engineers pioneered what were known as 'gravitation schemes'. As part of these, they built large reservoirs, submerging entire valleys above the city to be served, then transported water through pipes with the aid of gravitational pressure, to supply individual households in the city. Replacing traditional water sources such as wells, this system was supposed to contribute not only to hygiene (by preventing 'miasmas', thought to emerge from impure, standing water), but also to the moral uplift of the urban poor—who, according to prevailing wisdom, led unclean lives and fell prey to alcoholism as they didn't have access to potable water.

In the latter part of the nineteenth century, British engineers tried to replicate such systems in cities across the Empire. John Bateman, the leading exponent of gravitation schemes in Britain, inspired engineers like Henry Conybeare and Alexander Binnie, who were serving in India. Conybeare supervised the construction of a gigantic water-supply project for the city of Bombay in the 1850s, while Binnie completed a gravitation scheme serving Nagpur in 1872.[44]

These schemes came into being amidst rising concerns about the number of British soldiers losing their lives to disease in India. This was the context in which Florence Nightingale had urged into being the Royal Sanitary Commission (1863), which insisted on the introduction of modernized waterworks and drainage systems. In subsequent decades, historian Madhu Kelkar writes, the city of Bombay's 'traditional water management systems . . . [which] consisted of tanks and wells constructed by charitable people of all creeds' were marginalized. The old sources of water began to be portrayed as 'sources of pollution'. The new projects, which were advertised as promoting hygiene and combating disease, centralized power in the hands of engineers rather than local communities, and turned water into a commodity.[45]

Poona too received a new source of drinking water with the construction of Lake Fife and the Mutha Canals, which began serving it in the 1870s.[46] However, this merely supplemented the existing sources, which included a Peshwa-era tank at nearby Katraj, and 'three private supplies' owned by local chieftains.[47] Despite the increasing importance given to sanitary engineering from the 1880s onwards, the Indian-controlled municipality in Poona was seen as reluctant to modernize the city's sanitary works.[48]

It was the plague outbreak of the late 1890s that brought about a sense of urgency. The journal *Indian Engineering* pointed out that the people of Poona still relied to a large extent on wells for their drinking water in the summers, and argued that the use of this ground water, contaminated by sewage in the absence of a drainage system, had probably contributed to the severe impact of plague in the city.[49] (Plague was still thought of as a water-borne disease at the time.)[50] It was in this context that J.C. Pottinger, then sanitary engineer to the Bombay government, submitted in 1899 a plan for a water supply-cum-drainage scheme for Poona.[51] The following year, he updated his proposals after receiving advice from a visiting authority on sanitary engineering, the aptly named Santo Crimp.[52] But the proposed scheme foundered on the question of funds. The cash-strapped Poona municipality (headed at this time by that prominent Deccan Club member, Dorabjee Pudumjee) was not in a position to take a loan, and the Government of India declined to support the project.[53]

Pottinger retired in 1901,[54] and a few years later, Visvesvaraya, now sanitary engineer, put forward his own proposals for a 'combined drainage and waterworks scheme' for Poona. Like the expatriate engineers who came before him, Visvesvaraya was enamoured of grand gravitation schemes. He went even further, proposing to power the works by electricity generated using water from the dam at Bhatghar. (This was part of an ambitious plan he developed to supply hydroelectric power to Poona, Kirkee, and industries in the region.) But the Government of India rejected the proposal once more, arguing 'that such works should be left to private enterprise'.

Visvesvaraya went back to the drawing board. In 1906, he tabled a relatively modest scheme, which would be limited to supplying water to Kirkee and greater Poona. This too was a gravitation scheme. He planned to construct tanks and filters in the hilly terrain adjoining the Parvati temple complex of the Peshwas, 'enabling ample pressure to be maintained in the water mains which feed Kirkee and Poona cantonments, city and suburban areas'. The scheme would require two new lakes to be created upstream of Lake Fife at Khadakwasla, and was also capital intensive, although, at Rs 16 lakh, its estimated cost was a fraction of Pottinger's earlier scheme (which was to cost Rs 44 lakh). Nevertheless, it was to be built and put into operation over a time frame of thirty years, at the end of which Poona would cease entirely to depend on water from the pre-colonial tank at Katraj.[55]

This plan also seems to have caused panic in the Poona municipality. The *Mahratta*, the Tilak-run nationalist newspaper, hinted that Visvesvaraya should devise a still more modest scheme. Asking him and 'the Municipal Sub-Committee' to meet each other halfway, it declared:

> . . . we are perfectly sure that Mr Vishvesvaraya is no faddist but is very anxious to serve the Municipality if he can do so by anything which he may also consciencIously [sic] do in his capacity as Sanitary Engineer to Government.[56]

The statement, of course, suggests that there were those who *did* consider Visvesvaraya a 'faddist', believing as he did in the most up-to-date Western principles of sanitation. In any case, he seems to have worked further on his design, subsequently adding on a drainage component. We know that in September 1906, the Bombay government forwarded to the central government a proposed system for water supply and drainage in Poona city. Possibly the Government of India offered some support, for in 1909, the *Mahratta* reported that the project had, '[a]fter the lapse of nearly two years, . . . once more come before the Poona City Municipality and the Poona public, though this time under more favourable auspices than ever before.'[57]

Visvesvaraya's state-of-the-art water supply system for Poona does not seem to have been commissioned, but we do know that his plan for carrying away sewage through pipes was approved by the Poona Municipal Board under the presidentship of his friend Gopal Krishna Gokhale. The implementation of a drainage scheme, however, had to wait until 1919, much after Visvesvaraya's departure from the Bombay Presidency.[58]

Visvesvaraya's contribution to sanitary works in Poona—where his role was more to conceptualize than to execute—set the template for many of his future engagements as an engineer. Increasingly, as sanitary engineer and otherwise, he would work as an itinerant expert, inspecting a site, providing suggestions, and leaving the personnel on the spot to carry them out. This was of course a natural consequence of his rise in the bureaucratic hierarchy, but it also reflected his growing professional reputation. As Bombay's Sanitary Engineer he advised on projects not just across the presidency but also outside it. In the process he became an evangelist for large-scale, centralized waterworks and sewerage systems.

In 1906, Visvesvaraya was asked to provide advice on drainage and water supply in the port city of Aden (in present-day Yemen). Aden was then a key stop on the sea route between Britain and India, and was jointly administered by the Bombay government and the colonial Government of India.[59] Visvesvaraya surveyed the location before suggesting the use of gravitation to carry away sewage to the sea through pipes. Drinking water was at a premium in Aden, which had low rainfall and relied on sea water purified by distillation. Visvesvaraya recommended building a new system of water supply, apparently endorsing an existing plan. This involved building a well at a location in the nearby sultanate of Lahej, which received substantial rainfall, and then piping the water to Aden.[60]

In Bombay Presidency, the waterworks of Karachi, Ahmedabad, Dharwar and Bijapur benefited from Visvesvaraya's counsel. When the water reservoir of the princely state of Kolhapur was found to have an unstable wall, Lt. Col. W.B. Ferris, the British Political Agent in that state, wrote to the Bombay government that the Maharaja of Kolhapur 'is most anxious that Government may be pleased to let him have the services of an experienced European engineer' to advise on the problem. The maharaja had clearly internalized the belief that only a white engineer could be trusted with important matters. In the event, it was Visvesvaraya who went to Kolhapur to investigate the dam, and guided the engineers there in successfully repairing the leak, earning the thanks of Col. Ferris.[61]

The jury is still out on how successful the gravitation-scheme approach, devised in Britain, was in the rather different climatic and environmental conditions of Asian countries. Bombay city's Vihar waterworks (which had been commissioned much before Visvesvaraya's time) faced problems when its main pipe began to be eaten away by rust, while the warm weather caused the spread of algae, choking the reservoir. Such projects also displaced entire villages and changed traditional ways of life, from religious practices to the use of wells. They consolidated power over water resources in the hands of the colonial state. This consolidation of power, and the disruption caused by the new schemes, was opposed by local populations in almost every instance, but to little avail. The modernizing imperative of the colonial state won out almost everywhere.[62] It was an imperative that Visvesvaraya internalized almost completely, and one that undoubtedly laid the foundation for new patterns of urban living—'reflect[ing] the ideas,' as John Broich puts it, 'that access to urban utilities should be easy and widespread, that former limitations on health, growth and the free circulation imposed by nature should be overcome'.[63] In the process, the Bombay Presidency's first Indian sanitary engineer also assembled a sparkling resumé.

*

Throughout his years in Poona, Visvesvaraya enjoyed considerable respect within the public works establishment. The surviving scraps of correspondence between him and his superiors suggest a largely cordial relationship. He was respected not only for his technical and administrative innovations, but also for his punctiliousness as a bureaucrat, though he could take it to extremes. In 1900, Bombay's Examiner of Public Works Accounts noted that the accounts related to famine projects in Visvesvaraya's office were 'very thorough and satisfactory' and 'quite up to date'. This was a remarkable achievement, especially in such trying times. He gently drew attention, however, to the fact that Visvesvaraya's staff had been working 'from 10 to 12 hours a day' to make this possible, and suggested that the engineer ask for one more clerk.[64]

Although Visvesvaraya himself was always fastidious and correct, his bosses were often friendly and informal.[65] One might say he was treated almost as an honorary Englishman. When the members of the Irrigation Commission visited Poona in 1901, he accompanied them on a boat ride on the Nira Canal to show them the headworks near Bhatghar. The wife of the commission's chairman, Colin Scott-Moncrieff, was on the trip too, and discreetly took a photograph of Visvesvaraya in conversation with her husband, sending it later to the Indian engineer as a keepsake.[66] Several years later, C.A. Kincaid, a senior official in the Bombay government, came across Visvesvaraya while visiting the Qutb Minar in Delhi. Bantering with the engineer, Kincaid

> asked him at what cost he would undertake to build another Kutub Minar. Without a moment's hesitation [Visvesvaraya] pulled out a pocket-book, made a few abstruse calculations, and in all seriousness undertook to build another one for fourteen lakhs![67]

While he was bold and forthright, it is clear that Visvesvaraya was sensitive about his image and cared about the approval of his superiors. He collected and preserved the comments they made every time he undertook an assignment. In memoranda, communiques, letters, and speeches, governors of Bombay and other senior officials within and without the bureaucracy showered encomiums on him. On various occasions, they referred to his 'timely suggestions', his 'valuable report', and his ability to give 'admirable advice'. They called him 'that excellent engineer'; 'that most talented and experienced engineer'; even, towards the end of his time in Poona, 'one of the ablest officers, European or Indian, of the Public Works Department, with whom it has been my pleasure and honour to work'.[68] In 1907, when there were discussions about reserving Poona's engineering college for students of Bombay domicile, the director of public instruction opposed the idea, for 'no doubt the Public Works Department would have been the poorer if a man like Mr. Visveshvaraiya was not eligible for admission into it'.[69]

When an all-India conference of irrigation engineers was organized in Simla in September 1904, Visvesvaraya was among only three engineers (and the only Indian) selected to represent the Bombay PWD. His superior, W.L. Cameron, suggested that he speak about his automatic gates and his irrigation module, adding: 'I hope . . . that you will get some good models made.'[70] Visvesvaraya submitted four papers, including one each on Reinold's gates at Bhatghar, his own gates at Khadakwasla, and his irrigation module. A single delegate sending in so many papers was probably unusual: Visvesvaraya was asked to mention which papers he was most keen on presenting.[71] In the event, he presented all four papers.[72]

Keen to observe and absorb new developments in engineering, Visvesvaraya sought, and was granted, additional leave to go from the conference at Simla to various irrigation works he wished to study in the northern provinces. He wrote to his chief engineer in Bombay that he also planned 'to inspect the working of the electric light installations at Calcutta & Darjeeling if time permits', and applied for the services of a peon who could accompany him on his travels.[73] Visvesvaraya's interest in the electrical works in Bengal was connected to his proposals for the electrification of Poona. The Bengal works were among the earliest such projects in India,[74] and Visvesvaraya had been keen to see if he could gain any pointers from them. (No doubt he was also inspired by the hydroelectric works established on the Cauvery in his home state of Mysore in 1902; on which see Chapters 8 and 9 below.)[75]

Meanwhile, other honours came Visvesvaraya's way. In December 1904 he was promoted from associate member to full member of the London-based Institution of Civil Engineers. This required his candidature to be supported by no fewer than ten corporate members of that institution; his sponsors included a number of his senior colleagues in the PWD.[76] The same year he was made a Fellow of the Bombay University. In 1905 he delivered a series of lectures on the subject of sanitary engineering at his alma mater, the Poona College of Science. Also around this time, he was placed on a committee to revamp the engineering syllabus at the same college (the committee renamed it the College of Engineering).[77] He was even courted by private companies, who sought his technical advice. In 1904, Burjorji Padshah, a top executive of the Tata group of companies,[78] was keen to have Visvesvaraya work with David Gostling, an engineer engaged in prospecting for sites for the Tatas' proposed hydroelectric works in the Western Ghats.[79]

In Poona, Visvesvaraya became a part of the social life of two worlds. First there was the official, largely white world of government officers, governors and the armed forces in the cantonment. Visvesvaraya's home was in the posh Queen's Gardens,[80] which a contemporary report described as 'the most fashionable part of Poona', which 'has grown into a Mayfair or Belgravia'.[81] He played host to important visitors, including P.N. Krishnamurthy, the Dewan of Mysore, and V.P. Madhava Rao, a future Dewan of Mysore.[82] He also mingled with prominent citizens and officials from across the presidency who converged on Poona to attend the monsoon session of the Bombay Legislative Council each year.[83] He participated in the social events that acted as a glue for colonial society: in 1905 he won a prize for zinnias in the Poona Flower Show at the Empress Gardens, a couple of miles from his home.[84]

But Visvesvaraya was also well known to and respected by the Indian elite of Poona, including social reformers, nationalist thinkers, and municipal leaders. He frequently made the journey to the older part of the city to spend time at the Deccan Club. Also part of his ambit was the Fergusson College, redoubt of figures like Gokhale, Agarkar, and Principal R.P. Paranjpye, renowned as the first Indian Senior Wrangler at Cambridge.[85] The journalist-turned-Mysore official K. Subba Rao, who was part of Madhava Rao's entourage when he stayed with Visvesvaraya, remarked on the engineer's '[supreme] regard for his countrymen of all castes and creeds and [implicit] regard and esteem for eminent non-official leaders of public opinion, in spite of their unpopularity with the British Government or sections of the Indian population—very rare quality to be found in hide bound official life'.[86]

*

Visvesvaraya could have been excused for feeling pride at the way his career had progressed thus far. Still in his forties, he held the exalted rank of superintending engineer and was also sanitary engineer to the Bombay Presidency. In fact, he had been promoted over the heads of several engineers who had served longer in the Bombay PWD.[87] As he noted, his European superiors were 'broadminded and generous' in their dealings with him.[88] Yet he was unable to rid himself of a vague sense of unease over whether he was getting his due. This feeling came to the fore during what ought to have been the highlight of his official career in the Bombay Presidency—his selection for the Kaisar-i-Hind medal in 1906.[89]

The Kaisar-i-Hind (Emperor of India) medal was an honour that had been instituted in 1900 by order of Queen Victoria, and could be conferred on 'any person without distinction of race, occupation, position, or sex, . . . who shall have distinguished himself (or herself) by important and useful service in the advancement of the public interest in India'.[90] It was clearly a prestigious award. But when Visvesvaraya learnt that he had been chosen for it, he was more disappointed than elated. The problem, it appears, was that although the award was meant to be race-blind, it nevertheless came in two 'classes'. First Class awards were signified by a gold medal, awarded on the recommendation of the Secretary of State for India. Second Class awards, for which one received a silver medal, were handed out by the governor-general (viceroy) in India.[91] Visvesvaraya had got the silver. And Visvesvaraya was always sensitive to distinctions of this kind.

Writing to an unnamed superior, he said that friends, both European and Indian, had been writing to him, and that they '[spoke] disparagingly of the new honour'. His correspondent had suggested that they try and get the medal changed to a gold; but, Visvesvaraya wrote, 'I feel that would be making the occasion a pretext for seeking a higher honour. My own view is that it would be most satisfactory if, without causing displeasure, the medal could be cancelled.'[92] In June 1906, the Commissioner of the Central Division in the Bombay Presidency wrote to ask if a 'Durbar' could be held in Poona on 5 July to bestow the Kaisar-i-Hind medal on Visvesvaraya, and if he wanted invitations for the function to be sent to anyone.[93] The latter protested—if somewhat feebly. 'I have begged you, if possible, to dispense with a public presentation, more particularly, if you have no other presentations to make on the same occasion; but I will be guided by any arrangements you may see fit to make for the occasion.'[94] In the event, it appears, a ceremony did take place.[95]

Why did Visvesvaraya and his friends consider the silver medal a slight? Very probably he read it as a sign that as an Indian, he would never be a first-class citizen in the colonial bureaucracy. When, the following year, two prominent princely states indicated they would like to appoint him as chief engineer, the doubts began to crystallize. No Indian had ever risen to the position of chief engineer in a British Indian province, and Visvesvaraya felt that, especially with the existence of 'political feeling in the country at the time', he could not expect to make it to the top spot 'except when my regular turn came according to my original rank'. He decided to quit the Bombay PWD, leaving his friends and colleagues flummoxed. Some of them warned him that he might be endangering his government pension by taking early retirement. In the event, the Bombay government convinced the Government of India to make an exception to the rules, and Visvesvaraya was assured of his pension.[96] He was also allowed to take two whole years off, beginning in 1908 (three months' privilege leave and a furlough of twenty-one months), 'with permission to retire at the end of the combined leave'.[97]

Thus ended a formative chapter in Visvesvaraya's life, which had begun nearly three decades earlier with his arrival at the Poona College of Science. Now he was leaving the Bombay PWD on his own terms. He had retired from his job, but not from his vocation.

7

In the Land of the Nizams

At a time when orthodox Indians feared 'crossing the black waters', Visvesvaraya made a career of doing so. When he decided to retire from the Bombay PWD, he had nearly two years of paid leave to use up. He chose to use the time not to visit his elderly mother or to put his feet up at a hill station, but to undertake his second international study tour (he had visited Japan in 1898). He would visit the well-off countries of Europe and North America and observe their cities, their engineering works, and, in general, the lineaments of his favourite thing—'modern' life. He would drop the elements of this modernity into his professional toolkit and attempt to put them to good use in his homeland.

Thus, in 1908, Visvesvaraya based himself in London and asked Thomas Cook & Son to handle his travel arrangements. Money was no object: he was single, and he continued to draw the salary of a superintending engineer. He made several journeys through Europe, the United States, and Canada, 'examining engineering developments in water-supply, dams, drainage, irrigation and other works'. He visited the Scandinavian countries, and even sailed to Russia, going to St. Petersburg and Moscow. (This was just a couple of years after the humbling Russo-Japanese war and the resulting disaffection among the Russian people; Visvesvaraya later noted laconically that Russia appeared to have 'the same standard of civilisation . . . as in the rest of Europe, but the rule was autocratic and discontent prevailed against the Czar's Government'.) In North America he saw dams and irrigation works and met Indian merchants, touching down at Ottawa, New York, and Detroit, home to the Ford Motor Company.

Before he crossed the Atlantic, Visvesvaraya studied the subterranean drainage systems of several European cities. Forty years before Orson Welles ran through the Viennese sewers in *The Third Man*, Visvesvaraya trudged along drains in the bowels of London, Paris, and Dusseldorf. When he visited Milan—the headquarters of the well-to-do, industrializing Italian north and host to international industrial exhibitions in 1881 and 1906—he may or may not have visited its imposing marble cathedral or viewed Leonardo da Vinci's *Last Supper*, but he did descend into the sewers running below the city. The chief engineer of the city's drainage system, who showed him around, was surprised to see Visvesvaraya taking an active interest in the design of the works. Wasn't the design and construction of challenging works in colonial India the preserve of British engineers?[1]

As if in answer to the Italian's query, Visvesvaraya received an unexpected message while still in Milan. The Nizam's government in the princely state of Hyderabad in southern India had asked the Bombay government to lend them Visvesvaraya's services for a critical, high-profile assignment. The Governor of Bombay sent this information on to Visvesvaraya via the India Office in London. 'We would willingly lend him,' the governor wrote. 'Would you ascertain whether he would return to India immediately for the purpose? . . . The matter is urgent.'[2]

*

Hyderabad was among the largest princely states in colonial India. Famed for its diamond mines and its fabulously rich rulers, the state was set in peninsular India's rocky Deccan plateau, flanked by the British Indian provinces of Bombay and Madras. The populace, most of which spoke Telugu, Marathi, or Kannada, had been ruled since the early eighteenth century by the Urdu-speaking Nizams of the Asaf Jah dynasty. The Nizams had started out as viceroys of the Delhi-based Mughals in the Deccan. After a brief dalliance with the French in India, they had, in the mid-nineteenth century, established themselves as loyal allies of the British.[3]

The state's capital was the eponymous city of Hyderabad, built on the banks of the river Musi (named after the prophet Musa or Moses, shared by the Abrahamic religions). Arising in the Anantagiri hills some fifty miles away, the Musi ran through the city from west to east. On its southern bank was the old, walled city, founded in the late sixteenth century by Muhammad Quli of the Qutb Shahi dynasty. This subsequently became the seat of the Nizam and the Hyderabadi nobility.[4]

In time, the settlement expanded far beyond the walled city, to an area north of the Musi known as Chadarghat (see Figure 7.1 below). Four bridges connected the two sides of the city. Adjoining Chadarghat was the Residency, home to the British Resident and his establishment, stationed there to oversee the Nizam's rule and mediate between the state and the colonial Government of India. Also on the northern side, separated from the rest of the city by the sixteenth-century tank known as Hussain Sagar, was the British garrison town of Secunderabad. Within the city, the river was lined on both sides by houses packed close together.[5]

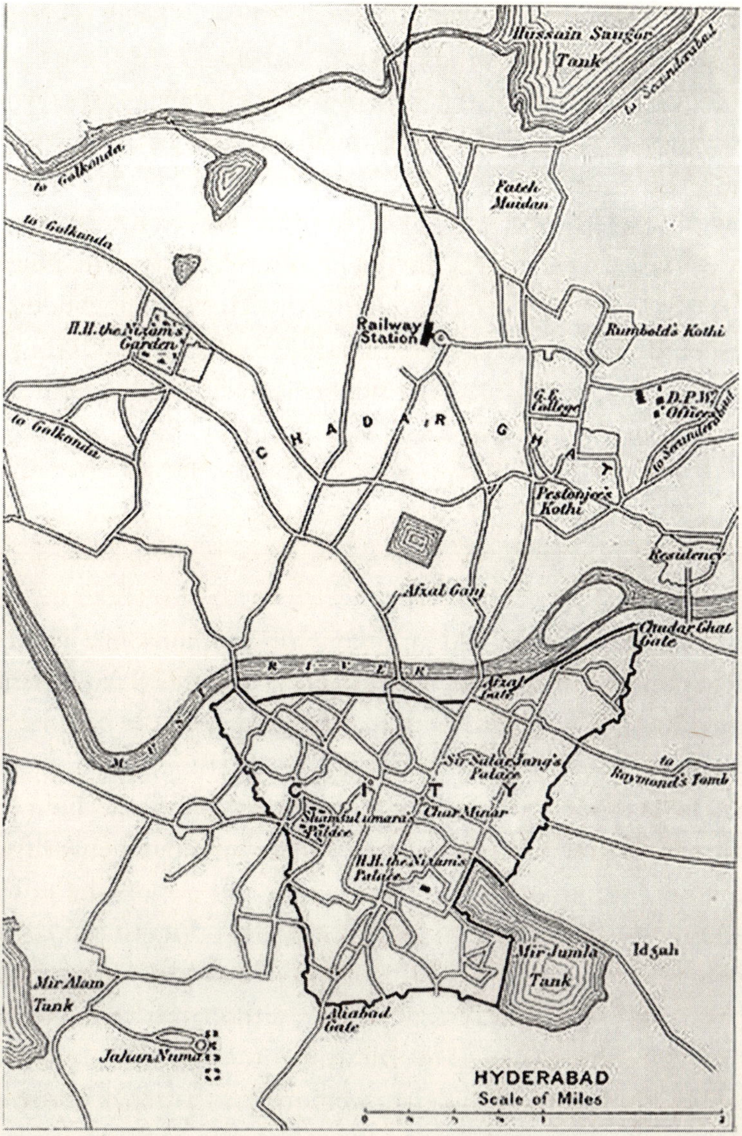

Fig. 7.1. Hyderabad city, early twentieth century

Source: https://commons.wikimedia.org/wiki/File:Hyderabad_map_1911.jpg (accessed 28 May 2024).

The city, resting on a plateau more than 1,600 feet above sea level,[6] was '[e]ncircled by great rocks and crags'.[7] At these higher altitudes to the west of the city were the catchment areas of the Musi and its twin, the Easi (named after Isa or Jesus), which joined the river three miles upstream of Hyderabad. A dense network of nearly 800 tanks of varying sizes served to regulate the flow of these rivers over a catchment area of 862 square miles.[8]

It was an arid area, and ordinarily the Musi dribbled down its channel. But once every few decades, the river swelled during the monsoon, burst its banks, and flooded the city. Such events had been recorded several times in the city's history. But none of them was as devastating as the one that occurred in 1908.[9]

*

That year, Hyderabad had an unremarkable monsoon. Then, in late September, a cyclone originating above the Bay of Bengal homed in on the region, causing torrential rain. On Sunday, 27 September, the correspondent of the *Times of India* reported that it had been raining for ten days; over the last thirty-two hours the entire state had witnessed 'one heavy incessant downpour without a minute's abatement'. The lashing rain had cut off the railway line from Secunderabad to Bezvada (today's Vijayawada). Near Begumpet in the new city, 'the country [was] descended as one huge roaring sea'. The Hussain Sagar, although it was equipped with sluices, threatened to overflow.[10]

The unrelenting thundershowers meant the tanks above the city were filled to the brim. In the wee hours of 28 September, the tanks began to rupture, until more than 200 of them had been breached. The Musi swelled, and a hurtling mass of water swept furiously through the city.[11] The Afzul Ganj and Chadarghat bridges came crashing down, and the river waters razed a nearby hospital to the ground. 'Houses collapsed like packs of cards,' the

Times of India reported, 'and thousands fled panic stricken and terrified before the roaring avalanche.'[12] In desperation, people scaled the walls of the old city, hung on to trees, and gathered in large houses. Most were washed away. In the end, some 19,000 dwellings were destroyed, with around 80,000 citizens cast out onto the streets. A scarcely imaginable 10,000 to 15,000 Hyderabadis lost their lives.[13]

The floods left a deep scar on the city's spirit. The Urdu poet Amjad Hyderabadi, who survived the disaster, painted in verse a picture that would live long in the minds of many:

Wo raat ka sannata wo ghanghore ghatain
Barish ki lagatar jhadi, sard hawain
Girna wo makanon ka, wo cheeqon ki sadain
Wo mangna har ek ka ro-ro ke duain

The sepulchral silence of night, the sinister clouds
The unrelenting rain, the freezing winds
The uprooting of houses, the screaming sounds
Praying with teary eyes, anguished minds.[14]

Over the weeks that followed, relief efforts were organized, while wishes and monetary contributions poured in from across the country.[15] But the scale of the disaster meant that something had to be done beyond the immediate rehabilitation of those affected. The government had to take steps to protect the city against possible flooding in the future.[16]

*

This, then, was the challenge the Nizam's government offered Visvesvaraya when they tracked him down in Milan. He was to use the powers of engineering to subdue the Musi, rendering it incapable of wreaking such havoc on Hyderabad in the future. They also wanted him to design a system of drainage for the city—this would both improve its sanitation and ensure that the sewers, which emptied into the Musi, didn't add to the risk of floods. For good measure, he was also to make general suggestions on rebuilding the city.[17]

The seeking of an external expert was not without precedent. Princely states had a tradition of appointing civil servants and engineers from neighbouring British Indian provinces for special tasks, as they were considered to have more extensive experience in a more advanced system of administration. Except that this time, the engineer chosen was not a white man. Ibrahim Ahmadi, a fellow engineer who had been a year ahead of Visvesvaraya at the Poona College of Science, wrote to him later: 'I was glad to read of your engagement in Hyderabad not because you got the post but because they have thought fit to confer this appointment on an Indian.'[18]

Hyderabad's interest in getting Visvesvaraya's services may be put down to a number of factors. His reputation as an engineer had reached its zenith in his final decade of service in the Bombay PWD. He was an outsider to the state, so his solutions would be seen as unbiased. Further, 'he was both palatable to the Nizam as a fellow Indian and to British officials as one with European training'.[19] Significantly, he came recommended by Akbar Hydari, a respected member of the Indian Finance Department, who was then Accountant General of Hyderabad. Hydari (1869–1942), who hailed from Bombay, was a nephew of Badruddin Tyabji, one of the founding members of the Indian National Congress, and may have been known to Visvesvaraya through his statesman friends in Poona.[20] Finally, it is probable, as historian Raj Sekhar Basu argues, that the ruling classes of Hyderabad—who had, over several decades of British influence, absorbed Western ideals of urban planning—saw in Visvesvaraya a modernizer who could help them expedite the realization of those ideals in their capital.[21]

Despite all these factors, Visvesvaraya was well aware that as an Indian he was an unusual choice. He wanted to make sure he was really wanted and valued, not chosen as an afterthought. By his own admission, he played hard to get. He had not yet begun the North American leg of his world tour, and had no intention of abandoning it; after all, his assignment in Hyderabad was not time-sensitive. He wrote back to the Nizam's government saying he would be willing to take on the job, but only after five months. When he did not hear back for a couple of weeks, he even withdrew his acceptance of the offer. But the Nizam's government persisted, and, as Visvesvaraya delicately put it, 'made some necessary modifications in the terms offered to make them convenient and attractive to me'.

Convinced that he was indeed Hyderabad's first choice and that his services were not being undervalued, Visvesvaraya relented. He spent the next several months travelling the US and Canada, before reporting to Hyderabad in April 1909.[22]

*

While Visvesvaraya wrapped up his travels, valuable work was being undertaken by local engineers in Hyderabad. From January 1909, the assistant superintending engineer, M. Ahmed Ali, led his fellow Hyderabad PWD officers in preliminary surveys to study the course of events during the floods. (Ali, who had been trained at the famed Cooper's Hill engineering college in London, would later become chief engineer in the Hyderabad PWD and be known by the title of Nawab Ali Nawaz Jung Bahadur.)[23]

When he arrived in April, Visvesvaraya began to assemble his own team, comprising engineers of the Hyderabad PWD and others from among his Bombay contacts. At the helm of the Hyderabad PWD was an engineer named A.T. Mackenzie. Understandably, Mackenzie was not pleased at having an outside expert brought in; but he came around eventually and cooperated with Visvesvaraya. Ahmed Ali remained a key member of the new team.[24]

Visvesvaraya's first priority was to ensure that any floods in the future could not sweep away en masse the crowded settlements along the banks of the Musi. One option would be to disallow the construction of houses within a certain distance (on average half a mile) of the river on either side. But since floods occurred but rarely, buildings were likely to spill over into the prohibited zone over the years. Moreover, such a measure would involve a substantial 'loss to the people and Government'. Nor did the topography permit the river to be diverted away from the populated areas. Instead, he recommended increasing the capacity of the river channel. 'To this end some of the more prominent obstructions in the river bed will be removed and the waterways of existing bridges enlarged. Embankments will be provided on both banks to close all spill outlets.'[25]

Visvesvaraya also noted the connection between deforestation and floods. Citing the example of Italy, which he had visited during his recent international tour, he recommended that '[s] teps should be taken to extend forests and plantations, within the Musi catchment above Hyderabad'.[26]

But relieving blocks in the river channel would only partially solve the problem in the event of gigantic floods, whose effects, as seen in 1908, were hardly limited to the houses along the river.[27] Likewise, afforestation would help reduce the impact of floods, but could not prevent them entirely.[28] To deal with the threat of large-scale floods, Visvesvaraya's team first had to understand the underlying causes of the recent disaster. Systematic and data-driven as his approach was, this meant reliving the horrors of the last September in minute detail. Approaching a scene of such devastation—even much after the event—Visvesvaraya, Ahmed Ali, and their colleagues must have needed nerves of steel and the calmness of battle-hardened military surgeons. Blocking out—for the moment—emotions and the stories of individuals, they set about reducing the problem to one of physics and hydraulics.

Visvesvaraya despatched officers to collect relevant data from various locations in the catchment and channel of the Musi. He analysed historical rainfall records to establish that the intensity of rain in September 1908 outstripped anything recorded in recent decades. The team also traced the contours of the floods, helping Visvesvaraya painstakingly reconstruct the sequence of events. He calculated that on 28 September 1908, the flood waters had come charging down at 4,25,000 cubic feet per second, more than four times the carrying capacity of the Musi. 'There is no record,' he wrote, 'of a run-off of such intensity for a catchment of this size in any part of the world.'[29]

Having crunched the data, Visvesvaraya concluded that the destructiveness of the floods was chiefly due to the inadequacy of the tanks in the Easi-Musi catchment area: that fateful weekend in 1908, 221 out of the 788 tanks had been breached.[30] He emphasized this point in his report: 'The fall of rain was no doubt heavy, but had the tanks not burst simultaneously, the flood would not have risen to the great height it did.'[31] These old, crumbling tanks could not be relied upon any more to regulate the flow of a river in spate. What was required, therefore, was the construction of two large reservoirs upstream of Hyderabad City, one on the river Musi and one on its tributary, the Easi.[32] This solution was chosen on the basis of the local topography, which was amenable to the building of flood reservoirs 'because of the limited extent of the catchment and the existence of suitable reservoir sites in the valley'.[33]

As a believer in scale and centralized solutions and an engineer who derived inspiration from international precedents, Visvesvaraya envisioned these reservoirs as gigantic, multipurpose tanks. 'The larger a storage reservoir is made,' he wrote, 'the cheaper will be the cost of the water stored.'[34] The reservoirs would be used not only for flood control but also to provide water for irrigation and household use. Hyderabad, at this time, got its drinking water from two older lakes located in the city itself: the sixteenth-century Hussain Sagar and the nineteenth-century Mir Alam tank. It could now look forward to a more plentiful supply from the two new reservoirs. In fact, the new projects, located at a higher altitude than the city, would double up as a gravitation scheme, the like of which Visvesvaraya had championed so often as sanitary engineer in the Bombay Presidency.[35] In fact, the revenue-generating potential of the irrigation and water supply components of these projects, as Raj Sekhar Basu has emphasized, may have appealed to Visvesvaraya as much as their primary function of flood control.[36]

Citing the recommendations made some years earlier by a commission tasked with controlling floods in the Passaic river valley in the United States, Visvesvaraya held that the reservoirs should be designed with '[a]n extremely wide margin of safety'.[37] He provided the relevant calculations, concluding that the reservoirs should have the following capacities:

(Million cubic feet)	Flood storage	Irrigation storage	Total storage
Reservoir on the Easi	8,379	3,571	11,950
Reservoir on the Musi	5,360	3,079	8,439
Total	13,739	6,650	20,389

Table 7.1. Capacities of flood reservoirs near Hyderabad proposed by Visvesvaraya

Source: Table reproduced (with labels edited for clarity) from [M. Visvesvaraya], *The Flood of 1908 at Hyderabad: An Account of the Flood, its Causes and Proposed Preventive Measures* (Hyderabad (Deccan): [Hyderabad Government], [1909]), para 39.

Taken together, the reservoirs would have a total capacity of 20,389 million cubic feet, or 20.389 TMC (thousand million cubic feet) in today's parlance.[38] The flood storage would be left unfilled except during emergencies, when the excess water from the river would be diverted there safely (it would be drained away slowly at a later time).[39] Thus, the floods would be tackled at the source, several miles before the point where the Musi sliced through the city.

*

During his stay of half a year in Hyderabad, Visvesvaraya also studied the problems of drainage. At the time, Hyderabad's sewage was dumped in the Musi. In densely populated localities, residents 'used to dig pits in front of their houses' and dispose of their household waste in them. 'The pits sometimes overflowed and sometimes dried up'. Visvesvaraya noted wryly: 'It was remarked at the time that a stranger visiting the city for the first time and insufficiently acquainted with the habits of the people, might suspect that "mosquito breeding" was one of the industries of the city.'[40]

Here was fertile ground—metaphorically speaking, of course—for Visvesvaraya to draw on the learnings from his subterranean sorties in Europe. But it was not an underground network he proposed for Hyderabad, but rather a system to carry away waste by pipes. His plan was an ambitious one covering the entire city, but it was beyond the budget of the government in the immediate future, and only parts of it were implemented to begin with. For good measure, he also submitted a report to the British Resident with suggestions for a system of drainage for the cantonment of Secunderabad.[41]

Visvesvaraya's scheme for Hyderabad centred on a sewage farm—where the city's waste would be converted to agricultural manure—created on the northern bank of the Musi, downstream of the city. The sewers on both sides of the river were to be guided through 'pipe ducts' to this farm. The sewage from the southern side of the city would be carried across the river near the Chadarghat Bridge to join the waste coming from the northern side; both streams would be combined and 'conveyed to the farm . . . in an earthen channel'.[42] At the supply end of the system, the scheme, as it evolved, was to provide for waste to be carried from individual houses to sewers at the street or district level, all of which would eventually be guided towards the sewage farm.[43] In other words, what Visvesvaraya had in mind was the counterpart of a gravitation scheme. When the project was completed, there would be a seamless path from the individual household to the communal sewage farm.

Visvesvaraya's plans were handed over to Hyderabad's engineers after he left the city in November 1909, but he was to return several times in the 1920s and 1930s to assess the project's progress and make suggestions. He specified the type of sewers to be installed in the streets; stipulated that households wishing to link up with the sewage system must use flushing WCs; and suggested that loans could be arranged for residents to encourage them to undertake the expenses required to plug into the drainage system. By the time of his final visit, Hyderabad's drainage works, which were executed under the supervision of the high-ranking Hyderabad PWD engineers Nawab Karamat Jung and M.A. Zeman, had made substantial progress, though the task of getting more households connected to it remained.[44]

*

The third part of Visvesvaraya's assignment came under the nebulous head of 'the reconstruction of Hyderabad City'.[45] The first step in this direction was beautification, the creation of a modern aesthetic along the riverbanks.

The engineer in Visvesvaraya could sometimes sound ruthlessly instrumental. He now declared: 'It is usual to take advantage of the devastation by a flood to rebuild and improve the area affected on a proper building plan . . . It is of the greatest importance that Government should [not miss] this opportunity to render the river front healthy and [picturesque].'[46]

A modern city, for Visvesvaraya, was one with a secularized public space, where the needs of sanitation, neatness, and public spirit trumped other requirements. He recommended the shifting of slaughterhouses from the riverside to covered areas elsewhere in the city, and the banning of ritual activities such as 'the burial and burning of dead bodies in the river bed within the City limits'.[47] (This was a sweeping suggestion, unmindful perhaps of the religious significance the Musi had for both Hindus and Muslims.)[48] The river channel was to be fortified by high embankments, and tree-lined boulevards built along the banks. Gardens would be laid out on the riverfront in regular geometric patterns.[49]

Before the floods, the banks of the Musi had been chock-a-block with houses. Now, the government should take care that 'squalid insanitary dwellings' did not spring back up. What the riverfront needed, instead, was '[l]arge shops and houses with small front gardens'. Visvesvaraya approached the problem in a utilitarian spirit—his solution would provide the greatest good for the greatest number. Even though some poorer citizens who could not afford to build large houses would have to move, they would be able to use the riverside walkways and enjoy the green boulevards, which would purify the air. Moreover, they were to be offered land in other locations, along with funds to help them rebuild their homes; and such exchanges of land were to be accomplished 'with a tender regard for the people displaced'.[50]

This, of course, was easier said than done; and it did not seem to occur to him that people might be attached to the localities or communities they originally belonged to.

To his credit, Visvesvaraya spared nobody from this utilitarian logic. His plans included a boulevard on the stretch of the riverbank connecting the Afzul and Oliphant Bridges. This boulevard, however, would have to run alongside the periphery of the Baradari[51] of Nawab Salar Jung III, a prominent noble whose father and grandfather had served as prime ministers of the state (he himself would do so a few years later). 'While the Nawab's garden along the river bank,' Visvesvaraya wrote,

> will perhaps lose its importance as a pleasure ground, the property will acquire a frontage along a wide promenade which will add to its value. As this is an essential part of the improvement scheme, it is hoped, in view of the important public purpose it will serve, the Nawab will co-operate with Government and come forward to part with the land on receipt of liberal compensation.[52]

*

Visvesvaraya's stay in Hyderabad came towards the end of the decades-long reign of the sixth Nizam, Mir Mahboob Ali Khan.[53] A friendly British chronicler recorded that the ruler was said to be 'a very small man, but one who had "a kingly presence and a regal eye." He wrote poetry, he was a great shikari, he had a kind heart, and he was generous to a fault.'[54] The Nizam's prime minister was Maharaja Sir Kishen Pershad,[55] who was descended from a long line of nobles and embodied the syncretic 'Hindu-Muslim culture' characteristic of the Hyderabadi elite.[56] The finance minister was an Englishman, Sir George Casson Walker.[57] Visvesvaraya met Pershad and Walker a number of times to discuss the schemes he had suggested.[58] Their total projected cost was Rs 137 lakh: 119 lakh for the multipurpose reservoirs and 18 lakh for the embankments, boulevards, and other works on the riverfront.[59] The necessary funds had not yet been sanctioned when he completed his stint in Hyderabad in November 1909,[60] but it was only a matter of time, for the state's leaders appear to have determined after 1908 to undertake far-reaching renovations to their capital city.[61]

Soon after Visvesvaraya's departure, the government sought an independent opinion on his schemes from P. Roscoe Allen, an experienced engineer of the Madras PWD who had also served in Hyderabad in the past. Allen gave his approval promptly, advising the government to start implementing the schemes immediately.[62]

By the time construction began, however, there was a new Nizam. Mahboob Ali Khan died in 1911, and his son, Mir Osman Ali Khan, ascended the throne. Nevertheless, there was continuity in policy, as the new ruler extended his father's plans to invest large sums of money in the renovation of Hyderabad City.[63] It was under Osman Ali's rule that the first of Visvesvaraya's projected reservoirs was begun.

*

On a Sunday in March 1913, the seventh Nizam stood surveying a vast open site along the Musi at Gandipet, a village around fourteen miles west of Hyderabad city. Alongside him were top officials of his government, the British Resident, and the great and the good of Hyderabad. Gandipet was the site chosen for the first of the two flood-control reservoirs, and the party assembled there had come to witness the inauguration of its construction.

First, the Superintending Engineer for Irrigation, A.T. Mackenzie, stepped forward to address the gathering. He began by recounting the unfortunate sequence of events that had led to the decision to create this reservoir. After the catastrophic floods of 1908, the government had invited an outside expert to help devise a system to ensure such an event did not recur. Mackenzie may have been privately miffed at this move at the time, but now he said graciously: 'The choice fell upon Mr. Visvesvaraya, one of the ablest of India's engineers, a man who would make his mark in any walk of life . . . It is to him that we are indebted for the scheme we are now commencing.' He mentioned the stellar contribution of the Hyderabadi engineer Ahmed Ali, and introduced C.T. Dalal, the engineer who had been chosen to work with him (Mackenzie) to execute the new project. Dalal had recently helped build the gigantic Marikanave dam in the state of Mysore.

Mackenzie spoke of the stupendous scale of the structure that was now to be built.

> In no part of the world would it be a small matter to dam up a river draining nearly 300 sq. miles of country and subject to violent floods, with a wall 125 feet high, to transform it into a placid lake three or four times the area of the Husain Saugar, and capable of containing ten times the quantity of water, to construct a covered conduit twelve miles long, and a pipe system for nearly a million people. . . . This . . . is by far the biggest thing ever done in Hyderabad.

He then announced that the reservoir would bear the incumbent Nizam's name: it would be known as the Osman Sagar. The Nizam now delivered a speech in Urdu before symbolically laying the inaugural stone. Three cheers were raised, and 101 celebratory shots of dynamite exploded across a ravine.[64]

*

The Osman Sagar was completed in 1920. The second reservoir, built on the river Easi, was finished in 1927, and was named Himayat Sagar after the Nizam's son.[65] While Visvesvaraya inspected their progress on subsequent visits to Hyderabad, the execution of these monumental works was the achievement of other accomplished engineers. C.T. Dalal, who had worked with A.T. Mackenzie on the Osman Sagar, subsequently combined with another British engineer, C.T. Mullings, to build the Himayat Sagar. (Mullings would later go on to take charge of the spectacular Mettur Dam in the Madras Presidency.)[66]

When it was commissioned, the Osman Sagar became the principal source of water for the city of Hyderabad in place of the Hussain Sagar and Mir Alam tanks. The system was complex, involving filtration plants and supply through pipes. But the increasing demand for water meant that within a decade, even this new source was insufficient. The Himayat Sagar was now pressed into service. As part of a project to renovate the water supply in the 1930s, the existing filtration plants at Asifnagar and Mir Alam were expanded, several new tanks and pumping stations were set up, and the Osman Sagar and Himayat Sagar were earmarked to provide 14 million gallons and 13 million gallons of water a day, respectively. This arrangement worked well until the 1950s, when a burgeoning population made it necessary to expand the supply once more. As a result, in the 1960s, a new project, the Manjira Barrage, was created around forty miles from the city.[67] Through all these changes, however, the Osman Sagar remained synonymous with drinking water in the popular Hyderabadi imagination. To this day, the Dakhni saying is heard: '*Gandipet ka pani piye toh Hyderabadi hogaye.*' (If you drink the water of Gandipet, you become a Hyderabadi.)[68]

As for the twin reservoirs' effectiveness at preventing floods—which, after all, was their primary purpose—nature lost little time in putting it to the test. In October 1931, heavy rains reminiscent of the storm of 1908 were witnessed: four inches of rain fell in a two-hour period in the Musi/Easi catchment. Some of the older tanks in the catchment area were breached again. Several sluice gates were opened in the Osman Sagar and Himayat Sagar dams to let out excess water, but the reservoirs held fast. The *Times of India* reported: 'Experts are of opinion that but for the existence of the two big reservoirs, the tragedy of 1908 would have been repeated this year.'[69]

*

The floods of 1908 prompted a series of projects that helped transform the urban landscape of Hyderabad.[70] It led not only to the creation of flood control and water supply measures but also to a decades-long drive to modernize the city, now more than four centuries old. In 1912, the government set up a City Improvement Board.[71]

Although Visvesvaraya had been engaged temporarily in 1909 as a 'Special Consulting Engineer', he did not simply provide recommendations and vanish from the scene. As we have seen, he was invited back a number of times to oversee the progress of projects he had suggested in 1909. Over the years, Osman Ali's government also made Visvesvaraya a long-term partner in its modernization plan, relying on his advice at frequent intervals.

Around 1930, they enlarged his remit, asking him to provide his views on city planning in general. The government could not have picked a more enthusiastic modernizer. By now, Visvesvaraya was in his late sixties and already known for having led the transformation of his home state of Mysore. He now undertook a detailed survey of the city, producing an ambitious report that heralded his vision of a completely transformed Hyderabad. A news correspondent described it as 'a comprehensive report . . . for the [sic] remodelling and modernising the Capital of the Nizams, which is an old and irregularly built city, whose population is frequently in the grip of malaria and plague and where the death rate is high'. Visvesvaraya's report covered multiple aspects of urban planning, including 'road construction, drainage, major and minor city improvements, municipal utilities, financing of improvement schemes and their organisation and administration', and tried to integrate a number of existing plans 'into a connected practical working programme'.

In Visvesvaraya's imagination, a neat, geometrical rationality was what Hyderabad required. It was not a heavy population that made the city look crowded, but the 'narrow and crooked' gallis and the 'old fashioned and irregularly built' homes. He envisioned a city divided into zones, each dedicated to a particular type of function: one zone for business, another for homes, yet another for playgrounds. The areas alongside the river were to be developed into 'a Civic Centre for Hyderabad', and the city was to be filled with 'parks and parkways'. Individual localities could have their own markets, provided they were kept clean and hygienic; but there was to be one large, principal market near the river in the heart of the city, modelled on Western department stores. The city needed granaries that were not overrun by rats. It needed sheds for dairy animals. It needed to be more welcoming of travellers, with 'hackney carriage stands and hotels, serais and dharamsalas'.[72] Visvesvaraya also dealt with transport: he suggested that two-thirds of Hyderabad should be covered by 'cement-concrete' roads (which were laid by the Drainage Department) and the other one-third by asphalt roads (the City Improvement Board was in charge of building these).[73] He even appears to have envisioned a railway line going around the circumference of the city.[74] In order to see through all these works, the municipality, which was then toothless, had to be given more powers.[75]

In all, these works were expected to cost around Rs 4.5 crore over a period of ten years. Visvesvaraya anticipated that there would be objections, but by now (as we shall see in later chapters) he was an old hand at justifying large investments by the state. He argued that many of the new works would themselves generate revenues; that the Hyderabad government was in the pink of health financially; and that 'no more worthy object can be thought of for utilising the surplus revenues of Government than making the City, which was the seat of H. E. H. the Nizam's Government, healthy and efficient according to accepted modern standards of city life'.[76]

*

In November 1932, Pingle Venkat Rama Reddi, the vice-president of the Hyderabad municipality, invited Visvesvaraya to a 'garden party' where he was received by prominent citizens including Sir Kishen Pershad. The garden in question was one of those that had been cultivated along the riverfront, as Visvesvaraya had envisaged nearly a quarter of a century earlier. After Reddi's welcome address, the guest rose to speak. In a nostalgic mood, he recalled his many visits to the city and summarized the progress that had been made over the years and the steps that remained to be taken. He also deflected some of the praise that had fallen to him. 'I do not wish to convey any exaggerated idea of my own share in these works,' he said;

> I merely outlined some of the more important schemes . . . and have been in communication with the Engineers who executed them. The works have all been done, and many of them designed independently, by the Engineers of the State Public Works Department. His Excellency The Maharaja Sir Kishen Pershad Bahadur has given the works encouragement at every stage. During my first visit to design the flood protection works, I received considerable support from the late Sir George

> Casson Walker. I am personally indebted for much kind help and advice to my friend Sir Akbar Hydari.[77]

Visvesvaraya had clearly formed a good working relationship with the Nizam's government as well as with Hyderabad's engineers. He had come to consider A.T. Mackenzie, now no more, 'one of the best friends I had in the engineering service'.[78] Mackenzie—like Ali Nawaz Jung, who had been assisting Visvesvaraya from 1909—was a graduate of the Cooper's Hill College in London.[79] So, almost certainly, were Karamat Jung and M.A. Zeman, who played key roles in the drainage works.[80] C.T. Dalal, who had led the Osman Sagar project, was an alumnus of Visvesvaraya's own alma mater, the engineering college at Poona.[81] Visvesvaraya was at ease with this anglicized cohort who, along with the Nizam, seemed to share his modernizing impulse. It was an impulse that Visvesvaraya articulated neatly as he concluded his speech at the garden party: 'When the remaining projected improvements are all satisfactorily carried out, Hyderabad will have completely emerged from a medieval into a modern city.'[82]

While today's Hyderabad still bears the marks of Visvesvaraya's interventions, it did not quite become the city he envisioned. As early as the interwar years, landmark buildings rose along the Musi, such as the High Court and City College (on the southern side) and the Osmania Hospital and the Asafiya Library (on the northern side). The section of the river from the Purana Pul to the Chadarghat Bridge—the epicentre of the 1908 floods—had its banks elevated thirty feet.[83] Sections of the riverfront were beautified. But the banks of the Musi never became the 'Civic Centre' Visvesvaraya had in mind. (Today, while the tank bund—the road alongside the Hussain Sagar—is still thought of as a place of leisure and relaxation, boulevards and gardens are conspicuous by their absence on the banks of the river.) Meanwhile, the spectre of flooding, combined with the opportunity to build 'newer and more "modern" palaces', encouraged Hyderabad's traditional nobles to move their residences to the northern side of the city. The development of roads and automobile traffic also contributed to the city's centre of gravity moving northwards over the years, 'away from the cramped old city'.[84]

For the rest of the twentieth century, the gigantic multipurpose reservoirs insulated the city successfully from destructive floods. But they have had an unexpected impact too. With large amounts of water from the reservoirs being taken away for irrigation upstream of the city, what is left for Hyderabad is 'a river with little or no water passing through a city that holds its nose when downwind' (for despite the drainage schemes of the 1920s and 1930s, sewage is being dumped once more into the Musi).[85]

*

Visvesvaraya's work in Hyderabad gives us an insight into the way the canvas of his professional expertise expanded over the course of his career. As sanitary engineer in the Bombay Presidency, he had cut his teeth on water supply and drainage schemes. In Hyderabad he not only deployed this expertise in hydraulic engineering, but also ranged beyond it to pronounce on much broader issues in urban planning. Both to him and to the Nizam's government which employed him, this did not seem an undue leap. In fact, his primary qualification for the task was the fact of his having travelled extensively in the metropolises of the West. His philosophy of town planning involved a direct recreation of what he had gathered as an admiring visitor in those cities. Indeed, his vision of an ultra-modern Hyderabad 'equipped with clean houses, flush-down lavatories, dustless roads, paved footpaths and a plentiful supply of open spaces, parks and gardens'[86] was reminiscent of Sinclair Lewis's fictional American town of Zenith in *Babbitt* (1922), with the difference that he had none of Lewis's sense of foreboding about the numbing effects of this monochrome modernity. It was an era when engineers saw themselves as equipped to remake the world, and in keeping with the times, Visvesvaraya never thought of consulting sociologists or anthropologists when undertaking changes that would fundamentally alter the social fabric of a centuries-old city like Hyderabad.[87] Nevertheless, he was emerging as an amateur sociologist himself, with definite views not only on the spatial characteristics of a modern city, but on the features of a modern society. These views would shape his engagements in the next phase of his life, back in his home state of Mysore.

PART II

Becoming a Statesman

8

'The Land of Your Birth'

Throughout his career in Bombay, the press in Mysore had kept track of Visvesvaraya's progress. In 1901, when he first officiated as sanitary engineer to the Bombay government, the *Daily Post* of Bangalore congratulated him on becoming 'the first native of India . . . elevated to such a position of trust and responsibility'. Calling him 'the pioneer from this Province [Mysore] in the matter of study outside the State', the paper went on to remark: 'It is a pity that the services of such an able Irrigation and Sanitary Officer should not have been availed of by the Government of the Province which is his home.'[1]

His home province did not, however, forget Visvesvaraya altogether. Leading Mysore officials, as we have seen, sometimes stayed with him when they visited Poona.[2] In 1908, soon after he had decided to quit the Bombay PWD, he heard from V.P. Madhava Rao, the Dewan of Mysore, who was attempting to Indianize the top rungs of the Mysore PWD. The chief engineer, William McHutchin, was retiring that year. Would Visvesvaraya—who had reached within one step of the chief engineership in Bombay—be interested in taking up the equivalent position in Mysore?

Visvesvaraya initially declined. He recorded in his memoirs that he was not interested in the job. Perhaps he was playing hard to get once more. More likely, he wanted to explore his options rather than jump into a full-time position so soon after quitting the Bombay service.

Mysore was undeterred. In May 1909, V.P. Madhava Rao's successor, T. Ananda Row, wrote to Visvesvaraya again. The new dewan repeated the offer of the position of chief engineer, appealing to his love for 'the land of your birth' and adding strategically that the Maharaja of Mysore 'is aware that you attach greater importance to opportunities for rendering public service than to mere official emoluments. Such opportunities will be open to you in works and projects which have to be carried out in Mysore.'[3]

This was precisely what Visvesvaraya, with his zeal for reform, would have wanted to hear. He wrote back, asking specifically if he would have the opportunity to work in two fields in addition to his regular duties. These were the promotion of technical education on the one hand, and industries on the other. He received a positive response, and accepted the job. This meant he had a position waiting for him as soon as he completed his sojourn in Hyderabad. He wound up his work there in November 1909. That same month he was back in Bangalore, the city of his youth, as Chief Engineer and Secretary to Government in charge of the Mysore Public Works Department and railways.[4]

*

Mysore presented an attractive field of work for Visvesvaraya, and not just because it was the home he had been away from for nearly three decades, the state that had launched his engineering career with a scholarship to Poona all those years ago.[5] It was also gaining a reputation as a 'progressive' or 'model state', with an enlightened administration that the British felt could serve as an example to other Indian princes, often characterized as oriental despots and vainglorious playboys. It was a princely state that, for all its observance of long-held traditions, had been set on the path towards modernization and Westernization by more than a century of British influence (direct and indirect) and a series of reformist Indian administrators.[6] And yet, from the point of view of an inveterate modernizer like Visvesvaraya, there was much more to be done.

Situated in the southern half of the Indian peninsula, the region that formed Mysore comprised two distinct ecological zones: the *malnad* (*male:* Kannada for mountain; *nadu:* country), the hilly, wet, and wooded western districts such as Chickmagalur and Shimoga, dotted with plantations; and the *maidan*, the plains to the east, which included the cities of Mysore and Bangalore.[7] Several dynasties had marked their presence in the region since antiquity, including the Chalukyas, the Rashtrakutas, the Cholas, and the Hoysalas. In 1399, the Wadiyar (also spelt Wodeyar) dynasty was established near present-day Mysore city by Yadu Raya, a warrior of the Yadava clan who hailed from Dwaraka in Gujarat. His successors continued to rule the region, their presence a complex dance involving conflicts with neighbouring powers, dominion over the local chieftains or *palegars*, and, at various points, feudatory status to the Vijayanagara Empire in the south and the Mughals in the north.[8]

In 1761, Hyder Ali, a military officer in the Mysore army, usurped power. He jailed the incumbent Wadiyar king (Krishnaraja II) and ruled in all but name. His son and successor Tipu went a step further, declaring himself Sultan. Hyder and Tipu enlarged the kingdom through military campaigns, all the while battling the forces of the English East India Company—which was growing increasingly powerful in the subcontinent—and other rivals including the Marathas and the Nizam of Hyderabad. Tipu eventually died in action in 1799, when the British laid siege to his fort in Srirangapatnam, around ten miles from Mysore city.[9]

Fig. 8.1. Map from 1808, showing the borders of Mysore after the defeat of Tipu Sultan

Source: https://en.wikipedia.org/wiki/Political_history_of_Mysore_and_Coorg_%281800%E2%80%931947%29#/media/File:SouthernIndiaWilkinson1808a.jpg, accessed 27 June 2024.

The East India Company and their ally, the Nizam, took over some sections of the vanquished sultan's territories, but they handed the core of the Mysore kingdom back to the Wadiyars in the person of their scion, Krishnaraja III, then barely five years old. Needless to say, the Company still held the strings to the administration. For the post of dewan they chose the experienced administrator Purnaiya, who had earlier served both Hyder and Tipu, and surrendered after the latter's death. For the next twelve years, Purnaiya served as regent as well as dewan.[10]

According to some accounts, the Wadiyars' historic fort in Mysore had been flattened and the foundations of a new city, Nazarabad, laid adjacent to it during Tipu's reign. The British now began the process of restoring Mysore city. The walls of the old fort were rebuilt, as was the palace within it.[11]

But the restored Wadiyar king was destined to lose power again. Lacking competent counsel in the post-Purnaiya era, the monarch was capricious in the management of his finances, leading to uprisings in various pockets of the kingdom. Arguing that the maharaja was not competent to rule the state, the British took direct control of Mysore in 1831. The indigenous system of government was replaced by a British-run bureaucracy, headed by two officials styled commissioners. Within a few years, this was reduced to a single commissioner, while the office of dewan was dissolved.[12]

Of these commissioners, who ruled from the newly established British settlement in Bangalore, the most influential were Col. Mark Cubbon, who held the office from 1834 to 1861, and Lewin Bowring, who served from 1862 to 1870.[13] Cubbon was a 'conservative' administrator content during his long tenure with 'maintaining law and order and collecting the revenue', whereas the state under Bowring played a much more active role. Investments were made in improving irrigation and transport networks; the cultivation of coffee, a cash crop, was encouraged; and there was increased spending on education.[14] It was also under Bowring that a grand new Greco-Roman complex of government offices was opened in Bangalore, at the edge of what was to become a vast park named after Cubbon.[15] This period set the template for the administrative organization of Mysore.

Meanwhile, British policy towards the princely states was undergoing a shift. In the aftermath of 1857, the British Crown had taken over the rule of John Company's Indian territories. The British began to look upon the princes as potential allies, as buffers against the possibility of further uprisings. They were less keen now to annex these states outright. It was this climate, combined with the deposed Wadiyar king Krishnaraja III's loyalty during the events of 1857, that influenced the British to rethink their role in Mysore. For his part, the ageing king, who had no heirs, adopted a son in 1865. When this son (the future Chamarajendra Wadiyar X) came of age in 1881, the colonial government turned the reins of the kingdom over to him.[16]

But the Rendition, as this move was called, was accompanied by humiliating, almost crippling conditions under a unilateral 'Instrument of Transfer'. In return for military protection and the privilege of ruling themselves, Mysore was asked to pay an enhanced 'subsidy' of Rs 35 lakh every year to the Government of India. The royals were tutored by British officials, ensuring they imbibed a worldview congenial to their overlords' interests. The government's performance was overseen by the British Resident, who was the link between the Mysore government and the Viceroy of India and could in practice clip the former's wings when it was expedient to do so. Finally, the British brought in upper-caste civil servants from the neighbouring British-administered province of Madras. The Madras Brahmins constituted a check on the power of the locally dominant Hebbar Iyengar community. (This, incidentally, was the start of a long-drawn conflict between the so-called Mysore and Madras Brahmins.)

Despite these controls, however, the Rendition did represent an opening up of spaces of autonomy for the local ruling elite. The maharaja, who was beholden to the British as far as external affairs were concerned, was nevertheless the ultimate authority within the state. The traditional post of dewan, or prime minister, was revived. The dewan and at least two other officials would form a council that advised the king.[17] This arrangement, according to one view, 'was the closest thing to independence experienced by any part of the subcontinent' after the British had become the dominant power.[18] It was also the start of an era in which the dewan would emerge as the most powerful influence in the state. In particular, the first two men to occupy that position were larger-than-life figures who left behind a legacy of important political, industrial, and public works initiatives that Visvesvaraya was to inherit when he returned to Mysore.

*

The first dewan after Rendition was C.V. Rangacharlu. Rangacharlu was born in 1831 in the Chingleput district near Madras, in an Iyengar family that had its roots in the Andhra country. The son of a government clerk, he attended Pachaiyappa's School and the Madras High School (forerunner to the Presidency College)—there was no university in Madras at the time. Beginning his official career at nineteen, he worked in the Madras and Mysore bureaucracies for eighteen and thirteen years respectively before he was made Dewan of Mysore in 1881.[19]

Rangacharlu set the tone for post-Rendition Mysore when, that very year, he presided over the state's first tentative step towards responsible government: the formation of a Representative Assembly.[20] The Assembly met in Mysore after the Dasara festivities each year, its members a select group of businessmen and landlords to whom the government presented a report of progress in the state. The members could, in turn, place their concerns before the government. While this was not a popularly constituted parliament, it was nevertheless an audacious move at a time when no such assemblies existed in the British Indian provinces.[21]

The dewan started out by tightening the state's purse-strings, as Mysore was recovering from the effects of a major famine that had struck the region in 1876–77. But his government subsequently invested in capital projects such as the construction of railway lines. The railroads were meant to facilitate the transport of natural resources for the use of industries, and of food in times of drought. The line between Bangalore and Mysore was completed under his watch; he also flagged off the construction of a new line between Bangalore and Tiptur. Rangacharlu told the Representative Assembly that this line, which was to continue west up to Tarikere, where the *malnad* began, would 'tap the great coffee and arecanut producing districts of Hassan, Kadur and Shimoga, [and] bring all remote parts of the province within easier reach of Bangalore'. It would 'provide against future famines' and 'be invaluable for promoting industry and cultivation and the general development of the Province'.[22] Indeed, Rangacharlu was strongly committed to the development of industries. In his insistence that mechanization alone would help labourers—both agricultural and artisanal—produce a surplus and escape the Malthusian trap of poverty and famine,[23] he echoed the thinking of M.G. Ranade, his near-contemporary in the Bombay Presidency.

Rangacharlu was reputed to be a tough, no-nonsense administrator who would not tolerate nepotism or corruption among his subordinates. His 'blistering tongue' spared no one in such instances.[24] Other stories were told, of his refusing to promote a relative out of turn, of the high standards he set for his subordinates, of his appetite for work, of his 'impatien[ce with] dawdlers, drones and the dilettanti' and his 'passion for gathering information',[25] that foreshadowed to a remarkable extent the image that would spring up around Visvesvaraya three decades later.

*

Rangacharlu died in 1883, having served as dewan for two short but impactful years.[26] On his deathbed he is believed to have recommended to the maharaja a relatively junior officer, still in his thirties, as his successor.[27] This was K. Seshadri Iyer (1845–1901), a Palghat Iyer who had been educated in Calicut and at the Presidency College, Madras. He had joined the Mysore government in 1868, at the same time as Rangacharlu, and even served as the latter's Personal Assistant.

The ailing dewan's advice was heeded, and Seshadri Iyer succeeded him. Iyer became the longest-serving Mysore dewan, holding that office for seventeen years (1883–1900),[28] whereas (as a near-contemporary observer put it) 'it was difficult for most Dewans to endure the agony of Dewanship even for five years'.[29]

Seshadri Iyer was a consummate administrator who had a firm grasp of subjects as wide-ranging 'as the European medical system, the Indian Ayurvedic system, the system of baths and water cures, railway construction, fruit diet, astronomy, astrology, communal organizations, orthodox rituals, the fast cure, [and] the traditional history of various sects and sub-sects of all communities in various parts of India'. He commanded the respect of Europeans and Indians alike, whether they were professionals such as engineers or lawyers, commercial men such as coffee planters, or even peasants or religious figures. But he also ruled with an iron fist, 'great in autocracy, in his despotic methods and the manner in which he put down his political opponents'.[30]

In his economic policies, the development scholar Bjørn Hettne argues, Seshadri Iyer's main objectives were to keep famine at bay and to '[facilitate] the exploitation of the natural resources of Mysore, primarily through the help of foreign capital, expertise and man-power', thus presiding over the '*opening up of Mysore*'.[31] The imputation is that Seshadri Iyer worked, consciously or unconsciously, in ways that served the colonial government's interests.[32]

British capital did indeed dominate such industries as existed in Mysore at this time. The emerging railway network was built with the help of private railway companies operating from British India, and was eventually entrusted to these companies to manage.[33] But the most important industry in Mysore was gold mining. Beginning in the 1870s, British expatriates and companies had been granted licences to drill for gold in the Kolar region in the south-eastern part of the state. After several efforts, mining became viable from the mid-1880s. Banding together under the management of a British mining firm, John Taylor and Sons, these companies established several large mines and built townships around them in what came to be known as the Kolar Gold Fields. Much like the railway towns that were springing up around the subcontinent at the same time, these were racially segregated enclaves where life revolved entirely around the company. Although the labourers in their thousands were mostly Tamil speakers from the neighbouring districts of the Madras Presidency, the operations were directed almost entirely by foreign experts using imported machinery. The industry, on the whole, contributed handsomely to the Mysore government's annual revenues in the form of royalties.[34]

As these companies stepped up production, their need for energy increased. The Mysore government realized that if the state could produce electricity, the mining companies would make for ready customers. With the backing of the Resident,

British engineers set out to assess the potential for setting up a hydroelectric plant. Their choice fell upon the scenic island of Sivasamudram on the river Cauvery, around forty-five miles downstream of Srirangapatnam, where the water fell hundreds of feet in two majestic cataracts. In 1899, the Mysore government approved the project as formulated by the deputy chief engineer, Captain A.J. de Lotbiniere. Two companies, General Electric of New York and Escher Wyss of Zurich, were contracted to provide the machinery and build the generating plant. The scheme was inaugurated in 1902. The mining companies thus became the exclusive buyers of the power generated by the Mysore government at Sivasamudram.[35]

The Cauvery Power Scheme, as it was known, became a symbol of Seshadri Iyer's contributions to the modernization of Mysore. It was one of the earliest hydroelectric power installations in the subcontinent, preceded only by a modest one set up for lighting purposes in Darjeeling in 1897.[36] Because of it, Bangalore became the first Indian city to be lit up by electric lamps in 1905.[37] But the project had its challenges. Despite some early success, the plant was not able consistently to generate the amount of power aimed for, as the volume of water in the river was not always sufficient. As a result, the Mysore government ended up losing several thousand pounds in fines and concessions to the gold mining companies for failing to keep up its end of the contract.[38]

The other major project associated with Seshadri Iyer's administration was a large reservoir at Marikanave. The site, near Hiriyur in the heart of Mysore state, was—as the word 'kanave' or 'kanive' indicates—a natural ravine, through which the river Vedavathi flowed. The British had been interested in the site since the mid-nineteenth century, but it was not until the tail end of Seshadri Iyer's tenure that the Mysore government resolved to build a dam there. It was to be a 'protective' irrigation work, its main purpose being to provide insurance for cultivators during drought years rather than to enable them to grow high-value crops that would increase the revenue to the state. Constructed under British engineers in the employ of Mysore, the reservoir began functioning in 1906. The original estimate was Rs 39 lakh, but more than Rs 44 lakh had been spent on it by 1911. It was a spectacular structure. The dam rose to a height of 172 feet, and the lake it created had a capacity of more than 30 TMC: only the Aswan reservoir on the Nile was larger. However, as we shall see later, this was another instance of hopes outpacing reality, for the lake was nowhere close to full at any time, and the agricultural outcomes were debatable.[39]

Seshadri Iyer was a vigorous man, but a diabetic condition wore him down until he passed away in 1901, a year before the Cauvery Power Scheme was inaugurated. A deputy, T.R.A. Thumboo Chetty, had officiated in his place towards the end of his tenure.[40] The next dewan was P.N. Krishnamurthi, who belonged to the clan of Purnaiya, marking the first time after Rendition that a native Mysorean had become dewan. He was followed, however, by two more 'Madrasis'. These were the Tanjore Marathas V.P. Madhava Rao (who served from 1906–09) and T. Ananda Row (1909–12). Madhava Rao's tenure was notable for the creation of a Legislative Council in 1907 to complement the Representative Assembly, but he also took controversial decisions, especially when he tried to gag the press.[41] It was during Ananda Row's dewanship that Visvesvaraya was to join the Mysore administration as chief engineer.

*

While the dewans controlled the administration from the secretariat in Bangalore, the state's symbolic seat was in the city of Mysore. It was in Mysore that the royals had their palaces and organized grand ceremonial events—such as the lavish Dasara celebrations—designed to legitimize their rule in the eyes of the public.[42] The city also began to get new landmarks as a new regnal period began. Chamarajendra X, the first king after the Rendition, died in 1894 at the age of thirty-one, leaving behind an heir who was all of ten years old. His queen, Kempananjammani (widely known by the title Vani Vilasa Sannidhana), ruled as regent until their son, Krishnaraja Wadiyar IV, took charge in 1902. Known as 'Nalwadi' (The Fourth), he was to rule Mysore for close to four decades.[43]

In 1897, substantial portions of the palace inside the fort had burned down in an accidental fire, and the royal family had moved to the nearby Jaganmohan Palace. It was here that the weddings of Krishnaraja IV and his younger brother, the yuvaraja, were held; and it was here that the former's investiture took place in 1902, Viceroy Curzon in attendance. The main palace was rebuilt to the plan of Henry Irwin, the architect responsible for Simla's Viceregal Lodge, and in 1912 the monarch and his family moved back there. The new Mysore Palace was a sprawling Indo-Saracenic edifice with Hoysala-style embellishments. In addition to living quarters for the royals, it had sumptuously adorned halls and a grand, open darbar. Over the next two decades, various old buildings near the palace (including the houses of some of the maharaja's relatives) were razed and replaced with landscaped gardens and lawns. The palace compound was thus redesigned as a model of rationality, its periphery dotted with temples to various deities. As historian Janaki Nair notes, this contributed to 'a museumized landscape' that emphasized the grandeur of Mysore's royals.[44]

As they had done for his father, the British took charge of Krishnaraja's education from his boyhood. A special school was set up within the palace for the prince and other children of the royal family. (The class included a commoner, the grandson of a wealthy horse dealer who had moved from Persia to Bangalore some decades previously. This was Mirza Ismail, whose career would be intertwined with that of the king.) The prince's specially chosen tutor was Stuart Fraser, an Indian Civil Service officer and alumnus of Balliol College, Oxford. In addition to classroom study of subjects related to statecraft, Krishnaraja was taken on chaperoned tours, to give him a sense of what lay within and beyond his kingdom. He was brought up to occupy two worlds. In one he played the traditional monarch to his people, complete with all the rituals and symbols that tied him to the land; in the other he displayed the Western learning and anglicized bearing required in dealing with British officialdom and his fellow princes from other states. It is telling that it is in English rather than his mother tongue, Kannada, that he appears to have been most comfortable. (The other languages he was exposed to were Urdu and Sanskrit.)[45] He also grew up to be a consummate player of the piano, the violin, and the cello, 'with a preference for severely classical music'.[46]

As maharaja, Krishnaraja IV presided over a period of great social and economic change in Mysore. He showed considerable political nous in dealing with conflict within his kingdom. He was more than a figurehead, keeping up to date with affairs of the state and taking decisions at critical junctures. For close to two decades, his evolving relationship with Visvesvaraya was to be pivotal to Mysorean policymaking.[47]

*

No sooner had Visvesvaraya settled into his new office than he was confronted with an organizational challenge. A high-ranking PWD colleague wanted to recruit a number of new officers on the basis of their family connections to existing Mysorean bureaucrats. Visvesvaraya returned the list made out by his colleague, asking him to do some research and order the candidates 'according to [their] precise technical and educational qualifications'. Eventually, the decision was made on the basis of 'merit and qualifications as far as they could be ascertained'.[48]

This was only the first of several run-ins Visvesvaraya had with the organizational culture of the Mysore administration. For all its status as a model state, Mysore's bureaucracy had a distinctly non-modern character. While competitive exams for the civil service had been instituted in the 1890s, many positions were still filled by 'nomination'—which often amounted to relying on kinship and patronage networks.[49] The upper echelons were almost entirely populated by Brahmins, as the profusion of Iyers, Iyengars, Raos, -achars, and -ayyas in any account of the period indicates. But this homogeneity did not prevent the forming of factions, notably what were known as the Mysore and Madras Parties, which officials were expected to adhere to, based on their place of origin.[50] In an environment where professional opportunities were few and far between, bureaucrats jockeyed jealously for promotions and favourable postings (getting out of a *malnad* posting, with its prospect of heavy rains and malarial conditions, was a common preoccupation).[51] One of them recalled 'the exceedingly vicious system of morning and evening Durbars in the gardens or spacious grounds of . . . high officers where the district officers[,] leading non-officials and others used to wait to catch a glimpse of the august personage to exchange a few words with him and if possible to better their own prospects'.[52] Excessive deference was expected: contractual officials were expected to remain standing when talking to gazetted officers.[53] Pomp and show were important adjuncts of governance. Being able to put on a grand entertainment for a visiting higher-up was an important career skill for civil servants in the districts.[54]

All of this was anathema to Visvesvaraya, who wanted 'a more efficient bureaucracy'. As the scholar Narendar Pani has argued, Visvesvaraya defined this as a bureaucracy 'more in tune with Western ideals'.[55] For him, a true bureaucrat must, following the Weberian model, be disinterested, unmoved by personal connections, driven by duty, and governed by rules and procedures.[56] This was evident in his insistence on punctuality, his preference for Western dress with its connotations of modernity, and his admonishment to his relatives that they must not ask any favours of him.[57]

Visvesvaraya had none of the art of circumlocution that was part of the prevailing work culture. Instead, he was gruff and direct, while (to his mind at least) being fair and objective. He ruffled feathers from the very start and caused apprehensiveness among officers accustomed to a much more leisurely pace of work. He was not unduly concerned about his colleagues' feelings when delivering what he believed were opinions or orders necessary for the work at hand. Early in Visvesvaraya's tenure as chief engineer, the dewan asked him to assess a plan drawn up by a civil servant in his early thirties. This officer—Navaratna Rama Rao, who went on to become a prominent bureaucrat as well as a renowned litterateur—had put down proposals for improving the sanitary and economic well-being of a knot of malarious villages in the Sulekere region near Shimoga. Visvesvaraya visited the spot with a retinue of engineer officers and set up a meeting with Rama Rao. The junior bureaucrat remembered Visvesvaraya as

> [treating] me with marked dislike and casualness throughout the discussions, and after a series of uncomplimentary observations about my essay, observation about my reaction, etc., . . . he wound up with 'And have you anything more to say than that your dignity is offended?' I protested angrily at his gratuitously offensive manner; and this only made him smile and say that bad temper was not an argument.

The disagreement was not personal, though, for Visvesvaraya later invited Rama Rao and his colleague to lunch, chatted with him about the Central College, of which they were both alumni, and asked after his relatives, whom he happened to know. He also gave Rama Rao important assignments later on in his career.[58]

Within the Public Works Department, of which he was the head, Visvesvaraya quickly established a reputation for being exacting and idealistic. He personally addressed the annual conference of the Mysore Engineers' Association, an annual gathering of the state's PWD engineers that had been held from the time of his predecessor.[59] There was no doubting the fact that Visvesvaraya was aware of his stature as a celebrity engineer who had won plaudits in British India. His speeches were didactic: now exhorting, now cajoling, now admonishing. He urged the engineers of Mysore to show zeal for work: 'character,' he insisted, 'is more important than cleverness'.[60] He lamented that there were some lackadaisical PWD engineers who 'are always in arrears . . .' They feared being transferred. 'We are,' he declared, 'too much accustomed to soft conditions.' The solution was 'a resolve to work hard. . . . With industry and by studying technical books and papers, even men of mediocre talent can excel'.[61] He quoted Moberly Bell, a writer in *The Times* of London, who said: 'If your business is only to sweep a crossing, remember that it is your duty to make that crossing the best swept in the world.'[62] (In our time, the words are often mistakenly attributed to Visvesvaraya himself, and emblazoned on posters next to his stern visage.) On another occasion, Visvesvaraya asked his audience to

> [work] longer hours and [do] everything on a system. Successful engineers everywhere work harder than we do. We should dismiss from our mind the idea that any great work can be accomplished, that any reputation in the profession can be made, without drill, discipline and iron labour.[63]

In these addresses, Visvesvaraya introduced one of his favourite themes: 'initiative'.[64] The good bureaucrat should not be content with keeping the wheels moving. 'Taking the initiative,' he told his engineer subordinates, 'does not mean, doing things according to your whims and fancies, or exceeding your powers, or incurring expenditure without authority. It only means that you should work in advance of what is to be done, and instead of waiting for others to move first, bring your best judgement into action.'[65] He expected each engineer to pick an area of specialization and study the latest developments and literature in that area.[66] When they failed to do this, he did not hesitate to upbraid them. In 1917 he declared: 'The past year was not by any means remarkable for initiative or enterprise on the part of our Engineers.' They had been asked to look into the renovation of small and large tanks; that was proceeding slowly. Their work on 'town planning, drainage and water-supply [had] been spasmodic', and their 'progress on specialization studies has been inconsiderable. No wonder that instances of engineering research, fore-thought, initiative and enterprise are so few, and I have to complain about a conspicuous lack of organization and co-operative effort among you.' He urged them 'to prepare a very precise programme for the new year and treat it as a debt of honour and put forth your best efforts to give effect to it'.[67]

There was an unremitting earnestness in Visvesvaraya's messages to his subordinates, a refusal to contemplate ordinary human foibles. Along with pride in seeing a native Mysorean speak with the authority and vision of a reformer, his audience must have had a mild sense of foreboding, for here was someone who meant to shake things up. Life in the Mysore PWD would not be the same again.

*

In June 1911, Krishnaraja Wadiyar IV inaugurated the first session of a newly created institution, the Mysore Economic Conference. 'The need for greater attention to industrial and commercial development is beginning to be recognised in British India,' he said. 'We have, in this State, our own problems to work out and my Government have, therefore, resolved to provide a proper organization so that both the officials and the public might give to such questions the increasing attention demanded by them.'

Anyone listening closely to the maharaja's speech would have had no doubt who was the moving force behind the conference, for it had all the characteristic rhetorical moves of Visvesvaraya's public addresses.[68] The monarch began by comparing Mysore against international benchmarks on the basis of three key statistics. The yearly per capita income of European countries was around Rs 400 as against a measly Rs 30 in Mysore. The literacy rate was above 80 per cent in Japan and above 90 per cent in Britain and Germany; in Mysore it was a paltry 5 per cent. The rate of mortality in Mysore was higher than in European countries. This showed 'the extent of poverty, ignorance and low vitality prevailing in our midst'; it was 'a striking reminder of the economic inefficiency of our people.' To catch up, Mysore had to emulate these model nations. Agriculture and crafts were to be systematized, while '[m]anufactures and trade, the chief instruments for increasing wealth, should be specially encouraged'.

This, then, was the task of the Economic Conference: to help reinvigorate the economy of the state; to provide a fillip to industrialization; to evangelize for new initiatives. The bedrock of these activities would be the amassing of relevant data.[69] The Conference, as it took shape, consisted of committees focusing on three subjects: Agriculture, Education, and Industries and Commerce. There were, of course, separate executive departments of government devoted to each of these fields; the committees of the Economic Conference served as advisory bodies. The main task of the committees was to gather detailed statistics about the existing state of affairs and prepare reports suggesting new measures that could be taken to further develop their respective fields.[70] In the first year, the three committees were allotted a combined sum of Rs 1 lakh 'to cover the cost of establishments, experiments, demonstrations and the collection of statistics and data'.[71]

Crucially, the committees were composed not only of top bureaucrats but also of *non-officials*, as individuals outside of government employ were known. That is to say, members of the public, including representatives of agriculture, commerce, and the intelligentsia, were invited to sit on the committees alongside government officers.[72] However, there were no elected representatives. As of 1912, the Conference as a whole had forty-four members, of whom eight were non-officials, twenty-three were government officers, and the remaining thirteen either belonged to the Legislative Council or were retired civil servants.[73]

The committees worked throughout the year, and gathered at common sessions of the Economic Conference chaired by the dewan.[74] Resolutions drafted by the committees were placed before the Conference at these sittings, and those that won the assent of two-thirds of the body were passed on to the government for implementation. The resolutions that were thus passed in 1912 included those 'for opening new elementary schools, for appointing female teachers in girls' schools, for providing facilities for the education of the depressed classes, for the creation of a teaching and residential University for Mysore, and for the establishment of a State-aided Bank'.[75] Many of these, as we shall see later, eventually led to the establishment of transformative institutions.

The committee on Industries and Commerce, headed by Visvesvaraya,[76] was the centrepiece of the Economic Conference. It had a number of sub-committees, divided by type of industry. Each would have a superintendent with expert understanding of the field in question, who would 'travel for at least six months in the year studying the resources of every locality in the way of raw material, capital, labour and local enthusiasm for the purpose'. He would furnish each district with 'the latest business information, business methods, [and details of] machinery and plant pertaining to each principal industry'.[77] In July 1912, this committee also welcomed a member from outside the state, Alfred Chatterton, whom the Mysore government had appointed as special adviser for Industries and Commerce. Chatterton was a British engineer who served in the Madras Presidency as head of its Bureau of Industrial Information, and initially came to Mysore for a period of six months on loan from Madras.[78] Over the next few years, Chatterton would form an important partnership with Visvesvaraya (see Chapter 12 below).

Not everyone in the Mysore establishment was convinced of the necessity or wisdom of creating an Economic Conference. The deputy commissioner of Kadur, K.R. Srinivasa Iyengar, who was present at the inaugural session in June 1911, noted in his diary on the last day: 'After all, to the immence [sic] relief of everybody, the Conference terminated today. The business done by the 3 days sitting consisted of nothing more than selecting the subjects and forming the committees.' It was evident to Srinivasa Iyengar that Visvesvaraya was the moving force behind the Conference. He noted that '[s]ome of the propositions which Visvesvarayya had raised and had been decided against him by the Conference came subsequently in the shape of orders from His Highness'. The chief engineer's bearing at the conference did not impress Srinivasa Iyengar, who noted that he had come away with 'a poor opinion of Visvesvarayya's . . . capacity and a worse one of his behaviour and manners'.[79]

Navaratna Rama Rao, who shortly thereafter became the secretary of the committee on Agriculture, described how Mysore's bureaucrats viewed the Economic Conference in its early days. They thought it was merely a talking shop with no tangible outcomes, that 'it claimed credit for sunshine and rainfall, and had raised report writing to a fine art'. The head of the Agriculture Committee, the veteran bureaucrat K. Doraswami Iyer, 'made no secret of regarding the Economic Conference as a huge and costly joke'.[80] Doraswami Iyer, who happened to be the son of the former dewan, Seshadri Iyer, was well-known for his irreverent manner, and was no fan of Visvesvaraya's.[81]

*

It was not only his penchant for data-gathering, his autocratic manner, and his determination to push the bureaucracy out of its comfort zone that made Visvesvaraya the cynosure of all eyes in the Mysore establishment. He also showed remarkable energy and great daring in the practical work he took on. Within a year of his taking over as chief engineer, Visvesvaraya was putting forward large, ambitious projects for government approval. In October 1910, he put up a note to the dewan proposing four major initiatives.[82]

The first was to expand the railroad network within the state. There had been a lull in railroad construction after the dewanships of Rangacharlu and Seshadri Iyer, and Mysore had to 'make up for lost time'. Visvesvaraya wanted to build two new metre-gauge lines, from Arsikere to Mysore city, and from Nanjangud to Erode. These lines would span the length of the state and connect it to the Bombay Presidency in the north and the Madras Presidency in the south. He also proposed two light railways, Bangalore–Hosur and Bowringpet–Kolar. The latter would connect the gold fields of Kolar to the railway network. He envisaged running electric trains on these lines, inspired by such lines in the United States and the London Underground system.[83] Finally, he wanted to create a tram service for the city of Bangalore to boost commercial activity.[84]

The second initiative was the revamping of irrigation in the state. The gigantic and expensive Marikanave reservoir was in the red, while the interest due on the capital spent continued to mount. Visvesvaraya suggested building new canals to increase its effectiveness. As for Mysore's many tanks, large and small, they were currently 'managed by [rule] of thumb'. What was needed instead was 'scientific regulation of the water' after systematically analysing rainfall patterns and the areas served by each tank.[85]

A third project was the fostering of industries. Visvesvaraya wanted Mysore to manufacture steel through electric smelting, produce nitrates as fertilizer, and further develop its cotton and silk textile industries. A Director of Industries should be appointed, endowed with funds to lay the groundwork. In addition to boosting the state's economic well-being, these industries would also serve as consumers of the electricity produced by the government.[86]

This last point was connected with Visvesvaraya's final—and most ambitious—proposal. This was to build an enormous multipurpose dam on the river Cauvery. This would irrigate vast swathes of land, enabling commercial agriculture on a large scale; it would also enhance the state's capacity to produce electricity, which could not only be sold to the mining companies of Kolar, but also be provided to the new industries Visvesvaraya proposed to promote in the state.[87]

These initiatives, then, were all part of Visvesvaraya's integrated vision for a productive, prosperous, and industrialized Mysore. It was a vision that was as costly as it was ambitious. Taken together, Visvesvaraya's four proposals would require a humongous investment of Rs 254 lakh,[88] an unprecedented level of expenditure on public works.

Unsurprisingly, the proposals faced stiff opposition from various quarters. In particular, the reservoir project, which formed the centrepiece of Visvesvaraya's plans and accounted for the bulk of the projected cost, was to become a *cause célèbre.* The stage was set for one of the biggest battles of his Mysorean career.

9

Reservoir of Hopes[1]

Paris and the Eiffel Tower, San Francisco and the Golden Gate Bridge, Kolkata and the Howrah Bridge: some cities are synonymous with iconic engineering works. If the more modestly sized city of Mysuru has such a symbol, it is the Krishnarajasagara (KRS) reservoir and dam, constructed across the river Cauvery between 1911 and 1932.

The KRS, located about twenty kilometres north of the city, is a constant presence in the lives of Mysoreans. Every summer, the newspapers are full of reports about the water levels in the reservoir, which irrigates large agricultural tracts and supplies drinking water across Karnataka. Locals and tourists encounter the KRS when they picnic at the Brindavan Gardens, laid out with shimmering lights and musical fountains in the shadow of the towering 130-foot dam.[2] In the rains, the more adventurous among them drive up to the dam's waste weir to watch the water gush through the open sluices. Behind the dam lies the reservoir, a gigantic sea of blue—the *sagara* named after Krishnaraja Wadiyar IV.

If the erstwhile monarch of Mysore lends the KRS his name, Visvesvaraya is undoubtedly its face. It was during his time as

Chief Engineer of Mysore that the project was green-lighted; it was during his subsequent tenure as dewan that the early phases were constructed. In the villages and towns of Karnataka, the KRS is inseparable from Visvesvaraya. As one *jaanapada geete*, or folk song, has it:

Kaṭṭide Kannambaḍi kaṭṭeya
Koṭṭihe usiranu koṭi jīvake
Huṭṭali ninnanta
Nūrāru Cetana
Kāveri jaladhāra Visvesvaraya.[3]

You built the dam at Kannambadi
And breathed life into crores of people
May hundreds of inspirations like you be born
O embodiment of the Kaveri, Visvesvaraya.[4]

As a public project, the KRS was unprecedented, and not just by the standards of a princely state in colonial India. When it was sanctioned, even the Tennessee Valley Authority—the grand American project that was to inspire the Nehruvian 'temples of modern India'—was two decades away.[5] The British had, of course, constructed large canals across the subcontinent from the nineteenth century onwards. But dam building was relatively new territory even for colonial engineers. They had built dam-and-reservoir projects in the preceding decades, but only a handful, and none as large[6] as the project that Mysore was contemplating near the village of Kannambadi.[7]

What is truly intriguing about the KRS is not its design or execution, but that it exists at all. What possessed a princely state and its cadre of Indian engineers to undertake it? The answer is a complex one, but Visvesvaraya is at its centre. The KRS was, after all, at the heart of his grand project of modernizing and industrializing Mysore. It took him well over a year of driving complex debates and negotiations just to get started on this ambitious—some said reckless—project. He had to reckon with a wide variety of issues: technical, financial, and political.

*

The village of Kannambadi lay eight miles upstream of Srirangapatnam, the pre-colonial capital of Mysore.[8] It was here that the river, having emerged in the rain-fed hills near Coorg in the *malnad*, began its unimpeded flow eastward through the *maidan* lands of Mysore.

For centuries, this stretch of the river valley had appealed to rulers as a suitable site for irrigation works. A Persian inscription, unearthed near Kannambadi and dating from the reign of Tipu Sultan in the late eighteenth century, declares that the ruler 'laid the foundation of the Mohyi Dam across the river Cauvery to the West of the Capital' with the aim of expanding agriculture in the region.[9] But Tipu's efforts came to naught, probably because he had his hands full with various battles to protect his territories.[10]

In subsequent years, Dewan Purnaiya is believed to have tried, also without success, to carry water from this site to the city of Mysore through a canal. From the 1870s onwards, Mysore's British engineers tried on and off to identify a suitable location for a dam.[11] Meanwhile, plans took shape for a different reservoir project, the Marikanave, on the river Vedavathi. This was a large and expensive project, and once the government undertook to build it, plans for a Cauvery reservoir were put on the backburner.[12]

Before long, however, the Cauvery reservoir idea returned in a different context: electricity generation. As we have seen, Mysore established the Cauvery Power Scheme in 1902, a pioneering hydroelectric project located at Sivasamudram, an island downstream of Srirangapatnam. This allowed the government to supply electricity to the mining companies of Kolar, promoting the gold-mining industry and bringing in valuable revenue.

But it turned out that during summer, the water levels in the Cauvery were too low to permit the plant to function at full capacity. This ended up becoming a nuisance for the state, which often defaulted on its commitments and had to pay large fines to the mining companies.[13]

The government tried to address this issue through what it called 'conservancy measures', which involved using sandbags to shore up the water at various check dams along the river. But this wasn't enough, and soon, officials decided that building a large reservoir upstream of Sivasamudram might solve the issue.[14] In the monsoon, it would capture rainwater before it ran off to the sea. Come summer, the water could be released downstream, providing the hydroelectric works with a flow steady enough for its turbines.[15]

Mysore's Public Works Department, headed by its long-serving chief engineer William McHutchin, now began systematic surveys of the region. These were conducted by his young deputy, Captain N.B.E. Dawes of the Royal Engineer corps. In 1908, Dawes drew up an ambitious proposal for a multipurpose reservoir at a site more than fifty miles upstream of Sivasamudram: Kannambadi.[16]

Dawes's proposed project was gargantuan. According to a later Mysore engineer, it involved carrying water all the way from the dam to the power station at Sivasamudram through a pipe made of reinforced concrete.[17] The ultimate aim was to produce 70,000 HP of electricity, for sale not only to the gold mines of Kolar, but also to the industrial belts of Madras and Coimbatore outside the state; and to provide water to 3,00,000 acres of fields along the Cauvery. Although Dawes's plan was to begin with a power-generating stage and plough the profits from it back into the further expansion of the reservoir, the estimated cost of the project as a whole was stupendous, at Rs 440 lakh. This fact, combined with the complications involved in building a project that would extend beyond the boundaries of Mysore, meant that the government bided its time, unwilling to act immediately on the scheme.[18]

In 1909, McHutchin reached the age of retirement,[19] and Captain Dawes was asked to officiate as chief engineer until a replacement was identified (the government had decided to appoint an Indian).[20] In the normal course of events, Dawes would have reverted to the position of deputy chief engineer when Visvesvaraya succeeded McHutchin in November that year. But this was not to be.

On 30 July, Dawes went out to oversee repair work being undertaken on the Krishnarajakatte anicut (a small check dam) on the Cauvery. As he and his team were going back to shore, their boat overturned. All but one of them swam to safety. Dawes struck out at once to save the labourer who remained trapped in the river. The man survived, but Dawes was sucked into the current, hurtling through the gap in the damaged anicut, and eventually drowned.

Dawes's poignant death—he was only thirty-one—was widely mourned in Mysore. When the funeral service at St Mark's Church in Bangalore was over, Mysore was left without its highest-ranking engineer, and the Cauvery reservoir project without a potential champion.[21] Visvesvaraya, who had already agreed to take over as Chief Engineer of Mysore that year, heard the news in Bombay during a break from his consulting assignment in Hyderabad. On 5 August he wrote to the dewan, T. Ananda Row: 'I am deeply grieved to hear of the death of Capt. Dawes under such tragic circumstances. It is some satisfaction to read in the papers that the Mysore Government acted with great promptitude in all matters connected with that distressing event.' Possibly he had looked forward to working with Dawes. Now, he gently enquired of the dewan 'what arrangements you contemplate making to fill the vacancy caused by the sad death of Capt. Dawes'.[22]

*

When Visvesvaraya took over the reins of the Mysore PWD, he lost no time in reviving the idea of damming the Cauvery. In the Deccan, he'd studied and worked on the big dams at Bhatghar and Khadakwasla. The experience had convinced him that in regions without perennial, snow-fed rivers—in other words, most of peninsular India—large reservoirs were necessary to rationalize irrigation. He knew of the great multipurpose projects emerging around the world, and was especially inspired by the Aswan Dam on the Nile, which he had seen during his travels.[23]

In 1910, Visvesvaraya had his team of Indian engineers undertake fresh surveys for a dam-and-reservoir project at Kannambadi. They included B. Subba Rao, a superintending engineer, and two younger colleagues, M. Ananthalwar and K.R. Seshachar. Mysore's chief electrical engineer, an American named H.P. Gibbs, investigated the possibility of an additional installation to increase the capacity of the Sivasamudram power plant, and concluded that one could be built for Rs 8.5 lakh.[24]

These investigations formed the basis for Visvesvaraya's preliminary proposals for a dam and reservoir project. This plan, which he sketched out in the ensuing months, differed from Captain Dawes's proposals on some key points. Most importantly, Visvesvaraya abandoned the idea of a concrete pipe carrying the water all the way from the dam to the power plant at Sivasamudram. Instead, sluices would allow large volumes of water to flow down the regular course of the river towards the hydroelectric station. Unlike the earlier plan, Visvesvaraya proposed ways to make the project generate revenues without having to transport and sell electric power to buyers outside the state of Mysore.[25]

Visvesvaraya had come up with a more practical and potentially less expensive plan than the one Dawes had drawn up, but it was still extremely ambitious. It was part of his grand vision for Mysore—one that involved a modernized system of irrigation, the promotion of commercial agriculture and a market economy, and the fostering of industrial enterprises.

Visvesvaraya's reservoir was to be built in stages over a decade, finally reaching a capacity of around 39 thousand million cubic feet (39 TMC). It would bring up to 2,00,000 acres of land under irrigation, staving off famine in drought years and allowing cultivators to grow cash crops like sugarcane. It would also boost the flow at Sivasamudram so that the state could generate more electric power—not just for the mining companies but also for the new industries that he planned to promote in Mysore.[26]

The chief engineer made astoundingly confident predictions about his project. In around a decade, he argued, 'the return on the irrigation share of the capital may amount to as much as 8 per cent,' and at that stage Mysore 'may get produce valued at about 1½ crores from irrigation alone'. He also thought the project would help generate enough power to net the government more than Rs 30 lakh per year in revenue.[27]

For some four decades, the creation of a Cauvery reservoir had remained in the realm of theoretical possibility. It is easy to see why: the implications were manifold and the challenges—financial, legal, and logistical—enormous. But Visvesvaraya was a man in a hurry. Over the next year, he threw himself into the task of getting the project under way. In the process, he got involved in multiple, simultaneous, and frenetic negotiations.

*

The first set of negotiations was with John Taylor and Sons, the firm that represented the mining companies of the Kolar Gold Fields. When they realized the Sivasamudram plant was struggling to meet their need for electric power, the companies had begun to fret. They pressed the Mysore government to build a reservoir to shore up power generation, and tried to negotiate a fresh deal.

Strictly speaking, it should have been the dewan, T. Ananda Row, who negotiated on behalf of Mysore; but so complete was Visvesvaraya's identification with the reservoir project that he took on the job himself. He drove a hard bargain. On the afternoon of 30 November 1910, the mining companies' London-based representative, Arthur Taylor, along with a local emissary, called on Visvesvaraya at his office in Bangalore. Taylor was prepared to offer £11 per horsepower of electricity supplied each year—a small increase over the £10 the companies were currently paying—when the new reservoir was put into operation. He hinted that if the government didn't accept this offer, the companies had the option of producing their own power using oil engines.

Visvesvaraya did not bite. According to his note on the meeting, he told Taylor 'that if he had not come here to assure us of the willingness of the Company to pay £2 more per H.P. for power already supplied and £12 per H.P. for any additional power they might want, he need not waste his breath in carrying on negotiations with this Government'.[28]

Visvesvaraya didn't want the deal to fall through, for his reservoir project depended on it. But he was no pushover either. Over the next few weeks, the parties went back and forth several times, Visvesvaraya consulting H.P. Gibbs and the dewan when necessary. Eventually, the mining companies agreed to pay £12 per horsepower for the first ten years following the commissioning of a reservoir. In the interim, they would buy an additional 3,000 horsepower at the current rate of £10.[29]

Yet, after all this, Mysore was unable to guarantee that they would build a reservoir. As the months rolled on without a decision, the mining companies grew restive.[30] But Mysore's ability to get started depended on a number of other negotiations which were playing out simultaneously. Of these, the main challenge came from the government of the neighbouring Madras Presidency.

*

For decades, Mysore and Madras had been locked in battle over the major river they shared. Flowing eastward through the plains of Mysore, the Cauvery entered Madras territory, where the river and its tributaries irrigated a fertile delta in the vicinity of Tanjore before emptying into the Bay of Bengal. According to an agreement signed in 1892, Mysore was to seek Madras's go-ahead before constructing any irrigation works that impounded water before the Cauvery entered Madras. Madras, meanwhile, was bound to give its approval unless there was a threat to any 'prescriptive rights already acquired and actually in existence'.[31]

In October 1910, the Dewan of Mysore informed the Madras government about his state's plans to build a dam on the Cauvery. Madras, unsurprisingly, raised concerns. They argued that the project would seriously deplete the volume of the Cauvery as it entered Madras and endanger the welfare of farmers across the sprawling Tanjore delta.

But this was not the only objection. It emerged that Madras had been planning their own reservoir on the Cauvery—a much larger one than Mysore's—at Mettur, near Salem. Now they worried there wouldn't be enough water left in the river at Mettur to make this a viable proposition.[32]

In late November, Visvesvaraya travelled to Madras, where he parleyed with his counterparts in the PWD. A million acres of land were being irrigated in the Cauvery delta, the Madras engineers told him. To safeguard crops, they needed water to flow into the delta at a particular rate, represented by a reading of 7 feet on the gauge at the Upper Anicut near Trichy. In years when the flow measured less than this, the proposed reservoir in Mysore should not be permitted to store water.

Visvesvaraya replied that they had no cause for worry: Mysore's reservoir project would not materially reduce the flow of water into Madras. Figures showed that around 150–300 TMC of water 'was going to waste into the sea' each year. The proposed Mysore reservoir would only store 40–50 TMC.

Visvesvaraya was confident he'd made out a convincing case to the Madras engineers, who had been affable in meetings. Reporting to the dewan after returning to Bangalore, he praised them for their 'fair dealing'.[33]

But he soon found they had dug in their heels. Around ten days later, the office of Madras chief engineer C.A. Smith wrote that they could not proceed without seeing the complete design of Mysore's proposed reservoir and its irrigation system.[34] Smith worried that Mysore would impound water in drought years, precisely when Madras most needed it. If a strict system of monitoring was not put in place, Mysore's farmers might take more than their fair share of water from the canals.[35]

A long and tortuous correspondence followed. Ananda Row took the lead for Mysore, while Visvesvaraya continued to advise him on technical details. (There was an irony in this: Ananda Row was a Tanjore Maratha by lineage, his family hailing from the very delta Madras was trying to protect.) Mysore's Resident, Col. Hugh Daly, acted as an intermediary.

Ananda Row pointed out that irrigation in the Cauvery delta could hardly be under threat if the Madras government themselves had plans to construct an 80-TMC reservoir upstream of the delta.[36] The inference was that Madras was not just trying to safeguard its existing irrigation in the Cauvery delta, which was its legal right, but also its proposed expansion of irrigation in the future.[37] Visvesvaraya added impishly that 'any objection to the construction of a reservoir [at Kannambadi] . . . must apply with greater force to the Madras proposal': their Mettur reservoir was to be much larger.[38]

Both sides argued adroitly, indulging occasionally in sophistry, tossing out the odd red herring. Madras stalled; Mysore pressed. Finally, Mysore asked the Government of India to intervene. This initially backfired. The Inspector-General of Irrigation in India, John Benton, looked into the papers on the subject and issued an extensive note in which he came down heavily on the side of Madras's claims.[39]

All this while, pressure from the mining companies was mounting. As the prospect of an improved and assured supply of electricity receded, John Taylor and Sons hinted once again that they might withdraw their custom and set up their own diesel-based generating station in the gold fields. This would have dire financial consequences for Mysore.[40]

Finally, around September 1911, things began to move. It appears that Hugh Daly was able to put in a word with the Viceroy, Lord Hardinge, garnering some support for Mysore.[41] Hardinge's government suggested that Madras might be amenable to Mysore building a smaller reservoir, equivalent to their planned first stage (with a capacity of around 11 TMC). Mysore put this to Madras, while deciding that even if they built a smaller reservoir, they would lay the foundations of the dam wide enough to allow for the raising of its height later.[42]

In late September, the Madras government relented—partially. They agreed that Mysore could build a reservoir with a capacity of 11.03 TMC, provided the extent of the lands irrigated under it did not exceed 25,000 acres. They also made it clear that if Mysore went ahead and built the wider foundations, they could not use that fact later to demand permission to raise the dam.[43]

Mysore accepted these conditions, and the Government of India gave its blessing.[44]

There were to be many more disputes in working out the water-sharing arrangements in subsequent years, as Mysore and then Madras got down to constructing their respective reservoirs.[45] For the moment, though, Visvesvaraya and Ananda Row had won their first battle: they could now begin to build their dam. But they could do so only because they had, in parallel, wrestled successfully with a third challenge: to convince stakeholders *within* the Mysore government to approve the project.

*

Visvesvaraya's proposals for a reservoir first came before his colleagues in October 1910, as part of his comprehensive programme of public works. He had whittled down Dawes's previous estimates, but the projected costs were still enormous: Rs 160 lakh for the complete reservoir (an estimate that would later be revised upwards), Rs 94 lakh for expanding Mysore's railway network, and a few lakhs each year for sundry other projects.[46]

Mysore's Financial Department and the executive branch of government—the dewan and his councillors—had to scrutinize these projects before they could be green-lighted. Taken together, they formed an array of influential and spirited individuals with their own worldviews and institutional interests. While the dewan was firmly in his corner, Visvesvaraya had to work hard to win the others over.[47] In particular, he was up against a formidable opponent in the financial secretary, J.S. Chakravarti.

Jnan Saran Chakravarti was a precocious thirty-five-year-old official with a sterling academic and professional background. A Bengali Brahmin descended from a long line of pandits and teachers, he had been a star student and something of a prodigy at Presidency College in Calcutta, equally adept at the sciences and the humanities. In addition to his formal qualifications—a BA in science subjects, an MA in mathematics at the age of just twenty, and special commendations for research work in mathematics and chemistry—he was considered an exceptional scholar of English and Sanskrit, and had dabbled in legal studies.[48] He began his career as a teacher, but soon joined the Imperial Finance Department after topping its nationwide selection exams. He served for a decade in Rangoon, Allahabad and Calcutta before being deputed to Mysore, on generous terms, in 1908.[49]

Chakravarti was reared on principles of financial prudence, and challenged Visvesvaraya's attempts to rush through proposals requiring large expenditures. On 22 November 1910, he produced a painstaking memo scrutinizing every argument raised by Visvesvaraya in favour of the reservoir and other projects.

Was it really necessary to spend scores of lakhs on a reservoir, he asked, just to augment slightly the power available to the mining companies? Would it not be much less expensive, and equally effective, to strengthen existing efforts at river conservancy? Gold deposits were finite, he pointed out. Data suggested 'that Mysore gold mining has in all probability passed its zenith . . . the chances of the demand for power increasing considerably beyond the present standard are very remote indeed'.

As for the extra capacity (at a huge extra cost) contemplated for irrigation purposes, Chakravarti insisted it was unnecessary. Visvesvaraya had claimed that the project would irrigate 1,25,000 acres, resulting in substantial agricultural revenues a few years down the line. Chakravarti thought this was unrealistic, because the Cauvery valley in Mysore did not have the density of population needed for labour-intensive farming of the kind Visvesvaraya had in mind. Citing the report of the Indian Irrigation Commission issued some years previously, he emphasized that storage reservoirs designed to capture rainwater were expensive to build and unlikely to yield high returns. Nor was a reservoir strictly necessary to keep famine at bay: the tracts in question were well served by railways, so the procurement of food would not be a problem.

Most importantly, the projected cost of Rs 160 lakh was unthinkable. The government coffers contained around Rs 124 lakh, of which Rs 54 lakh was available for investment, assuming—and this was a crucial point—that they spent no money on anything else. Visvesvaraya and the dewan wanted to borrow money from public deposits in savings banks in order to make up some of the shortfall. This Chakravarti opposed, 'for such a course really amounts to incurring a loan which should quickly be repaid to avoid possible embarrassment'. In sum, the reservoir project would drain the treasury while preventing the state from addressing other necessary issues.[50]

Visvesvaraya responded in writing a few weeks later. He said Chakravarti had 'grievously misunderstood' the situation. Irrigated land would not depend solely upon water from the reservoir; that was only in addition to the water available in the river during the rainy season. As for the argument that intensive cultivation needed a larger population, he thought that people 'will come whenever there are chances of getting food and making money'. His ego had been pricked because the younger man had opposed his arguments by citing the report of the Irrigation Commission, the same body Visvesvaraya had so impressed a decade previously. 'I am not likely,' he wrote, 'to recommend any proposal which the Irrigation Commission would not have approved.'

Having indirectly chastised the financial secretary for stepping on his turf, Visvesvaraya proceeded to return the favour, lecturing him on the principles of finance in progressive countries. 'Whatever may be the case in old-fashioned Native States, modern Governments do not accumulate money. State accumulations are not meant to be locked up as they are in Mysore, earning a low rate of interest, but to be utilized to the fullest extent in attracting capital and developing the resources of the country.'

If they waited until Madras had built its reservoir at Mettur, Visvesvaraya warned, Mysore's hopes of proceeding with its project would diminish. The mining companies would not wait endlessly either. 'If counsels of inaction and timidity should prevail, a great opportunity would slip out of our hands.'[51] Clearly, Visvesvaraya was not above employing pressure tactics in negotiating with his Mysore colleagues. He also demanded from them a certain degree of trust and deference on the basis of his experience and standing, and didn't always bother to give detailed defences of his projections.[52]

Besides, he had the backing of the dewan. Although his contemporaries sometimes saw Ananda Row as an indecisive, status-quoist dewan,[53] his actions in the case of the reservoir project suggest a different picture. He supported it energetically. Informing the maharaja of progress in December 1910, he wrote that it was 'now or never' for the reservoir project. The chief engineer was 'no mean authority in a matter of this kind' and 'a most capable Engineer . . . , better than whom we never had before'. Ananda Row was in favour of removing the cap on individual savings bank accounts, so that the government could utilize them to help fund the project. The financial secretary's 'criticisms, even if correct in all respects, prove too much, and if ideas of that kind had prevailed in the past, or should yet prevail, the Mysore Government and the Mysore people should rest content with remaining on a dead level of mediocrity through the ages to come'.[54]

Visvesvaraya and his team did make some revisions to their plans as the discussions wore on (the negotiations with Madras, which were taking place in parallel, also had an impact on this). They had initially planned to build the reservoir in two stages, starting with a capacity of 28.72 TMC and increasing it later to 39.27 TMC. By December 1910, Visvesvaraya was suggesting three stages (7 TMC, rising to 29 and then 39 TMC), possibly as a means to lower the initial requirement of funds. As of March

1911, he had reverted to a two-stage plan. Now the first stage was to have a capacity of 11 TMC, going up in the second stage to 41.5 TMC.[55]

But Chakravarti was neither cowed by Visvesvaraya's manner nor mollified by his minor concessions. He protested that he was not given all the relevant papers to see, and when he was, he was given very little time to digest them.[56] He asked indirectly why the Financial Department had not been involved in the negotiations with the mining companies.[57] Over the next few months, in the midst of meetings and discussions, Chakravarti produced a series of further memos, arguing eloquently against hasty decisions, demanding justifications, and trying to safeguard—as it was his job to do—the financial security of the state.

Chakravarti eventually conceded that the state might need a reservoir, at least to guarantee electricity to the mining companies. He was still unconvinced about the irrigation component, a huge waste of money in his view. Visvesvaraya had claimed the combined project would be profitable. This, Chakravarti argued, was a sleight of hand. 'It is financially fallacious,' he argued, 'to couple the returns of the electric side and the irrigation side of the scheme and say that the return will be so much on the whole.'[58]

When Visvesvaraya and the dewan proposed building a first stage with foundations large enough to permit the eventual raising of the dam, Chakravarti argued this was risky unless they were absolutely sure that Madras was going to allow them to build a bigger reservoir eventually. Otherwise, it would mean a loss of Rs 30–40 lakh.[59]

Both combatants were equally spirited. The financial secretary thought Visvesvaraya's plans seductive but irresponsible. '[T]he idea of almost unlimited future development has a very powerful charm; and an advocate of the less expensive scheme runs the risk of appearing in the light of a narrow and short-sighted individual.' But huge expenditures required scrutiny.[60] Visvesvaraya pressed his point in his response: Chakravarti, he said, was unable to see the larger social and economic benefits of the proposed projects, '[concerning] himself solely with debt heads, cash balances and interest charges'.[61]

At the heart of the debate lay a difference of worldviews and temperaments. The finance officer was careful and scholarly; the engineer was expansive and impatient, not wanting to miss the wood for the trees. The former thought the state's primary responsibility was to maintain enough funds to care for its citizens in times of distress; the latter believed the state must take bold steps that would make such a need redundant.

*

The stalemate could easily have continued for years. But Mysore, for all the checks and balances in its systems of government, was a monarchy. So after a marathon run of correspondence, meetings, and negotiations, it fell to the maharaja to take a final decision. And Visvesvaraya had his ear. Although no decision was forthcoming for several months, Krishnaraja IV finally sanctioned the first stage of the reservoir project in October 1911.[62]

Visvesvaraya later described his role in precipitating the decision. As the proposals languished for months, he had, for all his bluster, grown disheartened, and even contemplated quitting. He went on leave instead. Seeing the situation unaltered upon his return, he went into a sulk. 'I kept aloof,' he recorded in his memoirs, 'and confined my activities for some time only to the punctual execution of the routine duties of my office.'

The maharaja, sensing something was amiss, asked what was troubling him. 'I told his Highness the truth,' the engineer recalled,

> that I was disappointed with the facilities given me to carry on new works and progressive developments. As there was no work in the State to be enthusiastic about, I wanted to leave

the service. His Highness' reply was: 'Don't be hasty, I will do what you want.'[63]

*

The table below shows the plans and projected costs for the project when construction began. It was to be carried out in two stages (the second stage being subject to negotiations with Madras). The first stage would create a reservoir of 11.03 TMC capacity in order to augment power generation at Sivasamudram; in the second, the reservoir would be enlarged to hold 41.5 TMC of water, and a network of irrigation canals would be constructed below it.

	At the completion of the first stage	**At the completion of the second stage**
Height of dam above riverbed	97 feet	124 feet
Maximum water level	80 feet	118 feet
Storage capacity	11.03 TMC	41.5 TMC
Length of dam	4,200 feet	6,300 feet
Length of waste weir	1,800 feet	2,600 feet
Other works	Increasing the capacity of the power station at Sivasamudram	Canal network serving 150,000 acres
Cost	Rs 81 lakh (dam) + Rs 8 lakh (additions to power station)	First stage cost + Rs 58 lakh (for raising the dam) + Rs 106 lakh for irrigation canals
Total cost		**Rs 253 lakh**

Table 9.1. Details of Mysore's Cauvery Reservoir Project as of November 1911

Sources: 'Cauvery Works: Great Extensions', TOI, 3 November 1911, p. 9. See also 'Cauvery Reservoir Works', KSA-MV-VOL, pp. 14–15.

A dedicated division of the PWD was set up to execute the reservoir project, and construction began in November 1911.[64] Several thousand migrant workers poured in from nearby provinces, and were engaged in earthwork, quarrying, and other tasks.[65] A sizeable settlement sprang up over the next few years, complete with offices, homes, a workshop, a hospital, a club, and a school.[66] Before long, various challenges arose: cholera struck the site, and unexpected topographical features made it complicated to lay the foundations of the dam. Nevertheless, work progressed. By the second year, masonry had begun to go up for the lower sections of the dam.[67] The government also formulated a plan for the rehabilitation of the peasants whose villages would be swallowed up by the new reservoir. Instead of simply buying them out, they would resettle the villagers in fresh tracts where they could benefit from the new irrigation works.[68]

Meanwhile, Visvesvaraya's star was rising: in 1912, he succeeded Ananda Row as dewan. His successors in the PWD took over the everyday management of the project, but he kept abreast of its progress, even making personal inspections. 'Mr. Visvesvaraya is a terror to the slack and the slow,' wrote a journalist in 1913. Labourers at the site told the correspondent 'how on a recent visit [Visvesvaraya's] keen eye sighted, at some distance, a micacious stone that some overseer had allowed to be welded into the mass of the foundations, having first smeared it over with cement when he heard the Dewan was coming. "Out with it," said the Dewan . . .'[69]

Mysore's gamble in building a large foundation paid off when an arbitrator appointed by the Government of India ruled, in 1914, that Madras must not stand in the way of their raising the dam. Although further disputes were to arise through the 1920s, there was no turning back now.[70] As the dam rose, it began to fulfil its projected functions. By 1915–16, the reservoir held enough water to keep all four installations (the fourth one having just been completed) of the Cauvery Power Scheme active, and the government was able to discontinue river conservancy works. Simultaneously, the canal works had progressed far enough to enable farmers to grow sugarcane.[71] By 1917–18, the PWD had begun 'work . . . [related] to the second stage' of the reservoir, which had recently been christened the Krishnarajasagara in honour of Mysore's ruler.[72]

The progress achieved in these early years represented a stupendous engineering achievement. A vivid description of the period is to be found in *New India's Rivers*, a book brought out in 1956 by Henry C. Hart, an American political scientist. To begin with, the engineers were in a race against time: Mysore had undertaken to supply additional electric power to the Kolar mining companies by 1915. Further, they were almost entirely reliant on manual labour and animal power. Stones were transported to the site in bullock carts. There they were cut and laid in the emerging structure by hand. To set them, the engineers used not cement but *surki,* an inexpensive traditional mixture of limestone and clay. Finally, the dam had to be put up in a section 'where the Cauvery flows swiftly through its rocky bed'. This meant clearing the foundations and erecting the masonry in small stretches during the dry season each year, and safeguarding the emerging structure from the swollen river during the monsoons. The year leading up to the deadline saw frenetic activity. 'In that last hectic year,' Hart writes,

> it was the zeal of the huge team Sir M Visvesvaraya had drawn to the dam-site that saved the day. The senior engineers shared his own determination; . . . their self-respect was at stake. Their assistants were Mysoreans fresh from engineering college, and the physical energy and zeal of those youths seemed to grow with the obstacles. Thousands of ordinary workmen in that fourth year paid back to the job the loyalty created by three years of steady work at fair pay.[73]

As is evident from Hart's almost gushing tone, he was enraptured by modern India's embrace of ambitious dam projects. His account appears to gloss over the likelihood of any friction between the officers and the labourers at a time when extraordinary demands were placed on the latter. Nevertheless, it gives a valuable sense of the manifold pressures under which Mysore's engineers worked, and the pioneering nature of their work: it was probably the first project on such a large scale to be undertaken in colonial India without the involvement of British engineers.

Indeed, there were to be many more legal, financial, and engineering challenges as the project continued, spanning the tenures of multiple chief engineers and dewans. There were further negotiations with Madras over the use of the Cauvery waters; issues with ballooning costs; and technical problems such as the creation of a 1.75-mile-long tunnel to take the principal canal to agricultural lands situated beyond the hilly terrain at Hulikere, around 25 miles from the reservoir. At one point, Visvesvaraya himself—long retired from the dewanship—was invited back to head a committee overseeing the construction of the principal irrigation canal. It was during the administration of Mirza Mohammed Ismail, a dewan whose vision was substantially aligned to Visvesvaraya's, that the project finally reached completion; the canals alone cost Rs 2 crore. The year was 1932.[74]

*

In subsequent decades, the finished KRS project became a symbol of a progressive Mysore, and helped transform the Cauvery valley—the district of Mandya in particular—into an affluent sugar belt.[75] On a visit to the district in the summer of 2019, I saw sprawling green fields of cane and paddy under a glorious blue sky.

Locals told me that their ancestors initially grew rain-fed crops like ragi and maize. They had been able to switch to lucrative crops like rice and sugarcane only after irrigation began under the KRS project. On the highway near the village of Dudda, an enthusiastic young man told me that India depended on Mandya for its food grains, and if there had been no canal water, there would be no hope of grain in Mandya.[76]

The KRS and its irrigation canals are clearly central to the lives of many, for whom Visvesvaraya remains the face of the project. The district reportedly has hundreds of memorials to the engineer.[77] In one village, I saw a small Ganesha temple with busts of Visvesvaraya and Krishnaraja Wadiyar IV in the yard. The former was described as *annadaata*, provider of food. In a public park in the centre of Mandya town stands a towering statue of the former dewan, sponsored by the government-owned Mysore Sugar Company.

All of this suggests a near-deification of Visvesvaraya in the present day. But his legacy is not without its opponents. One set of critics claims that he has received too much credit for the KRS. When, in 2020, the Karnataka government decided to put up statues of Visvesvaraya and Krishnaraja IV at the South Gate of the KRS, protestors argued against placing the two men on the same footing. The benevolent and far-sighted maharaja was the key figure behind the project, they said; Visvesvaraya only carried out his wishes as a part of his job. Moreover, he only played a peripheral role in a project that took two decades to complete. He was not even the originator of the project; that honour should go to the intrepid Captain Dawes.[78]

There is no doubt that the execution of the KRS was the work of several capable engineers.[79] Even in Visvesvaraya's time, his subordinates played key roles in the studies that undergirded his proposals. It is also true that Dawes had prepared a scheme for a multipurpose project before Visvesvaraya.

Yet, as the above narrative indicates, the idea was languishing, before Visvesvaraya showed how it could be implemented in a relatively practical and self-contained manner. Moreover, only someone with Visvesvaraya's nationwide reputation as an engineer, his clout, and his immense drive could have ensured the project got under way in the face of the numerous obstacles it faced. In this sense, he was undoubtedly the pivotal figure behind the project.

Ultimately, the more important debate about the KRS is not who should be celebrated for it, but whether the outcomes justified the massive costs—not just financial, as Chakravarti had pointed out, but also social and environmental. Some of these questions would be raised by persistent critics in the 1920s, testing the strength of Visvesvaraya's convictions. Before that, however, he threw himself into many other, equally transformative undertakings in Mysore.

10

At the Helm

With construction on the Cauvery Reservoir Project finally under way, Visvesvaraya had ticked a key item off his list by 1911. But he was also making progress on the other components of his public works agenda. Surveys and blueprints were being prepared for the new railway lines he had proposed from Mysore to Hassan and Nanjangud to Erode.[1] Visvesvaraya had also made plans to revamp the working of the Marikanave, the large irrigation reservoir near Hiriyur that had been commissioned before his tenure: he proposed to add a new canal to the project and implement his block system of irrigation in the command area.[2]

By his third year as chief engineer, then, Visvesvaraya had wrought enormous changes. Although it was too early to judge of their success, his initiatives were legion. Gigantic engineering projects were under way; new organizations had sprung up; the bureaucracy had been jolted awake. It was widely known that it was Visvesvaraya who had pushed through the Kannambadi project, and that the Economic Conference was his brainchild. He had also received commendations from the governments of Mysore and India. At the Imperial Durbar held in Delhi in December 1911, he was made a Commander in the Order of the Indian Empire (CIE),[3] an honour for which he had been recommended by the British Resident in Mysore.[4] The following year the Mysore government publicly lauded 'the energy with which certain large and important projects have been prepared by the Chief Engineer, Mr. Visvesvaraya'.[5]

Soon there were murmurs in the corridors of government that the Chief Engineer was destined for—or at least interested in—bigger things. Some believed he was already pulling the strings of government, the dewan having been reduced to a figurehead. Now, as T. Ananda Row neared retirement, the grapevine had it that the maharaja had no choice but to offer Visvesvaraya the dewan's post: otherwise he would quit the government, leaving the Kannambadi project without its leader and Mysore without its chief engineer.[6]

The suggestion that Visvesvaraya was angling for the dewan's position was probably a trifle uncharitable. But it does appear that he was not entirely averse to the possibility.[7] Although he later recorded that he would have been content with being a councillor overseeing education and industries, he knew that the dewanship would give him unrivalled powers to undertake far-reaching development programmes in Mysore.

In any case, Mysore officialdom had sensed the maharaja's mood correctly. When the monarch pressed him to accept the position, Visvesvaraya allowed himself to be convinced.[8] By October 1912, it was public knowledge that he was waiting in the wings.[9] The following month, Ananda Row called curtains on a four-decade-long Mysorean career. Krishnaraja IV issued a royal decree:

> we, placing trust and confidence in the loyalty, ability and judgment of Mokshagundam Visvesvaraya, C.I.E., do hereby appoint the said Mokshagundam Visvesvaraya, C.I.E., to be the Dewan of Mysore, and we do further appoint the said

> Mokshagundam Visvesvaraya, C.I.E., to be *ex-officio* President of the Council.[10]

At a Durbar organized at the Mysore Palace on 10 November, Visvesvaraya received his *sanad* (the royal deed of his appointment) and ceremonial robes. The next day, he was back at the secretariat in Bangalore to begin his innings as dewan.[11]

*

Visvesvaraya's appointment as dewan was unprecedented in many ways. Never before had an engineer officer risen to the pinnacle of the Mysore administration. The dewans since the Rendition of 1881 had all come from literary or legal backgrounds. They were members of the Mysore Civil Service who had typically served in non-technical areas of government. All of them had spent years, usually decades, in the Mysore service before being appointed to the dewanship.[12] Under normal circumstances, the senior-most member of Ananda Row's council, H.V. Nanjundayya,[13] would have expected to succeed him. Nanjundayya was a distinguished civil servant and scholar, a former Chief Judge of Mysore's Chief Court.[14] But Visvesvaraya, who had only arrived in Mysore three years previously and had never served on the dewan's council, had vaulted over him.

These circumstances meant that Visvesvaraya laboured from the start against a simmering resentment in some quarters.[15] But he had the maharaja's backing, for he was the right man in the right place at the right time. Having arrived recently from Bombay, he did not belong to any of the Durbar's competing factions. At the same time, he was a native Mysorean, which meant that in the context of the long-standing Mysorean-Madrasi rivalry, his appointment would be welcomed by the majority of the populace.[16] He had already proved to be a dynamic leader in the office of chief engineer. And although the British Resident, Hugh Daly, thought Visvesvaraya 'rather wanting in tact', he endorsed the choice, noting that the engineer was 'liberal-minded &. . . free from any taint of nepotism'.[17]

The Anglo-Indian press welcomed the development. Ananda Row had been a competent but unadventurous dewan, the *Times of India* opined. On the other hand, Visvesvaraya, in his time as chief engineer,

> has infused a considerable part of his restless enthusiasm even in departments which did not strictly belong to him. His mind is full of ideas as to what should be done to instil the spirit of progress among his own people, and his position as Dewan will give him a rare opportunity of converting them into facts.

Although some observers had questioned the wisdom of making a prime minister of an engineer, 'this objection . . . does not apply to Mr Visveswarayya who has a wide knowledge of affairs, and is not likely to deal with men as if they were brick, mortar or road-metal.' Moreover, Visvesvaraya 'is understood to have some large schemes for the economic and industrial development of Mysore, and his term of office promises to be one of strenuous activity'.[18]

There were other kinds of expectations too. An oft-repeated anecdote has it that when Visvesvaraya was offered the dewanship, he first gathered his kith and kin, warning them that he would only take up the position if they all agreed never to come to him for favours of any kind.[19] The story may be apocryphal, but it illustrates the traditional assumptions of patronage that came with high office.

*

Soon, Visvesvaraya was being welcomed by various groups within the state. Fittingly, it was the Mysore Civil Engineers' Association that organized one of the first public functions in honour of the new dewan. The meeting, held on 30 November 1912, was chaired by a former dewan, V.P. Madhava Rao, and attended by the serving British Resident, Hugh Daly. Visvesvaraya got down to brass tacks immediately. Addressing his fellow engineers—who, as employees of the Public Works Department, were usually generalists—he urged each of them to pick a specialism. Many large projects were under way in Mysore, he said, in the areas of irrigation, railways, waterworks, and the construction of buildings. 'No single engineer can be an expert in more than one, two or three of these great branches of engineering, and if the works are to be carried out and maintained efficiently and economically, we require specialists who are at the top, or very near the top of their profession.'[20]

When prominent residents of the city of Mysore felicitated him—aptly, it was at the Rangacharlu Memorial Hall, named for the former dewan most in sync with Visvesvaraya's thinking—the new dewan delivered a sermon. He provided a laundry list of areas in which work was yet to be done in Mysore—education, rail connectivity, commercial agriculture, cottage industries—and stressed that progress in these areas would depend on 'local initiative, enthusiasm and enterprise on the part of the people'. He then reeled off various statistics, speaking of Mysore's illiteracy and reliance on agriculture. He told his audience to let go of '[t]he Hindu ideal [which] is that this world is a preparation for the next and not a place to stay in and make oneself comfortable'. They must instead observe how

> [t]he nationality of Western countries . . . rests on an economic basis. Their activities, political, industrial and social, are subordinated to their resources at command, and they all aim at

> the creation of more wealth and increased comfort . . . we must compare ourselves with, and be guided by the experience of, progressive countries. The comparison brings to light certain startling truths . . .[21]

In Bangalore, a reception was organized in the Glass House—then known as the Albert Victor Conservatory—in Lalbagh, the British-run botanical garden dating from the days of Hyder Ali. As a crusader for industries, Visvesvaraya would have appreciated the unintended symbolism, for the conservatory was modelled on London's Crystal Palace, which had housed the Great Exhibition of 1851, Britain's paean to industrialism.[22] As his predecessor, Ananda Row, looked on, representatives of various communities, organizations and interest groups presented formal addresses to Visvesvaraya. Among them were spokespersons of the Muslims, Jains, Lingayats, Vokkaligas, and Arya Vaisyas.[23]

No fewer than ten speakers placed before the new dewan their wish lists for what his administration should undertake. They asked for more railways, for a government-run bank, for improvements to primary and industrial education, and much more. These were, in fact, of a piece with the many measures Visvesvaraya was himself interested in, and he responded with a resumé of initiatives the government was considering. But then he fired an unexpected salvo. 'In all the addresses you have been pleased to read to me,' he intoned,

> you state what, in your opinion, His Highness' Government should do, or what I should do, but there is not one word said of what you yourselves are going to do, not one word even of offer of co-operation on your part. I can make no promise or response on such terms. If the public ask me what His Highness' Government is going to accomplish during my term of office, I will only say it will depend on what the people themselves may

> help to build up. . . . We have able officers, both European and Indian, in the service of the State, to help us, and if the people also give evidence of a disposition to move, to awaken from the lethargy of years and show capacity to undertake reforms and improvements, Government will be prepared to guide and direct their activities into healthy and profitable channels.[24]

If the audience bristled at this ambush, they did not show it: a newspaper report of the event recorded that the speech was greeted by '[p]rolonged applause'.[25] What is unmistakable is that they had received a clear and early indication of Visvesvaraya's approach to the dewanship. He, and the experts he relied on, would work tirelessly to improve the material basis of the people's lives; but they would do so from on high, didactically. They knew what a modern, productive society should look like; they would show the way ahead. They would seek the people's inputs, but the latter must first bestir themselves and become worthy followers.

*

Visvesvaraya's paternalistic tone was not merely an expression of his personality. It also reflected the accepted position of the dewan as second only to the maharaja in the state. The dewan controlled the levers of government. He addressed the annual sessions of the Representative Assembly, and presided over the sessions of the Legislative Council. While the Legislative Council was comprised almost entirely of nominated members and officials, the older Representative Assembly did contain some elected members (although these tended to be mostly rich landowners or businessmen elected on a limited franchise).[26] Yet both were piloted by the dewan, himself an unelected official.

The dewan also had his own council consisting of two senior civil servants, which formed the executive arm of government.

At the start of Visvesvaraya's tenure, the First and Second Members of Council were H.V. Nanjundayya and D. Devaraj Urs respectively. The latter died unexpectedly in December 1912, and was replaced by M. Kantharaj Urs, an official who happened to be the uncle of the maharaja.[27] In 1914, they were joined by a third colleague, styled Extraordinary Member of Council. This was Krishnaraja IV's younger brother, Kantirava Narasimharaja Wadiyar, known as the yuvaraja.[28] The yuvaraja was in his mid-twenties, and had recently returned from an educational tour of Europe. His appointment to the council was an unusual move, designed to give him some administrative experience.[29] Possibly he also functioned as the eyes and ears of the maharaja.

Between them, the dewan and his councillors supervised the various departments of government devoted to agriculture, finance, the police, the judiciary, forests, public works, public health, education, and many other subjects.[30] Although there were two legislative bodies, their ability to hold the executive accountable was severely circumscribed.[31] The dewan also headed the Economic Conference, which functioned as a sort of shadow bureaucracy, advising the relevant departments of government. The powers of the dewan, then, were vast. He was a sort of super-bureaucrat in command of the officers running the business of government.[32]

The dewan's position also came with grand perks and untold prestige. Even a man as unsentimental as Visvesvaraya cannot have been entirely immune to these attractions. While his office continued to be in the secretariat in Bangalore, his accommodation was upgraded significantly. He now occupied a grand colonial bungalow a few miles north of the secretariat and a couple of miles south of the palace the Wadiyars had built for their stays in Bangalore. Surrounded by large grounds, it was a two-storeyed house with a grand, pillared porch and spacious verandahs. Its first resident was the Reverend John Garrett of the Wesleyan

Mission, who in 1858 established a school that developed into the Central College, Visvesvaraya's alma mater. Garrett, who hailed from the Isle of Man, had given the bungalow the Manx name of Ballabrooie (meaning a farm or house bordered by a river). In 1897, the state government bought the house from Garrett's son-in-law, and designated it the home of the serving dewan.[33]

It is safe to assume that Visvesvaraya had a phalanx of servants to help him run Ballabrooie and entertain official guests. When his predecessor, Ananda Row, retired, the maharaja granted him 'a permanent establishment of two harikars, one jamedar, one daffedar, and six dalayets'—the terms refer to errand boys, head footmen, and liveried servants—along with 'the existing guard of infantry' at his home.[34] If this was the staff of a retired official, one can imagine a serving dewan's retinue. Visvesvaraya also maintained a working office at home, and often conducted meetings and other official work there.[35]

When in Mysore city, the dewan stayed in Lake View, a bungalow on the Yelwal Road that faced the Kukkarahalli tank. (Today it is called the Jaladarshini Guest House, and the road it is situated on is known as the Hunsur Road.)[36] In Mysore, his regular ambit encompassed the maharaja's spectacular palace; the Public Offices, where the Representative Assembly sat; and Government House, where British officials and European guests stayed when they were in Mysore.[37]

*

To legitimize themselves, monarchies through the ages have relied on rituals designed to invoke a hoary genealogy.[38] The Wadiyars did this, of course, but they were also embedded in the British Empire, which itself was adept at using the language of spectacle to bolster its all-powerful image.[39] As a result, Visvesvaraya, as Mysore's highest executive officer, functioned in a culture suffused with ceremony. In an often-reproduced photograph from the period, he is dressed in the Mysore dewan's traditional costume for the durbar: lace-edged turban, dark long coat with gold-embroidered lapels and cuffs, satin sash across the left shoulder, creased trousers, and gleaming shoes of black leather. Slight of frame and slender of face, sporting a wispy moustache, he looks unreasonably young for a man in his fifties. He stands straight, his feet close together, his hands clasped before his stomach, his shoulders slightly hunched. The body language and the faraway look in his eye give little indication of the assertive man within.[40]

If the costume was dictated by tradition, his role on ceremonial occasions was governed by intricate protocols. These ranged from where he sat (usually next to the maharaja) when he accompanied the monarch on visits outside the state, to who should present him with *pan* and *attar* upon their arrival.[41] When the British Resident attended the Dasara festivities, he sat to the right of the maharaja, and it was the dewan's duty to offer him *pan, attar* and garlands. All this was part of an elaborate sequence that was carefully negotiated between the palace, the Residency, and the Government of India over many years.[42]

A stickler for discipline and bureaucratic formality, Visvesvaraya embraced the ritualistic aspects of his role as dewan. The pomp and ceremony may well have appealed to him, for he was a great believer in the importance of dress and comportment.[43] Whether he enjoyed entirely the shows of deference to the maharaja that were part of official protocol we do not know, but he did share a cordial relationship with the king, who gave him considerable elbow room at the start of his tenure.

When it came to relations with the British, however, Visvesvaraya was very sensitive to any perceived slights (although in his public utterances and policies he reiterated Mysore's loyalty and gratitude to its colonial suzerain).[44] One anecdote, which has passed into legend, illustrates this nicely. It concerns the tradition by which the Mysore royals invited the Resident and other prominent British officials to the palace for a 'European Durbar Day' during the annual Dasara festival. The Resident, as noted earlier, sat to the king's right. The European invitees were provided with chairs on one side of the Durbar Hall, while the Indian courtiers, including the dewan, were seated on the floor on the other side.

When Visvesvaraya first saw this arrangement after becoming chief engineer, it stuck in his craw. Whatever its origins, he could not abide the implication of a possible differentiation in status. He declined to attend the function the following year, and when pressed, explained his reasoning. The result was a change in the protocol, so that from then on, everyone sat on chairs.

The story has the ring of truth, and was recorded by at least two contemporaries of Visvesvaraya's in the Mysore service.[45] In fact, the concerns ran both ways: anthropologist Aya Ikegame's incisive work shows that British officials were equally anxious about the symbolism of each step in the function. They were not pleased that the Resident had to wait for the maharaja to sit before he could take his seat; that he was asked to walk on the monarch's left when they entered the royal gallery; that the dimensions of his chair were such as to leave his feet dangling above the floor.[46] Visvesvaraya's intervention, however, was the more remarkable for having come from the less powerful side of the equation.

On another occasion later in his dewanship, Visvesvaraya entered into a correspondence with H.V. Cobb (an ICS man who was appointed Mysore's British Resident in 1916)[47] over the question of the correct mode of address for the dewan. Cobb had opened a demi-official letter with the salutation 'My dear Dewan'. Visvesvaraya objected to this, writing:

> As important matters are discussed between your office and mine, I personally think it is better to retain a dignified style of

> address and, besides, it is not usual to address a person by his office whatever may have been the practice in the remote past. The alternative to the form hitherto used will be 'My dear Sir' or 'Dear '. I hope you will not mind my inviting attention to this matter.[48]

The Resident was taken aback. It was as a mark of respect, he said, that he had 'adopted the use of "Dewan" instead of "Sir", the former seeming to me the more ceremonious'. He assured Visvesvaraya that 'it is a common English practice today in Ecclesiastical, legal & political circles to address persons by their office', but offered to change the way he addressed the dewan in future letters.[49]

Visvesvaraya could be prickly, but his concern for self-respect did not stop at his own person. In an era when titles and post-nominals abounded, some of his junior staff were referred to in official contexts simply by their names. Visvesvaraya decreed that any government employee with a university degree or drawing a monthly salary of Rs 50 or more must be referred to as 'Mr'. (It seems not to have occurred to him, however, that *every* employee—they were all men—deserved to be called 'Mr'.)[50]

*

In November 1913, a year after Visvesvaraya had taken over as dewan, Mysore had a guest vastly more powerful than the Resident who came down from Bangalore every Dasara: the Viceroy of India, Lord Hardinge.

The 'viceregal special' pulled into Mysore's railway station on the morning of 6 November. The viceroy and Lady Hardinge were received by the maharaja, the yuvaraja, the Resident, the dewan, and many other notables. As they emerged from their saloon, a thirty-one-gun salute was fired from the Fort. There were guards of honour, public addresses, and much fanfare as the entourage proceeded to Government House, 'the escort to the procession [being] formed by a squadron of Imperial Service Lancers and His Highness's own Bodyguard who looked very well with their panther skin schabragues [sic] and were beautifully mounted'.[51]

That evening, the Viceroy announced at a formal banquet that the Instrument of Transfer—under which the Rendition had been carried out in 1881—was to be superseded by a bilateral treaty between Mysore and the Government of India. This treaty, he said, 'will place the relations between us on a footing more in consonance with Your Highness' actual position among the Feudatory Chiefs in India'.[52] This was, on paper at least, a transformative moment in the relationship between the state and the colonial government.

The rest of the viceregal tour was occupied with the twin objectives of finalizing the treaty and cementing the ties between maharaja and viceroy. The Hardinges were entertained lavishly. Lord Hardinge camped with Krishnaraja Wadiyar in Karapur to watch the traditional *Khedda*, the trapping of wild elephants that would later be sold or added to the royal stables.[53] He went on a bison hunt with the maharaja and R.H. Campbell, the monarch's private secretary. (They found no bison; the herds, ironically, had fled the jungles of Mysore as a consequence of the upheaval caused by the Khedda.)[54] He visited the construction site of the Kannambadi reservoir.[55] He was shown the breathtaking Gersoppa Falls, the historic city of Srirangapatnam, and the gold mines of Kolar.[56] On 19 November, the viceregal train arrived in Bangalore station to even greater fanfare than they had witnessed on first reaching Mysore. Once again, Visvesvaraya was a part of the welcoming party. The guests stayed at the Residency, located on the High Ground, not far from the dewan's house.[57] During his stay, the viceroy called on Visvesvaraya at Ballabrooie.[58]

A few days later, the Hardinges concluded their tour. On 26 November, the Resident Hugh Daly and the maharaja signed the new treaty in Mysore city.[59] The terms had been finalized during the intervals between trapping elephants and hunting for bison in the jungles of Karapur. The viceroy, the maharaja, Visvesvaraya, and Daly had all taken part in the discussions.[60]

In theory, the treaty 'gave full powers of internal administration in the State to His Highness'.[61] But as an official chronicler later acknowledged, it did not radically alter the position of Mysore vis-à-vis the Government of India. Nor did it change the fact that Mysore had to pay a subsidy of Rs 35 lakh each year to the colonial government. It was, however, of great symbolic importance, being a reciprocal agreement in place of a decree from above. Moreover, certain egregious provisions of the erstwhile Instrument of Transfer were toned down or eliminated. For instance, a clause allowing the Government of India to take over the state in specific circumstances was deleted.[62]

Visvesvaraya later referred with faux modesty to 'the small part I had taken in the evolution of the new Treaty'.[63] Krishnaraja Wadiyar had written to him on 22 November: 'I fully realise the fact that the success of my representation to the Viceroy [about the need for a new treaty] was in no small measure due to the able and convincing manner in which you put the case before him.' He complimented the dewan on '[having] won not only this lasting honour for Mysore, but accomplished so much for the State in several other directions'.[64]

The maharaja's praise is perhaps not to be read literally, for tact and diplomacy were not Visvesvaraya's strong points. He does appear to have got on well with Lord Hardinge—who had earlier intervened to resolve the deadlock with Madras over the Kannambadi project—and he was certainly involved in the deliberations. But correspondence from this period suggests that it was the sympathetic Resident, Hugh Daly, who had played the more influential role, smoothing negotiations over several months between the maharaja and the colonial government.[65]

In any case, the change from Instrument to Treaty was hardly achieved by force of personality alone. Instead, as Bjørn Hettne shows, it must be viewed in the light of the larger political context in the Indian subcontinent. The British were wary of the emerging popular base of the Indian National Congress after the Swadeshi movement in the first decade of the twentieth century. They began to woo the rulers of princely India, granting them concessions to cement their allegiance as a counter to nationalist sentiment. In this situation, the Treaty could be presented as a pat on the back to Mysore for its administrative record, and recognition of its royals as political allies.[66]

*

Whatever its causes, the symbolic boost to Mysore's status came at a useful time for Visvesvaraya, who was anxious to transform the kingdom into a modern, self-sufficient, and prosperous state, and needed all the elbow room he could get for his ambitious projects.[67]

The first and most important site of intervention, he decided, must be the village. He gave an early indication of his thinking during his first speech to the Representative Assembly, made a month before the Viceroy's visit. Addressing the members of the assembly at Mysore's Public Offices, he first gave the customary précis of the government's activities in the year past.[68] He then expressed his personal views on the needs of the state. The people's standard of living had shown some improvement in recent years, but still:

> Only one person in every sixteen is able to read and write. The cultivators are not fully occupied even in normal seasons; in

> years of scarcity, for months at a time, they are left without occupation and without hope. Three-fourths of our population are dependent on agriculture and the great bulk of them live in villages without activities or aspirations outside their individual households. Our land-owners are small men, our business is conducted by small traders and artisans, each working singly for himself. The lessons of co-operation and organization have not permeated even the top strata of society.[69]

Mysore's leaders 'must develop the life and capacity of our people by encouraging in them self-help, power of initiative, courage to change, courage to create new things, spirit of co-operation and a capacity for organization'. The Economic Conference was a step in that direction, but its impact was largely in urban centres; now 'a special effort is necessary to stimulate economic activity in rural areas'. In each village in the state, more children must go to school; each family must save either cash or food grain for use in the eventuality of famine; they must also have a trade to fall back on during the off-season for farming, or in times of famine. Finally, '[t]he villages may be called upon to publish once a year a few essential statistics of their economic growth'.[70]

Soon after, he codified these ideas into a formal 'village improvement scheme', having consulted civil servants and members of the Representative Assembly. A pro forma was created specifying the kinds of statistics individual villages must collect. If village residents put forward proposals for projects related to education, trade, and basic amenities, the state would provide 50 per cent of the funds.[71] In the first year of the scheme's operation, 79 per cent of the 13,360 villages in the state had set up committees to consider development projects. The state's official report for the year 1914–15 recorded that these committees had raised the equivalent of Rs 93,953 in funds and voluntary labour, while the government had granted a total of Rs 84,005.

Under the committee's guidance, the rural citizenry had donated their labour to construct roads and wells. Well-to-do individuals had put up money for the building of schools and travellers' inns. In the principal districts of the state, the village committees had come together for conferences.[72]

Similar results were recorded in subsequent years. Government officials met individual Village Improvement Committees and gave talks 'on co-operation, sanitation, education and other elements of village improvement'. Committees from different villages continued to meet at conferences.[73] In thousands of villages, the committees 'subscribed for [sic] newspapers, . . . held weekly meetings for instruction and recreation, and . . . devoted half a day a week to labour for communal purposes'.[74]

Visvesvaraya himself made extensive tours through the state's districts, and urged his councillors to do likewise.[75] He travelled frequently: in just one seven-month period, between September 1915 and April of the following year, he travelled through the Kolar, Chitaldrug, Tumkur, Mysore, and Hassan districts.[76] A colleague described his meticulous preparation for each of these tours.

> Several weeks before a District tour commenced, a few officers were set to collect factual and statistical information relating to the state of official business in the District, its agricultural features, irrigational facilities, industrial activities, educational progress and general economic conditions. The major and minor wants of each Taluk, as revealed by official records, proceedings of the Representative Assembly and the Economic Conference, were tabulated. There thus emerged a miniature Gazetteer of the District and an aide-memoire of matters which required attention at Government level. These preparations ensured the most economical and fruitful use of the time which the Dewan was able to spend in the District. The results of

> personal inspections and decisions taken at conferences with local officers and leading citizens completed the record. Along with these comprehensive tour notes, responsibility sheets were issued, indicating which officer or officers were expected to pursue matters that called for further examination or action.[77]

In all, with his frequent personal appearances and the creation of village committees, conferences, and statistical returns, Visvesvaraya was a palpable presence in the villages of Mysore. But there was another aspect in which the people's interaction with the state was transformed. This was in the increasing voice given to citizens in matters of local importance.

Until the early twentieth century, the figure of *amildar* ruled the roost in the talukas of Mysore, just as deputy commissioners loomed large at the district level. Amildars liked to think of themselves as swashbuckling figures as they rode around the countryside, simultaneously playing the roles of revenue collector, magistrate, policeman, and administrator. As agents of the maharaja, they inspired awe. They administered their territories with a firm hand, sometimes harsh and sometimes benevolent.[78] Under Visvesvaraya, however, they had to take a step back and listen to citizen leaders. The dewan believed firmly that 'non-officials', in the parlance of the day, should take responsibility in matters of local development. As a result, merchants and other independent citizens not employed by the state sat alongside government officials on the village committees and the committees of the Economic Conference.[79]

This created a stir. A contemporary in the Mysore bureaucracy recalled that '[f]or a time the officials thought they had even lost caste with the Dewan'. The sight of 'District and Taluk Officers and the Secretaries to Government and . . . non-officials' sitting 'on the same public platform' was a novel one, and likely unnerved those who were used to lording it over the public. Some of these officials thought the citizens were being emboldened to the point where they couldn't be governed. One reported the story of a village headman whose house Visvesvaraya had visited. The headman, swelling with importance, defied the Amildar the next day—a thing previously unheard of. A second story, also unverified, had it that Visvesvaraya once convened a gathering in the Kolar district where he asked locals about their needs. One resident fearlessly criticized the officers of the area on many counts.

> The Dewan was taken up with this man's public spirit and he asked him to produce proof of his allegations in the afternoon. In the evening when the gathering again assembled, the Dewan called upon the chief speaker of the morning to come forward. The Amildar or the police chief most reverentially submitted to the Dewan that the non-official speaker was wanted in several criminal cases, that so long he was absconding, that fortunately that morning his presence at the meeting was welcome and when he came out, the police took him to the lock-up![80]

The tenor of the official records, however, should not be taken to mean that the new endeavours found universal favour. As might be expected, there were those who did not buy into the idea of voluntary work for common ends. This was acknowledged by Visvesvaraya himself in 1914, when he told the Representative Assembly he did not want 'penal or coercive measures' for those who played truant; instead, 'lists of defaulters [could be] sent to the Amildars and, if necessary, also posted in the village *chavadi*'.[81]

Like most of Visvesvaraya's ideas, the Village Improvement Scheme was essentially a top-down process. Local initiative and the participation of citizens notwithstanding, the vision of what constituted progressive projects came entirely from the government. It was formulated by Visvesvaraya and others he had trained, and then disseminated through official visits, speeches, and conferences. Besides, the government would only fund projects it deemed to be in line with this vision. The idea that village dwellers might possess traditional know-how—what we would now call indigenous knowledge—of some value was never seriously considered.[82]

*

Visvesvaraya, then, had democratic inclinations, albeit within limits. He had arrived in a kingdom ruled by bureaucrats at the command of a monarch. He wanted to turn it into something more responsive to the public, if not responsible to it. At the same time, he was instinctively wary of the prolonged negotiations, criticisms, and roadblocks to development (as he saw it) that would inevitably accompany a largely representative system. He saw polities as being somewhere on an evolutionary timescale towards modernity. Democratization was important but must proceed step by step. People must be trained in the ways of parliamentary debate and prove themselves responsible enough to handle real legislative power.

This philosophy informed the political reforms Visvesvaraya brought in during his dewanship. He set about giving some teeth to the Representative Assembly. Its members, who were previously allowed only to make speeches detailing their needs, were now permitted to discuss Mysore's budget. A précis of the budget was drawn up in Kannada for the benefit of members who were not conversant with English. From 1917, a second session of the Assembly was organized for this purpose, as the existing annual meeting at around Dasara came after the budget was passed each year. Members were now allowed to ask questions of the government, and were granted 'the right to elect four members to the Legislative Council instead of only two'. Meanwhile, the

Legislative Council was expanded from eighteen to twenty-four members. More space was found for elected members, although government nominees and state officials continued to be in the majority. Here too, members were allowed to discuss the budget and pose questions (they were later also allowed supplementaries).

These were small, incremental reforms, and Visvesvaraya was well aware of this when he looked back on them decades later. However, he insisted that 'they marked a definite advance over the previous position [and] were highly prized at the time they were sanctioned'.[83]

*

Visvesvaraya had begun his tenure by comparing conditions in Mysore to what he had observed on his travels abroad in 1899 and 1908–09. His diagnosis was that the Mysorean populace was ill-educated, disorganized, dismally poor, and in need of strong leadership. 'My one aim, therefore, was to plan, promote and encourage developments chiefly in education, industries, commerce, and public works to enable the people to work well, earn well and live well.'[84]

Work well, earn well and live well: a remarkably pithy condensation of Visvesvaraya's materialist credo. True to his word, he focused his energies on education, industries, and economic development generally. These were not piecemeal initiatives, but formed part of a grand plan. Implementing the plan, however, would come with its own challenges.

11

From Universal Education to University

Even as Visvesvaraya carved out a space for himself in the Mysore administration, his old Poona friend, Gopal Krishna Gokhale, was soaring in stature. Since the days when the two had fraternized at the Deccan Club, Gokhale had held many influential positions. He had entered first the Bombay Legislative Council and then the Imperial Legislative Council. He had set up the Servants of India Society. He had served as president not only of the Poona municipality, but also of the Banaras session (1905) of the Indian National Congress. He had become a renowned leader and educationist, and gained the mantle of a spokesperson for India both within the country and in Britain.[1]

It was in the Imperial Legislative Council that Gokhale found a platform to press the colonial government for the reforms he held dear. In 1911, he placed before the house a bill on primary education.[2] '[I]n almost every civilised country,' he told his fellow legislators, 'the State to-day accepts the education of the children as a primary duty resting upon it.' Educating the entire population would lead to 'a keener enjoyment of life and a more refined standard of living. It means the greater moral and economic efficiency of the individual. It means a higher level of intelligence for the whole community generally.' Only if it paid attention to this basic need of the populace could the colonial Government of India 'take its proper place among the civilised Governments of the world'.

India's literacy rate was an abysmal 6 per cent, whereas in North America, Australia, and several parts of Europe it was close to 100 per cent. In several countries across the world, primary education was either free, or compulsory, or both. In the USA, Canada, Australia, Japan, Britain, and a host of European nations large and small, it was free *and* compulsory, usually for a period of six years. Even countries outside the prosperous West had been able to implement mass education—Gokhale gave the examples of the Philippines under American rule, Ceylon under British rule, and, within India, the princely state of Baroda. Since 1906, Baroda had provided free and compulsory education for boys aged six to twelve and girls aged six to ten (later eleven).

Citing various historical precedents, Gokhale argued that for elementary education to be effective, it had to be made compulsory. But he knew there would be objections, and tried to pre-empt some of them by making concessions in the bill. Rather than stipulating that the central government should make education compulsory at one go, the bill merely sought to give local bodies (i.e. municipalities and district boards) across the country the power to introduce compulsory education in their jurisdictions, provided they fulfilled certain conditions. This meant that the measure would only be introduced gradually. Instead of a compulsory period of six years, Gokhale's bill asked only for four. Although he was strongly in support of girls' education, he anticipated a great deal of opposition, and was willing to see the policy implemented first for boys. While the central government would need to provide two-thirds or more of the funds required, the bill proposed to ease the financial burden on local bodies by allowing them to charge fees except where the student came from an impoverished family. Finally, there was 'ample provision for exemption from compulsory attendance on reasonable grounds, such as sickness, domestic necessity or the seasonal needs of agriculture'.[3]

Despite these concessions, Gokhale's bill proved abortive. Government officials and other members of the council raised various objections. The people would not want to be compelled, they said; the rural population was not interested in education; suitable teachers could not be found; there were not enough buildings for schools; the situation in British India was not comparable to that in Baroda or the foreign countries Gokhale had mentioned. Crucially, the Education Member of the Viceroy's Executive Council declared that the government could not find the money.[4]

Although his efforts were ultimately in vain, Gokhale put a brave face on things. '[W]e, of the present generation in India, can only hope to serve our country by our failures,' he said. 'The men and women who will be privileged to serve her by their successes will come later . . . This Bill, thrown out today, will come back again and again . . .'[5]

Gokhale's optimism was to prove unfounded when it came to British India. But there was some consolation for him from another quarter. Barely a year after his efforts at the Centre, one of India's largest princely states embarked on a move to make education compulsory. It is perhaps no coincidence that the programme was piloted in large part by Gokhale's friend and associate, Mokshagundam Visvesvaraya.

*

Visvesvaraya had grown up in a Mysore administered directly by British commissioners. Although he attended a government-run school in Chikkaballapur before moving to Bangalore in the

1870s, state intervention in primary education was then a very recent phenomenon. Mark Cubbon, Commissioner of Mysore from 1834 to 1861, was unenthusiastic about education for the masses, arguing that the people did not know how to value it. On his government's low investment in education, he once remarked that '[i]n an abstract point of view this is to be regretted, but subject nations are not kept in order and good humour on abstract principles'. It was under the Commissionership of Lewin Bowring (1862–70) that the Mysore government began to invest in schools. In 1868 they instituted the 'Hobli School Scheme', undertaking to establish a school for every *hobli*, or set of villages, whose residents were willing to set aside a building for the purpose. In addition, a number of institutions were set up to provide secondary and collegiate education, while 'Normal Schools' were established to train teachers. At the time of the Rendition of 1881, Mysore had 1087 schools (907 of them at the primary level) run or supported by the state, and another 1000 private schools.[6]

A similar policy continued after the Rendition. State investment in education continued to rise, and successive dewans further modernized the system. The government created a number of industrial schools to provide vocational training, and in the first decade of the twentieth century, consultants were brought in from America and England respectively to help institute 'manual training' (especially on the Swedish 'sloyd' system of woodwork and handicrafts) in schools at the secondary level, and the Kindergarten system for lower classes.[7]

By the year 1910–11, Mysore had 2460 public schools—most of them at primary level—with around 1.15 lakh students, and 1807 private schools (traditional village schools receiving no support from the state) with close to 23,000 students. While the bulk of the public schools taught in Kannada at the primary level, there were schools of other types too, including Sanskrit, Anglo-Kanarese, Anglo-Tamil, and Anglo-Hindustani. At the middle school level there were English, Kannada, Hindustani, Telugu, and Tamil institutions.[8] In addition, there were special schools for Europeans and Eurasians, for Muslims, and for historically disadvantaged groups like the Untouchables.[9]

Thus, when Visvesvaraya returned to Mysore, there was an established system of education of nearly forty years' standing. But its reach was still low. As of 1910–11, only 27.9 per cent of boys of school-going age were at school; the number for girls was a meagre 5.6 per cent.[10] Visvesvaraya, like Gokhale, was apt to set as his benchmark those countries where literacy was close to 100 per cent, countries where nearly every child had some years of schooling.[11]

Pulling Mysore up to those standards was one of the main aims of his pet organization, the Economic Conference. At its inauguration in 1911, Maharaja Krishnaraja Wadiyar IV declared that '[e]ducation is the sovereign remedy for all economic evils'.[12] Within a year, the Conference's Education Committee had set ambitious targets for the government. These included:

> (1) the improvement and extension of primary education, (2) the supply of trained teachers, (3) the opening in the course of five years a thousand new elementary schools, (4) the encouragement of female education and appointment of an inspectress of schools, and (5) the establishment of model middle schools with boarding establishments for girls.[13]

Investment on this ambitious scale, however, would not be worth making unless the facilities were going to be used by a large number of students.[14] The most crucial recommendation of the Education Committee, therefore, was that a system of compulsory education should be instituted.[15]

*

Thus it came about that the year after Gokhale had floated his bill at the Centre, a bill to make education compulsory was placed before Mysore's Legislative Council.

The Elementary Education Bill, as it was called, was published in the *Mysore Gazette Extraordinary* in October 1912. Under its provisions, the Mysore government was to make education compulsory for children aged seven to eleven in certain zones on a trial basis, while retaining the power to extend it to other parts of the state later on. Parents not sending eligible children to school would first be warned and then charged a fine, beginning at Rs 2 and rising to Rs 10, if they continued to ignore the rule. The bill also forbade employers from hiring children who were eligible for but not attending school, and prescribed a fine of Rs 20 for failing to obey this rule. This, as the *Times of India* noted, was a crucial feature, since the prospect of adding to the family income was one of the main reasons parents did not send their children to school.

Like Gokhale, the framers of the bill had provided for many exceptions in order to make it politically palatable. The bill asked the government to make education compulsory only for boys to begin with, although it provided for its extension to girls in selected areas. Moreover, a boy could stay away from school if he was unwell, if he had farming duties at particular times of the year, if there was no school within a mile of his home, or if family circumstances prevented him from attending. He could also skip religious lessons if his parents were against them.[16]

Unlike Gokhale's proposal at the centre, this was a bill introduced by the government itself, and had the support of influential officials. As a result, it was never in danger of being held up by the Mysore Legislative Council. The Elementary Education Regulation came into force in 1913.[17] By this time Visvesvaraya was dewan, and it fell to his administration to implement the new law. They decided to make a beginning in fifteen 'centres'. In 1914–15 they compiled a roster of boys in the relevant age-group, set up a mechanism to monitor attendance, and inaugurated the measure in these centres. The programme had what Visvesvaraya called 'a modest start'. By the end of the first year, 10,800 out of 16,000 eligible boys in the chosen centres were in school. From then on, the number of centres with compulsory education grew rapidly, reaching forty in 1915–16, sixty-eight in 1916–17, and 238 the following year. In 1917–18, compulsory education was also piloted for girls aged seven to ten, in Mysore city and Bangalore.[18]

*

As it turned out, compulsory education was never fully realized in princely Mysore. According to a survey published in 1949, only around 58 per cent of the state's 9,00,000 children in the relevant age-group were enrolled in a school. Compulsory education in the strict sense was being implemented only in nine districts. In large parts of the state, the government, while providing schools, did not attempt to ensure that all eligible children attended.[19] Political scientist James Manor has argued that the compulsory education programme was little more than a cosmetic measure, one of several the Mysore royals took in order to create for themselves a 'progressive image'. He suggests that the project's proponents knew from the start it was financially unsustainable, and that a move to place primary and secondary schools under district boards in the 1930s was really a way for the state government to duck the responsibility for compulsory education.[20]

There is no doubt that Visvesvaraya and the Mysore royals had a penchant for big, symbolic projects, and it is very likely that these benefited the urban elite disproportionately. But it is surely reductive to see the compulsory education law as just a public relations exercise, for the measure undoubtedly helped them scale up primary education massively. In 1911–12, the year before

Visvesvaraya became dewan, only 30.1 per cent of boys of school-going age in Mysore were enrolled in a school. For girls, the figure was a meagre 6.2 per cent; combined, it was 18.3 per cent. These figures rose steadily over the next couple of years, and dramatically after the introduction of compulsory education. As of 1917–18, 68 per cent of eligible boys and 14.2 per cent of eligible girls were at school. Taken together, the fraction was 41.4 per cent.

	1911–12	**1912–13**	**1914–15**	**1915–16**	**1917–18**
Public schools	2,567	2,725	4,279	5,346	9,633
Students in public schools	1,23,491	1,31,539	1,91,172	-	3,38,872
Private schools	1,911	1,843	1,859	1,822	1,107
Students in private schools	25,723	24,901	26,825	-	14,989
Enrolment (boys)	30.1%	29.8%	41.7%	45.8%	68%
Enrolment (girls)	6.2%	6.4%	8.9%	9.7%	14.2%
Enrolment (combined)	18.3%	18%	25.5%	27.9%	41.4%
Schools per capita	1 per 1,274	1 per 1,249	-	1 per 786	1 per 531
School density	1 per 6.58 sq. miles	1 per 6.44 sq. miles	-	1 per [4] sq. miles [unclear in source]	1 per 2.75 sq. miles
Money spent on education (public)	Rs 19.48 lakh	Rs 20.01 lakh	Rs 23.07 lakh	Rs 27.85 lakh	Rs 31.43 lakh

	1911–12	1912–13	1914–15	1915–16	1917–18
Of the above, state government funded	60.25%	60.1%	58.27%	54.69%	61.54%
Money spent on girls'/ women's education	Rs 2.31 lakh	Rs 2.4 lakh	-	Rs 2.96 lakh	Rs 3.64 lakh
Grants-in-aid	-	Rs 1.44 lakh	Rs 2.52 lakh	Rs 3.44 lakh	Rs 4.55 lakh
Schools for 'depressed castes'/ 'backward classes'. Mostly government-run or aided.	102	120	203	264	496

Table 11.1. Education statistics, Mysore, 1910s

Source: Compiled from *Report on the Administration of Mysore*, various years. Blanks indicate that the relevant information was not found in the source.

In fact, the emphasis on mass education was not confined to centres where compulsory education was implemented. In 1911–12 and subsequent years, a substantial sum (usually Rs 1 lakh or more) was budgeted for the building of schoolhouses, and a similar sum to promote primary education. Village residents were encouraged to raise some of the money for new schools, and in some instances, well-to-do individuals made over buildings to the government for use as schools.[21] As Table 11.1 indicates, the net expenditure on education rose from Rs 19.48 lakh in 1911–12 to Rs 31.43 lakh in 1917–18—an increase of 61.34 per cent.

Thousands of new schools were established: as the table shows, the number of public schools increased almost four-fold during Visvesvaraya's tenure as dewan. The number of students enrolled in these institutions grew by over 170 per cent. While private institutions (informal village schools) declined in number by several hundred, they accounted for a relatively small proportion of the students in the state, and the fall was probably a reflection of the increasing access to state-run and state-aided schools. Other statistics in Table 11.1 further illustrate the broad trend, namely a substantial scaling up of primary education.

*

Several other features mark out Mysore's education policies under Visvesvaraya. These include an emphasis on female education, an insistence on the importance of 'manual training' at all levels, modernization of the school curriculum using the Kindergarten and sloyd systems, the spread of English language teaching, and the creation of special institutions for students of the 'backward classes'. Most of these features existed in Mysore's education system before Visvesvaraya's time, but his administration scaled them up rapidly. In other areas—notably technical and commercial education, and physical training—Visvesvaraya introduced new priorities.

Education historian Parimala Rao has shown, based on archival records, that Visvesvaraya was a keen promoter of schooling for girls. Although earlier dewans had supported women's education,[22] the subject had always remained on the fringes of the state's consciousness. What is more, it had always had its opponents. In Visvesvaraya's time too, senior government officials were reluctant to move on matters concerning female education. Some did not want compulsory education to be applied to girls; others did not want them to be taught English, maths, and science.

Sometimes they opposed female education by insidious means, by blocking the construction of hostel buildings or arguing against the appointment of male instructors. But Visvesvaraya overruled specious objections and saw to it that compulsory education for girls was begun. According to Parimala Rao, he made it a point to inspect girls' schools when he toured the districts, and did his best to support them. In at least one instance '[h]e . . . directed the local officials of the education department to ensure the admission of girls from untouchable communities'.[23] Through these years, around forty scholarships were awarded each year to 'widow pupils'.[24] In 1917–18, as many as 700 scholarships were offered in primary and secondary schools for girls.[25]

The latter provision may have had its origins in a proposal that came from First Councillor H.V. Nanjundayya, one of the officials who agreed with Visvesvaraya on the need to promote female education. In 1914–15, Nanjundayya had floated the idea of setting aside Rs 9,200 per year for prizes and scholarships for girls in vernacular and Anglo-vernacular schools. At Visvesvaraya's suggestion, a further stipulation was added: a third of the funds would be reserved 'for the encouragement of such classes of people as have not hitherto availed themselves of the existing facilities for female education'.[26] Official correspondence indicates that Visvesvaraya and Nanjundayya were also keen to promote female education at the secondary, vocational, and collegiate levels.[27]

Another noticeable trend from the 1910s is the steady increase in the number of schools for students from minority communities. Mysore had a network of Anglo-Hindustani schools, Hindustani middle schools, and primary schools for Muslim students. Between 1911–12 and 1917–18, the number of primary schools for Muslim boys rose from 180 to 600, and for Muslim girls from 59 to 122. In the same period, the number of schools for the 'depressed castes' (i.e. Untouchables) had risen from 102 to 496. Most of them were either state-run or supported by the state.[28] Boarding schools for

Panchamas (another term for Untouchables) were established in Tumkur and Chikmagalur.[29]

While the rapid increase of educational facilities for minorities was an achievement, it would have caused mixed feelings in Visvesvaraya. For, a corollary of special schools for disadvantaged communities was that students from these backgrounds were segregated. His ideal was a single, common education system accessible to all students irrespective of their background. He once told the Central Mahomedan Association of Mysore that elsewhere in India, Muslims were increasingly opting to join 'institutions meant for the general public, as they seem to realise that it is in this way, rather than in multiplying special institutions, that the permanent interests of the Mahomedan community will be best served'.[30] On a visit to the temple town of Nanjangud in 1914, he remarked that the villagers of the district were enthusiastic about education, but bemoaned the fact that society was rife with divisions. A village could do well for itself if all its residents came together to establish a single school for 'all classes and creeds and all grades of education'. But they were fragmented—'Hindu and Mahomedan, high caste and low caste, "left-hand" class and "right-hand" class . . . The Mahomedans want separate schools and a separate organization even to a separate Inspectress of Schools. In some places, the Thoreyas are not allowed to attend the common school. The Panchamas are not allowed to associate with the Thoreyas. None of these communities will drink out of the same well, or allow their children to drink out of the same fountain of learning.'[31]

Why, then, did Visvesvaraya not dismantle the system of schools for particular communities? Possibly he calculated that there would be too much opposition to his vision of a casteless society, and that for the time being, special schools were the best way to ensure everyone had access to education.

For Visvesvaraya, education had to be practical in orientation. He was not enamoured of the system of 'religious and moral instruction' that had been inaugurated in schools and colleges in 1908.[32] These were non-sectarian but Hindu-centric, 'based on the *Sanathana Dharma* text-books' at the higher levels and on works such as the *Dharmabodhini* at the primary level.[33] The year he took over as dewan, the state's administration report described the religious lessons in most primary schools as 'more or less dull and stereotyped'.[34] Had it been up to him, Visvesvaraya would have abolished these classes, but public opinion, as embodied in the Representative Assembly, was for their continuation. Visvesvaraya acquiesced, but not without a rider. In 1915 he told the Assembly that 'Government have no desire to disturb existing arrangements [for religious lessons]. If possible, the present arrangements will be improved by providing for business education in addition.'[35] It was almost as if he was administering an antidote along with the potion.

This business-like orientation found expression in other ways too. While Mysore already ran industrial schools for students opting for vocational education, the government now introduced a system of 'Practical Instruction' in regular schools (this was in addition to the sloyd system of training already in place). The aim was to provide students a taste of industrial arts such as woodwork, ironwork, and weaving, so that those who discovered an interest in such pursuits could move on to dedicated industrial schools.[36]

There was a marked emphasis on physical activity. Sports had always been an integral part of student life in the Maharaja's and Maharani's Colleges, Mysore and the Central College, Bangalore. In these institutions—which had students from high school up to undergraduate level—hockey, tennis, football, cricket, gymnastics, and badminton thrived. Now, the government took steps to promote physical culture across the schools of the state. They made drill exercises mandatory for students seeking the Secondary School-Leaving Certificate, established a 'Scout training scheme', and invested in the training of physical education instructors.[37]

Finally, Visvesvaraya's government revamped and strengthened the Education Department, which was directly in charge of public schools. They increased the salaries of government-employed teachers. They enlarged the staff of educational inspectors, who in turn toured the countryside, organized conferences on education, helped set up local 'teachers' associations', and in general evangelized for the cause of primary education.[38]

*

Along with primary education, Visvesvaraya had a special interest in technical and commercial education. In October 1910, when he was Chief Engineer of Mysore, he had been appointed head of a committee to overhaul the system of industrial education. The committee submitted its report in September 1912.[39] The committee's recommendations were influential in the establishment of 'a comprehensive scheme of elementary and advanced technical and commercial education' in 1913. At the heart of this system were three new institutions: the Chamarajendra Technical Institute (CTI), a Commercial School, and a Mechanical Engineering School. The first of these was in Mysore city, and the other two in Bangalore.[40]

The CTI was formed by combining two existing institutions at Mysore—an industrial school and an engineering school which trained subordinates for the Public Works Department. Furnished with an impressive new building on Mysore's central Sayyaji Rao Road, the CTI was divided into five sections: engineering; industries and crafts; fine arts; commercial school; and workshop.[41] The engineering section trained students for jobs as senior and junior sub-overseers and *shekdars* (junior officers) in the Public Works Department. Other sections taught arts such as carpentry, fitting, and smithy.[42]

The other industrial schools in the state, whose numbers fluctuated between around twenty and thirty, continued to operate as before. They were scattered across the state, in places like Holenarsipur, Chikkanayakanahalli, Channapatna, Tiptur, Molakalmuru, and Melkote, in addition to Mysore and Bangalore. Most of these schools were government-run or government-aided, while some were run by missionaries or other private groups. The subjects taught in the various industrial schools included carpentry, weaving, smithy, wood-carving, lacquer work, toy-making, and metal work. There were a handful of schools especially for girls, although the subjects taught—knitting, sewing, needlework and embroidery—reflected contemporary notions of women as largely belonging to the domestic realm. A few industrial schools were exclusively for Panchamas.[43] Many of the students trained in these schools took what were known as the Madras Technical exams in order to certify their skills.[44]

The Mechanical Engineering School in Bangalore, which opened in July 1913, trained students in subjects more suited to mechanized industry and transportation systems, such as the maintenance of oil engines and the installation of mill machinery. Soon, it began classes for permanent way inspectors, telegraph signallers, and drivers of motor vehicles (some of these were later shifted to the government's railway department). For working students, evening classes were organized in 'technical drawing, electric wiring and motor mechanics'. By 1917–18, there were 170 students enrolled in the school.[45] The school's superintendent was a Mysorean with an unusual CV: S.V. Setty, a Roorkee alumnus who had studied electrical engineering at Faraday House, London, before spending an exciting year as a trainee designing and flying aeroplanes at the Avro Company's airfield in Surrey.[46]

Alongside these industrial schools, Mysore also established an agricultural school in Hebbal, near Bangalore, in 1913. It was started at the site of an existing experimental farm, and emanated from a proposal put forward by a Canadian expert in Mysore's employ, Dr Leslie Coleman. The aim was to train the sons of landed farmers in science-based agricultural techniques. A few years later, a private donation enabled the government to start another agricultural school, teaching in Kannada, at Chikkanahalli in the Tumkur district.[47]

Also focusing on the imparting of employable skills were the commercial schools run or supported by the Mysore government. In addition to the existing government-aided schools (one in Bangalore and another, the Hardwicke Commercial School, in Mysore), two new government-run schools were started in 1913–14: the Government Commercial School in Bangalore and the commercial section of the Chamarajendra Technical Institute in Mysore. Subjects included bookkeeping, banking, shorthand, and typewriting. Individual classes in commercial subjects were also begun at Tumkur, Shimoga, Hassan, Channapatna and Chikmaglur. In order to obtain instructors for some of these institutions, the government sent graduates and advanced students to two Bombay institutions, the Government College of Commerce and Davar's College of Commerce.[48]

If craft skills and business education formed two key components of Mysore's strategy for developing human resources, the trifecta was completed by higher scientific and technological education. As Mysore had few institutions that could provide such training, funds were set aside for sending students outside the state. Each year, a handful of students travelled to Britain, continental Europe, and the United States to study subjects such as electrical and mechanical engineering, agricultural chemistry, medicine, soap-making, organic chemistry, mining and metallurgy, and forestry. They were supported by scholarships or loans from the state. There were also a number of scholarships to attend institutions in other parts of India, such as the Veterinary College and the Victoria Jubilee Technical Institute in Bombay.[49]

Visvesvaraya's government eventually determined that when it came to engineering degrees, sending Mysoreans outside the state for training was no longer sufficient for their needs. The result was the establishment, in 1917, of the College of Engineering in Bangalore. Its inaugural batch of forty students began their studies on the premises of the Mechanical Engineering School overseen by S.V. Setty. The new college had as its first principal the Mysore PWD engineer K.R. Seshachar, who had worked closely with Visvesvaraya on the Kannambadi project.[50]

*

There was one final element in Visvesvaraya's plans for Mysore.[51] As a student at the Central College in Bangalore in the 1880s, he had taken the examinations of the Madras University, since Mysore did not have its own university. Three decades later, that was still the case. For Visvesvaraya, however, the existence of at least one university was a fundamental requirement of a progressive polity.

He first spelt out his vision for a Mysorean university in March 1912, when he was invited to the College Day function at his Bangalore alma mater and addressed the students there. First, as always, came a statistical comparison to establish the need for the new measure. Countries like the United Kingdom, Germany, and Canada were dense with universities. 'The population of Canada is scarcely 25 [per cent] more than that of Mysore and yet that country has 18 universities. I do not see why we should not have at least one university in Mysore.' The comparison was telling, for it treated Mysore not just as a component of British-ruled India, but as an entity to be measured against other autonomous countries in the world. Next, Visvesvaraya specified the kind of university he had in mind: one with a practical bent. He wanted the new university to focus on 'the imparting of technical and commercial education . . . for that is the most profitable form of education you can impart to the rising generation nowadays'. Further, it should be a universal institution, defined by its quality; Visvesvaraya was not interested in the revival of an ethnic Indian or communitarian identity. Referring to contemporary efforts to establish what would become the Banaras Hindu University and the Aligarh Muslim University in northern India, he said: 'My interest in the great Hindu and Mahomedan University movements of to-day is not for the reason that they are either Hindu or Mahomedan but because we want more first class universities in the country.' Finally, Mysore must act quickly. They must forge ahead boldly with a belief in the intrinsic worth of university education, and not worry too much about external ratification. '[I]f we are to wait till we are assured of future recognition by other employers of labour, we may have to wait till the Greek Kalends.'[52]

This was an audacious move. No princely state in India—not even Baroda, which had implemented compulsory primary education some years previously—had as yet established a university.[53] Even the vast territories of British India were served by only a handful of universities, established in the nineteenth century at Bombay, Calcutta, Madras, Allahabad, and Lahore. Until the first decade of the twentieth century, these were not centres of teaching. Actual instruction usually took place in the many standalone colleges affiliated to each of these universities, which determined the colleges' syllabi and examined their students. The universities, in turn, were governed ultimately by the colonial Government of India. Although the princely states were technically autonomous in internal matters, this meant that the colonial government controlled their systems of education, for their colleges would have to be affiliated to one of the universities in British India.[54] As the move to create a university within Mysore would disturb this balance of power, the Government of India was not likely to look upon it favourably.

Visvesvaraya's message may have been bold, but his intended audience—which extended far beyond the students he was addressing that day—was well primed for it. As historian Manu Bhagavan has shown, contemporary debates in the press (including publications as diverse as the *Indian Patriot* of Madras, the *Daily Post* of Bangalore, and the *Times of India* of Bombay) had begun to focus on the idea of education as central to the creation of a 'modern' Mysore. Various commentators stressed the need for practical education that would serve the needs of economic development. The impediment, according to some, was a refusal to break out of the traditional Indian conception of education. Others argued that it was in fact the colonial university system—in this case, Madras University, which indirectly controlled the standards and syllabi of Mysore institutions—that was overly focused on theoretical subjects and examinations, thus holding the state back from participation in the modern world.[55]

To such critics of the existing state of education, Visvesvaraya's suggestion signalled an opportunity for much-needed reform. A new, local, university could—as Visvesvaraya indicated in his speech—be oriented towards the needs of economic progress and industrial modernity. Again, unlike Madras University, the new institution would be directly responsible for instructing students, who, like the professors, would live on campus. As Bhagavan argues, this context imbued the demand for a Mysore University with a 'potentially subversive' slant. It was, in effect, a demand for an institution not just on par with those in British India, but better. In that sense it was a palpable critique of the colonial government, a challenge to the colonizers' claims to superiority and to their supposed monopoly on modernity.[56]

As a result, the prospect of a new university was seen as a threat both by the Government of India, to which it acted as a direct challenge, and by Madras University, which feared the emergence of a competing institution in the region. For Visvesvaraya, veteran of the Kannambadi negotiations, these were familiar sparring partners.

*

When Visvesvaraya made his speech in March 1912, he was speaking on matters above his pay grade. He was then still chief engineer, and had no official locus standi to pronounce on higher education policy. But by then it had become quite clear that his ambitions for Mysore—and indeed his influence—went far beyond the efficient running of the Public Works Department. Around the time of Visvesvaraya's speech, the question of a university was being investigated in detail by the Economic Conference, which was in essence his own creation. By November of that year, he had become dewan, and from that point on, he took over directly the task of piloting the university proposals. Thus, while he may not have been the sole originator of the idea of a university for Mysore,[57] he was certainly one of the earliest to articulate it, and the most influential person to promote it.

In June 1912, the Economic Conference, announcing the results of its deliberations, recommended that 'a local university on the model of modern teaching and residential universities be established as soon as funds and facilities can be made available'.[58] In August, the government set up a committee to consider the issue. Chaired by the scholarly First Councillor H.V. Nanjundayya, it was composed of prominent officials and professors in Mysore's existing colleges. The Nanjundayya Committee's recommendations came in around a year later. They declared that Madras University was ill-placed to serve the requirements of education in Mysore, while emphasizing the quality of Mysore's existing colleges (and hence their ability to form the kernel of a new university).[59]

The government now sent two professors from the Maharaja's College—C.R. Reddy and Thomas Denham, the Principal—abroad, to study the university system in what were seen as advanced countries. (It is telling that they were not asked to study the universities of British India.) Denham travelled to Australia, while Reddy—who had been part of the Nanjundayya Committee—toured Japan, England, and the United States.[60] Sometime around 1914–15, the two professors returned and submitted their reports to the Mysore government.[61]

When the proposals for a new university were first communicated to the Government of India in 1913, their reaction was hostile. This was unsurprising, given the context discussed earlier. But over the next three years, Visvesvaraya and his team revised their proposal multiple times, adding explanations and details, and kept up negotiations with the colonial government, both by correspondence and in person. They did not waver from their argument that Madras University could not adequately serve Mysore's requirements. At the same time, they took care to stress that their proposal was 'not put forward in any spirit of rivalry or dissatisfaction with any of the existing Universities, least of all with the Madras University'. They also insisted that the university project did not mean that Mysore would neglect school-level education. At one point, a Government of India official insisted that their university must be of the 'Unitary type' (an integrated campus-type university in a single location). Visvesvaraya replied that their plan was in essence for a unitary-type university that would grow up around the Maharaja's College in Mysore. Although the university would include an outstation entity in Bangalore's Central College (the government being loath to leave out this well-established institution), students of both colleges would have opportunities 'to come together as frequently as possible for common lectures, the annual Convocation, the University week, sports and other similar objects'. By 1916, the central government had come around. In April, the Viceroy gave his approval for a new university.[62]

Clearly, it was not Visvesvaraya's persuasiveness alone that swayed the colonial government. Manu Bhagavan suggests two possible reasons for their change of heart. First, the colonial government may have calculated that after several years of public debate that had dented the image of British India's universities, little further harm could be done. Mysore's university, when realized, would probably come nowhere close to its proponents' ideals, and would therefore pose little threat. Second—and this is perhaps the more concrete and plausible explanation—the outbreak of the First World War had altered the context. The colonial government now had more pressing battles to fight. Furthermore, Mysore supported the war effort substantially, a stance which required some reciprocal gesture.[63] Mysore also had a sympathetic go-between in the form of the Resident, Sir Hugh Daly, who shared a good relationship with the dewan and the maharaja.[64] Daly mediated the correspondence with the colonial government; he even accompanied Visvesvaraya when the latter travelled to Simla to meet leading officials of the Government of India.[65]

Having received the colonial government's go-ahead, Mysore resolved to inaugurate the new university by July 1916. But another hurdle now arose. The Madras government and its university had been brought into the discussion, and the Government of India wanted Mysore to address their reservations. By the time these details reached Mysore, it was late in May. Visvesvaraya and Daly now managed to convince leading officials of Madras University to expedite matters through an emergency face-to-face meeting. On 31 May, the parties met at the Government House in the hill station of Ooty, the summer capital of Madras, and thrashed out various points. While they were outwardly affable, Madras University's officials were wary, and tried to stall. Mysore made some concessions. For instance, they agreed not to eat into the older university's clientele. They would place a cap on the number of students from Madras Presidency entering the new Mysore University (no more than 10 per cent of the incoming class) and ensure that their fees were in line with those charged in Madras. But on other demands, which were likely to delay the starting of the new university if acceded to, they stood firm.[66]

*

In parallel with the negotiations with Simla and Madras, the Mysore government had taken care to build support for their university project among the local population. From the start, the composition of the relevant committees and delegations had been made carefully, in such a way as to pre-empt possible criticisms of the project as an elitist one likely to further Brahmin hegemony in the state.[67] In 1916, the government released a draft of the university scheme to the public, inviting suggestions;[68] in May that year, Visvesvaraya and other leading officials met at Ballabrooie to discuss the points arising from this exercise.[69]

On 29 June 1916, a Bill for the creation of a university in Mysore was tabled in the Mysore Legislative Council. Held at the Public Offices in Bangalore, the deliberations were spirited, and spilled over into a second session on 17 July.[70] On both occasions, Visvesvaraya made important speeches that revealed further his conception of the new university. Speaking to a packed house of members and spectators on 29 June, he stressed that the university would not be a standalone prestige project, but an integral part of the state's larger education policy. To those who argued that a university was superfluous in a state with such a low literacy level, Visvesvaraya replied that this made a university all the more necessary. 'Education promotes education and, without higher education, no appreciable expansion of secondary or elementary education can be looked for.' Further, the university would bring many benefits, tangible and intangible. 'The general object [of a university] in the broadest sense,' he said, 'is to encourage learning, to promote higher education, to create a centre of culture, to light a torch that would dispel the gloom of ignorance from the remotest corners of the country.' Mysore's university would do this, but it would also help (and here Visvesvaraya quoted an earlier speech of his own) to 'prepare future manufacturers, merchants, businessmen, economists, lawyers, sanitarians, engineers, statesmen, etc., for the country'.[71]

This secular, practical orientation was apparent also in Visvesvaraya's approach to questions of language, religion, and location. In his speech on 17 July, he stated that the new university would function primarily through the mediums of English and Kannada. While many other languages were spoken in the state—Visvesvaraya himself, it should be recalled, was a Telugu-speaker—it was not practical to give all of them a prominent place in the university's curriculum. 'English is the language of civilization, Kannada is the language of the Court and of the great majority of the population. These two languages should suffice for our purpose,' Visvesvaraya said. If they tried to find a place for every language, they would 'be spending more time on language than on matter'.

Similarly, he was not in favour of 'religious training' in the new university, for 'it would be difficult to satisfy all denominations and the attempt to help to develop religious sentiment through the University would, I fear, end in failure.' He was willing to consider the *academic* study of religion—in the form of a Faculty of Theology—at some point in the future, but stressed that Mysore University was to be non-denominational.

As for its location, the new university would have the Maharaja's College (on the edge of Mysore city) as its nucleus. In other words, it would be an urban university, not a bucolic sanctuary. 'I do not believe in segregating the students and allowing them to grow up as it were in a cloistered life. They will be at a disadvantage when they come back to the hard realities of this work-a-day world.' Finally, the university was to play the role of a leveller. 'It is . . . His Highness' wish that under its fostering care all classes of His Highness' subjects should profit and that it should contribute to the uplift of all strata of society, the rich and the poor, the forward as well as the backward.'

The bill was passed without the need for a vote.[72] On 25 July, the state gazette declared the creation of Mysore University.[73]

*

Mysore University thus began its career in 1916. H.V. Nanjundayya was appointed the first vice-chancellor, and Thomas Denham the registrar.[74] The various parts of the university were coordinated by a council (which included the principals and some professors at the constituent colleges) and a senate (comprising, at least initially, every single professor in the university). Students' unions were to be established both in Mysore and in Bangalore.[75] Although the university received fees and some private endowments, the bulk of its expenses were borne by the government.[76] In 1917, the government also instituted sixty scholarships (each worth Rs 15 in addition to a tuition fee waiver) for non-Brahmin students.[77]

The main offerings at the start were the BA in Arts, based in the Maharaja's College at Mysore, and the BA in Sciences, based in the Central College at Bangalore. Arts students could choose their optional subjects from a list that included history, political science, economics, and philosophy. Science students could study either mathematics, physics and chemistry, or zoology, geology and botany. All students had to study English and one other language, which could be Kannada, Telugu, Tamil, Hindustani, Sanskrit, Persian, or French.

A BSc degree was also offered, and required the student to take more science courses.[78] From 1917, women students could also join the BA, studying for it in the Maharani's College at Mysore.[79] In order to gain admission to the university, high school graduates had to complete an additional year in one of the designated 'Collegiate High Schools' across the state, and then take an entrance exam.[80]

As Visvesvaraya had envisaged, Mysore University rapidly grew to encompass other fields, including professional courses. Within a few years, a number of new or existing institutions had been folded into the university. These included the new Government Engineering College at Bangalore, and a Medical College established in the same city in 1924. In 1917, a Commerce course was started at the Maharaja's College. Exams for the BA degree were first conducted in 1917–18; for the BCom in 1919–20; and for the BE in 1920–21.[81]

At the same time, the university's physical infrastructure was growing. In Bangalore, additions were made to the edifice of the Central College, and a new students' union building was provided. In Mysore city, new lecture theatres for the Maharaja's College came up, as did hostels, libraries (including one repurposed building), a students' union building, a pavilion for cricket, a swimming pool, and housing for faculty members,[82] forming a bustling integrated campus occupying parkland atop a hill. Writing in 1930, an observer remarked on the 'many acres of playing fields, fields thronged every evening by cricket, football and hockey players and by scores of interested spectators'.[83]

Soon after its establishment, the University attracted a number of accomplished scholars from across India, who joined its faculty. From Bengal came the polyglot philosopher

Brajendranath Seal and the historian Radhakumud Mookerji; from Madras the philosopher Sarvepalli Radhakrishnan; and from Bombay the economist K.T. Shah. (Seal served as Vice-Chancellor from 1920 to 1930.)[84] By the late 1920s, Mysore University's degrees were recognized by the Universities of Bombay, Madras, Punjab, Lucknow, Dacca, London, Oxford, and Cambridge, and also by the Benares Hindu University and the Aligarh Muslim University.[85]

*

It was in October 1918, in the midst of a world war and a global influenza epidemic, that Mysore University held its first convocation. The Maharaja, speaking as the Chancellor of the University, paid tribute to Visvesvaraya's role in enabling its creation. 'It was chiefly [Visvesvaraya's] patriotism, his enthusiasm, and his unflinching advocacy which converted, what was once little more than a dream of the future into a living creation,' the monarch declared, 'and his name will always be remembered, above all others, as the man to whom our University owes its being.'[86]

The chief guest at the event was the eminent mathematician, judge, and educationist, Sir Asutosh Mookerjee. It had been something of a coup to get the former Vice-Chancellor of Calcutta University to preside. On the one hand he had been concerned about the influenza situation in Mysore; on the other he was keen on combining his trip with visits to Bangalore and the Kolar Gold Fields. ('He seems,' Visvesvaraya wryly remarked to a colleague, 'to want to kill a whole flock of birds with one stone.')[87]

Now, listening to Sir Asutosh speak at the convocation, Visvesvaraya must have felt it had been well worth the effort to arrange his visit. In stirring tones, the chief guest urged the graduates to use their education to serve the larger community. He stressed the connections between all branches of learning—'the kinship of the arts and sciences'—and the particular importance of practical subjects. 'Furnaces and foundries, studios and workshops, must be deemed as honourable and made as abundant as the offices of the learned professions'. He waxed lyrical about the prospect of the 'utilization of our boundless natural resources', praising Visvesvaraya for having established projects to that end. While emphasising that an Indian university must serve Indian needs and not be a mere facsimile of a Western ideal, he cautioned that Indians must keep abreast of the latest knowledge and not bury their heads in the sands of their 'glorious past'.[88]

Mookerjee could hardly have spelt out a vision more in consonance with Visvesvaraya's views on the role of a university.

12

Manufactured in Mysore

At the start of Visvesvaraya's tenure as dewan, mechanized industries played a minor role in Mysore's economy. Outside of the European-controlled gold mines of Kolar and government-led infrastructure projects such as the Cauvery Power Scheme, large-scale works were scarce.[1] Most manufacturing took place in small units started with private capital, or in cottage industries engaged in traditional craft-based production. Among them were a couple of textile mills in Bangalore and Mysore, a few tanneries, a handful of sugarcane mills and sugar factories, oil mills, tile factories, and indigenous brass and copper works. In 1910–11, only eighty-five units in the entire state (not counting the gold mines) were classified as 'large factories', and the definition was liberal: the average number of employees in each of these factories was forty-nine.[2]

This state of affairs contrasted sharply with Visvesvaraya's vision of a Mysore pulsing with industries large and small, a state hospitable to the industrial entrepreneur and the commercial traveller. In his ideal Mysore, there would be 'no town or village without a hotel or inn run on modern business lines'. Each town would have space marked off for industrial units, a museum showcasing 'agricultural and commercial products' alongside 'industrial machinery and plant', and '[a] library, a reading room, and a bureau of information . . . There should be no town without half a dozen industries and no village without one or more rural industries.'[3]

The establishment of an Industries and Commerce Committee under the Economic Conference was Visvesvaraya's first step towards effecting the necessary transformation. But it was in bringing to Mysore the English engineer and Madras official Alfred Chatterton that he made his most decisive move. For Chatterton had spent the best part of two decades promoting the development of industries in the Madras Presidency. If Visvesvaraya was a zealot when it came to industrialization, Chatterton was no less than an evangelist. Doctrinal differences notwithstanding, they were to form a momentous partnership over the next four years.

*

Alfred Chatterton was born in 1866, five years after Visvesvaraya.[4] He was scarcely twenty-two when he was selected for the Indian Educational Service and appointed a professor in the College of Engineering at Guindy near Madras. Unlike most colonial engineers of his generation, he came neither from a military background nor from Cooper's Hill, the special college near London that trained engineers for the Indian PWD. Instead, he was trained at a couple of London institutions with a marked vocational bent: the Finsbury Technical College and the Central Institution in South Kensington.[5] For good measure, Chatterton spent time in the locomotive works of the London and South Western Railway before coming out to India.

Perhaps it was due to this background that Chatterton took a keen interest in practical engineering problems alongside his academic pursuits. At various points he held additional charge of the PWD workshops and the Madras School of Arts, a government-run industrial school. Chatterton served at Guindy until 1900, and held various positions in the Madras government thereafter. In 1906 he was appointed Director of Industrial and Technical Enquiries; in 1908 he became Director of Industries. Throughout his time in Madras, Chatterton strove to encourage small-scale industries employing local artisans. At the Madras School of Arts he poured his energies into experimental work in the production of aluminium utensils and chrome-tanned leather, and the use of fly-shuttle looms for handloom weaving. In 1906 he got the government to shift these looms from Madras city to Salem and set up a weaving factory there, as 'an experiment to ascertain whether it is possible to improve the condition of the hand-weavers in Southern India'.[6]

Chatterton was conversant with the work of Indian economic thinkers like M.G. Ranade, and shared their view of Indian industries as struggling in the face of foreign competition.[7] He also believed that industries founded with foreign capital were of little help to the Indian economy, as their profits were channelled outside the country, and they afforded few opportunities for the development of 'native industrial leaders'.[8] He thought the remedy was for governments in India to invest in new ventures, acting as a spur to Indian capitalists to enter these fields.

These views were unusual in many ways for a Briton in India. For one thing, his compatriots found the idea of direct government intervention in the economy abhorrent. For another, his emphasis on local capital and jobs for locals bore an affinity to Swadeshi thinking. Chatterton, however, was no radical. His interest in improving the lives of the Indian masses was sincere, but he was proud of the imperial connection and derisive of the leaders of the Swadeshi movement, questioning whether 'their capacity for production extends beyond the manufacture of verbiage'.[9] Instead, it was well-meaning colonials like himself who should lead the reform of the Indian economy. They were qualified to do so, and would not fall prey to grand delusions. Chatterton rejected the idea that India was ready for large-scale industries driven by complex technologies. Given India's 'greatest asset—abundant cheap labour', he thought the greatest impact could be made by focusing 'on the decaying indigenous industries: hand-weaving, working in metals, tanning and leather manufactures, on all the petty industries which supply the simple needs of the people'. Such industries should be revived and made more efficient by educating artisans, giving them improved tools, and encouraging them to move from manufacturing within the home to a system of 'cooperative working or . . . small factories'.[10]

On this last point his beliefs differed from Visvesvaraya, who was keen that Mysore should have the latest technologies and the kind of large-scale industries that existed in the rich countries of the West. The Indian preached in the cathedral of industrialization; the Englishman preferred the chapel.

Many scholars have remarked on this difference, which was to come to the fore later on.[11] But the similarities in the two men's thinking are much more striking. Chatterton found the Indian masses too passive, 'content with an extremely low standard of living and . . . averse to more exertion than is required to provide themselves with what is generally more than the bare necessities of life'.[12] Visvesvaraya echoed this sentiment, declaring that '[t]he nationality of our people rests on a religious and fatalistic basis, not on an economic basis'.[13] The two belonged to the same generation. Both saw the state as having to play a role in improving the lives of the masses. Engineers both, their visions were technocratic, involving the application of better techniques, the eradication of superstition, and the creation of a rational citizenry.[14] Like Visvesvaraya, Chatterton believed in the need to make education more practical, and in the importance of foreign travel in widening citizens' perspectives.[15] Like Visvesvaraya again, Chatterton was driven by a sense of public service, but could be paternalistic and even imperious.[16]

Visvesvaraya, then, could not have found a more like-minded candidate to direct his project of industrialization in Mysore. The timing was right too. By around 1910, Chatterton was beginning to outstay his welcome in Madras, as his imperial bosses decided it was not the government's job to establish industries.[17] But Mysore, being a princely state with some independence, did not face such restrictions.[18] In July 1912, a few months before he became dewan, Visvesvaraya brought Chatterton to Mysore as Special Adviser to the Industries and Commerce committee of the Economic Conference (Chatterton came on secondment from the British Indian Educational Service).[19] The Economic Conference in turn recommended the establishment of a new government department devoted to industries. In 1913, Visvesvaraya's government created a Department of Industries and Commerce (DIC), and appointed Chatterton its director.[20]

*

The DIC was charged with transforming Mysore's economy. As the scholar Bjørn Hettne has observed, it was a top-down project 'to foster the growth of industrial capitalism in a society where very little spontaneous development of capitalism was to be found'.[21] The DIC was to provide finance, information, and guidance to industrial entrepreneurs; set up demonstration factories; compile statistics; carry out industrial surveys; and establish an industrial museum.[22] The Department would work in tandem with the Industries and Commerce Committee of the Economic Conference. Some of their members overlapped, and others served sequentially in each.[23] Visvesvaraya kept a close watch on both organizations.

The first duty of this Industries bureaucracy was to set up model factories in sectors that promised a good return while utilizing the state's natural resources. Typically, these were operations which involved technologies new to the state, and struggled to attract private capital.[24] When private efforts to use powered machinery to crush sugarcane floundered, the DIC designed a new type of furnace that optimized the amount of fuel required and reduced labour costs. To modernize the textile industry, a Government Weaving Factory was established in Bangalore, a move that mirrored Chatterton's earlier work in Madras. Its personnel experimented with new designs for looms, and demonstrators travelled across the state to promote the use of fly-shuttle slays.[25]

The most prominent of the DIC's demonstration factories were the ones it established to manufacture soap and sandalwood oil. Sandalwood grew abundantly in the state of Mysore, and the government had exclusive rights over its commercial exploitation. Sandalwood oil was much sought after in the world's markets for use in the production of perfumes, soaps, and medicines. But Mysore made no attempt to manufacture the oil, since they were able to generate adequate revenues by selling the wood itself. This they did through auctions. Most of the wood was then exported to Germany, which had the know-how and the plant to undertake its distillation. When the First World War broke out, that avenue was closed. Alfred Chatterton saw that the time was ripe for sandalwood oil to be produced within Mysore. The state could thus move up the value chain, and also make huge savings on transport costs when exporting it, since it took one ton of wood to make every 100 pounds of oil. Working closely with J.J. Sudborough and H.E. Watson, scientists at the Indian Institute of Science in Bangalore, he organized experiments to determine an optimal distillation process. In May 1916, a sandalwood oil factory was started in Bangalore, with machinery produced in India (as the war had cut off imports). Its success prompted the establishment of a bigger factory in Mysore City the following year.

The process used produced remarkably pure oil which was in high demand in several countries. It was also a propitious time to establish the industry, the price of sandalwood oil having risen from 21 to 50 shillings per pound between 1914 and 1917. In 1916–17 the state sold around Rs 7.6 lakh worth of sandalwood oil; the following year the figure was Rs 27.5 lakh. The factories had got off to a roaring start (although the collapse of the market after the war was to create challenges in the early 1920s).[26]

Under Visvesvaraya and Chatterton, the government also decided to establish the viability of soap manufacture in Mysore. In 1915, they placed an order for machinery with an English firm, George Scott & Sons, but once again the war came in the way of it being shipped. The DIC then undertook to produce the equipment in its workshop, and had made considerable progress when the machinery from England finally arrived in 1917. The soap factory was inaugurated in Bangalore in February 1918. It produced soap from vegetable oils. The government had to import many of the raw materials required: coconut oil from Cochin, salt from Madras, and caustic soda from Calcutta. In April 1918, a scientist named S.G. Sastry, who had been sent to England to study soap manufacture, was employed as Industrial Chemist in the Department of Industries. Later that year he took over the management of the soap factory. By the 1930s, the soap factory had developed into a highly profitable enterprise, manufacturing perfumes in addition to soap. A market for its products was created across India and even in some African countries. It also succeeded as a demonstration factory, encouraging many private players to embark on soap-making.[27]

Another such undertaking was a filature established in Channapatna under Chatterton's supervision, with the aim of mechanizing silk reeling.[28] Earlier governments had already begun efforts to modernize the silk industry, supporting, for instance, a silk farm established in Bangalore in the late 1890s by the Bombay industrialist J.N. Tata.[29] These efforts were intensified under Visvesvaraya and Chatterton, both of whom had strong views on the need to replace traditional modes of sericulture with what they saw as scientific measures.[30] In the Channapatna filature, Chatterton installed Japanese machinery of the kind used in the Tata Silk Farm; but the eventual aim was to set up a facility in Bangalore with Italian machinery, which was considered even more advanced.[31] Towards the end of 1913, an Italian named Washington Mari was appointed Mysore's 'silk expert' on a one-year contract. Mari was asked to make a study of Mysore's silk industry and suggest possible improvements; train Mysoreans in sericulture; and run the Channapatna filature, now styled the Central Sericultural Farm.[32] Mari spent a further year in Mysore from June 1916, this time as Director of Sericulture. He experimented with different breeds of silkworm and tried to popularise Italian silk rearing practices. However, his attempts to import reeling machines from Italy came to nought owing to the ongoing World War.[33]

A second function of the DIC was to give out loans to private parties or cooperative societies who wanted to mechanize their businesses, whether in the agricultural or the industrial sector. In some cases, the Department even installed the machinery for the client. Alternatively, clients could procure machinery from the Department on a hire-purchase scheme. Under this system, a wide variety of industries emerged, including pumping installations (for irrigation), sugar factories, oil mills, grinding mills, and printing presses. In most cases, the owners did very well for themselves. But this required a complete transformation in the style of their operations, whether or not they had signed up for this. As a top Department official noted: 'The leisurely habits of doing business, which did not matter when production was on a small scale, become dangerous directly [as soon as] machinery is installed.' Those mechanizing their businesses soon found that they had to keep their plant running for longer periods, hire more workers, and make other investments if they were to earn a profit.[34] In a sense, this was part of the Department's objective: to introduce the discipline of the market to the commercial life of the state.

Finally, the DIC undertook the construction and maintenance of machinery used in government and private organizations. For this purpose, it took charge of a PWD workshop and established new ones in the districts of Shimoga and Tumkur. It took over the state's industrial schools from the Education Department. It helped make blankets for the army during the war. A dedicated Commerce section, established in 1917, brought out statistics on the trade being carried out via railways, and assisted the state in the rationing of various items during the war years.[35]

*

The DIC was only one part of the institutional scaffolding Visvesvaraya installed for the erection of an industrial economy. In addition to providing machinery and expertise to entrepreneurs, it was necessary to train an industrial workforce, to establish channels for the financing of industries, and to create a platform for the traders and industrialists of the state to compare notes and lobby for their common needs. The first of these requirements was addressed through a revamped system of industrial and engineering education, as we saw in the last chapter. To fulfil the second and third, the government promoted two new institutions: a bank and a chamber of commerce.

The decision to establish a government-backed bank had first been taken under the aegis of the Economic Conference by a committee led by Visvesvaraya, shortly before he became dewan.[36] As dewan, Visvesvaraya sought the help of his old friend Sir Vithaldas Thackersey to conceptualize the new bank. Thackersey, whom he had got to know via the Deccan Club in his Poona years, was a cotton tycoon belonging to a prominent Kathiawari Bhatia family of Bombay. He was a pillar of the mercantile world, serving at various times as President of the Bombay Corporation and as member of the Bombay and Imperial Legislative Councils. He was also active in the world of banking, and had helped the princely state of Baroda set up a commercial bank in the first decade of the twentieth century.[37]

As it happened, Thackersey had just suffered a serious setback: the Indian Specie Bank, which he had promoted in 1905, collapsed in 1913 as a result of speculative activity. It was generally believed that the directors of the bank, Thackersey among them, had failed to exercise oversight over its adventurous managing director, thus precipitating a crisis.[38] But none of this made a difference to Visvesvaraya, who trusted Thackersey implicitly. He had sought the businessman's advice since his days as chief engineer on matters such as Mysore's railway works and the Kannambadi dam project, and did not hesitate to do so again. The first chairman of Mysore's new bank, K.P. Puttanna Chetty, wrote to Thackersey in 1913, requesting him to suggest the name of an Indian who could serve as manager of the bank. Thackersey suggested instead that they appoint '[a] European manager of good standing and with plenty of experience', and provided three alternatives. One of them, W.C. Rose (a Jersey-born banker who had served for many years in the Delhi and London Bank), became the first manager.[39]

The Bank of Mysore, as the new institution was called, was registered in May 1913, and began functioning that October. It had an authorized capital of Rs 20 lakh, the state putting in half that amount to begin with. The remaining 10 lakh was raised from an enthusiastic public. The government also committed to making further investments and contributions for the first decade of the bank's life. In return they had oversight of the bank's functioning.[40]

Three years after the establishment of the Bank of Mysore, the government led the creation of a Chamber of Commerce for Mysore. As with the Bank, the idea for the Chamber had originated in the Economic Conference; W.C. Rose and Alfred Chatterton were among those who then worked on implementing it. Rose was elected President of the Chamber when it came into being. The Chamber was inaugurated on 8 May 1916 at Bangalore's Government High School. As Visvesvaraya declared that day, the Chamber was meant to 'safeguard and promote the special interests of trade and industry in Mysore.' In particular, he was concerned that well organized and resourceful 'outsiders'—most probably a reference to Marwari merchants—controlled much of Mysore's commerce, while their Mysorean counterparts, owing to their 'apathy . . . , their prejudice, lack of enterprise and unwillingness to move with the times', were left by the wayside.

Visvesvaraya thought the indigenous businessmen were untrained, poorly informed, and unwilling to work together to further their common interests; this was what the Chamber of Commerce would help them do. 'An individual having a grievance may be snubbed, . . . but no public authority can afford to ignore the joint representation of 500 merchants.' He wanted the Chamber to not only represent their needs to the government and public bodies, but also popularize the views of the business community on particular issues, collect statistics, publish a trade directory, encourage the founding of joint-stock and partnership firms, and push merchants to widen their horizons through travel.[41]

Both Bank and Chamber bore the mark of Visvesvaraya's zeal to catalogue and rationalize resources, his eagerness to instruct and guide the business class. The outcomes were more ambiguous. The Bank of Mysore, for instance, was only moderately successful in promoting industry and commerce. It lent generously to Mysore's merchants—the loans issued up to 1917 amounted to Rs 50 lakh. But it was not very effective at supporting industrialists, and this was partly a consequence of its structure. It was created as a commercial rather than an investment bank, which meant it could only '[take] short-term deposits and [lend] invariably for short periods'.[42] Visvesvaraya was aware of this shortcoming; possibly his aim had been to get the bank started on a small scale before ramping up operations. By 1918 he was discussing with Thackersey the possibility of creating a separate industrial section within the bank. But neither this nor subsequent attempts in the 1920s to restructure the bank came to fruition.[43]

Mysore also had another institution that aligned with Visvesvaraya's project of instructing the state's merchants, peasants, and workers and guiding them towards the Elysium of industrial society. This was the Industrial and Agricultural Exhibition held in Mysore city each year during the Dasara festival. It pre-dated his arrival in Mysore: it had become an annual event in 1907, when Visvesvaraya was still in the Bombay PWD. As the historian Janaki Nair has shown vividly, Mysore's officials conceived the exhibition primarily as a means to educate the state's peasants and skilled labourers. Improved farming tools and machinery were displayed to encourage cultivators to modernize their operations. Lectures were organized and prizes awarded for impressive exhibits. In its first five years, however, the exhibition had a negligible impact on its intended audience, and attendance fluctuated.[44]

Visvesvaraya's response was not to reassess the aims of the exhibition, but to ask his colleagues to redouble their efforts. At the inauguration of the exhibition in 1913, the secretary of the organizing committee, G.H. Krumbiegel (a German horticulturist who spent many years working in Mysore) remarked that there were few exhibitors from Mysore. 'This,' Visvesvaraya responded, 'is probably because the objects and uses of the Exhibition are not fully brought to the notice of the people in the districts and interest is not kept alive. There should be a network of organization[s] for bringing the labours and interests of all people, who are likely to profit by the Exhibition, to bear on the year's work.' Visvesvaraya saw the exhibition as 'a fitting corollary' to the many other measures his government was taking: the creation of the Department of Industries and Commerce, the activities of the Economic Conference, and the founding of new industrial and commercial schools. He wanted the exhibition to expand its relevance through the 'add[ition of] a permanent hall of industrial and agricultural machinery in connection with the Chamarajendra Technical Institute', which would welcome visitors at any time of the year.[45] The exhibition venue was built up further, and the government allocated Rs 30,000 to fill the new rooms with machinery.[46]

Although the next few years coincided with the First World War, the exhibition continued to be held. Machinery produced by British and expatriate engineering firms was placed on view alongside contraptions that Alfred Chatterton wanted to popularize, including the fly shuttle and 'a deep well pump' that he had patented.[47] Visvesvaraya tried to spread his ideas about the importance of statistics, inviting Gilbert Slater, an economics professor at Madras University, to lecture on the topic at the exhibition.[48] Despite these efforts, it is difficult to say how successful the exhibition was in its didactic ambitions. By 1920—two years after Visvesvaraya's tenure as dewan ended—the government had given it up as a lost cause, deciding instead to organize a 'Dasara Fair' whose sole aim was to provide merriment for visitors to the royal capital. The exhibition was, however, resurrected in 1927, and grew in scope and size in the following decades.[49]

*

All these institutions notwithstanding, Mysore still suffered from one serious drawback in its quest to boost its industries and commerce.[50] The state, bordered by the provinces of Madras to the east and Bombay to the west, had no coastline, and hence no port of its own. This made it logistically difficult and uneconomical for Mysore to export its products beyond Indian shores, or even to principal Indian centres of commerce such as Bombay: in both cases they had to transport goods over several hundred miles of railroad. Almost from the time of the Rendition, the state's officials had tried to get access to a port on the west coast of the Indian peninsula.

The demand was taken up seriously again during Visvesvaraya's dewanship. Mysore now singled out as a potential port the small town of Bhatkal, which lay along the Arabian Sea near the southern tip of the Bombay Presidency, just fourteen miles west of the Mysore border (see Figure 12.1 below). In 1915, they engaged a prominent colonial engineer,

Sir Francis Spring, of the Madras Port Trust, to report on the feasibility and cost of building an up-to-date harbour at Bhatkal. In subsequent years, a posse of other experts from Mysore, Bombay, and even London made further studies of the question, coming up with varying plans and estimates. Mysore also planned to connect Bhatkal by rail to Shimoga, a prominent town in the *malnad* region.

The catch, of course, was that Mysore needed the Bombay government to agree to the plan. To make the Bhatkal port viable, Mysore needed legal and administrative jurisdiction over an area of around three square miles, covering the prospective port and the strip of land required to connect it with their railway network. The Bombay government did not oppose Mysore's plan to build a port, but they were unwilling to grant jurisdiction over their lands to Mysore. Meanwhile, British officials stressed that that the project was unlikely to recover its costs.

The Bhatkal plan was a vital part of Visvesvaraya's agenda. It was to assume particular significance in relation to Mysore's efforts—discussed below—to produce and export iron. Visvesvaraya's keenness on the project was evidenced by his government's heavy investment in expert opinion and feasibility studies, and by his own active involvement: along with the Mysore Resident, he attended meetings with the Governor of Bombay and officials in Delhi.

Ultimately, Visvesvaraya failed to make headway with Bombay and the Government of India. In fact, Mysore would continue to make representations over the next three decades, with little success. Nevertheless, the state's commitment to the Bhatkal idea was clearly a legacy of Visvesvaraya's determination to seek export markets for Mysore's industries.

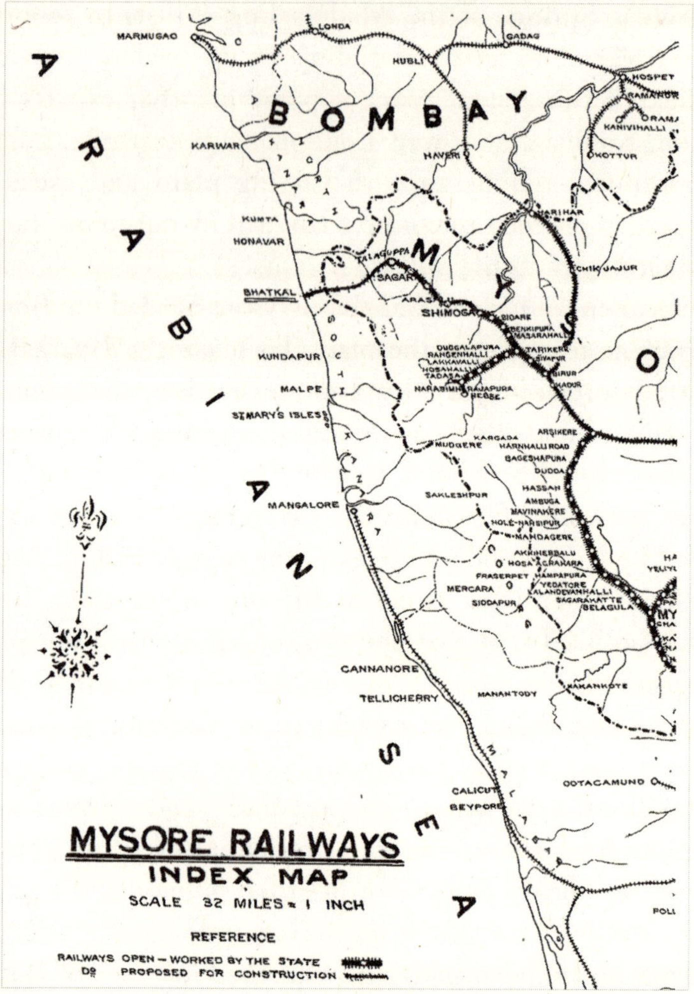

Fig. 12.1. Map showing the location of Bhatkal relative to Mysore territory as of the 1940s

Source: 'Development of the Bhatkal Harbour and Construction of the Chamarajanagar-Mettupalaiyam Ry.', [Railway Department, Mysore], 1945–46, File No. 217/[9], KSA-DIGITIZED (https://archives.karnataka.gov.in/home/viewdocument?doc_id=RGVlcGFrMzczNzQ=&doc_location=RGVlcGFrMQ==). The map follows the note by H. Rangachar, General Manager, Mysore State Railway (4 November 1945) titled 'The Bhatkal Harbour Project'.

*

As the war progressed, the colonial government began to reconsider their traditional laissez-faire approach to the Indian economy. It became clear to them that steps must be taken to support Indian industry, if only in the strategic interests of the Empire. In 1916, they instituted the Indian Industrial Commission under the Chairmanship of Sir Thomas Holland, who had served as Director of the Geological Survey of India earlier in his career.[51] Among those invited to sit on the Commission was Alfred Chatterton.[52]

By this time Chatterton had spent around four years in Mysore, three of them as director of industries. His work was remarkably successful in the arenas he was committed to: the mechanization of small-scale and agrarian industries. The sandalwood oil factory not only generated useful revenue for the state, it also became a symbol of Mysorean industry. Visvesvaraya appreciated his efforts in these fields, and acknowledged his contributions on many public occasions, while lauding his 'energy' and his 'wide experience . . . in industrial matters'.[53] The two engineer-bureaucrats respected each other and shared a solid working relationship.[54]

But Chatterton did not share Visvesvaraya's enthusiasm for rapid industrialization and gargantuan projects like the Kannambadi reservoir. He believed that in a predominantly agrarian country like India, industrialization must be undertaken incrementally.[55] This sometimes irritated the dewan, who once wrote to his director of industries that 'it is not your business to point out the backwardness of Mysore industries, but to indicate its possibilities and stimulate efforts'.[56] He was particularly disappointed at Chatterton's indifference to his plans to establish an iron works in the state. In later years he was to remember Chatterton as 'a highly qualified and able officer' who 'interested himself in some specific industries only . . . He could not be induced to take interest in iron and other mechanical engineering industries which the State wanted to establish'.[57]

It was in this climate that Chatterton received the invitation to join the Indian Industrial Commission. It was a prestigious opportunity, one that would allow him to make an impact on an all-India scale. Quite possibly he saw it as a good time to step away from Mysore, where the potential for conflict with Visvesvaraya was becoming apparent. He agreed to serve on the Commission. This took him away from Mysore for two years, although he would later return as Industrial Adviser and head of the sandalwood oil factories.[58]

*

With Chatterton gone, Visvesvaraya was left to pursue his own unfettered vision of an iron works for Mysore. The production of iron was a crucial part of his programme: if new factories were to spring up across the state, they would need iron and steel.[59] Iron production was an audacious goal, but Visvesvaraya may have been encouraged by the recent success of the Tatas, with whom he had been in contact in his days in the Bombay Presidency.[60] The Tata Iron and Steel Company (TISCO) had successfully raised capital from the public and gone into production in 1912.[61]

The existence of substantial deposits of iron ore in the Bababudan Hills, located in Kadur District in Mysore's *malnad* region, was well known. For centuries, communities across Mysore had smelted iron using traditional charcoal furnaces. These were still in use in in some parts of the Chitaldrug District, but on the whole the availability of inexpensive imported iron had made them unviable. More than one Mysore administration in the past had flirted with the idea of establishing a modern iron-manufacturing industry.[62]

There was, however, one major impediment in the way of producing iron on an industrial scale: Mysore didn't have coal deposits. Coke, a derivative of coal, is an essential ingredient, referred to as the *fuel*, in the manufacture of iron. Along with *flux* (usually limestone), it is added to the iron ore in a blast furnace, where it reduces the oxides of iron to the metal in elemental form. If the state had to import coal, it would make the resulting iron very expensive and unable to compete with other Indian producers.[63]

One way out of this conundrum was to use a different source of carbon, namely charcoal, instead of coke. Charcoal could be produced by burning wood, and there was plenty of wood available in the forests of Kadur and Shimoga districts, not far from the iron ore deposits.

It was to this option that Visvesvaraya turned. Looking back on this time in later life, he noted that 'resort was had to the use of wood charcoal . . . on the model of charcoal iron factories in the United States of America and Sweden'.[64] Perhaps it is this that has led to the impression—although Visvesvaraya himself did not claim it—that the use of charcoal was a breakthrough idea, one that only he could have had since he had travelled to the countries in question.[65] In fact, it was a fairly obvious choice. It was charcoal that the traditional village smelters used; charcoal was the fuel envisaged in earlier discussions on the possibility of starting an iron works in Mysore. A few years before Visvesvaraya came to Mysore from the Bombay PWD, the government had sent Dr W.F. Smeeth, the Irishman who headed its Geological Department, to Italy to see the working of the Stassano furnace in Turin. This was an electric furnace for the conversion of iron ore to pig iron and steel using charcoal.[66] However, this process was not replicated in Mysore. To produce electricity on the required scale at a location close to Mysore's iron belt would have been too expensive.[67] In addition, Smeeth was not convinced that charcoal could be procured economically.[68]

What Visvesvaraya brought to the table, then, was a conviction that charcoal could feasibly be used for the production of iron on an industrial scale. In 1915, his government commissioned experiments to determine the most efficient method of converting timber to charcoal.[69] That year, the dewan told the Representative Assembly that '[t]here are possibilities in the iron deposits of the Bababudans and a profitable industry in iron and steel may be created if the problem of smelting iron ore with charcoal on a commercial scale is satisfactorily solved'.[70]

The prospect of plundering the state's forests—what he tellingly described as 'the redundant wood supply of our dense *Malnad* forests'—for timber to produce charcoal aligned perfectly with Visvesvaraya's view of natural resources.[71] To him, the forests served little purpose if the resources they contained were not converted into industrially useful or commercially valuable products.[72] In fact, he saw the *malnad*, through Orientalist eyes, as a backward, malarious region overrun by vegetation.[73] The taming of its forests tied in with his plans to make the region healthier for human settlements as part of what he called the Malnad Improvement Scheme.[74]

Similarly, the mineral deposits of the state could not be allowed to lie idle under the earth's surface. Visvesvaraya thought the Department of Geology, which had been established during Seshadri Iyer's dewanship with the aim of drawing up a geological map of Mysore, was not earning its keep. '[I]t is high time,' he wrote in December 1914, 'that the Department was made to subserve the economic interests of the State instead of confining its activities to matters of subsidiary importance or interests.'[75] In February 1915, the Department was restructured and renamed the Department of Mines and Geology. Among other objects, it was to work on the '[p]roduction of minerals and development of metallurgical industries on a commercial scale', working in conjunction with the Department of Industries and other government bodies to attract private investment.[76]

W.F. Smeeth, who continued as director of the department in its new avatar, now embarked on an exhaustive survey with this goal. An alumnus of Trinity College, Dublin and an Associate of the Royal School of Mines, London, he had served in the Mysore Geological Department since 1898.[77] Working with a junior colleague, P. Sampat Iyengar, Smeeth brought out a report in 1916 titled *Mineral Resources of Mysore: A Brief Account of the More Important Economic Minerals, their Occurrence and Distribution with Notes on their Mining and Metallurgical Treatment and Uses*.[78]

Alongside gold, manganese, and chromium, iron was one of the chief minerals the report dealt with. The authors noted that the peaks of the Bababudan range consisted of iron-bearing rocks, mostly haematite. Pits were dug across this area, samples extracted, and a series of tests conducted. The report identified the ores of a peak known as Kemmangundi (the name itself indicating the reddish haematite ores found there) as significant from a commercial point of view. While remarking on 'the very complex character of these deposits' and the difficulty of assessing how economical it would be to extract them, the geologists estimated that millions of tons of ore could be got in the vicinity. The ore could then be hauled down the slopes of Kemmangundi, 'probably by a wire ropeway, and thence by a light railway to a smelting works' in the region.[79]

Smeeth and Iyengar thought a charcoal iron works was feasible. Having consulted the Conservator of Forests, they suggested that 1,00,000 tons of wood could be hauled out of the *malnad* forests each year by '150 to 200 miles of light railways or tramways'. This would yield 20,000 tons of charcoal, which would be sufficient to turn out 20,000 tons of pig iron. Since the impurities present in coke—ash and phosphorus—were not found in charcoal, the resulting iron would be of a higher quality than that produced using coke. The authors estimated that a reasonable amount of charcoal iron could be sold not only in India, but also in Japan and Australia.[80]

These projections regarding a possible iron works seem to reflect discussions that Smeeth had held with a visiting American consulting engineer named Charles Page Perin, whose opinion Visvesvaraya had sought in 1915. The New York-based Perin was a veteran of the iron and steel industry, and had, only a few years earlier, helped put up TISCO's factory in Sakchi, a village located a couple of hundred miles west of Calcutta.[81]

During his visit to Mysore, Perin consulted Smeeth and saw the forests of Kadur and Shimoga in the company of M.G. Rama Rao, the Conservator of Forests. His report, which he sent to Visvesvaraya in May 1916, was encouraging. It contained a plan for the establishment of a factory that would produce 20,000 tons of charcoal iron a year using a blast furnace. A number of incidental products were mentioned. Perin proposed to use 'modern by-product recovery kilns' in the production of charcoal from wood, and to produce calcium carbide from 'the charcoal breeze, or such portions of the charcoal as cannot be used in the blast furnace'. The entire cost of establishing the works, he said, would be around Rs 64 lakh.[82] Perin was confident it would be a profitable venture with a range of knock-on benefits to the state's economy. He even suggested that if, in the future, electricity could be supplied economically to the factory, it might be possible to go one step further and produce steel.[83]

The iron works would need to be situated at a reasonable distance from Kemmangundi and from the forests. The site would also need an adequate supply of water. Although Shimoga and Lakkavalli were also considered, the most favoured site, by 1916, was Benkipur (later renamed Bhadravati) on the banks of the Bhadra river.[84]

*

Although he now had a favourable report from an established expert, Visvesvaraya knew he would have to fight battles on several fronts to get an iron works sanctioned and running. As in the case of the Krishnarajasagara project (see Chapter 9), he had to win over multiple stakeholders, not least his own colleagues in the government. He began by sending his correspondence with Perin to the members of the dewan's council for their perusal in September 1916.[85]

Next, he approached TISCO for technical assistance in the running of the proposed factory. The manufacture of iron was still a nascent industry in India, and if Mysore were to enter the field, they would need technical guidance. TISCO was one of only two companies producing iron in the country,[86] and Visvesvaraya had contacts with the Tatas from his days in the Bombay Presidency (see Chapter 6). In December 1916, he travelled to Sakchi, where he sounded out TISCO's directors.[87] (Vithaldas Thackersey accompanied him, no doubt tendering unofficial advice.)[88] He then made his way to Bombay to try and hammer out an agreement with representatives of the parent company, Tata and Sons. On Christmas Day, he had a meeting with his old acquaintance, the Tata official B.J. Padshah, and Lallubhai Samaldas, a prominent Bombay businessman who served as a director in various Tata companies.

The three men discussed the terms under which TISCO would undertake the task of establishing and running the new works. Mysore was to furnish the whole of the capital for putting up the factory, and pay TISCO a 10 per cent commission on the total costs incurred during construction. TISCO would continue to be managing agents of the new factory for a fixed period after it went into operation: Padshah pushed for a thirty-year agreement, while Visvesvaraya leaned towards twenty. (They would eventually settle on twenty-five years.) Samaldas and Padshah also made it plain to the Mysore dewan that the capital and operating expenses were likely to be much higher than the estimates he had at present.

Clearly, the TISCO representatives saw the issue through the cold lens of business logic, whereas Visvesvaraya was keen to realize the project at (almost) any cost. He told Padshah and Samaldas that the Mysore government was approaching the venture not merely as a business, but also to provide an opportunity for local engineers and workers to acquire the experience of working in a basic industry. The Tata representatives responded

> that this object perhaps could be better carried out by making the primary aim, in the first instance, to get profit and to get the best skilled labour, imported or native, to get running traditions of mutual loyalty, co-operation and discipline and hard work, and then when traditions began to be established and the profits began to be earned, make the employment of Indian and particularly Mysorian [sic] labour and intellect a primary aim.[89]

The meeting ended on a hopeful note. Partly as a result of Padshah's counsel, Visvesvaraya revised the estimated cost of establishing an iron works to Rs 90 lakh. On 2 January 1917, he wrote to the Mysore maharaja, formally proposing (among other works) a factory for '[w]ood distillation and manufacture of pig iron'. As usual, he made sanguine predictions about the profits that the government would get from the new ventures in a few years' time. True, the machinery needed for the iron works would be unusually expensive (this being the time of the First World War); but Visvesvaraya insisted it was a good time to get into the business. '[S]hrewd businessmen have assured me,' he wrote, 'that it would take four or five years after the war before foreign competition returns to normal conditions.'

Still, as the discussions in Bombay showed, Visvesvaraya knew that a foolproof business case had not been made out for the iron manufacturing project. This did not perturb him unduly. He now told the maharaja: 'We should be prepared for difficulties and losses in some directions . . . Every commercial scheme has an element of chance in it. If we are to go into business we must take some chances.'[90]

The proposal then went to the dewan's council, where it was discussed over the course of a couple of meetings in January 1917. Financial officers were also consulted, including J.S. Chakravarti, Visvesvaraya's one-time nemesis in the matter of the Kannambadi dam. This time Chakravarti raised no objection, and the maharaja okayed the project on 21 January.[91] In February, the council empowered Perin to place orders abroad for machinery, even as Padshah sent Mysore a draft of the agreement to be drawn up with TISCO.[92]

In March, however, Second Councillor Albion Banerji—a Bengali ICS officer serving in Mysore—raised a red flag. Asserting that he had not had access to the full details of the project at the time of the council's earlier decisions, he now turned against the project. He pointed to the lack of solid numbers suggesting that the venture would be profitable, argued that maintenance costs on the tramways had not been factored in, and alleged that the Forest Department would lose money in the process of supplying fuel to the iron works. He also argued that there was no need for the state to hand over the actual manufacture of iron to an external body (TISCO), on terms particularly favourable to the latter.

In notes submitted to the maharaja, Visvesvaraya furnished circumstantial evidence to establish that although Banerji had missed the first January meeting, he had indeed had access to the relevant information before the council decided on the project.[93] He also rebutted Banerji's arguments point by point. He emphasized that Perin had spent a year preparing his report, that the Conservator of Forests had calculated that the project would not be financially injurious to his department, and that there was a strong need to enlist TISCO's expertise, as '[i]ron-making is not by any means the easy process which Mr. Banerji assumes it to be'.[94]

In the months that followed, Visvesvaraya's colleagues raised other questions, prompting the maharaja to caution the dewan that he should pay heed to their concerns. Camping in the Fern Hill Palace at Ooty that summer, the monarch's private secretary, R.H. Campbell, wrote to Visvesvaraya that 'it is [the king's] earnest wish that there should be absolute unanimity between yourself and the Council in regard to any further important steps'. Visvesvaraya, also billeted at Fern Hill, responded with his usual bluster, telling Campbell that this was out of the question, since Banerji was clearly opposed to the project. 'If *absolute unanimity*, as you state, is to be insisted on, the better course will be to issue an order to cancel the understanding with the Tatas and stop the work.'[95] In the end, he had his way.

That was not all, however. The Government of India, catching wind of Mysore's plans for an iron factory, were trying to slow them down, for they feared that a project like this would interfere with their wartime priorities.[96] Communicating via Resident H.V. Cobb and his staff, they insisted that their approval should be sought before Mysore invested in such a project. Letters went back and forth between the Residency and Visvesvaraya's government, the latter emphasizing Mysore's right to autonomy, especially now that they were governed by a Treaty rather than an Instrument of Transfer. Although the Durbar did share various details with the colonial government—the draft agreement with TISCO, financial estimates, C.P. Perin's report—they did so months after they had ordered machinery in America through Perin. They now used these sunk costs as a bargaining chip, telling the Government of India that if they did not sanction the project, and quickly, Mysore would incur losses and lose good business opportunities while iron prices were high.[97]

By the second half of the year, the colonial government had been painted into a corner. In October, they protested weakly that Mysore had not given them enough time to conduct an independent analysis of the project proposals, which of course they would have carried out in the state's best interests. They still thought Mysore should proceed cautiously; but if the durbar wanted to go ahead, they would not stand in the way.[98]

The agreement with the Tatas was finalized the same year, and the Mysore Distillation and Iron Works came into being soon after. It was supervised by a board containing three directors appointed by Mysore and two by TISCO, the latter company being designated managing agents. Perin and Marshall, the New York-based firm run by Charles Perin and his partner, were appointed consulting engineers for the construction of the plant. Under Perin's supervision, the factory and the surrounding township began to come up in 1919.[99]

Once more, Visvesvaraya had succeeded in pushing through an ambitious project by his sheer conviction and force of personality. Yet there were many question marks over the project. The prospect of exporting pig iron at competitive rates depended on access to a seaport, and the negotiations over Bhatkal were stuck. Meanwhile, Banerji's instinct that the agreement was generous to TISCO was not misplaced, for it was Mysore that bore all the financial risks while the managing agents only stood to gain. Visvesvaraya was aware of this, but TISCO's assistance was indispensable if he was to realize his goal of setting up an iron works. Visvesvaraya also realized that Perin's initial estimate of costs was too low, but he was content to trust the consultant's optimistic predictions as to the likely market they would enjoy for charcoal pig iron.[100] Although Visvesvaraya stepped down as dewan in 1918 for unrelated reasons (see Chapter 13), these questions would come back to haunt him in later years (see Chapter 16).[101]

For the moment, however, Visvesvaraya could look back at his dewan years with some satisfaction. As the world returned to a semblance of stability after four battle-scarred years, his administration had established the foundations of an industrial economy in Mysore. A large multipurpose dam project was partially functional; new railway lines had been built; a government department was in place to foster industries; and a new factory was gearing up to turn out charcoal iron from locally sourced raw materials. It remained to be seen how stable these foundations were, and at what cost they had been laid.

13

A Dewan at Work

In 1913, S. Hiriannaiya, a civil servant with a law degree, was selected as the dewan's private secretary. Hiriannaiya's friends and relatives were delighted by the news, but cautioned him that the work would be 'arduous', the duties 'onerous'. 'I have little doubt,' wrote one colleague, 'that you will do full justice to your new duties though you are certain to find them somewhat taxing. It is a trite saying that the place is not a bed of roses.'[1]

Perhaps Hiriannaiya recalled these words as he first arrived at Visvesvaraya's office in Bangalore's secretariat, the grand Greco-Roman edifice at the edge of Cubbon Park. Everything about it screamed briskness, efficiency, and toil. On the dewan's desk was an electric calling system, inherited from his predecessor, which could summon minions from various rooms. Visvesvaraya had added a 'Roneophone', a dictaphone purchased from the Roneo Company of Holborn, London, and advertised as 'a busy man's right hand—ACCURATE, SPEEDY, ENDURING AND ECONOMIC'. In his official stable were three cars: a 1913 Wolseley with a 'limousine landaulette body' for daily use; a Hotchkiss for the dewan's tours in the countryside; and a 'run-about' in which his staff accompanied him on such travels.[2]

It was well known that the dewan's office barely slept. The day's work was conducted in two sessions, the first from around 7 a.m. until lunch, and the second from 3 p.m. until late evening. In the first session, which was usually held in his home office at Ballabrooie, Visvesvaraya met with bureaucrats to assign and evaluate tasks. In the second, he dealt with paperwork at the secretariat. Work continued seven days a week, a portion of the staff in attendance on any given holiday.[3]

Visvesvaraya was an exacting boss. He insisted his staff be punctual, well turned out, and active. He favoured Western attire and expected them to adopt it too: he once pointed out to a young civil servant that his collar button was showing behind the knot of his tie. The four clerks who worked directly under the dewan, handling his correspondence and sundry other tasks, were kept on their toes. Letters and notes he dictated would go through multiple drafts. Envelopes had to be sealed and stamps affixed without the gum smudging. Telephone calls received in the secretariat had to be attended to at once. One of his personal clerks recalled that he worked alongside the dewan seven days a week—the exception being 'important festival days', when Visvesvaraya asked him to stay home so that his family was not upset.[4]

But the boss was not without a kindly streak. He made sure lunch was available at Ballabrooie for any of his staff who wanted it. Having begun work early in the day, they were served coffee and a snack at 11 a.m. He also secured additional allowances for his clerks,[5] and wrote to the maharaja multiple times requesting that the allowances be extended. In one case he even asked for the allowance to be increased, as the clerk in question 'does confidential work' and his workload 'has been exceptionally heavy'.[6]

It was a similar story when it came to Visvesvaraya's private secretary. Visvesvaraya worked him especially hard. Hiriannaiya's family members tell anecdotes of his exchanges with the dewan. Once, when Visvesvaraya called him 'lazy', Hiriannaiya had to protest that he worked such long hours that his own son hardly knew him. On another occasion, when the two were on a train journey, Visvesvaraya drily observed to Hiriannaiya, who was looking out of the window, that he appeared to be interested in nature. The younger man denied the charge; the dewan downed the shutters and began to dictate notes.[7] On the other hand, he made sure Hiriannaiya was compensated for his sacrifices, getting the government to give him better terms for his allowances.[8] Hiriannaiya became one of Visvesvaraya's most trusted aides, and they remained in contact for decades after they had ceased to work together.[9]

Occasionally, Visvesvaraya acknowledged that Sunday was not a weekday. He did this not by taking the day off, but by varying his routine. Escaping the hustle and bustle of Bangalore and the secretariat, he would take the Wolseley down on Saturday evening to Muddenahalli, the village of his birth, where his mother still spent most of her time. He took with him a stack of files, working on them in the relative peace of his telephone-free ancestral home. Often he was joined by his brother, nephew and niece. (This brother, also based in Bangalore, was M. Ramachandra Rao, a jurist who went on to serve as a judge in the post-Independence Mysore High Court.)

As the nephew, M.S. Murthy, recalled, Visvesvaraya was fastidious about the use of government property. In the village one weekend, the young Murthy asked his uncle if he could borrow his 'red and blue pencil' (presumably Visvesvaraya used it to mark up his files). Visvesvaraya hesitated: the pencil came from his office supplies. 'I sensed that my request had embarrassed him,' Murthy later remembered. 'To my great delight on the following trip I found among other things a cane basket marked "personal stationery for children's use".' When they returned to Bangalore on Monday mornings, the dewan's relatives would have to get off at Ballabrooie. The journey from there to Ramachandra Rao's home was made in Visvesvaraya's personal car; the Wolseley was an official car to be used for official business alone.

On his visits to Muddenahalli, Visvesvaraya took neither motorcade nor police escort. He did not play the dewan with his neighbours in the village. Yet he was his usual didactic self. He discussed with them 'their living conditions, food habits, education of the adults and children, sanitation, drinking water facilities, cattle welfare etc.' He got newspapers delivered to the village and asked the literate residents to read them out to the rest. He urged the villagers to send their children, boys and girls alike, to school.[10]

*

A benevolent dictator he may have been to his immediate subordinates, but plenty of bureaucrats in Visvesvaraya's government disliked the way he functioned. This was often compounded by disagreement with his policies.

One of his least popular innovations was what he called the Efficiency Audit. In his very first address to the Dasara Representative Assembly as dewan, Visvesvaraya described this measure, which was to 'provide for more frequent and systematic inspections, . . . improve the office manuals and standing orders, and . . . ensure that the rules and orders in force are properly worked . . . that beneficent activities of every kind receive stimulus, that serious irregularities receive prompt attention'. The Mysorean government was run 'on the European model', but its 'staff . . . have not fully adopted European business habits'. Hence 'an "efficiency audit" is as much a necessity as a "financial audit"'.[11]

The Efficiency Audit was made operational in 1914. Its officials could be requisitioned by government departments or district officials 'for the investigation of irregularities'. Rules were codified and 'office manuals' created. Every office was to undergo inspections, sometimes without prior notice. Also introduced was '[a] new system of qualification reports', which would 'enable Government to obtain, from time to time, more detailed information than what has been hitherto available regarding the work and capacity of the several officers'.[12]

The Efficiency Audit was integral to Visvesvaraya's vision of a lean government machinery. But many took it as an affront to their dignity. For some senior government officials, the prospect of unannounced inspections and secret reports on their productivity was too much to contemplate. At a meeting in 1913 where Visvesvaraya spoke about the Efficiency Audit, one colleague reportedly 'denounced it as a system of spying'.[13]

There were other grievances too. High-ranking colleagues sometimes complained they were being railroaded into certain decisions, denied time to consider them. His councillors were said to be unhappy at Visvesvaraya's habit of going above their heads and getting an outside opinion on some matters.[14] There was a general feeling that he was profligate in awarding bonuses, raises and allowances to employees at various levels, and that some of them were taking him for a ride by paying lip service to ideals they did not really believe in. H.V. Nanjundayya, who worked closely with Visvesvaraya, was at one point irked enough to write a letter of complaint to the maharaja's secretary, R.H. Campbell. In the letter, which his son made public after his death, Nanjundayya wrote:

> I do not envy the man who will succeed to the task of reintroducing sober economy in the public expenditure of this State. Offices are being multiplied every day, and pay and allowances increased on every side to men who play up to the fads of the hour. Phrases and shibboleths pass from mouth to mouth and are caught by every one who wishes to get on. . . . It

> is the present Dewan's fortune to have come at the nick of time [i.e., at a time of prosperity] to scatter largesses all around. Not only officials but also non-officials are drawn into the golden rain. But when the lean years succeed, how difficult it would be to bring men down again to earth and get [from] them the usual work for the usual pay.[15]

For his part, Visvesvaraya was conscious that he had his critics, some of them virulent. And while he was strong-willed, he was also sensitive to criticism. 'One consequence of the unfriendly atmosphere,' a junior colleague noted, 'was that he [Visvesvaraya] distrusted all disagreement.'[16]

His touchiness, and the difficulty that long-serving bureaucrats—already socialized into a particular mode and culture of work—experienced in working with him, come through vividly in the diary kept by a colleague, K.R. Srinivasa Iyengar. Serving in the Mysore civil service from the 1890s to the 1940s, Srinivasa Iyengar was a deputy commissioner in Kadur before being transferred to Bangalore as Secretary of the General and Revenue Branch of the state government around the time Visvesvaraya became dewan. He thus had occasion to work in close proximity to Visvesvaraya for a couple of years. His diary, which deals largely with office politics, was edited and published in 1982 by the scholar Narendar Pani.[17]

Iyengar had a tumultuous relationship with Visvesvaraya. He was scrupulous in recording the latter's good points, but also made clear the frustration he often felt in working with him. A dyed-in-the-wool bureaucrat, he was wary of Visvesvaraya right from the time people started talking of him as the dewan-in-waiting. He did not agree with Visvesvaraya's bold policies and expensive projects as dewan, preferring a more financially conservative approach. He thought 'the Dewan had lots of ideas but they were flighty and superficial'.[18]

Iyengar also took exception to what he saw as Visvesvaraya's abrasive personality. One colleague reported to him that the dewan had been brusque with him. Apparently, Visvesvaraya had said: 'I know to be very polite: but I am very sorry I have no time for it,' before granting an interview for only a few minutes.[19] In January 1913—when Visvesvaraya had only been in office a couple of months—his colleagues arrived half an hour late for a meeting of the dewan's council, as a previous engagement had run over time. 'The Dewan told them that he would like them to be more punctual,' Srinivasa Iyengar noted. 'Mr. HVN [H.V. Nanjundayya, the First Councillor] said that they were delayed in hearing appeals and that it was an [sic] usual thing.' At that meeting, there was also an argument between Visvesvaraya and Nanjundayya about the proposal to set up a new Department of Industries with Alfred Chatterton as its head.[20]

But what Iyengar found particularly difficult was having to report on a daily basis to Visvesvaraya in his role as general and revenue secretary. Visvesvaraya wanted him to be dynamic, to follow up on files and issues, and to come up with ideas of his own. But Iyengar, conscious of bureaucratic rank and vintage, was loath to send reminders or suggestions to those whom he considered his superiors. Early on in his tenure, Visvesvaraya summoned him and asked him to speed up the processing of various files. Iyengar replied that some of them were pending with the councillors and the dewan himself: how could he say anything to them? The dewan replied that he would welcome a reminder if that was the case.[21]

Once, Visvesvaraya arrived at the office forty-five minutes later than his usual time. Fifteen minutes later, he rang for Iyengar and asked why he had not come over immediately. Another time, Iyengar recorded that Visvesvaraya 'was in a nasty mood finding fault with me for everything saying that I had not done many things that he wanted. After having been a Deputy

Commissioner for years, I found the treatment accorded to me by the Dewan so galling that I was extremely mortified over it.' On a third occasion, Visvesvaraya asked Iyengar to take notes when a number of people came to the office with petitions for the dewan. '[F]or this silly dirty work,' Iyengar fumed, 'the time of the Secretary to Government had to be wasted for 3 hours.'[22]

One day, around seven months into their working relationship, there was a showdown. Visvesvaraya censured Iyengar for being passive, saying he 'had not done anything original and shown initiative'. Iyengar retorted that Visvesvaraya 'probably judged of a man's work by the amount of fuss and noise he made about it; that it had always been my habit not to make fuss or noise about my work, but to go on with it smoothly and quietly and that I had not considered it worthwhile to worry or annoy him with all kinds of matters simply for the sake of being in evidence before him'. That evening, Visvesvaraya unbent a little, acknowledging 'that he had been rude to me [Iyengar] in the morning'.[23]

From Srinivasa Iyengar's perspective, Visvesvaraya blew hot and cold. One moment he was scolding him for not doing enough; the next he was telling him not to push himself too hard.[24] When Iyengar declined to give his opinion on who would be suitable for a particular post, he was seen as passive, but when he did, the Dewan thought he was promoting his friends.[25] Iyengar craved Visvesvaraya's trust, but in vain. He spoke to H.V. Nanjundayya about it. He also spoke to the dewan's private secretary, who assured him 'that the Dewan had no feeling of dislike towards me and that it was his nature not to trust anybody'.[26]

Over the course of a year and a half, the working relationship became untenable. Iyengar occasionally introspected, wondering whether in fact he could perform his duties better. At other times he fretted and poured out his frustrations to anyone in Mysore officialdom he thought would share his grievances—including R.H. Campbell, the maharaja's private secretary. He sometimes thought the dewan was trying to sideline him because he was a Tamil Brahmin and not a native Mysorean.[27] He had a number of conversations with the dewan, both trying to articulate their points of view. Eventually, almost to his relief, Srinivasa Iyengar was transferred out of the position of general and revenue secretary. Later he became a deputy commissioner again, and was posted to Tumkur. Distance acted as a salve, and the relationship become more friendly.[28]

Iyengar's diary naturally privileges his own point of view. But even taking into account the one-sidedness of the resulting picture, it is clear that Visvesvaraya, while wanting to be fair to those he dealt with, was unable to look at things from their perspective. He was willing to listen to their grievances, and saw himself as an objective person who did not hold grudges against anyone for having a difference of opinion. In practice, he found it very difficult to work with anyone who didn't share his perspective (or at least profess to do so). Yet he was unable to be entirely ruthless. He tried to balance official strictness with personal kindness as he understood it, but this sometimes confused matters further. It is also apparent that there were several high-ranking people in the bureaucracy who were unnerved by Visvesvaraya's policies and his ideas of efficient functioning. Gossip flowed freely about him. He himself was not infallible. He was extremely sensitive to criticism, and found it difficult to empathize with his subordinates.

As Narendar Pani shows in his masterly introduction to Srinivasa Iyengar's diary, the larger significance of Iyengar's clashes with Visvesvaraya lies in what they tell us about two very different conceptions of bureaucracy. Iyengar had thoroughly imbibed the long-standing culture of Mysore's government services, where the distinction between the official and the personal were blurred. There was much jockeying for positions; officials visited their superiors' homes to place requests; and club life appears to have been an extension of office politics. Promotions and plum postings were understood as resulting from seniority rather than exceptional ability or performance. Visvesvaraya, on the other hand, believed in an idealized, Weberian form of bureaucracy in which the personal and the official did not mix, where procedure was paramount. He was obsessed with efficiency. In sum, he wanted to remake Mysore's government services in the image of a Western bureaucracy as he understood it.[29]

*

Visvesvaraya's Western sensibilities, on the other hand, seem to have smoothed his relationships with many—though by no means all—of the British officials he came into contact with. As dewan, he had occasion to meet a wide range of them, from viceroys to provincial governors. But the one he had to work with most frequently was the Resident. In Hugh Daly, who occupied that position from 1910 to 1916, he found a relatively sympathetic Resident, even an ally.[30] This was not a circumstance to be taken for granted, for Residents in princely states were there mainly to watch the administration with a critical eye, ensuring it was conducted in a way that aligned with the Government of India's interests.

Educated at Winchester—a leading English public school—and Oxford's Balliol College, Daly had served in the British army, seeing action in Burma in the 1880s, before joining the Government of India's Foreign Department. He spent many years in the department, which dealt largely with the princely states and the empires neighbouring India, before he came to Mysore as Resident.[31] Daly had recommended Visvesvaraya for a C.I.E. in 1911 when the latter was serving as chief engineer in Mysore, and supported the decision to appoint him dewan in 1912. Daly knew the engineer could be a bull in a china shop, but he appreciated his straightforwardness.[32] When it came to many of Visvesvaraya's projects, the Mysore government relied on Daly to act as an intermediary between them and the Government of India.[33]

Daly was well liked in Mysore circles. S. Hiriannaiya, Visvesvaraya's private secretary, described him as 'a high-minded Englishman and one of the finest political officers ever accredited to the Mysore Court'.[34] In Daly's last year in Mysore, Visvesvaraya declared at a public meeting that the Resident and his wife 'have been a centre of concord and harmony among us and we have come to regard them as safe advisers and very valued friends'.[35] The year after Daly's tenure as Resident ended, a new building was constructed for the Mythic Society (an institution for Indological studies) with the support of the government, and named the Daly Memorial Hall.[36] Daly himself appears to have remained close at hand, settling down for a while at nearby Ooty at the maharaja's invitation.[37]

It is highly probable that Daly was responsible for another important honour that came Visvesvaraya's way in these years. The news came one day in June 1915, when Visvesvaraya was at Ooty. The dewan and Hiriannaiya sat down to a full day's work at the Fern Hill Palace, the Mysore maharaja's residence in the hill station. That evening, Mirza Ismail, who was then Palace Secretary, came over to announce that Visvesvaraya had been put down for a knighthood in the King's Birthday Honours list. At 9 p.m., a congratulatory missive from the maharaja arrived. A little while later came a note from the yuvaraja. 'The honour was long overdue—' Hiriannaiya noted, 'that is from our stand point—because the Dewan does not very much care for it.' Nevertheless, tears welled up. 'Dewan received the honour with mixed feelings and really broke down at about 11 p.m.—the first time I saw him overpowered by emotions & feelings.'[38] More than a century later, Hiriannaiya's daughter reflected that in that moment, Visvesvaraya had no family to share the news with.[39]

Knighthoods were, of course, one means the British Empire used to cement the loyalty of influential individuals in colonial locations. Top officials of princely states seem to have got them almost as a matter of course. At one point or another, Kantaraj Urs, Albion Banerjee, and Mirza Ismail (the dewans who succeeded Visvesvaraya), the maharaja, the yuvaraja, and K.P. Puttanna Chetty (a member of the dewan's council before his retirement in 1913) were all knighted.[40] Nevertheless, it was an honour that moved Visvesvaraya to tears.

The investiture was held the following month at the grand Viceregal Lodge in Simla, perched atop a knoll in the Himalayan hill station. On 13 July, Visvesvaraya, and others being honoured that day, dined with the viceroy before they repaired to the venue for the ceremony.[41] It is fitting to think that it must have been Visvesvaraya's old acquaintance, Lord Hardinge, who uttered the words 'Arise, Sir Mokshagundam', as Sir Hugh Daly and the Yuvaraja of Mysore looked on.[42] Perhaps scenes from Hardinge's 1913 visit to Mysore and his interventions in the matter of the Kannambadi project flashed before the dewan's eyes in that moment.

Characteristically, Visvesvaraya combined the trip to Simla with state business. It was during this visit that he and Daly held parleys with Government of India officials on the proposed Mysore University and other matters. On the way back, the newly knighted dewan met officials of the Bombay government to talk about Mysore's proposed port at Bhatkal.[43]

*

Less than two years into Visvesvaraya's tenure as dewan, long-simmering tensions in Europe boiled over. Since unification in 1871, Germany had emerged as a formidable industrial and imperial power, making her rivals wary. Meanwhile, self-determination movements were threatening to pull apart the Austro-Hungarian and Russian Empires in the Balkan region.

On 28 June 1914, Franz Ferdinand, next in line to be emperor of Austria-Hungary, and Sophie, his wife, were shot dead by an assassin as they rode through the streets of Sarajevo. The spark thus lit grew rapidly into a conflagration. By late August, almost all the major European countries, bound in various combinations by treaties, were involved in military conflict. On one side were the Allied or Entente Powers (including Britain, France and Russia); on the other, the Central Powers (including Germany, Austria-Hungary, and Turkey under the Ottomans).[44] As a war between imperial powers with possessions on various continents, it had ramifications around the world. From India, more than a million soldiers crossed the seas to fight on behalf of the British Empire.[45]

Princely states, eager to demonstrate their loyalty, rushed to the aid of their colonial overlords. On behalf of Mysore, Krishnaraja Wadiyar IV donated Rs 50 lakh to the Government of India in aid of the British war effort. He gave a further Rs 2 lakh to the Imperial Indian Relief Fund.[46] Mysore's Imperial Service Lancers were sent to battle in Aden and Mesopotamia, fully kitted out, accompanied by their horses and mules. The Mysore government allocated carts for use as ambulances, and provided free electricity to the colonial government for the production of munitions in Bangalore or at the Kolar Gold Fields.[47]

Prominent citizens made sizeable donations to the Mysore Imperial Service Lancers War Fund, beginning with the maharaja (Rs 1000) and the dewan (Rs 400). Ordinary residents of various districts also contributed via their amildars.[48] Leading residents of the state donated socks, jerseys, balaclavas, pillow cases, and khaki shirts.[49] European planters signed up for war service and were shipped out to the front lines.[50] As dewan, Visvesvaraya was also involved in other measures in support of the war effort. In April 1916, he endorsed the new Resident H.V. Cobb's request that the Mysore government officially encourage the recruitment of Anglo-Indians in the state for war service.[51] That July, the government went out of their way to help a battalion of the Royal Sussex Regiment during its march up and down between Bangalore and Mysore. Village wells along the route were cleaned ahead of the march. Government officials escorted the battalion along various stretches. In Mysore city, the soldiers marched past admiring throngs. They were feted at Government House and welcomed at the royal palace. Krishnaraja IV himself received the battalion, inspected it, and invited them to explore the palace, lit up against the night sky.[52]

Outwardly, Visvesvaraya did all that was expected of the dewan of a vassal state during the war. He contributed personally to the Mysore Imperial Service Lancers War Fund.[53] He worked with the Resident on the modalities of transferring the Rs 50 lakh the maharaja had pledged to the Government of India.[54] He exhorted the public to contribute monetarily, whether in the form of donations to the St John Ambulance Association (a local philanthropic organisation aiding Mysorean soldiers at the war front) or subscriptions to a War Loan taken out by the Government of India. At public meetings, he made gallant references to the relief work undertaken by the European ladies of Mysore, and waxed eloquent about Britain's noble quest to save the world. 'England,' he said, '. . . has shouldered the burdens of the weaker nations and made untold sacrifices in men and money to uphold the cause of civilization. . . . The extraordinary self-sacrifice and tenacity of purpose shown by England compels our warmest admiration. It has always been so with the British Nation.'[55]

Visvesvaraya was no pacifist, and he knew it was in Mysore's best interests, politically if not strategically, to demonstrate its loyalty to the British Empire by contributing conspicuously to the war effort. But as an economic nationalist, he did not relish the prospect of his projects for industrial development being interrupted or shelved. The Government of India frowned upon the starting of large non-military projects at this time: the industrial capacity of the land was to be placed first and foremost in the service of the war effort. Visvesvaraya, however, was unwilling to sit tight until the war ended. He continued to push the sandalwood oil and soap factory projects, and the proposals for manufacturing iron at Bhadravati. He even expedited the building of a planned railway line between Mysore and Arsikere before the supplies could be commandeered for war purposes. When the Government of India asked Mysore for land to establish an acetone factory, Visvesvaraya's government expressed concern that the undertaking 'would mean the planting of a new quasi-military interest in the midst of a civil population', and stressed that the land, if granted, should be returned to Mysore at the end of the war.[56]

Visvesvaraya's stance in these matters increasingly became a matter of concern for the Government of India. He had also begun to assert his independence in other domains, notably in Mysore's relations with foreign governments.[57] To make matters worse, he never really got on with H.V. Cobb, who had replaced Hugh Daly as Resident in 1916.[58] The colonial government began to keep a close watch on the Mysore administration.

In 1916, Visvesvaraya's government sent two of their officials, along with a team of seven businessmen, to Japan. Their brief was to 'study the conditions of industry and trade' there, in order to boost economic ties between Mysore and Japan while drawing lessons relevant to the fostering of industries in Mysore.[59] While the delegation was in Japan, however, the British Ambassador in Tokyo became suspicious of them. Breathless intelligence reports were generated, including one by an Indian spy known simply as 'Agent P.' This man befriended the Mysoreans while they were in Japan, and reported that they had little interest in business or industry, hardly visited any commercial undertakings, and were keener on meeting Japan-based Indians with revolutionary tendencies. They also had an audience with the recent Japanese prime minister, Marquis Okuma, who reportedly expressed his sympathy with Indian nationalist aspirations. The Resident, who had approved the trip without consulting the Government of India, was admonished, and told to block any such delegations to Japan in the future. A chastised Cobb set to work on Visvesvaraya, who was preparing to send a second delegation to Japan in 1917. The dewan, however, stuck to his guns, until the Government of India sent a communication forbidding further trips to Japan.[60]

The British also kept a close watch on any Japanese citizens visiting Mysore.[61] The First Councillor, Kantaraj Urs, reportedly had two Japanese servants.[62] In one case, Visvesvaraya requested permission to appoint a Japanese 'silk expert' for Mysore a couple of days after the arrival in Bangalore of a Japanese man whom the British suspected of being a political agent.[63] On another occasion, he was reported to have corresponded directly with Japan's Foreign Office, which, under the terms of Mysore's treaty with the colonial government, he was not supposed to do.[64] The British were nervous about the relations between Mysore and Japan, but they could not quite put their finger on what they objected to. The best they could come up with was this: 'On the part of the Japanese it probably means some plan for getting into closer commercial relations with the State and its resources; while on the part of the Mysoreans it probably means some vague idea of development on Japanese lines in some vague direction.'[65] Indian revolutionaries certainly existed in Japan,[66] but it is hard to escape the conclusion that in the case of Mysore's contacts with that country, the British were making a mountain out of a molehill.

Meanwhile, in Bangalore and Mysore, tempers were frayed. The Government of India's political secretary, Sir John Wood, visited Bangalore in the middle of 1917. He reported confidentially that 'the relations between the Residency and the

Durbar were far from happy'. Resident Cobb had a somewhat abrasive manner, and letters from his office were sometimes (as Wood conceded) 'unfortunately worded'. Cobb's 'reputation' had preceded him, for he had been unpopular in his previous appointment in Baroda. Finally, he suffered by comparison to his predecessor, Hugh Daly, who had been a great favourite of the durbar and was still close to the maharaja. Krishnaraja Wadiyar was very keen to see Cobb replaced; Visvesvaraya found him unsympathetic to his projects.[67]

For his part, Cobb believed that Krishnaraja, Visvesvaraya, and Daly were out to 'make things unpleasant for him and hound him out of the State'. Wood found this fanciful. Nevertheless, Wood reported,

> Mr Cobb says that he finds [Visvesvaraya] absolutely impossible to deal with: that if his proposals are not accepted at once, he flies into a passion and reasonable discussion becomes impossible: that he is autocratic to an astounding degree and resents opposition as though he were a Napoleon. An instance of his unreasonableness was his complaint that the Resident omitted to see him to his carriage when he had paid a private call upon him. Though touchy about his own dignity, he showed an airy disregard of that of others. For instance, when Mr. Cobb attended the meeting of the Representative Assembly, he was given flowers at the close of the proceedings, not by the Dewan but by his Private Secretary.[68]

Cobb also made the usual criticisms of Visvesvaraya's impetuosity in undertaking projects such as the planned iron works at Bhadravati, which he considered risky.[69]

The visiting political secretary tried to calm both sides. He told Cobb to be cautious in his choice of words when talking or writing to Visvesvaraya and others. He pointed out to Visvesvaraya

> that he . . . was apt to show impatience of criticism in discussions with the Government of India officials (notably in connection with the Mysore University and the Bhatkal project) and not only in his personal relations with the Resident. The Dewan admitted that, in his eagerness to get something done, he might have been impatient but said that it was 'impossible to get anything done without treading on somebody's corns'.[70]

By the fifth year of his dewanship, then, the Government of India had surely begun to consider Visvesvaraya something of a problem. He had a mind of his own; he was hypersensitive; he did not toe their line on matters of war or foreign policy. This left him more than usually dependent on the goodwill of the maharaja.

*

His equation with the maharaja was, of course, the most important of Visvesvaraya's official relationships. Krishnaraja Wadiyar did more than adorn the throne: from the start of his formal reign in 1902, he had kept himself informed of the day-to-day affairs of his government. His first private secretary, an ICS officer named Evan Maconochie, recorded that the monarch put in an appearance every day at his office in the Mysore Palace, staying until the files submitted to him had been processed.[71] A glance at the archival records generated by the Mysore government's official work in the following decades confirms that a wide range of cases went up to the maharaja for his final approval or sanction, especially when it came to financial matters. He did not make notings on the files but spoke in person with the top bureaucrats of the state, and was otherwise kept informed.[72]

When he chose Visvesvaraya as his dewan, Krishnaraja Wadiyar was not yet thirty. Visvesvaraya was over fifty, but he treated the maharaja with the deference due to a superior. The maharaja shared Visvesvaraya's modernising outlook to a large extent, and was generally sympathetic to his projects, even when they called for heavy expenditure. He was also supportive in other ways: he usually approved Visvesvaraya's unconventional requests to raise the pay or allowances of various government officers. While Krishnaraja kept his distance—his world revolved around the palace at Mysore rather than the secretariat in Bangalore—Visvesvaraya called on him from time to time, and they were thrown together on ceremonial occasions like the Dasara Durbar and the king's annual birthday celebrations.

This happy state of affairs continued until around 1916. By that time, stray sources of dissatisfaction had begun to emerge on either side. An old hand in an unnamed princely state once described the general pattern of a dewan's tenure. Initially, there was a 'period of honeymoon between the Maharaja and the Dewan', and they would meet as frequently as possible. Over time, though, they would begin to doubt each other.

> In the third year a desire for something like judicial separation makes itself felt. And during the next two years there is a tug of war and during this period various disintegrating influences which surround the Dewan and the Maharaja make their voices and influences felt till at-last [sic] when the fifth year is reached it looks as if the State coach requires immediate change of the executive horse.[73]

In the case of Visvesvaraya, the honeymoon lasted longer. But 'disintegrating influences' did indeed appear. One of them, as we have just seen, was the growing suspicion of the colonial government, which found the dewan intractable on many fronts. Now, in addition to Resident Cobb, the maharaja's British private secretary, R.H. Campbell, reportedly made life difficult for Visvesvaraya.[74]

Another centrifugal force came in the form of an emerging political movement, to which Visvesvaraya and the maharaja responded in different ways. This was the Non-Brahmin Movement launched in the neighbouring Madras Presidency during the war years. Spearheaded by well-to-do representatives of the mercantile classes which occupied the middle ranks of the caste hierarchy, the movement arose in opposition to the disproportionate influence of Brahmins in government jobs and public life. Forming just over 3 per cent of the presidency's population, Brahmins nevertheless accounted for the vast majority of positions in government. They were also prominent in nationalist causes such as the Home Rule League. Forming a political group known as the 'Justice Party', the non-Brahmin leaders argued that in order to redress this imbalance, posts should be set aside for their communities in the government bureaucracies and legislative bodies. In contrast to many of the Brahmins, they adopted a pro-British stance, and were supported by the influential British editor of the *Madras Mail*, T.E. Welby.

In Mysore too, Brahmins formed a minuscule proportion of the population (3.8 per cent in 1918) but held the majority (65 per cent) of 'gazetted' jobs in the government. The numerically important Vokkaliga and Lingayat communities had begun to mobilize from the first decade of the twentieth century, but it was after the rise of the Non-Brahmin Movement in Madras that political agitation gathered steam in Mysore. In 1917, the Madras Presidency-born C.R. Reddy—the Maharaja's College professor who had earlier been sent to various Western countries to survey their systems of education—established a non-Brahmin political body in Mysore, the Praja Mithra Mandali.

As elected representatives had relatively little power in Mysore's system of government, the Mysore non-Brahmin leaders exerted pressure on the palace, cultivating influential figures in the royal family. They appealed to the maharaja, who, as a member of the royal Urs caste, was a non-Brahmin himself. They found backers in two members of the dewan's council. These were the maharaja's younger brother, the yuvaraja, and M. Kantaraj Urs, who was married to the maharaja's sister in addition to being his uncle.[75]

Visvesvaraya viewed these developments with dismay. He was dead against reserving posts for particular communities, and saw the Non-Brahmin Movement as focused on ousting Brahmins from positions of responsibility rather than enabling others to compete for them. He insisted that he was for the promotion of education among all communities. His administration, as we have seen, had indeed done a great deal to spread primary education. It had also set up scholarships and special schools for the 'backward' and 'depressed classes'. Nor was Visvesvaraya entirely opposed to certain kinds of affirmative action.[76] He argued that with these measures, members of other communities would over time be able to compete on an equal footing with the Brahmins for various positions.

His protestations, however, showed a lack of sociological insight or imagination. In characterizing the Brahmin community as a 'progressive community' the pre-eminence of which was due to 'its own special enterprise',[77] he was refusing to acknowledge the historical inequities Brahmins had benefited from. The hierarchical caste system had, for centuries, freed them of the need to engage in the world of production, allowing them to form an intellectual class of priests, scholars, and teachers. They were naturally much better placed to make use of opportunities for formal education under colonial rule. In addition to enjoying connections and social capital, Brahmins also benefited from the patronage of British officialdom.[78] In these circumstances, the case for intervention was by no means illogical.

Visvesvaraya was no communalist, and had no sentimental attachment to Brahminical culture. He was an unequivocal critic of the caste system,[79] and abhorred discriminatory social customs.[80]

However, his refusal to look beyond what he characterized as 'merit and capacity'—categories that were more culturally determined than he would care to admit—and his warning that affirmative action would negatively impact 'production . . . and the efficiency of the administration'[81] made him appear like a reactionary. To imagine what these arguments sounded like to his opponents, one need only note that almost identical language was used in this period by expatriate British officials when faced with the necessity of increasing the representation of 'native' Indians in the upper ranks of the engineering and other government services, and that Indian nationalists—among whom were many Brahmins—were having none of it.[82]

The arbitrariness of conceptions of 'merit' has been demonstrated effectively by scholars in our time, although such arguments remain in vogue.[83] More than a century ago, public discourse had yet to examine these assumptions in such detail, and Visvesvaraya genuinely believed he was taking a principled stand. He could afford to do this because he was not a politician responsible to the people. An arch-technocrat, he mainly had to keep the maharaja and his councillors on his side.

The Wadiyars, on the other hand, led a precarious existence. They ruled at the pleasure of the British; at the same time, they had to retain the confidence of their subjects. The maharaja could not afford to ignore the political currents of the time. To give him his due, self-interest may not have been the only factor at play: Krishnaraja may genuinely have wanted to create a more level playing field.

Either way, the maharaja and his dewan were now at loggerheads. In December 1916, the maharaja instructed Visvesvaraya that in selecting the next batch of probationary revenue officers, he should ensure that at least one-third of them were non-Brahmin candidates. In another instance, when Visvesvaraya proposed two names for membership of the senate of Mysore University, Krishnaraja overruled him. The maharaja's alternative nominees included M. Basavaiah, a politician who belonged to the Non-Brahmin Movement. He also indicated that Visvesvaraya should have thought of appointing a member of the Wesleyan Mission to the senate. Visvesvaraya was incensed.[84] He wrote icily to R.H. Campbell in the palace that 'the Senate is not a body created for honouring people but to promote a specific object, namely, the development of university education'.[85]

The dewan now began to feel that he no longer had the maharaja's ear, and resented having to route his communications through palace officials including Mirza Ismail, who was then serving as Huzur Secretary. His pride hurt, he told Campbell around the start of 1917 that he would like to resign. Letters zipped back and forth between Visvesvaraya, Campbell, and Mirza.[86] In one of them, written in January 1917, Visvesvaraya protested to Mirza that '. . . you have played me many tricks'. He added: 'The cat & dog [official] life I have been forced into for the past one year is perfectly impossible.'[87] Mirza and Campbell tried to placate the dewan. Visvesvaraya later sent the monarch a long letter which—going by the summary provided by an early biographer who had access to it—veered from indignation to an uncharacteristic abjection. He was then granted an audience with the maharaja. The upshot was that Visvesvaraya agreed to continue in office.[88]

But that was not the end of the matter. By July, Visvesvaraya had regained his confidence sufficiently to send the maharaja an extensive memorandum demanding substantial changes in the structure of the executive branch of government. The maharaja sent the memo back with his comments.[89] He acknowledged Visvesvaraya's basic concerns and agreed with some of his suggestions. But in other instances, he administered the equivalent of a rap on the knuckles, letting the dewan know who was boss.

Visvesvaraya began by arguing that the volume of day-to-day work handled by the dewan had increased enormously since the start of his tenure. To help reduce his burden and enable him to concentrate on important matters, he suggested the expansion of the Executive Council. The three existing councillors should be joined by two 'Additional Members', one of them being from the government services and the other being a 'non-official'. These members would perform similar functions to the other councillors (they would oversee various government departments) but would not be a part of the Cabinet—that would still be made up of the dewan and the first three councillors. Finally, the number of departments under the Extraordinary Member of Council (the yuvaraja) should be reduced, as he 'has other social duties connected with his high position'. Given the context, it would be reasonable to speculate that Visvesvaraya was trying to reduce the scope for what he saw as interference by the yuvaraja. Krishnaraja Wadiyar turned down Visvesvaraya's suggestion to expand the council, insisting that to ease bottlenecks it would be necessary for the dewan to delegate responsibilities and streamline processes rather than add more members.

The words 'efficient' and 'efficiency' cropped up with remarkable frequency in Visvesvaraya's memorandum. Not running the affairs of the state efficiently, he contended, would lead to 'grave consequences'. To avoid such a situation, 'special merit in all departments should be recognised and promotion, at least to the top appointments, regulated invariably by merit and not exclusively by seniority'. Although Visvesvaraya made no mention here of demands for reservation, the subtext was clear enough. Krishnaraja's reply: promoting promising officers was well and good, but they must 'be careful not to overdo it, for, in trying to encourage one good man, we may be discouraging many others perhaps just as good.'

Visvesvaraya's next suggestion clearly reflected the difficulties he was facing. '[W]henever a new Dewan is appointed,' he said, '. . . the majority of the Members of Council . . . should be men who would sympathise with his views or who are selected in consultation with him. Otherwise there will be unhealthy rivalries and the Ministry will not be able to attempt large improvements or carry on a progressive administration.' To this, Krishnaraja responded by reminding Visvesvaraya that in actuality 'the Council is that of His Highness the Maharaja who is supposed to, and does in fact, take an active part in the administration and the Council which consists of the Dewan and 2 or 3 Members is expected to be guided and controlled by him.' He also stressed that councillors could not be selected on the basis of their alignment with the dewan's views: 'difference of opinion must exist . . . It is hardly reasonable to expect the Councillors to support the Dewan's proposals in every case.'[90]

In 1918, members of the Praja Mithra Mandali formally petitioned the maharaja to institute measures against the Brahmin domination of government services.[91] As a result, a committee was constituted to investigate the issue. Headed by Sir Leslie Miller, the British chief judge of Mysore's Chief Court, the committee was asked to 'consider steps necessary for the adequate representation of communities in the public service'. Defining 'backward communities' as those of which less than 5 per cent of the members were literate in English, the committee essentially placed all communities (with the exception of Europeans and Anglo-Indians, whom they treated as a special case) other than the Brahmins in that category.[92] In the report they eventually submitted in 1919, they recommended that '[w]ithin a period of not more than seven years, not less than half of the higher, and two-thirds of the lower appointments in each grade of the service and so far as possible in each office, are to be held by members of communities other than the Brahmin community, preference being given to duly qualified candidates of the depressed [Untouchable] classes when [such] are available'.[93] These targets were made operational from 1921.[94]

Although the Miller Committee's approach had some limitations (for instance, it largely declined to address the vast variations within the capaciously defined 'backward' category),[95] its constitution and its report marked the introduction of some important arguments into the discourse on 'efficiency'. The terms of reference given to the committee asked them to keep in mind, when considering the meaning of efficiency, that an increased proportion of government officers from less privileged communities would be beneficial to Mysore as it would spark 'a wider diffusion of education [and] a feeling of increased status . . . in the backward communities'.[96] The committee itself argued in its report that '[e]fficiency . . . is not to be measured solely or even mainly by academic qualifications and it will not be denied that there are many important branches of the administration in which other qualities such as sympathy, [honesty] of purpose, energy and common sense go as far to make an efficient officer as literary superiority'.[97]

With the appointment of the Miller Committee, the writing was on the wall for Visvesvaraya. Mysore politics was entering a new era, and the dewan was increasingly out of place in it.[98]

*

The dewan-maharaja saga continued through 1917 and 1918, bordering at times on melodrama. From time to time Visvesvaraya would threaten to resign. But he could not quite bring himself to do so, both because he feared that he would be accused of abandoning ship while his ambitious projects were still under way, and because he himself was keen on advancing them. At one point he suggested, as a way out, that he would quit as dewan if he could be made an unpaid Member of Council with charge of some of these projects. The unorthodox suggestion was rejected. Meanwhile, the Government of India agreed to turn over a number of company-run railway lines in Mysore to the state government. This was something Visvesvaraya had been working towards, and the maharaja now increased his salary in recognition of the achievement. Visvesvaraya protested that he did not want a raise, but it was a fait accompli.

Visvesvaraya continued to harp on his many grievances. The maharaja did not trust him, he said; he bypassed the dewan and sided with those working under Visvesvaraya; he frequently vetoed the dewan's decisions. At one point an exasperated Krishnaraja responded: 'As long as you get your own way in matters great or small, I find that everything is plain sailing but the moment I differ from you in the slightest degree, you resent my interference and refuse to be controlled. You accuse me of ignorance and in fact you assume the position of a complete autocrat who is not to be interfered with on any pretence.' On the question of reservations, he declared: 'I refuse to believe that we are sacrificing efficiency by introducing non-Brahmins into the service. I am convinced that my policy in this matter is the only right one and I intend to pursue it.'[99]

As the Great War in Europe entered its last months, Visvesvaraya and Krishnaraja Wadiyar finally reached a truce of their own. There came a day when Visvesvaraya made up his mind to resign in actuality, and the maharaja to accept his resignation. A date was mutually agreed upon. On 9 December 1918, barely a month after Armistice Day, the dewan left his office for the last time. He would technically be on leave for the next six months, after which he would cease to be an officer in the Mysore service.[100]

Before leaving the secretariat that day, Visvesvaraya gave a farewell address to his colleagues. 'I hope it is pardonable for me to claim,' he said,

> that so far as the exigencies of the time permitted, there has been no discrepancy between the principles I professed and the

> practice of them. It is occasionally stated in private circles that I am *pro* this or *anti* that community. Time will show that I have tried to hold the scales even . . . I am disappointed that much that could have been done has not been accomplished. But I am thankful that the public have been well disposed and no single untoward event or incident has occurred to mar the even tenor of administration these six years. I have found the people of Mysore extremely reasonable and responsive—the vast rural population no less than the accredited public leaders. They have been trustful, I believe not because of any marked successes in the administration, but because they knew Government were sincere and anxious to serve them.[101]

*

Remarkably, the denouement of Visvesvaraya's tussle with the maharaja was playing out while the state wrestled with the most devastating epidemic in living memory. In May 1918, the so-called Spanish flu, having run through the battlefields of Europe, made its appearance in the port cities of Bombay and Calcutta. Cases were first detected in Mysore in June, but the epidemic peaked there in September and October. By the time it subsided a few months later, it had taken more than 1,95,000 lives in the state. Across India, as many as 12.5 million are said to have died.

As the flu spread through Mysore in September–October 1918, an official noted that hospitals and clinics were overwhelmed. 'The doctors and their staff are so heavily overworked that it is a wonder they have not turned mad. The lot of the compounders is indeed pitiable.' Coming on the heels of a poor monsoon and the economic stresses caused by the Great War, the virus compounded the people's misery.[102]

It also came at a time when Visvesvaraya's resignation letter was virtually in his pocket and on the point of being whipped out. Yet his administration acted with alacrity. The sanitary commissioner put out detailed instructions for the public in English and Kannada, emphasizing the importance of fresh air, rest, and oral medication in the form of thymol, a compound with disinfectant properties. Medical officers and junior bureaucrats were asked to travel through the countryside, working with sanitary officials and traditional healers to hand out medicine. District officials and the heads of Bangalore and Mysore's municipalities were instructed to submit reports every single day, in addition to weekly summaries. In both cities, makeshift open-air clinics were set up. The city of Bangalore, under the energetic direction of its municipal president K.P. Puttanna Chetty—a veteran of plague relief operations from earlier decades—saw a great collective effort to tackle the epidemic. Retired doctors, missionary organizations, and medical students stepped in to render or organize service. Porridge was cooked in the *anna chattram* (public kitchen) and distributed, along with thymol, to affected citizens in their homes. Similar steps were taken in Mysore.[103]

There were challenges galore, not all of them epidemiological. Visvesvaraya noted grimly that some traders had begun to hoard grain, and the government responded by controlling prices. Across the state, not everyone had confidence in the efficacy of institutional medicine. In some districts, the people initially fobbed off health officials.[104] In late October, the government approved a proposal to conduct a twenty-four-day long *samputi karana jvara japam* in the temple on Mysore's Chamundi Hill to ward off the virus, since 'the proposed Japam is calculated to put heart into the people, particularly the masses'. (The approval was given by a member of the dewan's council and not by Visvesvaraya, though he did endorse it.)[105]

Meanwhile, Visvesvaraya collated and forwarded to the maharaja, almost on a daily basis, reports received by telegram and telephone from the districts as well as the principal cities of the state. This he did initially from Mysore, where, remarkably, the Dasara ceremonies and the session of the Representative Assembly were held as usual in October (although barely a third of the members were present at the latter, the rest being occupied with relief work in their constituencies).

Back in Bangalore by the last week of October, Visvesvaraya visited the poorer sections of the city. He continued to relay updates to the maharaja almost on an everyday basis until early November, when he switched to weekly reports. His last update was in early December, barely a week before he left office. By then the situation had stabilized to a large extent.[106]

Although there were some shortcomings (including a perception that it had prioritized the cities of Bangalore and Mysore over the districts), the state had done a commendable job on the whole. 'The well-organized administrative machinery and the existing health infrastructure,' writes T.V. Sekher, who has studied the episode in depth, 'made it possible to control the influenza pandemic.'[107] As this statement indicates, this success—such as it was—owed a great deal to the institutional capacity built up over several years. Nevertheless, the leadership of the day had acquitted itself well.

*

The last couple of years of Visvesvaraya's dewanship had been full of drama and intrigue. In the midst of all the manoeuvrings and the brief tumult caused by the Spanish flu, the ordinary business of state had continued. The dam at Kannambadi continued to rise; Charles Perin's engineers staked out the site for the iron factory at Bhadravati; Mysore University had its first convocation ceremony; the Dasara festivities and the annual agricultural and industrial exhibition were held as usual.[108]

Taken as a whole, Visvesvaraya's six years as dewan were filled with frenetic activity. His ambitions, as we've seen, were stunningly wide. He set out to rebuild Mysore's villages, introduce compulsory education, establish a new university, provide a fillip to small-scale industries, open an iron works, extend the state's railway network, and build a new port—all at a time when Mysore was feeling the echoes of cataclysmic global events.

In order to chase these goals, Visvesvaraya wrought a transformation in the structure and culture of the government bureaucracy. He often rode roughshod over convention. In his own formulation, he trod on a good many corns. But he also won the devoted following of some colleagues and subordinates, and balanced a wide range of competing interests with considerable success for much of his tenure.

A decade previously, he had embarked on a new phase of his career after quitting the Bombay PWD. Now it was time to reinvent himself again.

PART III

On the National Stage

14

Setting Sail

Although Visvesvaraya parted ways with the Mysore government in November 1918, he did not sever all ties.[1] He also maintained good relations with his contacts in the Government of India. Despite their private reservations about him during the latter years of his dewanship, the colonial authorities now gave him a letter establishing his bonafides, which could smooth the way for him to obtain appointments with business leaders, bureaucrats, and statesmen in various foreign countries—for he had decided once more to undertake a study tour abroad.

This time the impetus came from his friend Vithaldas Thackersey and another Bombay-based textile magnate, Mulraj Khatau. With the cessation of hostilities in Europe in 1918, it was safe once more for civilians to take to the seas. Thackersey, Khatau, and their associates had decided to take the opportunity to travel abroad, most likely to renew their business contacts in various countries. They invited Visvesvaraya to join them. The plan was to circumnavigate the globe, visiting Japan, the United States, and Europe. (Vithaldas's wife, Premlila Thackersey, who also went on the trip, later recalled that the original plan had been to go to Europe; Japan and the US had been added to the itinerary at Visvesvaraya's urging.) Visvesvaraya was no tycoon, but as a single man who had been drawing a healthy salary for decades, such a trip was within his means. It would also be a good change of scene after the difficult time he had had of late in Mysore.

The company left Bombay in March 1919 on a liner of the Peninsular & Oriental Company, the S.S. *Dunera*, sailing down the west coast of India before turning eastward. They docked at Colombo, Singapore, Hong Kong, and Shanghai before heading to Japan on another vessel, the S.S. *Kumana Maru*. It was probably the first time Visvesvaraya was travelling abroad with a group of friends, but he had no time for frivolities at sea. 'When we used to sit on the deck in the mornings and evenings,' Premlila Thackersey observed, 'he narrated his past experiences. He was not interested in playing bridge or in sports.' Docking in Kobe on 8 April, the travellers checked into the Oriental Hotel. They stuck with each other for the first few days and then explored the country separately.[2]

*

On his first visit, more than two decades earlier, Visvesvaraya had seen Japan mark thirty years since the start of the Meiji Era.[3] Now, in 1919, the country was nearly seven years into a new regnal period, the Taisho Era.[4] Having played a modest but successful role in the Allies' victory in the First World War, Japan was poised to sit at the negotiating table at Versailles as one of the world's dominant forces. The nation was clearly an imperial power in East Asia, although the militarism that would contribute to a second world war was yet to manifest itself overtly.[5]

Visvesvaraya spent three months in the country. His aim was to 'study modern developments in education, industries, commerce, and politics'.[6] The British Embassy in Tokyo provided him with introductions to various organizations (no doubt their secret agents were simultaneously keeping an eye on his movements). Visvesvaraya also enlisted the support of the Indo-Japanese Association, a body that had become well known for hosting visiting Indian notables and businessmen.[7] Established in 1903 in the context of a growing trade between the two countries, the association had influential patrons in Japan. Since 1906, it had been presided over by Marquis Okuma Shigenobu (who also served for two spells as Prime Minister of Japan, in 1898 and 1914–16).[8] In an era when Indians and Japanese were discovering affinities in various fields under the umbrella of 'pan-Asianism', the British viewed this association with some wariness. The association, in turn, stressed its apolitical nature.[9]

Visvesvaraya was particularly taken with what he saw of the Japanese system of government in the villages. At the time, Japan had around 72,000 villages organized into 12,000 units called unions. Usually consisting of a few thousand residents each and helmed by an elected official known as the Soncho, the unions were placed under prefectures (equivalent to districts), which in turn reported to the government at the centre. But the unions themselves were autonomous in their internal functioning, and run by elected bodies. In search of a model for rural government in India, Visvesvaraya visited one of these Japanese unions and studied in detail its workings.

He also assiduously collected statistics on Japan's industrial and educational progress and information on economic policies since the Meiji Restoration. He appears to have met leading government officials and visited universities and technical institutions. He took notes on the country's systems of banking, education, agriculture, and commercial law. He was particularly impressed by the Japanese system of sending selected students to other countries, so that they could absorb the state of the art in various fields, thus providing a vital input to policymaking in Japan.[10] Somewhat uncharacteristically, he even spent some time trying to understand Japan's ancient history. In this he was guided by Junjiro Takakusu, an Oxford-trained scholar of Buddhism and professor at the Tokyo Imperial University, whom he had first met on his 1898 trip. In the old imperial capital of Kyoto, Professor Takakusu enabled Visvesvaraya 'to witness in a Buddhist temple . . . numerous manuscripts written both in Indian and Japanese characters, stated to be over 700 years old'.[11]

Towards the end of his stay, Visvesvaraya and his Indian colleagues were invited to a reception by the Indo-Japanese Association. A surviving photograph, probably from this occasion, shows rows of dark-suited Japanese businessmen and a handful of Indians, the men in suits and the women in saris, in a manicured garden. Seated in the centre of the front row are the Association's president, Marquis Okuma, and Visvesvaraya.[12]

At the function, Okuma gave a speech in Japanese, an interpreter translating as he spoke. Visvesvaraya then rose to reply. He thanked the association and complimented it for '[helping] to promote the trade and cement the good relations between our two countries'. He referred to the growing Indian business community in Japan, and spoke of the historic connections binding the two countries, which were 'as old as the Buddhist religion which you have adopted from India'. He spoke nostalgically about his first visit two decades earlier. Probably for the benefit of any British agents or invitees in the audience, he took care to make some flattering remarks about measures the British were then taking towards constitutional reform in India. 'Ladies and gentlemen,' he concluded, 'I have no intention to detain you with a long speech on this occasion. We have had an enjoyable afternoon. We have made new friends. We are grateful for the hospitality extended to us. . . . I may assure you we shall carry with us very pleasant memories of our visit to your great country.'[13]

*

Visvesvaraya and his friends were due to go to the United States next. But places on ships were still hard to come by, and the party had to split up. Visvesvaraya decided to follow an alternative route. Departing from Yokohama, he sailed for Victoria, British Columbia, on Canada's west coast. He then crossed over to the United States, where he was reunited with his friends. They observed factories producing cement, paper, and—in Detroit, Michigan—automobiles. Detroit was, at this time, consolidating its position as the world's leading car manufacturing centre. Fantastic economies of scale were being achieved through assembly-line production, and Ford's revolutionary Model T was being put on the market at lower and lower prices.[14]

Visvesvaraya also spent some time in Chicago, where, among other things, he met some supporters of *Chicago Commerce*, a periodical of which he was a regular reader. While there, he ordered something that he needed urgently from a shop. The item was ready in time, and he added a dollar to the agreed price when he paid for it. The following day, the shop's proprietor, who had been away when Visvesvaraya collected his goods, tracked him down at his hotel and handed back the additional dollar, earning the Indian's admiration.[15] The incident appealed to Visvesvaraya for its didactic potential, and in later years he would often relate the anecdote.[16]

Visvesvaraya approached America with the reverence of a pilgrim. He sought meetings with heads of universities and government departments and hung on to their every word, eager to read lessons into their remarks. Unconsciously perhaps, he sought echoes of his own opinions. Harvard's president, asked if the university specialized in any fields, told him: 'We ride all horses abreast.'[17] At an unidentified mid-western university, he learnt that indigent students put themselves through school by working alongside their studies. In Washington, D.C., he asked the chief of the Federal Reserve Board what he thought about

India's financial policies. The official was reluctant to commit himself. When pressed, he indicated that his suggestions would be of little use as long as India didn't have an autonomous government. Visvesvaraya seems to have understood this as a statement of support for Indian self-government.[18]

In his memoirs, Visvesvaraya also describes a meeting with Herbert Hoover, who he notes was serving as the United States Secretary for Commerce. As Hoover actually entered this office in 1921 as part of incoming President Warren G. Harding's administration, Visvesvaraya may have got his dates mixed up. In any case, Hoover was already an influential man in Washington. During the First World War, he had achieved fame and acclaim for organizing food supplies for affected populations in Europe before heading the Food Administration back in the US. By 1920 he was seen as a possible presidential candidate. Like Visvesvaraya, Hoover was a professional engineer who had risen to the position of a statesman: before the war, he had made millions working as a mining engineer across the world.[19] Visvesvaraya engaged Hoover in conversation about the state of industrial development in America before pressing him for his views on what ailed India. Hoover apparently told him: 'You people have no hustle in you.' On what basis the future American President came to this judgement we do not know—Hoover had no first-hand knowledge of any part of India—but once again, Visvesvaraya saw in it a confirmation of his own view that his compatriots were not driven enough to seek material prosperity.[20]

*

Thus Visvesvaraya spent most of 1919 abroad. Back home, it turned out to be a year of tumultuous political developments, a year that historians Barbara Metcalf and Thomas Metcalf have described as 'a watershed in the modern history of India'. It was the year the

Government of India Bill containing the Montagu-Chelmsford constitutional reforms was introduced in the British Parliament. It was also a year when the British in India took extreme measures in the face of popular unrest. They pushed through the infamous Rowlatt Act (which allowed for the arrest without trial of allegedly seditious individuals), while in Amritsar, General Reginald Dyer ordered his troops to fire on a massive gathering of unarmed protesters in a public park, Jallianwala Bagh. Meanwhile, M.K. Gandhi, back in India after two decades in South Africa, was winning a wider following than ever before for the Indian National Congress and for the broader nationalist movement.[21]

In the midst of his visits to captains of industry and world leaders, Visvesvaraya kept track of these events. By the end of the year, he had left the United States and was billetted in London. (Vithaldas Thackersey, who had fallen ill in America, also travelled to England, but returned to Bombay after a couple of months there.) In late November, a report via Reuters noted that 'eminent Indians' then in the imperial capital, including V.S. Srinivasa Sastri, Annie Besant and Visvesvaraya, were pleased with the report of the Joint Committee of Parliament established to comment on the Government of India Bill, which was then under consideration. The reforms proposed a division of power in the provinces by placing selected subjects of governance ('transferred subjects') under elected Indian ministers, while others ('reserved subjects') remained under British-appointed governors—a system known as 'dyarchy'. At the centre, power continued to be concentrated in British hands.

The Indian National Congress and other nationalist leaders were unimpressed; they felt the reforms were a far cry from the self-government they had sought at both provincial and central levels. Visvesvaraya, on the other hand, was among those who believed the reforms constituted a good beginning.[22] This was consistent with his long-standing affinity with Moderate opinion in India. He also had some slight acquaintance with the pilot of the reforms, the Liberal statesman and Secretary of State for India, Edwin Montagu. Montagu had visited Mysore in 1913 when a new treaty with the Government of India was being contemplated. Visvesvaraya had also met him in Madras in December 1917, when the secretary of state was in India to thrash out with Viceroy Lord Chelmsford the details of the constitutional reforms they were considering.[23]

In December 1919, the British parliament passed the Government of India Bill. Visvesvaraya was part of a group of prominent Indians who marked the occasion by organizing a dinner to felicitate Montagu. Among those who joined Montagu and his wife at the banquet—held at the Savoy Hotel in London—were the Aga Khan, leader of the Ismailis in India and beyond, who chaired the event; the Calcutta physicist Sir Jagadish Chandra Bose and his wife; Sir M. Bhownaggree, only the second Indian to be elected a British MP; the poet and Congress leader Sarojini Naidu; and the legal luminary and former Congress President, Sir C. Sankaran Nair. Several British guests attended too, including the popular science-fiction writer, H.G. Wells.[24] It is amusing to imagine a conversation between Visvesvaraya and Wells that evening: both men who, in their own fashion, were given to imagining the future.[25]

*

These events marked an apt beginning to Visvesvaraya's stay in London. For his next project was to write a short book expressing his views on the policies required for India's overall development in the new, post-war era that brought with it an increase in the scope for Indians to manage their own affairs. Into the book he would distill the learnings from his year abroad. He would also bolster his arguments with copious statistical data available in the

India Office Library, housed in the grand classical building in Whitehall from which the Secretary of State for India functioned. For this purpose, he stayed in London for the next ten months.[26]

In this, he was following in the footsteps of an intellectual ancestor. Half a century earlier, the legendary Indian Liberal Dadabhai Naoroji had spent countless hours in the same library, collecting the data that would underpin his famous argument that British economic policies were 'draining' India's wealth. There was another parallel too. For several years in the late nineteenth century, Naoroji had made London's National Liberal Club his home and his base.[27] Visvesvaraya was a member of the same club, having joined it when he was in London in 1908. His candidature had been recommended by his friend Gokhale, one of the intellectuals through whom he had been exposed to the Naoroji school of thought in his Poona days.[28] We do not know where Visvesvaraya stayed in 1919–20, but it is possible that he too found the club in Whitehall Place a useful place to work and organize meetings: it was situated but half a mile from the India Office.[29]

As usual, Visvesvaraya seems to have worked methodically and to a schedule. Before the year was out, his book was published by the firm of P.S. King and Son (another Westminster-based organization, located a few hundred yards from the India Office). It was titled *Reconstructing India.*[30]

The title was a nod to the shared need of nations across the world to pick up the pieces after the receding hurricane that was the First World War. For Visvesvaraya, however, repairing the damage caused by the war was secondary to a much larger project of reconstruction. 'India,' he conceded in the first chapter, ' . . . has had no devastated cities to reconstruct, no ruined homesteads to restore, and no sunken ships to replace.' There were problems of food supply and inflation, but the real reason India needed '[r]econstruction on an extensive scale' was that 'political, social and economic developments have been insufficiently considered for many years past, and because, in consequence of such neglect, the standard of living has reached a level far below the minimum recognized in civilized communities as necessary for decent existence.'[31] The implication was clear. The British had never bothered to draw up a comprehensive programme of economic development in India. It was from this longer 'neglect' and not just from wartime suffering that the country must now emerge.

Visvesvaraya's pamphlet had the concision and careful organization of an engineer's report. He suggested measures for reconstruction under three heads, *political, economic* and *social,* rounding off his disquisition with his thoughts on 'nation-building'.[32]

On the political side, he complimented his friend Montagu once more on the recent constitutional reforms. But he also criticized the 1919 legislation for not promoting real federalism in India, for failing to effectively integrate the people of the princely states into the national polity, and for conceding no power to elected representatives at the centre. He made detailed remarks on the various provisions of the new constitutional system. The crux of his suggestions was as follows. Decentralization was key: power must be devolved as much as possible from the central to the provincial level, and in turn from the provincial to the local level. Political institutions must be moulded along the lines of those in countries like Canada and Australia at the higher and intermediate levels, and Japan at the village level.[33] All things considered, the litmus test for the colonial government would be the extent to which it enabled the Indian system of governance to mirror that in the settler dominions—Canada being the prime exemplar—of the British Empire.[34]

Visvesvaraya emphasized that the principle of autonomy must also be extended to the realm of fiscal policy. The god-like fiscal powers of the secretary of state must be curtailed. A financial commission should look into the system to ensure it was not unduly geared towards British interests. The gold standard should be introduced, and '[a] central State bank or a federal reserve banking system . . . should maintain the necessary reserve against the issue of currency notes'.[35]

On the economic side, Visvesvaraya's programme of reconstruction was premised on a call to promote industrialization across the nation. Using historical examples, he gave the lie to the supposed free-market principles of the industrialized nations, which were honoured more in the breach than in the observance. Their experience, along with that of Japan since the Meiji Restoration, showed clearly 'that industries and trade do not grow of themselves, but have to be willed, planned and systematically developed'.[36]

Like his intellectual mentor Ranade, Visvesvaraya insisted that the government must intervene to promote Indian industries. In particular, every province should have a department of industries, rather like the one he had created in Mysore in 1913. Each province should establish museums of industry and 'experimental stations', promote technical education, and maintain industrial statistics. Meanwhile the central government should protect and support fledgling Indian industries through tariffs and concessions; it should even take it upon itself to start 'large and difficult industries, including the manufacture of railway materials and shipbuilding'.[37]

In order to build an industrial nation, Indians must make the most of their country's natural resources. These Visvesvaraya viewed through a thoroughly anthropocentric lens. Not only minerals but also forest resources existed, in this view, to serve humankind. Reflecting his approach to Mysore's wooded *malnad*, he declared that 'a forest is a crop . . . wood will rot unless cut and removed at the proper intervals'.[38]

His interest in large-scale industrialization notwithstanding, Visvesvaraya did not neglect the problem of poverty in villages. To address this, he recommended measures to make agriculture more 'scientific'. Farmers should be encouraged to form cooperative societies and use improved equipment, high quality seeds and chemical fertilizers. They must also be equipped with skills that would enable them to run cottage industries as a fallback during lean agricultural years.[39]

On education, Visvesvaraya reprised the views he had articulated as Dewan of Mysore. Once more, he emphasized the need for a utilitarian focus. Primary education should be scaled up enormously, and supplemented by vocational training for students who did not move on to secondary school. For those unable to study full-time, universities must provide 'extension courses' in 'languages, finance, natural science, music, painting, etc. . . . to enable students to take a leading part in a specific trade, art, or profession'. The universities themselves should have a strong practical orientation, focusing on 'medicine, architecture, civil, mechanical and electrical engineering, chemistry, mining and metallurgy, scientific agriculture, forestry, ship-building, economics, finance and statistics'. Following the Japanese example, students from each province must be sent abroad for industrial training and research.[40]

Visvesvaraya came next to the question of social reconstruction. He began by articulating a strong critique of traditional Indian society. The Indian idea 'that life is merely a transitory stage in the passage of the soul to another world . . . chills enthusiasm, kills joy, and promotes fatalism'. He was scathing in his criticisms of the caste system and the practice of untouchability. 'No country outside India,' he wrote, 'has . . . a social system which cuts at the very root of human brotherhood, condemns millions of persons to perpetual degradation, makes people hyper-exclusive, magnifies religious differences, and disorganizes society.' He enumerated the other social ills: strict endogamy, early marriages, the relegation of women to the home, the prohibition of foreign travel. Significantly, he noted that one of the reasons reformers from Raja Rammohan Roy downwards had had a limited impact was that 'Government, not being of the people, could not themselves seriously undertake social reform, and at times even felt constrained to discourage Indian reformers from doing so'.[41]

What was to be done? Promote literacy. Encourage intercaste marriages. Raise the minimum age for marriage. Put an end to 'enforced widowhood and its attendance inhumanities and barbarous practices'. Open up all levels of education to women so they could enter the formal economy. Encourage inter-dining and foreign travel. De-ritualize religion and reimagine it as a form of moral education emphasizing 'service to fellow-beings, discipline, patriotism, clean life, and clean practices, tolerance and adherence to principle'.[42]

Social institutions, and not just political ones, were to be made self-governing. In the wake of the Great War, Western nations had understood that '[e]mployers must meet their workpeople in council. Parents must give their children reasons. Women claim equality with men and have already secured equal opportunities of entry into most professions and occupations.' Likewise, India needed co-operatives in the villages and trade unions in the industries: organizations that would provide representation while fostering 'social discipline'.[43]

All of these measures for reconstruction, Visvesvaraya held, would need something to weld them together—and that was 'a spirit of nationhood'. For him, there was no necessary contradiction between nationhood and being (an autonomous) part of the British Empire. His whole programme of reconstruction implicitly assumed the existence of an Indian nation: a well-defined political entity whose people must put their collective interests first in their interactions with the outside world.

In addition to the formulation of 'national plans and programmes in the political, economic and social spheres', a sense of national identity required a sort of cultural homogenization—something along the lines of the United States' efforts at 'Americanization'. 'India,' he remarked, 'must recognize that certain standards of taste, thought and sentiment are necessary to union, and should devise and carry out a comprehensive scheme of "Indianization," with a view to creating a new type of Indian citizenship.' Each province should have one language for official purposes, English forming the link language. All parts of the country should commit to providing compulsory education at the primary level followed by vocational training.[44]

But who was to establish these common tastes and ideals? Here Visvesvaraya fell back on the solution most familiar to him from his official career: the expert committee. 'A committee or board of leading men should be appointed in each province', and, aided by expert advice, produce a programme for 'Indianization'. Finally, a sense of national and civic responsibility should be encouraged through the dissemination of messages through newspapers, pamphlets, movie houses, folk singers, and books.[45]

Towards the end of his book, Visvesvaraya allowed himself a moment of florid rhetoric that neatly summarized his message. At this historic juncture, Indians must decide

> whether they will be educated or remain ignorant; whether they will come into closer touch with the outer world and become responsive to its influences, or remain secluded and indifferent; whether they will be organized or disunited, bold or timid, enterprising or passive; an industrial or an agricultural nation; rich or poor; strong and respected, or weak and dominated by forward nations.[46]

*

Reconstructing India was a vehicle for Visvesvaraya's views developed over a thirty-five-year official career. They were not, however, lightly tossed off. In the Preface, he took care to mention his many journeys abroad 'for the purpose of obtaining first-hand knowledge of world conditions and problems'.[47] In the book, he made an effort to knit together his thoughts into an integrated vision. He took the trouble to search far and wide for statistics and historical precedents to back up his arguments. He was well informed on current debates, and prescient on some points: the Government of India set up a Fiscal Commission in 1921, and India got a Reserve Bank in 1935.[48] Nevertheless, the book was more call to action than scholarly treatise. Some of the solutions proposed were simplistic: Visvesvaraya did not seriously reckon with the complexity of human behaviour and the conflicting interests of the various groups and classes in society. There were also inherent contradictions. On the one hand, Visvesvaraya wanted to encourage—somewhat more readily than he had as a functioning administrator—democratization, the freedom of expression, and decentralization. On the other, he favoured a sort of homogenization that could only be achieved by a top-down process driven by a largely unrepresentative elite.

In the context of its time, however, *Reconstructing India* was hailed as an unusually lucid, comprehensive, and practical plan. It was taken note of not only in England and India, but also in Australia. Commentators appreciated the book for a variety of reasons, which were often linked to their own backgrounds.

Visvesvaraya's British and Australian reviewers were struck first by the fact that he was a prominent Indian advising his countrymen to work within the reformed constitutional system, eschewing the politics of protest. At a time when Mohandas Gandhi's Congress was gearing up to launch the Non-Cooperation Movement, Visvesvaraya's criticisms of the British were made much more palatable by his insistence on cooperation. Secondly, his blunt admonishment of his fellow Indians—not only for the medievalism of some of their social customs, but also for what he saw as their lack of ambition and drive—convinced British and colonial reviewers that he was an objective and impartial analyst. As the *Western Mail* of Perth, Australia, put it, Visvesvaraya 'is not of the menacing class of agitators like Gandhi, and is quite fearless in the criticism of the Indian people whose caste, traditions, religions, and dreamy pessimistic outlook make up the barriers to progress. Of British rule he is a fair critic, though he puts no limit to his claims for capital and help from the British people.'[49] Thirdly, he was lauded for offering not just a critique, but also solutions. The *Queenslander* of Brisbane declared: 'Many books have been written about Indian problems, but this is the first that we have seen which sets out a great national programme of constructive development.'[50] A columnist for London's *Pall Mall Gazette*, who may have run into Visvesvaraya in one of the many clubs on the street after which the paper was named, described him gushingly as 'one of the most constructive Indians I have had the pleasure of meeting'.[51]

In the Anglo-Indian press, too, Visvesvaraya was praised for his conciliatory and forward-looking approach. The *Times of India*, which had access to a précis of Visvesvaraya's book, declared that 'it is patent that he is convinced that non-co-operation will lead not to progress but to chaos'. It also welcomed the fact that he did not hark back to a golden past, for 'to-day there are too many prophets of the glories of the past for India's well-being'.[52]

Compliments also poured in, for different reasons, from the Indian reformist press. *Reconstructing India* was discussed in great detail in the *Servant of India* by K.G. Limaye (soon-to-be editor of the Servant of India Society's Marathi newspaper *Dnyanprakash*). Limaye differed from Visvesvaraya slightly on some points, but was largely approving. He noted that 'unlike

Mr. Gandhi, the idea of the author is to bring within easy reach of even an ordinary Indian peasant all the comforts and conveniences of modern civilized life'. He called *Reconstructing India* 'a remarkable book that ought to be studied with keen interest by every student of Indian administration as well as by . . . responsible statesmen who aspire to be at the helm of affairs . . . under the Reform Act'.[53]

Also appearing in the *Servant of India* was a broader discussion of 'Economic Reconstruction in India' by the economist V.G. Kale of Fergusson College in Poona, in the course of which the author declared that Visvesvaraya's book was a good guide to understanding 'the problem to be solved and . . . the correct methods of solving it'. He pointed out the genealogy of Visvesvaraya's views, noting that '[h]e restates the case of India's patriotic economists in favour of a comprehensive programme of work to be undertaken and carried out by a "national" Government in this country with the active co-operation of the people'. The argument that the government must intervene to promote industries was 'one which has been hammered by Indian publicists for years together'. What made Visvesvaraya's intervention important was his 'several concrete suggestions' and the fact that he was 'not a doctrinaire economist or an armchair critic' but 'a man of affairs'.[54]

There is no doubt that the book served to place Visvesvaraya—already a well-known public figure—on an entirely new footing in Indian intellectual and elite administrative circles. Free for the first time in his life to express his opinions without fear of ticking off an employer, he had staked out a clear position in national life: one that was in consonance with the nationalist school of economics and the fast-growing demands for Indian autonomy, while hewing closely to the constitutionalist position of a now-receding generation of Moderate politicians who did not subscribe to Gandhi's mode of mass politics. He also had an unusual background: no other professional engineer had entered the Indian public sphere in quite the same way.

It is fair to say that all this was no accident, but a result of deliberate positioning. The confidence with which he made all of India his subject (and not just Mysore or Bombay, of which he had direct experience) catapulted Visvesvaraya onto a much larger stage than before. It must have been no light decision to incur the expense of staying in London for almost an entire year, while foregoing opportunities to earn an income, in order to write his book. Although the availability of data in London was a factor, the decision to publish his views through a metropolitan publisher turned out to have been astute, ensuring Visvesvaraya visibility not only in India but also in Britain and its wider empire. The long stint in London also allowed him to spend time in influential company. On one occasion, he attended a talk at the Royal Society of Arts by a well-known engineer, George Buchanan, on ports in India. Montagu presided. (Visvesvaraya participated in the discussion that followed, taking the opportunity to press the case for a port at Bhatkal.)[55] In September, the outgoing Under-Secretary for India, Lord Sinha, prepared to leave for his next assignment as Governor of Bihar and Orissa. Visvesvaraya was once again among a group of Indians felicitating him at the Savoy. Again, the secretary of state was in the chair.[56]

It is not entirely surprising, therefore, that during the course of the year—as Visvesvaraya records in his memoirs—Secretary of State Montagu invited Visvesvaraya to join his council. Visvesvaraya declined. He noted retrospectively that '[i]t did not fit in with the plans I had in view to accept that office, where opportunities to an Indian for doing any useful work were very limited'.[57] Perhaps he felt the position—that of one adviser among many to the secretary of state—was largely ornamental. He may also have thought that as a token Indian on the council, his views were likely to hold limited weight.[58] Nevertheless, the offer was a clear sign of his growing stature.

*

By the end of 1920, Visvesvaraya was back in India.[59] It was the beginning of a new phase in his life, devoid of the structure imposed by an official position. Nor would he have the accommodation and the many perquisites of a top government official. He would have to design a new lifestyle and routine for himself.

Characteristically, he had already given some thought to this before travelling abroad. In 1918, he had made notes in his diary under the heading 'System of Work on return from Tour'. Under 'Residence', he planned the following:

1. To live in Bangalore in a clean bungalow—a small one neatly maintained. (To build one if necessary)
2. To build a couple of rooms more if necessary for visitors in the village [Muddenahalli]
3. To arrange to retain a couple of rooms in a bungalow in Bombay always for residence
4. Occasionally to go for a fortnight or so to the Hills.[60]

He now followed up on these plans. In Bangalore he didn't move far—he rented out a bungalow called 'Uplands' in the upmarket High Ground, only a short walk from Ballabrooie. In Bombay, he obtained the long-term use of a section of a house belonging to a friend, Balakrishna Agarkar.[61] The address was Warden Road—a prime location in south Bombay—and the house itself, in the words of one visitor, was a 'cosy nook on the sea'.[62]

For some three decades thereafter, Visvesvaraya would maintain two establishments and divide his time between

Bangalore and Bombay. In Bangalore he would keep in touch with issues relating to Mysore state, and maintain his connections with friends and family. In Bombay he would keep in contact with statesmen and industrialists of British India. From these two bases, he would pursue a dual career. On the one hand, he would work as an independent consulting engineer. These assignments would form his primary source of income, supplementing nicely the generous pensions he drew from the governments of Bombay and Mysore.[63] Secondly, he would take up opportunities for public service—this largely meant serving on committees and commissions—arising from his growing reputation as a public intellectual devoted to the cause of India's economic development.[64] As it turned out, these two strands of his post-retirement life would often overlap.

*

Visvesvaraya didn't have to wait long. In February 1921, barely a couple of months after he returned to India, he received his first independent assignment. It came from the Bombay government, which asked him to chair a committee to overhaul the system of technical education at multiple levels in the presidency.

The opportunity came as a direct result of the new system of 'dyarchy', under which his old Poona friend, R.P. Paranjpye, had just become Bombay's Minister for Education. Paranjpye was a celebrated scholar and educationist. In 1899, he had become the first Indian to win the prestigious title of Senior Wrangler at Cambridge (awarded to the top scorer in the Mathematics Tripos). From 1902, he had served as principal of Poona's Fergusson College. But the professor, who identified politically as a Liberal, had also been a member of the Bombay Legislative Council for many years, initially by nomination and later by election to the seat reserved for Bombay University. It was when he was re-elected in 1920 that he took charge of Education, one of the subjects that had been 'transferred' to Indian hands under the constitutional reforms.[65]

Among the professor's electoral promises had been the development of industrial schools and the fostering of industrial ventures.[66] From Paranjpye's perspective, Visvesvaraya was a natural choice as chairman of the committee he now instituted.[67] As Liberals, as followers of Ranade and Gokhale, as prominent denizens (past and present) of the city of Poona, the two men had much in common, and knew each other well.[68] Since those days, of course, Visvesvaraya's fame had grown considerably. What is more, the symbolism of having a 'native' Indian head the committee was unmissable: earlier committees on technical education in colonial India had generally been headed by Britons.[69]

The terms of reference handed to the new Technical and Industrial Education Committee were capacious. The committee was to suggest how to provide or improve facilities for the training of the industrial workforce at all levels—including top management, supervisory positions, technicians, and shop-floor workers. Unusually for the times, they were also tasked with 'suggest[ing] practical measures for training girls and women to qualify them for industrial careers suited to their special aptitudes'. (The reference to 'special aptitudes', of course, hinted at a conventional view of the gendered division of labour. It is also noteworthy that there were no women on the committee.)[70]

The committee was made up of professors, government officials (including Bombay's director of industries), and men representing various railway companies, industrial enterprises, and mercantile associations. As constituted initially, it had six Indian and eight British members. Over time, a few members were added or subtracted for various reasons. At the time the deliberations came to an end, there were six Indian and ten British members.[71]

Beginning in March 1921, the committee held no less than twenty meetings over the course of a year. Between meetings, members collected relevant data and did other work individually or in sub-committees.

The minutes of the committee's meetings indicate that Visvesvaraya led with a light touch, not voicing his own views too frequently. However, he was firm at junctures when he felt it was time for the members to come to a conclusion on particular points. Proceedings were cordial for the most part, but Visvesvaraya noted a rift in the committee by the end of August. In spite of all efforts to arrive at a consensus, the committee eventually split. An interim report was submitted in October, but the final report took a few months longer. By the time it was ready for submission in March 1922, it had taken the form of two separate statements: a majority report signed by all the British members, and a minority report signed by all the Indians including Visvesvaraya.[72]

The Visvesvaraya-led minority recommended an elaborate system of technical and industrial education catering to students at all levels and various ages. This would include (a) university-level courses to train industrial executives; (b) polytechnics with less emphasis on theory, to train shop-floor managers; (c) 'Middle Industrial Schools', designed to produce self-employed 'skilled craftsmen'; (d) 'Lower Industrial Schools', whose graduates 'should be able to start life as journeymen'; (e) 'Mass Industrial Classes', which would provide brief vocational courses to teenagers with minimal or no basic schooling; and (f) industrial schools and colleges for girls and women (more on this below).[73] Categories (a), (b), and (c) would serve 3950 students, while (d) and (e) would serve a further 27,000 students each year in the presidency. Through this system, they wanted to reach as large a section of the population as possible, including village residents.[74]

Diagram II

Relation between General and Technical Education.

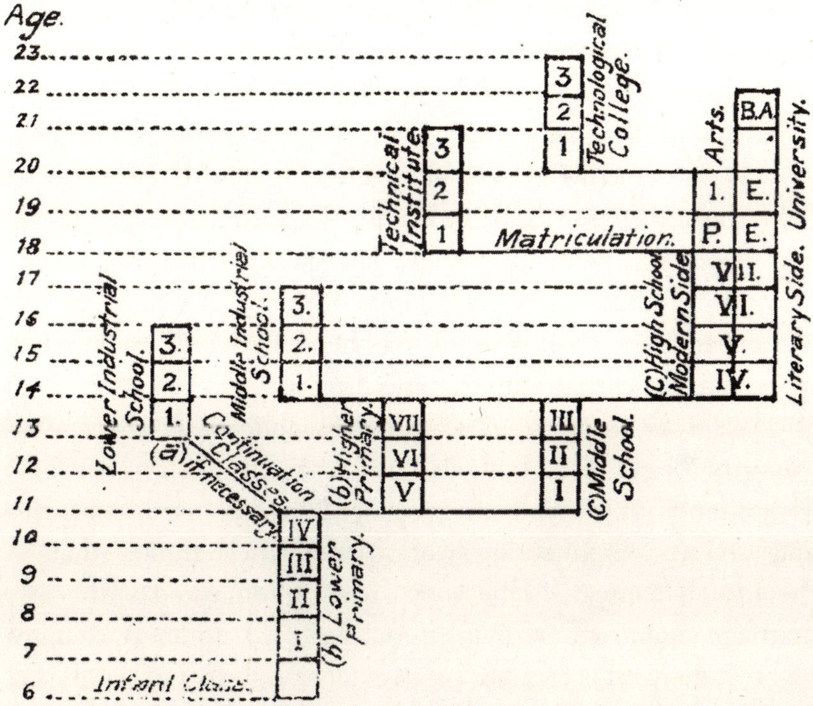

(a) ***Minimum age of admission 13.***
(b) ***Vernacular.***
(c) ***Anglo-Vernacular.***

Fig. 14.1. The Indian members' suggested programme of technical education in Bombay

Source: Reproduced from 'Minority Report', in *Technical and Industrial Education in the Bombay Presidency: Final Report of the Committee appointed by Government, 1921–22* (Bombay: Government Central Press, 1923), pp. 73–163, here p. 150. Accessed via http://dspace.gipe.ac.in/.

The British members, on the other hand, held that there would not be enough takers for such an elaborate system. They argued that the best solution, and the one that industries preferred, was training by apprenticeship within and alongside commercial factories—a scheme which could only accommodate around 600 students.[75] 'There cannot,' they wrote, 'be an immediate leap from the technical instruction of a few hundreds to provision for many thousands.'[76]

Another difference came at the administrative level. The Indian members of the committee recommended the establishment of 'a Development Council and a Development Committee' to help the Education and Industries Departments, businesses, and workers to work in concert. They wanted the government to commit to 'a ten-year programme of progressive development and expenditure'. The Britons, on the other hand, preferred to work with the current bureaucratic structure.[77]

As far as women's education was concerned, the Indian minority began by acknowledging that in western nations, '[t]housands of women are employed in organised industries and even on engineering works'. Yet, they argued that in the Indian context, '[t]he social usages connected with early marriage, standard of living, etc., have to undergo changes before a demand is created for an extensive system of vocational education for women'. As a result, they recommended a rather conservative system of training that assumed women would largely be homemakers. The subjects included domestic arts such as cookery, sewing, and laundry; and crafts such as embroidery, basketry, knitting, and lacquer-work. They suggested the establishment of one Higher Industrial and Art School for women; two Middle Industrial Schools; and Mass Industrial Classes, though the last of these would cater to no more than 4000 female students a year. Women who decided to seek technical education at the university level would join the existing colleges for men.[78]

These were tentative measures—they probably didn't go as far as Visvesvaraya would have liked personally, if we go by the views he expressed in *Reconstructing India* and elsewhere.[79] Yet they represented a progressive attitude compared to that of the British faction. The latter were reluctant to make any proposals for female education, arguing that they did not have enough relevant information.[80] (They nevertheless felt qualified to say that the Indians' view of 'the demand among women for "mass industrial classes" and for the special schools which they advocate is highly optimistic'.)[81]

Finally, when it came to university-level education, the Indians proposed the creation of a College of Technology in Bombay city, affiliated to a new Faculty of Technology within the University of Bombay. Its function would be to 'train technical experts and captains of industry'. They wanted the college to be modelled on the Manchester College of Technology and the Massachussetts Institute of Technology.[82] While the British members went along with the proposal for a College of Technology, they were less enthusiastic about it, taking care to note that it needed 'further investigation'.[83]

In summary, the split in the committee followed a familiar pattern in colonial-era debates. Indian thinkers, nationalist or loyalist, wanted the most advanced technical education facilities. The colonial establishment, on the other hand, was sceptical—on the grounds of cost; out of a fear of creating a dissatisfied, overqualified and under-employed class of Indian; and owing in some cases to a biased assessment that doubted the capacity or readiness of Indians to take on the most prestigious or responsible roles in an organisation.[84] No doubt Visvesvaraya and his Indian colleagues were ambitious, even utopian, in some of their recommendations. Equally striking, though, was the conservative approach of the majority faction.

Visvesvaraya was left frustrated by the outcome. He later recounted a private conversation with Lord Lloyd, Bombay's Governor at the time, who hinted to him that he 'should be content with putting forward proposals for the training of apprentices'. Reading between the lines, it appears that Visvesvaraya may have attributed the British members' final stance to pressure from the government. At any rate, he concluded that the Bombay government was doing its best to undercut the efforts of its elected minister, and 'had no intention of developing higher technological education in the Province. In the end I found I had wasted nearly a year on profitless work'.[85]

Indeed, the committee's report went the way of most such efforts, decorating the shelves of government libraries without being implemented in any meaningful form.[86] There, however, it provided an important and public record of the Indian desire for a more wide-ranging and progressive industrial education policy.

There was also a coda. While the Government of Bombay was not keen on ambitious steps such as creating a College of Technology, key officials in the University of Bombay were taken with the idea. After more discussion in the years that followed, the university's academic council created its own committee in 1930 to consider how the idea of a technological institution might be realized given the difficulty of raising funds. This committee, too, was headed by Visvesvaraya. As a result of its report, the university eventually established a Department of Chemical Technology. The focus on one kind of technology made the new institution less expensive to set up. The choice of chemical technology was made with a view to achieve synergies with the flourishing cotton textile industry of Bombay. A two-year BSc (Tech) course began in 1934. It admitted candidates who had already earned a BSc or equivalent. They could specialize either in chemical engineering (the design of chemical plants) or textile chemistry (the study of the processes carried out within such plants). Over time, the new department received support from individual donors, enabling it to move from its temporary location in Bombay's Esplanade to a more expansive, purpose-built campus in Matunga in 1943.[87]

*

A less taxing and more pleasant assignment came Visvesvaraya's way a year after his work on the Bombay committee: an invitation to preside over the 1923 session of the Indian Science Congress, to be held at Lucknow.[88] This was a signal honour. The Science Congress had been established on the eve of the First World War as the result of the efforts of P.S. MacMahon and J.L. Simonsen, two expatriate professors of chemistry teaching in Indian colleges. Set up to encourage individuals working in universities as well as government departments to present their research, the annual congress quickly became a prestigious platform. In its first decade, its presidents included such luminaries as Asutosh Mookerjee and P.C. Ray.[89]

Visvesvaraya began his Presidential Address in Lucknow by acknowledging that he had been invited as a representative of engineering, a field which did not yet have its own section in the Science Congress. Yet, given that '[a]dvance in Science has . . . become the criterion of a nation's standing', he decided to speak not on engineering, but on the state of science, more broadly defined, in India vis-à-vis the world. He wanted 'to invite attention to the present deficiencies of Science and research in this country, and to plead for greater organized effort to promote its interests in future'.[90] He had begun by striking a nationalist note even in a learned organization that, theoretically, ought not to have been limited by political boundaries.[91]

After an exhaustive (and likely exhaust*ing* for his audience, so thorough was it) survey of the colleges and research institutions across India engaged in various branches of science, Visvesvaraya came down to brass tacks. Those engaged in scientific work in the country must pool their resources and work together. Various associations and institutions published their own journals and bulletins; instead, they should combine to establish, in each field, one scientific journal of national scope and international renown. This would encourage scientists to publish locally rather than in foreign journals. He asked:

> [W]hy should not all the chemists in India, officials and non-officials alike, band together to run an Indian Journal of Chemical Research and forswear the habit of seeking publicity in foreign publications which brings no credit to India? . . . Why cannot the Meteorologists, the officials of the Survey of India, the Directors of Observatories, and the University and College Professors and Lecturers of Physics in India, jointly run a good Indian Journal of Physics and Astronomy?

'The point,' Visvesvaraya continued, 'is that it would be an immense advantage if all good work done in India in a particular subject should appear together in a single publication so that workers in countries abroad may know where to look for it and find it.'[92]

Also needed at the national level were coordinating institutions. The Indian Science Congress itself should go beyond being a yearly convention, assemble an administrative team, and take on other functions during the rest of the year. Citing Britain's Department of Scientific and Industrial Research and the USA's National Research Council, both set up in 1916, he suggested that India should have 'a Central Scientific Advisory Council'. Eventually the Science Congress would serve to generate new knowledge, while the new council would help translate this knowledge into solutions to various problems. As he put it, '[t]he one body will show what is theoretically possible and the other what may be practically expedient'.[93]

Visvesvaraya also wanted 'an all India centralized laboratory to help industry' along the lines of the UK's National Physical Laboratory, the US's Bureau of Standards, and Japan's National Laboratory for Scientific and Industrial Research.[94] (His wish was to come true much later, with the establishment of the Council of Scientific and Industrial Research in the 1940s.)[95]

Finally, the scientific community in India should focus on solving issues related to industrialization, agriculture, food, and the exploitation of resources: in other words, their work should be guided by utilitarian objectives, chief among them the eradication of poverty, which was 'a preventable disease'.[96]

Visvesvaraya rounded out his speech with a summary of recent theories and inventions from across the world, ranging from Einstein's concept of relativity to the thermionic valve and its use in the wireless transmission of speech. But the crux of his speech lay in his exhortations to promote applied science for the national well-being. 'We have every variety of culture and talent in this country . . . With the enormous numbers of our population chronically ill-fed or underfed the country can hardly afford to neglect the study of Science or scientific research.'[97]

*

A clear line ran through Visvesvaraya's initiatives in Mysore, his vision for national development as expressed in *Reconstructing India*, his approach to technical education while serving on the Bombay committee, and his address to the Indian Science Congress. In every instance, he saw the ultimate goal as improving the material well-being of the masses. The solutions were presented as apolitical, the crux being the use of scientific techniques to harness natural resources efficiently. But as he entered the new, self-employed phase of his life, he was to find that these interests drew him inexorably into the realm of the political.

15

Among the Politicians

Across India, it was a time of political ferment. Since the start of the First World War, the Indian National Congress and other nationalists had stepped up demands for *swaraj*, or 'self-government' for Indians. To most of these activists, swaraj, as conceptualized in the 1910s and early 1920s, meant a representative government, run almost entirely by Indians, while maintaining allegiance to the British Crown and remaining a part of the Empire. More specifically, what they sought was 'dominion status' for India.[1]

In other words, they wanted India to have the same rights and level of autonomy as the British dominions of Australia, New Zealand, Canada and South Africa (and later Ireland). The term 'Dominion' as applied to these countries had come to mean that they governed themselves, and '[a] resolution of the Imperial War Conference in 1917 referred to "full recognition of the Dominions as autonomous nations of an Imperial Commonwealth"'.[2] Although the precise position of the dominions within the Empire underwent further changes during the 1920s and 1930s,[3] Indian nationalists of various hues continued to measure India's constitutional status with reference to them.

As he made quite evident in his 1920 book *Reconstructing India*, Visvesvaraya shared the hope that India would achieve dominion status in the near future. Laying down the gauntlet, he declared that the colonial government would be judged on whether this became a reality in the coming ten years.[4] His interest in the subject of constitutional reform, along with his commitment to questions of industrialization and technical education, now brought him into regular contact with two leaders of the Indian National Congress.

The first of these was the veteran leader and former Congress President Madan Mohan Malaviya (1861–1946), a lawyer from Allahabad who also served in the Imperial Legislative Council from 1909 to 1920 and helped establish the Benares Hindu University (BHU) in 1916.[5] Visvesvaraya had first met Malaviya in December 1910, when he took leave from his work as chief engineer in Mysore to attend the Allahabad session of the Indian National Congress. A year or so later, he had seen Malaviya deliver a speech in Hindi of 'great force and eloquence' at a meeting in Calcutta held to raise funds for BHU. When BHU became a reality, it had a direct link with Mysore in the person of Krishnaraja Wadiyar, who served as the Benares institution's first chancellor.

Although he did not share Malaviya's specific interest in the revival of Hindu culture, Visvesvaraya appreciated the latter's role 'in moulding the thoughts of his orthodox audiences'—in other words, in liberalizing their views.[6] One point in particular drew the two men together, and that was a fervent belief in the need for policies that would encourage industrialization in India. As a member of the Indian Industrial Commission (1916–18) appointed by the Government of India, Malaviya had written a searing dissenting note in which he emphasized India's pre-colonial industrial heritage, and argued that Japan and Germany rather than Britain must serve as exemplars for the country's industrial reinvigoration.[7]

The second Congress politician whom Visvesvaraya got to know well in these years was Mukund Ramrao Jayakar (1873–1959). Educated at St. Xavier's and Elphinstone Colleges in Bombay, Jayakar had qualified as a barrister in London in 1905 before registering as an advocate in the Bombay High Court.[8] In the years that followed, he combined his legal practice with social reform work and regular attendance at Congress meetings. He also participated in the Home Rule movement and was one of the members of the committee appointed by the Congress to inquire into the infamous Jalliwanwala Bagh massacre of 1919.[9]

Jayakar and Visvesvaraya had common friends. When Jayakar was unwell in 1917, these friends took him to Bangalore to convalesce. The party stayed with Visvesvaraya, who was then still dewan, at Ballabrooie, and saw some of the local sights. Jayakar was as impressed by his 'dignified, unobtrusive, considerate' host as he was by the electricity-generating town of Sivasamudram and the reservoir under construction at Kannambadi. A few years later, when Visvesvaraya moved into his Bombay house on Warden Road, the two men became neighbours, in a manner of speaking, as Jayakar lived in nearby Thakurdwar.[10]

Malaviya and Jayakar were active participants in the movement for swaraj. Although they were intimate comrades of Mohandas Gandhi—the rising star of the Congress, and by 1919, its most important leader—they remained wedded to the Liberal or Moderate credo. This, as we saw in Chapter 14, involved engaging in dialogue and negotiation with the colonial powers while working within the existing legislative machinery.[11] Gandhi, on the other hand, had converted the nationalist agitation into a mass movement, and his preferred mode of political mobilization was 'non-cooperation'. This involved refusing to participate in colonial institutions (courts, legislative bodies, schools, colleges), boycotting British goods, and organizing nationwide *hartals* or strikes. All these measures were to be undertaken nonviolently. He also formed an alliance with the leaders of the Khilafat agitation, a protest by Indian Muslims against the Allies' post-war policies related to some of the sacred sites of Islam that had been ruled by the now-defeated Ottomans.

In 1920–21, Gandhi launched a massive non-cooperation drive across the country to protest the inadequacy of the postwar constitutional reforms and the subsequent draconian actions of the colonial government, which had been cracking down mercilessly on dissidents—sometimes violently, as in the case of the horrific shooting at Jallianwalla Bagh. The Congress now demanded that the British grant India swaraj while making amends for their actions in Punjab.

Although its unprecedented scale and fervour rattled the colonial government, the non-cooperation movement did not ultimately make much headway.[12] It was in this context that Malaviya decided to adopt a different approach. In December 1921, he took a group of like-minded political leaders and public figures to Calcutta to meet the viceroy, Lord Reading. Visvesvaraya was a part of this group, as was Annie Besant. They requested the viceroy to organize a 'round table conference', at which the various stakeholders would try and thrash out the question of self-government and dominion status.

But the viceroy declined to hold talks unless the Congress agreed to suspend its non-cooperation activities. This was unacceptable to Gandhi.[13] At its annual session in Ahmedabad the same month, the Congress responded by resolving 'to continue the programme of non-violent non-cooperation with greater vigour than hitherto'. It also encouraged its members to be ready to undertake 'civil disobedience', which involved volunteers courting arrest by deliberately breaking what they deemed to be unjust laws.[14] Nevertheless, Gandhi made it clear at the Ahmedabad Congress that the aim of swaraj was not to break away entirely from the British Empire.[15]

Despite the outcome of the Ahmedabad Congress, Malaviya, Jayakar and their associates—who included the lawyer-politician M.A. Jinnah—did not give up their efforts to bring about a round table conference with British and Indian stakeholders. In preparation, they organized a multipartisan meeting in Bombay in January 1922. Held at the Cowasji Jehangir Hall of Bombay University, the meeting was attended by hundreds of prominent individuals (including Gandhi, who was present unofficially and declined to vote on any of the resolutions). They came from all over India: from Bombay, from the United Provinces, from Punjab, from Sind, from Madras, from Bengal. They included not only politicians of various hues, but also scientists, industrialists, and businessmen. Visvesvaraya was a key invitee.

On the second day, the chairman of the conference, C. Sankaran Nair, resigned over a disagreement with Gandhi (who reiterated that as far as he was concerned, there could be no talks with the viceroy unless the government released some political prisoners). Visvesvaraya was voted chairman in Nair's place.[16] He thus found himself chairing a meeting of the most influential political leaders of the time. It was a scene Visvesvaraya could hardly have imagined when, nearly forty years previously, he had received his engineering degree in the same hall.[17]

The resolutions of the Malaviya Conference, as this meeting later came to be called, condemned the colonial government's recent use of sedition laws to carry out 'wholesale arrests and imprisonments, including those of some of the most respected leaders and citizens'. However, the consensus was against undertaking civil disobedience (as the Ahmedabad Congress had resolved to do) until all alternative solutions to the crisis had been explored. Proposed instead was 'a Round Table Conference between the Government and the popular representatives' to discuss 'the demand for Swaraj or full responsible Government on the Dominion basis' along with other grievances. But this could only proceed if the government agreed to arbitration with a view to the release of political detainees.[18]

The conference set up a twenty-strong committee to liaise between political figures and the viceroy with the aim of organizing the desired round table conference. Among its members were the Calcutta chemist P.C. Ray, the Ahmedabad industrialist Ambalal Sarabhai, Visvesvaraya's former Mysore colleague C.R. Reddy, and political leaders from across India, including Malaviya himself. Visvesvaraya was once again made chairman of the committee, while Jayakar and Jinnah served as its secretaries.[19] In addition to his closeness to Malaviya and Jayakar, Visvesvaraya's formal neutrality—not being a party man—may have contributed to his being chosen as chairman.

The committee met daily for several days thereafter. They telegraphed the resolutions of the Malaviya Conference to the Viceroy's Private Secretary, with a note saying that Visvesvaraya, along with the committee's secretaries, was ready to meet the Viceroy to offer additional clarifications if needed.[20]

But the viceroy did not respond to these overtures. Meanwhile, Gandhi went ahead with his plans for a programme of civil disobedience, only to call it off in February 1922 after protestors turned violent in Chauri Chaura in the United Provinces. The state moved to arrest Gandhi, who was sentenced to six years in prison.[21] Under these circumstances, the committee emerging from the Malaviya Conference was rendered moot, and Visvesvaraya formally resigned as chairman in May 1922.[22]

In the end, the conference in Bombay was more symbolic than effective. As one critic pointed out, the viceroy and Gandhi had already reached a stalemate over the non-cooperation movement and the release of political detainees, and unless it could break that stalemate, the conference would achieve nothing concrete, resolutions notwithstanding.[23]

One important point, however, had emerged from the failed negotiations and manoeuvrings. The Malaviya Conference had demonstrated the existence of a wide consensus among Indian leaders that dominion status for India was their chief political aim. To this end, many leaders were prepared to engage in dialogue with the Government of India and the British government.

As for Visvesvaraya, his role in the proceedings was surely another indication of his growing reputation as a statesman at the all-India level. In particular, he was now seen as someone who had a keen interest in, and understanding of, the constitutional relationship between Britain and India.

*

Although the efforts of the committee arising out of the Malaviya Conference had been in vain, Visvesvaraya continued to play an important role in the quest for dominion status. He remained involved in discussions with Jayakar, Malaviya, and others in Bombay.[24] Around this time, Jayakar also encouraged him to draw up a document that would detail the modalities of a dominion form of government, should India be granted that status. In March 1922, Visvesvaraya produced a short 'Draft Scheme' titled 'Dominion Status for India'.[25]

Visvesvaraya's document (he did not append his name, but it is quite clear he was its author)[26] began by noting that Britain had given its word to grant India dominion status. 'Indians,' he wrote, 'desire that they should no longer be excluded from the higher offices and occupations in their own country.' In the very next sentence, he added what for him—as an engineer and evangelist for industrialization—was of paramount concern: Indians also wanted 'the opportunity to handle their country's resources; to train, equip and put to work the vast population now insufficiently employed, in order to increase production and redeem the country from its great and abject poverty'.[27]

Visvesvaraya wanted 'full responsible Government of the federal type' to be instituted by the start of 1927, rendering India 'an equal member of the British [Commonwealth]'.[28] His scheme was divided into three sections. The first section described the institutional framework that would have to be created; the second emphasized the urgent need to implement dominion status; and the third spoke of the need for 'National Organisation' in order 'to develop a disciplined combination and effort among the people to prepare for self-Government and nationhood'.[29]

The system of government proposed by Visvesvaraya was as follows. At the centre would be an Indian Parliament made up of an upper house (the Senate) and a lower house (the House of Commons). The former would replace the existing Council of State, while the latter would replace the Central Legislative Assembly. The head of Parliament would be the British monarch's appointee, styled Governor-General as before. The governor-general would set up a 'Cabinet from members of the Indian legislature possessing the confidence of that legislature, and dependent for their offices on the support of a majority in the Lower House'.[30]

The House of Commons would have around 250 members (significantly more than the existing Central Legislative Assembly, which had a strength of 144). The franchise would be based on '[l]iteracy or ownership of property', so that the Parliament 'should represent the great mass of public opinion, not merely the propertied classes and interests'. The House would function for a minimum of 180 days each year. The legislature was to be professionalized by offering salaries to Members of Parliament along with free railway travel.[31]

Along similar lines, 'Full responsible Government' was to be introduced at the provincial level at the end of three years from the promulgation of the Montagu-Chelmsford Reforms of 1919. Serving as the legislature would be a popularly elected Legislative Assembly in place of the existing Legislative Councils, which had a significant proportion of appointed members.[32]

The government would thus be federal in character. Visvesvaraya's insistence on this point was significant, and flowed from his belief that given the vast size and population of most provinces, they would be best placed to develop their natural resources and industries if given greater autonomy. It was also a reflection of the system in Canada and Australia. The provinces should be in charge of subjects such as industries, education, public works, and irrigation, while the centre 'should deal with all questions that are of common import to all the provinces', including the army, railways, shipping, and telegraphs.[33]

The government in Britain, referred to as the Imperial Government, would be in charge of India's 'international arrangements' with countries outside the British Empire (subject to the approval of the Indian Parliament in certain cases). Within the Empire, 'Imperial Conferences' would be held to discuss issues common to all the dominions, but '[a]ny action based on such consultations must rest on the deliberate choice of each Dominion and not on the vote of a majority of the Dominion representatives comprising the Conference'.[34]

Visvesvaraya next came to a key point: the relationship of the proposed Indian dominion with Britain. In this respect, India's position would be identical to that of the white settler dominions such as Canada and Australia. When it came to Empire-wide matters, the dominion governments could not pass laws that contravened those of the 'Imperial Parliament'. On the other hand, Britain's treaties with nations outside the Empire were not applicable to the individual dominions unless they wished to be party to them.

In Canada, the British government appointed the governor-general, although the choice had to be approved by the dominion government. Visvesvaraya appeared to suggest a similar system for India. The provincial governors would also be chosen on the recommendation of the central government in India.

Crucially, the army would be under the full control of the Indian dominion government, as would the framing of laws on 'currency, exchange, banking and regulation of fiscal policy'. However, the British navy would continue to 'protect the Dominions as well as Dominion shipping', and the British government had oversight of the naval laws of the dominions.

In most respects, then, the dominions would function like independent nations except in wartime, when they were expected to come to Britain's and each other's aid. [35]

The latter parts of the draft scheme were concerned with more subjective matters, such as a description of the current political scenario in India, and the need for training the population to become responsible citizens who understood the significance and features of the coming dominion status. They showed Visvesvaraya's evolving view of what it meant to be a citizen of the British Empire: one's duty to the nation and its autonomy must come before one's obligations to the Empire as a whole.

On the political situation, Visvesvaraya did not mince words. He declared that '[i]n almost every department of Governmental activity which affects the people's interests, the attitude and methods of the present system have been unnational and far below accepted standards of civilised administration.' India's literacy rate was below 8 per cent, as opposed to 80–90 per cent 'in civilised countries'; yet the government had ignored long-standing requests for compulsory education 'on the ground that money cannot be found for it, although money . . . has always been found for the army and various less important objects'.

Visvesvaraya emphasized the need for protectionist policies to nurture Indian industries, and the importance of technical and commercial education.[36] He stated emphatically that the people were in no way lacking in potential; what they needed was a clear programme of training. Given that, nothing could stop India from 'supplying all the administrators, generals, engineers, and technical and scientific experts she needs in 10 or 15 years time'. Crucially, the required steps would be taken 'only [by] a national government'.[37] He stated baldly: 'The main obstacle . . . to Indian freedom is British vested interests.' Britons occupied the highest reaches of government bureaucracies, and owned or ran the lucrative industries in India; British industries had a captive market in the country.[38]

He was prepared to reach '[a] compromise'. The career prospects and pensions of long-serving British government employees would be secured; British industries already operating in India would likewise receive some safeguards. The British, for their part, must understand that 'permanent co-operation . . . must be based on self interest'. It was in the interest of British trade to make 'substantial concessions to Indian sentiment'.[39]

Meanwhile, in preparation for dominion status, the army and civil service would need to be Indianized swiftly; the railways nationalized; and 'the machinery, traditions, principles and methods characteristic of a dependency' replaced by 'those of a Dominion form'. India must emulate Japan, which had sent officials and students across the world to learn from other countries. Visvesvaraya described an ambitious plan by which Indians would set up 'National Councils' and 'Provincial Councils' as a civil society effort during the transition to dominion status. There should be 'a Citizen Committee and Association' in each 'district, city, town and village'. Big cities could also have 'societies, leagues, clubs, etc.' These various bodies would lobby for an early establishment of democratic government at all levels, educate officials on the 'policies, machinery, and practices of responsible Government as understood in the self-Governing Dominions', and 'promote the feeling of nationality, self-help, spirit of service and mass co-operative effort among the people'.[40]

These measures bear the mark of Visvesvaraya's belief in committees and top-down reform. He stressed the need to work out change 'in conciliation and compromise',[41] mirroring the approach of the Congress Moderates. Yet his impatience with the colonial government frequently made itself apparent. The various citizens' bodies, for instance, were to meet weekly, and '[a] resolution should be passed once a week in every city, town and village demanding responsible Government until the same is conceded and actually established in the country'.[42] Towards the end of the document, he pointed out that there were 12,000 or more political prisoners in the country. 'How long can this state of things last?' He concluded: 'The country as a whole does not desire to break off the British connection; it wants to be relieved of its heavy handicaps. The aim is not that Englishmen should lose, but that the far larger population of India should not starve. The country wants freedom to develop her own destiny.'[43]

Just as he had in *Reconstructing India*, Visvesvaraya was adopting a position that was not opposed to British-style institutions, but to the British policy of holding India in a dependent position. His model for a rejuvenated India was a country like Canada or Australia—namely a country with a British-style parliamentary democracy and institutional arrangements, but with autonomy as a nation.

*

Visvesvaraya had asked Jayakar to use his dominion scheme as he saw fit without revealing his name as its author, as he '[did] not want advertisement'.[44] Jayakar tried to recruit allies to the Indian cause on the basis of this document. In 1924, he showed the scheme informally to Leslie Wilson, the Governor of Bombay. (Jayakar had got to know Wilson while serving as leader of opposition in the Bombay Legislative Council, to which he had been elected in 1923 as a candidate of the Swaraj Party—a sub-group within the Congress which, unlike the Gandhians, decided to participate in elections at the provincial and central levels.)[45]

Wilson perused the scheme carefully. Although he made encouraging noises ('this is the first time that I have seen on paper proposals of any sort dealing with this all-important question [of dominion status]'), he raised several objections. He argued that six years was too short a timeframe for such a fundamental change as that envisaged by the scheme. He said India's case was different from that of Australia or Canada, 'particularly with regard to defence and to religious, communal and class differences'.[46]

Visvesvaraya, who was shown a copy of Wilson's letter by Jayakar, remarked that despite the 'geniality and sociability' of its tone, it 'makes no admissions while it raises numerous small difficulties'. He was confident, however, that the objections could be met, and offered to meet Jayakar to discuss how the latter could respond to Wilson.[47] In the event, Jayakar decided not to debate these points further with Wilson, although the governor did apparently send the scheme on to his political bosses.[48]

Jayakar also sent the scheme to Major Graham Pole, a British Labour politician whom he had met in Bombay. His hope was to influence the Labour Party (whose leader, Ramsay MacDonald, had become prime minister in Britain that year) to champion the cause of dominion status for India. Jayakar engaged with Pole over several months, but stopped writing to him when it became clear that the latter's interventions in England were having no tangible results.[49]

In 1927, the Simon Commission was created to assess the impact of the 1919 constitutional reforms and suggest steps for the future. Indian nationalists were incensed that the commission did not have a single Indian member. Pulling together, they convened all-party conferences in 1928 (like the Malaviya Conference of 1922), as part of which a committee was appointed to draw up a draft constitution for India embodying the demands of the nationalists as a whole.[50] The resulting report, known as the Nehru Report (1928) after its chairman Motilal Nehru, was much more detailed than Visvesvaraya's scheme, but agreed with it in its essential features.[51] (Jayakar was invited to sit on the committee, but was not in a position to do so. However, he was a signatory to the 'Supplementary Report' issued later.)[52]

The Nehru Report, in turn, led to key developments. In December 1928, the Congress declared dominion status within one year as its aim. When the demand was not met, they called for 'complete independence' ('*purna swarajya*') in December 1929, although this did not imply a complete dissociation from the British Commonwealth. Eventually, three Round Table Conferences were organized in London beginning in 1930, leading to further constitutional reform under the Government of India Act 1935. Even this, however, stopped short of granting India the status of a fully autonomous dominion. It was only with Independence in 1947 (coming after the British Empire was weighed down by the strains of the Second World War) that India finally got dominion status. This was short-lived, because in 1950—as the British Empire's dissolution proceeded—India took on the form of a sovereign republic.[53]

*

Visvesvaraya's role in the deliberations on dominion status is little known. To be sure, several others at the time were applying themselves to the question. Many of them came from a legal background and were better equipped to tackle it. Yet the sequence of events indicates that Visvesvaraya, while staying in the background, had a crucial input. His interest in the mechanics of dominion status stemmed from a combination of influences. On the one hand, he was the product of a Victorian education and an admirer of British institutions; on the other, he was an economic nationalist who was growing increasingly impatient with colonial apathy towards Indian aspirations.

16

Critics, and Bhadravati Again

Even as Visvesvaraya was establishing himself on the national stage, his successors in Mysore were trying to steer the state through the choppy waters of the early postwar years.

When Visvesvaraya resigned as dewan in 1918, the seniormost member of his council,[1] M. Kantaraj Urs, was chosen to replace him. The circumstances were propitious for Kantaraj Urs. Not only was he a close relative of the maharaja; he was also Mysore's first non-Brahmin dewan, making him a welcome choice at a time when the political movement opposing Brahmin domination was coming to a head. His tenure, however, was marred by ill health. Even before he could take over as dewan, his fellow councillor Albion Banerji had to deputize for him. Urs finally occupied his office in 1919, but had to step down just three years later, after suffering a stroke. This time Banerji took over as full-time dewan, a post he held until 1926.[2]

Although they were known to be more financially conservative than Visvesvaraya, neither Urs nor Banerji cut back on his ambitious development projects in any significant way. The government kept construction going on the Kannambadi reservoir project, and got on with the task of building the iron works and an associated industrial township in Bhadravati.[3] But spiralling costs and an economic downturn that came in the wake of the war years soon left Mysore in a financial bind: the state found itself taking out loans worth Rs 335 lakh. In February 1922, the government set up a Special Finance Committee to study the situation and suggest remedies.[4]

Mysore's journalists sniffed a major story. Over the next few months, the newspapers were awash with articles on the possible reasons for Mysore's financial woes. Many commentators traced the problems to the years of Visvesvaraya's dewanship. His ambitious projects and his indiscriminate expansion of the bureaucratic apparatus, they held, had weighed down the state with gigantic liabilities. 'The frenzied finance of that brilliant but irresponsible Dewan,' declared a *Times of India* correspondent, ' . . . left the State in a very serious condition financially, and to this day that position has not been fairly faced.'[5] Even sympathetic observers reinforced this argument. The prominent journalist D.V. Gundappa, while lauding Visvesvaraya for the 'high idealism' he displayed during his tenure, noted that his projects were marred by 'hurry, over enthusiasm and unreliable assistance'.[6] The *Daily Post* of Bangalore granted that Visvesvaraya's regime had been progressive; '[b]ut however valuable this educative aspect of his strenuous Dewanship may have been, there is no denying that it was purchased at an almost prohibitive cost, and the resulting strain, combined with other unforeseen circumstances, has proved to be too much for the State'.[7]

Always sensitive to criticism and protective of his reputation, Visvesvaraya decided to staunch the flow of adverse commentary. Billeted in his Bangalore bungalow, he drafted a statement of rebuttal, releasing it to the press on 5 July 1922. When he stepped down as dewan, he noted in this statement, there had been no complaints about his financial management. The whispers had begun around eighteen months after he left. 'Since then, as criticisms have been appearing from time to time both in the public press and elsewhere, I feel a brief explanation is due from me to the public.'[8]

Visvesvaraya began by enumerating the charges against him. They were:

> (1) that the finances were in a disorganised condition when I relinquished office . . . (2) that during my term of office the current expenditure went up by leaps and bounds . . . (3) that the productive public works and industrial schemes initiated by me forced the hands of Government to contract huge loans which have resulted in the present financial debacle.[9]

Replying to the first criticism, he argued that official figures showed a surplus in the state's accounts in every complete year of his dewanship. In other words, the state's revenues exceeded its ordinary expenditures (this head didn't include money spent on capital works) in each of the six years he was at the helm. In his last full year as dewan (1917–18), the surplus was as high as Rs 60 lakh. In 1917, he had invited a retired financial officer of the Government of India to go over the government's books; this officer had endorsed Visvesvaraya's policies. Months after Visvesvaraya's departure, Albion Banerji, then acting dewan, had announced in the Representative Assembly that the state's 'finances are in a prosperous condition'. All this showed that the outgoing dewan had left the state in robust financial health.[10]

Visvesvaraya came next to the allegation that bureaucratic bloat during his time had caused the state's expenditures to soar. He pointed out that the annual 'Service expenditure' had gone up by a modest Rs 58 lakh between his first and sixth years. In contrast, over the next three years, this annual figure had gone up by around Rs 84 lakh.[11]

Finally, Visvesvaraya addressed the question of the many new projects started in his time. The figures showed that except in one year (1914–15), the expenditure on capital works (including railway expansion, the Sivasamudram plant, and the Kannambadi project) never exceeded the surplus for the corresponding year.[12] Taken as a whole, Rs 289 lakh was spent on these works in Visvesvaraya's six years as dewan, whereas the total surplus earned in those years was Rs 311 lakh. In other words, the surpluses—the difference between revenues and ordinary expenditures—'more than covered the capital outlay on productive works'. By contrast, in the four years that followed (1918–22), capital expenditure had amounted to around Rs 394 lakh, whereas there was, instead of a surplus, a deficit of around Rs 30 lakh. He granted that in spending so lavishly on the new projects, his successors had 'made a plucky attempt and presumably their object was mainly to secure a larger revenue speedily from the new works'. But given the recessionary post-war economy, he thought they could have slowed down work on these projects, spending no more than Rs 25 lakh per year on them.[13]

In summary, then, the real surge in expenditure had come after the end of the First World War and Visvesvaraya's dewanship. This was a period of 'rising costs and falling revenues; high prices of supplies and services, slump in trade, decline in sterling revenues[,] in railway earnings, in forest receipts, etc., nearly all attributable to change in world conditions and policies'.[14] Behind the diplomatic wording, the implication was clear—global events had created a challenge for Mysore in the years after his tenure, and it was the Urs/Banerji administration that had failed to manage the situation.

On the face of it, Visvesvaraya had presented a convincing defence. More than one newspaper complimented him for taking the trouble to address his critics, and for doing so without rancour.[15] Leader-writers observed that post-war conditions had indeed had a significant impact on Mysore's economy.[16]

Some analysts, however, pointed out flaws in Visvesvaraya's reasoning. Faced with complaints about the 'alleged disorganised conditions of finances during his time', he had merely shown that the treasury was always in surplus.[17] 'That Mysore finances were sound in the sense that there were funds enough to meet liabilities when Sir M. Visveswarayya left, may easily be accepted', *The Hindu* commented, 'but if it is sought to prove that they were then in a well-ordered state, that capital and revenue receipts and permanent revenues and windfalls were clearly distinguished, that the financial accounting in vogue was up-to-date and incapable of improvement and that service expenditure was regulated in due correspondence to normal revenues, then, we think the endeavour will be made in vain.'[18] A member of the Mysore Legislative Council, Hosakoppa Krishna Rao, wrote to the *Daily Express* of Madras that while he was sympathetic to Visvesvaraya's policies and projects, the former dewan could not absolve himself of responsibility for difficulties faced after his regime. 'Shrewd man that he was, he ought to have known that his Dewanship could not be interminable and that a financial crisis might at any time crop up. He ought to have clearly laid the future financial policy of the State for the guidance of his followers who might not after all be blessed with the master mind he inherited.'[19]

Perhaps more damagingly, some writers pointed out that the figures Visvesvaraya had presented were difficult to square with publicly available data. 'M.S.', a columnist writing in the *Vokkaligara Patrike,* noted that it wasn't clear how Visvesvaraya came to the figure of Rs 60 lakh as a surplus for the year 1917–18. Subtracting the expenditures from the revenues as per the official figures gave a figure of no more than Rs 1.79 lakh.[20] (M.S. was right: perusal of a government publication summarizing the accounts from 1909 to 1919 reveals that while Visvesvaraya's figures for expenditure on capital works generally agreed with the official data, his surplus figures differed substantially.)[21] 'We presume,' M.S. continued, 'that the sale proceeds of the bonds in which the accumulated surplus of the State were invested is taken into account and credited to the ordinary revenues and the expenditure on capital works is added to the ordinary expenditure and by this process a surplus of Rs. 60 lakhs has been shown. This is no surplus at all.'[22] (Two years later, the Resident of Mysore, who had been requested by Visvesvaraya to forward his defence to the Government of India, remarked privately that 'the sixty lakhs surplus seems to rest largely on the imagination of the writer'.)[23]

Other commentators implied that Visvesvaraya had been disingenuous in excluding the year 1918–19 from his analysis. Although he had retired in the middle of the financial year, it was he who had drawn up the budget for the entire year. (According to Visvesvaraya's own statement, the surplus fell from Rs 60 lakh to a much lower Rs 7 lakh in 1918–19, while the capital expenditure was well over Rs 40 lakh for the year.) Administrative spending had also risen dramatically during that last year.[24]

Critics also took issue with Visvesvaraya's assertion that his successors could have limited expenditure on the projects he started. In fact, Urs and Banerji had been committed to a certain outlay by Visvesvaraya's own decisions, such as the terms of the tie-up with the Tatas to set up the steel plant at Bhadravati. In the case of the KRS reservoir, they could not afford to slow down the pace of construction, for if they had, the stability of the dam would have been compromised.[25]

Finally, even if Visvesvaraya's calculations of the yearly surplus were correct, it was simplistic to argue that just because these surpluses were large enough to meet the required annual investment in development projects, the state's financial policy was sound. This argument assumed that the state had no need of substantial funds for other purposes. As the state's financial secretary J.S. Chakravarti had argued in back in 1910–11, Visvesvaraya's policy left little leeway for the government to spend on other, more modest programmes, and little liquidity to deal with unexpected situations such as famine.[26]

Visvesvaraya made careful note of these reactions. In September 1922, he responded with a second statement.[27] Even though he had helped draw up the budget for 1918–19, he stressed, he could not be held accountable for expenditures made after his departure in December 1918.[28] It was not true that his successors had been compelled to take out loans because of the sheer scale of the projects he had launched; in fact, Dewan Kantaraj Urs had explicitly told the Legislative Council in 1920 that the government had decided to take out a loan '*solely and simply* because we wish to develop the resources of the State at a rate much quicker than would ever be possible, with the aid of the surplus revenues of the State alone'.[29]

Notably, Visvesvaraya made no attempt to support his calculation of a Rs 60 lakh surplus in 1917–18; instead, he confidently repeated the claim as part of a rousing summing-up.[30] He even issued a challenge. 'I am prepared to discuss this matter further,' he declared, 'with any responsible person or body of persons like the Members of the Legislative Council. There is nothing to hide. The more the matter is examined the better it would be for all concerned.'[31]

His critics held fire. Visvesvaraya had gone on the front foot, challenging them while conceding no misjudgement on his own part. True, he had sidestepped the odd point. But he had made a compelling (if not quite watertight) case that the state's expenditures had risen sharply *after* his tenure, largely owing to post-war fluctuations in the economy. In the end, though, the debate hinged on a subjective question: what was the right balance for a government between saving for a rainy day and investing in capital-intensive, revenue-generating public works?

The exchanges may have been inconclusive, but the intense press scrutiny of Visvesvaraya's policies and his vigorous defence of them had one somewhat unexpected result: it caused him to return to the service of the Mysore government in a new role. In 1923, he was given charge of the iron works at Bhadravati.

*

Established towards the end of Visvesvaraya's tenure as dewan, the Mysore Distillation and Iron Works was bankrolled by the Mysore government, while—as we have seen in an earlier chapter—the Tata Iron and Steel Company (TISCO) served as its managing agents. Under the managing agency system, in vogue across the subcontinent at this time, a firm possessing technical or market expertise could undertake to direct the operations of another company in return for a fee guaranteed by a contract. In this case, TISCO was responsible for building the Mysore company's factory at Benkipur/Bhadravati, working it, and marketing its products. The Mysore government, on the other hand, was in charge of sourcing and transporting all the raw materials to the plant. The enterprise as a whole was overseen by a board consisting of three Mysore-appointed members and two TISCO nominees.[32]

According to the initial projections, the plant would be operational by late 1919. By then the Mysore government was to complete all arrangements for carting the necessary iron ore, wood, and limestone to Bhadravati, while TISCO and their consulting engineers (the New York-based Charles Perin and his partner, S.M. Marshall) were to have finished constructing the plant and installing the machinery.

In practice, things were not so smooth. In the immediate aftermath of the Great War, importing machinery proved no easy task. The costs of equipment soared. The consulting engineers could only make sporadic visits to the site; they were also busy with a much larger assignment—an ambitious programme of expansion that they were heading, simultaneously, at TISCO's own works in Sakchi.

Meanwhile, the Mysore government had to solve a number of practical problems. These included the installation of a ropeway to haul the iron ore down the hill from Kemmangundi, and a railway line to carry it from there to the plant. Rail and tram lines were also needed to bring the necessary wood and limestone to Bhadravati from the surrounding regions. Scampering to fulfil these requirements were top officials of Mysore's geology, railway, and forestry departments; but by the government's own admission, there was a lack of coordination. 1919 came and went, as did the next two calendar years. First Kantaraj Urs and then Albion Banerji kept pushing back the expected date of inauguration. Banerji conceded in 1922 that the projected costs now stood at more than *thrice* the original estimate. Moreover, the managing agents were now painting a gloomy picture of the plant's prospects. They noted that pig iron prices had plummeted, and that Indian buyers were not looking for charcoal iron or the by-products of wood distillation that the new plant was going to produce.[33]

But Mysore was too far committed to scrap the project, or even to put it on hold. The only option, the dewan felt, was to complete it and hope that it would start earning profits sooner rather than later. It was also a matter of prestige, for the people of the state were watching the project's progress keenly.[34] So on they ploughed. Late in 1922, Charles Perin came to Bhadravati for one final push. On 18 January 1923, the first lot of pig iron poured out of the blast furnace.[35]

But the opening of the works was a muted affair, overshadowed as it was by worries about the future. Perin would not be available forever—he left for New York at the end of March—and the executives at Bhadravati neither exuded nor inspired confidence, struggling with untrained workers and breaks in production. The two entities responsible for the entire operation—the Mysore government on the raw materials side, and TISCO and its consulting engineers on the manufacturing and marketing side—were not in sync. The Board of Management showed little initiative. It was evident that the company lacked a clear leader who could take responsibility for its fortunes.[36]

It was in this context that Visvesvaraya's battle with his critics in the press was playing out. His recent statements to the press had contained implicit criticisms of the way the Bhadravati project had been handled after his departure. Would he now be ready to walk the talk, and show how the job should be done? Dewan Albion Banerji, casting about for ways to salvage the project he had once opposed, was willing to find out. In March, with the maharaja's blessing, he sought out Visvesvaraya in Bombay and asked him if he would take charge of his own pet project, serving as chairman of a revamped Board of Management.[37]

Cynics might have surmised that the government was trying to make Visvesvaraya the fall guy for what they feared would be a massive failure. He was the original author of the mess; it was up to him to clean it up or bear the wrath of the people. A more charitable interpretation would be that Krishnaraja Wadiyar and Banerji had the maturity to look past personal disagreements and identify the best person for the job. After all, few individuals knew the background of the project as well as its original promoter.

For Visvesvaraya, the proposal must have come as something of a surprise. He was just settling into his wider role as a public intellectual and enjoying the freedom that came with being self-employed. On the other hand, it was a tempting opportunity to clear his name by demonstrating that the project of his conception was indeed a viable one.

He agreed to take up the challenge, but not before laying down certain conditions. First: he, who had once stood at the apex of the state machinery, must not be ordered about by relatively junior civil servants. In his dealings with the government, he told Banerji, 'nothing should be said or done . . . inconsistent with the consideration due to my status as an ex-Dewan'.[38]

Second, he demanded autonomy. Allow me the freedom to make far-reaching changes, he seemed to say, and I will deliver results. This much was clear from the order issued by the government on 11 April 1923, creating a new Board of Management with Visvesvaraya as chairman. N. Madhava Rao, the secretary of the existing board, would now be styled Government Director, reporting to Visvesvaraya. A third Mysore nominee would join the two men on the board. Although TISCO continued to be represented on the board, it was plain that the reorganization placed the government members, the chairman especially, in the driver's seat. Visvesvaraya was to visit the works at least once a month; Madhava Rao would work full-time at Bhadravati, overseeing operations and keeping the chairman informed of developments. Rao, who had worked closely with Visvesvaraya in the past and was loyal to him, would also act as his point of contact with the government departments on the one hand, and the managing agents on the other. Visvesvaraya was also empowered to issue orders to government departments on matters concerning their work for the iron factory. Finally, his board had carte blanche to make further refinements to the organization, 'only such reforms as involve radical changes or fresh [capital] outlay being reported for the approval of Government'.[39]

*

The arrangement suited Visvesvaraya perfectly. He was in a position of strength, for it was the government that had approached him. Not only did he have a free hand at Bhadravati; he could remain at his bases in Bombay and Bangalore, and didn't have to give up his other professional commitments. For his part, he declined to collect his salary as chairman until the iron works had been established as viable.[40] This gesture gave him the moral high ground, emphasizing that he had taken up the job purely for the public good.

The terms agreed, Visvesvaraya lost no time in getting to work. On 16 April, a mere five days after the government order was released, he was at Bhadravati, meeting his fellow board members, company executives, and government officials. In a note he released soon afterwards, he declared that the board would begin by rationalizing operations, cutting costs, and focusing on revenues: in other words, they would bring a business-like approach to the project. He outlined a new organization structure, with well-defined divisions and sections, clear lines of control, and a centralized authority (the board). Each division was asked to supply a detailed statement on its current status, followed by weekly and monthly reports detailing its transactions and activities, challenges faced, and possible improvements.[41]

In his first few months in the saddle, Visvesvaraya made multiple visits to Bhadravati. He had conversations with W.F. Smeeth of Mysore's Geology department, who was in charge of transporting iron ore from the mines to the factory; B.V. Ramiengar, the Conservator of Forests; and V.J. Gudkov, the Russian American engineer who served as general superintendent of the iron works. He conferred with Madhava Rao and the other board members. Together, they catalogued the various challenges facing the factory, including inefficiencies in the blast furnace, the saw mill, and the charcoal retorts used for distilling wood. The biggest concern was the blast furnace. Designed to yield 60 tons of pig iron a day, it was producing only 35 tons. Gudkov was asked to make rough drawings for a new furnace. Smeeth, who was due to retire at the end of June 1923, was asked to hand over all information regarding the ropeway under construction at Kemmangundi so that the work continued smoothly after his departure.[42]

Within three months, the various departments and their activities had been 'brought under one unified control'.[43] But a new set of challenges arose. In the monsoon, a swollen Bhadra river caused flooding in the factory. The furnace packed up, bringing the production of pig iron to a grinding halt for seven weeks in July and August.[44] Gudkov recited a litany of problems afflicting the works, and suggested that the plant be shuttered for six months while they were addressed. Soon after, Visvesvaraya reported Gudkov's 'retirement': a euphemism for being sacked. Madhava Rao was brought in to oversee repairs and improvements.[45] Although he was not an engineer himself, Rao almost certainly had access to expert advice from Charles Perin's firm.[46] Despite some further problems, the blast furnace was in good working order by November.[47]

As Visvesvaraya and his trusted lieutenants got to grips with the entire process, TISCO's role diminished further, culminating in the ending of their contract as managing agents in 1924. The split was amicable: TISCO even waived their commission as agents for the period following the plant's inauguration.[48] The reason for this parting of ways is not entirely clear. Possibly TISCO's top brass, some of whom had not been predisposed to the partnership in the first place,[49] preferred to concentrate on their operations in Jamshedpur (as Sakchi was now known), which were going through a make-or-break phase themselves.[50]

*

Visvesvaraya continued as chairman of the board for nearly six and a half years. His role was essentially managerial, for although he was an engineer and had studied many iron works across the world, he had no experience of working in them, and little formal training in metallurgy. What he did bring to the job was a clear vision, a sense of purpose, and an aura that enabled him to demand sacrifices of his staff.[51] Initially, he and his team focused on streamlining processes, increasing efficiency throughout the plant, and cutting costs. He spent a few days in Bhadravati each month, inspecting operations and giving pep talks to the managers, reportedly telling them that the works were 'a national asset, [that] they should be real patriots, not think of their salaries and emoluments but make the project a business success'.[52]

The most significant achievement during Visvesvaraya's first three years as chairman was the complete Indianization of the factory's personnel. From the early 1920s, Mysore had been sending some students to TISCO's in-house training facility, the Jamshedpur Technical Institute. It is very likely that some of them returned to work in Bhadravati.[53] Others may have been sent abroad for training.[54] The result was that by 1925, all the foreign technical experts in the Bhadravati works had been replaced by executives from Mysore's bureaucratic cadres.[55]

While focusing on reducing costs wherever possible, the board also made a few investments, upgrading the plant with a view to improving the saleability of its products. In 1924, they established four sales offices across the subcontinent, and geared up to install alcohol refining and tar distillation equipment to further process the by-products of the wood distillation plant. They also upgraded the foundry so that they could manufacture cast-iron pipes from some of the pig iron produced. This went into operation in 1926.[56]

The same year, Visvesvaraya travelled to London on an unrelated assignment. He used the chance to visit charcoal iron factories and wood distillation plants in England, continental Europe (especially Sweden), and North America.[57] In addition to gathering ideas for further improvements to the Bhadravati works, he set out to find American buyers for Bhadravati's iron.[58]

By this time the plant was functioning smoothly. In 1926 it nearly met the annual target of 20,000 tons of pig iron.[59] By the following year it was turning out 58 tons of pig iron per day, not to speak of 15 tons of pipes, 5 tons of acetate, 7.5 tons of tar, and 500 gallons of alcohol. Wood, iron ore and limestone were arriving at the works in adequate quantities.[60]

Despite all these accomplishments, however, the company was still running up losses. The reason was simple: market conditions were extremely unfavourable. Across the world, the prices of iron were taking a nosedive. Hundreds of iron works had gone out of operation in Britain and the United States. In India, pig iron sold at Rs 94.5 per ton when the plant began functioning in 1923; by 1927 it was down to Rs 45.9 per ton. No matter how much pig the plant produced and how efficiently, the revenue generated at these prices wasn't enough to cover its costs and other liabilities.[61] Within India, the firm was competing with TISCO and the Indian Iron and Steel Company (managed by Burn & Co. of Calcutta), both of which were many times its size.[62] Bhadravati had hoped to command higher prices for its iron, as charcoal iron was of superior quality to coke-fuelled iron, but this did not come to pass.[63] For some observers, all of this raised the question: was the undertaking, impressive as it was, an exercise in foolhardiness?

*

Around the time Visvesvaraya was settling into his new role in Bhadravati, the critics of his tenure as dewan had returned to the fight with renewed vigour. In 1924, when the Bombay Corporation engaged him as a consultant to advise them on cutting costs (more on this in Chapter 17), a Bangalore-based reader wrote to the *Times of India* that it was ironic that the man who had committed vast sums of Mysore's money to grand projects was now giving lessons in economy.[64] In November that year, Visvesvaraya issued yet another press statement defending his record as dewan.[65]

One critic in particular was extraordinarily persistent. Going by various noms de plume including 'Mysore', 'Fact', and 'Truth',[66] he bombarded the press—ranging from *The Hindu* of Madras to the *Daily Post* of Bangalore and the *Times of India* of Bombay—with detailed analyses of Visvesvaraya's projects with a view to exposing them as albatrosses around the government's neck.[67] He carried on the campaign for several years. His aim was not just to prove that Visvesvaraya had been profligate during his dewanship, but to establish that some of the works he had helped start should now be abandoned if the state was to be saved from financial disaster. His prime targets were the Bhadravati iron works and the second (irrigation) stage of the Krishnarajasagara project. The critic, who appeared to have sources in the government and quoted extensively from official data and reports, was understood to be a retired bureaucrat of high standing.[68]

This critic—let us call him *Mysore*, in italics—made a series of claims about the two projects in question. On the KRS reservoir, he argued that while its contribution to the generation of electricity at Sivasamudram was not in question, its use via a system of canals to irrigate vast swathes of agricultural land was unviable. He claimed that Visvesvaraya and his team had seriously (and on purpose) underestimated the cost of the project—not factoring in, for instance, the cost of a technically challenging requirement, the construction of an underground tunnel, to take the canal to fields on the far side of a hillock at Hulikere. The costs had kept on rising since. The project would not bring in the projected revenues; there were flaws in its design.[69] When, in 1925, the government formed a committee to examine his allegations, he objected to its composition, as it contained engineers who had formerly worked under Visvesvaraya on the KRS project.[70]

On the Bhadravati project, *Mysore* made the point that Visvesvaraya, as dewan, had pushed the iron works proposal through at a time when

> the Great War was at its fiercest . . . The Submarine campaign was in full swing, England was being nearly starved to surrender, all iron and machinery had been commandeered for the War, the production of iron and steel in England . . . was utilised solely for the War, and it was at such a time (May, 1918), that Sir V. with unique daring sanctioned his scheme and ordered machinery from England!! The shrunken production and the sudden world-wide demand following upon the armistice necessarily led to profiteering, and the cost of the Works rose from a crore to two crores . . .

He claimed that consulting engineer S.M. Marshall had declared in 1922 that the high phosphorus content of Mysore's iron deposits would seriously damage the prospects of fetching high prices for the charcoal iron produced; in spite of this, the government had gone ahead with the works. He accused the government of hiding details of the firm's financial performance from the Legislative Council and the Representative Assembly, and of making misleading assumptions in the figures it did release. For much of this he held Visvesvaraya responsible. 'Sir V. is not a mere Chairman of a Committee or Board. He dominates them and the other members are merely items.' *Mysore* demanded that the government set up an enquiry committee to examine the Bhadravati works.[71]

Visvesvaraya and the Mysore government appeared unfazed, coolly countering some of these claims in the press through letters and statements.[72] But beneath the unruffled exterior,

Visvesvaraya was deeply troubled. He was cut to the quick by some of the ad hominem attacks made by his arch-critic. In 1923, *Mysore* remarked snidely in *The Madras Mail* that Visvesvaraya's 'patriot[ism]' in agreeing to take charge of the Bhadravati works came at a cost—his salary of Rs 20,000 per year. This must have stung, and may have been one of the factors prompting the ex-dewan not to draw his salary until he had set the firm right. So upset was Visvesvaraya by the continuous barbs that at one point he compiled a painstaking collection of possibly libellous extracts from *Mysore's* many articles with a view to taking legal action.[73] The critic had said he was 'as slippery as an eel'; referred to his 'inordinate vanity'; called him a 'pinch-tongued fraudulent celebrite [sic]'; accused him of 'dodges, casuistry and sooth-saying'. He had declared: 'Sir V has missed his vocation. He was made to be a prospectus writer, [propagandist], statistician to speculative companies.' And there was much more in this vein. With reference to one of *Mysore's* lengthy diatribes, Visvesvaraya (or his secretary) merely typed the words: 'Difficult to read.'[74]

Around 1927, the critic unmasked himself.[75] His name was T. Paramasiva Iyer, and he was a retired judge of the Chief Court of Mysore, having served in that office during Visvesvaraya's dewanship.[76] Hailing from the Tanjore district in Madras Presidency, he came from a prominent Tamil Brahmin family.[77] His older brother, T. Sadasiva Iyer, served as Chief Judge of the Travancore High Court and later as Additional Judge in the Madras High Court;[78] his son, T.P. Kailasam, would later achieve renown as a Kannada playwright.[79] Paramasiva Iyer was an erudite man, steeped in Sanskrit as well as Western literature. He was also an amateur geologist who yearned to use his Western-style education to re-interpret Vedic literature. In the preface to a book he published on the topic in 1911, he recalled how exposure to a British professor's science lessons 'facilitated my realising nearly a quarter of a century later the identity of Vēdic and Puranic stories with geological and chemical phenomena'.[80] His studies, ambitious and painstaking as they were, sometimes tended to the fanciful.[81] A colleague once recalled him declaring 'that within a few years half of Europe will be destroyed by volcanoes and earth quakes [sic] and that in India the sea will encroach on and submerge a great part of the country and that Mysore and Tibet alone will escape the catastrophe on account of their high situation'.[82]

Paramasiva Iyer had not always been at loggerheads with Visvesvaraya. In the late 1910s, he had written to him appreciatively, praised him in public, and even shared with him his pet geological theories ('I am quite convinced though you may laugh at me that our old Rishis & Pauraniks were expert Geologists, that the country was once under a continuous sheet of laterite . . .').[83] It is not clear what led to his extraordinary animus against Visvesvaraya just a few years later. Possibly he had always been critical, but kept his counsel while Visvesvaraya was in power. Alternatively, he may have been disillusioned with Visvesvaraya's approach as he saw Mysore enter a financial crisis in the early 1920s. Envy may well have played a part too. Paramasiva Iyer was one of the many long-serving bureaucrats who saw Visvesvaraya, having spent the majority of his career outside Mysore, waltz in to become chief engineer, then dewan, and proceed to overturn the established way of doing things. What is more, the interloper was a philistine, an out-and-out modernizer who, unlike Iyer, had no time for traditional learning.

Some observers saw the attacks on Visvesvaraya as a bitter expression of the Madrasi-Mysorean conflict. This interpretation was offered even before the main critic's identity had been revealed (although those in the know may have had their suspicions). Whenever a son of Mysore achieved prominence, the *Mysore Chronicle* opined in 1924, he was defamed 'by a clique . . . [comprising] a few place-hunters . . . who are worse than Mir Sadaks and Umaichands'[84]—the reference being to alleged traitors in the time of Tipu Sultan and Nawab Sirajuddaulah respectively. In the context of *Mysore's* criticisms of the Krishnarajasagara project, which had long been opposed by agriculturists in the Tanjore delta,[85] a correspondent wrote to the *Guardian* that the people of Mysore had good reason to '[suspect] that after all "Mysore" may be an enemy masquerading as a friend[,] possibly a land-holder of Tanjore, whose feelings towards Sir M. V. are embittered because of personal reasons'.[86] In 1928, a Bangalore lawyer named S. Venkatapathaiya wrote an impassioned pamphlet refuting Paramasiva Iyer's arguments against the Bhadravati works. Claiming to have no personal connection with Visvesvaraya, Venkatapathaiya was nevertheless incensed by Iyer's activities. He took particular exception to the former judge's 'nauseating and nasty jargon', his 'dirty language'. He painted Iyer as a jealous outsider and countered his tenor by writing in a sarcastic and vehement tone himself.[87]

Others took a more sober line in rebutting Paramasiva Iyer's analyses. A retired public works engineer from Dharwar wrote in *The Hindu* in 1927 that Iyer, 'from the way he reviews the finances, seems to assume perfection in human estimates, which is the chief defect in his argument. It betrays an utter lack of experience in engineering a project to completion.'[88] In August 1928, the General Manager of the Bhadravati Iron Works issued point-by-point rebuttals of the allegations Iyer levelled against the Bhadravati Board.[89]

Some of these allegations were as follows. The geologist W.F. Smeeth had been against the project from the start, and his counsel had been ignored. The Forest Department was supplying wood free of cost to the iron works in a bid to mask the true cost of running it. High value timber was being used to make charcoal. Visvesvaraya's reports of the firm's financial performance did not take into account depreciation of the plant. The *malnad* was being stripped bare of its forests. Government agencies at the local level were being induced to buy cast iron pipes from Bhadravati at high rates, thus subsidizing the works at a loss to themselves.

The government showed with quotations that Smeeth had been positively disposed to the project, and that he had participated actively in it until his retirement. They asserted that the iron works was paying the Forest Department for all the wood procured; that only trees incapable of providing high quality timber were incinerated to produce charcoal; that the forest resources were utilized in a sustainable manner, as attested by an expert from the Forest Research Institute in Dehra Dun; that depreciation was very much accounted for; and that the iron pipes sold to municipalities were competitively priced and of high quality.[90]

*

The summer of 1927 found Mysore playing host to a prominent visitor: Mahatma Gandhi. He had fallen ill, and was asked to recuperate in a cool place. Gandhi spent the next few months in the Nandi Hills and in nearby Bangalore, where he stayed in a bungalow named Kumara Park, which had once been the residence of the former dewan Seshadri Iyer.[91] Paramasiva Iyer now tried to recruit him to the cause, plying him with letters about the KRS and Bhadravati projects. Possibly he was counting on Gandhi's reputation for opposing large-scale industrialization. On 29 July, Gandhi wrote a terse reply:

> What do you think can be the motive prompting him to falsehoods, etc., which you ascribe to Sir M. Vishveshvarayya? Everything I have heard about his character is entirely in his favour. Outside Karnatak he is known as a very patriotic man. Personally I am totally opposed to him in his ambition for

> Americanizing India. . . . But this fundamental difference does not blind me to his great abilities and his great services. I would require positive unchallengeable proof to dislodge him from the position he occupies in my estimation.[92]

During his time in the state, Gandhi went to see both the KRS reservoir and the Bhadravati works. Visvesvaraya was not in Bhadravati when Gandhi visited, but he deputed the general manager of the works, M. Venkatanaranappa, to take care of the honoured guest.

Gandhi and his entourage reached Bhadravati at 9.30 p.m. on 17 August. At six the next morning, he went on a walk in the industrial township, escorted by Venkatanaranappa. As they walked, Gandhi asked his host about the possible reason for Paramasiva Iyer's opposition to the industrial enterprise, and what his standing was in Mysore. 'I explained the circumstances as far as I knew,' Venkatanaranappa later reported to Visvesvaraya, 'and told him that there is hardly any following [for Iyer] except possibly a very small section of outsiders who had no real stake in the country.' Gandhi proceeded to probe discreetly, asking about the company's origins and current performance, and why Visvesvaraya had retired from the dewanship while his major projects were still in progress. He showed interest in Visvesvaraya's 'improvement scheme' for the *malnad*.

Later that morning, Gandhi addressed a crowd of a thousand. The people made contributions worth Rs 500, which was given to Gandhi in a casket of charcoal iron produced in the foundry at Bhadravati. Speaking in Hindi (with a Kannada interpreter by his side), he stated that contrary to his image, he thought factories like theirs were a national good, and noted the role of this one in providing employment to thousands. At the same time, he urged the employees present to spin and to buy khaddar so as to support the impoverished weavers who produced it; and to stay away from liquor and gambling.[93] The speaker was then taken on a guided tour of the various sections of the factory. In the evening, he spent close to an hour discussing further aspects of Visvesvaraya's work with Venkatanaranappa before heading for Chickmagalur, the next stop in his itinerary.[94]

Ten days later, Gandhi addressed a gathering in Bangalore in what was possibly his last public appearance before leaving the state. He paid tribute to the Mysore government's many initiatives. 'I saw with wonder and admiration Krishnarajasagar and the Bhadravati Iron Works,' he said, 'the two great monuments of Sir M. Vishveshvarayya's zeal and skill. . . . These great undertakings have an undoubted place in your march towards economic progress.' Gandhi did caution, however, that the state's 'progress . . . seems to me to be confined to the middle class and not to take enough note of the peasantry', and advocated the propagation of hand-spinning.[95]

*

In Gandhi's pronouncements—couched as they were in caveats—Visvesvaraya had found public support from an unexpected quarter. But the stark fact remained that the iron works were in straitened circumstances, and some action had to be taken to pull it out of the red.

Visvesvaraya responded to the situation in his usual way. Shutting down operations was never an option for him, both because it would be a personal defeat and because it would go against the logic of progress and modernization that defined his vision for Mysore.[96] Instead, he suggested making further investments to allow the firm to pivot to more profitable markets. In 1927, he put forward a series of ten proposed upgrades to the factory that would collectively cost Rs 55 lakh.[97] He wanted to *step up* the production of pig iron, thereby achieving economies of scale. The blast furnace was to be upgraded to increase its capacity to 80 tons of pig iron a day. The pipe foundry was to be extended, since they could sell cast iron pipes more easily than pig iron (the latter had to be exported, and transportation was costly). More pig iron required more charcoal, so the distillation apparatus was to be expanded too. There was a market for steel: it was time the works began to manufacture it. An open-hearth furnace—to convert pig iron to steel—and a rolling mill—to shape the steel into sheets—should be set up alongside the blast furnace so it could consume the pig iron produced, converting it to steel to the extent of 25 tons a day.[98]

Visvesvaraya did not stop at this. He wanted to use the sawmill at Bhadravati to cut timber from the neighbouring forests to commercial sizes. He also wanted to serve the market for railway sleepers by treating wood with one of the by-products of the distillation process—an oil with preservative properties. Thus, they could dispose of the 'wood preservative oil produced at Bhadravati and the inferior timber available in the forests near by' at one stroke. The state should also produce bobbins from this low-quality wood, and 'put up a paper mill to utilize bamboos which grow wild in the forests along the tramway lines'. In the future, the industrial complex at Bhadravati could produce a number of new products, including acetic acid, formaldehyde, and stainless steel. Power could be brought from the Gersoppa Falls (also known as the Jog Falls), situated around eighty miles to the west; this could also help industrialize the surrounding area. Everything he laid eyes on was grist to the mill of Visvesvaraya's industrializing vision.[99]

Some of these suggestions were quickly translated into action. In 1928–29, a 'timber creosoting plant' was set up to coat wood with preservatives, and managed by the Forest Department. The blast furnace was expanded to a capacity of 80 tons a day as Visvesvaraya had wanted, and inaugurated in September 1928. An additional pipe foundry was under construction.[100]

But the government did not want to rush into the heavier investments he had suggested, particularly the establishment of a steel plant. Even as Visvesvaraya got the works' engineers to conduct experiments in preparation for steel manufacture, the government kept him in limbo for over a year. They eventually declined to sanction the addition, reportedly leaving him frustrated. Around this time, his relationship with Dewan Mirza Ismail was also growing fractious (the tension was related to Visvesvaraya's role in investigating a riot in Bangalore the previous year, an episode discussed in Chapter 18 below). One way or another, he decided he had had enough. In September 1929, he quit as chairman of Bhadravati's Board of Management.[101]

The company's health was far from ideal when Visvesvaraya left. But he had hauled it out of the ICU. From a personal point of view, he had done enough to prove his point, that the industry could be run economically (if not very profitably). As he noted in a statement he issued as he left, the company had not faced losses for the last three years; if one ignored depreciation costs, it had even turned a profit of Rs 2 lakh in 1928–29. Raw materials were being hauled to the plant much more economically, production was steady and more cost-efficient, and '[a] local staff [had] been trained for the various positions'.[102]

*

Many of the things Visvesvaraya had dreamt of did eventually come to pass, years after he resigned. A steel plant, comprising an open-hearth furnace and a rolling mill, was finally installed in 1934. Electric supply to the steel plant was established the following year (not from the Gersoppa Falls, but from the existing generating plant at Sivasamudram). By 1940, the settlement at

Bhadravati had matured into a well-organized township with 'up-to-date sanitary arrangements, . . . free hospitals, schools and club houses'.[103]

But even the most sympathetic analysts could not deny the fact that the works never became a business success. Iron and steel prices never picked up: they were hit once more in the 1930s by the effects of the Great Depression. An important market disappeared in 1933, when Japan, under pressure from its own iron manufacturers, banned the import of pig iron from India. New technology had enabled competitors to produce coke-fuelled iron of improved quality, which meant that Bhadravati's charcoal iron (which had been expected to command higher prices owing to its superior quality) did not find the aimed-for niche in the market. The by-products of wood distillation were no longer in demand abroad, as less expensive synthetic substitutes took off in Europe in the 1930s. This meant the wood distillation shop had to be run at one-fourth of its rated capacity, and the company resorted to producing charcoal by incinerating wood in kilns set up in the forests themselves. In fact, by the late 1930s, the collapsing markets meant that 'all sections of the plant [were] being operated on a restricted scale'.[104]

Some of these challenges, such as the effects of the Great Depression or Japan's import ban, could not have been foreseen. But Perin, Visvesvaraya, and company should arguably have accounted for likely technological developments abroad which would render their products obsolete. They knew that Mysore was cut off from major markets and did not have easy access to a seaport, which would make exports less viable.[105]

What is more, Visvesvaraya's aggressive response to crises meant that the government threw good money after bad, tying itself into further knots with each expansion. Even as the losses mounted, they were investing large amounts of capital in electrification and steel manufacture. Here again, Visvesvaraya knew well that steel prices were likely to go down in the 1930s, but convinced the government to plough on regardless.[106] It was not until the 1940s that the Bhadravati works reportedly turned the corner, and then largely because of the windfall that came with increased demand from the colonial government during the Second World War.[107]

*

Once more, Visvesvaraya had ended a six-year stint on a contentious note. In many ways, his official association with Mysore in the 1920s was suffused by the reverberations from his dewan years a decade earlier. If anything, his critics had grown more vocal. And not entirely without reason. No doubt Paramasiva Iyer frequently went over the top with his criticisms. He suffered from the very fault he was tasking Visvesvaraya with: imagining himself to be a polymathic expert in fields as wide as business, finance, structural engineering, geology, and chemistry. But despite these excesses, critics like Iyer performed an important function. They demonstrated the need for greater public scrutiny of expensive undertakings that used public money. They pressured Visvesvaraya and the government to be more transparent. And although their criticisms usually rested on the financial implications of these large development schemes, they may have opened up a space for the questioning of Visvesvaraya's totalizing vision: one that set about remaking Mysore's geography and environment as well as its society.

In an insightful reading, cultural historian Chandan Gowda has argued that it was a vision that prioritized the attainment of 'civilisational recognition on the global stage' over everything else. Visvesvaraya and his fellow travellers believed that all nations aiming to be developed must pass through a standard series of stages, just as the industrialized nations of the West had done, and that Mysore was as yet in one of the earliest stages. Their efforts were guided towards an imagined *telos*, a Mysore that would be accepted by the world as modern and civilized. For this, no price was too high to pay.[108]

17

Reclaiming the Metropolis

Even as he managed the fortunes of the iron works in Bhadravati through monthly visits, Visvesvaraya was becoming a fixture in Bombay circles. Not only was he a veteran of the presidency's Public Works Department, he was now an ex-dewan, a Knight Commander of the Indian Empire, and a bonafide celebrity. Ensconced in his sea-facing cottage on Warden Road, he was situated within hailing distance of top colonial officials, leading nationalist politicians, and the city's textile magnates. Soon he was being called upon by various authorities to tender advice on sundry matters. When, in 1921–22, he chaired a committee on technical education, it had been at the behest of the provincial government.[1] His next assignment came from the Bombay Municipal Corporation, which engaged him to help streamline its activities during an economic downturn in 1924. In 1926, it was the Government of India that called on him, asking him to help investigate a controversial engineering project that promised to alter dramatically the landscape of South Bombay. These engagements allowed Visvesvaraya once more to ponder questions of urban development, a subject he had first grappled with in his work for the city of Hyderabad more than fifteen years previously.[2]

*

Immediately after the First World War, real estate prices in Bombay had gone through the roof. Flush with funds, the municipal corporation had begun ambitious and expensive projects. When a recession subsequently hit in 1922–23, they found themselves strapped for cash, with large commitments on their hands. They established a Retrenchment Committee to address the situation. Since a lot of the corporation's work was engineering-related, the committee, in turn, asked Visvesvaraya for advice.[3]

In June 1924, Visvesvaraya, having undertaken some initial research, provided the committee with a 'programme of retrenchment and reform', which the corporation subsequently endorsed. He then worked with them over a period of six months before tabling a report in early 1925, by which time many of the reforms had been implemented, slashing costs by about Rs 11 lakh.[4] In addition to the reduction of posts deemed redundant,[5] the suggested reforms included better accounting practices, more stringent auditing, and organizational changes within the corporation to help decentralize responsibilities.[6] Efficiency was not a goal to be sought only in times of financial distress, Visvesvaraya believed; it should be an ongoing effort. For this purpose, a Municipal Research Bureau should be established, which, among other duties, would keep track of how 'progressive foreign city administrations like those of Birmingham, Glasgow, Toronto and Tokyo' were being run.[7]

Characteristically, Visvesvaraya did not content himself with discussing measures of economy. Instead, he expanded the scope of his report to spell out his vision for the future of Bombay city. The corporation should do more, he said, to promote industries. Free and compulsory education was to be arranged at the lower levels.

There must be playgrounds in every locality. The city should be organized into zones for various purposes (industrial, commercial, residential, leisure). More housing should be provided; suburbs should be developed and connected effectively to the city.[8]

The press reported appreciatively on Visvesvaraya's efforts, running summaries of his report as well as extracts from it.[9] There were some caveats. A writer in the *Times of India* remarked that it was one thing to point out what needed to be done, but the real challenge was to implement reforms in the face of 'conflicting tastes on the part of a heterogeneous community . . . and all manner of racial and religious prejudices as well as vested rights'.[10] *The Hindu*, while complimenting Visvesvaraya on his 'valuable suggestions', observed that 'there is a danger in over-estimating the value of Western experience and importing Western methods *en masse* for solving all our civil problems, some of which are uniquely indigenous in their nature and origin'.[11]

These comments notwithstanding, the municipality appears to have found Visvesvaraya's work—at any rate the cost cutting and streamlining measures he initiated—useful. In quick succession, he received offers to take on similar assignments with the municipalities of Karachi and Madras.[12] By the mid-1920s, Visvesvaraya was being seen as an authority on urban development.

*

While Visvesvaraya was giving his attention to the future of Bombay city as a whole, an urban engineering project of spectacular dimensions was being carried out a few kilometres down the coast from his home on Warden Road. Known as the Back Bay Reclamation scheme, the aim of the project—sanctioned in 1920—was to claw back more than a thousand acres of land from the waters of the Back Bay, the stretch of the Arabian Sea that flanked the west coast of Bombay between Marine Lines and Colaba. (The docks that formed Bombay's harbour were on the eastern side of the island, sheltered from the open sea). A dredger roamed the waters of Bombay Harbour, sucking up clay from the seabed before it was pumped through pipes to the other side of the island and emptied into the Back Bay. A retaining wall was being built in the bay to hold in place the filling material.[13]

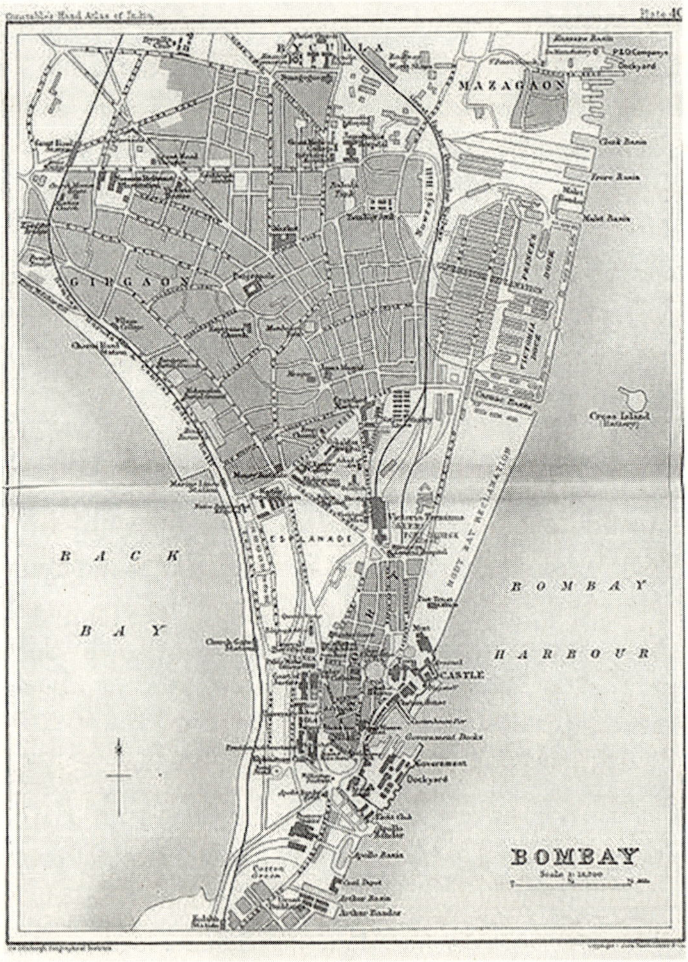

Fig. 17.1. The southern part of Bombay showing Back Bay and the harbour, c. 1893

Source: https://upload.wikimedia.org/wikipedia/commons/9/93/Bombay_City_map_%281893%29.jpg, accessed 1 July 2024.

Bombay had a long history of land reclamation projects. Indeed, the metropolis had come into being through a series of reclamations since the sixteenth century, as Portuguese and British settlers colonized the stretches of sea and the marshes that separated what was originally a cluster of small islands. The Back Bay project itself had been long in the making. After an abortive attempt by a private company in the 1860s, it was seriously considered once more in 1905 by the Bombay government's Public Works Department.[14]

Two factors now pushed the project centre stage. These were overcrowding and a susceptibility to epidemics, both related to the rapid growth of the textile industry and the massive influx of industrial labourers into the city. The 1911 Census revealed that 80 per cent of the city's population was housed in single-room lodgings, often packed several to a room. Slums proliferated, and frequent outbreaks of cholera and malaria were accompanied by the ever-present danger of plague, which had devastated the city in the 1890s. All this was in close proximity to the commercial heart of the city, which suffered from clogged roads.[15] The Bombay government hoped that the Back Bay project, by adding a large amount of land to this part of the city, would allow the building of new offices and homes for the elite, ease the traffic situation, and open up more space in the interior to house industrial labour.[16]

In 1911–12, the Bombay government obtained permission from the Government of India to ask a private engineering firm, Lowther and Kidd, to examine the location and draw up a report. The firm obliged, carrying out over 1,314 borings on the harbour side to assess the clay available on the seabed (they had determined that the ocean floor on the Back Bay side was not amenable to dredging). They concluded that 1,145 acres of land could be reclaimed in the Back Bay at a cost of around Rs 325 lakh by depositing clay retrieved from the harbour. A committee of local notables, headed by Visvesvaraya's friend Vithaldas Thackersey, endorsed the idea of reclamation in 1913. But the Government of India hesitated to sanction the scheme, and it went into limbo during the First World War.

In 1918, a high-powered group of Bombay businessmen (Vithaldas Thackersey once again among them) teamed up with the firm of Tata and Sons and approached the Bombay government, offering to carry out the reclamation on a commercial basis. The government, encouraged by this interest, preferred instead to execute the project themselves. In the midst of a bullish real estate market, they anticipated huge windfalls from the sale of land, which they could then use for various public purposes.[17]

In December 1918, the Bombay Presidency got a new British governor, Sir George Lloyd. Before leaving London, Lloyd had done some reading at the India Office, and was convinced that housing and public health were Bombay's biggest concerns. His concern was shared by the Secretary of State for India, Edwin Montagu, who virtually commanded him to get on with reclamation in the Back Bay. Lloyd's resolve to act swiftly was further strengthened when, soon after his arrival in Bombay, he visited the slums, noting the squalor and the terrible lack of sanitation.[18]

Lloyd was a supremely confident man, imbued with a strong belief in the white man's burden.[19] He made it his mission to kickstart the Back Bay project as quickly as possible. In April 1919, he asked the Government of India to nominate an engineer to examine and update Lowther and Kidd's 1912 proposals, but urged that the engineer chosen should reach India by the third week of May. When—unsurprisingly—this did not prove possible, Lloyd took matters into his own hands and hired Sir George Buchanan, a consulting engineer who had earlier directed river training works in Burma and helped renovate the port of Basra in Mesopotamia.[20]

THE TIMES, WEDNESDAY, MAY 24, 1911.

A CITY WON FROM THE SEA: THE GREAT RECLAMATION SCHEME AT BOMBAY.

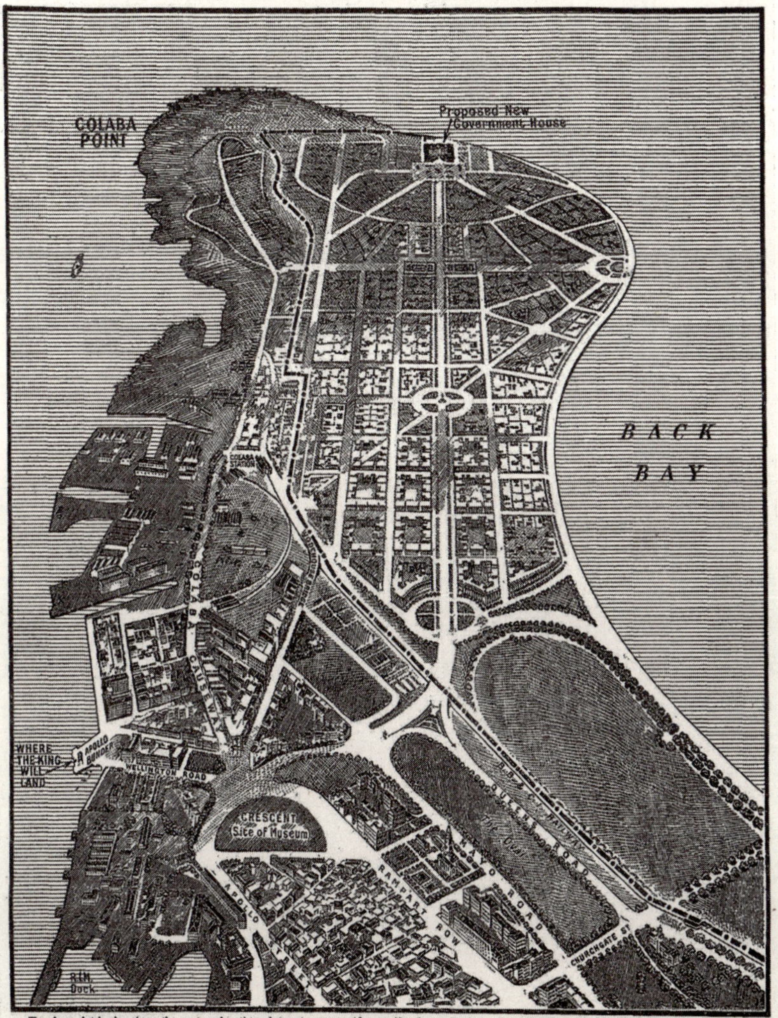

The above sketch plan shows the great reclamation scheme at present under consideration at Bombay. The Bombay Government propose to reclaim from the sea the area shown on the right hand side of the line of dots and dashes. The total area thus created will be 973 acres, the scheme is expected to pay for itself in 60 years, and the Government will then enter into possession of a vast new estate free of cost. A small portion of the scheme, near Wodehouse Bridge, is already complete. The land is rocky and is only submerged at high water.

Fig. 17.2. An artist's conception of the Back Bay Reclamation as of 1911. Bombay harbour is on the left, and the area to the right of the dotted line is the part to be reclaimed from the sea. The view is roughly from north to south

Source: https://upload.wikimedia.org/wikipedia/commons/a/a2/Bombay Reclamation_1911.jpg, accessed 1 July 2024.

Buchanan spent some time on site before proceeding to London in June, where he partnered an established engineering firm to form a new company named Meik & Buchanan. He also met an official from Simon & Co., a Scottish firm that could construct a dredger for use in the Bombay Harbour. Returning to Bombay in November 1919, Buchanan submitted his report on Lowther and Kidd's earlier scheme.[21] In it he estimated that the dredger would need to excavate 25 million cubic yards of material, and that this could be done in five years. The Government of India endorsed Buchanan's report in April 1920, and in May, the secretary of state green-lighted the project. George Lloyd then got it approved in the Bombay Legislative Council, while Buchanan's firm was asked to direct the reclamation.[22]

Lloyd took a crucial decision at this stage. Convinced that Indian landlords were opposed to the freeing up of more land for housing as it would bring down rents, he resolved to bypass the Bombay Municipal Corporation, on which the Indians' interests were represented, by creating a new agency, the Bombay Development Directorate. Along with other urban development projects, he entrusted the reclamation project to the BDD.[23] This meant that while Meik & Buchanan advised on the dredging and filling, it would be carried out by engineers in the employ of the BDD.[24]

*

The project began in 1921 with the hauling of rock from a quarry in uptown Kandivli for use in the building of the sea wall. Journalists reported excitedly as work on the enormous wall of rubble and concrete progressed simultaneously from the northern and southern ends. The government launched a publicity campaign advertising the engineering wonders that were making the project possible, and describing in heady terms the future uses of the reclaimed land.[25]

But there were problems and delays from the start. Buchanan's initial estimate of the project's cost had been Rs 367 lakh, a figure that seemed to ignore the enormous increase in the price of equipment and labour since Lowther and Kidd had produced their estimate of Rs 325 lakh. Now, just a year after the project had begun, Buchanan's firm raised their estimate dramatically, to Rs 669 lakh.[26] The dredger—named the 'Sir George Lloyd' in typically sycophantic fashion—and a booster named the 'Colaba' (which would help pump the extracted clay through pipelines) arrived in Bombay in the first half of 1922. But the building of the sea wall had not progressed enough to create an enclosed area in the bay. As a consequence, dredging began only in December 1923—coinciding almost exactly with the end of Lloyd's tenure as governor.[27] The coup de grace came in 1924, when it emerged that the dredger equipment was working at just over half the expected rate. Moreover, the sea wall turned out to be permeable, allowing large quantities of the material dunked in the Bay to be washed away. The prospects of this mind-bogglingly expensive scheme now looked bleak.[28]

Loud public criticism erupted. The most energetic critic was Khurshed F. Nariman, a local lawyer who became a member of the Bombay Legislative Council in 1922. When Nariman insisted on a probe into the reclamation project in 1924, a toothless 'advisory committee' was constituted to look into the Bombay Development Directorate's work and suggest ways forward. Even this defanged committee created a furore. One of its members, the businessman Manu Subedar, produced a ferociously critical individual note, while a subsection of the committee computed that at the current rate of progress the project would take another twenty years to complete, by which time the expense would have reached Rs 1,100 lakh. In December 1925, shortly before these results were made public, the Bombay government decided to bin their contract with Buchanan's firm.

Meanwhile K.F. Nariman launched a blizzard of attacks in the *Bombay Chronicle*, an anti-establishment newspaper run by B.G. Horniman, a fierce critic of colonial rule. He lambasted the BDD and its handling of the reclamation. He made eye-popping allegations of incompetence and graft in high places, delivering impassioned speeches in the Legislative Council and at gatherings of the public.[29] Soon, the phrases 'Back Bay Bungle' and 'Lloyd's Folly' had become the staples of newspaper headlines.[30]

The Bombay government belatedly moved to allay the public's concerns. They set up local committees to look into the engineering aspects of the reclamation and whether it made business sense to proceed with some sections of the project. For good measure, they also asked the Government of India to step in.[31]

*

In July 1926, the Government of India established an enquiry committee with wide powers to investigate how the reclamation project had been handled so far, and to suggest future steps. As chairman of the committee they appointed Sir Grimwood Mears, Chief Justice of the Allahabad High Court. Two engineers formed the core of the committee. Visvesvaraya was the first. The other was Sir Frederick Hopkinson, director in a London-based engineering firm, who had recently built a dam and irrigation works in Sudan. S.B. Billimoria, a prominent Bombay auditor, was the fourth member, while an ICS officer, R.B. Ewbank, acted as secretary. When Mears was laid up with malaria for a few weeks in August and September, it was Visvesvaraya who deputized for him as chairman.[32]

Visvesvaraya was almost an inevitable choice for the Back Bay enquiry committee. He was fresh from his study of the working of the Bombay municipality, in the course of which he had identified the issues of housing and overcrowding as key to the future of the city. But his acquaintance with these problems stretched back further, to his time as sanitary engineer to the Bombay government in the first decade of the twentieth century. Further, as a civil engineer with experience of large projects, he was well suited to examine the reclamation scheme. His status as a former Dewan of Mysore added weight to his opinions.

But there was also a delicious irony in the situation. In Mysore, Visvesvaraya was just then working overtime to prove that the Bhadravati iron works and the Krishnarajasagara irrigation project were more than ill-considered, unproductive extravagances. Now, in Bombay, Visvesvaraya found himself on the other side of the table, investigating a grand project that was not quite going to plan.[33] In fact, the Back Bay Reclamation was just the sort of project that would have caught his fancy. It was a technological solution to a social problem. It promised to generate huge revenues for the state, which could be re-invested in public projects. His respected friend Vithaldas Thackersey, since deceased, had seen merit in the scheme some years previously. Very likely the two men discussed it at the time. Visvesvaraya, then, was almost certainly sympathetic to the aims of the project. His job now was to assess why its execution had gone awry.

*

The committee began work in Bombay, where they examined the wall in the Back Bay, visited the quarry in Kandivli, and inspected the dredger and booster. Then they sat down to their chief task.

Between August and November 1926, they spoke to thirty-eight witnesses in Bombay and nineteen in London, submitting their final report in December.[34] The witnesses included government officials, public works engineers, consulting engineers, vendors of machinery, corporators, legislators—virtually everyone who had been concerned with the project, whether as initiator, participant, supplier, critic, or staunch opponent.

Among those interviewed in Bombay were dredging masters working aboard the 'Sir George Lloyd', the project's chief critic K.F. Nariman, and the unfortunately named Sir Lawless Hepper, the Director of the BDD. In London the committee was able to examine not only George Buchanan, but also George Lloyd—now Lord Lloyd, serving as British High Commissioner in Egypt—and other colonial officials who had returned to Britain upon retirement. They also interviewed Llewellyn Lewis, who had served as chief engineer on the reclamation works, reporting to the BDD, until July 1924.[35]

In both India and England, the committee's sessions were organized in grand surroundings. The Bombay sessions were held in the library of the Secretariat, an imposing Venetian Gothic edifice. In London, the committee began holding their sessions at Richmond Terrace in Whitehall, before moving half a mile down the Victoria Embankment to a committee room of the House of Lords. Wherever they were held, the hearings attracted a great deal of attention. They were attended by sections of the public, prominent figures in the world of Anglo-Indian officialdom, and newspaper correspondents who filed vivid reports.[36] And there was plenty to report on. The proceedings were often intense. Witnesses, having submitted written statements and documents beforehand, were grilled for hours, in some cases for days.[37]

Visvesvaraya was generally courteous yet persistent in his examination of the witnesses. He played the devil's advocate.

When interviewing key participants in the project, he challenged them with criticisms made by other stakeholders.[38] When interviewing opponents of the scheme, he asked them if they would consider alternative interpretations that were more forgiving of the protagonists.[39] It was delicate work for the entire committee, but particularly so for the Indian members, Visvesvaraya and Billimoria, who had to question many individuals who were higher in the racialized pecking order of colonial society. At various points, Visvesvaraya found himself examining W.L. Cameron, who had been his last boss (and a kind one at that) in the Bombay PWD, and Sir Sydney Crookshank, who had been PWD Secretary to the Government of India some years later. Most challenging, perhaps, was the task of questioning George Lloyd.[40]

Lord Lloyd (as he was now styled), though much younger to Visvesvaraya, had an imposing presence. Usually sporting a 'clipped moustache, brilliantined black hair, and faultless attire', he was to the manor born, an Eton man and a Cambridge Blue.[41] He spoke with the moral certitude of one who belonged to a ruling race. But Visvesvaraya did not shirk from asking him difficult questions. He pressed the former governor on why he had not consulted other engineers for technical advice before settling on George Buchanan; why other authorities with rights over the harbour, such as the Royal Indian Marine (the predecessor of the Indian Navy), had not been spoken to; whether Lloyd's government had not rushed the project and pressured the Government of India to sanction it swiftly. Lloyd replied airily: 'Anybody who commits a crime against inaction in the East commits a grave crime . . . I have committed that crime, I am afraid, by trying to get something done; I am not ashamed of it; I am very proud of it.' As for the absence of records of his government having taken competent advice, he declared: 'Everything is not on record in any Government where you are very driven.'[42]

Visvesvaraya also asked why the revised project estimate of 1922 had not been placed before the Bombay Legislative Council; whether Lloyd had not relied too heavily on George Buchanan; whether due process was followed in choosing a vendor for the dredger. Lloyd did not, on the whole, evade questions, but countered them with a mixture of plain-talking and bluster. When Visvesvaraya said the BDD should have worked with the PWD, Lloyd teased him for being too fond of his former department. ('I left the Department eighteen years ago,' came the deadpan reply.) When he complained that certain questions were premised on assumptions he could not verify, Visvesvaraya offered to show him the relevant documents. When Lloyd refused to address what he considered rumours, Visvesvaraya simply replied that it would be in his best interests to clarify matters anyway.[43]

*

The Government of India did well by its committee members. They were assisted by a large team of assistants and remunerated for their efforts. Visvesvaraya was paid Rs 1,500 per month while in India and £100 per month in Britain, in addition to allowances.[44] In London, he stayed at the Hotel Cecil, which overlooked the Thames on one side and the Strand on the other.[45] In the midst of his work on the committee, he found time for plenty of other meetings. He located a potential buyer for the methanol produced as a by-product at Bhadravati. He had informal meetings with Lord Birkenhead, the Secretary of State for India, to discuss the possibility of a reduction in the subsidy that Mysore paid the Government of India annually. (This he did on behalf of his friend Mirza Ismail, who had recently taken over as dewan, although the latter seems to have had second thoughts about using Visvesvaraya as an

A late nineteenth-century view of the College of Science, Poona, where Visvesvaraya studied civil engineering

Source: Courtesy of T. Derek V. Cooke

M.G. Ranade, Visvesvaraya's intellectual mentor during his Poona days

Source: G.A. Mankar, *A Sketch of the Life and Works of the Late Mr. Justice M.G. Ranade*, vol. 1 (Bombay: Caxton Printing Works, 1902).

G.K. Gokhale, Visvesvaraya's close associate during his Poona days

Source: https://commons.wikimedia.org/wiki/File:The_honourable_professor_G_K_Gokhale.jpg

Krishnaraja Wadiyar IV, soon after he became Maharaja of Mysore

Source: https://commons.wikimedia.org/wiki/File:Nalvadi_Krishnaraja_Wodeyar_c1903.jpg

A postcard showing the Public Offices (secretariat), Bangalore, workplace of key government officials of princely Mysore

Source: https://commons.wikimedia.org/wiki/File:Mysore_Government_Offices,_Cubbon_Park,_Bangalore.jpg

The author near the Sandalwood Oil Factory, established in Mysore during Visvesvaraya's dewanship

Source: Courtesy of Akshaya Vijayalakshmi

Portrait of Visvesvaraya, 1924

Source: Proceedings of the Seventh Indian Economic Conference, Bombay (Bombay: H.L. Kaji, 1924).

Visvesvaraya as president of the Indian Economic Conference, Bombay, 1924 (front row, eighth from the right)

Source: Proceedings of the Seventh Indian Economic Conference, Bombay (Bombay: H.L. Kaji, 1924).

Economist V.G. Kale, who was favourably impressed by Visvesvaraya's *Reconstructing India*

Source: Souvenir of the Silver Jubilee Session of the Indian Economic Conference … 31st December, 1941 (via dspace.gipe.ac.in)

Industrialist Walchand Hirachand, with whom Visvesvaraya worked closely in the 1930s

Source: https://commons.wikimedia.org/wiki/File:Mr._Walchand_Hirachand.jpg

Visvesvaraya being awarded the Bharat Ratna, 1955. On the right is President Rajendra Prasad

Source: https://commons.wikimedia.org/wiki/File:Sir_M._Visveswarayya_receiving_the_Bharat_Ratna_award_from_President_Dr._Prasad.jpg

Visvesvaraya as 'annadaata' (provider of food), bust adjoining Ganapati temple, Mandya District

Source: Author's photograph

Fresco depicting Visvesvaraya, flyover outside the College of Engineering, Pune (formerly College of Science, Poona; Visvesvaraya's alma mater)

Source: Author's photograph

interlocutor.) He met the engineer Charles Perin, who was about to leave for India and was keen to visit Bhadravati. He bumped into the former Mysore dewan, Albion Banerji. ('He is not in a position to do me any more harm,' Visvesvaraya wrote of his one-time opponent, 'so I have asked him to lunch with me here . . .'). In October, Visvesvaraya wrote to Mirza that the committee's 'work is going on smoothly', although '[t]here may be troubles in the report stage one cannot tell'. He was itching to get to other matters, especially to do with his responsibilities at Bhadravati.[46] When the work of the committee ended, he would travel on to Europe and America in his quest to study the latest developments in the manufacture of charcoal iron.[47] For the next couple of months, though, his duty lay in the committee room.

*

Back at the House of Lords, the committee's most searching examination was reserved for George Buchanan, the figure at the centre of the controversy. Perhaps anticipating that he would be put on the spot, Buchanan came to the sessions accompanied by a lawyer.[48] Although the lawyer emphasized that his client was 'a busy man, whose time is money',[49] the examination went on for several days.[50]

Chairman Mears went into elaborate detail to establish whether Buchanan had taken into account the nature of the clay to be found in Bombay Harbour before ordering the dredgers to be used there. It emerged that Buchanan had not taken any independent borings, going instead by Lowther and Kidd's data from 1912. While that report had described the clay in the harbour as 'stiff and unctuous'—a rather poetic description that prompted much discussion—Buchanan had ordered a dredger guaranteed to work at the required speed only in 'soft clay'. The semantic gymnastics he subsequently undertook in order to justify his decision did not satisfy the committee.[51]

Following up on a related point, Visvesvaraya asked Buchanan why he didn't insist that the manufacturers of the dredger would have to test it on site in Bombay to see if it functioned at the advertised rate.

'I have never done such a thing in my life,' said Buchanan, 'and I do not know any place where it has ever been done.'

'If you did not do it in your life, ought not you to take a leaf from the lives of other people and inquire whether other engineers did it?'

'They do not do it.'

'Then people take a very serious risk in entrusting work to you.'[52]

This was only one exchange from Visvesvaraya's long and sustained examination of Buchanan, whom he questioned on a wide range of seeming irregularities. Why had Buchanan not considered dry filling (pouring *moorum*, or pulverized rock, into the bay) as an alternative method before recommending suction dredging? Dry filling, Visvesvaraya contended, may well have proved cheaper than the dredging project in its final form. Why had Buchanan said nothing about the poor output of the 'Sir George Lloyd'? Why had he taken a hands-off attitude, travelling around the world and leaving the works in the hands of Lewis, the BDD's engineer, and not producing the kinds of detailed plans he should have as technical adviser? Why had he not called formally for competitive tenders before deciding on the firm that would sell the dredger? Why had he not done anything when it was brought to his notice that the sea wall was leaking mud?[53]

In his defence, Buchanan claimed that Lewis, the BDD's Chief Engineer in charge of the reclamation project, had shut him out; that since he didn't have control over Lewis and the other staff, he (Buchanan) could not be held responsible for the execution of the project; that the main reason for the dredger's poor output was that the crew were not paid bonuses and therefore didn't give it their all.[54] Buchanan adopted a defiant attitude, often declining to discuss certain details. Typical of his responses was the answer he gave when Visvesvaraya asked if his firm's method of calling for tenders for the sea wall did not deviate from standard practice: 'I will not say anything about it. We thought that was the best way to do the work.'[55] Visvesvaraya, however, was persistent in the face of this stonewalling, and skilful in his cross-examination. At one point an exasperated Buchanan said, turning to Grimwood Mears: 'There again I cannot answer these questions, Mr. Chairman. I am very sorry; possibly I am very stupid.'[56]

*

The final session concluded on 15 November. Over the next two weeks, the committee members drafted a unanimous report over a hundred pages long, to go with several hundred pages' worth of transcripts of the testimony of the fifty-seven witnesses.[57]

The report concluded that there had been errors of omission on the part of several actors. While Governor George Lloyd could not be faulted for relying on the advice of his chosen expert, Buchanan, he ought to have noticed that Buchanan's 1919 estimate of costs was extremely low. He had also failed to spot that Buchanan, in his report, had 'described the clay as hard, whilst Messrs. Simons & Co. [the suppliers of machinery] were putting forward an offer for a soft clay dredger'. Lloyd's explanation that this was a technical point and hence beyond his purview was not accepted.[58] The crucial point about the clay had also been missed by officials of the

Bombay government and the Government of India, neither of whom examined the Lowther/Kidd and Buchanan reports 'with due and proper care'.[59]

The committee also held that the Bombay government had confused matters by not making it clear who was responsible for the actual results. Assuming they thought Meik and Buchanan should be in charge of the actual 'execution of the works, nothing was easier than to say so in plain and simple words, and as a necessary corollary to put the Resident Engineer [Lewis] entirely under the control of [that] firm'. The confusion had resulted in a situation where the BDD and Buchanan's firm pointed fingers at each other, neither willing to take ultimate responsibility.[60] Lawless Hepper, the Director of the BDD, had not been transparent with the public regarding the (lack of) results after the dredging had begun. His 'reports . . . did not present a true picture of the progress of the work and concealed material circumstances'.[61]

As for George Buchanan, he had spent too little time surveying the conditions in Bombay before drafting his report in 1919. He was careless in specifying the kind of dredger he wanted from Simons & Co., and did not obtain a written guarantee from them that it would work at the rate the project required. The primary reason for the dredger's unsatisfactory output was that it was built to work in soft clay. *Contra* Buchanan, it was not down to the operators: 'no crew, however skilful and diligent, ever can or will get anything like five million cubic yards of material from the Harbour in any one season [the calculated requirement for the project] by the agency of the "Sir George Lloyd".' Buchanan also misinterpreted his position in the project. He did not take the trouble to inform the Bombay government when he disagreed with the BDD's handling of the project, conveniently assuming that they were in charge. His firm was passive; they 'did not prepare proper programmes of work nor adhere to any fixed programme'.[62]

As for the utility of the project itself, the committee disagreed with the claim 'that the Reclamation of Back Bay would, by providing more land in the business and residential area, in some way relieve housing conditions of the poorer classes'—a veiled reference to George Lloyd's roundabout logic. But they were sympathetic to the idea that the project, if it had proved as profitable as initially hoped, would have allowed the government to fund other public works.[63] (The latter was somewhat analogous to Visvesvaraya's ideas on productive irrigation: the idea that focusing on commercially valuable crops would allow a local government to avert famine in a drought year by generating profits that could be used to buy food from outside.)[64] Therefore they advised the government to continue with the reclamation, albeit on a reduced scale for the time being. They should first finish reclaiming land in the blocks marked 1, 2, 7, and 8 (at the two ends, as shown in Figure 17.3), through a mixture of dry filling and dredging. A 300-foot-wide band was to be filled along blocks 3, 4, 5, and 6, in a way that would connect blocks 2 and 7. This 'strip of 300 feet', they wrote, 'will afford facilities for a marine drive which would run from Marine Lines to Colaba; together with footpaths, roads, parks, playing fields and recreation grounds'. The work should be taken out of the purview of the BDD, and executed by a contractor. The contractor would be supervised by an engineer reporting directly to the Bombay government (Visvesvaraya's individual view was that the contractor should be overseen by the Public Works Department).[65]

As it happened, the government followed the committee's advice in reclaiming blocks 1, 2, and 8 over the following decade. Also constructed during this time was a spectacular

Marine Drive, though it ran not along the rim of Blocks 3-6, but towards the north from Block 1, hemming the curved coastline from the vicinity of Churchgate station to Malabar Hill (see Figure 17.4). It was only in the 1960s and '70s that land was eventually reclaimed in the remaining blocks.[66]

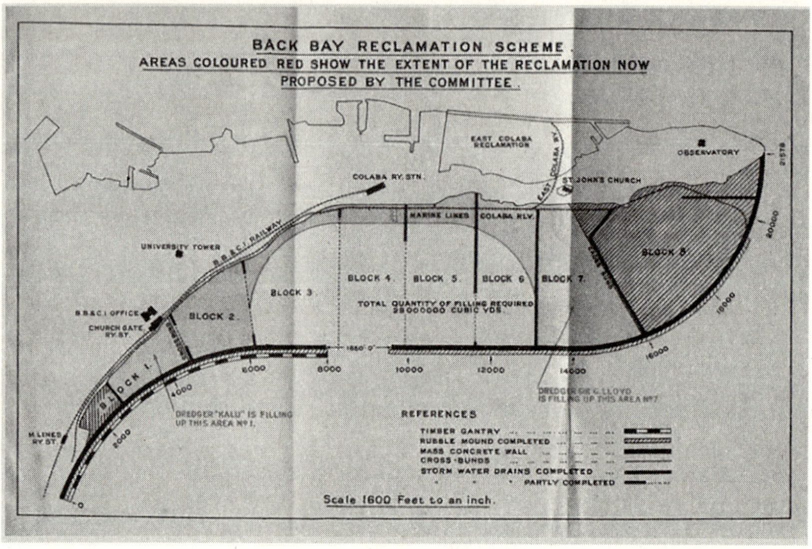

Fig. 17.3. The eight blocks of land to be reclaimed, as envisaged in the reclamation scheme begun in the 1920s. The top of this map represents the east

Source: *Report of the Committee appointed by the Government of India to enquire into the Bombay Back Bay Reclamation Scheme 1926* (Bombay: Government Central Press, 1927), front matter. Accessed via archive.org.

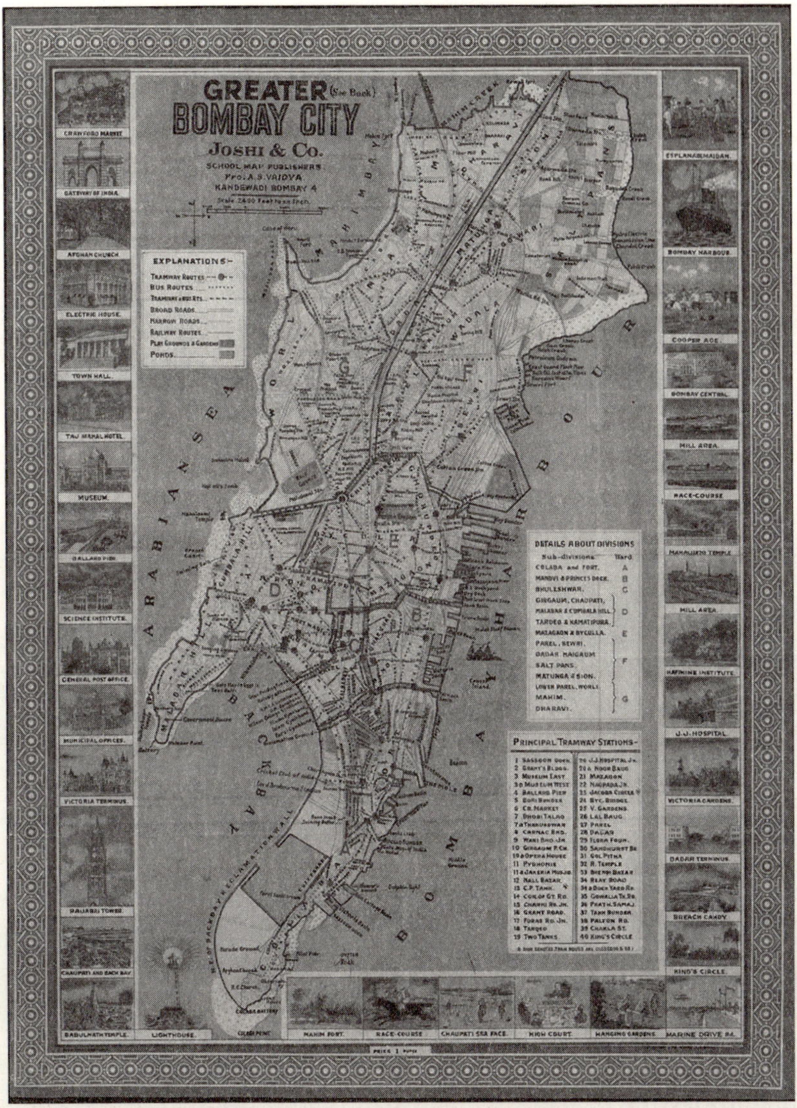

Fig. 17.4. Map of South Bombay showing the Back Bay Reclamation and the coastline north of it where Marine Drive was built

Source: Section of a map by Joshi & Co. [1940], via https://www.geographicus.com/P/AntiqueMap/bombay-joshi-1940-2, accessed 1 July 2024.

*

All in all, the Back Bay Enquiry Committee of 1926 had done an excellent job of unravelling the tangled strands of the story. They had produced, from the masses of evidence collected, a lucid reconstruction of the sequence of events, along with an analysis of what had gone wrong. Even as a government-appointed body, they had not omitted to call out the provincial and central governments for mistakes made. In England, the report was greeted with approval by *The Times*, the *Financial Times*, and the *Birmingham Gazette*. The last of these made the perceptive comment that the report had exposed how decision-makers were in thrall to experts and their claims to specialist knowledge, whereas experts were not infallible.[67]

However, it is undeniable that in their conclusions, the committee toned down their criticisms of top government officials. Having mentioned the points that George Lloyd missed, they nevertheless declared that he had 'acted throughout with the highest motives, anxious only to make good his undertaking to Mr Montagu and to benefit the City of Bombay'.[68] Having castigated the BDD Director, Lawless Hepper, for misleading the public, they added the caveat that he was overworked: the BDD had several other projects, and Hepper 'could only have carried out [his] duty as regards the Reclamation by neglecting other duties related to the other schemes'.[69] Nariman's general allegations notwithstanding, they concluded that there was no evidence of corruption on the part of any government officials.[70]

This soft-pedalling earned the ire of the project's opponents in Bombay. H.P. Mody, Chairman of the Bombay Millowners' Association, called the report 'wishy-washy . . . All that the Committee have done is to make a scape goat of Sir George Buchanan and to let down gently, very gently, everyone else connected with the project'. Mody, who had given evidence before the committee, complained that when Visvesvaraya was examining him on a particular point, Frederick Hopkinson had tried to cut short the discussion on the grounds that it was not germane to the committee's enquiry.[71] Hopkinson had also been hostile to Nariman when the latter was giving evidence.[72]

Whether Hopkinson had played a part in the leniency of the report's comments on government officials, and what Visvesvaraya's views were on the point, it is impossible to say, since the members took joint responsibility for the report. But anyone who cared to read the entirety of the report or the published proceedings of the inquiry would have been left in no doubt that the whole affair was a fiasco on all sides. The point was driven home more emphatically by an event that began just days after the committee's report was released. This was a court case for defamation brought by a BDD official against Nariman. After dramatic proceedings that were once again followed avidly by the press, Nariman was acquitted amidst great public rejoicing. As historian Gyan Prakash has observed, what Nariman had achieved was 'to place colonialism on trial. According to him [i.e. Nariman], the underlying cause of graft and incompetence was the arbitrary exercise of British power. The real scandal, the muckraker charged, was colonialism'.[73]

It was a point that Visvesvaraya may have been loath to make in such bald terms, but it would certainly have rung true at some level. In later years, he was to become increasingly outspoken in his critique of the colonial government.

18

Constitutional Adventures

1927 was a good year for Mysore and its ruling elite. Mirza Ismail was settling into the role of dewan with aplomb. He was close to the maharaja, with whom he had grown up—they had been classmates in the special school set up for the Mysore royals—and, as a Muslim, had the sympathy of the non-Brahmin party, which was then in the ascendancy in Mysore. That year his relatively new administration pulled off a coup by getting the British to commute the annual subsidy payable by Mysore from Rs 35 lakh to around Rs 25 lakh.

Meanwhile, Visvesvaraya had returned to India, having completed his sojourn in London as part of the Back Bay Enquiry Committee and his subsequent tours in Europe and the United States. From his bases in Bombay and Bangalore, he continued overseeing the iron factory at Bhadravati. In Bangalore, he played elder statesman and mentor to Mirza, who was attempting to revive the former dewan's industrial policies.[1] In July of the same year, Visvesvaraya gave a widely publicized lecture under the aegis of the Mysore Chamber of Commerce titled 'Vision of a Prosperous Mysore'. It was in essence a recap of his many addresses as dewan a decade earlier, harping on the importance of industrialization and self-sufficiency. Yet it was received rapturously by the press, the *Evening Mail* declaring it a 'great speech' by a speaker who was 'patriotism-incarnate'.[2] It was around this time that Mahatma Gandhi, while recuperating from an illness in Mysore, paid glowing tributes to the state's administration and the great projects associated with Visvesvaraya.[3] To cap it all, August and September 1927 witnessed the celebration, with great pomp, of the Golden Jubilee of the reign of Krishnaraja Wadiyar IV.[4]

*

Below the surface, however, the fissures in Mysorean society were deepening. One manifestation was a communal conflict that developed over a few weeks in the middle of 1928 in the old city of Bangalore. Known locally as the *Ganapathi Galabhe* and in official circles as the Bangalore Disturbances, the affair had its origins in a seemingly innocuous circumstance: the existence of a Ganesha idol in the premises of a government-run Anglo-Vernacular school in Sultanpet, a Muslim-majority locality. Goaded by the *Veerakesari*, a majoritarian Kannada newspaper, the students demanded the construction of an alcove to house the idol. One was duly built, at which point the local authorities intervened to prevent the reinstallation of the idol within it, deeming the school a secular space.

Word spread that the decision not to reinstall the idol had the backing of Abbas Khan, the Muslim president of the Bangalore City Municipality and a prominent leader of the non-Brahmins, who happened to live near the school. The Brahmin-dominated Kannada papers insinuated that Khan, who was an acquaintance of Mirza Ismail (also a Muslim), enjoyed the dewan's support in the matter. The situation was soon politicized by a group of reactionary leaders identifying themselves with the Congress.[5] As the British Resident wrote in a confidential report to his bosses in Simla, 'local Congress leaders . . . took an active part in fomenting [a] schoolboys' strike and endeavoured to give it an anti-Mahommedan and anti-Dewan bias'.[6]

The Congress leaders in question were Ram Lal Tiwari, a sweet-shop owner with north Indian roots; H.V. Subrahmanyam, the son of former First Councillor H.V. Nanjundayya; and J. Bhima Rao, hailing from Jamkhandi, a small princely state in the Deccan. While they stoked passions in a series of public meetings held in the vicinity of Sultanpet, their supporters described them as 'satyagrahis', appropriating the Gandhian idiom at a time when the Bardoli Satyagraha was taking place in the Bombay Presidency.[7]

On 29 July, the government arrested the Congress trio. On 30 July, thousands of students thronged the Central Jail (where the leaders were held), Carlton House (the dewan's residence), and the government secretariat. The crowds, armed with tree branches and stones, grew aggressive, and the government had to engage the Mysore Lancers to control them. Amidst thundering hooves, flying stones and shattering window panes, the City Magistrate decided to release the trio of Tiwari, Bhima Rao and Subrahmanyam. Emerging from the jail after 6.30 p.m.,[8] they were brought by their rejoicing supporters to the school in Sultanpet, where preparations had been made for the consecration of the idol (it had been reinstalled the previous day).[9] As night fell, thousands of Hindus gathered in the grounds, and local Muslim residents braced themselves for conflict. It was not long before the tinderbox was lit. As the police watched indecisively, locals rushed out of the shadows with *lathis*, while the crowd flung stones. Shots were heard, allegedly from the general direction of Abbas Khan's house. Miraculously, nobody was killed, but many citizens and police officers were injured.[10] The following day, the government tasked a magistrate, rather than the police, with investigating the riot. The situation remained tense in the days and weeks that followed. Sensational rumours flew about. The nationalist press criticized the government virulently, and was temporarily muzzled.[11]

*

It was late August before the increasingly beleaguered government formally instituted an enquiry committee. Its seven members included D.K. Rama Rao, a judge of Mysore's Chief Court; B. Nagappa, the government's legal remembrancer; and members of the Legislative Council. They came from varied backgrounds: Hindu Brahmin, Hindu non-Brahmin, Muslim, and European. But the most high-profile member was Visvesvaraya, who was appointed chairman of the committee.[12] Aware that Visvesvaraya was close to Mirza Ismail, some sections of the public saw this as a move to protect the reputation of the dewan and his government. Visvesvaraya's supporters shot back that this was an insult to his impartiality and sense of duty.[13]

Between September and November, Visvesvaraya and his colleagues examined 156 witnesses, most of them in public and a few *in camera*.[14] The witnesses included police officers, government officials, and members of the public who had been on the spot.[15] The hearings were conducted in the Daly Memorial Hall. For two months, the hall, built a decade previously for the much more pleasant labours of the scholars of the Mythic Society, was transformed into a sombre theatre.[16]

The press covered the proceedings in lurid detail. The statements made by key witnesses, the admonishments and repartee of the committee members, snippets from their exchanges—all appeared in print day after day. Having begun by promising the witnesses they would not be penalized in any way for speaking out, Visvesvaraya proceeded to interrogate them fiercely, apparently keen to remove any suspicion that the government was controlling the committee.[17] 'You can not economise truth,' he warned one witness. 'God help the city,' he exclaimed at another point in the proceedings. He remarked wryly that the district superintendent of police, who believed he had no authority to take decisions at the time of the clashes, 'appeared to be a gentleman at large'.[18] He also permitted himself the odd wisecrack. When the journalist D.V. Gundappa stepped up to give evidence, Visvesvaraya's first question was, 'What is wrong with Mysore?' It was the title of an article Gundappa had written a few days earlier.[19]

Sifting through the piles of evidence they received, including implausible statements and contradictory accounts, the committee produced a ninety-nine-page final report in December. One member, Gulam Ahmed Kalami, appended a note in January 1929 expressing his disagreement on some points.[20] The committee's report began with the sequence of events in July 1928, presenting the points that were generally agreed upon. Then, in separate chapters, it discussed the general Hindu and Muslim views, respectively, of the riots. These were followed by the committee's own analysis and interpretations, including a discussion on the long-term causes of the conflict and the steps that the government should take to avoid such episodes in the future.[21]

The report was organized, then, in such a way as to present and examine multiple viewpoints before delivering a verdict. Its analysis, too, was even-handed on the whole. Almost all the parties involved came in for criticism: the authorities for permitting an alcove to be built for the idol in the first place, the students for their hooliganism, the Hindu leaders for their rabble-rousing, the Muslim residents of Sultanpet for resorting to violence, the police for their passivity, and the government for their delay in launching an investigation.[22]

Of these, it was the police, the magistrates and the government that bore the brunt of the committee's criticism. They had bungled the whole affair, the report held. They had failed to anticipate a clash even though they knew large crowds were proceeding to the school on an emotive occasion, failed to search houses in Sultanpet where individuals with lathis and firearms were allegedly sheltered, and made no arrests. In short, there had been a 'breakdown of the Government machinery' on 30 July.[23]

The committee now came to the causes of the tensions. Some witnesses had put forward a 'conspiracy theory'—a secret cabal in the state was seeking to bring down the government. The inference was that the cabal was made up mostly of disaffected Brahmins who could not stomach the appointment of a Muslim as dewan.[24] This was, in fact, an extreme version of a quite plausible explanation. The British Resident in Bangalore certainly subscribed to a version of it. Historians of princely Mysore, too, have stressed the calculated nature of the events leading up to the Ganapathi affair, and understood it as an expression of a wider conflict between rival power groups (especially Brahmin versus non-Brahmin) in the state.[25]

As it turned out, the Visvesvaraya Committee rejected the conspiracy theory, concluding that there was no concerted plan to overthrow the government, even though there may have been disaffected individuals.[26] Their alternative explanation, however, did acknowledge that sections of the public had grievances against the government. They explained the riot as a symptom of the growing tensions within Mysorean society. Among the main causes were the reservation policy for non-Brahmins inaugurated by the Miller Report of 1919, and the creation of separate electorates for different communities in the central legislature and the British Indian provinces. These policies, they said, had caused people to think in sectarian terms, and bred animosity.[27] This argument had a personal resonance for Visvesvaraya: the appointment of the Miller Committee had, after all, been one of the factors precipitating his resignation as dewan in 1918.[28]

The solution suggested—which, once again, bore the stamp of Visvesvaraya's thinking—was the creation of a melting pot. Mysore's residents, irrespective of their religious, linguistic and caste backgrounds, should adopt a homogeneous culture, rather like Turkey was doing under Kemal Atatürk. 'Standards, when established, will facilitate business, promote social intercourse, create good understanding and mutual trust, and cheapen the cost of necessities and amenities for all.'[29] (While this argument emphasized secularization, it did place the burden of assimilation on minorities. Generalizing freely while describing the pan-Indian context, the committee claimed that '[t]he Mussalmans who formerly were tolerant to the customs of the preponderatingly Hindu population among whom they lived have in recent years been showing a tendency to stand apart'.)[30]

Also contributing to the clashes, the committee argued, was the economic situation: growing unemployment among the educated meant they had time on their hands and grievances to nurse. The suggested remedy was, again, typical of Visvesvaraya's views: increased investment in industries, more facilities for technical education, and the creation of more job opportunities outside the government services.[31]

Finally, the committee argued that there was growing dissatisfaction because the people had inadequate means of participating in their own government. Although Mysore had a Representative Assembly and a Legislative Council, what 'the politically-minded public' wanted was 'a fuller and truer form of responsible Government'. If this was a legitimate aspiration for the people of the British Indian provinces—who already had elected ministers in charge of some subjects—it was no less so for the people in a princely state, even one with an enlightened ruler.[32]

*

The Bangalore Disturbances had a long-lasting political impact in Mysore. The coalition that had developed in the preceding years between leaders of the Hindu non-Brahmins and the Muslims was riven. Mirza's administration had to tread very carefully in the future in undertaking affirmative action that might benefit either Muslims or Hindu non-Brahmins.[33]

But perhaps the most unexpected outcome, from Mirza's point of view, was the Visvesvaraya Committee's strong endorsement of the people's democratic aspirations. While the Mysore government enjoyed a cordial relationship with the Congress at the national level, Mirza never warmed to the Mysore Congress, and was loath to devolve power to elected representatives.[34] Now his own ally and mentor had cut the ground from beneath his feet by endorsing the political aims of the Mysore Congress. Visvesvaraya's committee had gone so far as to ask for a transition to a constitutional monarchy, with the king reduced to a figurehead and the dewan replaced by an elected chief minister (though they had provided for the incumbent dewan to serve for a time as the first chief minister).[35]

Would Visvesvaraya have accepted a similar suggestion in 1917 or 1918, when *he* was the unelected dewan? It seems unlikely, although he had introduced some constitutional reforms during his tenure. A decade later, his views seem to have been influenced by the developing political situation in British India, his own interaction with nationalist politicians in the 1920s, and his strong involvement in the movement for dominion status at the national level.

These connections also paved the way for Visvesvaraya to assume another new role: that of spokesperson for what was known as the states people's movement. The movement dealt with the political rights of the citizenry of India's princely states, and was closely tied up with issues of constitutional reform and the broader Indian quest for dominion status.

Visvesvaraya was no stranger to negotiations between the princely states and the British. It was in his years as dewan that the old Instrument of Transfer had been replaced by a more equitable treaty between Mysore and the Government of India. The latter's receptiveness to Mysore's overtures was of a piece with British strategy towards princely states at the time: from the early twentieth century, they had resolved to cultivate the princes as a buffer against the emerging nationalist movement. They complimented the princely rulers for their cooperation during the First World War. In 1921, they sanctioned the establishment of a Chamber of Princes, a forum at which the princely rulers could consult each other and place before the government their views and needs. The British continued to court the princes through the 1930s, when constitutional reforms were being debated. For much of this period, they hoped that the princes would agree to become part of an all-India federation of provinces and states.[36]

But the relationship between the British and the Indian princes was only half the story. Even as the ruling elites were engaged in negotiation, activists in princely India began to demand political reform within their respective states—a demand directed at the maharajas, most of whom ran their fiefs autocratically.

These activists organized themselves on a regional basis. Prominent among their leaders in the Deccan was the pleader (later law professor) and Servants of India Society member G.R. Abhyankar, who hailed from the princely state of Sangli near Kolhapur.[37] Around 1917, Abhyankar sent the viceroy and the Secretary of State for India a pamphlet entitled *Native States and Post-War Reforms*. While seeking more autonomy for the princely rulers, he noted that they in turn must grant basic rights and representation to their subjects. The people 'are not associated with the administration,' he wrote, 'and there are no self-governing institutions in these States. The press does not wield any appreciable influence'. There was an urgent need for 'some constitutional machinery' to allow the people 'to voice their feelings and sentiments'.[38] His own suggestion was that in parallel with the provincial and all-India forums at which the princely rulers met each other, 'there should be conferences of the subjects of Native States, for the same areas', featuring elected representatives of the people.[39] Abhyankar was serious about these ideas: he or his associates were involved in the establishment and running of the Deccan States People's Conference (first held in 1921 in Pune) and the Sangli State Praja Parishad [People's Council] (set up in 1922).[40]

The work of Abhyankar and his associates was part of a nationwide trend. In the interwar period, citizens' organizations sprouted across princely India. In states large (Mysore, Baroda) and small (the principalities of Punjab, Kathiawad, Rajputana, and Orissa), *praja mandals* and *lok parishads* became the order of the day.[41] But they failed to secure the outright support of the one political organization in British India that might have formed a natural ally: the Indian National Congress. The Congress, which came into its own under the leadership of Gandhi around the time of the First World War, took a hands-off approach to the princely states. Its leaders were loath to do battle with the princes while their energies were directed towards agitating against the excesses of colonial rule at the national level. At the Nagpur Congress of 1920, the party declared that it would not meddle in the princely states' domestic issues.[42]

Nevertheless, the Congress could not completely ignore the popular movements in the princely states. Over the following decade, the party tried to walk a tightrope, acknowledging the princely subjects' aspiration to political rights while declining to get directly involved in their battles. It was only in the late 1920s that the Congress publicly pushed the maharajas to grant their subjects fundamental rights.[43] As the various praja mandal movements led to cooperation at the national level, the Congress finally gave the resulting organizations its implicit blessing. On 17 and 18 December 1927, delegates from across the subcontinent attended an Indian States People's Conference (ISPC) in Bombay. In the chair was Mocherla Ramachandra Rao, a lawyer hailing from the Andhra region. On 27 December, a similar gathering, styled the All-India States Subjects Conference, was held in Madras on the sidelines of the annual session of the Indian National Congress, which took place in the same city from 26–28 December. The Bombay and Madras conferences emphasized the need for representative government in the princely states. On the last day of its Madras session, the Congress took cognizance of these developments by passing a resolution[44] that said the princes 'should establish representative institutions and responsible Governments in their States at an early date'.[45]

In the following years, the Indian (sometimes styled All-India) States People's Conference[46] became a regular event. Its organizers maintained an office in South Bombay (ironically, the address was Princess Street).[47] While the ISPC spoke for the people of princely India as a whole, their own membership was predominantly middle-class.[48] The organization had strong links with the Servants of India Society. G.R. Abhyankar was an active participant, as was his colleague from the society, the engineer-turned-social worker A.V. Thakkar.[49] Another stalwart of the society, V.S. Srinivasa Sastri, had been the first choice for president of the inaugural conference in 1927 (he was otherwise occupied, so the job went to Ramachandra Rao).[50] In the early days, meetings were frequently held at the Servants of India Society's premises on Bombay's Sandhurst Road.[51]

The states people's movement was playing out against a background of political debate on a larger question: the future constitutional status of India as a whole. The Simon Commission (infamous for its failure to include a single Indian member) had been instituted by the British Parliament in November 1927 to assess the success of the constitutional reforms of 1919 and suggest future steps. The following month, a parallel committee was established to examine the constitutional relationship between the princely states and the Government of India. Headed by Sir Harcourt Butler (a former Education Member in the colonial government), the committee visited India in the first half of 1928 before repairing to London. In July, several princely rulers travelled to London to present their case before the committee.[52] They also tried to drum up public support for their concerns: November saw the Jamsaheb of Nawanagar—better known to the British public as the sublime cricketer Ranji—give a talk titled 'Playing the Game' at the National Liberal Club, referring to the obligation of the British to do right by the princely rulers.[53]

Not to be outdone, the ISPC also sent a delegation to England. Ramachandra Rao and Abhyankar were among its three members. The Butler Committee declined to meet them, saying the question of the form of government *within* the states was not within its purview. The delegation responded by submitting a memorandum to the committee. In their two months in London, the delegation worked energetically to advertise their cause. They lobbied influential personalities, including Labour politicians such as Colonel Josiah Wedgwood and Major Graham Pole, known to be sympathetic to Indian nationalist demands. They got Labour MPs to ask questions in the British Parliament regarding the position of the states' people. They addressed the Indian Majlis in London and Cambridge. They arranged for wide press coverage of their views.[54] They even tried, with limited success, to open a dialogue with the princes camping in London.[55]

*

Visvesvaraya was well informed on the states people's movements and their demands. For one thing, Abhyankar was in touch with him. The leader from Sangli had studied history at Poona's Fergusson College in the 1890s when G.K. Gokhale was a professor there, and later joined the latter's Servants of India Society. He may well have made Visvesvaraya's acquaintance through Gokhale in those years.[56] In 1918, Abhyankar sent Visvesvaraya some literature—probably the pamphlet on princely India which he had submitted the previous year to the viceroy and secretary of state. Visvesvaraya, then still Dewan of Mysore, sent him a guarded but encouraging reply. 'I have read portions of your book with much interest,' he wrote. 'But I am not in a position to frankly say what I feel on the questions dealt with without raising controversial issues.' He was, after all, still in the employ of a princely ruler himself. But he was clearly sympathetic. 'Indian Princes are making a move in the direction you have in view,' he noted. The state of Bhavnagar had just set up a Representative Assembly. 'I can only say if you keep on agitating, some good may come of your labours.'[57]

There were other connections too. Visvesvaraya's friend M.R. Jayakar also took an interest in the movement, presiding over the third annual meeting of the Deccan States People's Conference in the early 1920s.[58] Closer to home, the Mysorean journalist and writer D.V. Gundappa was actively involved in the states people's agitation. Gundappa had occasionally clashed with Visvesvaraya during the latter's years as dewan, but respected him for his refusal to clamp down on the press even when it proved an irritant to his administration.[59] As the two men continued to move in similar circles long after Visvesvaraya had ceased to be dewan, they would have had opportunities to discuss the status of the subjects of princely states.[60]

Visvesvaraya's sympathy with the subjects of princely India (in the abstract) did not initially come in the way of his good relations with the Mysore establishment and the state's ruler. As we have seen, he was in charge of the Bhadravati Iron Works for much of the 1920s, and on very good terms with Mirza Ismail, who became dewan in 1926. As a result, it was Visvesvaraya (and not a government official) who was selected to represent the Mysore Durbar when the Butler Committee visited the state in March 1928. Deposing before the committee for twenty-five minutes in the ballroom of Bangalore's Residency, he clarified the terms of a memorandum the Mysore government had submitted earlier.[61]

By the end of 1928, however, his relationship with Mirza Ismail and the durbar had soured somewhat. Not only had Visvesvaraya been openly critical of Mirza's administration in the aftermath of the Bangalore Disturbances; he was also at loggerheads with the dewan over the question of adding a steel plant to the Bhadravati works.[62]

Around the same time, representatives of the princely subjects of southern India were banding together along the lines of other such regional associations. They decided to organize the first South Indian States People's Conference (SISPC) in Trivandrum, capital of Travancore state. It was to include representatives from the states of Travancore, Cochin, Hyderabad, Mysore, and Pudukottah. Casting about for a suitably eminent person to preside over the conference, the organizers alighted on Visvesvaraya: he was not only a south Indian but also a princely subject and an ex-dewan associated with progressive constitutional reforms in Mysore.[63] Quite possibly D.V. Gundappa had something to do with the choice: he was Secretary of the SISPC as of November 1929, and may well have been involved in the first conference.[64]

For Visvesvaraya, the opportunity to campaign for greater democracy in the princely states came close on the heels of his own public statement along those lines after the Bangalore riot of 1928. Following 'a protracted discussion . . . regarding the policy and scope of the conference', he accepted the invitation.[65]

*

Visvesvaraya arrived in Trivandrum on 12 January 1929, a couple of days before the start of the conference. The Travancore administration treated him as an official guest, and the state's dewan made arrangements to be present at the first day of the conference.[66] 'I came here as an agitator,' Visvesvaraya would say later, 'but they treated me as a State guest.'[67] His impeccably bourgeois credentials probably reassured the royals that he was not there to rabble-rouse.

More than 900 delegates attended the conference, which began at noon on 14 January.[68] As usual, Visvesvaraya's presidential address was a model of clarity. Significantly, he widened the scope of his speech beyond the direct concerns of his constituents, placing the issue of the states' subjects and their needs in the context of the broader political movements in India. '[W]e should not overlook the fundamental fact,' he said, 'that the problem of Indian Reforms is one and indivisible.'[69]

In his address, Visvesvaraya listed the different stakeholders in the debates on constitutional reform. These were '(i) the British Government and the British people; (ii) The Indians residing in British India; (iii) the Princes ruling the Indian States: and (iv) The Subject People of the States.' The first of these groups was status-quoist. The second was fighting for dominion status. The third—the princely rulers—did not want to give up any of their powers, and were 'disinclined to come under any future Government of India', for they preferred to deal directly with the British. The fourth group—the states' people—sought 'some form of responsible Government for themselves in their respective States and a fair share of voice in any future constitution of the Government of India which may exercise control over their affairs'.[70] Visvesvaraya's sympathies lay with the second and fourth groups.

As we have seen in an earlier chapter, Visvesvaraya had himself been involved in the movement for dominion status in the past. Now he reminded his audience of the work of political leaders in British India, who had recently protested against the Simon Commission, organized All-Parties Conferences, and sketched the outline of a dominion constitution as embodied in the (Motilal) Nehru Report of 1928. True, the Nehru report had skated over the question of the position of the princely states (not to mention their subjects) in a future Indian federation. But this was justified, Visvesvaraya insisted, as it had a larger and more pressing goal. He asked the people of the states not to rock the boat, but to support the politicians of British India in their quest for dominion status.[71]

Nevertheless, the states' people were amply justified in their efforts to come together and demand their rights, for they had no one else to turn to.[72] The colonial government did not care for them. The Butler Committee was concerned only with the narrow question of the equation between the princely governments and the paramount power; they had shown no interest in 'the needs of the 70 millions of people [living in princely India] whose good government is, or ought to be, their primary concern'. The functioning of the Butler Committee, as with the Simon Commission, had shown 'no open dealing, no largeness, no magnanimity, no gesture of generous treatment'.[73] The princes, on the whole, were no better. They gave their tax-paying subjects no say in how public funds should be used. They curtailed the people's freedoms and were reluctant to democratize their systems of government. 'There is no instance,' Visvesvaraya declared, 'of any State in any part of the world which is ruled on the medieval principles that the Indian States at present are, that has risen to a position of power, wealth or enlightenment in the commonwealth of States. . . . Even China, Persia and Afghanistan have become or are fast becoming democratic.' It would be in the best interests of the princes themselves to adopt a liberal policy towards their people and take on the role of 'constitutional Sovereigns'.[74]

Next, Visvesvaraya proposed a detailed programme of constitutional reform, both within the states and at the all-India level. Every state, he said, must have an elected legislature, the executive being a 'cabinet composed only of members . . . who can command the support of the majority of the members of that legislature'. The legislature would need to approve any out-of-the-ordinary expenditures by the monarch. The judiciary should be separated from the executive. Rights relating to property and assembly, free speech, and a free press should be granted to the people. And finally, a Visvesvaraya special: 'Among the obligatory duties of each State should be included certain minimum nation-building activities on its part necessary for a self-supporting State in respect of education, industries, defence and self-government. . . . results under these activities should be published at least once a year in each State.'[75]

As for the federal government to be formed at the centre in the future, Visvesvaraya proposed a Central Legislature with two houses, both of which would have elected representatives of the states as well as the provinces. The members from the princely states would not participate in debates and decisions on matters exclusively concerning British India (he cited precedents from the USA and Australia for such an arrangement). Of course, it would not be possible for every one of the hundreds of princely states to have a seat in the legislature. The less prominent ones could be 'grouped together, and representatives elected from the groups'.[76]

Visvesvaraya knew that the system he was advocating would be a hard sell to the princes as much as to the British.[77] He tried to sweeten the pill with a number of concessions.[78] For instance, he suggested the Chamber of Princes would not be dissolved, but be turned into a forum for the princes to take care of 'their dynastic claims, and their personal rights and privileges'.[79] Furthermore, states would be given a grace period of fifteen years to establish democracy internally,[80] and in the meantime they would not be barred from having a representative in the central legislature.[81] An autonomous, dominion form of government at the centre need not spell the end for British businesses and employees in India: 'British interests' would be treated with 'scrupulous justice'.[82]

Visvesvaraya's address was well received by his compatriots. The *Bengalee*, a Calcutta-based newspaper that represented the worldview of the Congress Moderates,[83] supported his proposals and praised '[t]he extreme moderation with which [he had] put forward his views'.[84] The General Secretary of the ISPC sent a cable of congratulations, declaring that '[t]he line shown' in Visvesvaraya's address 'will be our definite future programme'.[85] On the second and final day of the conference in Trivandrum, resolutions were passed endorsing Visvesvaraya's principal proposals, and creating a long-term committee that would raise awareness on issues relating to the states' subjects.[86] A document was prepared, which became known as the 'Visvesvaraya Memorandum'.[87] Arriving in Madras a few days later from his sojourn in England, Ramachandra Rao supported the stance taken by the conference.[88]

*

Around this time, the demand for a round table conference to discuss a constitution for India—a demand first made in the early 1920s at the time of the Malaviya Conference over which Visvesvaraya had ended up presiding—came to the fore again. Both the ISPC and the SISPC argued that when a round table conference was held, it must give a seat at the negotiating table to representatives of the subjects of the princely states, not just their rulers.[89] Gundappa, as Honorary Secretary of the SISPC, specifically suggested Visvesvaraya's name.[90]

But the British authorities insisted that only their relations with the princes, and not the internal affairs of the states, were relevant to the question of constitutional reform.[91] When a Round Table Conference[92] was finally inaugurated in London in November 1930, the princely states were represented by a contingent of maharajas and administrators headed by Mirza Ismail, Visvesvaraya's estranged friend. M. Ramachandra Rao was the only attendee who could be said to represent the states' people.

Visvesvaraya was not invited.[93] This did not, however, stop him from putting forward his views. Along with his friend K. Natarajan, editor of the *Indian Social Reformer*, he released a document laying down the measures that would be needed for India to achieve dominion status. Its provisions were very similar to those in the document Visvesvaraya had prepared anonymously for M.R. Jayakar some years previously. This time, he was prepared to be identified publicly with these views.[94]

The meeting that began that November was the first of three RTCs held in London from 1930 to 1932. The participants included large contingents of princely rulers, Indian Liberals, industrialists, and leaders representing the Hindus, the Muslims, and the Untouchables. While this made for an impressive spectacle—concentric circles of notables, suited, turbanned, and brilliantined, seated in a sumptuous hall at St James' Palace—the RTCs were undermined by the absence of key stakeholders.[95] They were held against the backdrop of popular upheaval across India, a start-stop Civil Disobedience Movement led by Gandhi, and the frequent imprisonment of Congress leaders. As a result, the Congress—arguably one of the most important parties interested in the issue of constitutional reform—boycotted the first RTC; was represented by Gandhi alone in the second; and skipped the third.[96]

The British negotiators also changed midway. Just before the second RTC, the balance of power in the British government shifted, and a Conservative Secretary of State for India, Samuel Hoare, succeeded his more India-friendly Labour counterpart, William Wedgwood Benn.[97] These complications notwithstanding, enough points were agreed on to enable the organizers to bring out, in March 1933, a White Paper that embodied the results of the parleys. This was to form the basis for the drafting of a new constitution for India.[98]

As the cycle of Round Table Conferences drew to a close, there was keen speculation in India on the contents of the forthcoming White Paper.[99] In Bombay, Visvesvaraya and other influential residents kept tabs on the developments. In January 1933, they spent three days together discussing the outcomes of the recently concluded third conference. Here Visvesvaraya rubbed shoulders with Liberal leaders such as Chimanlal Setalvad and Phiroze Sethna; businessmen such as Manu Subedar, Lallubhai Samaldas and Chunilal V. Mehta; and professionals such as cardiologist and Congressman Manchersha Gilder, and journalist K. Natarajan of the *Indian Social Reformer*.[100] M.R. Jayakar, who had attended the third RTC, briefed the participants.[101]

The Bombay eminences concluded that the reforms likely to be announced were entirely inadequate, and released a statement to that effect. It was also signed by dozens of leaders from across Bombay and India who could not join the discussions. Among them were the Liberals V.S. Srinivasa Sastri and C.Y. Chintamani, industrialist Ambalal Sarabhai, economist V.G. Kale, leader of the Untouchables Baloo Palwankar, and states people's champions Ramachandra Rao and A.V. Patwardhan. The statement pointed out that the British government had laid down an onerous condition for setting up a federal government in India: more than fifty per cent of the princely states (together making up at least fifty per cent of the *population* of princely India) had to elect to join the federation. The British were also proposing 'safeguards' or discretionary powers for their officials (including the viceroy and provincial governors) during the shift to a federal form of government, without specifying how long this might last. Such provisions interfered with the federal legislature's control over finance-related legislation. No time-bound commitments had been made to Indianize the army in India.[102]

On 9 February, a public meeting was organized by more or less the same group in Bombay's Cowasji Jehangir Hall. The organizers issued a resolution echoing their earlier statement. The reforms in their current form were unsatisfactory, they said, and would not suffice to 'allay the discontent and disaffection so widely prevalent in the country'. The measures needed to be refined substantially. Moreover, discussion on the reforms could only proceed if all those imprisoned on political grounds in recent times were freed at once.[103]

*

The Round Table Conferences had turned out to be a damp squib. Federation was never achieved. The people of the princely states were never consulted. Yet the debates brought to light several questions that were to be crucial for the incipient Indian nation. And Visvesvaraya, generally thought of as an apolitical administrator, was extensively involved in them.

Indeed, there was one aspect of constitutional reform that Visvesvaraya arguably thought about more deeply than many of his politician friends. This was its connection with economic development. When, in March 1933, the White Paper emanating from the third RTC was eventually published,[104] Visvesvaraya produced an individual critique that focused on the economic ramifications of the constitutional system envisaged in it. In the article, which he sent out to several newspapers,[105] Visvesvaraya argued that the new system would do nothing to alleviate the abject poverty in which most of the Indian population lived. If the state was to be anything more than a 'policeman's Government', the new constitution must incorporate some key measures. A National Economic Council must be created at the centre, 'composed of leading industrial experts and agriculturists, business men and bankers from all parts of India'. This body would 'advise in regard to the country's trade and industries and economic interests generally'. There should be additional developmental bodies, with a similar purpose, at the local and municipal levels. Visvesvaraya wanted the new federal legislature to take charge of economic policy 'without any interference from London'. The legislature should be in charge of setting up the planned Reserve Bank, running the Railway Board, and formulating policy of a fiscal nature (which would involve protective tariffs).[106]

In essence, Visvesvaraya was asking for a *planned* economy that would be *national* in its priorities. This was not a position he came to overnight, but the result—as the next chapter will show—of a long engagement with economists and economic ideas.

19

An Engineer among the Economists

January 1924. Cowasji Jehangir Hall, Bombay University: a venue Visvesvaraya knew like the back of his hand. Here he had received his engineering degree forty years previously; here he had chaired the famous Malaviya Conference a couple of years ago. This time he was on stage with the newly arrived Governor of Bombay, Sir Leslie Wilson. The occasion was the inauguration of the seventh Indian Economic Conference, the flagship meeting of the Indian Economic Association (IEA). Visvesvaraya was to preside over the proceedings.[1]

The IEA had been established during the First World War by a group of British professors working in India: H. Stanley Jevons of Allahabad University, C.J. Hamilton of Calcutta University, and Percy Anstey of the Sydenham College of Commerce and Economics in Bombay.[2] Since then, it had rapidly achieved prominence. The expatriate professors were joined not only by prominent Indian academics from across the country, but also by representatives of big business.[3] The Indian Economic Conference, as the IEA's annual event was known, quickly became India's preeminent gathering of academic economists and professionals interested in economic policy. Held in a different city of the subcontinent each year, its proceedings were covered at length in the national press.[4] The IEA's periodical, the *Indian Journal of Economics* (which had been started by Jevons at Allahabad University) grew into a venue for influential interventions in Indian economics during the interwar years.[5]

The meeting in Bombay in 1924 marked the seventh edition of the annual conference. The IEA's president for the year was V.G. Kale, Professor of Economics at Poona's Fergusson College; but he was tied up that January and unavailable to preside over the conference. It was in this context that the organizers turned to Visvesvaraya, who agreed to travel from Bangalore to oversee the event.[6]

This was a remarkable choice, even if it came as an afterthought. The association had turned not to an economist, but to an engineer, a man who had only the previous year presided over a very different gathering, the Indian *Science* Congress. Yet it seems to have raised few eyebrows, for Visvesvaraya had long been known in economics circles. As a young man in Poona he had sat at the feet of Ranade and his circle of thinkers; in his home state he had overseen the establishment of the Mysore Economic Conference and its organ, the *Mysore Economic Journal*.[7] He had been in contact with economic thinkers such as Gilbert Slater of Madras University,[8] and his *Reconstructing India*, which boldly prescribed economic reforms on an all-India scale, had attracted the attention of V.G. Kale himself.[9] Visvesvaraya had also maintained a relationship with Sydenham College in Bombay, which served as a sort of nucleus for the Indian Economic Association.[10] Established in 1913 at the initiative of Bombay's business leaders and subsequently named after the serving Governor of Bombay, the college was a pioneer in providing commercial education at the university level.[11] This was the institution that Visvesvaraya held up as his model when he stressed the need for commercial education in his home state; it was where he sent advanced

Mysorean students of commerce to complete their training.[12] Visvesvaraya had even tried—unsuccessfully—to recruit M.L. Tannan (who later became Principal of Sydenham) to head a commerce college in Mysore.[13]

All in all, Visvesvaraya was well known to the influential Indian economists of the day. Yet he was an outsider to the profession, and this was the first time he would interact with them en masse.

*

At the opening of the Economic Conference, K. Subramani Aiyar, the Chairman of the Reception Committee, spoke first. Aiyar, a former principal of Sydenham,[14] assured Governor Wilson that 'we have no lists of grievances to enumerate, and there will be no direct or covert appeals for financial aid from Your Excellency's Government'.[15]

The governor appreciated the sentiment, formally inaugurated the conference, and left to attend to other business. Visvesvaraya now rose to give the presidential address. Immediately contradicting Subramani Aiyar's conciliatory tone, he declared that it was a challenge 'to discourse on Indian Economics in a practical spirit without coming up against controversial topics. . . . Indian Economics has been in a state of complaint ever since the subject came to be handled by men of courage, ability and independent thought. Questions germane to the subject have been discussed with great candour in the past in the writings of eminent men like Dadabhai Naoroji, Romesh Chunder Dutt, William Digby and others'.[16]

It was a tradition he sought to continue. Very deliberately, he listed all that was wrong with the Indian economy, laying the blame for much of it at the door of the colonial government.

First, commerce and industries had been neglected, and colonial claims about improved economic conditions were to be taken with a pinch of salt. The outgoing Bombay Governor, Sir George Lloyd, had emphasized the improvement in agricultural output in recent decades. But 'Sir George . . . has adopted a wrong basis for his comparisons. A progressive Government would take pride in the growth of production from industries, of volume of commerce, of science, of arts and crafts and of technical education.' Instead, Lloyd harped on agriculture. Visvesvaraya also objected to Lloyd's benchmarks: India's progress should be assessed not with reference to its own dismal past, but against the economically advanced nations.[17]

The indifference to industry was also reflected in colonial policies on technical education, a subject in which neither central nor provincial governments had shown enough interest. Visvesvaraya referred to the 1921 committee he had headed on technical education in the Bombay Presidency; the suggestions of its Indian members had gone unheeded by the government. Similarly, the pro-industrial measures suggested by the Indian Industrial Commission of 1916–18 had largely been ignored.[18]

Visvesvaraya was particularly concerned by 'the unsatisfactory state of . . . economic statistics' in India. Local governments didn't have data on agricultural production at the village and district levels. Industrial investment and output was unquantified, as was the percentage contribution of indigenous firms. The little data that did exist suggested a country in the direst economic health. 'The masses of the population are steeped in poverty bordering on destitution.' In such a situation, the government's failure to collect and publish statistics 'creates the suspicion that their maintenance is inconvenient'.[19]

Having detailed his diagnosis, Visvesvaraya laid out his ideas for 'a new economic structure'. This was largely a reiteration of the vision he had put forth four years previously in *Reconstructing India*. This time, however, he had a captive audience of influential economists and businesspersons. He observed that the provincial

Boards of Industries should be made more representative and should cooperate with voluntary organizations like chambers of commerce and industrialist groups. Following the Japanese model, there should be panchayats at town and village levels 'to attend to increase of production under agriculture and industries and the spread of education, including vocational education and discipline'. Provincial governments should not hesitate to take out loans for 'development projects'. There was a need for 'an economic survey for the Provinces', following which statistics related to education and local businesses should be made public at regular intervals.[20]

Visvesvaraya envisioned a self-sufficient, autarkic Indian economy. This required, first, a change in the fiscal relationship with Great Britain. The colonial Indian government must stop ordering equipment from Britain for the Indian railways; they should instead promote and patronize local manufacturers. India must have 'fiscal autonomy'. The country should adopt the gold standard instead of the existing 'system of sterling exchange'. The need for economic protection, especially in sectors like steel, was so obvious that the ongoing investigations of the Indian Tariff Board (which was tasked with assessing the case for protective tariffs) were a waste of time. In sum, the future relationship between Britain and India should be built on 'mutual benefit and healthy common interests'. With political will and the right measures, he declared, India could increase agricultural production by 100 per cent and industrial production by 300 per cent within the next fifteen years.[21]

The speakers at the conference that followed dealt with many of the themes Visvesvaraya had mentioned. There were papers on the Indian government's policy on currency, the cooperative movement, tariffs and protection, the challenges of overpopulation, and economics as a subject in India. Visvesvaraya stayed for all four days of the conference, offering at the end his comments on the papers presented. He also added some fresh suggestions and anecdotes to the points he had made in his opening speech. In closing, he encouraged the IEA to establish branches at the provincial level to raise awareness about economic issues. By the time the attendees boarded the S.S. *Begum* for a valedictory cruise in Bombay harbour, the engineer had well and truly arrived among the economists.[22]

*

Central to Visvesvaraya's prescriptions for the Indian economy was the effective use of statistics. The colonial state did, of course, collect data, as evidenced by the luxuriant detail in which the imperial gazetteers described each district and province. But it did so for its own administrative purposes, which did not include pulling the masses out of poverty.[23] Raising the standard of living and developing the country industrially would require different kinds of data. To begin with, there was an urgent need to obtain an accurate quantitative picture of the current situation.

This point was endorsed by Indian members of the Central Legislative Assembly in the mid-1920s, when the colonial government contemplated levying new taxes on the public. The legislators argued that the government must first undertake an economic survey to establish the people's economic position, and whether they could indeed afford to pay taxes.[24] Among the assembly's members at this time were a number of Visvesvaraya's friends, including the Congress leader Madan Mohan Malaviya, the industrialist Purshotamdas Thakurdas, and the new president of the Indian Economic Association, Lallubhai Samaldas.[25]

The colonial government's Finance Department responded by setting up a committee. The Indian Economic Enquiry Committee, as it became known, was tasked not with reporting on the actual well-being of the people, but with specifying *how* such a study might be carried out, and what additional sources of data might be required for the exercise. Indian legislators and industrialists naturally considered this a dodge. But the establishment of the committee, even with this narrower mandate, was nevertheless an important step.[26] Visvesvaraya was named its chairman.

Given his growing profile as an expert on matters economic and the fact that he was a trusted friend of many in the legislature, the choice of Visvesvaraya was not entirely surprising. His two colleagues on the committee were more conventional appointments: Pandit Hari Kishan Kaul, a retired civil servant and former Commissioner of Lahore, and A.R. Burnett-Hurst, professor of commerce at the Muir Central College in Allahabad University.[27]

Visvesvaraya, Kaul, and Burnett-Hurst gathered in Delhi in February 1925. There they met legislators and held discussions. They even found time to dine at the Viceregal Lodge at Simla, where they were presumably briefed by Government of India staff. They then travelled to various provinces, where they interviewed witnesses and spoke to government officials. In April and May, this work took them to Allahabad, Calcutta, Rangoon (Burma then being administered along with British India), Madras, Poona, Bombay, and back to Simla.[28] 108 witnesses submitted written responses; eighty-one gave their views in person. They included professors and lecturers of economics, government officials, legislators, business journalists, and representatives of chambers of commerce.[29]

The committee investigated a crucial theoretical question: what were the appropriate measures of a country's economic status? After discussing this and related questions threadbare with scores of witnesses,[30] they concluded that the key measures were 'income (including production), consumption (including cost of living), and wealth'. While the government was already collecting some demographic data and statistics related to agricultural and industrial production, there were no systems in place to calculate parameters such as 'income, wealth, cost of living, indebtedness, wages and prices'. The committee recommended 'intensive enquiries . . . in limited areas in every district' to measure these parameters. They also suggested '[a] detailed quinquennial census of industrial production', '[a] comprehensive quinquennial wage census', and the drawing up of '[c]ost of living index numbers . . . for the principal industrial centres'. They urged that '[a]ll statistical work should . . . be co-ordinated and centralized, the aim being to provide a common purpose and give the statistics an economic trend by means of a central thinking office.' A bureaucratic machinery was to be created to give effect to these steps, including Central and Provincial Statistical Bureaus.[31]

These recommendations largely embodied Visvesvaraya and Kaul's thinking. Visvesvaraya, in particular, had long nursed an almost fanatical devotion to quantitative data and statistics. The compilation of statistics, we recall, had been one of the key activities underpinning the Mysore Economic Conference during his years as dewan. He wrote articles about the need for statistics,[32] harped on it in his various publications, and peppered his speeches and writings with comparative figures, sometimes to the point of tedium.

Burnett-Hurst, the British member of the Economic Enquiry Committee, did not share Visvesvaraya's unbridled enthusiasm for statistics in the Indian context. He appended a dissenting note to the committee's report. 'As a statistician and economist' (which his colleagues were not), he disagreed with '[s]ome of the principles and most of the details of [the report's] recommendations'. He found his colleagues' suggestions too ambitious, and criticized them for aiming to model the collection of statistics on the practices prevailing in the British Dominions (such as Canada and Australia). India was much larger, and the costs of collecting data would be exponentially greater. The population was predominantly rural, making it difficult to obtain data; the people were largely illiterate; there were too many 'scattered unorganised undertakings' when it came to the industrial sector. Burnett-Hurst also disagreed with the measures his colleagues had chosen. There would be little use in the government calculating the national income, which in any case was 'very largely an academic exercise which should continue to be left to statisticians, economists and other non-officials'. Individual incomes were not as relevant to measure in India as family incomes. Moreover, 'the money value of the income of a family is no true index of its economic condition'. What the government should focus on was obtaining 'a full and detailed description of the standard of living of different classes of the people', which could be done 'by collecting and analysing a large number of family budgets'.[33]

This was a fairly common British reaction to Visvesvaraya's enthusiasm for new methods. British officials and expat professors tended to distrust any data originating in forms or ledgers compiled by Indian clerks, suspecting that they simply made them up.[34] They were also convinced that Indian society was fundamentally *different* from those of the settler colonies, and therefore required different methods.

Burnett-Hurst's critique notwithstanding, Visvesvaraya's involvement in the Economic Enquiry Committee would have given him a detailed understanding of the kinds of debates economists and statisticians were conducting at the time. What is more, the committee's exertions had established the existence of 'a wide-spread desire in the country for an economic enquiry'.[35] Even though the Government of India did its best to put its recommendations in cold storage, it became increasingly hard to ignore the appeal for a statistical organization. The Royal Commissions on Agriculture (1928) and Labour (1931) endorsed the principle, and in the early 1930s the central government set up a Statistical Research Bureau. Although plans for a Central Statistical Organization were mooted and dropped, the Bureau continued to function through the 1930s in different forms.[36]

The Economic Enquiry Committee, in other words, was an important milestone in the evolution of the state's statistical apparatus.[37] Visvesvaraya himself continued to champion the discipline of statistics. In the early 1930s, he served as one of the vice-presidents of the Indian Statistical Institute, which had just been established in Calcutta by the physicist-turned-statistician P.C. Mahalanobis.[38]

There was also a larger significance to the work of Visvesvaraya's 1925 Committee. It reinforced the principle that the purpose of collecting and processing economic statistics would be to 'facilitate the shaping of the economic policies and the solution of current economic problems with a view to meet existing deficiencies, improve resources and increase the country's prosperity generally'.[39] This was, in effect, an early expression of the need for economic planning.[40]

*

Visvesvaraya was a keen follower of economic policies across the globe, and no doubt the *Zeitgeist* in the 1920s and '30s further strengthened his belief in what was now being termed *planning*, just as it influenced other prominent Indians like the physicist Meghnad Saha.[41] Around the world, interwar debates on economic policy centred on the concept of planning, although there was no consensus on what exactly it meant. Proponents of planning came from different ideological backgrounds, and interpreted it in various ways. Lionel Robbins, an economics professor at the London School of Economics, noted in 1937:

> 'Planning' is the grand panacea of our age. But unfortunately its meaning is highly ambiguous. In popular discussion it stands for almost any policy which it is wished to present as desirable. . . . When the average citizen, be he Nazi or Communist or Summer School Liberal, warms to the statement that 'What the world needs is planning', what he really feels is that the world needs that which is satisfactory.[42]

Planning was as much a feature of the Nazi German economy as it was of the Soviet economy.[43] Even within a single country, different kinds of planning were conceived of and debated over. Daniel Ritschel refers to varieties such as 'National Planning', 'Socialist Planning', 'Capitalist Planning', and 'Progressive Planning' in 1930s Britain.[44] Marcia Balisciano, writing of debates at a similar time in the United States, posits that there were four different conceptions of planning—'Social Management Planning', 'Technical-Industrial Planning', 'Business Economy Planning', and 'Macroeconomic Planning'.[45] In India too, as historian Medha Kudaisya argues, different schools of thought were to emerge. Communist thinkers wanted a form of planning with complete nationalization of industries. Jawaharlal Nehru and others were not averse to some form of private capital. The colonial government, too, formulated a version of planning. Only Gandhi, who believed in a decentralized, village-based economy, opposed the idea of planning. But Visvesvaraya, who vigorously promoted planning before most of these actors, fell into none of these categories. For him, industrialization was to be at the core of planning.[46] He was far from apolitical—his consistent insistence on fiscal autonomy and representative government marked him out as a critic of the colonial state—but, as historian Benjamin Zachariah puts it, he was 'less committed to questions of social organization in terms of capitalism or socialism'.[47]

Visvesvaraya's conception of planning, in other words, was fundamentally technocratic. Possibly he was influenced by trends in the United States, where sociologist Thorstein Veblen had called for engineers, rather than business managers, to helm industrial development. American mechanical engineers like Morris Cooke and Henry Gantt evinced a strong interest in social engineering; with Herbert Hoover's ascent to the Presidency in 1929, the reins of the nation were in the hands of a mining engineer.[48] According to Balisciano, emerging views of planning were also strongly influenced by the industrial doctrine of scientific management, associated with another engineer, F.W. Taylor.[49]

Visvesvaraya, a man of action, rarely spent time discussing the genealogy of his beliefs. So we do not know if he read Veblen, or what he thought of Taylorism. We do know, of course, that he once met Hoover in America. Visvesvaraya, who had long internalized the Orientalist trope about tropical climates inducing sloth,[50] seemed to concur with Hoover's throwaway remark, made at their meeting, that Indians lacked 'hustle'.[51] To the Indian engineer, industry—in both senses of the word—was the answer to economic problems.

Through the interwar years, Visvesvaraya articulated this belief at various public forums. The key to increasing national wealth was to establish more industries, provide them with government support and economic protection, and train up an army of industrial workers through courses in technical and commercial subjects.[52] Speaking at the valedictory function of the All-India Swadeshi Bazaar and Industrial Exhibition held in Poona in 1927, he urged Indian universities to place less emphasis on 'literary and theoretical courses', promoting instead 'degrees in agriculture, engineering, technology and commerce'.[53] Three years later, speaking at a function at Sydenham College, he made a similar point.[54]

At the 1931 convocation ceremony of the Andhra University at Waltair, Visvesvaraya again stressed the importance of 'bring[ing] education closer to business'. On the same occasion, he made one of his first public endorsements of planning. 'You have all heard of the famous Five-Year Plan of Soviet-Russia,' he said to the graduating students in Waltair, 'which is a programme to cover year by year and item by item the economic development of the Union commencing from the year 1928-29.' India could fruitfully follow the Soviet example. 'We are not concerned,' Visvesvaraya was quick to add, 'with the Soviet methods creating a classless society or promoting collective ownership, but their principle of conscious planning conveys a much-needed lesson to this country.' He proceeded to sketch out how a hypothetical Andhra administration (the region was in reality part of the Madras Presidency) might establish a five-year plan for education.[55]

*

Barely three years later, with the Round Table Conferences in London leading up towards the drafting of a new Indian constitution, Visvesvaraya gave systematic expression to his ideas on planning in a book titled *Planned Economy for India*. The book was first published in December 1934, and his intervention owed not a little to his frustration with '[t]he prolonged delay in constitution-framing and the absence of any move to grapple with the unemployment problem'.[56]

Although this was probably the first attempt by an Indian to draw up a nationwide plan, Visvesvaraya's contribution did not take place in a vacuum. As Raghabendra Chattopadhyay has shown, the colonial government had proposed their own steps towards economic planning in 1930, when they set up an Economic Advisory Council. Ideas of state intervention were in the air as a result of the Great Depression and Franklin

Roosevelt's New Deal in America. The colonial government calculated that an initiative of this kind might stem the political unrest they were contending with at the time. In the next four years, various provincial governments established similar advisory bodies to help steer them out of the depression. Prominent individuals, including the business tycoon G.D. Birla, began to talk of planning.[57] These developments must have encouraged Visvesvaraya to organize his thoughts on planning as they had evolved over the preceding decade.

In *Planned Economy for India*, Visvesvaraya revisited many of the themes he had discussed in his 1920 book, *Reconstructing India*. This time, however, he made explicit his endorsement of formal economic planning. Planning was now the norm rather than the exception around the world, he argued. Most countries had historically used 'some sort of plan, but plans were usually kept secret' until the Soviet Union came out publicly with its first plan in 1928. Other countries had brought out plans (Italy, Turkey, China, Denmark), and yet others were considering planning in some form (Mexico, Germany, Sweden). In addition, many Western industrialized countries had Economic Councils. India too must have these two measures, namely 'economic planning and economic organization'.

Visvesvaraya suggested the following institutional arrangements. At the national level there would be an Economic Council made up of 'expert economists and leading business men [sic]' from across India. The council, which was to assess the needs of the Indian economy and suggest policy measures to increase the nation's wealth, would have a small Standing Committee in Delhi. The central government would create a Development Department, overseen by a cabinet minister. This department would have a Development Committee made up of civil servants 'approved by the Economic Council and the Legislature', which would work with the Economic Council's Standing Committee to recommend policies and ensure that planning goals were being met. Analogous institutions (an Economic Council and a Development Department) would be set up at the provincial level, while provinces would prepare five-year plans.

Thus, there was a sort of expert body, the Central Economic Council, which helped formulate plans; and an official body, the Central Development Department, responsible for the success of the plans. The actual implementation of the plans, however, would occur at the level of districts and cities, and would be taken care of by the regular administrative departments of the provincial governments.[58] This was clearly a technocratic set-up, for none of the personnel involved in planning—except the Development Minister—was democratically elected (though the legislature would have some say in the choice of civil servants in the Development Committee).

Visvesvaraya sketched the lineaments of a ten-year plan for the country as a whole. (He suggested a ten-year plan because the economic data available was insufficient to form the more accurate estimates required for a shorter plan).[59] The aim of Visvesvaraya's prototype plan was 'to double the income of the country within ten years'. Targets were set under various heads—industries, agriculture, public works and infrastructure, commerce, finance/banking, (combating) unemployment, and education/training.[60]

A sum of Rs 700 crore (Rs 7 billion) would need to be invested in fresh industrial ventures. Increasingly, mechanized agriculture and cooperative farming were to help raise agricultural income by 25 per cent, while moving 20 per cent of the agricultural workforce to industrial occupations. Roadways would be nearly doubled in extent, as would the installed electric power capacity. Rail coverage would be increased by around 29 per cent.[61] The literacy rate—languishing at 8 per cent—would be brought up to 50 per cent. Targets were also set, inter alia, for the production of coal, iron and steel, automobiles, shipping capacity, the capacity of the cotton textile industry, and the number of students in universities.[62]

Some of this would be undertaken directly by the government and some of it by capitalists, whom the government would help with financing. Naturally, the government would need funds for this. For this purpose, they should take out 'loans to the extent necessary either from the local public or from foreign countries'. By appealing to their sense of public duty, people hoarding wealth should be encouraged to invest it in productive undertakings.[63]

In order for economic planning to be successful, Visvesvaraya stressed, India must have political autonomy. In his seventies now, he had become much more direct in his criticism of the colonial setup, at least as far as the economic relationship between India and Britain was concerned. 'Great Britain wants India as a market for her manufactured products; so there is no incentive to the growth of industries in this country.' The consequence of 'Dependency Rule', he argued, 'has been to lower the country in almost every field of human activity, to foster special interests and to impede the well-being of the vast masses of the population.' The remedy was one he had been advocating for years: India must have a new Constitution giving it the same level of autonomy as the British Empire's settler dominions.

Indians, too, he argued, must reform their attitude. Measures were needed 'to change the outlook of the people, modernise their business practices and habits, prepare them for independent thinking and collective self-help and bring them into the company of the progressive nations of the world'.[64]

Visvesvaraya would expand on this point in a different tract, published three years later. There he wrote that besides the economy, India needed 'reforms and reconstruction in other spheres of national life—political, social, intellectual and spiritual'.[65] Education was essential to the creation of an efficient workforce. Women must be empowered to participate in the formal economy. Indian towns must have 'better libraries, hotels, inns, travel bureaux, chambers of commerce, banks, business houses, co-operative stores': all the accoutrements of a commercially vibrant society. He even went to the extent of suggesting the advantages of 'a standard dress, a uniform language, besides certain well-recognised international habits and practices in matters pertaining to business, society, travel and self-defence'.[66]

*

In 1937, provincial elections were held under the provisions of the reformed constitution as defined by the Government of India Act of 1935. The Indian National Congress came to power in a majority of the provinces, where previously colonial governors had held the bulk of executive power.[67] It was in this context that Visvesvaraya published a pamphlet titled *Nation Building*. It was addressed to the new Congress governments, and purported to advise them on running a planned economy. He reiterated the institutional set-up he had outlined in *Planned Economy*, focusing this time on how the provincial governments should go about creating their five-year plans.

As before, Visvesvaraya emphasized that the purpose of these plans was to fight poverty and raise the standard of living of the masses. Now he made an estimate of how much people's incomes would need to be raised. He concluded, based on some back-of-the-envelope calculations, that the average per capita income was Rs 60 per year. One of the aims of economic planning should be to boost this figure by 50 per cent within a decade.[68]

In addition to his usual advocacy of heavy industries, Visvesvaraya stressed the importance of rural industries and the need for 'real Self-Government in villages'.[69] He suggested the formation of District Committees, with whose guidance the inhabitants of each village 'would start improving their existing occupations and creating new units of work . . . The bulk of the increase in occupations should come from cottage and small-scale industries, particularly those intended to supply goods for which there is a demand within the district itself'. Each district would need to produce some essential items such as clothing, utensils, furniture, and agricultural tools.[70] If this vision of self-sufficient villages sounded vaguely Gandhian, it may not have been entirely coincidental. As other remarks in the text show, Visvesvaraya was keen to emphasize that his vision was not incompatible with Gandhian thinking, which held sway over the Congress to a substantial extent.[71]

On the face of it, Visvesvaraya was the antithesis of Gandhi. The former wore suits of imported cloth, championed rapid industrialization, and had a firmly materialist conception of national well-being; the latter wore a khaddar dhoti, promoted the spinning wheel, and emphasized self-respect and self-reliance over material wealth. Visvesvaraya spent the 1920s and '30s arguing for dominion status and economic planning; Gandhi led tumultuous popular uprisings while institutionalizing his programme of hand-spinning and village industries (the All India Spinners' Association was established in 1925, and the All India Village Industries Association, or AIVIA, in 1934).[72] As Gandhi once wrote, the pair '[held] perhaps diametrically opposite views'.[73]

Yet there was genuine respect between them. Gandhi had praised Visvesvaraya during his sojourn in Mysore in 1927 (see Chapter 16). In the following decades, they corresponded off and on, attempting to thrash out their differences, and tried to find ways to work together. Visvesvaraya, who sent Gandhi a copy of *Planned Economy*, declared that he was not against village industrialization. 'You are for developing village industries and

I favour both heavy industries and village industries,' he wrote. 'To the extent that you propose to advance village Industries, I am at one with you.'[74] This was more than mere politeness or expediency: Visvesvaraya had indeed made provision for rural industries in all his blueprints for development starting from his Mysore days. As he put it in *Nation Building*, he believed that '[t]he development of heavy and cottage industries must go on *pari passu* if the country is to prosper economically and be self-sufficient. Advanced countries have established a close relationship between the two . . .'[75]

Gandhi, for his part, was willing to concede a temporary role to large-scale industries such as the Bhadravati Iron and Steel Works in Mysore.[76] He was even prepared to countenance 'power-driven machinery' in heavy industries, so long as it did not '[displace] human labour without providing displaced hands with a substitute at least as good as displaced labour'.[77] He also assured Visvesvaraya of (political) support in the latter's bid to promote automobile manufacture in India (see Chapter 21 below).[78]

Ultimately, however, the two failed to find any real common ground. Visvesvaraya continued to send Gandhi his tracts and information on the rural industrialization schemes he and his associates formulated in the 1940s. But his vision of rural industry, for all its resemblance to Gandhi's idea of self-sufficient villages, had one fundamental difference: he saw rural industries not as an end in themselves but as a stepping stone to further mechanisation.[79] In the last letter on record between the two, an exasperated Gandhi wrote that

> verbally our objectives appear the same but when I look at our means, the difference seems to me to be unbridgeable. . . . Much as I would love to work as a humble co-worker side by side with you, I cannot.

> Your detailed, patient replies carefully prepared, fail to convince me. What is the use of taxing you further with my questions?[80]

*

Visvesvaraya's programme, however, was more palatable to Gandhi's younger colleagues in the Congress. His overtures in *Nation Building*, in addition to *Planned Economy* and his earlier work, made him an obvious candidate for the Congress's ambitious National Planning Committee (NPC), established in 1938 by Subhas Chandra Bose, the party's president, with Jawaharlal Nehru as its chairman. Its establishment was a clear indication that the Congress was preparing for a time in the not-too-distant future when they would form an autonomous all-India government. In its first session, held in Bombay in December 1938, the NPC worked on preparing a questionnaire to be sent out, *inter alia*, to the governments of the various provinces and princely states. In the second session, held the following June, they constituted twenty-seven sub-committees to collect and interpret data under various heads.

Packed with industrialists, scientists, and academics, the NPC was unabashedly expert-driven and urban-centric. Bose and Nehru, who initiated and led the effort, were part of the young guard of the Congress. Despite opposition from some sections of the party, the Nehru-led committee insisted on the importance of promoting large-scale industries alongside cottage industries. This was very much in tune with Visvesvaraya's approach. But the veteran engineer soon grew impatient with what he saw as its ponderous progress. In the first session, he asked that the NPC instruct each provincial government to establish at least one significant industrial venture forthwith. His colleagues, however, felt that the committee's role was to advise, not order. At the second session, Visvesvaraya made a similar demand, only for Nehru to stress the importance of collecting and analysing data thoroughly before proposing action. Visvesvaraya resigned from the NPC some time later.

In September 1939, war broke out in Europe. India was quickly swept up in the currents of what became the Second World War. Soon after, the Congress governments in the provinces quit, objecting to Britain dragging India into the conflict. The NPC continued to function for another year, during which time nineteen of its sub-committees tabled their reports. But with the war on and Nehru in and out of prison for opposing India's involvement in the war, the committee's work went into limbo for the next few years. It reconvened after the war, and a full set of the sub-committees' reports was published a few years later.[81] The results of the NPC's labours, then, arrived more with a whimper than a bang. Nevertheless, it served as a template for a far more influential body that would be created in 1950 by the government of independent India: the Planning Commission.[82]

*

Meanwhile, Visvesvaraya kept up his interest in planning, especially its industrial aspect. During the war years he became president of a new industrialists' body, the All India Manufacturers' Organization (AIMO), based in Bombay (more on this in Chapter 22). Under the aegis of the AIMO, he brought out a number of manifestoes on planning and industrial policy.[83]

In 1944–45, a high-profile plan was released by leading Indian industrialists (including G.D. Birla, J.R.D. Tata, and Kasturbhai Lalbhai) and a few economists. Known as the Bombay Plan, it was undertaken in clear anticipation of an independent Indian government at the end of the war. In it, the industrial class saw itself as working closely with the state to double the per capita income of the Indian population in a fifteen-year period. The state would provide essential infrastructural services and establish heavy industries, while private business would step up the production of goods.[84]

This was in tune with Visvesvaraya's thinking. He was largely in favour of capitalism and what he saw as the civilizing influence of a business-friendly environment, but he was not a free-market Liberal of the classical type either, for he clearly believed in large-scale public investment by a strong and decisive state. In the 1930s, he had stated that he wanted his proposed plan for India to 'avoid *communistic* tendencies; its basic policy should encourage collective effort without interfering with individual initiative'.[85]

It is not clear whether Visvesvaraya was approached by the Bombay Planners to be a part of their endeavour. He was certainly well acquainted with some of India's big industrialists, and had strong ties with the Tatas (he served as a director in their steel company for several years).[86] In any case, he was in sympathy with their effort, and endorsed it heartily. Some months after the Bombay Plan was released, Visvesvaraya published his own views in a pamphlet titled *Reconstruction in Post-War India: A plan of development all round.*[87]

Incensed by the colonial government's lack of encouragement to Indian industry during the Second World War, he contrasted the Bombay Plan favourably with the government's preparations for post-war reconstruction.[88] The government had set up committees, but these had only come up with 'piecemeal proposals . . . ; proposals mostly unproductive which have no relation to one another and which give no ideas of the aggregate financial liability involved'.[89] What India needed instead was planned, coordinated policies. His own suggestions were compatible with those of the Bombay Plan.[90] The Bombay Plan had been drawn up for a period of fifteen years. Visvesvaraya suggested that '[f]rom the Fifteen-Year Plan, a plan for five years can be deduced and put forward in complete detail'. Both the longer and the shorter plan should be refined after seeking expert and public opinion.[91]

The historian Medha Kudaisya has argued that the Bombay Plan established the template for the Nehruvian Five-Year Plans and the post-Independence 'mixed economy'. Among the important ideas they emphasized was the need to calculate, and improve, the per capita income of the population; and the concept of 'deficit financing' (the idea that it was legitimate and desirable for the state to incur debt in order to stimulate economically productive activity).[92] As the preceding discussion shows, Visvesvaraya's 1934 book, *Planned Economy for India*, anticipated the Bombay Plan on both these issues.[93]

*

Visvesvaraya's views on planning were generally treated with deference, but they were not without their lacunae. Several criticisms can be made (and many were) of his conception of planning.

First, it lacked theoretical sophistication. Reviewing his *Planned Economy for India* in 1936, the young Cambridge-educated economist D.R. Gadgil agreed with Visvesvaraya on the need for a cogent economic policy and thorough statistical data, and was glad that 'one of India's most renowned engineers and administrators' had lent his weight to these causes. On the other hand, he noted that '[the book's] merits are such as could not easily be appreciated by the academic economist. It adds nothing to either our knowledge of economic facts or to our interpretation of them.' It contained many unsubstantiated assertions and simplistic analyses.[94] Indeed, Visvesvaraya's writings on planning were more manifestoes than scientific treatises. They cited international precedents and Visvesvaraya's own observations from his travels, but they did not engage with the debates that economists of the time were involved in, such as the one between Hayek and Keynes in the 1940s.[95]

Second, Visvesvaraya assumed that the experience of the industrial nations of the West provided the only blueprint for development. He did not take into account the global nature of industrialization and the exploitation—especially of colonial societies—that had historically accompanied it.[96] Could the experience of the West be replicated in India without giving rise to some form of imperialism? And would an India with no colonies to exploit be able to industrialize as rapidly as the countries he held up as exemplars?

Third, as one prominent Marxist critic pointed out, his conception of planning focused on the generation of wealth without giving due attention to 'the question of distribution'. The critic in question was G.D. Parikh, an economics professor at Bombay's Ruia College,[97] and his remarks were made in the context of the Bombay Plan and Visvesvaraya's *Post-War Reconstruction* (1944), which endorsed it. For Parikh—a close associate of communist revolutionary M.N. Roy and co-author of a *People's Plan for Economic Development of India*[98]—it was simplistic to assume that Indians of all stripes should unite for the purpose of national production without questioning existing hierarchies or entering into class conflict. Visvesvaraya, he wrote, 'has never heard of the antagonisms between the cultivator and the rackrenteer, the primary producer and the middleman or the worker and the capitalist.' To critics like Parikh, Visvesvaraya and the authors of the Bombay Plan were really pleading for the further enrichment of capitalists under the cloak of national development.[99]

Fourth—and this was another point raised by Parikh—Visvesvaraya often appeared to flirt with militarism and authoritarianism. In his pronouncements on planning, he gave a prominent place to production and training for defence purposes,[100] and stressed the need for a 'citizen army'. 'Every man capable of wielding arms,' he said, 'should be trained in the modern methods of warfare as is done in Germany, Italy, Russia and Japan.' His rationale was that economic development was of no use to a nation if it could not defend itself.[101]

Referring to such views, Parikh wrote that '[t]he bogey of defence is a familiar note in nationalist planning. It provides a cover for the desire or ambition of offence. It had been a familiar cry of Hitler, Mussolini and others . . .'[102] He implied that it also created a lucrative business opportunity for the capitalists, who could step up the industrial manufacture of weapons and other military requirements.[103] With its emphasis on defence and its proposed alliance between the state and big business, Parikh argued, Visvesvaraya's vision was 'typically fascist'.[104]

It is not unlikely that authoritarian states held some subliminal appeal for Visvesvaraya, a man who wanted citizens to dress and talk alike and would certainly have appreciated trains that ran on time. In the late 1930s, with Japanese militarism on the rise, the National Socialists running amok in Germany, and Mussolini entrenched in Italy, Visvesvaraya told the graduating students of the Benares Hindu University:

> Men with patriotic fervour should be invited to lead in order to secure the degree of discipline and regimentation necessary for a directed economy. . . . In totalitarian States under dictators in Germany, in Italy, in Soviet Russia, people's lives are regulated by various restrictions with the object of consolidating and augmenting national power and raising the standards of income and comfort of the nation as a whole. People have reconciled themselves to curtailment of liberties for the sake of the collective security and common economic advantage which it brings to them.[105]

If there was a hint of admiration in those lines, however, Visvesvaraya immediately sought to balance the record with his next words:

> The people should be free to plan as they will, produce what they want, increase efficiency in directions in which they feel they are deficient, and mobilise the country's resources in materials and man-power for all their rightful tasks.[106]

To argue that Visvesvaraya was a fascist or that he wanted India to turn into a belligerent imperial power was an exaggeration. There may have been contradictions and inconsistencies in his thinking, but in his considered views he never departed from his espousal of democratic institutions. Nor do we have any grounds to believe he had the faintest interest in domination over other lands. Nevertheless, he was surprisingly unmindful of the evils bound up with the kinds of industrialism that prevailed in the countries he cited as role models. It is also true that he underestimated 'social complexities'.[107] As Parikh put it, 'the problems [planning] involves are not merely or mainly the technical problems; . . . they are pre-eminently social'.[108]

*

Despite the problematic elements in his economic thinking, and even though he never became part of the planning machinery in post-Independence India (see Chapter 23), it is undeniable that Visvesvaraya's interventions deeply impacted the evolution of policies on economic development. As we've seen, his works prefigured the notions of mixed economy, deficit financing, and income measurement. In addition, scholars have argued that his writings and his career in Mysore were an important influence on Jawaharlal Nehru's policies after Independence. Visvesvaraya's belief that the state should manage key industries (which in turn would promote the growth of other industrial sectors) found expression in the Nehruvian public sector units. His establishment of educational and banking institutions (Mysore University, the Bank of Mysore) with a view to promoting industrial development was mirrored by Nehru's creation of the Indian Institutes of Technology and the State Bank of India with a similar objective. His Mysore Economic Conference was a precursor to the Planning Commission.[109]

The interwar years, then, were a time when Visvesvaraya, slowly but surely, established himself as a public intellectual at a pan-Indian level. In his sixties and seventies, he had fashioned a new public identity. Remarkably—as we shall see in the chapters to come—he did this while keeping up his earlier roles as civil engineer and industrial cheerleader.

20

Rivers Gear

Since 1912, the year he became Dewan of Mysore, Visvesvaraya had been more administrator than engineer. Over the next fifteen years, he had ridden his various hobbyhorses—economic development, statistics, industrial management, education policy—so consistently that he could have passed for a jockey. Yet he didn't lose touch entirely with his original field—hydraulic engineering. While he no longer took charge of executing projects, he was offered, and accepted, several short-term consulting assignments in the interwar years.

These assignments drew on his expertise in irrigation, water supply, and flood control. They took him across the length and breadth of the subcontinent. In the 1920s, Visvesvaraya headed a committee that recommended a water supply scheme for the city of Bangalore. The scheme involved the creation of a reservoir on the river Arkavathi at Thippagondanahalli, around twenty miles outside the city. Visvesvaraya continued to take an interest in the project until it was commissioned in 1933.[1] In the early 1930s, he continued to advise the Hyderabad government on the drainage system being built for their capital.[2] In the same decade, he was consulted by Nagpur and Indore on issues such as water supply, drainage, and urban development.[3] Even the Portuguese administration of Goa sought his advice.[4]

In 1937, Mahatma Gandhi requested Visvesvaraya to advise the newly formed Congress government of Orissa on ways to tackle the scourge of recurrent flooding in the Mahanadi delta (there had been a massive flood that year).[5] Visvesvaraya obliged. He began by analysing gazetteer and census data alongside the report of a 1928 committee that had looked into the question of floods in Orissa. The result was a 'preliminary note' he submitted to the government in November 1937.[6]

True to form, he favoured decisive and large-scale engineering interventions. These included 'protective embankments, . . . judicious dredging, flood escapes, . . . opening out estuaries and making cuts through sand banks'. Although the 1928 committee had opined that it was not feasible to build flood control reservoirs on Orissa's rivers, Visvesvaraya—citing current proposals to build reservoirs on the Mississippi and Ohio rivers in the USA, and the ones he himself had initiated on the Easi and Musi in Hyderabad—asked the government to investigate this option once more. As in Hyderabad, he foresaw the possibility of turning a flood control measure into a multipurpose project serving additional purposes such as irrigation and the production of electricity.

For the moment, Visvesvaraya recommended the appointment of two engineers to gather current and historical hydrological data, and '[a] committee of three expert engineers . . . as an advisory body to supervise the technical side of the work of the special staff and maintain a continuous study of flood problems'.[7] Such a committee was created in 1938. At least two of the members—the Mysore engineer M.G. Rangaiya, and the Bombay irrigation specialist C.C. Inglis—knew Visvesvaraya's work and worldview well.[8] In April 1939, Visvesvaraya was able to go see the Mahanadi delta for himself. He spent ten days inspecting the area, and produced a second note, which the expert committee took into account in its deliberations.[9] The committee, whose members also investigated the conditions in various parts of the state, concluded that reservoirs need not be considered until less expensive options had been explored. They provided the government with a list of engineering works they believed should be undertaken.[10]

The issue was eventually passed on to the central government in 1945. The Chairman of the Central Waterways, Irrigation and Navigation Commission, the Roorkee-educated civil engineer A.N. Khosla, ultimately pushed for a multipurpose reservoir, just as Visvesvaraya had. This was the genesis of the Hirakud Dam project, on which work began in 1946.[11] When it came time to appoint a chief engineer for the project, the state turned to Visvesvaraya once more, asking him to recommend a suitable candidate.[12]

*

In addition to these miscellaneous jobs, the interwar years saw Visvesvaraya take on two high-profile assignments that afforded him the opportunity to revisit the philosophy of irrigation he had first developed during his years as a PWD engineer. In both cases, he served as chairman of enquiry committees reporting to the Bombay government. Decades after he had retired from the Bombay service, he was in a position once more to leave an imprint on irrigation policy in the presidency.

The first of these appointments came in 1929, the year Visvesvaraya stepped down from the chairmanship of the Bhadravati iron factory. That year he was asked to head a two-member committee set up to audit the Lloyd Barrage, a spectacular new irrigation project in Sind that had been under construction since 1923. Visvesvaraya's colleague on the committee was his old friend from the Nizam's PWD, M. Ahmed Ali, who now went by the title of Nawab Ali Nawaz Jung Bahadur. The assignment took

Visvesvaraya back to Sukkur, the sleepy town where, thirty-five years earlier, he had been in charge of building a water supply system. It also resulted in his second brush with the Indus, Sind's most important river.[13]

Emerging from the snows near Mount Kailash in Tibet, the Indus rushed and skipped through the mountainous regions of Kashmir and the North West Frontier Province, then swelled as it was fed by the five rivers of the Punjab. It proceeded southward to create a vast alluvial basin in Sind before draining into the Arabian Sea, having traversed a distance of around 2,000 miles in all.[14] The river was of crucial importance to agriculture in Sind, which received little rain. Cultivators in the region traditionally used inundation canals to harness its waters in the hot months, when the river overflowed its banks. But the supply was unpredictable at the best of times, and the canals were of little help in winter. The province also experienced extremes of weather, with sweltering summers and frosty winters.

As a result, colonial bureaucrats thought of Sind as an insalubrious and laggard region, peopled by unlettered peasants incapable of carrying out organized, settled agriculture. They decided it was the state's duty to guide the cultivators towards more efficient, commercially-oriented farming using perennial irrigation. To this end, over several decades, 'projects for the control of the Indus at Sukkur were mooted, considered and rejected'. But it was only towards the end of the First World War that, for a combination of reasons, the authorities finally took the plunge.[15]

In 1923, proposals for a colossal irrigation works were approved by the Secretary of State for India and the Bombay Legislative Council. Its centrepiece would be a barrage at Sukkur in northern Sind, close to the point where the Indus entered the province. This structure, unlike a dam, would not impound water; instead, its purpose was to regulate the flow of the river. The barrage would feed an intricate network of canals thousands of miles long, doubling the irrigable area of Sind from 3.5 to an astounding 7 million acres. 5,500 million cubic feet of earth would need to be dug out to accomplish this: enough to fill a medium-sized reservoir. It was 'the biggest irrigation scheme of its kind undertaken in any part of the world'. The projected cost was a humongous Rs 18.35 crore (an estimate later revised to over Rs 20 crore). To put this in perspective, the total amount expended on *all* 'productive' irrigation projects *since the inception* of the colonial state was approximately Rs 75 crore.[16] The Barrage Administration, a specially created unit within the Bombay PWD, began construction work in July 1923.[17]

The barrage project came to bear the name of George Lloyd, then Governor of Bombay. As with the Back Bay Reclamation project, which was also sanctioned during Lloyd's tenure, it proved a controversial proposition. The most obvious reason was the enormous expense involved. Recent constitutional reforms meant it was the Bombay government, not the Government of India, that would have to stump up the funds. But Sind's residents formed less than one-fifth of the Presidency's population, and taxpayers in other parts of Bombay were loath to have their money spent on a project that would not benefit them in any tangible manner.[18] Nor was support for the project unanimous among Sindhis themselves. Landowners in the northern part of the province worried that under the new system the state would keep a closer watch on the amount of water taken from the canals. Their counterparts in Lower Sind districts like Hyderabad (distinct from its namesake in the Deccan) and Karachi were concerned that the new works centred on Sukkur in the north would reduce the amount of water available in their part of the province. Finally, a number of colonial engineers unconnected with the project questioned its design and implementation on technical grounds.[19]

By 1929, the voices of dissent had become so loud that the Bombay government could no longer afford to ignore them. This was the context in which Visvesvaraya and Ali Nawaz Jung were invited to examine and submit a report on the Lloyd Barrage's 'engineering aspects, both technical and administrative'.[20] 'The public', the *Times of India* opined,

> will welcome [their] appointment . . . Since the Back Bay reclamation scheme was so grossly mismanaged, there is some justification for fearing that mistakes may be made in this larger undertaking. Sir M. Visweswaraya and Nawab Ali Nawaz Jung Bahadur are two experienced engineers . . . Weight will be given to their opinion because they are independent of the Government of Bombay or of any other Government.[21]

The Mysorean-Hyderabadi duo began work in June 1929. They started out in Bombay, where they pored over the relevant PWD files. They then embarked on a tour of Sind, visiting Karachi, Larkana, Hyderabad, and other places. They spent a week in Sukkur observing the barrage as it took shape: 39 of its 66 spans had been built already. They spoke to engineers at various levels of the Barrage Administration, and held discussions with its chief engineer, Charles Harrison. They also met other irrigation officers of the Sind PWD who were not directly connected with the new project, and consulted 'several leading public men, representative Zamindars and cultivators'.[22] Returning to Bombay, the engineers submitted their views in September.[23]

The report submitted by Visvesvaraya and Ali Nawaz went into great technical detail, evaluating the layout of the barrage and canals, the techniques and materials being used in their construction, and the management of the project. The authors identified a number of areas of concern. The composition of the cement-and-concrete sludge used in the apron of the barrage was not appropriate. The dredgers employed at the main site were proving ineffectual, leading to ballooning labour costs. The canals, as designed, were not capacious enough to serve the needs of the crops grown in the province.[24] The procurement of expensive construction machinery should have been carried out with the aid of private consultants or a committee of experts, who could have helped get it at better prices. The Barrage engineers should have taken more time to carry out background studies before starting to build: this, too, would have helped them avoid cost overruns.[25]

Most of these points dealt with matters of detail, suggesting ways in which the construction of the project could be made more efficient. The sixty-page report contained several more suggestions of this kind.[26] But there was a larger question at stake: whether the barrage and canals project was justified in the first place. As the statistics quoted earlier make clear, the Lloyd Barrage project was an unprecedented intervention in the natural regime of the Indus and the agrarian society of Sind. There were massive environmental risks involved, some affecting particular sites and others applicable to the project as a whole.

Visvesvaraya and Ali Nawaz were conscious of these. They noted, for instance, that there was a bar, or shallow section, in the river around the barrage site. This meant there was a real danger of silting and even, conceivably, of the river being violently diverted by the obstruction in the vicinity of the barrage.[27] Silting was also probable in the canals.[28] The Indus, the report observed, 'constantly shifts its course, its behaviour is uncertain and treacherous and its hydrography is not correctly known'.[29]

Another key challenge was the possibility of the project leading to salt accumulation and waterlogging in the agricultural tracts served by the canals. Visvesvaraya was well acquainted with these problems, both of which had bedevilled the (much smaller) works in the Deccan during his time there decades earlier. Now, he and Ali Nawaz pointed out that in neighbouring Punjab, with its manifold irrigation projects, waterlogging was proving to be a major challenge. In Sind itself, there had been '[n]o systematic subsoil survey', but the available data suggested that the province would be highly susceptible to the same problems.[30]

Some of these observations were potentially damning. How could the world's largest irrigation project have been undertaken without a careful study of the soil conditions and the likelihood of waterlogging? How could the state have set out to change the characteristics of the Indus without fully understanding its existing regime?

Remarkably, these questions did not alarm Visvesvaraya and Ali Nawaz. To them, they were points that could be worked out in real time. Concerns notwithstanding, they held firmly that the barrage was a necessity. The proliferating irrigation works in Punjab were siphoning off large amounts of water from the Indus before it entered Sind. This was 'a menace to the future of Sind agriculture', and the only way to counter it was to 'make arrangements in Sind to raise the level of supply of river water and control its distribution by constructing a barrage'.[31] Moreover, the barrage project would dramatically boost the agricultural output of the region and 'bring prosperity to Sind'. If its construction was a gamble, it was a gamble worth taking.

> It is not to be expected that a great complicated scheme of this magnitude will be perfect in all its details. Natural conditions will not lend themselves favourably in every direction and no big undertaking of this size can be carried out without risks and without interfering with some local interest or other.

'Should unforeseen risks or difficulties arise in future', they added sanguinely, 'the resources of engineering should be able to cope with them.'[32]

This was a classic statement of the engineer's supreme faith in man's dominion over nature. The bias towards getting on with things and dealing with issues as they arose also echoed Visvesvaraya's approach to the negotiations surrounding the Krishnarajasagara dam nearly two decades earlier. Now, he and Ali Nawaz declared that the Lloyd Barrage was 'a *fait accompli* and no useful purpose will be served by prolonging controversies. It is now the duty of every official and of every patriotic citizen not to dwell on old objections but to accept conditions as they are and offer constructive suggestions'.[33]

They proceeded to fulfil their own patriotic obligations by offering recommendations for the future execution of the project. To reduce the likelihood of waterlogging and salinity, they suggested that the intensity of irrigation on the Lloyd Barrage project—the proportion of actually watered land to the area under the command of the canals—be reduced from the proposed figure of 74 per cent to 60 per cent or lower.[34] Officials must keep an eye out for instances of waterlogging, increasing the frequency of their water-table measurements, and be prepared with 'projects for the necessary drainage cuts and channels' as a remedy.[35] The Barrage staff must also regularly monitor the flow of the Indus and watch for any disruptions in its course.[36] In particular, they should carry out '[s]ections of the river bed . . . annually both above and below the Barrage and at selected points for about 15 miles above the river to watch the effect of Barrage operation on the river course'. These steps would also help them tackle potential floods.[37]

Having dealt with the most pressing concerns, Visvesvaraya and Ali Nawaz focused on measures that would be required to realize the positive potential of the project. Some of these reflected Visvesvaraya's long-standing views on commercial agriculture and how it could dovetail with the fostering of industries. 'A Bureau of Research' was to be set up in order to conduct 'scientific investigation . . . in irrigation and agriculture'. Technical training should be stepped up, and education in Sind was to be 'given an agricultural and business bias'. Further, '[c]omplete agricultural statistics should be maintained from year to year', and 'a few model villages' could be created 'to serve as patterns for others in village planning and scientific agriculture'.[38]

On the whole, Visvesvaraya and Ali Nawaz had pulled off a fine balancing act. They had been conscientious in noting the uncertainties associated with the Lloyd Barrage project, environmental and otherwise. They had spelt out clearly where further investigation and vigilance was required. They had even left, buried in the fine print, indications of the haste and hubris that had accompanied the barrage project's execution. Despite all this, the authors had come down strongly in favour of the continuation of the project. For good measure, they had handsomely complimented the Bombay PWD engineers in charge of it and lauded Chief Engineer Harrison for his 'admirable devotion and energy'.[39] They had even argued that, given the sheer scale of the project, the Government of India should relieve the Bombay government of the financial responsibility for it.[40]

All this must have come as music to the Bombay government's ears. In setting up the committee, they must have known that although Visvesvaraya and Ali Nawaz were disinterested parties, they were both pro-PWD in their orientation and positively disposed towards large, ambitious engineering projects. Shortly after their report was submitted, the Governor of Bombay, Sir Frederick Sykes, wrote to Visvesvaraya. 'The report is obviously an excellent one,' he remarked, 'and the amount of interest which you and the Nawab Saheb [Ali Nawaz] have taken in trying to ensure that it should be a really useful contribution to the interests of a great scheme is very clear.'[41]

*

If Sind was on the brink of getting its first modern irrigation project at the end of the 1920s, the situation was somewhat different in other parts of the Bombay Presidency. The Deccan, in particular, had benefited from major irrigation works as early as the late nineteenth century. Cultivation had become especially profitable from the first decade of the twentieth (around the time Visvesvaraya's block system had been introduced), with a substantial increase in the area under high-value crops like sugarcane.[42]

But the picture turned less rosy in the 1920s, when crop prices plateaued, even as the undesirable side effects of perennial irrigation—waterlogging and the accumulation of salts in the soil—became increasingly apparent. The idyll was positively shattered around 1930, when prices crashed in the wake of the Great Depression. The decline affected both dry crops such as jowar and bajri, and wet crops such as rice, wheat, and sugarcane. By the late 1930s, sugarcane cultivation and the production of *gul* (the Marathi term for jaggery) had dropped. Cultivators were going into debt, and struggled to pay the charges for canal water. They were also reluctant to use canal water because of the red tape involved.[43]

There was a paradox, however. Even as individual growers of sugarcane faced problems, private companies were establishing sugar mills on the canals taking off from the Nira, Pravara, and Girna rivers.[44] The main reason was a change in fiscal policy at the all-India level: in 1932, the colonial government had, among other pro-sugar measures, granted economic protection to the sugar industry. The Bombay government offered further concessions in the early 1930s, hoping to boost canal revenues by attracting sugar companies to the command areas. The result was that a number of entrepreneurs—among them the family of Walchand Hirachand, who happened to be a close associate of Visvesvaraya's—embarked on the production of white sugar in the Deccan. The Bombay Presidency was by no means the sugar heartland of India—that honour belonged to the United Provinces and Bihar & Orissa—but by 1937–38, it hosted no fewer than seven sugar factories. These companies, which grew their own sugarcane, wanted to increase their land holdings, and demanded canal water at concessional rates.[45]

Such was the agrarian situation in Bombay when the Presidency—minus Sind, which had been hived off the previous year—got its first Congress government in 1937, following constitutional reforms that increased provincial autonomy. Faced with indebted farmers, waterlogged fields, and the new requirements of sugar factories, the new Bombay government, headed by B.G. Kher, established a committee of inquiry in the dying days of 1937. The eleven-member committee included engineers, members of the legislative assembly, and agricultural scientists. It was chaired by Visvesvaraya.[46]

The choice of Visvesvaraya as Chairman of the Committee was a straightforward one. Now in his mid-seventies, he was a national figure known as much for his espousal of economic planning as for his engineering credentials. That very year, he had advised the Kher government on how they might draw up a five-year plan for the Bombay Presidency.[47] He knew the Bombay irrigation system as well as anyone, having spent twenty-five years as a part of it in his earlier years. In other words, he was a man of nationwide standing, well known to the government, and well-versed in the problems of the region.

Visvesvaraya and his colleagues were asked to advise the government on a number of related questions. What principles should govern the supply of canal water to individual cultivators, sugar factories, and other buyers such as municipalities? What rates should they be charged for the water? What could be done to relieve the effects of waterlogging?[48]

Assembling in Bombay in January 1938, the committee spent two months collecting data and opinions through questionnaires, memoranda, conversations, and first-hand observations made while travelling across the Presidency, covering Ahmednagar, Poona, Dharwar, Ahmedabad, and other districts. They heard from farmers, sugar companies, and agricultural 'experts' before finalizing their recommendations.[49] These clearly bore the imprint of Visvesvaraya's thinking.

The committee's central recommendation was to make the block system of irrigation—which Visvesvaraya had pioneered on the Niral Canal three decades earlier—the default mode on the major canals of the Deccan. It was designed to encourage crop rotation, allow more farmers the opportunity to grow sugarcane, and distribute canal water rationally across a large number of villages. Its widespread adoption, the committee argued, would reduce wastage of water.[50]

Addressing the question of water rates, the committee emphasized the need to shift towards volumetric pricing—again, a point Visvesvaraya had raised in the first decade of the twentieth century. Under the existing system, farmers were charged for canal water on the basis of the size of the field irrigated and the type of crop raised: an arrangement which encouraged indiscriminate watering whenever canal water was made available. If users were instead charged on the basis of the volume of water supplied, they would use it much more carefully.[51]

However, volumetric pricing would take time to implement; so in the meantime, the committee suggested some changes in the rates charged under the existing system. For instance, they recommended concessions in the water rates charged for seasonal crops, including a discounted rate on two struggling canals, the Girna and the Nira Right Bank, presumably to encourage the use of canal water.[52]

As for the scourge of waterlogging, the committee noted it was partly due to water seeping out from the canals into adjoining fields: a possible solution was 'sealing [the canal walls and bed] by puddling and lining'. But the problem owed much more to the excessive watering of fields by cultivators. Farmers should be educated about the dangers of this practice. In addition, they should be barred from growing sugarcane 'in shallow soil unless the natural drainage is good' or 'in large concentrations' in areas with 'deep [soil]'. In already waterlogged fields, basic drainage works would need to be undertaken. The affected farmers would need to take the lead in constructing these, while the government could guide them.[53]

Visvesvaraya and his colleagues took special pains to analyse the requirements of the sugar companies in the presidency. These companies had worked out that in order to operate successfully, they needed to grow their own sugarcane. Accordingly, they occupied land on the canals, where they were charged the same water rate for sugarcane as ordinary cultivators, although they were exempt from the block system. They also paid the government for drainage works within their territories, along with other miscellaneous charges.[54]

The committee noted sympathetically the various challenges facing these sugar factories and stressed the positive contribution they made to the local economy. They generated jobs for labourers during the agricultural off-season, 'provided schools, dispensaries and other amenities in areas in which they were formerly unknown', and 'introduced fluid capital into the areas in which they operate'. A range of policies was needed to encourage these companies. The government should share the cost of drainage measures, help the companies acquire consolidated blocks of land by negotiating with individual landowners, require farmers in factory areas to sell their cane to the companies at specified prices, and freeze the current water rate for the companies (Rs 45 per acre per year) for a period of thirty years.[55] In one case, that of the Ravalgaon factory, they suggested an even lower rate (Rs 28 per acre per year), arguing that its presence on the Girna Canal helped salvage that otherwise unsuccessful irrigation work.[56]

*

The Visvesvaraya Committee's recommendations were well received,[57] and the Bombay government agreed to implement most of them.[58] But the markedly pro-sugar company views it espoused were not unanimously shared within the committee. One member—J.G. More, a prominent non-Brahmin leader and MLA—appended a dissenting note to the committee's report.[59] He argued that the Bombay government's recent policies had been geared towards '[replacing] the indigenous agriculturist by the capitalist', and that his colleagues on the committee were continuing that approach. The crux of his criticisms was that the emphasis on making the canal systems generate revenue 'runs counter to the protective purposes of the canals': they were intended primarily to save the region from famines, not to enable the production of commercial crops.[60]

More pointed out that Visvesvaraya's block system had had problems in the past, reiterating earlier criticisms of the system. Selecting specific blocks of land in a village for irrigation would mean that some farmers—whose lands were outside the blocks—would have no access to irrigation. Visvesvaraya assumed that such farmers, if desirous of growing sugarcane, could swap lands with those in the blocks. But this was unrealistic, not least because 'cultivators have a natural ingrained attachment to their ancestral lands'. More also questioned the claim that the block system would reduce wastage of water, pointing out that a great deal of wastage actually occurred 'in transit from the main canal'.[61] What is more, it was unfair that the sugar companies should be exempt from the restrictions involved in the block system.[62]

More also disputed the accuracy of the data on which his colleagues had based their recommended water rates, and proposed further reductions for the benefit of the indebted farmers of the presidency. On the other hand, he questioned the concessions granted to the sugar companies. As profit-driven organisations, they contradicted the original purpose for which the canal systems of the Deccan had been built, namely to avert famine. Such being the case, the government should charge them a higher water rate.[63] In the case of the Ravalgaon Sugar Company, to which the committee wanted to grant a particularly low water rate, More pointed out a conflict of interest: 'The factory belongs to one of the members of the Irrigation Inquiry Committee [Lalchand Hirachand].'[64] Ravalgaon should be charged the same rate as the other sugar companies. The companies should be asked to pay the full cost of drainage works required for relieving waterlogging in their areas of operation. He also objected to the government adopting pressure tactics and siding with the factories in their efforts to acquire land from individual cultivators.[65]

Included in the report was Visvesvaraya's brief, almost disdainful rejoinder to More. Sugarcane had accounted for a large proportion of the crop value in recent years, and neglecting to promote it 'will strike at the root of the income of the cultivators and will bring about the financial ruin of the irrigation system as a whole'. He dismissed farmers opposing the block system as '[c]ultivators who are interested in the old ways of doing things or who have been profiting by the old order'. He concluded by remarking that 'Mr. More who had ample opportunities of bringing forward his questions at Committee meetings failed to do so, but announced his intention of writing a minute of dissent at the last moment'.[66]

Irrespective of the financial practicality of More's suggestions, however, he had put his finger on some of the blind spots in Visvesvaraya's thinking. Whether in the case of the Lloyd Barrage or the canals of the Deccan, he saw irrigation works as engines of economic growth rather than as an insurance against famine. For him, perennial irrigation and the rearing of commercial crops were the acme of agricultural progress. He hewed to his block system despite the many challenges it had encountered. While acknowledging the dangers of waterlogging and soil salinity, he traced these problems not to the massive interventions engineers had made in the local ecosystem, but to the unenlightened practices of unlettered cultivators. Moreover, he was confident that technical solutions could be found. Finally, his pro-industrial leanings meant he was soft on large landholders and commercial undertakings like the sugar companies of the Deccan. All in all, the septuagenarian's views on irrigation had remained remarkably consistent since his departure from the PWD thirty years previously.

21

The Motor of Progress

As a civil engineer, Visvesvaraya's days were spent at dams, reservoirs, irrigation canals and water works. But it was in the factory that his heart truly lay. The clang of metal, the sizzle of chemicals, the emergence of tangible products on a conveyor belt: these seem to have been his idea of Elysium. They represented progress and prosperity—especially if the products in question were gleaming automobiles. Motor vehicles were a key feature of American society, and it was America that Visvesvaraya saw as the foremost exemplar of modernity. During his foreign sojourn of 1908–09, he had made a pilgrimage to Detroit to see Henry Ford's factory; he went back to Detroit when he visited the US in 1919.[1] In India, Visvesvaraya had lived through the transition from horses to motor cars in official circles. In his days as Dewan of Mysore, he had spent many hours in his Wolseley and his Hotchkiss, travelling not only through the thoroughfares of Bangalore but also across country roads on his regular inspection tours of Mysore's villages.[2] Later on, he maintained a car at his Bombay residence too.[3]

By the 1930s, motor transport had gained substantial traction in India. While still outnumbered by bullock carts and *tonga*s, cars and buses were running not only in the cities but also between villages. For Visvesvaraya, they were an unalloyed good. Writing in 1934, he observed that motor transport had a positive economic effect, 'bringing village produce closer to markets', reducing 'the wide fluctuations that existed in different parts of the country in the prices of food grains, cotton piece-goods and yarn', and even 'having a distinct educative value in the villages' now that rural Indians could travel more easily and see something of the world.[4] For all their potential impact, however, the number of automobiles in the country was minuscule. As of 1932, Visvesvaraya noted, British India had around 2,00,000 automobiles as against 26.8 million in the US. Moreover, the entire stock of automobiles in India was imported, resulting in 'a huge drain of India's wealth'. If only cars and buses could be manufactured locally, India could save large amounts of foreign exchange while creating jobs for 'many thousands of her people'.[5]

These were more than academic arguments. Starting in the 1930s, Visvesvaraya networked actively with industrialists of his acquaintance, goading them to start an auto manufacturing unit on the one hand, and lobbying governments for concessions on the other. The quest for establishing a motor industry in India would consume him for the best part of a decade, although he had no financial stake in the matter.

*

Visvesvaraya set the ball rolling in May 1935, when he called a meeting of around forty business leaders in Bombay. No less than the Chairman of the Tata group, Sir Nowroji Saklatvala, agreed to chair the conclave, which was held at the Tatas' Bombay headquarters. Visvesvaraya presented his preliminary ideas about the prospects for an automobile factory, stressing that he had done his homework: his proposals were based on informal talks with dealers active in the import and sale of automobiles in Bombay. The possible locations he had in mind were Jamshedpur (where iron and steel and several ancillary industries were thriving) and Bombay; but he preferred the latter, for it was the largest internal market for cars. The idea was to establish a factory of medium size producing cars and buses, each of a single, standardized design. At the start, certain components would have to be imported. Others could be outsourced to workshops in Jamshedpur and Bombay, and a few would be made within the new factory, where the vehicles would finally be assembled. A sum of Rs 100–150 lakh would need to be invested. The government would be requested to aid the fledgling industry through protective tariffs and other concessions.[6]

Visvesvaraya had said enough to capture the initial interest of his audience. They decided that the plan was worth looking into, and that someone should travel abroad to gather information on functioning automobile factories (any new Indian factory at this stage would require technical assistance from established firms).[7] In the event, Visvesvaraya took on the task himself. According to an early biographer, he paid his own way,[8] and this was likely the case: there is no evidence to suggest that his industrialist friends offered to foot the bill, for despite their interest in the venture, they remained cautious.

Visvesvaraya set sail for England in June 1935. This was the first leg of a six-month tour that was to encompass Europe and America in addition. He went to Oxford, Birmingham, and other auto manufacturing centres, and consulted Lord Austin of the Austin Motor Company on the feasibility of producing cars in India. He travelled through Germany, France, and Italy, paying special attention to the Fiat factory in Turin. He then crossed the Atlantic. Passing through New York, he camped for a month in Detroit, where he met Charles E. Sorensen and W.S. Knudsen, high-profile executives at Ford and General Motors respectively. Visvesvaraya also found time to gather information by corresponding with W.A. Tookey, a Westminster-based consulting engineer and recent President of the UK's Institution of Automobile Engineers, and Frank F. Beall of Detroit, who had been part of the team that created the Gray, a $500 motor car, in the 1920s.[9]

Visvesvaraya completed his peregrinations in early 1936. In April, he organized another meeting of industrialists in Bombay, where he presented his updated plans. Three of them—Manu Subedar, A.D. Shroff, and Cursetjee Limjee—formed a subcommittee to evaluate his proposals.[10] While their report acknowledged the 'enormous trouble' the veteran engineer had gone to, they were circumspect in their evaluation of the plans, noting only that Visvesvaraya 'has certainly made out a prima facie case for the enquiry not to be abandoned'. They didn't agree entirely with his estimates. For instance, they thought the cost of manufacturing cars would considerably exceed Visvesvaraya's estimate of Rs 1,400 per unit. His calculations had been made on the model of large-scale American factories, whereas the proposed Indian one would be much smaller and would not enjoy the same economies of scale. Foreign companies, moreover, were likely to compete vigorously, lowering the prices of their cars being sold in India. They thought that much more detailed estimates were required, and argued that '[w]hile Sir M.V. seems very much enamoured of American conditions, we are of opinion that it would be safer to go on European model [sic]'.[11]

*

Evidently the Bombay industrialists were not going to be swayed by sentiment if they did not see a solid business case. Nevertheless, Visvesvaraya continued his efforts, leaning especially on one of his close associates, Walchand Hirachand.

Walchand (1882–1953) was a Jain businessman from Sholapur who had started out as a construction contractor before entering the sugar and shipping industries. He was known for his buccaneering ways and his outspoken manner, especially when it came to challenging entrenched expatriate commercial interests.[12] Visvesvaraya had known him from at least the 1920s, when one of Walchand's companies was working on the drainage system he had designed for Poona city. The businessman and the engineer were also part of the same social circles. When in Poona they would meet at Parnakuti, the home of Premlila Thackersey, the widow of Visvesvaraya's old friend Vithaldas Thackersey.[13] Now, in the 1930s, they were thrown together once more. The older man peppered Walchand with notes on his automobile scheme. They discussed potential directors for the new venture, and Visvesvaraya ran the names by the respected cotton tycoon Sir Purshotamdas Thakurdas. He tried to gather allies, introducing Walchand to other 'friends'—presumably industrialists—at the Willingdon Sports Club in Bombay.[14]

Around 1938–39, Walchand decided to take the plunge. He was probably encouraged by a momentous political development that had taken place in 1937. That year (as we have seen in earlier chapters) elections were held across British India on the basis of recent constitutional reforms, which provided for a significant measure of provincial autonomy. The Congress swept the elections, coming to power in eight provinces including Bombay, where B.G. Kher assumed office as the premier. Walchand knew that the Indian National Congress had long advocated the promotion of local manufactures, and that a Congress government was much more likely than one run by a British governor to support an Indian plan for a car factory. What is more, Bombay's new finance minister, A.B. Latthe, was known to him. To top it all, 1938 was the year the Congress established a pro-industries National Planning Committee, and both Visvesvaraya and Walchand were appointed to it.[15] All in all, there could hardly have been a more propitious time to make a move.

Walchand and Visvesvaraya now approached the Bombay government with their scheme, asking for support in the form of a guaranteed return of 3.5 per cent on investment for shareholders over a ten-year period.[16] Walchand called on Kher; Visvesvaraya wrote to Latthe; Walchand's brother, Lalchand Hirachand, met the finance secretary. The response was encouraging. The Bombay government even loaned Walchand the services of their director of industries, P.B. Advani, for four months, to help him look for technology partners abroad.[17] This was something of a coup: not only was Advani in a superb position to influence the government, he was also an old acquaintance of Visvesvaraya's. The two had got to know each other in the early 1920s, when Visvesvaraya established his second residence in Bombay, and they often went for evening walks together.[18]

Walchand sounded out his business partners and formulated plans to float a company. Visvesvaraya continued to correspond with Latthe with a view to meeting the government's stipulations on organizing the firm. Finally, a new company was established for the manufacture of motor vehicles, with Tulsidas Kilachand, D.M. Khatau, and Walchand himself as managing agents.[19]

August 1939 found Walchand and Advani in America, knocking on the doors of the Ford Motor Company in Detroit as they sought a technology partner. Advani's initial talks with Charles Sorensen at Ford were particularly promising. The Ford Company's own experts examined Visvesvaraya's plans and pronounced them viable. Walchand and Advani even gained an audience with Henry Ford himself. But the deal fell through when Ford's Canadian arm, which had jurisdiction over the company's affairs within the British Empire, demanded a 51 per cent stake in the Indian company.[20]

The Bombay duo—who had kept Walchand's aides in Bombay posted on their progress by telegram while instructing them to 'SEND COPIES ALL CABLES VISVESVARAYA'[21]—now turned to another American manufacturer. This was Chrysler, which produced extremely popular mid-range cars like the Plymouth and the De Soto. This time they had better luck. In November 1939, a month after they returned to India, Chrysler's own representative visited Bombay and reported positively to his principals. On 8 July 1940, Walchand's company signed an agreement with Chrysler's Export Division (Visvesvaraya was one of the witnesses to the agreement). Under its terms, they could produce cars for the subcontinent using Chrysler's technology. Chrysler would charge a fee, but sought no financial equity in the Indian company. Later that year, the agreement was forwarded to the Bombay government.[22]

By this time, however, Walchand had lost his trump card. For the Congress provincial governments had quit at the end of October 1939, protesting against Britain's autocratic decision to involve India in the war that had just broken out in Europe.[23] This meant a British governor was back in charge of industries in Bombay. He kicked the problem upstairs, telling Walchand and his colleagues that the Government of India would need to approve their project. The colonial government, in turn, maintained they would only approve new ventures that were essential to the prosecution of the war. They asked the Defence Department to evaluate the proposal on this basis.

Walchand now argued that his venture would be of direct benefit to the Allies' war effort. The government had decided to modernise the Indian Army, and was procuring thousands of automobiles for these purposes. Walchand said his factory could provide some of these—5000 automobiles per year—allowing the government to reduce its reliance on expensive imports. But the Defence Department was quite content to continue using the imported Fords and Chevrolets that had served them well in the past. In December 1940, the Government of India refused aid for Walchand's project, declaring that it was not relevant to the Empire's wartime needs. A week later Visvesvaraya brought out a tract criticizing their stance, but to no avail. In January 1941, the Bombay government washed its hands of the project.[24]

*

Curiously, this was the very moment when another ambitious proposal of Walchand's received the approval of the British. This was a plan to manufacture military aircraft in India.[25]

The venture was, in a sense, born out of the motor car campaign. According to Walchand's official biographer, it was on his way back to India after his talks with Ford and Chrysler in 1939 that Walchand met the man who would become his collaborator in the aircraft undertaking. On his flight from San Francisco to Hong Kong en route to Bombay, Walchand ran into William D. Pawley, a dapper American businessman in his early forties. Pawley was in the aeroplane business. The president of the New York-based Intercontinent Corporation, he was at this time director of an aircraft manufacturing plant in Kuomintang China supplying aircraft to the Chinese national government.

Heady from his recent experience of talking to Henry Ford and his ilk, Walchand immediately suggested that Pawley go into business with him and provide technical assistance for an aircraft factory in India. He also shot off a proposal to the colonial government. If they supported his venture, he said, he would supply aircraft to them for use in the war that was now under way in Europe.[26]

The proposal bobbed up and down the colonial hierarchy over the next year. Unlike with the motor car venture, however, it had a measure of support in the corridors of power. Perhaps unbeknownst to Walchand, the viceroy, Lord Linlithgow, had already begun to look at the possibility of having planes produced in India, and the government was examining a proposal presented by a group of businessmen from Calcutta. Linlithgow and the London-based Secretary of State for India, Leo Amery, calculated that India would need aircraft for strategic reasons, that there would be scope for a civilian industry after the war, and that keeping Indian manufacturers out of this vital sphere of wartime activity would sit poorly with the Indian public at a time of rising national consciousness.

This was the context in which Walchand's proposal arrived. The government was favourably disposed towards this option. They were encouraged especially by the involvement of Pawley, who had a successful track record manufacturing aircraft, as well as the contacts necessary to source parts from America. In July 1940, the Government of India offered in principle to buy $10 million worth of military aircraft from the putative company. Although the British premier, Winston Churchill, and his Minister for Aircraft Production, Lord Beaverbrook, opposed the scheme for a long time—they argued that it would interfere with Britain's wartime production of planes, which was also reliant on components from America—London too gave its approval that December.

Once again Walchand teamed up with Tulsidas Kilachand and D.M. Khatau to act as managing agents, this time to a new aeroplane manufacturing firm, Hindustan Aircraft, Limited (HAL). Pawley signed an agreement with HAL in December 1940, agreeing to help establish a factory, provide machinery and technical experts, and manage the new operation.

Walchand now had to decide where to locate the factory. Having burnt his fingers with the British-appointed Bombay government, he decided now to negotiate with princely states in which he had contacts. In the end, he struck a deal with Mysore, perhaps unsurprisingly given his closeness to Visvesvaraya. The state was still helmed by the pro-industries statesman Mirza Ismail, who was now in his fifteenth year as dewan and back on friendly terms with Visvesvaraya.[27] In early 1941, Mysore invested Rs 20 lakh in HAL, Walchand and his friends providing an equal amount. The Mysore government also exempted HAL from taxes on revenue flowing from the sale of aircraft to the colonial government, and assisted the company with grants of land and subsidized water and electricity. In April, the Government of India became the third major shareholder. Pawley and his team, along with engineers from Walchand's stable, rapidly erected the new factory in Bangalore. HAL supplied its first assembled aircraft—an Intercontinent-Harlow PC-5A trainer—to the colonial government in August 1941.

Visvesvaraya had no official position in HAL, but anecdotal evidence suggests he was in the thick of things. M.R. Varadarajan, one of the engineers who helped build the new plant, later recalled that Visvesvaraya played a mediating role 'in the discussion with the State Government that preceded the establishment of the factory at Bangalore . . . Many difficulties were to be overcome, and Sir M.V. with his personal intervention helped us a great deal'.[28] V.S.N. Rao, who wrote one of the early lives of Visvesvaraya, adds that the former dewan keenly followed the building of the factory too. He went frequently to the works, plying Maganlal Shah—another engineer involved in the construction of the plant—with 'searching questions about the machinery, equipment, raw materials, engine, wings and the type of the steel that was required', asking if the last of these could be sourced from the plant at Bhadravati. According to Rao, Maganlal Shah declared 'that he had yet to see any other man of Visvesvaraya's type, bubbling with enthusiasm, beaming with penetrating intelligence, upright in character, charming in courtesy and full of patriotic fervour'.[29] Hyperbole aside, the engineers on the spot—who might have been forgiven if they'd felt a twinge of irritation at having to indulge the seventy-nine-year-old's curiosity in the midst of their onerous duties—clearly felt gratitude for his enabling role. Visvesvaraya continued to be treated as a special guest at HAL for several years thereafter, a fact to which surviving photographs with the company's top brass attest.[30]

*

Walchand and friends had succeeded in setting up an aircraft factory less than two years since that first meeting with Pawley, and Mysore's assistance had been crucial to this success. In fact, around the time he approached Mysore, Walchand had also placed the automobile proposals—which were about to be turned down by the Bombay government—before the princely state.[31] Since the aircraft scheme was cleared, it was natural that he should fancy his chances in Mysore with his other pet project as well.[32]

Thus it came about that towards the end of 1940, Walchand made a couple of visits to Bangalore and discussed his automobile project with Mirza Ismail, who assured him of his support. For good measure, Walchand engaged a journalist he knew, a correspondent of *The Hindu* named Salivateeswaran, to set up a base in Bangalore the following summer, feel the pulse of officialdom, and prime the press.[33] Visvesvaraya was also overseeing the campaign from his base in Bangalore, feeding Mirza information and suggestions.[34]

Walchand asked Mysore for similar terms to the ones he'd been promised by B.G. Kher's government in Bombay. Would they guarantee 3.5 per cent on investment for ten years? Would they be willing to put in Rs 150 lakh out of the Rs 225 lakh required?[35] He also wanted the Mysore government to purchase the motor cars and trucks the company would manufacture, grant customs waivers for machinery brought into the state, and provide or arrange for land, electricity, and railway transport for their cargo at reduced rates.[36]

Walchand assured Mysore that the venture would yield rich dividends. Chrysler had already offered to provide technical assistance; his team were also in talks with the Austin Motor Company of Britain, which would help them produce 'low power cars up to 15 H.P.' In all he aimed, at the start, to manufacture (and not merely assemble, he stressed) 3,000 cars and 5,000 trucks annually. There was ample demand for motor vehicles in India: around 20,000 to 30,000 were imported annually for civilian use. In addition, at least 6,000 new trucks would be required for military use each year while the war lasted. Why not manufacture some of these in India? Since locally made cars and trucks would not incur duties or shipping and insurance costs, they would be less expensive than imported ones.[37]

Mirza Ismail backed the proposal strongly, forwarding Walchand's proposals to the maharaja in March 1941.[38] But Mirza no longer had the kind of influence over the ruler that he'd had for much of his dewanship. For the old monarch, his childhood friend Krishnaraja IV, had died the previous year. On the throne now was Krishnaraja's nephew, Jayachamaraja Wadiyar. Under the new dispensation, Mirza found he had to route his communications to the ruler through the latter's private secretary, Sir Charles Todhunter.[39] The writer R.K. Narayan, who grew up in Mysore and had a brother working in Todhunter's office, described him as 'an encrusted British administrator' who maintained a bunch of 'terrified and efficient clerks'.

> While Sir Charles kept his dogs, cats, and ducks sheltered in the main building, he housed his clerks in a derelict unventilated barnyard, under a smoky, verminous tiled roof, at the farthest corner of the compound, and summoned them to

> his presence with a buzzer. He glared at them over his narrow spectacles, thumped his huge fist on the desk, and drove them to slave for him twelve hours a day by sheer bullying. His main job was to see that the Maharaja did not lose his loyalty to the British Crown or establish any industry which might affect British interests.[40]

In the matter of the automobile project, Mirza found in Todhunter a formidable adversary.[41] Todhunter gave an early indication of the position when he wrote to Mirza on 26 March that the maharaja was looking at the proposals, but 'trusts that you will not commit the State in any way to the acceptance of the scheme'.[42] The next day he wrote a long letter explaining the maharaja's position, which was that he could not support a project that appeared 'to have little prospect of ultimate success'. Walchand's company, the maharaja thought, would be too reliant on imported components. He wouldn't be able to sell trucks to the colonial government, which had very particular requirements and had already identified vendors. Any machinery the factory required would be exorbitantly expensive as long as the war was on, and at the cessation of hostilities, the concern would have to reckon with 'a glut of trucks in the market'.

The letter pointed out several flaws in Walchand's calculations, which had led him to predict a tidy profit for the proposed venture. 'His Highness finds it difficult to make anything of the figures of estimated profit which Mr. Walchand Hirachand has borrowed from Sir. M. Visvesvaraya. He finds it hard to believe that there would be a sum available for profit of Rs. 1,350 when the whole cost of the car was only Rs. 1,400.' Walchand had assumed that dealers in India would agree to a lower commission than they got for the imported cars they sold. He had failed to factor in the royalties that would need to be paid to Chrysler and Austin Motors. On a recent trip to Bombay, the maharaja had discussed the automobile factory scheme in detail with Visvesvaraya and P.B. Advani. He had 'found their arguments, which seemed to him to avoid the concrete issues, singularly unconvincing'. Meanwhile, the Bombay manager of General Motors (which ran an import business in India) had indicated to the maharaja that car manufacture was not viable in India, which was why GM had not undertaken it. According to Todhunter, the maharaja felt that Walchand himself was not really confident of the company's success: why else would he ask Mysore for a ten-year guarantee to shareholders in addition to investing a majority of the capital? The automobile scheme had been debated for close to seven years, and had it had real potential it would have come to fruition much earlier.[43]

This was a devastating response, but Mirza was unruffled. He wrote back the very same day, saying that the maharaja's concerns arose because he had not seen all the relevant information, which he, Mirza, would be sending him shortly. In the meanwhile, he forwarded—no doubt with a glint in his eye—a cutting from an Australian journal, which he had received from Visvesvaraya. The article, dating from 1939, argued for the manufacture of cars and aeroplanes in Australia, declaring that '[a]ll human progress . . . consists in wise men doing what fools have declared cannot be done'.[44]

A week later, Mirza sent Todhunter a more detailed missive in which he answered the concerns he had raised. He acknowledged that some components would be imported, but only at the beginning, and only because it was the cheaper alternative. Eventually, once a motor industry was established in India, ancillary industries would come up and components would become available in the country. As for the difficulty of obtaining machinery and space on ships to bring it over during the war, the Chrysler Corporation's 'elaborate organization with considerable resources and equipment in America' would come to their aid.

The royalties owed to Chrysler and Austin would not be very high, and would 'work out eventually to about Rs. 25 a vehicle'.

Mirza also pointed out that General Motors, whose manager the maharaja had consulted, had competing interests. Along with Ford, GM controlled the market for cars in India and was happy to make large profits without undertaking *ab initio* manufacture of cars in India. Furthermore, 'it can hardly be said that they have any permanent interest in the country's future'.

As for its relevance to the war effort: the brand new aircraft factory in Bangalore had already been acknowledged as contributing to it, and it was not unlikely the motor factory would soon be seen in a similar light. In any case, it was important to 'take a long range view of the problem of the industrial development of the State'. A new automobile industry would create jobs and '[bring] a number of other incidental and indirect benefits'. What is more, there were synergies to be exploited by promoting aircraft and automobile manufacture simultaneously.

Finally, Mirza argued that just because nobody had stepped forward earlier to set up or support an automobile factory, one could not conclude that it was an unviable idea. 'Such an argument stretched to its logical conclusion would, I am afraid, cut at the root of all enterprise.'[45]

In the meanwhile, Visvesvaraya, a veteran of run-ins with the colonial authorities, had begun a media blitz. In late March, he wrote to twenty-one newspapers about the project and sounded out twelve other princely states (presumably to signal to Mysore that the promoters had other alternatives).[46] Walchand's publicist, Salivateeswaran, was also at work. A few weeks later, he reported to Mirza Ismail that newspapers across the country—no doubt prodded by him—were of the opinion that the project should be declared part of the war effort. They included the *Tribune* of Lahore, the *Hindustan Standard* of Calcutta, the *Bombay Chronicle*, and *The Hindu* of Madras.[47]

Walchand and his allies were cranking up the pressure. They knew what they were up against. It was not so much the maharaja they had to convince, but the representatives of the colonial government, who appear to have been pulling the puppet strings. The Mysore Resident, J.H. Gordon, had asked the dewan to keep him posted on developments, which he was within his rights to do. But he was also receiving information direct from Todhunter.[48] Gordon, in turn, sent regular updates to his bosses in New Delhi and Simla.

On 9 April, Gordon wrote confidentially to the office of the Crown Representative in New Delhi that he had met the maharaja the previous week. The ruler was 'definitely sceptical about the possibilities of success' and was unlikely to approve the project unless 'the commitments of the State are considerably modified and reduced'. Since Mirza was so committed to pushing the project through, Gordon expected 'trouble ahead between His Highness and the Dewan'.[49] On 23 April, the Resident reported to Simla that the climate in Mysore was tense. The dewan was adamant; his colleagues were 'sitting on the fence'. Gordon had heard from Jayachamaraja Wadiyar that 'the Dewan's insistence on his proposals amounted almost to truculence and that the Dewan has forced the issue to such an extent that if his proposals are not acceded to, His Highness will have no option but to ask him to resign if he does not do so of his own accord'.[50]

Gordon himself felt it would be for the best if the dewan were to quit and be replaced by a more passive official, but the Political Adviser in Simla did not want to precipitate matters, cabling the Resident that he should try and 'secure mutual accommodation of viewpoint as between His Highness and Dewan', both on the automobile project and on other governance-related matters in which they were at odds.[51]

While these confidential reports were zipping across the subcontinent, negotiations continued in Mysore. The maharaja sent the promoters' representative a long list of questions, and Todhunter annotated the responses with remarks based on close questioning of Walchand and Visvesvaraya at a meeting he had with them and the dewan on 13 April. The maharaja and Todhunter scrutinized the proposal and the agreement with Chrysler, covering intricate details and scenarios.[52] According to his notes, Todhunter even got Walchand to admit that it would be twenty years before a completely indigenous car could be manufactured in India.[53]

Mirza, for his part, continued to bolster his case. In a note dated 19 April, he expanded on the idea that an automobile factory would boost employment and stimulate the local economy. He went out of his way to allay the ruler's fears. The guaranteed interest the company sought was 'not an unconditional bounty or subsidy, but will be recovered from the company as soon as sufficient profits accrue'. An important compromise had been introduced: Mysore was now being asked to invest only Rs 30–40 lakh (as opposed to the original Rs 150 lakh), the shortfall to be made up from various sources including other princely states and the public.[54]

Pressure was applied from other directions too. C. Hayavadana Rao, President of the Mysore Chamber of Commerce, wanted to bring a delegation of prominent citizens to meet the maharaja and urge him to support the automobile project. After some back and forth with Todhunter, a meeting failed to materialize.[55] Instead, the chamber telegraphed their view that '[a]utomobile project is a great national and an economic question . . . Any adverse step in Mysore may, it is feared, lead to very unfavourable reactions'.[56]

Despite all these efforts, the maharaja (or his advisers) remained unmoved. The only question exercising Todhunter was how the durbar might reject the project without incurring the wrath of the press.[57] In the end, the Government of India provided them with an excuse by declaring that they could not guarantee the availability of foreign exchange, which the company would require in order to import components.[58] On 8 May, Todhunter wrote to Mirza conveying the final decision of the monarch 'that there is no purpose to be served by continuing the present negotiations with the promoters of the scheme'. The letter made it clear that the young maharaja was unwilling to go against the advice of the Government of India, which had simply repeated its position that irrespective of the scheme's prospects in the long run, it was not advisable or practicable to set up the factory in the midst of the war.[59]

Mirza saw the writing on the wall, but fired a closing salvo. 'The people of Mysore,' he told Todhunter, 'will not easily forget or forgive those responsible for deliberately missing such a splendid opportunity of establishing an industry of such far-reaching importance in the State.'[60] The next day, he submitted his resignation.[61]

*

Walchand and Visvesvaraya had drawn a blank in Mysore, but they continued their dogged efforts. Walchand now pulled out all the stops to try and get the manufacture of automobiles classified as a war industry. He persuaded sympathetic British MPs to put questions on the floor of the House of Commons. He got one of them, the Earl Winterton, to write to Secretary of State Leo Amery. He engaged a British officer on leave to lobby the colonial government in Simla on his behalf. He sought an audience with Claude Auchinleck, the Commander-in-Chief of the Indian Army, in Bangalore once again in Delhi, asking him to give his putative firm a chance to supply trucks to the army.[62]

Meanwhile, Visvesvaraya, now in his ninth decade, continued his public criticism of the colonial government. In February 1942, he wrote a letter to the viceroy's private secretary, shortly before publishing his entire correspondence with the Government of India over the preceding years on the topic of the automobile industry.[63]

In April 1942, the American Technical Mission, headed by Henry F. Grady, arrived in India. They were to suggest how India could ramp up the production of material and equipment required for the war, and how the United States might assist in that process.[64] Visvesvaraya was quick to publish a statement on the occasion, pointing out that the colonial government was thwarting attempts to manufacture automobiles in India even as it was poised to spend Rs 50 crore on importing 'trucks and other mechanized motor equipments'. It was time the government let Indian industrialists start enterprises to supply wartime equipment, especially now that the Grady Mission could help such entrepreneurs source industrial machinery and expertise from America.[65] Walchand, for his part, met the members of the Grady Mission during their time in India, and also wrote to its chairman at length. Their efforts, however, did not have any impact.[66]

As it happened, Walchand's aircraft factory also ceased to function as a production facility at around this time. Once Japan entered the war, the Government of India decided they must have full control of the factory. Among other considerations, they calculated that they might need to jettison the factory in the event of a Japanese incursion, so that the latter could not gain control of it. As a result, they took over the company entirely in 1942. Walchand and company were paid compensation in addition to the value of their shares (although Pawley was initially retained), while the Mysore government temporarily relinquished its interest in running the company.

Meanwhile, as aerial warfare took hold in Asia, the Grady Mission stressed that India should be used as a centre for assembling and servicing American military planes. The Allies, they indicated, were better off letting the US take care of the actual production of aircraft. In 1943, the plant was handed over to the Tenth United States Army Airforce. Manufacturing was stopped, and the factory became a massive maintenance operation for the rest of the war. Employing some 15,000 workers, it was used to service aero engines in addition to a wide range of American planes.[67]

*

From the perspective of Walchand, Visvesvaraya, and their friends, the colonial government had been diabolical as usual in their discouragement of indigenous industry while safeguarding the interests of foreign business, while the new Maharaja of Mysore had been craven in his subservience to the British.[68] As the foregoing account makes clear, there was more than a kernel of truth in this reading. The Government of India did indeed put a spanner in the works, and the correspondence makes it clear that Jayachamaraja Wadiyar was worried about incurring the displeasure of the British. It is also apparent that foreign businesses, such as GM, which had a flourishing import agency in Bombay, were nervous about the prospect of a new rival that might undercut them.[69] On the other hand, there were legitimate grounds for scepticism about the project. Mysore's ruler was well within his rights to think carefully about the huge investment and risk his state was being asked to shoulder. Walchand was asking Mysore to insulate his company from risk and grant it very substantial concessions.

Walchand was known for rushing headlong into new ventures.[70] It is quite likely that the automobile project, had it been okayed, would have run into difficulties. The business historian Gita Piramal notes that when the colonial government decided it wanted full control of Hindustan

Aircraft, Walchand, in his heart of hearts, was probably quite happy to sell his stake (at a handsome profit), because by this time the factory was facing many issues arising from a lack of planning.[71]

It was, in many ways, the story of the KRS and Bhadravati all over again. Visvesvaraya and Mirza wanted industrial development at all costs. They wanted the state to take the lead and bear the risks. The propriety or otherwise of allowing individual industrialists to reap the rewards did not occur to them: they were untroubled by what might now be referred to as 'crony capitalism'. As in the earlier cases, they were opposed by more conservative and cautious administrators. The difference this time, according to the scholar Bjørn Hettne, was that Mysorean politics had evolved. The massive government underwriting of large-scale industrial ventures was only made possible by 'squeezing the peasants' (as it was taxpayers' money that was being invested). This was just about possible to do in Visvesvaraya's time, but it became especially difficult once the peasantry became politically active, as it did during Mirza's long dewanship.[72]

*

In the end, Walchand did succeed in setting up an automobile factory, but it was to take him a few more years. By that time the war had ended, removing some of the complications. Crucially, the promoters stopped clamouring for government assistance and concessions on a large scale, and decided to take a chance, invest their own capital, and go to the markets for the rest. Their company, Premier Automobiles Limited (PAL), went public in 1944, and production began at its Bombay factory in 1947. PAL turned out Plymouths and Dodges with Chrysler's support, and, a few years later, began a similar collaboration with Fiat of Italy.[73] It had taken a dozen years after Visvesvaraya gathered his industrialist friends in Bombay, but the first Indian-built cars had finally hit the road.

22

Mentor to Manufacturers

In September 1939, as Visvesvaraya and his friends were in the midst of their efforts to set up an automobile factory, war broke out in Europe. Although the gravity of this development was unmistakable, the early years of the Second World War brought no immediate disruptions to the rhythms of Visvesvaraya's life in Bombay. As he neared the age of eighty, he kept up a steady routine of work and social engagements. His secretary at the time, Y.G. Krishnamurti, left a vivid description of Visvesvaraya's life in his Warden Road home. Cut off from the bustle of downtown Bombay, the bungalow had a patch of lawn with strains of birdsong, a book-filled drawing room, and a sea-facing 'glass-fronted study . . . [with] an atmosphere of its own attuned to the rhythm of the waves'. Visvesvaraya kept a dog—we are not told its name or breed—and employed a liveried servant. He guarded his time jealously, fobbing off admirers and socialites when he could. He did, however, host conclaves of 'wise men' dominated by serious conversation. He kept up with the latest literature, '[grubbing] about in book-shops for volumes the release of which is noticed in advance', and burying his nose in them as soon as he got into his car.[1] He travelled and lectured, eyes firmly fixed on the future,[2] except on one special occasion, when he made a nostalgic trip to the Deccan Club in Poona on the fiftieth anniversary of its founding.[3]

*

In 1941, four up-and-coming industrial entrepreneurs of Bombay decided to organize a conference featuring representatives of manufacturing firms from across India. They belonged to a body styled the Association of Indian Industries, but neither the association nor the businessmen themselves were household names. In need of an eminent figure to endorse their conference, they decided to request Visvesvaraya to preside. They went to meet him at his Warden Road home one Sunday. At the appointed hour, they were 'received at the door not by a servant, not by a secretary, but by Sir Visvesvaraya himself, immaculately dressed in western clothes and complete with the picturesque Mysore turban'. Visvesvaraya listened carefully to his visitors' requests before responding 'in unequivocal language and clipped sentences'.[4] He told them he would chair the conference if they assured him that they were committed to the cause of industrializing the nation, and that their involvement would go beyond organizing a one-off conference. He asked that they vow to work four hours a week towards the cause of promoting industrialization—a gesture reminiscent of his old friend Gokhale, who had asked his fellow Servants of India to take an oath atop the hill behind Poona's Fergusson College more than thirty-five years earlier. He wanted them to establish, once the conference was over, 'a permanent organization on an all-India basis representing manufacturers'.[5]

Thus was born the All-India Manufacturers' Organization (AIMO). An office was set up in Churchgate, Bombay, and Visvesvaraya became the AIMO's first president. (He would continue in that role for thirteen years.) Taking shape while the Second World War raged, the AIMO quickly achieved substantial recognition in western India. Its members came from a variety of industrial firms, ranging from family-run units to larger companies based in Bombay or Baroda, such as Godrej & Boyce Manufacturing, Cipla (Chemical, Industrial and Pharmaceutical Laboratories Ltd.), and Alembic Chemical Works.[6] After the inaugural event in Bombay in 1941, the organizers took the annual conference to various cities. In 1942 they met in Poona. For the third annual meeting, Visvesvaraya and his new associates travelled to Baroda in the midst of a blackout, eating their dinner on the train by candlelight. The next two conferences were held in Nagpur and New Delhi respectively.[7]

At one level, the AIMO was a business lobby like the various chambers of commerce. It provided a forum for the proprietors of small and medium industrial firms from across India to network, share information, and air their views on matters of economic policy that affected them. Visvesvaraya's presence lent heft to the organization, and brought it public attention. He became its guiding spirit and a fixture in its deliberations. Year after year he delivered the presidential address at the annual conference; sometimes he also spoke at the valedictory ceremony. His speeches were all variations on a theme he had been playing for decades: the need to act quickly and decisively in promoting the growth of industries in India. At the first conference in Bombay, Visvesvaraya urged private businesses to band together and begin without waiting for the government's help.[8] In Poona, he lamented that Indian industries were not given contracts to produce armaments for the ongoing war; instead the lucrative business went to Canada and Australia.[9] In Baroda, he urged the creation, under a five-year plan, of 'two heavy industries in every province after the war is over'.[10] In Nagpur, the conference concluded with a resolution that 'deplored Government's policy in not encouraging any large scale industry inspite [sic] of the war'.[11] In addition to making their views public, the AIMO reached out to the colonial government directly with suggestions. In November 1945, they sent the government a plan for the fostering of twenty-four basic industries across India, Visvesvaraya reportedly having 'informed the Viceroy and the Planning Department [which the colonial government had established in 1944] that his organisation has completed the spade work involved'.[12]

For Visvesvaraya, then, the AIMO was about more than networking or lobbying. After all, he neither owned nor had a personal stake in any firm. For him it was an educational forum: a medium for the propagation of his credo, a tool for spreading the industrial ethos. He wanted the organization to 'take stock of existing conditions, collect working data and information relating to industries in the various parts of the country'; in essence, 'to provide the industrially-minded public with the basic data needed to investigate and judge things for themselves'.[13] Although his younger colleagues were hard-headed businessmen, there does seem to have been an element of national consciousness that elevated their work beyond the plane of mere self-interest, galvanized as they were by their president's zeal.[14]

The AIMO, in turn, provided Visvesvaraya with a sort of organizational home in his ninth decade. Its frequent committee meetings[15] and annual conferences gave him a routine and a sense of community in Bombay. He had always felt comfortable in the company of industrialists, starting with his old friend Vithaldas Thackersey. Now he took on the role of mentor to his younger colleagues, who treated him with deference and indulged his fastidiousness. They allowed him to lecture them when he thought they were not dressed smartly enough;[16] waited as he worked on his speeches for weeks; scurried about liaising with the printer when he made last-minute revisions, only for him to point out a stray undotted 'i'.[17]

Visvesvaraya also used the AIMO as his soapbox. In the 1940s, he reeled off an astonishing number of pamphlets on his pet topics, all of them published by the organization. He wrote on the iron and steel industry, on rural industrialization, on how the government should approach economic planning after the war,[18] and on why industrialisation was the only route to national wealth. Representative of these publications was a slim tract, *Prosperity through Industry*, which he first brought out in 1942. Its thesis was obvious: it was contained in the title, and Visvesvaraya had been articulating it for decades. 'Why is India poor?' Visvesvaraya began. He gave his answer up front:

> It is because production is low, the country depends for its subsistence mainly on agriculture; industries which can increase income are neglected and gainful activities subsidiary to production are limited. Why is production low? Because man-power is untrained and unorganized, and Government policies which regulate and control the economic activities of the country are unprogressive and their method of approach to industrial problems is too piecemeal and parochial.[19]

The organization of the text was familiar. Visvesvaraya compared India to other countries on a statistical basis—in terms of literacy, per capita income, percentage of population in industrial occupations—and showed that the state of affairs was dismal. He blamed colonial economic policies, in particular the lack of protection and other forms of encouragement to local industries. The ongoing war had presented India with great opportunities to industrialize; once more the colonial government had thwarted those hopes. They had blocked his pet project of producing cars and buses in India, then proceeded to import automobiles worth more than Rs 50 crore.[20] If India was to become prosperous, all this must change. The government must set up a 'Post-war Reconstruction Committee or Board'. It must put in place five-year plans at the central and provincial levels, budgeting at least Rs 1,000 crore for heavy industries such as steel, auto and aircraft manufacture, shipbuilding, dye production, armaments, and armoured vehicles. Every province must establish a couple of these industries; in addition, 'subsistence industries' were to be set up in the villages. The people 'should be roused—and where possible electrified and vitalized—into an active purposeful life'. At a time when cries of 'Quit India' were resounding across the subcontinent, Visvesvaraya gave his audience a rather different slogan, one that focused on economic rather than political freedom: 'Industrialize or perish'.[21]

*

If the AIMO absorbed his energies in Bombay, there was no dearth of organizations in Bangalore that could serve as outlets for Visvesvaraya's zeal for industrialisation. From 1938 to 1947, he served as Chairman of the Court of the Indian Institute of Science.[22] His contacts with the institute went back a long way—its professors had carried out research for the sandalwood oil factory started during his dewanship—but now, as head of its governing body, he was in a position to influence the directions in which it would develop. Over the years, he felt, the institute's professors had started to see themselves more as fundamental scientists than as applied researchers. At meetings of the court and in his interactions with the faculty members, he insisted that the institute's raison d'etre was not the pursuit of 'pure science' but the carrying out of research that was applicable to industry.[23] M.S. Thacker, who taught at the institute from 1940 and spoke often with Visvesvaraya, put it succinctly: 'To him research is a production facility; it is intended to produce scientific data, inventions, new products, solutions for manufacturing problems, and other tangible things which are essential to industrial progress.'[24] During the war years, which overlapped with his time as Chairman of the Court, Visvesvaraya pushed for, or presided over, the inauguration of several new departments and workshops in fields such as metallurgy, mechanical engineering, and aeronautical engineering. The last of these was closely connected with the development of the HAL factory in Bangalore.[25]

The other Bangalore institution that took up Visvesvaraya's time was a new one, started at his urging in 1943. This was the Sri Jayachamarajendra Occupational Institute (SJOI), named for the maharaja who had succeeded Krishnaraja Wadiyar, and established with the help of a donation of Rs 2 lakh from Visvesvaraya himself. In his memoirs, Visvesvaraya noted that this was the equivalent of his fees for serving as chairman of the board that ran the Bhadravati iron works from 1923 to 1929 (he had not accepted a salary at the time). Visvesvaraya also submitted to the Mysore government a note embodying his vision for the new institute.[26] The state had an engineering college for the education of industrial leaders, and industrial schools to turn out skilled labour; the SJOI would produce the intervening layer, consisting of industrial foremen. The aim, according to P.H. Krishna Rao, the civil servant placed in charge, was 'to train practical workmen who could use modern machinery intelligently in their jobs and who in their turn would be capable of training others in their spheres'.

The SJOI offered Diploma and Certificate programmes for students who had specified school-level qualifications. In addition to 'the three branches of engineering—civil, mechanical and electrical', subjects covered would include 'sanitary engineering and plumbing, boilers and engines, draughtsmanship . . . and mining', and even 'new branches like radio engineering, cinematography and sound recording'. The instructors would be drawn from industrial enterprises as well as the government bureaucracies.[27] City municipalities and district bodies were encouraged to award scholarships of Rs 15 per month to students from their respective areas who received admission to the Occupational Institute. Many complied.[28]

By 1949, the SJOI was running nineteen diploma and seven certificate programmes in fields as diverse as 'automobile engineering, electrical and radio-technology, ceramics, glass technology, mining, printing, tailoring, [and] book-binding'. It had 800 students on its rolls, and was described by the University Education Commission of 1948–49 as 'one of the best' of its kind in the country.[29]

*

Throughout the war years, Visvesvaraya had urged governments, institutions, and industrialists to seize the opportunity to accelerate industrial development in India. When peace returned, he was able to go a step further. In 1946, the AIMO decided to send a delegation of industrialists on a four-month-long tour of the UK, Europe, and North America. These countries had made rapid advances in industrial production during the war; now the Indian businessmen wanted to see these developments for themselves, draw inspiration, and place orders for machinery. Their aim was to kickstart old ventures and establish new ones in the aftermath of the war, which had interrupted contact with foreign countries.[30]

The AIMO's move was not exceptional: many batches of Indian industrialists went on foreign trips of this kind at the end of the war. Most of them went privately, at their own expense. In the early months of 1945, a group went to Australia, their travels in that country aided by the Australian Trade Commissioner to India.[31] Later that year, another delegation travelled to Britain and the United States. It included such industrial heavyweights as G.D. Birla and N.R. Sarker from Calcutta, and J.R.D. Tata and A.D. Shroff from Bombay. Kasturbhai Lalbhai, the textile magnate from Ahmedabad, was slated to join them, but seems to have opted out as he was unwell.[32]

Unsurprisingly, it was Visvesvaraya, now a sprightly eighty-four, who was chosen to lead the AIMO's 1946 delegation. The other members were in their thirties, forties, or fifties, making Visvesvaraya by some distance the senior statesman on the tour. They included two of the Bombay businessmen who had first approached Visvesvaraya in 1941: Murarji Vaidya, who ran a silk mill, and G.V. Puranik, whose family business manufactured ayurvedic medicines. Among the other delegates were S.N. Haji, managing director of Scindia Steamships (Burma); Hansraj Dhanda, who ran a hosiery factory in Ludhiana; Sankalchand Shah of Bombay, who was associated with various mills and engineering works; and Hansraj Gupta, managing partner of the Delhi Iron Syndicate.[33]

Unlike the others, Visvesvaraya had no personal stake in a particular company, and came from a professional rather than a business background. From the start, he was ringmaster, conductor, and motivational speaker rolled into one. An AIMO colleague gave them a send-off lunch at Bombay's iconic Taj Mahal Hotel on 19 June. Two days later, the delegation set sail for Liverpool aboard the *Empress of Scotland*, a troopship carrying British army men home after their wartime service.

No sooner had they embarked than Visvesvaraya 'laid down a programme for the delegation'. He had decided they would compile a report in two parts at the end of their travels: the first would be a report of the places they had visited, and the second a snapshot of the current status of various Indian industries. For the latter part, each member had chosen one or more industries to examine. Now, on the journey out to England, he wanted them to place before him sketches of their individual reports. For this purpose the entire team was to meet twice every single day. The ship was crowded, but Visvesvaraya struck a deal with the captain to give them the use of the children's play area in the afternoons. This clashed with tea time in the dining room, so the delegates—no doubt muttering to themselves—had to content themselves with making their own tea in their cabins.[34]

*

The *Empress of Scotland* docked in Liverpool on 8 July. The AIMO delegates made their way to London, where the India Supply Commission (ISC), located in Mount Street, Mayfair, served as their local point of contact. The ISC, which had been established a few months earlier by the Government of India to help Indian buyers source industrial machinery from the UK, put the AIMO delegation in touch with British business associations such as the Federation of British Industries and the Board of Trade. With the help of these contacts, an itinerary was drawn up for the touring party to visit various manufacturers in Britain.[35]

Postwar Britain, as we have seen, was used to hosting such delegations. Just before the AIMO group, a party with a similar mission had arrived from the princely state of Hyderabad.[36] Always concerned with status and protocol, British officialdom was much exercised by the question of how to treat each of these visiting parties. To this end, the Federation of British Industries made enquiries about Visvesvaraya and his colleagues.[37] An India Office functionary noted that Visvesvaraya was 'an Indian of some standing although he is now getting on in years'.[38] While he had heard that the delegates 'are regarded as top-notchers', a fellow bureaucrat remarked that '[c]ompared with the industrial group which visited this country in 1945, this team looks like a second eleven'. The cricketing metaphor was not entirely off the mark, for the AIMO delegates were certainly not as influential as the likes of G.D. Birla and J.R.D. Tata. Nevertheless, the bureaucrat thought they 'represent a good cross section of the medium Indian business houses', and advised the Federation of British Industries to 'do something for them—a lunch would, I think, be the thing'.[39]

No doubt the AIMO delegates enjoyed their lunch at the federation. More importantly, they saw many factories over the next few weeks, travelling to Derby, Bristol, and the industrial towns of Lancashire. In Oldham, near Manchester, they visited Platt Brothers, makers of textile machinery.[40] In Derby they were shown around the Rolls-Royce factory, where they saw jet engines being assembled; they also went to a locomotive works and a factory producing chinaware. A photograph in a local newspaper showed a few of them in the Rolls-Royce works, their leader—rechristened 'Visvesvarama' in the accompanying article—bare-headed and white-haired but natty in a light double-breasted suit, looking over his slender nose at a jet engine while those around him engaged in conversation.[41] One can picture him dutifully entering in his notebook statistical nuggets mentioned by the hosts: for instance, 40 per cent of the officers in the plant were devoted to R&D.[42]

Energetic as they were, one wonders how much the delegation could have garnered from what seems to have been an endless series of rushed visits. The three factories in Derby, for instance, were covered in a single day.[43] The Director of Platt Brothers complained privately that the India Supply Commission had sent the delegation to his plant without ringing to confirm their visit. He had seen the itinerary the ISC had drawn up, and it was full of mistakes and logistical blunders. It was 'almost completely impossible of fulfilment, as firms as far apart as one side of Cheshire and another side of Lancashire were put down for visiting in one day, and then the next day the same district to be visited. Also certain firms had the name of the place where their works were given as 30 miles away from where they were really situated. Altogether honestly I have never seen such a muddle.'[44]

*

If indeed their programme was confused, the delegates took little notice of it. They continued their enthusiastic visits, Visvesvaraya declaring later that everyone had been most hospitable.[45] Although they were only a private party, they thought of themselves as important representatives of Indian economic interests, and sought to place their views before the British government. Through the good offices of the ISC, Visvesvaraya obtained for the delegation an audience with the Secretary of State for India, Lord Pethick-Lawrence.[46]

It is worth underlining that this was August 1946, when Britain, now under Clement Attlee's Labour government, had accepted that the end was nigh for the Raj. They were grappling with the delicate task of ensuring a smooth handover of the reins of the Indian state to local leaders at a time when Muhammad Ali Jinnah's Muslim League was pressing for the creation of a separate nation for South Asia's Muslims. In recent months the British had sent a Cabinet Mission to India and organized a summit in Simla to mediate between the Congress and the Muslim League. Now they were preparing to announce the creation of an interim government for India with Nehru at its head.[47] Pethick-Lawrence was in the thick of the action. It was extraordinary that he made the time to see the 'second eleven' from the AIMO in the midst of these frenetic negotiations. What's more, he must have been bemused to receive the letter Visvesvaraya sent him on behalf of the delegation. Couched in polite terms, it was a sermon on how the 'dependency form of government' (i.e. British colonial rule) was responsible for the dismal state of Indian industries. What was needed, then, was 'a radical change in the political situation'. Declaring that they were usually apolitical, the delegates nevertheless expressed the hope that Pethick-Lawrence's policies 'will in due course satisfy all the parties concerned and carry this age-old problem of India's self-government to a peaceful, harmonious and permanent settlement'.[48]

The meeting took place on 16 August. According to a summary prepared by an India Office employee, Visvesvaraya read aloud the letter he had already sent beforehand, 'and then the Delegation proceeded to cross [examine] the Secretary of State on a number of points'.[49] If Visvesvaraya, with his slow, deliberate manner, did read out the entire letter, which ran to several pages, Pethick-Lawrence must have had to exercise all his patience to sit through it. In the discussion that followed, Visvesvaraya's colleagues asked the secretary of state about likely policies related to business when the interim government came into being. They were also concerned that their orders of textile machinery from Britain were being delayed as the suppliers were being asked to serve British buyers first. They wanted a commission to be set up to expedite the building of industrial plants. Pethick-Lawrence and his staff gave sympathetic but non-committal replies.[50] According to the visiting delegation's notes, the secretary of state, while acknowledging the need for an early resolution of the political deadlock in India, opined that 'the real difficulty . . . was the lack of team-spirit among Indian leaders themselves'.[51]

The meeting achieved little. Yet it was important for the AIMO delegation to show that they had made contacts in high places. They were keen that the meeting should be reported in the press, but as Pethick-Lawrence insisted that the contents of their discussion were not for public consumption, they contented themselves with an announcement from the secretary of state that he had met them.[52]

*

A few days later, the team of industrialists sailed for America. Visvesvaraya impressed his younger colleagues by standing in line for upwards of ninety minutes while waiting to embark in Southampton, all the while carrying his own articles.[53] In the United States, the party made the rounds of engineering industries in Chicago, the car manufacturers of Detroit, and the hydroelectric power plant at the vertiginous Niagara Falls. Much of this was old hat for Visvesvaraya, who had been to companies like Ford and GM several times on previous visits to America. But the others in his party must have been wonderstruck at the sheer scale of some of the factories they saw. The section of their final report dealing with these factories was described by a reviewer in the *Indian Journal of Economics* as 'simply thrilling . . . the Ford Motor Company at Detroit produces as many as four thousand cars per day and has 85,000 employees. One of its many buildings in the plant is one mile long. The General Electric Company has 247 buildings extending over 1¾ miles, etc. etc.'[54] Visvesvaraya and his friends seem to have visited the Massachusetts Institute of Technology—by this point a much sought-after destination for elite Indian students studying abroad—and commented on its role in making the fruits of science available to American agriculture and industries.[55]

After accompanying his colleagues to an aircraft production facility close to New York, Visvesvaraya took off on his own to Knoxville to see the Tennessee Valley Authority, the grand hydraulic engineering scheme associated with Franklin Roosevelt and the New Deal years. The party then moved on to Canada, sailed back to Europe, where they travelled in smaller groups, and assembled once more in London for the British Trade Fair in December.[56]

Shortly thereafter, Visvesvaraya returned to Bombay. Disembarking from the *Stirling Castle*, he told the press that the delegation had been well looked after wherever they went. They had spoken to 'various industrial committees, and presidents, directors or other representatives of the local industries and trade' in the countries they had visited. All that remained for them to do was bring out their final report. To this end they would all meet in Bombay in January.[57]

The report was duly published that year, 1947. It received favourable if not ecstatic notices. The reviewer in the *Indian Journal of Economics* called it 'a valuable publication which should be read by every one interested in Indian industries'.[58] The *Bombay Chronicle* described it as 'a mine of information on various industries that need to be developed in India'.[59]

It marked the end of a decade of frenetic activity for Visvesvaraya. In 1935, he had sailed across the oceans in his quest to stimulate one particular industry, namely automobile manufacture. On the 1946 tour, he set his sights higher still: the aim this time was to create a ready reckoner that could spark not one but several new ventures. In the intervening years, he had produced pamphlets with the frequency and energy of a crusader, criss-crossed the country delivering his message from the AIMO podium, and taken the increasingly hapless colonial government to task on numerous occasions. He would soon have a different government to deal with, for the nation stood on the cusp of Independence.

23

An Ageing Gadfly in the New India

Visvesvaraya's return from the 1946 tour marked the end of a chapter in his life: it was to be his last trip abroad. He was now 85 years old. He began to scale back his responsibilities slightly, giving up, for instance, his position as Chairman of the Court of the Indian Institute of Science in June 1947.[1] He acknowledged the need for help at home: in Bangalore, his newly married nephew M.R. Krishnamurthy (son of Visvesvaraya's younger brother, M. Ramachandra Rao) moved in with him. Krishnamurthy, his wife Shakuntala, and their children Sheila and Satish were to give the former dewan a taste of the family life he had never had. In 1952, the family moved from Uplands to another house in the vicinity, a neat bungalow with a driveway, a spacious, sunlit front yard, and a veranda bordered by a trimmed hedge. This house, 5, Cubbon Road, would be Visvesvaraya's home for the rest of his life.[2]

Yet Visvesvaraya was not about to slow down more than was absolutely necessary. He had no ailments, and his mind was as sharp as ever. He still divided his time between Bombay and Bangalore, and would do so until he was well into his nineties. He continued to preside over the annual conference of the All-India Manufacturers' Organization, travelling to locations as far apart as Ernakulam, Nagpur, and Calcutta, until 1954.[3] In 1953, he decided to step back from the day-to-day business of the collective. But his younger colleagues were reluctant to let him go entirely. Visvesvaraya was, after all, synonymous with the AIMO. Declaring him 'permanent President', they created a fresh position, that of Chairman, the occupier of which would be in charge of regular business.[4]

This new phase of Visvesvaraya's life coincided with a new historical era. By 1946, Indian ministers elected on a limited franchise had formed an Interim Government under the leadership of Jawaharlal Nehru. The following year, amidst frenetic negotiations and deadly communal riots, the transfer of power was complete. India and Pakistan became self-governing Dominions of the British Commonwealth. In January 1950, the Indian nation became a republic.[5]

We have no record of where Visvesvaraya was at midnight on 14/15 August 1947. When the Indian tricolour replaced the Union Jack, when Nehru spoke of India awaking to freedom while the world slept, was Visvesvaraya in Bombay, Bangalore, or somewhere else altogether? Had he gone to bed as per his strict daily routine, or was he awake, listening to a radio broadcast? Few of his mentors or contemporaries had lived long enough to see this day. Not Gokhale, nor Tagore, nor Krishnaraja Wadiyar; certainly not Ranade or Naoroji, who belonged to earlier generations still. He himself had long campaigned for an economically independent India, and now the dream had become a reality. Yet the new polity wasn't quite the federation he had hoped for, and the fate of the princely states—including his own—still hung in the balance. Was he elated, cautiously optimistic, or nervous?

One thing became clear soon enough. Visvesvaraya was not sentimental about the change of government for its own sake. Merely the fact that Indians were at the helm did not enthuse him. His test for measuring the government's performance remained the same as it had always been: what was it doing to help India industrialize rapidly?

For much of his career, Visvesvaraya had been a celebrity. Now he was treated as a living legend. His every utterance seemed to make the headlines. And he had a ready and regular forum at which to express his opinions, in the form of the Central Committee meetings and annual conferences of the AIMO, which continued to grow in stature.

Under his guidance, the AIMO developed a well-defined stand on the government's economic policies. They were—unsurprisingly—against the more left-leaning of the Nehru government's policies. The prospect of large industries being nationalized left them anxious. They lobbied for lower taxes. They didn't want the public sector intruding upon their fields of activity, stressing that economic development could be achieved 'only through the institution of private enterprise supported in every conceivable way by the Government and the people'. They demanded, at the same time, that the government differentiate between local and foreign firms in providing aid.[6]

Visvesvaraya himself continued his old refrain: the government must do more to promote the manufacture of steel, cars, and planes, which would catalyse the growth of other industries. They were also essential for the nation's defence needs. He was dissatisfied with the first Five-Year Plan (1951–56), which prioritised food security and did not go far enough, to his mind, to encourage industry.[7]

The state must support industry, but also get out of the way. Visvesvaraya argued that the maze of government regulations bred corruption, thus anticipating common critiques of what became known as the Licence Raj. In opposing nationalization, he pointed to the government's tendency to manage through generalists rather than technical experts. When the government decided to take over Air India from the Tatas in 1953, he 'disapproved the proposed nationalisation of a highly technical enterprise like the air services'. Nationalization would also replace corporate efficiency by the '[c]orruption, nepotism and inefficiency' that characterized 'the Government machinery'.[8]

Visvesvaraya was clearly worried by what he saw as the declining standards of probity in official circles after Independence. While declining to criticize the Congress top brass, which included 'patriotic and self-sacrificing' statesmen, he maintained that 'under their administration there had been growth in nepotism, corruption, slackness and indiscipline.' This, combined with the doctrinaire views of the all-powerful party on a number of issues, led him to emphasize the necessity of a strong and united political opposition. Perhaps, he said, India should have a two-party system like the United States, where it led to 'less tendency towards partisan practices'.[9]

Visvesvaraya was also impatient with symbolic policies, such as the Congress's interest in outlawing the consumption of alcohol in honour of Mahatma Gandhi's ideas. The engineer himself touched neither liquor nor meat,[10] but that was a personal choice. He scoffed at the government for spending its energy on pushing for prohibition when it ought to be focusing on education.[11]

Visvesvaraya's politics after Independence, then, were characterized by principled opposition to the Nehru government on a number of points. He respected the Pandit and his colleagues on a personal level, and even praised them.[12] But he could not bring himself to accept their gestures towards socialism, an ideology which he counted, alongside the explosion in population and science-based warfare, as one of the 'threats to national security'.[13] Most of all, having spent a quarter of a century criticizing the colonial state on the grounds that an independent government would do much more to promote mass education and rapid, indigenous industrialization, he was deeply disappointed at the pace of change under the Congress regime.

Three other themes surfaced repeatedly in his interventions in public discourse during the 1940s and '50s. These were the need for economic autarky and hence the development of indigenous expertise; the importance of military readiness, both in terms of technology and personnel; and the urgency of controlling the spiralling population. When the government hired foreign (mostly American) engineers to build dams as part of two iconic new projects—the Damodar Valley Authority and the Bhakra dam—he stressed that there were several Indian engineers who could do the job just as well.[14] At a 1948 ceremony in which he received an honorary doctorate from Mysore University, he declared that 'every section of the population should know that their country's defences are efficient and safe, and compare favourably with corresponding arrangements in similarly situated modern countries.'[15] The following year he asked for the creation of 'a Public Defence Advisory Committee of about a dozen patriotic citizens to study and advise Government regarding the strength of equipment to be maintained in every branch or department of military operations'.[16]

*

The ageing Mysorean's participation in public affairs was not, however, confined to making public statements a few times a year. He continued to take on assignments as an engineering consultant. In 1948, he advised the Saurashtra government on irrigation projects in the region.[17] In 1952, he headed the Railway Board-appointed team of experts that chose Mokameh Ghat as the ideal location for a new bridge across the Ganga in Bihar.[18] But perhaps the most important assignment he accepted was the chairmanship of a 'board of arbitration' established in 1947 to resolve a long-standing controversy over a new dam that was being built on the river Tungabhadra.

The Tungabhadra dam had first been proposed by the colonial government of Madras Presidency in the first decade of the century, with a view to irrigating the arid Rayalaseema region. The river, however, was shared with the neighbouring princely state of Hyderabad, and the proposed reservoir could not be built without the latter's cooperation. The two sides had gone back and forth over four decades, Visvesvaraya's friend Nawab Ali Nawaz Jung being one of the key interlocutors on the Hyderabad side. They had finally agreed terms for a shared multipurpose project that would serve both states, and flagged off construction in February 1945. But they had found it difficult to coordinate their efforts. Who would be the chief engineer? What building materials would be used — *surki* or Portland cement? If the costs were shared, how could each side be sure that the other was exerting adequate measures of economy?

This was the situation when, a couple of months after Independence, the two states roped in Visvesvaraya. His arbitration board proposed pragmatic solutions to the various disagreements. They recommended the use of surki for most of the structure and cement for the spillway and around the sluices. While Visvesvaraya insisted on a unified design, appointing an engineer from Hyderabad to oversee its drafting, he addressed the question of expenses by asking each state to build half the dam and take responsibility for the cost of its half. According to a sympathetic chronicler, these provisions fostered 'a healthy competition' between the two teams, and eventually they were able to coordinate their work to such an extent that they could 'abandon the principle of independent halves and undertake genuine joint effort'. The dam was eventually inaugurated in 1953.[19]

Through these years, Visvesvaraya also continued to push his development schemes. In particular, he converted his ideas on village industrialization—inspired largely by his visits to Japan, and developed and articulated in his writings over several decades—

into a formal plan. In the 1950s, the Mysore government implemented this plan, referred to as the 'Visvesvaraya Rural Industrialisation Scheme', in stages across the state. Under the scheme, each district was divided into forty to sixty *group circles*, each circle being a cluster of fifteen to twenty-five villages. The residents of each circle would pool their funds, to be supplemented by government grants, and set up industries suited to their local resources. The idea was to provide employment opportunities and additional sources of income beyond the villagers' traditional agrarian and craft occupations, while making them self-sufficient. The industries Visvesvaraya had in mind were small undertakings that could provide the basic necessities of *roti* (bakeries, dairy farms, fisheries, jaggery production); *kapda* (blankets, shoes, hosiery); and *makaan* (brick-making, carpentry, ceramics, furniture production), and a few other wants (incense sticks, crayons, paints, matches, soaps).

By 1955, it was reported that close to '8,300 new industries, with a capital investment of about Rs. 120 lakhs, have been started under the scheme. . . . the Mysore Central Co-operative Rural Industrial Financing Bank, established to solve the problem of cheap rural finance, is today in a position to boast of large assets amounting to about Rs. 20 lakhs'.[20] That same year, the project, which had been launched in Bangalore and Kolar districts around 1950, was scaled up and implemented across all the districts of the state. Throughout this time, the ex-dewan kept close tabs on its progress, as is evident from a detailed report he placed before the public in 1956, when he was almost ninety-five.[21]

Visvesvaraya's scheme seems to have gained notice outside Mysore too. In 1955, the Bombay Government announced it would pilot a programme on the same model, starting with ten circles, each to be provided capital of Rs 5000.[22] A similar system of rural industrialization was envisaged at the national level under the first two Five-Year Plans in conjunction with the 'community development block' programme, although internal committees noted, well into the 1960s, that the Union government had done little to make these a success.[23]

*

By this time, Visvesvaraya was being seen as the 'Grand Old Man' of Indian industry as well as modern Mysore. He was much in demand on ceremonial occasions as an inspirational figure, a wise elder, and a link to eras past. In the 1950s, he gave speeches at organizations and institutions he had been a part of or helped establish, including the Mysore Iron and Steel Works at Bhadravati, the College of Engineering in Bangalore, and the Central College.[24]

Visvesvaraya undoubtedly enjoyed the respect and attention he received on these occasions, and responded with courtesy. Yet a dry remark was never far from his lips. On 16 October 1952, he was invited to inaugurate a marble statue of the erstwhile monarch, Krishnaraja Wadiyar IV, in Mysore. (The statue had been installed under an ornate canopy in K.R. Circle, a stone's throw from the palace.) That morning the photojournalist T.S. Satyan, then a young man making his way as a freelancer, sought Visvesvaraya out at the imposing Government House, where he was staying, and obtained permission to take a few photographs. Afterwards Satyan, whose father was an admirer of the ex-dewan, asked him for his blessings. 'Who am I to bless you?' his subject shot back, before gently telling Satyan it was his own efforts that would determine how he fared in life. The photographer later accompanied him to K.R. Circle. From there, Visvesvaraya walked a block to pay his respects at an older statue, a likeness of Krishnaraja's father, Chamaraja X. 'There was thunderous applause from the large crowds that had lined up on either side of the road,' recalled Satyan in his memoirs, 'as Sir MV walked past them with a slight stoop and folded hands.'[25]

A couple of days later, Visvesvaraya flew down to Coimbatore, then an emerging industrial centre, to address a gathering of students and businesspersons. He had been invited by the industrial entrepreneur G.D. Naidu, whose organization ran courses to train automobile and radio technicians. After Naidu introduced the guest of honour, he was welcomed, in terms ranging from the respectful to the rapturous, by representatives of local firms and institutions. One firm, which produced textile machinery, thanked Visvesvaraya for using his last AIMO tour to the UK to help them import equipment from that country. The Southern India Engineering Manufacturers' Association pleaded with Visvesvaraya to persuade the Union government to step up the production of pig iron, a crucial input for its member companies, whose products included pumps, motors, engines, and sewing machines.[26] In the course of his own speech, Visvesvaraya told his audience that to root out corruption in business transactions they should 'appoint a Committee of three of the most honest businessmen of the City in order to collect information of wrong practices, wherever they exist, and communicate them to the authorities in control'. The more worldly-wise Naidu interrupted, half-joking: 'If no honest men are available, what am I to do?' Pat came the reply: 'Mr. Naidu is manufacturing Engineers, why not manufacture honest men also?'[27]

*

As Visvesvaraya entered his tenth decade, his age became a source of veneration in itself. Governments and organizations vied with each other to mark his birthday every 15th of September. There were banquets, parties, and public meetings. A glittering array of officials paid tribute in person or sent in messages. Visvesvaraya dutifully attended many of these functions, occasionally permitting himself to look back on his life's work. More characteristically, he also used these occasions to air his opinions on current affairs.

In September 1950, at the start of his ninetieth year, Visvesvaraya's AIMO friends organized a bash for him at Bombay's Taj Mahal Hotel. The Union Commerce Minister, Hare Krushna Mahatab, presided over the function. Visvesvaraya was in reflective mood. 'We must take life as it is,' he said, '[as it] always has been and always will be, more or less of a struggle. No man should fool himself in this matter.' Was life worth living, then? The engineer responded with a quote from the nineteenth-century philosopher Ernest Renan: 'The existence which was given me without my having asked for it has been a beneficent one for me. Were it to be offered to me, I would gladly accept it over again.'[28]

Two years later, at a Bangalore function chaired by the Maharaja-turned-Governor of Mysore, Jayachamaraja Wadiyar, Visvesvaraya explained the habits that had kept him healthy: 'regulation of diet, six to eight hours of sleep a day, work, indoor or outdoor, eight hours a day on the average, and regular exercise walking three to four miles every evening'. The president, vice-president, prime minister, and other distinguished personages sent Visvesvaraya birthday greetings. The same afternoon, a hundred influential invitees from business circles attended a lunch in his honour organized by his AIMO colleagues at the upscale West End Hotel.[29]

In 1955, when he entered his 95th year, the AIMO organized a banquet in Bombay.[30] Visvesvaraya himself was in Bangalore. He was courtesy itself as he received visitors at his bungalow. 'You have taken too much trouble,' he said.[31] He gave an interview to the *Times of India*, summarizing his modernist creed. He talked of the need for the nation to undertake 'development . . . on western lines', the necessity of supporting industrial entrepreneurs, the perils of doing away with English as a lingua franca in the young republic, and the importance of taking stringent action against officials who promoted 'communalism and sectarianism'.[32]

But the most important felicitation had come a week earlier, when Visvesvaraya received the Bharat Ratna—the highest civilian honour in Independent India. The other recipients of the Bharat Ratna that year were Prime Minister Nehru and the Benares-based scholar of religion, Dr Bhagwan Das. The scholar-politician V.K. Krishna Menon and the industrialist J.R.D. Tata were among those decorated with the Padma Vibhushan. The awardees gathered on the evening of 7 September 1955 in the Durbar Hall at Rashtrapati Bhavan, New Delhi, 'lit by a magnificent chandelier'. At 6.30 p.m., President Rajendra Prasad and his entourage entered the hall. Dr Prasad sat down on a golden chair, in front of 'thick red and black hangings surmounted by a gold lion capital'. Also on the dais were the vice-president, the Supreme Court's chief justice, and the Lok Sabha speaker. In the audience were high-ranking civil servants and MPs, forming a sea of Gandhi caps. A couple of attendants accompanied each awardee to the stage, where they received their medals and scrolls from the president. Jawaharlal Nehru, 'dressed in a cream sherwani and [wearing] a pastel yellow rose', 'was warmly and affectionately cheered by a large gathering' as he strode to the stage.[33] (Nobody commented on the oddness of his receiving an award from his own government.) Soon it was Visvesvaraya's turn, elegant in a black long coat along with his usual white turban. As flashbulbs popped, he arose from his seat in the front row. Next to him, J.R.D. Tata, in a light sherwani and churidar, clapped delightedly. Visvesvaraya walked slowly up to the president and received his scroll, head bowed, while a liveried attendant fastened the sash bearing the medal.[34] The citation he received called him 'A Great Engineer, Industrialist and Statesman' and 'the father of the idea of planned development in India'.[35]

Amidst the pomp, however, there was a faint air of bathos. The band began playing the national anthem before the President had declared the ceremony closed. To the consternation of the *Times of India* correspondent covering the event, they compounded the gaffe by elongating the *jaya he*s at the end of the anthem, 'in contradiction to the authorised version of the music'. The exacting correspondent also noted that '[t]he acoustics were uniformly poor and nothing could be heard at all distinctly'.[36]

Visvesvaraya—who was in New Delhi as a guest of the President—added an eccentric note of his own when, a day or two later, he suddenly packed his bags and declared he was moving to a hotel. Why, asked Dr Prasad (who recounted the story five years later); were the arrangements not to his liking? That was not the problem, said Visvesvaraya. There was an official regulation that guests could stay at Rashtrapati Bhavan for a maximum of three days. He proceeded to take his leave.[37]

In bestowing the Bharat Ratna on Visvesvaraya, the Congress government had signalled that they did not hold a grudge against him for his frequent criticisms of their policies. Equally, they recognized that he was a widely revered figure, and it served their ends to include him in the pantheon of national heroes. Family lore has it that when he was told he had been chosen for the award, Visvesvaraya warned Nehru that he should not expect him to praise the government.[38] True to his word, he continued to voice criticisms of government policy in subsequent years.[39]

*

Back home in Bangalore, Visvesvaraya focused on staying healthy. Like everything else he cared about, he turned old age into a project. He took a regular constitutional, far from the bustle of the city.[40] He swore by a particular exercise for the eyes, and urged visitors to practise it too: it involved rotating the eyeballs in different directions before pressing the eyelids with one's fingertips.[41] When C. Rajagopalachari retired as Chief Minister of Madras in 1954 owing to poor health, Visvesvaraya advised the statesman, who was seventeen years his junior, to take it easy for a few months, and offered to host him for some days in the bucolic calm of Muddenahalli, in the shadow of the Nandi Hills.[42] He seems to have enjoyed answering questions from visitors and correspondents about the key to his longevity.[43]

Visvesvaraya enjoyed having his family around him in his final years. According to Shakuntala Krishnamurthy, who kindly spoke to me in 2019, he adjusted very well to their presence. He would meet Satish and Sheila in the mornings: one child brought him the newspaper, another gave him a flower.[44] The children picked up his habit of jotting down sundry items in his pocket notebook: they took to leaving 'small chits . . . on their father's table—"shoes and exercise books wanted," "jam very urgent"'.[45] There were a couple of golden retrievers on the premises (probably looked after by family retainers), to whom Visvesvaraya fed Marie biscuits in the evenings. Although he ate in moderation, he enjoyed his food, favouring *kadubu*s. He took to reading the *Bhagavad Gita*, marking certain passages.[46] But it is safe to assume he was not seeking solace in the promise of an afterlife. On his 98th birthday he told a reporter: 'I do believe in God. But religion for the most part is a show and perhaps a waste of time. What is the use of a religion which propagates a caste system?'[47]

One of Visvesvaraya's grand-nephews, Pandri Nath, has left a lively account of him in these years. He tells of convivial family gatherings, and of the patriarch regaling his grand-nephews and grand-nieces with stories from his younger days. He would mimic the Chicago trader who sought him out to return his gratuitous dollar in 1919: 'I don't take nothing that don't belong to me'. The children would retort, '[A]nd you don't give nothing that belong to you either'—a response that tickled him no end.[48]

Even in his late nineties, Visvesvaraya received visitors and gave the occasional interview to the press. He kept up with his correspondence, having letters typed for him and signing them in an increasingly unsteady hand. In April 1960, he thanked the Hyderabad engineer Dildar Husain for sending him a volume brought out by the Hyderabad Centre of the Institution of Engineers (India). He had to add, however: 'My eye sight [sic] has grown dim for the last six months.'[49] Inevitably, his hearing began to fade too. A Films Division documentary made towards the end of his life shows Visvesvaraya—in three-piece suit and turban as always—cupping his ears as he tries to hear something clearly.[50]

*

Despite his increasing infirmity, Visvesvaraya was wheeled out for one final public celebration on 15 September 1960. Although he had only turned ninety-nine, it was billed as his centenary (he was after all entering upon his 100th year). That day, Bangalore came to a grinding halt. Schools and colleges were shut. The state legislature paused proceedings. 5 Cubbon Road 'was turned into a place of pilgrimage' as '[t]housands of people streamed into the house', eager to pay their respects. A gala reception was held at the Glass House in Lalbagh, the same venue where, nearly five decades earlier, Visvesvaraya had been felicitated by leading citizens at the start of his dewanship. Now, as his car pulled into Lalbagh, he found Prime Minister Nehru, Mysore Governor Jayachamaraja Wadiyar, and Chief Minister B.D. Jatti awaiting him. He emerged to applause, and, unable to walk, was 'carried in a cane chair to the dais'.

The prime minister offered Visvesvaraya a flower before opening the proceedings. Praising the centenarian for his 'youthful idealism', he said he 'always reminded one of the modern world of science, industry and technology'; it was science that held the key to the nation's future. Governor Wadiyar and Chief Minister Jatti followed up with further encomiums. '[I]f Mahatma Gandhi forged the weapon which brought us our independence,' said Jatti, using a somewhat ill-judged metaphor, 'it was Dr. Visvesvaraya who fired the first shot in our fight for economic freedom.'

Visvesvaraya sat through the proceedings for an hour and a half, struggling to make out the words being spoken, accepting 'garlands and addresses with tremulous hands'. When his turn came to respond, he was too weak to speak for long. He made a few remarks, then allowed his friend Murarji Vaidya to read out the remainder of his speech. One final time, he reprised his pet themes. Industrialization was the need of the hour; Indians must work longer hours and toil harder; they must be trained to be brisk, punctual, and businesslike. He laid particular stress on the need for compulsory education at the school level.[51]

There were other honours aplenty. That day, a commemorative stamp worth 15 naye paise was released in Visvesvaraya's honour.[52] In Bombay, Maharashtra's education minister unveiled a portrait of the city's adopted son.[53] In New Delhi, President Rajendra Prasad addressed a function organized by the Karnataka Sangha.[54]

Back in Bangalore, Visvesvaraya's day was not done. One of his grand-nephews, Sheshadri Mokshagundam, remembers a gathering of the extended family at the Cubbon Road house that evening. The patriarch made it a point to talk to each child separately, telling them in Telugu: '*Chaala baaga chadivi, kashta padi, munduki raavaali*'. Study well, work hard, and come up in life.[55]

*

In early 1961, Visvesvaraya was laid low by gastritis and chronic hiccups that interfered with his sleep. From this point on, he was virtually confined to his bed.[56] By the time of his real centenary that September, he was not even able to put on his habitual suit. 'Resting in a couch in informal clothes,' a journalist reported, he 'received a stream of visitors at his bungalow. He recognised a few of them and spoke to them haltingly.'[57] By this time, a younger relative recalled, '[h]is eyesight had diminished considerably. His hearing was completely gone'. After a final two-week battle with a recalcitrant bout of hiccups, he passed away on the morning of 14 April 1962.[58]

Sixteen years previously, Visvesvaraya had prepared a note in preparation for what he then thought was his imminent passing. 'Should my death occur in Bangalore city,' the last paragraph read,

> it is my request to those around me at the time that my body should be quickly taken away in a motor car to my village (Muddenahalli) near Nandi Hill and cremated there. The ceremony may be plain, humble and simple.[59]

His wishes were followed. A government communique announced that the hearse would depart from Cubbon Road at 4 p.m. that day, 'march in front of the Vidhana Soudha, Mysore Bank Circle, Kempegowda Circle, Ananda Rao Circle and pass by the Congress Bhavan, Race Course Road, Ringwood Circle and in front of [Ballabrooie] reaching Muddenahalli *via* Sankey Road and Bellary Road Tollgate'.[60] That evening, the flames rose against the backdrop of the same hills that had witnessed the arrival of Visvesvaraya more than a century earlier.[61]

Epilogue

Engineering a Nation

The twentieth century was a century of engineers.[1] Across the globe, institutionally trained, professionally organized, and highly networked experts in mining, construction, railway-building, and industrial production rose to prominence. Taking up key roles in business corporations and governments, they transformed not only the material character of the world but also its economic and political organization. This was most vividly illustrated by what historians Israel Garcia Solares and Edward Beatty call 'a moment of notable convergence': between the two world wars, men with engineering backgrounds rose to be heads of government in the USA, Britain, Canada, and Mexico.[2]

More than any particular technical skills, these professionals brought a distinct engineering worldview to their work in governments and policy-making bodies. They were joined by other leaders—from Mustafa Kemal in Turkey to Lenin in the Soviet Union—who may not have shared their engineering background, but subscribed to the same modernist credo. It was a credo that emphasized progress through the application of science and technology to transform the natural world while bringing order and rationality to human affairs.[3]

Engineers in India were not immune to these global trends. In the interwar years in particular, they evolved a common language of economic nationalism, defining their task as the harnessing of the land's resources to develop the nation.[4] None did this more dramatically, more consistently, or more insistently than Visvesvaraya. His legacies are many and varied, but it is this advocacy that lies at the heart of them. It is the thread that ties together the two prominent sides of his persona: the professional engineer and the development thinker. Over a long career spanning more than seventy years, he sought, literally and figuratively, to engineer India.

*

Looking back at Visvesvaraya's life, it is clear that the seeds of his interest in *planning* and *development* were planted in the late nineteenth century when he was a young engineer, even though those precise terms were not yet in vogue. Formed in these years, his close friendships with the leading Indian theorists of national economics informed his worldview for the rest of his life. Visvesvaraya was well primed to imbibe the lessons of Ranade, Gokhale, and their ilk. As an engineer, he agreed with their advocacy of industries and technological education. He went even further, coming to see industries, urban as well as rural, as the beating heart of what would be a developed India. Taught by British schoolmasters and professors in the late-nineteenth century, he held a Victorian belief in *progress*, and a strongly materialist conception of what it entailed. While he spoke about the cultural and social aspects of nation-building, his canvas was fundamentally economic. He was appalled by the poverty and illiteracy he saw around him, and made it his life's mission to promote measures to raise the standard of living of the average Indian. This essentially meant more and better production. It required a modernized workforce that would shed the baggage of superstition and outmoded tradition and adopt methods that had proved successful elsewhere in the world.

This emphasis on modernization stemmed not only from his training in colonial educational institutions, but also from his professional socialization in the public works bureaucracy, which was premised on the state's dominion over nature and natural resources. His belief in the importance of an interventionist state was further deepened by his travels to, and lifelong admiration for, Japan in particular. His experience of famine while he was an irrigation engineer made him think deeply about the more efficient use of water; it also strengthened his conviction that it was folly for a nation to base its economy primarily on agriculture.

When he became chief engineer and then prime minister of the state of Mysore, he had the opportunity to implement some of his ideas on moulding society. He brought to the job his engineering worldview. Like an irrigation engineer who must draw up plans (designs), make estimates, and control variables, Visvesvaraya the dewan surveyed the scene (by amassing statistics), set targets, and put in place structures (institutions) that he believed would transform Mysorean society.

Visvesvaraya's engineering background was also crucial in lending credibility to his views on economics—an area in which he had no formal training. His engineering career gave him a reputation as a doer, not just a thinker. It gave him opportunities for foreign travel, endowed him with a materialist philosophy of progress, and led him, for better or worse, to see the industrialized West as the only worthwhile model for the rest of the world. Visvesvaraya frequently invoked his foreign travels and his knowledge of global affairs to lend legitimacy to his interventions in policy debates. He invested time and money to undertake personal study tours of the more prosperous industrial nations at a time when foreign travel was taboo to many of his compatriots.

He took notes assiduously and collected statistics obsessively, quoting them ad nauseam in his speeches and writings.

In the interwar years, Visvesvaraya's standing as an ex-Dewan of Mysore was key to his gaining acceptance as a spokesman on economic matters. His pioneering of the Mysore Economic Conference added to his credentials, as did the many visible achievements—institutions and engineering projects—associated with his tenure. His work as dewan gave him the experience of negotiating with individuals in powerful positions, from viceroys down to maharajas. It also (along with his stellar record in Bombay) made him a figure the colonial powers were willing to engage with, even if they didn't always trust him absolutely.

On the other hand, his friendship with leading nationalists (albeit of the Moderate variety) and his professional successes as an Indian in the expat-dominated field of engineering secured his status as a suitable symbol of the cause of national development. He also entered on his career as a public intellectual at a time when constitutional reforms were resulting in a greater degree of political representation at both provincial and central levels. This enabled a number of his associates to enter legislative bodies. They, in turn, frequently sought his services as a committee man and adviser, formal or informal. Nothing illustrates better his acceptance as the face of nationalist economics than his being invited, in 1924, to preside over the Indian Economic Conference.

*

In his own lifetime, Visvesvaraya was hailed as one of the trailblazers for planning in India.[5] As we've seen, he was by no means the only public figure to promote the concept of planning in the 1930s and '40s. But he was probably the most influential, and certainly the most persistent. Moreover, his interest in planning did not emerge overnight. His undertakings from the

1910s onwards (including the Economic Conference in Mysore and the Indian Economic Enquiry Committee, which he chaired in 1925) show that he had been thinking along such lines for nearly two decades before he published his landmark *Planned Economy for India* in 1934.[6]

To be sure, Visvesvaraya was not an academic economist. He did not engage directly with the ideas of prominent theorists of his time. He carried out no quantitative analyses of the statistics he amassed, using them instead to compare India's position on various indicators with that of the industrialized West. But he was a keen observer of development policies in various nations; and his insight that the assiduous collection of data must form the bedrock of economic policy was prescient.[7] In fact, one of the enduring legacies of Independent India's experiments with planning—one that long outlived the prestige and utility of the Five-Year Plans themselves—was to be the creation of a world-class institutional apparatus for statistical sampling and analysis.[8]

Visvesvaraya's influence in post-Independence India was less direct than it might have been: he was past his prime by then, and his dissatisfaction with Nehru's socialist leanings caused him to keep his distance from the corridors of power.[9] But his emphasis on heavy industry as the engine of growth became a tenet of the Five-Year Plans, especially the Second Plan associated with P.C. Mahalanobis.[10]

However, the mixed economy that emerged after Independence was, in his eyes, weighted too far in favour of the public sector. The early voices critiquing the government on these grounds came from the ranks of his friends and associates. Visvesvaraya's long-time colleague in the AIMO, Murarji Vaidya, was one of the founders of the Forum of Free Enterprise (1956). His friend and fellow Central College alumnus, C. Rajagopalachari, promoted the Swatantra Party (1959) on a similar plank.[11] The Indian economy after the liberalization of the 1980s and '90s is probably closer to what Visvesvaraya had envisioned. The field today is wide open for private players, and disinvestment is rhetorically equated to efficiency. Nevertheless, the state—despite the dismantling of the Planning Commission in 2014—continues to set targets and otherwise intervene actively in the economy.[12]

*

Visvesvaraya's background as an engineer, as we have established, was crucial in shaping his views on nation-building. But what of his legacy in the field of civil engineering itself?

We must first acknowledge what Visvesvaraya was not: he was not a creator of new theoretical knowledge in the field of engineering. He left behind no formulae, theorems, or other contributions that entered the corpus of engineering science.[13] Over many decades as a distinguished member of the Institution of Civil Engineers and other professional bodies, he seldom presented or communicated technical papers. In his days in the Bombay PWD, he was forward-thinking and innovative, but his reputation as an otherworldly genius is somewhat exaggerated. Not all of his innovations were successful: take the case of his module for irrigation, which did not pass muster with his PWD colleagues. His famous automatic gates at Khadakwasla were acknowledged as a valuable contribution, but they were not, as we have seen, a de novo invention. His achievement with the Krishnarajasagara project in Mysore lay not so much in its design and construction—many able colleagues also had a hand in those—as in his zeal to get it sanctioned and his ability to push on with it in the face of political and financial obstacles.

On the other hand, Visvesvaraya was undoubtedly a competent, confident, and uncommonly thorough engineer who could, from his PWD days, be relied on to execute a wide variety of projects. He ran a tight ship. He worked hard, and made sure his subordinates did likewise. Despite his image as something of a dandy—with his insistence on wearing a spotless suit at all times—he was a hands-on engineer: physically active and never one to shy away from spending time on site. He kept himself abreast of the latest developments in civil engineering. When he reached the higher echelons of his profession—as sanitary engineer in Bombay, chief engineer in Mysore, and consultant in myriad provinces and states—he was decisive and bold in the projects he drew up.

Above all, however, he was an Indian engineer who stood up for himself in a world of racial prejudice. He won rare tributes from his British superiors. He had confidence in his abilities, a distinct professional pride, and uncommon drive: qualities that made him stand out at a time when the colonial establishment held a dim view of 'native' engineers. This meant that he became a symbol of indigenous pride well within his lifetime.

But Visvesvaraya was more than just a role model. He also created a strong institutional basis for the engineering profession to expand. He was directly responsible for the establishment of educational institutions that continue to flourish today in various forms, such as the Government College in Bangalore and the Department of Chemical Technology at Bombay University. He even anticipated, in a way, the establishment of the IITs, via his recommendations in the 1920s to set up an Indian version of the Massachusetts Institute of Technology. He played an active role in the governance of the Indian Institute of Science, which had departments of engineering in addition to the physical sciences, and which he nudged towards a more applied orientation, insisting that the institute produce knowledge of direct relevance to industries. In addition to university-level courses, Visvesvaraya vigorously promoted commercial and technical training of a vocational nature. In his work as Dewan of Mysore, in his writings, and in his role as a committee man, he pressed for the creation of a range of training facilities, from industrial schools to diploma-granting institutions.

*

Visvesvaraya's work as civil engineer is linked to another area in which he had a deep impact: the shaping of urban India. As an agent of change, his imprint is still felt in cities large and small across the subcontinent. Many of them still use water supply systems designed or recommended by him—most notably Hyderabad, which continues to be served by the Himayatsagar and Osmansagar reservoirs. The city of Mysuru has an enduring monument to his efforts in the sprawling, green Manasagangotri campus that houses Mysore University. The town of Mandya owes much of its prosperity to the KRS project, which turned the district into a sugarcane belt. The eventual shape taken by Mumbai's Marine Drive was influenced by the recommendations of the Back Bay Enquiry Committee, of which Visvesvaraya was a key member. More than a century after he advocated the creation of a sanitized, beautified zone along Hyderabad's Musi river, riverfront projects—including one proposed for the Musi by the Telangana government in 2017—have become de rigueur across the country (although serious concerns have been raised about their ecological impact and their potential to exclude the less well off).[14]

Nowhere, though, is Visvesvaraya's influence more keenly felt than in Bengaluru (as Bangalore has been known officially since 2014). Today the city is a global landmark by virtue of its status as the nerve-centre of the Indian information technology industry and a development centre for the largest tech multinationals. As the twenty-first century dawned, commentators such as *New York Times* columnist Thomas Friedman popularized the city globally as 'India's Silicon Valley'.[15] When the outsourcing boom took place, Americans began to talk with dread of being 'Bangalored'—or replaced in their jobs by a call centre employee in Bangalore.[16]

None of this, however, happened overnight. As the social scientist James Heitzman's work shows in vivid detail, there were crucial continuities between the Bangalore of Visvesvaraya's era and the post-Independence city that became a nucleus of scientific research, a centre for public sector industries, and, eventually, a US-facing information technology hub. Several trends inaugurated or boosted by Visvesvaraya—a focus on engineering and technical education, heavy government investment in industrial ventures, urban planning by experts—were extended after his time. His focus on state-led industrialization was deepened during his friend Mirza Ismail's tenure as Dewan of Mysore, and continued by the state after Independence. In the 1930s and '40s, companies were set up, by the state or with its backing, to manufacture lamps, hosiery, glass, enamelware, porcelain ware, electrical and radio equipment. The largest new undertaking was Hindustan Aircraft Limited, set up with Visvesvaraya's moral and strategic support in 1940. It became a nationalized concern in the post-Independence period, central to the production of military aircraft for the Indian Air Force.[17] When Mysore was incorporated into the Indian republic, Bangalore and its environs continued to be a favoured location for public sector industrial firms and government agencies such as the Indian Space Research Organisation.[18]

Visvesvaraya foresaw that Bangalore would grow in size and population, and that city planners would need to keep pace with the changes. In 1953, he suggested that the city would need a ring road some day. He also wanted 'a road with a broad, paved foot-path' to be built between Lal Bagh and Cubbon Park so that the people may '[take] an evening drive or walk in open air', just as they did on Bombay's Marine Drive.[19] Several decades later, Bangalore has not one but two ring roads, although the Marine Drive equivalent has not come to pass. In other ways, too, Visvesvaraya may have underestimated the challenges of managing a growing city. For, ironically, the emergence of Bangalore as a research and industrial centre bore within it the seeds of the city's partial unravelling. Were Visvesvaraya to visit Bengaluru today, he would see all the markers of modernity he craved: gleaming offices and malls, not one or two but dozens of luxurious business hotels, a growing metro rail network (he had envisaged a tram system in 1910),[20] a city so dense with engineers you couldn't toss a pebble without it landing on one. It is cosmopolitan, largely welcoming of professionals from other parts of the country, and pulsing with energy and ambition. And yet, in the process, it has also become some of the things he wanted to avoid at all costs: unruly and congested in large part; besieged by traffic snarls and water shortages; plagued by stark inequalities; business-friendly, to be sure, but more hedonistic than Calvinist in spirit.

*

Bengaluru is only one of thousands of cities across the world struggling with the challenges of *sustainability*. A hundred years ago, that term was not a part of the public discourse.[21] The worldview underlying Visvesvaraya's interventions, whether in the urban sphere or in the form of his large infrastructure projects, was a quintessentially Baconian one. For him, science and technology must be used to subdue and tame nature, make regions more habitable and orderly, and, above all, help reduce *waste*.[22] Visvesvaraya's interest in multipurpose dams that would combine electricity generation, canal irrigation, and flood control reflected a worldwide pivot towards such projects. The KRS, his pet project, pre-dated the American New Deal and the Tennessee Valley Authority (TVA) by some two decades, but he had seen other gigantic projects, in particular the Aswan Dam, during his international travels. The TVA was later to become the inspiration for a fresh set of undertakings in 1940s India, most notably the Damodar Valley Project.[23]

These projects, needless to say, constituted enormous interventions in riverine ecosystems. They regulated the flow of rivers, changed or allowed the changing of their courses, submerged dozens of villages, displaced populations, and transformed the cropping patterns in their command areas. Even Nehru, who famously championed such projects in Independent India, had his moments of doubt about them. In the six decades following Independence, large dams dispossessed some 40 million citizens of their original dwellings. People's movements have fought, with varying levels of success, to highlight the environmental and sociological fallout of many of these projects.[24]

Visvesvaraya's views reflected the times he lived in. Leaders across the world looked to these mega projects to deliver their societies from poverty or economic stagnation; few foresaw the extent of the challenges that would arise (although, as in the case of waterlogging and salt accumulation in the soils of the Deccan, some of the problems were visible fairly early on). Today we know, as historian Rohan D' Souza puts it, 'that fluvial regimes are complex geomorphologic, chemical, and biological processes in motion . . . the beating heart that keeps alive the river's ecologial health and viability is its *natural-flow regime*'.[25] It is true that all human civilization of necessity involves some interventions in nature. But the need to debate the limits of such interventions has never been more urgent.

*

A popular anecdote from Visvesvaraya's Mysore years goes like this. The dewan had just concluded a strategic meeting with his councillors, the yuvaraja, and the maharaja's private secretary,

R.H. Campbell. At the end of the meeting, the participants were talking casually, when Visvesvaraya prefaced a remark thus: 'I am a democrat, and . . . '

'What did I hear you say, Dewan Saheb?' Campbell cut in, looking him in the eye. 'A democrat? You, a democrat! You are the greatest autocrat going!'

Everyone, Visvesvaraya himself included, had a merry laugh.[26]

The story, which is told by S. Hiriannaiya, the dewan's private secretary at the time, captures the tension at the heart of Visvesvaraya's approach to governance. His self-image was that of a democrat, and he was indeed committed to democratic norms. Yet he had an instinctive attraction towards systems that had clear chains of command and enabled decisive action—a preference that grew stronger as he grew older and more impatient to see his ideas on development implemented. His twin faces as a democrat and a technocrat are crucial to understanding his legacy.

We must begin with the former. One of the most under-appreciated aspects of Visvesvaraya's career is his association with Liberal politicians and his deep involvement in debates on constitutional reform in colonial India. His friendship with Ranade and Gokhale did not just introduce him to nationalist economics. It also made him an informal member of a network of thinkers—Gokhale himself, Srinivasa Sastri, Chimanlal Setalvad, and others—whose political orientation drew upon the tenets of British Liberalism. They supported British legal and constitutional norms, aimed to establish a parliamentary democracy, and saw the state as being composed not of communities but of citizens with individual rights. They believed in private property and the role of the market, tempered by state intervention. They were incrementalists when it came to political reform.[27] Although Visvesvaraya engaged with a wide range of political leaders during his career, he was most at home among the Liberals and those who were closely aligned to them. He even went so far as to join the National Liberal Club in London.

It is against this backdrop that we must note his active involvement with issues of constitutional reform. As Dewan of Mysore, he expanded the legislature and its powers, while allowing the press a fair degree of freedom. Although these were halting measures, they went significantly beyond the steps taken by some of his predecessors. At the national level, he took a stand against the colonial government's imprisonment of its political opponents. As this book has shown, he played a key role in pushing for dominion status for India, and a crucial if unheralded part in producing an outline for a dominion constitution. Even more remarkable, given his own connection with the princely rulers of Mysore, was the active support he lent to the states people's movement, which sought to assert the rights of the citizenry in the princely states. He was also an early proponent of federalism, insisting that provinces would be best placed to utilize their resources productively if they received greater autonomy.

Despite these interventions, there is no doubt that the more lasting impact of Visvesvaraya's career on Indian society has been in the popularization of technocratic thinking. The Indian middle class has long had a fascination for technocrats.[28] The term usually refers to unelected technical experts in government roles—individuals with a strong belief in the power of science and technology to solve the most pressing problems of society. The technocrat is seen as skilled and efficient, a counterpoint to the venal politican and the arrogant, generalist bureaucrat.[29] In the Nehru years, statistician P.C. Mahalanobis and his associates in the Planning Commission wielded enormous influence. In more recent decades, engineers such as Sam Pitroda and Nandan Nilekani have held positions of great power in government agencies, while Manmohan Singh was widely welcomed as finance minister and then prime minister on account of his brilliance as an economist, his lack of an electoral base notwithstanding. But they were all foreshadowed by Visvesvaraya, who became prime minister of an important state and adviser to national politicians without ever contesting an election himself.[30]

In fact, it was around the First World War, just as Visvesvaraya was transitioning into his role as a policymaker, that the term *technocracy* came into public discourse. It arose in the United States, where its connotations were much more specific than they are today. The term represented the views then being articulated by sociologist Thorstein Veblen and a group of influential American engineers. Arguing that business logic and the conventional economy ('the price system') were inefficient, they declared that technical experts were best placed to run large corporations and work out a system of planning for the national economy. Herbert Hoover, for instance, asked a group of fellow engineers in 1921 'to visualize the nation as a single organism and to examine its efficiency towards its only real objective—the maximum production'. These ideas were further modified and popularized during the Great Depression by a group of ideologues headed by an enigmatic autodidact named Howard Scott.[31]

Visvesvaraya, who regularly read foreign journals and had met Hoover, would surely have heard of the Technocracy movement. Unlike Veblen and Scott, he did not question the role of the market as a coordinating mechanism; but he did agree that production had to be planned and stimulated in a scientific manner by experts who knew what was good for society at large. If the Depression haunted his American counterparts, it was India's chronic poverty that obsessed Visvesvaraya. Poverty was the single most pressing problem, its continuation a blot on the incipient nation's conscience, but it had a simple solution: rapid industrialization. The recipe was to invest in the most advanced technologies, introduce the latest industrial processes, and make full use of the country's natural resources. Agriculture too, would be made more productive by the application of science. Policies in all these realms were to be formulated on a scientific basis, through the compilation and analysis of data.

All of this was to be supervised by highly qualified professionals and businesspersons, who would advise elected ministers. Visvesvaraya's technocratic sensibility was most evident in his lifelong belief in the efficacy of appointed committees. Similarly, he thought prominent industrialists should be cultivated by government and used as agents of modernization, since they had the organizational resources to drive industrialization. The fact that this privileged a chosen section of capitalists did not seem to concern him.

His own endeavours were never subjected to a formal, independent audit.[32] He harboured no doubts that his own vision for a modern, developed state was the right one, even though he was responsible to nobody but the monarch. In the 1930s, he advised provincial governments and (briefly) the Indian National Congress through its National Planning Committee. His exit from the NPC illustrated his impatience with his politician colleagues, who did not accept his proposals in their entirety.

Part of the appeal of technocracy is the apparent simplicity of the solutions proposed by its votaries, who tend to underestimate 'social complexities, individual motivations and political forces'.[33] CCTV cameras will ensure law and order. Digital attendance dashboards monitored in central war rooms will solve the problem of teacher absenteeism in rural government schools. A national ID card system, the linking of several databases, and the creation of a cashless economy will root out corruption and black money. All of this is to be achieved without the messiness of debate or the search for root causes.

Visvesvaraya's own tracts were full of such utopian thinking. They dripped with sincerity and patriotism, but a lack of engagement with humanistic schools led to blind spots. They spared little thought for ecological problems or social dynamics. In treating Japan and the early industrial nations as exemplars, they did not reflect on the link between the industrial prosperity of those nations and their status as imperial powers. They were the forerunners of the kinds of books produced, several decades later, by another engineer-turned-national leader: the charismatic and inspirational A.P.J. Abdul Kalam, who served as President of India from 2002–07. Kalam's best-known book, co-written with Y.S. Rajan, is *India 2020: A Vision for the New Millennium.* First published in 1998, it begins with a chapter titled: 'Can India Become a Developed Country?' The answer is that it can, and the solution focuses on technology and industrial production. A flowchart lays out the recipe: 'Sustained Efforts for Growth of Core Competence' will lead to 'Self Reliance in Critical Technologies' and 'Strategic Industrial Infrastructure', which in turn will culminate in 'Technology Leadership', giving India 'Economic Prosperity', 'National Security', and its 'Rightful Place in World'.[34] A final chapter (which begins with what's meant to be an inspirational quote from the rocket scientist Wernher von Braun, with no sense of irony despite his association with the Nazi regime) prescribes voluntary actions that individuals, NGOs, multinationals, the government, and the media must take to realize the goal of development. Individuals, for instance, are to '[d]evote a few days in a month to doing something better; something speedier; something of high quality . . . ', while the media must '[s]pread the message of success, however small the successes are'.[35]

The parallels are clear: the (admirable) emphasis on poverty alleviation, the quest for 'developed' status, the emphasis on self-reliance and military preparedness, the privileging of technological solutions, and the appeal to volunteerism rather than political engagement and systemic change. What Visvesvaraya and Kalam underemphasize is the fact that there are winners and losers in this kind of transformation; that conflicts are bound to arise between different social groupings; and that the model of development they prescribe has historically involved the state's dominance over nature and communities alike.

*

The appeal of technocracy has always cut across party lines, but it has been particularly strong since 2014, when the Bharatiya Janata Party's Narendra Modi first took over as India's prime minister. Since then, the BJP government has intensified the emphasis on technology and technocratic solutions that was already apparent under previous administrations. The Aadhaar, or universal ID card project, has been rolled out to the vast majority of the population despite widespread debates and concerns over its efficacy and its implications for privacy. Digital tools are increasingly deployed in the provision of everyday services, even as urban areas large and small vie for the tag of 'smart city'. There has been a concerted effort to expand the cashless economy, including a massive, unannounced, demonetization drive. Shiny new superfast trains, infrastructure projects, and other symbols of access to the latest technology crowd the headlines.[36]

During this time, the government has been keen to adopt Visvesvaraya as an icon of its vision of development, or *vikaas*. Prime Minister Modi and his colleagues have often released statements in praise of engineers in general, and Visvesvaraya in particular, on Engineer's Day. Visiting the poll-bound state of Karnataka in 2023, the prime minister offered flowers at Visvesvaraya's *samadhi*.[37] In 2022, when a swanky new air-conditioned terminal for long-distance trains was opened in a Bengaluru suburb, it was named the Sir M. Visvesvaraya Byappanahalli Terminal. 'India's first centralised AC railway terminal' created great excitement in the media and a public hungry for proof of the nation's arrival on the world stage.[38] The current establishment undoubtedly shares many aspects of Visvesvaraya's worldview. In its keenness to be seen as business-friendly, its emphasis on manufacturing-driven growth, and its enthusiasm for 'One Nation, One Language', it mirrors his orientation from a century ago.[39] But it is important to point out also the many areas of divergence.

Visvesvaraya had no interest in a culturally defined national identity. He never referred to the Vedas, the Puranas, or the Gita, even though he may have personally drawn inspiration from the last of them. He saw no place for religion or religious symbols in public life. He was an ardent nationalist in the sense of insisting on Indians' potential and Indians' interests in the midst of an imperialist system, but he was not an exceptionalist. He did not insist on India's moral superiority, or its status as the fount of all wisdom. He did not encourage chauvinistic delusions about Indians having invented twenty-first-century technologies in ancient times. As we progress through what is being called the 'Asian Century', this is an aspect of Visvesvaraya's legacy we would do well not to lose sight of.

*

At the heart of Visvesvaraya's life was a question that animated many intellectuals of his era: What does it mean to be a modern Indian?[40] For some, it meant going back to the ancient past to identify authentically Indian modes of thought. For others, it meant amalgamating, judiciously, Indian traditions with the fruits of modern science. For Visvesvaraya, it meant starting from scratch.[41] There was nothing inherently sacred about tradition. Science and technology had shown the universal path to development, and the nations of the world had to compete with each other to get on that path. It was a simplistic credo, no doubt. It underestimated people's sentimental attachments, the need for community, and the finitude of nature's bounty. It assumed that the world was ultimately a meritocracy. It assigned a leading role to elites like himself. But at its core, it was a humanist vision, born of the wish to see an end to poverty and suffering. Visvesvaraya's modern Indian was a cosmopolitan, rational, hard-working, responsible, and self-respecting individual with enough comforts to live a dignified life. His assumptions and prescriptions must certainly be rethought and refined by every generation, but those are still goals worth striving for.

Notes

Introduction

1 'India's Henry Ford. Brahmin Plans Big Car Scheme. He's Always Had his Own Way', *The Mirror*, 7 September 1935, p. 9 (accessed via trove.nla.gov.au).

2 There is a great deal of confusion about Visvesvaraya's date of birth, but in this book I go by the date in his official documents, which is 15 September 1861. I discuss the question in more detail in Chapter 1.

3 See Dhruv Raina, *Visvesvaraya as Engineer-Sociologist and the Evolution of His Techno-Economic Vision*, NIAS Lecture, L1-2001 (Bangalore: National Institute of Advanced Studies, 2001); Vinod Vyasulu, 'Nehru and the Visvesvaraya Legacy', *Economic and Political Weekly* 24, no. 30 (29 July 1989): 1700–1704.

4 'PhD Scheme: Visvesvaraya PhD Scheme for Electronics & IT', Ministry of Electronics & Information Technology, Government of India, https://www.meity.gov.in/phd-scheme (accessed 26 February 2024).

5 Visvesvaraya's speech on College Day, Sydenham College, 17 December 1930, in MV-PAPERS-IEI, Vol. 13.

6 Y.G. Krishnamurti, *Sir M. Visvesvaraya: A Study* (Bombay: Popular Book Depot, 1941). On Krishnamurti's career, see 'Y.G. Krishnamurti' (https://www.srikanta-sastri.org/ygkrishnamurti, accessed 13 January 2024).

7 V. Sitaramiah, *M. Visvesvaraya* (New Delhi: Ministry of Information and Broadcasting, Government of India, 1971); V.S. Narayana Rao, *Mokshagundam Visvesvaraya: His Life and Work* (Mysore: Geetha Book House, 1973). On Narayana Rao, see Shakuntala Krishnamurthy, *Sir Mokshagundam Visvesvaraya* (Bangalore: n.p., 1992 [1980]), Preface.

8 T.T. Sharma, *Bharata Ratna Sir M. Visvesvaraya (Jeevana-Saadhane)* (Bangalore: Ankita Pustaka, 2005 [1960]); Masti Venkatesa Iyengar (ed.), *Sir M. Visvesvaraya: Nooraneya Vardhantiya Poojane Lekhana Sangraha [Centenary Commemorative Articles]* (Bangalore: MVJK Trust, 2006).

9 Raina, *Visvesvaraya as Engineer-Sociologist*; Benjamin Zachariah, *Developing India: An Intellectual and Social History, c. 1930–50* (New Delhi: Oxford University Press, 2005). D.S. Jayappa Gowda did his doctoral research on Visvesvaraya's dewan years. See D.S. Jayappa Gowda, *Dewan Sir M. Visvesvarayanavara Karyasadhanegalu (1912–18)* (Mysore: Shubhodaya Prakashana, 1994). A rare academic study of the early part of Visvesvaraya's career is Raj Sekhar Basu, 'The World of an Engineer: M. Visvesvaraya and Irrigation Engineering in Twentieth-Century India', in Arun Bandopadhyay (ed.), *Science and Society in India 1750–2000* (Delhi: Manohar, 2010), pp. 249–98.

10 Sunil Khilnani, *Incarnations: India in 50 Lives* (London: Allen Lane, 2016), Chapter 33: 'Visvesvaraya: Extracting Moonbeams from Cucumbers'; Chandan Gowda, 'Visvesvaraya, an Engineer of Modernity', *The Hindu* (Bangalore, 15 September 2010).

11 Janaki Nair, *The Promise of the Metropolis: Bangalore's Twentieth Century* (New Delhi: Oxford University Press, 2007); Manu Bhagavan, *Sovereign Spheres: Princes, Education and Empire in Colonial India* (New Delhi: Oxford University Press, 2003); Bjørn Hettne, *The Political Economy of Indirect Rule: Mysore 1881–1947* (New Delhi: Ambika Publications, 1978); Gyan Prakash, *Mumbai Fables* (Noida: HarperCollins, 2010); Sunil Amrith, *Unruly Waters: How Mountain Rivers and Monsoons Have Shaped South Asia's History* (London: Penguin Books, 2018).

12 See discussion above. As also mentioned in an earlier endnote, a notable exception is R.S. Basu, 'The World of an Engineer'.

13 Ramachandra Guha, 'Gandhi's formative years', *Financial Times*, 20 September 2013 (https://www.ft.com/content/1ca11fd0-1fc6-11e3-aa36-00144feab7de, accessed 27 January 2024); conversation with Patrick French, c. 2017.

14 Chandan Gowda, 'A few tales of modern mythology', *Bangalore Mirror* (online), 10 April 2015 (https://bangaloremirror.indiatimes.com/opinion/views/dewan-of-mysore-sir-m-visvesvaraya/articleshow/46880728.cms, accessed 28 February 2024).

15 Quoted in William E. Leuchtenberg, *Herbert Hoover*, Kindle Edition (New York: Times Books, n.d. [2009]), p. 162.

1. From Halli to Nagara

1 *Halli* is Kannada for 'village'.

2 E.g. T.T. Sharma, *Bharataratna Sir M. Visvesvaraya (Jeevana-Saadhane)* (Bangalore: Ankita Pustaka, 2005 [1960]), Chapter 3 ('Janana-Baalya-Vidyaabhyaasa'), discusses the birthdate and says that 27 August 1860 is the date that accords with Visvesvaraya's horoscope. V. Sitaramaiah, *M. Visvesvaraya* (New Delhi: Ministry of Information and Broadcasting, Government of India, 1971), p. 152, gives the date as 15 September 1861. V.S. Narayana Rao, *Mokshagundam Visvesvaraya* (New Delhi: National Book Trust, 1995 [1988]), p. 1, gives the date as 28 August 1860. The date appearing in official forms is 15 September 1861. See for instance the nomination form ('Form A', proposer H.G. Palliser, 5 March 1887) for Visvesvaraya to be admitted as an Associate Member of the Institution of Civil Engineers (ICE), London (courtesy ICE Archives, London). [Cited hereafter as 'Form A', ICE.]

3 On India, see Barbara D. Metcalf and Thomas R. Metcalf, *A Concise History of Modern India*, 3rd edition (Cambridge: Cambridge University Press, 2012), Chapter 4. On America, see 'American Civil War', in *A Dictionary of World History*, 2nd edition (Oxford: Oxford University Press, 2006), p. 19. On Russia, see 'Emancipation Manifesto', *Encylopedia Britannica*, 25 February 2024 (https://www.britannica.com/event/Emancipation-Manifesto, accessed 1

March 2024); Peter N. Stearns, *The Industrial Revolution in World History*, 4th edition (Boulder, Colorado: Westview Press, 2012), p. 122. On Japan, see section titled 'The fall of the Tokugawa' in Fred G. Notehelfer *et al.*, 'Japan', *Encyclopedia Britannica*, 1 March 2024 (https://www.britannica.com/place/Japan/The-fall-of-the-Tokugawa, accessed 1 March 2024); Jeffrey R. Bernstein, 'Japanese Capitalism', in Thomas K. McCraw (ed.), *Creating Modern Capitalism: How Entrepreneurs, Companies, and Countries Triumphed in Three Industrial Revolutions* (Cambridge, MA and London: Harvard University Press, 1997), pp. 441–89, here p. 446.

4 Srinivasa Sastri also had one son, Thimmappa Sastri, from an earlier marriage. Family tree in T.V. Venkatachala Sastry, *Bharataratna Sir M. Visvesvarayanavara Poorvajaru,* 3rd edition (Bangalore: Sapna Book House, 2014), p. 93; interview with Sheshadri Mokshagundam (great-grandson of Thimmappa Sastri), Bengaluru, 19 June 2019. The description of the house and its surroundings is based on my impressions from my visit to Muddenahalli in 2018, and on photographs I have seen in various publications.

5 See Leela Krishnamurthy, *Bharata Ratna Sir M. Visvesvaraya—Naa Kandu Keledante* (Bangalore: Leela Krishnamurthy and Karnataka State Archives, 2010), Chapter 1; *Bharata Ratna Sir M. Visvesvaraya* (Bangalore: Pradeep Kumar T.V. for Vaibhavi Visions, n.d. [2019?]), pp. 1–2. The latter is a narrative in comic form with multiple contributors. I thank Mr Sheshadri Mokshagundam (who contributed the text to the comic) for giving me a copy of the publication.

6 Pandri Nath, *Mokshagundam Visvesvaraya: Life and Work* (Bombay: Bharatiya Vidya Bhavan, 1987), p. 1.

7 See S. Srikanta Sastri, 'Mulakas', *Quarterly Journal of the Mythic Society*, Vol. XXI, No. 1, reproduced at https://www.srikanta-sastri.org/mulakas-origins-of-the-mulakanadu-sect (accessed 31 December 2022).

8 *A Manual of the Kurnool District in the Presidency of Madras*, compiled by Narahari Gopalakristnamah Chetty (Madras: [Government Press?], 1886), pp. 221–2 (quoted text from here) and p. 311. While I have consulted the *Manual* directly, I learned

of its existence from Sastry, *Visvesvarayanavara Poorvajaru*, p. 102, which mentions it and cites/quotes from the same pages. See also Pandri Nath, *Mokshagundam Visvesvaraya*, p. 1 (this source, however, mentions five ponds rather than just one).

9 See the family tree in Sastry, *Visvesvarayanavara Poorvajaru*, pp. 89-92.

10 See for instance the numbers at the end of the nineteenth century in B. Lewis Rice, *Mysore: A Gazetteer Compiled for Government, Vol. I: Mysore in General*, revised edition (Westminster: Archibald Constable and Company, 1897), pp. 224–6.

11 See H. Rangachar and P. Kodanda Rao, 'A Brief Life Sketch', in CENT-VOL, pp. 293–334, here p. 294. On Srinivasa Sastri's connection with medicine, see for instance V. Sitaramiah, *M. Visvesvaraya* (New Delhi: Ministry of Information and Broadcasting, Government of India, 1971), p. 6.

12 See the transcript of the document printed in Sastry, *Visvesvarayanavara Poorvajaru*, pp. 79–81.

13 Leela Krishnamurthy, *Naa Kandu Keledante*, p. 4. Pandri Nath, *Mokashagundam Visvesvaraya,* Chapter 1 mentions that Visvesvaraya's mother lived in Chikkaballapur when he was studying in Bangalore.

14 See Visvesvaraya's speech in 'Mofussil News: Chikkaballapur Notes: High School Day Celebration', *Daily Post*, 28 December 1928, in MV-PAPERS-IEI, Vol. 21. That the medium of instruction was Kannada was indicated to me by Visvesvaraya's family in interviews. Interview with Shakuntala Krishnamurthy (with inputs from Satish Mokshagundam and Lakshmi M. Satish), Bengaluru, 26 June 2019; interview with Sheshadri Mokshagundam, Bengaluru, 19 June 2019.

15 For background, see Rice, *Mysore: A Gazetteer*, pp. 745–7; [S.N. Mukerji], 'India: Education under the East India Company', under 'Education', *Encyclopedia Britannica*, n.d. (https://www.britannica.com/topic/education/The-spread-of-Western-educational-practices-to-Asian-countries#ref303195, accessed 31 March 2024); and P.L. Rawat, *History of Indian Education* (Agra: Ram Prasad and Sons, 1973 [1956]), Chapters 12–14.

16 See Pandri Nath, *Mokshagundam Visvesvaraya*, pp. 2–3.

17 Quoted in 'Mofussil News: Chickballapur Notes: High School Day Celebration', *Daily Post*, 28 December 1928, in MV-PAPERS-IEI, Vol. 21. Visvesvaraya's nostalgic tone on the same occasion in 1928 is apparent from the account in Sharma, *Bharataratna Sir M. Visvesvaraya*, Chapter 3 ('Janana-Baalya-Vidyaabhyaasa'). On Visvesvaraya's early school days, see also Pandri Nath, *Mokshagundam Visvesvaraya*, p. 4; Shakuntala Krishnamurthy, *Sir Mokshagundam Visvesvaraya* (Bangalore: n.p., 1992 [1980]), p. 1; Rangachar and Rao, 'A Brief Life Sketch', p. 294.

18 Rangachar and Rao, 'A Brief Life Sketch', p. 294.

19 See ibid., pp. 294–5; V.S. Narayana Rao, *Mokshagundam Visvesvaraya* (New Delhi: National Book Trust, 1995 [1988]), p. 2. I have found no primary sources mentioning Ramaiah's designation, but his family members remember it as being that of assistant commissioner at the government secretariat. Interview with Shakuntala Krishnamurthy (with inputs from Satish Mokshagundam and Lakshmi M. Satish), Bengaluru, 26 June 2019. According to V. Sitaramiah, Visvesvaraya's 'maternal uncle H. Ramiah [sic] . . . held a modestly high place . . . in the Secretariat of the Government of Mysore'. Sitaramiah, *M. Visvesvaraya*, p. 6.

20 M.A. Sherring, *The History of Protestant Missions in India, from Their Commencement in 1706 to 1871* (London: Trübner & Co., 1875), p. 301; Wesleyan Church website (wesleyan.org/about, accessed 9 April 2019); 'John Wesley', *Encyclopedia Britannica*, 27 February 2024 (https://www.britannica.com/biography/John-Wesley, accessed 6 March 2024); *Wesleyan Juvenile Offering: A Miscellany of Missionary Information for Young Persons*, Volume 6 (London: Wesleyan Mission-House and John Mason, 1849), *passim*; Rice, *Mysore: A Gazetteer*, p. 485.

21 Sherring, *History of Protestant Missions*, pp. 301–2; Rice, *Mysore: A Gazetteer*, pp. 485–6; G.G. Findlay and W.W. Holdsworth, *History of the Wesleyan Methodist Missionary Society, Vol. V* (London: Epworth Press, 1924), p. 206.

22 The Wesleyan Mission High School celebrated its centenary in December 1934. See 'Speech at the Wesleyan Mission High School', in *Speeches by Amin-Ul-Mulk Sir Mirza M. Ismail, Kt., K.C.I.E., O.B.E., Dewan of Mysore, Vol. II: January 1931 to January*

1936 (Bangalore: Superintendent at the Govt. Press, 1936), pp. 390–5.

23 See the late nineteenth-century pencil sketch of the school now in the Basel Mission Archives: 'Wesleyan Mission High School in Bangalore', Basel Mission Archives, BMA QC-30.009.0008 (www.bmarchives.org/items/show/66396; accessed 9 April 2019).

24 'Speech at the Wesleyan Mission High School', 22 December 1934, in *Speeches by Amin-Ul-Mulk Sir Mirza M. Ismail*, pp. 390-5 (quoted text from p. 391).

25 Janaki Nair, *The Promise of the Metropolis: Bangalore's Twentieth Century* (New Delhi: Oxford University Press, 2007 [2005]), p. 28; map accompanying T.E. Slater, 'Our Missionary Districts. Bangalore', *The Chronicle of the London Missionary Society*, No. 81, New Series (September 1898), pp. 214–6. I found the map courtesy of a mention in Aliyeh Rizvi, 'Resident Rendezvoyeur: On a mission', *Bangalore Mirror* (online), 20 December 2015 (https://bangaloremirror.indiatimes.com/opinion/others/how-to-be-a-chick-after-the-funeral-the-truth-the-tragedy/articleshow/50238424.cms), accessed 15 April 2023.

26 https://bcu.ac.in/our-legacy/ (accessed 9 April 2019 and 14 February 2020); University of Madras, *The Calendar for 1892-93* (n.p.: n.d.), p. 154; University of Madras, *The Calendar for 1903–1904*, Volume II (Madras: Higginbotham & Co., 1903), pp. 39–41; Suresh Moona, 'Holds a century old Legacy', *The Hindu* (online), 11 October 2018 (https://www.thehindu.com/society/history-and-culture/holds-a-century-old-legacy/article25192106.ece, accessed 15 April 2023); Sherring, *History of Protestant Missions in India*, p. 304.

27 *The Madras University Calendar 1879–80* (Madras: Higginbothan & Co., n.d.), p. 122. Visvesvaraya was at the Central College from 1877 to 1880. See Recommendation form ('Form C') for Visvesvaraya's transfer from Associate Member to Member of the Institution of Civil Engineers (ICE), London, 11 April 1904, p. 1 (courtesy ICE Archives, London).

28 University of Madras, *The Calendar for 1892–93* (n.p.: n.d.), p. 154.

29 Two examples being the Mysore civil servant and writer Navaratna Rama Rao, and C. Rajagopalachari, who would serve as Governor-General of Independent India. See Navaratna Rama Rao, *The Vanished Raj: A Memoir of Princely India*, translated by Navaratna Rajaram and Rajeshwari Rao (Bengaluru: Prism Books Pvt. Ltd., 2014), Chapter 1.

30 *Madras University Calendar 1879–80*, p. 122 (for a list of the staff); untitled snippet, TOI, 15 May 1877, p. 3, col. 1; untitled editorial, TOI, 29 June 1880, p. 2, col. 4.

31 Description aided by author's visit in 2019.

32 Based on a photograph of Waters on display at the Visvesvaraya museum in Muddenahalli. Waters's Cambridge degree is mentioned in *Madras University Calendar 1879–80*, p. 122.

33 Untitled report, TOI, 14 October 1875, p. 3, col. 2.

34 'The Bangalore Regatta', TOI, 16 September 1881, p. 3.

35 'News-letters', TOI, 16 June 1874, p. 2.

36 See for instance Rangachar and Rao, 'A Brief Life Sketch', p. 295.

37 'Central College Day', *The Daily Post*, 19 March 1912, Visvesvaraya Papers (microfilm), Reel 2, NMML.

38 Rice, *Mysore: A Gazetteer*, p. 793. On the degrees offered, see for instance the section on 'Examinations for Degrees', *Madras University Calendar 1879–80*, pp. 223–84.

39 *The Madras University Calendar, 1877–78* (Madras: Higginbotham & Co., 1877), pp. 110–11 (for English syllabus for the 1880 exam—it was set in advance); 'Alphabetical List of Graduates', University of Madras, *The Calendar for 1903–1904*, Volume II (Madras: Higginbotham & Co., 1903), pp. 167–394, here p. 393 (for Visvesvaraya's choice of language and Optional Subjects); *Madras University Calendar 1879–80*, pp. 38–44 (for details of the BA subjects and exams as of 1879–80). Although I haven't been able to locate the Calendar for 1880–81 (when Visvesvaraya took his exams), it is highly unlikely that the BA regulations changed in any significant way from the previous year.

40 Mirza Ismail, *My Public Life* (London: George Allen and Unwin, 1954), pp. 13–14.

41 'News-letters'/'News Letters' from Bangalore appearing in the *Times of India* in the 1870s, e.g. on: 23 March 1874 (p. 2),

6 July 1874 (p. 3), and 13 April 1875 (p. 2); Meera Iyer (writer and editor), *Discovering Bengaluru. History. Neighbourhoods. Walks* (Bengaluru: INTACH Bengaluru Chapter, 2019), esp. Chapter 2.

42 Illustration facing p. 32, in H.S. Sreenath, *Bharata Ratna Sir M. Visvesvaraya: His Economic Contribution and Thought* (Bangalore: Select Book, 2013).

43 Pandri Nath, *Mokshagundam Visvesvaraya,* p. 4.

44 Ibid., pp. 2–3; Rangachar and Rao, 'A Brief Life Sketch', pp. 294–5; Narayana Rao, *Mokshagundam Visvesvaraya* (cited above), pp. 2–3.

45 *Madras University Calendar 1879–80*, p. 123.

46 The museum in Visvesvaraya's natal home in Muddenahalli displays some of the books from his collection. When I visited in 2018, the ones on display included *Thrift* and *Self Help* by Samuel Smiles; *What Life Should Mean to You* by Alfred Alder; *Public Speaking for Business Men* by S.F. Wicks; *Common Sense Business Leadership* by Fosbrooke; and *Don't be Tired* by Dr P. Schmidt (trans. M. Chadwick).

47 These authors' influence on Visvesvaraya is mentioned by Shakuntala Krishnamurthy, 'Sir M.—An Inside View', in CENT-VOL, pp. 280–92, here pp. 291–2. On Smiles, see 'Samuel Smiles', *Encyclopedia Britannica*, 19 December 2023 (https://www.britannica.com/biography/Samuel-Smiles, accessed 1 March 2024). For Todd's themes, see John Todd, *The Student's Manual: Designed, by specific directions, to aid in forming and strengthening the intellectual and moral character and habits of the student* (London: Simpkin, Marshall & Co. and Lancaster: L. and R. Willan, 1840). As noted above, a copy of Smiles's *Self-Help* is among Visvesvaraya's personal effects on display in the museum at his birthplace in Muddenahalli. The phrase 'self-help' was to punctuate his own addresses in later years. See MV-SPEECHES-VOL, *passim.*

48 'Form A', ICE; 'Alphabetical List of Graduates', University of Madras, *The Calendar for 1903–1904*, Volume II (Madras: Higginbotham & Co., 1903), pp. 167–394 (Visvesvaraya is mentioned on p. 393).

49 Shakuntala Krishnamurthy, *Sir Mokshagundam Visvesvaraya* (Bangalore: n.p., 1992 [1980]), pp. 2–3 reproduces a letter of recommendation from Charles Waters dated 1880 which indicates Visvesvaraya was looking for a job in the Mysore Public Works Department.

50 For more details on the political context, see Chapter 8 below.

51 'Sir M. Visvesvaraya', *The Indian Review* 28, no. 2 (February 1927), pp. 93–6, here p. 93; Shakuntala Krishnamurthy, 'Sir M.—An Inside View', p. 283; archival records from KSA-DIGITIZED, cited below. For more on Rangacharlu, see Chapter 8 below.

52 'Sir M. Visvesvaraya', *The Indian Review* 28, no. 2 (February 1927), pp. 93–6.

53 See various files in KSA-DIGITIZED: 'Applications for [. . .] Engineering Scholarships from N. Rama Rao and N.J. Gopala Iyengar', Education Department, Mysore, 1883–84, File No. 1, S. No. [8-9] (https://archives.karnataka.gov.in/home/viewdocument?doc_id=RGVlcGFrMTA3Nzc0&doc_location=RGVlcGFrMQ==); 'Provincial Engineering Scholarships for 1883', Education Department, Mysore, 1882–83, File No. 3, S. No. 18, 19, 21, 29 (https://archives.karnataka.gov.in/home/viewdocument?doc_id=RGVlcGFrMTA3NzY0&doc_location=RGVlcGFrMQ==); 'Scholarships to Engineering Students', Education Department, Mysore, 1884, File No. 6, S. No. 1–2 (https://archives.karnataka.gov.in/home/viewdocument?doc_id=RGVlcGFrMTA3Nzc4&doc_location=RGVlcGFrMQ==); 'Provincial Medical [sic] Scholarships for 1883', Education Department, Mysore, 1882–83, File No. 4, S. No. 21, 22, 26, 27, 28 (https://archives.karnataka.gov.in/home/viewdocument?doc_id=RGVlcGFrMTA3NzU2&doc_location=RGVlcGFrMQ==); 'Local Medical Sholarships [sic]', Education Department, Mysore, 1882–83, File No. 4, S. No. 1–20, 23–[25], 29–32 (https://archives.karnataka.gov.in/home/viewdocument?doc_id=RGVlcGFrMTA3NzYz&doc_location=RGVlcGFrMQ==); 'Agricultural Scholarships to Sheshappa & C. VenkobRao of [?] and Tumkur Dists.', Education Department, Mysore, 1882–83, File No. 5, S. No. [1–4] (https://archives.karnataka.gov.in/home/viewdocument?doc_id=RGVlcGFrMTQ2NDE0&doc_location=RGVlcGFrMQ==).

54 'Agricultural Scholarships to Sheshappa & C. VenkobRao of [?] and Tumkur Dists.', Education Department, Mysore, 1882–83, File No. 5, S. No. [1–4], Folios 13 and 16. Via KSA-DIGITIZED (https://archives.karnataka.gov.in/home/viewdocument?doc_id=RGVlcGFrMTQ2NDE0&doc_location=RGVlcGFrMQ==).

55 See David Arnold, *Science, Technology, and Medicine in Colonial India* (Cambridge: Cambridge University Press, 2000), Chapter 4; Gyan Prakash, *Another Reason: Science and the Imagination of Modern India* (Princeton: Princeton University Press, 1999), Chapter 6.

56 On Cotton, see Sunil Amrith, *Unruly Waters: How Mountain Rivers and Monsoons Have Shaped South Asia's History* (London: Penguin Books, 2018), Chapter 2.

57 On Smiles and Stephenson, see Samuel Smiles, *Self Help; With Illustrations of Character and Conduct* (Boston: Ticknor and Fields, 1861), p. vi. In the 1860s, Smiles published a three-volume study titled *Lives of the Engineers*; he expanded it to a five-volume edition the following decade. 'Samuel Smiles', *Encyclopedia Britannica.*

2. Becoming an Engineer

1 Some portions of an earlier version of this chapter were published as an article: Aparajith Ramnath, 'Engineers' Day: The Story of the Irishman Who Moulded Visvesvaraya's Alma Mater', The Wire, 15 September 2019 (https://thewire.in/the-sciences/engineers-day-theodore-cooke-mokshagundam-visvesvaraya-civil-engineering-college, accessed 23 March 2024).

2 See Visvesvaraya's educational history in the recommendation form ('Form C') for his transfer from Associate Member to Member of the Institution of Civil Engineers (ICE), London, 11 April 1904, p. 1 (courtesy ICE Archives, London).

3 Reconstruction based on author's visit to the site, 2019.

4 See for instance Aparajith Ramnath, *The Birth of an Indian Profession: Engineers, Industry, and the State, 1900–47* (Delhi: Oxford University Press, 2017), esp. Chapter 3; Brendan P. Cuddy, 'The Royal Indian Engineering College, Cooper's Hill (1871–1906): A Case Study of State Involvement in Civil

Engineering Education' (PhD thesis, London University, 1980); Daniel R. Headrick, *The Tentacles of Progress: Technology Transfer in the Age of Imperialism, 1850–1940* (New York and Oxford: Oxford University Press, 1988), pp. 317– 19.

5 *Technical and Industrial Education in the Bombay Presidency: Final Report of the Committee Appointed by Government, 1921–1922* (Bombay: Government Central Press, 1923), p. 77; 'Laying the Foundation Stone of the Poona Engineering College', TOI, 11 August 1865, p. 3; *The Bombay University Calendar for the Year 1884–85* (Bombay: Thacker & Co., 1884), p. 382; *Gazetteer: Bombay Presidency: Volume XVIII. Part III. Poona* (Bombay: Government Central Press, 1885), pp. 57–8; 'History', website of the College of Engineering Pune, https://www.coep.org.in/about/history (accessed 4 March 2020).

6 'Laying the Foundation Stone of the Poona Engineering College', TOI, 11 August 1865, p. 3 (including quoted text); *The Bombay University Calendar for the Year 1883–84* (Bombay: Thacker & Co., 1883), p. 354. The architect referred to was likely James Trubshawe: see Michael Mark Chrimes, 'Architectural Dilettantes: Construction Professionals in British India 1600–1910. Part 2. 1860–1910: The Advent of the Professional', *Construction History* 31, 1 (2016): 99–140. C.J. Readymoney was later to make donations to help erect the University Convocation Hall and the Elphinstone College building in Bombay city. Preeti Chopra, *A Joint Enterprise: Indian Elites and the Making of British Bombay* (Minneapolis and London: University of Minnesota Press, 2011), p. xiv.

7 Description based on the bust of Cooke at the Poona College, as shown in *Dr Visvesvaraya*, a Films Division documentary from c. 1961. The film is available on the YouTube channel of the Films Division, at https://www.youtube.com/watch?v=ng12ol-gvHg (accessed 23 March 2024), and Cooke's bust appears at 2:19 – 2:29 minutes.

8 'Dr. Theodore Cooke', *Nature*, Vol. 85, No. 2142 (17 November 1910), p. 82 (including quoted text); *Bombay University Calendar 1883–84*, p. 355; 'Cooke, Theodore', in IBD 1915, pp. 97–8; Bombay Governor's introductory speech at Sassoon Mechanics'

Institute in 'Lecture by Dr. Theodore Cooke', TOI, 11 February 1878, p. A1; 'The Engineering College, Poona', TOI, 27 August 1877, p. 2.

9 'Lecture by Dr. Theodore Cooke', TOI, 11 February 1878, p. A1. On Humphry Davy, see 'Our History', website of the Royal Institution (https://www.rigb.org/our-history/humphry-davy, accessed 4 March 2020).

10 Cooke's preface, quoted in 'Notices of Books', TOI, 10 August 1871, p. 3.

11 'The Engineering College', TOI, 27 August 1877, p. 2.

12 Quoted in 'Lecture by Dr. Theodore Cooke', TOI, 11 February 1878, p. A1.

13 *Bombay University Calendar 1883–84*, p. 353 (including quoted text); *Gazetteer: Bombay Presidency: Volume XVIII. Part III. Poona* (Bombay: Government Central Press, 1885), pp. 57–8. On the different classes at Roorkee, see for instance Ramnath, *Birth of an Indian Profession*, p. 101.

14 *Bombay University Calendar 1883–84*, pp. 354–5; nomination form ('Form A', proposer H.G. Palliser, 5 March 1887) for Visvesvaraya to be admitted as an Associate Member of the Institution of Civil Engineers (ICE), London (courtesy ICE Archives, London).

15 *Gazetteer: Bombay Presidency: Volume XVIII. Part III. Poona*, p. 57.

16 *Bombay University Calendar 1884–85*, p. 396; 'The Engineering College', TOI, 27 August 1877, p. 2; Government resolution printed in 'The Deccan College of Science [sic]', TOI, 24 January 1887, p. 3.

17 *Gazetteer: Bombay Presidency: Volume XVIII. Part III. Poona*, pp. 57–8.

18 T. Cooke (Principal, Poona Civil Engineering College) to Director of Public Instruction, 10 November 1871. Letter No. 323 of 1871/72, in 'Appointments. Prospectus of the Poona Civil Engineering College', PWD No. 954 (1871), in PWD Vol. No. 1970 (1868–89), MSA (Maharashtra State Archives). Commas are missing in some parts of the original text, and have been inserted in the quotation here for the sake of clarity.

19 T. Cooke to Director of Public Instruction, Bombay, [6] January 1872, No. 389 of 1871/72 [copy]; Resolution No. 181,

Educational Department, Bombay, 13 February 1872. Both in 'Appointments. Prospectus of the Poona Civil Engineering College', PWD No. 954 (1871), in PWD Vol. No. 1970 (1868–89), MSA.

20 Handwritten note (folios M-269ff) in 'Appointments. Prospectus of the Poona Civil Engineering College', PWD No. 954 (1871), in PWD Vol. No. 1970 (1868–89), MSA.

21 See the list of LCE graduates from 1873 to 1883 (inclusive), in *Bombay University Calendar 1883–84*, pp. 269–73.

22 See Chapter 3 below.

23 *Bombay University Calendar 1883–84*, p. 355.

24 'A Memorial to Dr. Cooke', *Homeward Mail from India, China and the East*, 13 August 1894, p. 1064.

25 See the discussion earlier in this chapter.

26 See Bombay Governor Bartle Frere's speech as reported in 'Laying the Foundation Stone of the Poona Engineering College', TOI, 11 August 1865, p. 3.

27 See ibid.; 'The Engineering College, Poona', TOI, 27 August 1877, p. 2.

28 *Bombay University Calendar 1883–84*, pp. 94–103; Lt.-Col. J.G. Medley, R.E. (compiler), *Roorkee Treatise on Civil Engineering in India*, Volume 1, 3rd edition (ed. Major A.M. Lang, R.E.) (Roorkee: Thomason College Press, 1873); William Rankine, *A Manual of Civil Engineering* (London: Griffin, Bohn, and Company, 1862).

29 *Bombay University Calendar 1884–85*, pp. cclvii–cclxxx. On which of these were optional papers, see *Bombay University Calendar 1883–84*, pp. 101–3.

30 *Bombay University Calendar 1884–85*, pp. cclxii, cclxiii, cclxv, cclxvi, cclxvii, cclxix, cclxx, cclxxiii, clv.

31 See Chapter 1 above.

32 A similar point about the challenge of being in a new place with a different local language is made by Mukund Dharashivkar, *Drashta Abhiyanta Sir Visvesvaraya: Vicharvant Bharat Ratna Dr. Sir Mokshagundam Visvesvaraya Yanche Vyaktimattva Darshan* (Pune: Manovikas Prakashan, 2017), p. 21.

3. Becoming an Officer

1 *The Bombay University Calendar for the Year 1884–85* (Bombay: Thacker & Co., 1884), pp. 393–6. A misprint ('Decree' for 'Degree') in the quoted text has been corrected. Visvesvaraya's name is often rendered as 'Visvesvaraiya' in documents relating to the early part of his life. On the Cowasjee Jehangir Hall, see Tanushree Venkatraman, 'Grandeur restored, a hallowed hall of learning sparkles again', *Indian Express* (online), 10 June 2014 (https://indianexpress.com/article/cities/mumbai/grandeur-restored-a-hallowed-hall-of-learning-sparkles-again/, accessed 26 April 2020).

2 Rita P. Bhambi, 'Great Indian Peninsula Railway Company and its Contractors (1853–1871)', *Proceedings of the Indian History Congress* 73 (2012): 880–7.

3 *Bombay University Calendar 1884–85*, p. 397; *The Bombay University Calendar for the Year 1883–84* (Bombay: Thacker & Co., 1883), p. 152.

4 M. Visvesvaraya, *Memoirs of my Working Life* (Bangalore: M. Visvesvaraya, 1951), p. 1.

5 Quoted in T.S. Satyan, *Alive and Clicking* (Gurgaon: Penguin, 2005), p. 74.

6 See Aparajith Ramnath, *The Birth of an Indian Profession: Engineers, Industry, and the State, 1900–47* (Delhi: Oxford University Press, 2017), Chapter 3. On ranks achieved by retirement, see also the career summaries in, for example, IOL 1905 (section titled 'Record of Services').

7 For the types of subordinate jobs in the Indian PWD, see Arun Kumar, 'Colonial Requirements and Engineering Education: The Public Works Department, 1847–1947', in Roy MacLeod and Deepak Kumar (eds.), *Technology and the Raj: Western Technology and Technical Transfers to India, 1700–1947* (New Delhi, Thousand Oaks and London: Sage, 1995), pp. 216–32, here p. 219.

8 Brendan P. Cuddy, 'The Royal Indian Engineering College, Cooper's Hill (1871–1906): A Case Study of State Involvement in Civil Engineering Education' (PhD thesis, London University,

1980), Chapter 1; R.A. Buchanan, 'Institutional Proliferation in the British Engineering Profession, 1847–1914', *The Economic History Review*, New Series 38, 1 (1985): 42–60.

9 Ramnath, *Birth of an Indian Profession*, esp. Chapter 3.

10 Visvesvaraya, *Memoirs*, pp. 1 and 4; Recommendation form ('Form C') for Visvesvaraya's transfer from Associate Member to Member of the Institution of Civil Engineers (ICE), London, 11 April 1904, p. 3 (courtesy ICE Archives, London). The latter source is cited hereafter as 'Form C', ICE.

11 Visvesvaraya, *Memoirs*, pp. 2–4 (quoted text on p. 4). Visvesvaraya's account is a little unclear on the identity of the executive engineer, though he seems to be referring to Palliser (whom he mentions a few lines later). But based on another source, we can conclude that Palliser was almost certainly the boss he was referring to: see Visvesvaraya's employment history in 'Form C', ICE, pp. 1 and 3.

12 Pandri Nath, *Mokshagundam Visvesvaraya: Life and Work* (Bombay: Bharatiya Vidya Bhavan, 1987), p. 8.

13 Visvesvaraya's memoirs do, however, list his achievements with pride. On expatriate engineers' self-presentation in their memoirs, see for instance the discussion of G.F. Hall and H.F. Merrington (who, however, worked in later decades) in Ramnath, *Birth of an Indian Profession*, Chapter 3.

14 Ramnath, *Birth of an Indian Profession*, Chapter 3.

15 Reports submitted by Bombay engineers, 1878, in PWD Vol. No. 1737 (1868–89), MSA (especially Folios M-161 to M-166). The quote is from Col. W.W. Goodfellow, Acting Superintending Engineer, Northern Division, in his report dated 6 August 1878 (Letter No. 2166 of 1878), and appears on Folio M-166. One must note, however, the sagacity of the Governor of Bombay, Richard Temple, in responding to these reports on Indian engineers. He felt that the superiors writing the reports, while they had grounds for their views, had not shown 'sufficient liberality of opinion, nor . . . sufficient allowance for the circumstances in which Natives are placed'. He observed that in several cases, the reports had described the Indian engineers' work fairly positively, but had declined to conclude that they were capable of functioning independently as executive engineers. In some cases, he agreed that those evaluated were lacking, but accepted

blame on behalf of the government: 'these failures probably arise in part from defects in professional training, which defects we should try to remedy'. Confidential Minute by Richard Temple, 'Qualifications of Native Engineers for Executive Charge of a District and for the Higher Grades in the Department of Public Works' (17 September 1878), in PWD Vol. No. 1737 (1868–89), MSA (Folios M-171 to M-174).

16 'CONFIDENTIAL report in respect of the official character, &c., of Executive and Assistant Engineers employed in the Khandesh Irrign. District during the year ending [blank]', in PWD Vol. No. 1736 (1868– 89), MSA. Although the form is undated, it is found along with other forms marked 1887. That date also tallies with the information on the form (Visvesvaraya's designation and his status as Associate Member of the Institution of Civil Engineers, on which more later in the chapter).

17 Visvesvaraya, *Memoirs*, pp. 4–5.

18 Nomination form ('Form A', proposer H.G. Palliser, 5 March 1887) for Visvesvaraya to be admitted as an Associate Member of the Institution of Civil Engineers (ICE), London (courtesy ICE Archives, London).

19 Satyan, *Alive and Clicking*, pp. 71–4.

20 Visvesvaraya, *Memoirs*, p. 5. For the timeline, see 'Form C', ICE, p. 3.

21 Interview with Satish Mokshagundam and Lakshmi M. Satish, Bengaluru, 21 June 2019; interview with Shakuntala Krishnamurthy (with inputs from Satish Mokshagundam and Lakshmi M. Satish), Bengaluru, 26 June 2019; Government of Mysore, Department of Public Instruction, *Bhagya Shilpi* (Mysore: 1968), pp. 23–7; H.V.R. Athre (ed.), *New Book on Bharatha Rathna Dr. M. Visvesvaraya's Biography* (Bangalore: The Mysore Economic Review, 1983), p. 104.

22 'Form No. 15 A. Article 993(b) of the C.S. Regulations' (signed M. Visvesvaraya, 26 October 1909), in Visvesvaraya Papers, microfilm, Reel 1, NMML.

23 Quoted in Hiralal Lallubhai Kaji, *Life and Speeches of Sir Vithaldas Thackersey* (Bombay: D.B. Taraporevala Sons & Co., 1934), p. 248.

24 Visvesvaraya, *Memoirs*, pp. 5–6. The quoted phrase is from Reinold's letter to Visvesvaraya, 22 March 1893, which is printed in ibid., p. 6.

25 Ibid., p. 6.

26 See note on 'A hill on the right of the Sukur Cantonment. 15 Dec. 1840' (watercolour by Thomas Studdert) on the website of the British Library (http://www.bl.uk/onlinegallery/onlineex/apac/other/019wdz000004203u00000000.html, accessed 23 May 2020) (includes quoted text). On the British occupation of Sukkur, see A.W. Hughes (compiler), *A Gazetteer of the Province of Sind*, 2nd edition (London: George Bell and Sons, 1876), pp. 37–8. For population of Sukkur, see 'Form C', ICE, p. 3.

27 Visvesvaraya, *Memoirs*, pp. 6–7 (quoted text on p. 7); Form 'C', ICE, p. 3.

28 See for instance the description in 'Sir MV: The Legendary Nation Builder', brochure accompanying exhibition, Nehru Science Centre, National Council of Science Museums (n.d. [2014?]), pp. 24–5.

29 Pirbaksh's speech is printed in 'The Governor's Tour', TOI, 16 December 1895, pp. 5–6. For Doig's full name, see IOL 1905, p. 481.

30 'The Viceroy's Tour', TOI, 3 November 1894, p. 5; 'Arrival of the Govervor [sic] at Sukkur', TOI, 5 December 1894, p. 5.

31 Sandhurst's speech is printed in 'The Governor's Tour', TOI, 16 December 1895, pp. 5–6.

32 Quoted in Visvesvaraya, *Memoirs*, p. 7.

33 'Form C', ICE, p. 3; Visvesvaraya, *Memoirs*, p. 8.

4. Poona Circles

1 M. Visvesvaraya, *Memoirs of My Working Life* (Bangalore: M. Visvesvaraya, 1951), p. 1 and Chapter IV. The quoted text is from p. 28.

2 'Major Khan Bahadur Dinshah D. Khambatta, V.D.', *The Homeward Mail*, 21 May 1910, p. 657 (profile reprinted from the *Pioneer*); 'Sirdar Khan Bahadur Dorabjee Puddumjee' (under 'Obituary Notices'), *The Homeward Mail*, 28 July 1902, p. 1003 (quoted text is from this source); Visvesvaraya, *Memoirs*, pp. 28–30.

3 The earliest mentions I have found are from 1879. Untitled editorial beginning 'The village Punchayet', TOI, 10 May 1879,

p. 2; 'The Public Meeting at the Town Hall (Heerabaugh)', TOI, 28 July 1879, p. 3.

4 Col. L.W. Shakespear, *A Local History of Poona and Its Battlefields* (London: Macmillan and Co., 1916), p. 19 (the quoted text is from here) and p. 51; Visvesvaraya, *Memoirs*, p. 30; *Gazetteer of Bombay State: District Series—Volume XX: Poona District* (Bombay: Government Central Press, 1954), pp. 666–8.

5 'Native Arts Exhibition at Poona', *Homeward Mail*, 6 June 1883, p. 535; Untitled paragraph, *Homeward Mail*, 6 January 1890, p. 8; 'Bombay and the Congress', *Homeward Mail*, 29 December 1891, p. 1641; 'Sivaji's Tomb', *Homeward Mail*, 2 June 1895; B. Pattabhi Sitaramayya, *The History of the Indian National Congress (1885–1935)* (n.p.: Congress Working Committee, 1935), pp. 24–7.

6 'Opening of the Deccan Club', TOI, 19 November 1891, p. 5.

7 Visvesvaraya, *Memoirs*, p. 29.

8 'Opening of the Deccan Club', TOI, 19 November 1891, p. 5.

9 G.A. Mankar, *A Sketch of the Life and Works of the Late Mr. Justice M. G. Ranade, M.A., LL.B., C.I.E., &c., Judge of Her Majesty's High Court of Judicature, Bombay*, Volume 1 (Bombay: Caxton Printing Works, 1902), pp. 99–100; Visvesvaraya, *Memoirs*, p. 28.

10 On these differences, see for instance Gordon Johnson, 'Chitpavan Brahmins and Politics in Western India in the Late Nineteenth and Early Twentieth Centuries', in Edmund Leach and S.N. Mukherjee (eds.), *Elites in South Asia* (Cambridge: Cambridge University Press, 1970), pp. 95–118.

11 David Gilmour, 'Class, Race and the Colonial Clubs of India: Members Only', *Open* magazine (online), 20 September 2018 (https://openthemagazine.com/essay/class-race-and-the-colonial-clubs-of-india/, accessed 24 April 2023).

12 Such as Sadashivpeth and Narayanpeth; see Gail Omvedt, 'Non-Brahmans and Nationalists in Poona', *Economic and Political Weekly* Annual Number (February 1974): 201–16, here p. 202.

13 Untitled paragraph, *Homeward Mail*, 23 March 1901, p. 359.

14 Untitled paragraph under 'G U P', *Homeward Mail*, 3 October 1904, p. 1392.

15 The *Pioneer* article is reprinted in 'Major Khan Bahadur Dinshah D. Khambatta, V.D.', *Homeward Mail*, 21 May 1910, p. 657.

16 See Johnson, 'Chitpavan Brahmins', p. 95; Ross Bassett, *The Technological Indian* (Cambridge, Massachusetts: Harvard University Press, 2016), pp. 16–17; Gail Omvedt, 'Development of the Maharashtrian Class Structure, 1818 to 1931', *Economic and Political Weekly* 8, no. 31/33, Special Number (1973): 1417–32, here p. 1422.

17 This is apparent from the brief mentions of Tilak in Visvesvaraya's memoirs, while it is clear (as this chapter elaborates) that he owed much to Ranade and Gokhale. Visvesvaraya, *Memoirs*, Chapters II and IV.

18 Mankar, *A Sketch*, Volume 1, Chapters I and II; James Kellock, *Mahadev Govind Ranade: Patriot and Social Servant* (Calcutta: Association Press, 1926), Chapters I, II and IV. (For title and author details of the Kellock book, see https://www.sanjeev.sabhlokcity.com/Misc/216508_Mahadev_Govind_Ranade_Patroit_And_Social_Servant.pdf, accessed 23 March 2024; the version consulted is from https://dspace.gipe.ac.in/xmlui/bitstream/handle/10973/29608/GIPE-005106.pdf?sequence=3&isAllowed=y, and does not have some of the front matter.)

19 Mankar, *A Sketch*, Volume 1, Chapters I and III; Kellock, *Mahadev Govind Ranade*, esp. p. 63; 'Prarthana Samaj', *Encyclopedia Britannica*, 2 June 2008 (https://www.britannica.com/topic/Prarthana-Samaj, accessed 6 March 2024).

20 E.L. Turnbull and H.G.D. Turnbull, *Gopal Krishna Gokhale (A Brief Biography)* (Trichur: V. Sundra Iyer & Sons, 1934), p. 21.

21 Mankar, *A Sketch*, Volume 1, pp. 28–32.

22 Kellock, *Mahadev Govind Ranade*, pp. 12–13.

23 Manorama Barnabas, 'Study in the Philosophy of Social Change: The Ideas of Some Liberal Thinkers of Nineteenth Century Maharashtra and Their Relevance to Modernization' (unpublished PhD thesis, University of Poona, 1974), pp. 288 and 293.

24 Quoted in ibid., p. 288.

25 Barnabas, 'Study in the Philosophy of Social Change', pp. 287–329.

26 Mankar, *A Sketch*, Volume 1, p. 112; Johnson, 'Chitpavan Brahmins', pp. 110–12.

27 See Mankar, *A Sketch*, Volume 1, p. 81.

28 T.K. Shahani, *Gopal Krishna Gokhale: A Historical Biography* (Bombay: R.K. Mody, [1929]), p. 40. Gokhale also spent some parts of his college career at the Deccan College in Poona and the Rajaram College in Kolhapur. Ibid., pp. 35–40. On the New English School, see below.

29 P.M. Limaye (author/compiler), *The History of the Deccan Education Society* ([Poona]: n.p., 1935), Chapters I, III and IV. On Fergusson's term in Bombay, see Peter Harnetty, 'Fergusson, Sir James, of Kilkerran, sixth baronet (1832–1907)', *Oxford Dictionary of National Biography*, 23 September 2004 (https://doi.org/10.1093/ref:odnb/33112, accessed 23 March 2024).

30 Shahani, *Gopal Krishna Gokhale*, Chapter II; Turnbull and Turnbull, *Gopal Krishna Gokhale*, pp. 18–20; V.S. Srinivasa Sastri, *Life of Gopal Krishna Gokhale (Mysore University Extension Lectures)* (Bangalore: Bangalore Printing and Publishing Co. Ltd., 1937), p. 7.

31 See Sastri, *Life of Gopal Krishna Gokhale*, esp. pp. 7–8 and Appendix (pp. 129–32).

32 Shahani, *Gopal Krishna Gokhale*, pp. 56–7.

33 V. S. Srinivasa Sastri, *Speeches and Writings of the Right Honourable V. S. Srinivasa Sastri*, vol. 2 ([Madras]: South Indian National Association/Srinivasa Sastri Endowment Fund, 1969), p. 242.

34 Shahani, *Gopal Krishna Gokhale*, esp. p. 41; Sastri, *Life of Gopal Krishna Gokhale*, p. 11 (quoted phrase from this source).

35 Shahani, *Gopal Krishna Gokhale*, pp. 37–8 and 43–4; Sastri, *Life of Gopal Krishna Gokhale*, p. 6.

36 Shahani, *Gopal Krishna Gokhale*, pp. 58–9.

37 Ibid., p. 67; Barnabas, 'Study in the Philosophy of Social Change', p. 295.

38 Johnson, 'Chitpavan Brahmins', p. 110.

39 See Barnabas, 'Study in the Philosophy of Social Change', pp. 266, 323, and 590; Shahani, *Gopal Krishna Gokhale,* Chapter II; Turnbull and Turnbull, *Gopal Krishna Gokhale*, Chapter 4; Johnson, 'Chitpavan Brahmins', pp. 110–11; Limaye (author/compiler), *The History of the Deccan Education Society*, Part I, Chapters II and V.

40 Johnson, 'Chitpavan Brahmins', pp. 111–13.
41 Quoted in Barnabas, 'Study in the Philosophy of Social Change', p. 323.
42 Quoted in Barnabas, 'Study in the Philosophy of Social Change', p. 325.
43 Barnabas, 'Study in the Philosophy of Social Change', pp. 326–7.
44 Turnbull and Turnbull, *Gopal Krishna Gokhale*, Chapter 5.
45 Sastri, *Life of Gopal Krishna Gokhale*, pp. 50–3 (quoted text from pp. 50–51); Barnabas, 'Study in the Philosophy of Social Change', pp. 330–8. On the instruction to Gandhi, see for instance Gandhi to Gokhale, 1 April 1914, in CWMG, Vol. 12, p. 401; see also Ramachandra Guha, *Gandhi: The years that changed the world: 1914–48* (Gurgaon: Allen Lane, 2018), p. 9.
46 Quoted in Barnabas, 'Study in the Philosophy of Social Change', p. 319.
47 G.A. Mankar, *A Sketch of the Life and Works of the Late Mr. Justice M. G. Ranade, M.A., LL.B., C.I.E., &c., Judge of Her Majesty's High Court of Judicature, Bombay*, vol. 2 (Bombay: Caxton Printing Works, 1902), chapter I. Another important influence on Ranade and Naoroji was the German economist Friedrich List. See Manu Goswami, 'From Swadeshi to Swaraj: Nation, Economy, Territory in Colonial South Asia, 1870 to 1907', *Comparative Studies in Society and History* 40, 4 (October 1998): 609–36.
48 Mankar, *A Sketch*, Volume 1, pp. 82–6.
49 Bassett, *The Technological Indian*, p. 38.
50 Mankar, *A Sketch,* Volume 2, pp. 29–30. Hirabaug was probably the regular venue for the Industrial Conference. We know definitely that it was the venue for the 1894 edition. See 'The Poona Industrial Conference', *Homeward Mail,* 8 October 1894, p, 1330.
51 Quoted in Mankar, *A Sketch,* Volume 2, p. 31.
52 Bassett, *The Technological Indian*, Chapter 1 (quoted text from p. 21).
53 On Tilak's orthodoxy as strategy, see Sumit Sarkar, *Modern India: 1885–1947* (Pearson: Delhi, 2014), p. 63.
54 Bassett, *The Technological Indian,* Chapter 1, *passim.*
55 T.S. Satyan, *Alive and Clicking* (Gurgaon: Penguin, 2005), pp. 70–1; Visvesvaraya's Foreword to *Sayings—Wise or Witty* (compiler

M. Visvesvaraya) (Bangalore: n.p., 1957). See also the nature of the collection in MV-PAPERS-IEI.

56 Visvesvaraya, *Memoirs*, p. 27.

57 See Chapter 14 below; see also Bassett, *The Technological Indian*, p. 78.

58 The quoted text is from Visvesvaraya's speech at the end of the Poona Swadeshi Bazaar and Industrial Exhibition, 1927, excerpted in 'Industrial Progress at a Standstill', newspaper cutting (date and name of newspaper not visible), in MV-PAPERS-IEI, Vol. 21. The year of the event is deduced from other newspaper cuttings in the same volume.

59 See his remarks on not publishing his observations based on his first Japan trip (of which more below). Visvesvaraya, *Memoirs*, p. 121.

60 For more on Visvesvaraya's residence in this locality, see Chapter 6 below.

61 Bassett, *The Technological Indian*, Chapter 2 (quoted text from p. 68); 'First Sino-Japanese War', *Encyclopedia Britannica*, 12 October 2023 (https://www.britannica.com/event/First-Sino-Japanese-War-1894-1895, accessed 6 March 2024). See also Puran Singh, *On Paths of Life* (Delhi: Uttar Chand Kapur & Sons, [1954]): this is a posthumously published memoir (completed in 1927) by an Indian who studied in Japan at the turn of the twentieth century.

62 Ernest F.G. Hatch, *Far Eastern Impressions: Japan—Korea—China* (London: Hutchinson and Co., 1904). Quoted text from pp. 1, 4, 17, and 25. On Hatch, see Stephen Bottomore, 'Sir Ernest Frederic George Hatch', 'Who's Who of Victorian Cinema' (https://www.victorian-cinema.net/hatch, accessed 7 January 2023).

63 G.H. Rittner, *Impressions of Japan* (New York: James Pott & Co., 1904), pp. 139–40.

64 Visvesvaraya, *Memoirs*, pp. 68–70.

65 M. Venkatesa Iyengar, 'A Hard Task-Master', in CENT-VOL, pp. 257–64, here pp. 259–60.

66 Sastri, *Speeches and Writings,* Volume 2, p. 231. On Sastri's position at the Hindu High School, see ibid., p. 235.

67 On Ranade's knowledge of the Marathi language and its literature, see Mankar, *A Sketch,* Volume 2, pp. 178–9 and *passim*.

68 'Speech at the Gokhale Condolence Meeting', 25 February 1915, MV-SPEECHES-VOL, pp. 215–8, here p. 217.
69 Sastri, *Speeches and Writings,* Volume 2, p. 231; 'Speech at the Gokhale Condolence Meeting', p. 216.
70 Visvesvaraya, *Memoirs,* p. 31.
71 Mankar, *A Sketch*, Volume 2, p. 210. Visvesvaraya is not named, but identified as 'a friend from Poona'. On Modak, see ibid., pp. 101–4. Visvesvaraya recounts the incident as being in 1898, but he was probably confusing it with another visit, as Modak died in 1897.
72 Barnabas, 'Study in the Philosophy of Social Change', pp. 316–21.
73 Quoted in ibid., p. 318.
74 Quoted in ibid., p. 320.
75 Mankar, *A Sketch*, Volume 1, Chapter V; Mankar, *A Sketch*, Volume 2, Chapter I.

5. Transforming Irrigation in the Deccan

1 J.M. Maclean, *A Guide to Bombay. Historical, Statistical, and Descriptive*, 31st edition (Bombay: The 'Bombay Gazette' Steam Press, 1906), pp. 321-4; Jean Drèze, 'Famine Prevention in India', WIDER Working Papers (World Institute for Development Economics Research, May 1988), p. 11; *Report of the Indian Famine Commission 1898* (Simla: Government Central Printing Office, 1898), especially para 142.
2 Drèze, 'Famine Prevention in India', pp. 7–9 and 21–7 (quoted text on p. 21); T. Higham, 'Notes on an Inspection of Famine Relief Works in the Bombay Presidency, by Mr. T. Higham, C.I.E., on Special Duty in Connection with Famine Relief Operations', 26 July 1897, in *Further Papers Regarding the Famine and the Relief Operations in India During the Years 1897–98: No. VII* (London: Her Majesty's Stationery Office, 1898), pp. 427–42.
3 Higham, 'Notes on an Inspection'; *Report of the Indian Famine Commission 1898* (Simla: Government Central Printing Office, 1898), paras 132–142.
4 M. Visvesvaraya, *Memoirs of My Working Life* (Bangalore: M. Visvesvaraya, 1951), p. 8; Recommendation form ('Form C') for Visvesvaraya's transfer from Associate Member to Member of the

Institution of Civil Engineers (ICE), London, 11 April 1904, p. 3 (courtesy ICE Archives, London). The latter source is cited hereafter as 'Form C', ICE.

5 Alex Bolding, Peter P. Mollinga, and Kees van Straaten, 'Modules for Modernisation: Colonial Irrigation in India and the Technological Dimension of Agrarian Change', *Journal of Development Studies* 31, 6 (1995): 805–44, here pp. 811–3.

6 Naresh Chandra Sourabh and Timo Myllyntaus, 'Famines in Late Nineteenth-Century India: Politics, Culture, and Environmental Justice', Environment & Society Portal, *Virtual Exhibitions* 2015, no. 2, Rachel Carson Center for Environment and Society (doi.org/10.5282/rcc/6812); Sunil Amrith, *Unruly Waters: How Mountain Rivers and Monsoons Have Shaped South Asia's History*, Kindle Edition (London: Penguin Books, 2018), p. 12.

7 Amrith, *Unruly Waters*, pp. 66-7; Jon Wilson, 'How Modernity Arrived to Godavari', *Modern Asian Studies* 51, 2 (2017): 399–431, esp. pp. 429–30; David Hardiman, 'The Politics of Water in Colonial India', *South Asia: Journal of South Asian Studies* 25, 2 (2002): 111–20, here p. 113.

8 Wilson, 'How Modernity Arrived' (quoted text from p. 430); Amrith, *Unruly Waters,* Chapter 2; 'Sir Arthur Thomas Cotton', *Encyclopaedia Britannica*, 23 February 2024 (https://www.britannica.com/biography/Arthur-Thomas-Cotton, accessed 6 March 2024); Hardiman, 'The Politics of Water in Colonial India'.

9 Hardiman, 'The Politics of Water in Colonial India'; David Gilmartin, 'Models of the Hydraulic Environment: Colonial Irrigation, State Power and Community in the Indus Basin', in David Arnold and Ramachandra Guha (eds.), *Nature, Culture, Imperialism: Essays on the Environmental History of South Asia* (Delhi and Oxford: Oxford University Press, 1995), pp. 210–36.

10 Drèze, 'Famine Prevention in India', p. 14.

11 Aditya Ramesh, 'The Value of Tanks: Maintenance, Ecology and the Colonial Economy in Nineteenth-Century South India', *Water History* 10, no. 4 (December 2018): 267–89; Bolding *et al.*, 'Modules for Modernisation' (quoted text from p. 811); Hardiman, 'The Politics of Water in Colonial India' (esp. pp. 114–5).

12 Bret Wallach, 'British Irrigation Works in India's Krishna Basin', *Journal of Historical Geography*, 11.2 (1985): 155–73.
13 Bolding *et al.*, 'Modules for Modernisation', pp. 811–12.
14 In 1901, H.F. Beale, a Superintending Engineer in the Bombay PWD, suggested that canals should be operated commercially as the railways could help alleviate famines by transporting foodgrains from other provinces/regions. Bolding *et al.*, 'Modules for Modernisation', p. 813.
15 Visvesvaraya, *Memoirs*, p. 9 (quoted text is from this source); Evidence of M. Visvesvaraya in *Report of the Indian Irrigation Commission, 1901–03: Appendix* (Calcutta: Office of the Superintendent of Government Printing, India, 1903), pp. 97–107, here p. 99. This source is hereinafter cited as Evidence of M. Visvesvaraya.
16 *Report of the Indian Irrigation Commission, 1901–1903: Part I—General* (Calcutta: Office of the Superintendent of Government Printing, India, 1903), Preface, para 1 (including quoted text); 'Bombay Irrigation Policy', letter to the editor from 'J.', TOI, 10 December 1901, p. 6; 'Scott-Moncrieff Commission', *Encyclopedia Britannica*, 2 November 2009 (https://www.britannica.com/topic/Scott-Moncrieff-Commission, accessed 6 March 2024). The first of these sources is hereinafter cited as Irrigation Commission Report Part I.
17 Irrigation Commission Report Part I, front matter. On Scott-Moncrieff, see 'The life of Sir Colin Scott-Moncrieff', *Scottish Geographical Magazine* 34, 6 (1918): 230–4; Mary Albright Hollings (ed.), *The Life of Sir Colin C. Scott-Moncrieff, K.C.S.I., K.C.M.G., R.E., LL.D., ETC.* (London: John Murray, 1917), pp. 297–9.
18 M. Visvesvaraya, 'Memorandum on Irrigation Works in the Bombay Presidency, Excluding Sind', November 1901, in File No. 101 of 1903, Part I, PWD Irrigation Vol. 164, 1899–1903, MSA; Visvesvaraya, *Memoirs*, p. 11. On the background of the memorandum, see: [Illegible] to [no initials] Thompson, 16 September 1898 (handwritten letter), and [Visvesvaraya] to [no initials] Davidson, 21 January 1899 (handwritten note), in PWD Irrigation, No. 77 Part I, 1899, in PWD Irrigation Vol. 165,

1899–1903, MSA. On Visvesvaraya's famine work under Joyner, see 'Form C', ICE, p. 3.

19 In this connection Visvesvaraya argued that since Sind, which also came under the Bombay Presidency and had its irrigation works run by members of the same cadre of PWD engineers, provided much greater revenue than the Deccan and Gujarat regions, 'it may be concluded that the comparative ill-success of the latter is not due to any lack of efficiency in the administration.' Visvesvaraya, 'Memorandum', para 48.

20 Visvesvaraya, 'Memorandum', paras 12–14 and 19.

21 Ibid., para 55, point 14.

22 Ibid., para 30.

23 Ibid., Section 4; quoted text from para 31.

24 Ibid., para 51.

25 Evidence of M. Visvesvaraya, p. 99.

26 Visvesvaraya, 'Memorandum', para 52.

27 Ibid., para 54.

28 Evidence of M. Visvesvaraya, p. 99.

29 Visvesvaraya, 'Memorandum', para 55, point 9; see also Evidence of M. Visvesvaraya, p. 99.

30 Evidence of M. Visvesvaraya. The (large) number of questions is also noted by Dildar Husain, *An Engineering Wizard of India (1861–1962)* (Hyderabad: Institution of Engineers (India), Andhra Pradesh Centre, 1966), p. 93.

31 Evidence of M. Visvesvaraya, *passim*. See also Husain, *An Engineering Wizard*, pp. 93–4.

32 Evidence of M. Visvesvaraya, p. 106 and p. 98.

33 Ibid., p. 99. On the instructions given to the Irrigation Commission, see Irrigation Commission Report Part I, Preface, para 1.

34 Husain, *An Engineering Wizard*, p. 93.

35 E.g. 'The Irrigation Commission. Inquiry at Ahmedabad', TOI, 6 December 1901, p. 5; 'The Irrigation Commission. Resumed Sitting at Poona', TOI, 23 December 1901, p. 5.

36 Husain, *An Engineering Wizard*, pp. 93–4.

37 Letter No. 154 of 1902, from Superintending Engineer, Indus Left Bank Division, to Secretary to Government, Public Works

Department, Bombay, 13/14 [?] January 1902, in PWD Irrigation Vol. 226, 1904–1909, MSA, Folios S13–S29.

38 See letters in PWD Irrigation Vol. 226, 1904–1909, MSA, Folios S33–S39 and S41–S45.

39 H.G. Palliser M.I.C.E., Chief Engineer, Indus Right Bank Division, to Secretary to Government, PWD, Bombay, 8 May 1902, in PWD Irrigation Vol. 226, 1904–1909, MSA, Folios S47–S49.

40 Chitale is listed as having passed the First Examination in Civil Engineering from the Poona College of Science in 1882. *The Bombay University Calendar for the Year 1883–84* (Bombay: Thacker & Co., 1883), p. 294.

41 [P.K.] Chitale, L.C.E., Executive Engineer, Jamrao Canal, Southern District to Superintending Engineer, Indus Left Bank Division, 5 June 1902 (Letter No. 2049 of 1902), in PWD Irrigation Vol. 226, 1904–1909, MSA, Folios S53–S63.

42 Ibid.

43 M. Visvesvaraya, 'Irrigation on the Block System: A description of the system with proposals for applying the same to the Nira Canal and two minor tanks in the Poona District' (printed pamphlet, April 1903), in File No. 101 of 1903, Part I, PWD Irrigation Vol. 164, 1899–1903, MSA.

44 See Visvesvaraya, 'Irrigation on the Block System', para 5; and Bolding *et al.*, 'Modules for Modernisation', p. 815.

45 Visvesvaraya, 'Irrigation on the Block System', para 5.

46 Ibid., paras 5 and 8; Bolding *et al.*, 'Modules for Modernisation', p. 815.

47 Visvesvaraya, 'Irrigation on the Block System', paras 7 and 13.

48 Ibid., para 21.

49 Ibid., paras 25–27.

50 Ibid., para 29.

51 Visvesvaraya, 'Irrigation on the Block System', para 36. See also G.O.W. Dunn, M.I.C.E., Superintending Engineer, Central Division, to PWD Secretary, Bombay, 24 April 1903, Letter No. 2186 of 1903, para 6. In PWD Irrigation Vol. 164, 1899–1903, MSA, Folios S279–S280.

52 *Report of the Indian Irrigation Commission, 1901–03: Part II.—Provincial* (Calcutta: Superintendent of Government Printing,

1903), para 144. This source is hereinafter cited as Irrigation Commission Report Part II.

53 Irrigation Commission Report Part II, paras 164–5 (quoted text from para 164).

54 Ibid., para 167.

55 Irrigation Commission Report Part I, para 291.

56 Ibid., paras 291–2; Bolding *et al.*, 'Modules for Modernisation', esp. pp. 815–19 (quoted terms are from this source).

57 Bombay PWD Resolution, No. W.I.—2894 of 1903, issued by H.O.B. Shoubridge, Under Secretary to Government, 17 December 1903, in PWD Irrigation Vol. 174, 1904–1909, MSA, Folios M85–M86.

58 Visvesvaraya's letter No. 7680, 29 October 1904, para 2. The letter is reproduced in full in Bombay PWD Resolution No. W.I.—3070 of 1904, issued by J.B. Chapman, Irrigation Under Secretary, 22 December 1904, in PWD Irrigation Vol. 174, 1904–1909, MSA, Folios S267–S270.

59 M. Visvesvaraya, 'Instructions to the Committee appointed to introduce the Block System', typed note dated 7 June 1904, in PWD Irrigation Vol. 174, 1904–1909, MSA, Folios S151–S161.

60 M. Visvesvaraya, Executive Engineer for Irrigation, Poona District, to the Superintending Engineer, Central Division, 26 June 1904 (typed copy), in PWD Irrigation Vol. 174, 1904–1909, MSA, Folios S163–S173.

61 R.I. No. 9843, 'Rules under the Irrigation Act. Modifications in the _ to legalize the introduction of Irrign by Block System', handwritten note, in PWD Irrigation Vol. 174, 1904–1909, MSA, Folio M192.

62 Visvesvaraya's letter No. 7680, 29 October 1904, paras 1, 5 and 7. In PWD Irrigation Vol. 174, 1904–1909, MSA, Folios S235–S248.

63 Donald W. Attwood, *Raising Cane: The Political Economy of Sugar in Western India* (Delhi: Oxford University Press, 1993), p. 62.

64 Ibid., pp. 62–6 (quoted text from p. 66). See also Bolding *et al.*, 'Modules for Modernisation', pp. 825–7.

65 Bolding *et al.*, 'Modules for Modernisation', pp. 821–5.

66 Ibid., p. 827; C.C. Inglis, *Note on Irrigation on the Block System in the Deccan Canal Tracts*, Bombay PWD Technical Paper No. 16

(Bombay: Government Central Press, 1927), paras 7 (quoted text is from here) and 15–16.

67 Raj Sekhar Basu, 'The World of an Engineer: M. Visvesvaraya and Irrigation Engineering in Twentieth-century India', in Arun Bandopadhyay (ed.), *Science and Society in India: 1750–2000* (New Delhi: Manohar, 2010), pp. 249–98, here pp. 259–60 and 256 (quoted text from this page).

68 Bolding *et al.*, 'Modules for Modernisation', p. 821.

69 Inglis, *Note on Irrigation on the Block System*, para 8.

70 Ibid., paras 21, 22 and 25.

71 Ibid., paras 33, 34 and 38.

72 Bolding *et al.*, 'Modules for Modernisation', p. 825.

73 Ibid., pp. 828–9.

74 Attwood, *Raising Cane*, pp. 65-6 and *passim*.

75 Irrigation Commission Report Part I, para 291.

76 Bolding *et al.*, 'Modules for Modernisation', p. 813.

6. Poona's All-Rounder

1 Aparajith Ramnath, *The Birth of an Indian Profession: Engineers, Industry, and the State, 1900–47* (Delhi: Oxford University Press, 2017), Chapter 3.

2 See Chapter 5 above.

3 R.B. Buckley, *The Irrigation Works of India*, 2nd edition (London: E. & F. N. Spon, 1905), pp. 81–2; E.W.C. Sandes, *The Military Engineer in India*, Volume 2 (Chatham: Institution of Royal Engineers, 1935), p. 32; [M. Visvesvaraya], 'Paper No. 2: Automatic waste weir gates of Bhatghar reservoir (Lake Whiting)' and [M. Visvesvaraya], 'Paper No. 3: Automatic waste weir gates of Lake Fife, near Poona', in *The Irrigation Conference, Simla. 1904*, Volume 1 (Calcutta: Superintendent of Government Printing, 1905), pp. 3–6 and 7–11 respectively.

4 Buckley, *Irrigation Works of India*, pp. 195–6. See also [Visvesvaraya], 'Paper No. 3'.

5 Buckley, *Irrigation Works of India*, p. 196; [Visvesvaraya], 'Paper No. 2'. For the date of Reinold's patent, see Letter No. 713 of 1906, from Secretary to Government, General Department

(Bombay) to A. Hill, PWD Joint Secretary, 2 February 1906, in PWD Irrigation Vol. 226, 1904–1909, MSA, Folio S179.

6 Buckley, *Irrigation Works of India*, pp. 196–8; [Visvesvaraya], 'Paper No. 2'.

7 [Visvesvaraya], 'Paper No. 2', p. 4.

8 [Visvesvaraya], 'Paper No. 2'.

9 [Visvesvaraya], 'Paper No. 3', pp. 7–8.

10 Ibid.; M. Visvesvaraya, *Memoirs of My Working Life* (Bangalore: M. Visvesvaraya, 1951), pp. 14–15; 'A note by Mr. Visvesvaraya on the project for Automatic Sluice gates for Lake Fife Waste weir', December 1900, para 11; A. Hill, Executive Engineer, Bombay PWD, to Superintending Engineer, Central Division, Bombay PWD, 9 and 10 February 1901; 'Proceedings of a Committee appointed by the Chief Engineer, Public Works Department, in his No. C.E.-27, dated 28th January 1901, to examine the plans and model of the modified "Reinold" gates devised by Mr. Visvesvaraya, Executive Engineer, for use on the weir at Lake Fife, and report on certain points in connection therewith', [February 1901?]; M. Visvesvaraya, 'Project for automatic sluice gates for Waste Weir of Lake Fife, 1902', 18 February 1902, para 10. The last four of these sources are available in MV-PAPERS-IEI, Vol. 1.

11 Unless otherwise specified, the description that follows is based on the following sources: V.B. Priyani, *The Fundamental Principles of Irrigation Engineering [A Basic Text Book for Engineering Students]*, 3rd edition (Anand: Charotar Book Stall, 1957), pp. 91–3; Buckley, *Irrigation Works of India*, pp. 198–201.

12 A. Hill, Executive Engineer, Bombay PWD, to Superintending Engineer, Central Division, Bombay PWD, 9 and 10 February 1901, para 2. In MV-PAPERS-IEI, Vol. 1.

13 [Visvesvaraya], 'Paper No. 3', p. 10.

14 C.N. Clifton, Superintending Engineer, Central Division, to Chief Engineer, Bombay PWD, 24 February 1902 (PWD letter No. 1176 of 1902), para 5. In MV-PAPERS-IEI, Vol. 1.

15 Buckley, *Irrigation Works of India*, p. 200.

16 Visvesvaraya, *Memoirs*, p. 15.

17 His boss put it thus: 'Mr. Visvesvaraya has taken out a patent, but being connected with this particular work wishes it to be

mentioned that he does not wish to charge for the gates.' Clifton to Chief Engineer, Bombay PWD, 24 February 1902, para 12. In MV-PAPERS-IEI, Vol. 1.

18 'A Visit to Lake Fife', *Deccan Herald*, [23?] July 1904, cutting in MV-PAPERS-IEI, Vol. 1.

19 V.S. Narayana Rao, *Mokshagundam Visvesvaraya* (New Delhi: National Book Trust, 1995 [1988]), p. 8 (mentions the Tigra Dam); C.G. Karve, 'Makers of Poona', in R.V. Oturkar (ed.), *Poona: Look and Outlook, 1951* (Poona City: Poona Municipal Corporation, 1951), pp. 18–22, here p. 21 (mentions the Panama Canal).

20 The only account I have found that discusses the gates in the context of the state of contemporary engineering knowledge is by a practising civil engineer: N. Shankarappa, *Sir M. Visvesvaraya: Dismantling the Myths: Critical Examination of Sir M.V as a Civil Engineer,* E-book (Bengaluru: Kavya Kala Prakashana, n.d.). The book carries out a similar exercise for other projects associated with Visvesvaraya. I am grateful to Mr Shankarappa for meeting with me and explaining various technical points. In the discussion that follows, however, I have relied largely on primary sources.

21 As described on the the first page of the hand-lettered licence agreement between Visvesvaraya and George Gahagan and Co., 17 December 1902, reproduced in H.S. Sreenath, *Bharata Ratna Sir M. Visvesvaraya: His Economic Contribution and Thought* (Bangalore: Select Book, 2013), Plate III (between pp. 32 and 33).

22 M. Visvesvaraya, 'Project for automatic sluice gates for Waste Weir of Lake Fife, 1902', 18 February 1902, para 10.

23 [Visvesvaraya], 'Paper No. 3', p. 8.

24 'Proceedings of a Committee appointed by the Chief Engineer, Public Works Department, in his No. C.E.-27, dated 28th January 1901, to examine the plans and model of the modified "Reinold" gates devised by Mr. Visvesvaraya, Executive Engineer, for use on the weir at Lake Fife, and report on certain points in connection therewith', [February 1901?]; C.N. Clifton, Superintending Engineer, Central Division, to Chief Engineer, Bombay PWD, 24 February 1902 (PWD letter No. 1176 of 1902); A. Hill, Executive Engineer, Bombay PWD, to Superintending Engineer, Central

Division, Bombay PWD, 9 and 10 February 1901. All the above sources are available in MV-PAPERS-IEI, Vol. 1.

25 '*Office Note*' [handwritten], R.I. No. 6316, [June 1904], PWD Irrigation Vol. 226, 1904–1909, MSA, Folios S158–S160.

26 A.T. Mirza, Municipal Officer, Jamnagar, to Joint Secretary to Government, PWD, Bombay, 21 April 1904; handwritten office note, RI No. 4586; Ardeshir T. Mirza to M. Visvesvaraya, 3 May 1904; M. Visvesvaraya (Executive Engineer, Poona) to Superintending Engineer, Central Division, 5 August 1904; C.N. Clifton, Superintending Engineer, Central Division to Chief Engineer, PWD, Irrigation, Bombay (Letter No. 5692 of 1904), 26 October 1904. In PWD Irrigation Vol. 232, 1904–1909, MSA, Folios S11, S14–S15, S19–S20, S33–S34, S89–S90.

27 The Tigra dam in Gwalior state, and the Krishnarajasagara dam in Mysore state. Visvesvaraya, *Memoirs*, p. 15.

28 C.N. Clifton, Superintending Engineer, Central Division, to the Chief Engineer for Irrigation, PWD, Bombay, 4 January 1905. In PWD Irrigation Vol. 232, 1904–1909, MSA, Folio S-67.

29 Visvesvaraya, *Memoirs*, pp. 14–15; [Visvesvaraya], 'Paper No. 3'.

30 The coverage in *Indian Engineering* is mentioned in 'The Waste Weir Gates', *Deccan Herald*, 12 January 1905, cutting in MV-PAPERS-IEI, Vol. 1.

31 Buckley, *Irrigation Works of India*, pp. 198–201.

32 'Irrigation at Poona', TOI, 30 March 1903, p. 7; Visvesvaraya, *Memoirs*, p. 16; 'Horatio Herbert Kitchener, 1st Earl Kitchener', *Encyclopedia Britannica*, 31 January 2024 (https://www.britannica.com/biography/Horatio-Herbert-Kitchener-1st-Earl-Kitchener, accessed 6 March 2024); IOL 1905, pp. 7 and 592; 'Lord and Lady Lamington at Kharakwasla', *Deccan Herald*, 21 July 1904 and 'The Fife Lake: Visited by Lord and Lady Lamington', *Advocate,* 21 July 1904 (cuttings in MV-PAPERS-IEI, Vol. 1). The report in the *Deccan Herald* mentions that Lord Lamington and his wife saw the functioning not only of Visvesvaraya's gates, but also of A.T. Mirza's and E.O. Mawson's gates.

33 Alex Bolding, Peter P. Mollinga, and Kees Van Straaten, 'Modules for Modernisation: Colonial Irrigation in India and the Technological Dimension of Agrarian Change', *Journal*

of Development Studies 31, no. 6 (August 1995): 805–44, esp. p. 821.

34 [M. Visvesvaraya], 'Paper No. 21: Self Acting Module for Regulating Irrigation', in *The Irrigation Conference, Simla. 1904*, Volume 1 (Calcutta: Superintendent of Government Printing, 1905), pp. 72–4 (quoted text on p. 72); Bolding *et al.*, 'Modules for Modernisation', p. 822.

35 [Visvesvaraya], 'Paper No. 21', p. 74.

36 Sidney Preston (Secretary to PWD, Irrigation, Roads and Buildings, Government of India) to PWD Secretary, Bombay, 2 June 1904; handwritten 'Office Note' (R.I. No. 6316); handwritten note by [illegible] dated 9 July. In PWD Irrigation Vol. 226, 1904-1909, MSA, Folios S155, S158–160, and leaf after S160.

37 W.L. Cameron to M. Visvesvaraya, [7 July] 1904, MV-PAPERS-IEI, Vol. 1.

38 Bolding *et al.*, 'Modules for Modernisation', pp. 821–4; 'The Irrigation Conference: President's Final Address', TOI, 12 September 1904, p. 8.

39 Bolding *et al.*, 'Modules for Modernisation', p. 825.

40 Ibid., *passim.*

41 Visvesvaraya, *Memoirs*, p. 18.

42 Bombay PWD notification dated 12 September 1905, in *The Bombay Government Gazette*, 14 September 1905. Copy in MV-PAPERS-IEI, Vol. 1.

43 Mark Harrison, *Public Health in British India: Anglo-Indian Preventive Medicine 1859–1914* (Cambridge: Cambridge University Press, 1994), pp. 181–2. On Koch, see Lloyd Grenfell Stevenson, 'Robert Koch', *Encyclopedia Britannica*, 19 January 2024 (https://www.britannica.com/biography/Robert-Koch, accessed 6 March 2024); Steve M. Blevins and Michael S. Bronze, 'Robert Koch and the "golden age" of bacteriology', *International Journal of Infectious Diseases*, 14, 9 (September 2010): e744-e751.

44 John Broich, 'Engineering the Empire: British Water Supply Systems and Colonial Societies, 1850–1900', *Journal of British Studies* 46, 2 (2007): 346–65.

45 Madhu Kelkar, 'Sanitizing Heritage—Hydraulic Water Supply and the Erosion of the Traditional Water Management System

in Colonial Bombay City (1860–1947)', *Journal of Heritage Management* 4, 2 (2019): 123–40, especially pp. 125–6 and 123 (quoted text from Abstract on p. 123).

46 *Gazetteer: Bombay Presidency: Volume XVIII. Part II* (Bombay: Government Central Press, 1885), pp. 14–18. See also 'The Sewerage and Water Supply of Poona', *Indian Engineering*, 25 August 1900, pp. 116–8. [Via Google Books.]

47 G.M. Khopkar, 'Poona under the Municipality and under the Corporation', in R.V. Oturkar (ed.), *Poona: Look and Outlook, 1951* (Poona City: Poona Municipal Corporation, 1951), pp. 23–41, here p. 29.

48 See Harrison, *Public Health in British India*, pp. 180–1.

49 'The Sewerage and Water Supply of Poona'.

50 Paul-Louis Simond had argued in 1898 that fleas were involved in carrying the plague from rats to humans, but it was some years before his theory was widely accepted. See Marc Simond, Margaret L. Godley, and Pierre D.E. Mouriquand, 'Paul-Louis Simond and his discovery of plague transmission by rat fleas: a centenary', *Journal of the Royal Society of Medicine*, 91 (1998): 101–4.

51 '[Poona] Water Supply. New Reservoir Scheme', TOI, 13 March 1906, p. 7.

52 'The Sewerage and Water Supply of Poona'. See also obituary for William Santo Crimp in *Minutes of the Proceedings of the Institution of Civil Engineers*, Volume 145 (1901): 343–6.

53 'The Sewerage and Water Supply of Poona'; '[Poona] Water Supply. New Reservoir Scheme'.

54 IOL 1905, p. 591.

55 '[Poona] Water Supply. New Reservoir Scheme', TOI, 13 March 1906, p. 7. On Visvesvaraya's plans for electrifying Poona, see M. Visvesvaraya, 'Preliminary Report on a Project for Electric Light and Power Supply to Poona', 15 September 1902, in MV-PAPERS-IEI, Vol. 1.

56 'The Poona Water-Works Scheme. II', *Mahratta*, 25 March 1906, pp. 137–8, here p. 138. In MV-PAPERS-IEI, Vol. 1.

57 'The Poona Drainage Scheme', *Mahratta*, 14 February 1909, pp. 78–9. Consulted at the library of the Gokhale Institute of Politics and Economics, Pune.

58 Visvesvaraya, *Memoirs*, p. 16; Khopkar, 'Poona under the Municipality', p. 31.

59 Visvesvaraya, *Memoirs*, p. 18; Om Marathe, 'Explained: Aden, the war-torn Yemeni port's deep India connections', *Indian Express* (online), 14 August 2019 (https://indianexpress.com/article/explained/aden-the-war-torn-yemeni-ports-deep-india-connections-5904398/, accessed 17 March 2021).

60 Visvesvaraya, *Memoirs*, pp. 19–21.

61 Visvesvaraya, *Memoirs*, Chapter III (Ferris's letter is quoted on pp. 21–22).

62 Broich, 'Engineering the Empire', *passim*.

63 Ibid., p. 360.

64 F. Hutchinson, Examiner, Public Works Accounts, to M. Visvesvaraya, Executive Engineer, Poona Irrigation District, 14 July 1900 (handwritten copy), MV-PAPERS-IEI, Vol. 1.

65 See for instance various letters from W.L. Cameron of the Bombay PWD in MV-PAPERS-IEI, Vol. 1.

66 Visvesvaraya, *Memoirs*, p. 12.

67 C.A. Kincaid, *Forty-Four Years a Public Servant* (Edinburgh and London: William Blackwood & Sons, 1934), p. 151. Kincaid recalls this incident as having occurred at the time of the Delhi Durbar of 1911. Visvesvaraya would also have attended the event, for he received a C.I.E. that year (see Chapter 10 below), but Kincaid may have been misremembering some details as he refers to Visvesvaraya as a superintending engineer in Bombay although he had retired from that position in 1909.

68 Quotes appear in Visvesvaraya, *Memoirs*, pp. 14 and 21–25.

69 Quoted in typed copy of a letter, Education Department No. 1366, 24 July 1907, Visvesvaraya Papers, microfilm Reel 1, NMML.

70 W.L. Cameron to M. Visvesvaraya, [7 July] 1904, MV-PAPERS-IEI, Vol. 1.

71 [Name illegible], Superintending Engineer, Gandak Circle, Bengal PWD, to M. Visvesvaraya, [August 1904?], MV-PAPERS-IEI, Vol. 1.

72 'Programme of the Subjects to be Discussed at the Irrigation Conference, 1904', MV-PAPERS-IEI, Vol. 1.

73 M. Visvesvaraya to Chief Engineer for Irrigation, Bombay PWD, 15[?] September 1904, MV-PAPERS-IEI, Vol. 1.

74 See for instance S.M. Rutnagur, 'Preface', in S.M. Rutnagur (ed.), *Electricity in India: Being a History of the Tata Hydro-Electric Project: With Notes on the Mill Industry in Bombay and the Progress of Electric Drive in Indian Factories* (Bombay: The Proprietors, Indian Textile Journal, [1912]).

75 M. Visvesvaraya, 'Preliminary Report on a Project for Electric Light and Power Supply to Poona', 15 September 1902. MV-PAPERS-IEI, Vol. 1.

76 See Recommendation form ('Form C') for Visvesvaraya's transfer from Associate Member to Member of the Institution of Civil Engineers (ICE), London, 11 April 1904, p. 1 (courtesy ICE Archives, London).

77 Registrar, Bombay University to Visvesvaraya, No. 1789 [?] of 1904–1905, 17 September 1904, in Visvesvaraya Papers, microfilm Reel 1, NMML; Visvesvaraya, *Memoirs*, pp. 24–5; M. Visvesvaraya, Appendix I: 'Annual Report of the Sanitary Board for the Bombay Presidency for the Year 1905', in *Forty-Second Annual Report of the Sanitary Commissioner for the Government of Bombay, 1905, with Appendices* (Bombay: Government Central Press, 1906).

78 See 'Burjorji Jamaspji Padshah (1864–1941)', under 'Tata Luminaries' (https://www.tatacentralarchives.com/tata-legacy/luminaries.html, accessed 24 March 2024).

79 D. Gostling to B. Padshah (typed copy), 31 March 1904; B.J. Padshah to M. Visvesvaraya, 7 April 1904. In MV-PAPERS-IEI, Vol. 1. On Gostling's connection with the Tatas, see 'Speech by Sir Dorab Tata', in Rutnagur (ed.), *Electricity in India*, pp. 25–32.

80 His address, 10 Queen's Gardens, is mentioned on the envelope bearing a 1903 letter from the Governor of Bombay; a copy of it is available in MV-PAPERS-IEI, Vol. 1.

81 'The Evolution of Poona. Twenty-Five Years of Change', TOI, 20 December 1901, p. 4.

82 'Dewan of Mysore', TOI, 15 December 1902, p. 7; K. Subba Rao, *Revived Memories* (Madras: Ganesh & Co., 1933), p. 429.

83 Visvesvaraya, *Memoirs*, p. 17.

84 'Poona Flower Show: Prize List', TOI, 29 September 1905, p. 5.

85 Visvesvaraya, *Memoirs*, pp. 10 and 17. On Paranjpye, see 'Mr. Paranjpe', TOI, 9 December 1901, p. 6.

86 Subba Rao, *Revived Memories,* p. 429.
87 Visvesvaraya, *Memoirs*, p. 32.
88 Ibid., p. 17.
89 'New Year Honours. Kaisar-i-Hind Medal', *The Homeward Mail,* 20 January 1906, p. 88.
90 Royal proclamation printed in *The London Gazette*, 11 May 1900, p. 2996ff. Consulted via https://www.thegazette.co.uk/London/issue/27191/page/2996, accessed 24 March 2024.
91 Ibid.
92 M. Visvesvaraya, handwritten [draft?] letter, c. 1906, addressee not specified, in Visvesvaraya Papers, microfilm Reel 1, NMML.
93 [M.C.?] Gibb, Commissioner, Central Division, to M. Visvesvaraya, 20 June 1906, in Visvesvaraya Papers, microfilm Reel 1, NMML.
94 Visvesvaraya, typed draft letter to Gibb [Commissioner, Central Division], June 1906, in Visvesvaraya Papers, microfilm Reel 1, NMML.
95 [S.W. Edgerley?], Political Department, Bombay, to M. Visvesvaraya, 29 June 1906, in Visvesvaraya Papers, microfilm Reel 1, NMML.
96 Visvesvaraya, *Memoirs*, p. 32.
97 Bombay PWD notification, in *The Bombay Government Gazette*, 21 May 1908, p. 714. In MV-PAPERS-IEI, Vol. 1.

7. In the Land of the Nizams

1 'The Expositions in Milan (1881 and 1906)', Storie Milanesi project (Fondazione Adolfo Pini), curated by Rosanna Pavoni (https://www.storiemilanesi.org/en/insight/esposizioni-milano-1881-1906/, accessed 6 April 2021); M. Visvesvaraya, *Memoirs of My Working Life* (Bangalore: M. Visvesvaraya, 1951), pp. 35, 105 and 121–3 (quoted text from p. 122; on p. 35 Visvesvaraya mentions that a letter was forwarded to him care of Thomas Cook & Son).
2 Quoted in Visvesvaraya, *Memoirs*, pp. 34–5.
3 John Law, *Modern Hyderabad (Deccan)* (Calcutta: Thacker, Spink & Co., 1914), ch. III and ch. VII.

4 Law, *Modern Hyderabad*, p. 17; [M. Visvesvaraya], *The Flood of 1908 at Hyderabad: An Account of the Flood, its Causes and Proposed Preventive Measures* (Hyderabad (Deccan): [Hyderabad Government], [1909]), paras 4 and 6. The latter source was consulted at the Telangana State Archives, Hyderabad. On the name Musi, see Benjamin Cohen, 'Modernising the Urban Environment: The Musi River Flood of 1908 in Hyderabad, India', *Environment and History* 17, 3 (2011): 409–32, here p. 409 (footnote 1).

5 *Flood of 1908*, paras 1, 4, and 5.

6 *Flood of 1908,* para 4.

7 Law, *Modern Hyderabad*, p. 1.

8 *Flood of 1908*, paras 6–7; Visvesvaraya, *Memoirs*, pp. 34–6. On the name Easi, see Cohen, 'Modernising the Urban Environment', p. 409 (footnote 1).

9 *Flood of 1908*, paras 1 and 19.

10 *Flood of 1908*, paras 8 and 20; 'Disaster by Flood. Hyderabad Overwhelmed. A Deplorable Situation', TOI, 29 September 1908, p. 7.

11 *Flood of 1908*, paras 10 and 28; Visvesvaraya, *Memoirs*, p. 34.

12 'Disaster by Flood', TOI, 29 September 1908, p. 7.

13 *Flood of 1908*, paras 14–18.

14 J.S. Ifthekhar, 'Musi floods: a page from past', *Telangana Today* (online), 29 September 2019 (https://telanganatoday.com/musi-floods-a-page-from-past, accessed 6 May 2021). The transliteration as well as the translation into English are as provided by Ifthekhar.

15 'Order Being Restored: Heroic English Nurse', TOI, 3 October 1908, p. 9; 'The Hyderabad Floods. Progress of Relief Works' and Dwarkadas Dharamsey, 'Hyderabad Relief Fund', TOI, 9 October 1908, p. 7; 'Funds for Hyderabad. Madras Sympathy', TOI, 12 October 1908, p. 7.

16 *Flood of 1908*, para 3.

17 Visvesvaraya, *Memoirs*, p. 36.

18 Visvesvaraya, *Memoirs*, pp. 35–6 (Ahmadi is quoted on p. 36). Ahmadi is listed as an LCE graduate of 1883 in *The Bombay*

University Calendar for the Year 1883–84 (Bombay: Thacker & Co., 1883), p. 272.

19 Cohen, 'Modernising the Urban Environment', p. 426.

20 On Hydari, see 'Sir Akbar Hydari', under 'Attendees', in 'Conferencing the International', project page at the University of Nottingham (https://www.nottingham.ac.uk/research/groups/conferencing-the-international/delegates/people.aspx?id=52e91fac-5a0e-4db1-a0bb-909f71f8e3b0, accessed 1 April 2024). On Badruddin Tyabji, see 'Indian National Congress', Making Britain Database (https://www5.open.ac.uk/research-projects/making-britain/content/indian-national-congress, accessed 22 October 2023). That Hydari suggested Visvesvaraya's name is mentioned in 'Sir Akbar Hydari', *The Rajasthan*, n.d., cutting in MV-PAPERS-IEI, Vol. 23.

21 R.S. Basu, 'Modernising an old human settlement: Visveswaraya and the town planning in Hyderabad in the early twentieth century', esp. pp. 3 and 6–10. (The manuscript of this article was kindly shared with me by Professor Basu in 2023.)

22 Visvesvaraya, *Memoirs*, pp. 35–6.

23 *Flood of 1908*, para 71. This source mentions he was an 'F.C.H.', i.e. Fellow of Cooper's Hill. Ali Nawaz Jung is listed as chief engineer as of 1929 in *The Classified List of Officers of the Civil Departments of H.E.H. the Nizam's Government* (Hyderabad-Deccan: Superintendent, Government Central Press, 1930), p. 16. See also Visvesvaraya, *Memoirs*, p. 39.

24 Visvesvaraya, *Memoirs*, pp. 37–9. Visvesvaraya records the name as T.D. Mackenzie, but a perusal of the *India Office List* for 1905 suggests he must have been referring to A.T. Mackenzie. Law, *Modern Hyderabad*, p. 85 also identifies the engineer as A.T. Mackenzie.

25 *Flood of 1908*, paras 31–3.

26 Ibid., para 60, point 7.

27 See ibid., para 15.

28 Ibid., para 60, point 7.

29 Ibid., paras 20–25 (quoted text from para 25); Visvesvaraya, *Memoirs*, pp. 36–7.

30 *Flood of 1908*, para 28.

31 Ibid., para 25.
32 Ibid., para 34.
33 Ibid., para 40.
34 Ibid., para 40.
35 Ibid., para 39. On the Hussain Sagar and the Mir Alam tank, see: 'Hyderabad Water Supply: Increased Demand', TOI, 12 June 1930, p. 15; Mavin Kurve, 'Hyderabad Population Growth Outstrips Water Supply Increase', TOI, 17 March 1963, p. 7; 'Hussain Sagar Lake—Telangana Tourism' (https://tourism.telangana.gov.in/nature-discovery/HussainSagarLake, accessed 2 April 2024). On gravitation schemes, see Chapter 6 above.
36 Basu, 'Modernising an old human settlement', pp. 12–13.
37 *Flood of 1908*, para 38.
38 Ibid., para 39.
39 Ibid., para 34.
40 Visvesvaraya, *Memoirs*, p. 39.
41 Ibid., pp. 39–40.
42 Ibid., p. 40.
43 Ibid., pp. 39–41.
44 Basu, 'Modernising an old human settlement', esp. pp. 13-15 and 21-23; Visvesvaraya, *Memoirs*, pp. 39–41.
45 Visvesvaraya, *Memoirs*, p. 36.
46 *Flood of 1908*, para 56.
47 Ibid., para 57.
48 See Cohen, 'Modernising the Urban Environment', p. 412.
49 *Flood of 1908,* paras 49 and 58, and sketches accompanying the report (back matter).
50 Ibid., paras 55–6.
51 A pavilion with twelve arches.
52 *Flood of 1908*, para 66. On the Salar Jungs as prime ministers of Hyderabad, see 'A Brief History of the Salar Jung Family', under 'History of Salar Jung Museum', website of the Salar Jung Museum, Hyderabad (https://www.salarjungmuseum.in/History-of-SJM.html, accessed 2 April 2024).
53 His reign was officially from 1869–1911; however, the government was run by two regents until 1884, when he came of age. M. Fathulla Khan, *A History of Administrative Reforms in*

Hyderabad State (Secunderabad: New Hyderabad Press, 1935), pp. 68 and 73.

54 John Law, *Modern Hyderabad (Deccan)* (Calcutta: Thacker, Spink & Co, 1914), p. 2.

55 Kishen Pershad was prime minister from 1902 to 1912. Fathulla Khan, *History of Administrative Reforms*, pp. 81 and 85.

56 Mirza Ismail, *My Public Life* (London: George Allen and Unwin, 1954), p. 103.

57 Law, *Modern Hyderabad*, p. 75.

58 Visvesvaraya, *Memoirs*, p. 38.

59 *Flood of 1908*, paras 61–2.

60 Visvesvaraya, *Memoirs*, pp. 38 and 40.

61 Cohen, 'Modernising the Urban Environment', pp. 425--6.

62 Visvesvaraya, *Memoirs*, p. 38. Roscoe Allen had joined the Madras PWD in 1881. 'Allen, Parker Roscoe', in IOL 1905, p. 426.

63 Cohen, 'Modernising the Urban Environment', p. 427.

64 This account is based on Law, *Modern Hyderabad*, Chapter IX (pp. 82–92), and the quotations are from the speeches reproduced therein. The speeches were also reported in the *Times of India:* 'New Hyderabad Dam: Nizam Lays First Stone', TOI, 24 March 1913, p. 10. On Dalal, see the section titled 'The Gazettes' in *Indian Engineering*, 25 April 1903, p. xii, which describes him as 'Mr. C.T. Dalal, L.C.E., Superintending Engineer, Marikanave Works'.

65 Cohen, 'Modernising the Urban Environment', p. 426; Moses Tulasi, 'Hyderabad rains: Himayat Sagar floodgates opened', Firstpost, 15 October 2020 (https://www.firstpost.com/india/hyderabad-rains-himayat-sagar-floodgates-opened-8918191.html, accessed 27 May 2024).

66 See Visvesvaraya, *Memoirs*, pp. 38–9.

67 Mavin Kurve, 'Hyderabad Population Growth Outstrips Water Supply Increase', TOI, 17 March 1963, p. 7. See also 'Hyderabad Water Works to be Remodelled: Scheme to Cost Rs. 70 Lakhs', TOI, 27 December 1935, p. 21.

68 Asif Yar Khan, '100 years and still counting', *Telangana Today* (online), 8 March 2020 (https://telanganatoday.com/100-years-and-still-counting, accessed 5 May 2021).

69 'Torrential Rain in Hyderabad: Bursting of Tanks', TOI, 5 October 1931, p. 11.

70 According to Benjamin Cohen, 'the flood served as a watershed moment for the native rulers of Hyderabad State . . . to rebuild Hyderabad city, and the river, along modern, Western lines'. See Cohen, 'Modernising the Urban Environment', Abstract (p. 409).

71 Cohen, 'Modernising the Urban Environment', p. 427.

72 'Remodelling Hyderabad: 4 Crores Scheme: Sir M. Visvesvaraya's Report', TOI, 22 April 1930, p. 11; 'Improving Nizam's Capital: Big Markets Scheme', TOI, 21 May 1930, p. 11. The quoted text is from the first of these sources, which in turn describes Visvesvaraya's report.

73 'Engineering in Hyderabad: Road Problems: Important Progress in Capital', TOI, 18 June 1931, p. 11.

74 A newspaper report refers to his proposal for 'a circular railway'. 'Communications in Hyderabad: Elaborate Programme', TOI, 27 April 1933, p. 15.

75 'Remodelling Hyderabad', TOI, 22 April 1930.

76 'Remodelling Hyderabad', TOI, 22 April 1930. The quoted text is from the newspaper article's rendering of Visvesvaraya's position.

77 'Hyderabad City Improvement Schemes: Speech at the Garden Party on November 23, 1932 by Sir M. Visvesvaraya' (typescript), in MV-PAPERS-IEI, Vol. 23. A printed copy of Reddi's address on the occasion is also collected in the same volume.

78 'Hyderabad City Improvement Schemes: Speech at the Garden Party'.

79 'Mackenzie, Archibald Thomas', IOL 1905, p. 555.

80 One M. Karamat Ullah—probably the original name of Karamat Jung—studied at Cooper's Hill from 1895–98. See the list of Cooper's Hill graduates in Brendan P. Cuddy, 'The Royal Indian Engineering College, Cooper's Hill (1871–1906): A Case Study of State Involvement in Civil Engineering Education' (PhD thesis, London University, 1980), Appendix C, here p. 324. Visvesvaraya, *Memoirs*, p. 41, mentions that M.A. Zeman went on to receive the title of Nawab Ahsan Yar Jung. Zeman's Cooper's Hill qualification is mentioned on the title page of a technical paper of his: Nawab Ahsan Yar Jung Bahadur, 'Conservation of

Coal & Manufacture of Gasoline', presented at the Institution of Engineers (India), Hyderabad Centre, 27 June 1940 (consulted via https://archive.org/details/dli.ministry.01470/mode/2up, acessed 28 May 2024).

81 His LCE qualification is mentioned in the section titled 'The Gazettes', *Indian Engineering,* 25 April 1903, p. xii.

82 'Hyderabad City Improvement Schemes: Speech at the Garden Party'.

83 Cohen, 'Modernising the Urban Environment', p. 427.

84 Ibid., p. 428.

85 Ibid., p. 429.

86 Visvesvaraya, *Memoirs*, p. 41.

87 Raj Sekhar Basu writes, on Visvesvaraya's approach in general: 'There was very little idea that water planning needed to involve a multidisciplinary body of agricultural experts, peasant organizations, environmental scientists, economists, sociologists and lawyers.' Raj Sekhar Basu, 'The World of an Engineer: M. Visvesvaraya and Irrigation Engineering in Twentieth-century India', in Arun Bandopadhyay (ed.), *Science and Society in India: 1750–2000* (New Delhi: Manohar, 2010), pp. 249–98, here p. 285.

8. 'The Land of Your Birth'

1 Untitled clipping from *The Daily Post,* 19 November 1901, in MV-PAPERS-IEI, Vol. 1.

2 See Chapter 6 above.

3 M. Visvesvaraya, *Memoirs of My Working Life* (Bangalore: M. Visvesvaraya, 1951), p. 42 (including quote from Ananda Row). See also handwritten copy of Visvesvaraya's response to Ananda Row, dated 2 June 1909, in 'Sir MV: The Legendary Nation Builder', brochure accompanying exhibition, Nehru Science Centre, National Council of Science Museums (n.d. [2014?]), pp. 44–6. On the context of Madhava Rao's offer, see M.G. Rangaiya, 'Versatile Engineer-Administrator', in CENT-VOL, pp. 121–33, here p. 122. For McHutchin's full name, see IOL 1905, p. 555.

4 Visvesvaraya, *Memoirs*, pp. 42–3. On when he left Hyderabad, see ibid., p. 40. His designation as PWD secretary is mentioned in the printed official correspondence from 1910–11 collected in MV-PAPERS-IEI, Vol. 11.

5 See Chapter 1 above.

6 See Barbara Ramusack, *The Indian Princes and Their States* (New Delhi: Cambridge University Press, 2004), pp. 174–5.

7 B. Lewis Rice, *Mysore: A Gazetteer Compiled for Government, Vol. I: Mysore in General*, revised edition (Westminster: Archibald Constable and Company, 1897), pp. 2–3.

8 Rice, *Mysore: A Gazetteer*, Vol. I, pp. 356–7 and 361–9; Constance E. Parsons, *Mysore City* (London: Oxford University Press, 1930), p. 4.

9 'Hyder Ali', *Encyclopedia Britannica*, 1 January 2024 (https://www.britannica.com/biography/Hyder-Ali, accessed 6 Mar 2024); 'Tippu Sultan', *Encyclopedia Britannica*, 2 February 2024 (https://www.britannica.com/biography/Tippu-Sultan, accessed 6 March 2024); Rice, *Mysore: A Gazetteer*, Vol. I, pp. 362–3 and 412–15.

10 Rice, *Mysore: A Gazetteer*, Vol. I, pp. 417–21.

11 Parsons, *Mysore City*, pp. 158–9, 141, and 20. See also Rice, *Mysore: A Gazetteer*, Vol. I, pp. 400 and 418–19. Historian Janaki Nair takes a sceptical view of the claim that the palace was destroyed under Tipu, pointing out that the temples within the fort survived during his time. Janaki Nair, *Mysore Modern: Rethinking the Region under Princely Rule* (New Delhi: Orient Blackswan, 2012), pp. 130–1.

12 N.S. Chandrasekhara, *Dewan Rangacharlu* ([Delhi]: Publications Division, 1968), Chapter 3.

13 M.R. Vinitha, 'Politics of Development in Mysore 1881–1941' (unpublished MPhil thesis, University of Hyderabad, 2012), p. 17; Chandrasekhara, *Dewan Rangacharlu*, p. 37.

14 Bjørn Hettne, *The Political Economy of Indirect Rule: Mysore 1881–1947* (New Delhi: Ambika Publications, 1978), pp. 33–4.

15 'Attara Kacheri: Building that housed 18 public departments made way for Karnataka High Court', *Economic Times* (online), 28 August 2015 (https://economictimes.indiatimes.com/magazines/panache/attara-kacheri-building-that-housed-18-

public-departments-made-way-for-karnataka-high-court/articleshow/48713221.cms?from=mdr, accessed 23 May 2021); Meera Iyer (writer and editor), *Discovering Bengaluru. History. Neighbourhoods. Walks* (Bengalure: INTACH Bengaluru Chapter, 2019), pp. 88-90.

16 Hettne, *Political Economy of Indirect Rule*, Prologue and Chapter 1.

17 Ibid., Chapter 1; Chandrasekhara, *Dewan Rangacharlu*, p. 93. See also M. Shama Rao, *Modern Mysore: From the Coronation of Chamaraja Wodeyar X in 1868 to the present time* (Bangalore: Higginbothams, 1936), Chapter VIII.

18 Vinitha, 'Politics of Development', p. 10. Vinitha is here describing Donald Gustafson's views.

19 Chandrasekhara, *Dewan Rangacharlu*, Chapters 1–3 and p. 93.

20 Hettne, *Political Economy of Indirect Rule*, pp. 87–8.

21 Chandrasekhara, *Dewan Rangacharlu*, pp. 112–16.

22 Ibid., pp. 83 and 95–8. The quotes from Rangacharlu's address appear on pp. 97–8.

23 Ibid., pp. 100–101.

24 Ibid., pp. 103–4.

25 Ibid., pp. 104–7.

26 Ibid., pp. 103 and 143.

27 K. Subba Rao, *Revived Memories* (Madras: Ganesh & Co., 1933), p. 347.

28 'Aiyar, Sir Sheshadri (1845–1901)', in C.E. Buckland, *Dictionary of Indian Biography* (London: Swan Sonnenschein, 1906), p. 9.

29 Subba Rao, *Revived Memories*, p. 343.

30 Ibid., pp. 341–2.

31 Hettne, *Political Economy of Indirect Rule*, pp. 225–6. Emphasis in the original.

32 Ibid., Chapter 7, especially pp. 225–6.

33 Ibid., pp. 235–6.

34 See Basav Biradar's film *In Search of Gold*, available via Sahapedia's channel on YouTube (https://www.youtube.com/watch?v=rgwUnoZbAig); Deepa Alexander, 'KGF: Memories of a mining town', *The Hindu* (online), 22 April 2020 (https://www.thehindu.com/society/history-and-culture/kgf-memories-of-a-mining-town/article31406062.ece, accessed 28 May 2024);

Gilbert Slater, *Southern India: Its Political and Economic Problems* (London: George Allen and Unwin, 1936), pp. 254–5 (Slater describes the area as he saw it in 1918); Hettne, *Political Economy of Indirect Rule*, Chapter 7; Shama Rao, *Modern Mysore*, pp. 129–31.

35 Hettne, *Political Economy of Indirect Rule*, pp. 237–8; Shama Rao, *Modern Mysore*, pp. 180–2. On Sivasamudram, see A. Padmanabha Iyer, *Modern Mysore. Impressions Of A Visitor* (Trivandrum: Sridhara Printing House, 1936), p. 23, and J.V. Gayathri, 'Heritage of Mysore Division—Mysore, Mandya, Hassan, Chickmagalur, Kodagu, Dakshina Kannada, Udupi and Chamarajanagar Districts' (Mysore: Archaeology, Museums and Heritage Department, Mysore Palace, n.d), pp. 33–4. Via https://cdnbbsr.s3waas.gov.in/s3a29d1598024f9e87beab4b98411d48ce/uploads/2021/04/2021040634.pdf, accessed 27 May 2024.

36 Hydro-Electric Survey of India, *Preliminary Report on the Water Power Resources of India. Ascertained during the season 1918–1919 by the late G.T. Barlow, C.I.E., Chief Engineer, Hydro-Electric Surveys, Government of India, assisted by J.W. Meares, M.Inst.C.E., M.I.E.E., M.Am.I.E.E., Electrical Adviser to the Government of India. Compiled by J.W. Meares, Chief Engineer, Hydro-Electric Survey of India* (Calcutta: Superintendent Government Printing, India, 1919), p. i.

37 Shama Rao, *Modern Mysore*, p. 217.

38 Hettne, *Political Economy of Indirect Rule*, pp. 237–8; 'No. 6A.—Financial Secretary's note dated 22nd November 1910 on the programme of important productive public works in Mysore proposed by the Secretary, Public Works Department' (esp. Appendix II) in 'Section I. The Cauvery Reservoir Project (Mr. M. Visvesvaraya's Scheme)', in MV-PAPERS-IEI, Vol. 11.

39 'Note on the future of the Marikanave Reservoir Project by Mr. M. Visvesvaraya, M.I.C.E., Chief Engineer of Mysore, dated the 11th August 1911', MV-PAPERS-IEI, Vol. 11; Shama Rao, *Modern Mysore*, p. 178.

40 Subba Rao, *Revived Memories*, Chapter 29; Shama Rao, *Modern Mysore*, pp. 184–5.

41 See Subba Rao, *Revived Memories*, Chapters 31 and 32; Hettne, *Political Economy of Indirect Rule*, pp. 69–70, 78, 92–3. On the

1908 legislation related to the press, see also D.V. Gundappa, 'A Gentleman to the Press Too', in CENT-VOL, pp. 110–20, here pp. 114–5.

42 See Aya Ikegame, *Princely India Re-Imagined: A Historical Anthropology of Mysore from 1799 to the Present* (Abingdon, Oxon; New York: Routledge, 2015 [2013]), p. 15; Constance E. Parsons, *Mysore City* (London: Oxford University Press, 1930), Chapter XIV; Nair, *Mysore Modern,* pp. 134–5.

43 Shama Rao, *Modern Mysore,* pp. 165–74, 186–7, and 440–1. For the length of Krishnaraja IV's rule, see Hettne, *Political Economy of Indirect Rule*, p. 69.

44 Padmanabha Iyer, *Modern Mysore,* pp. 36–8; Parsons, *Mysore City*, Chapter III; Shama Rao, *Modern Mysore*, pp. 178–9 and 232; Nair, *Mysore Modern,* pp. 140–5 (quoted phrase on p. 145); Ikegame, *Princely India Re-Imagined*, Chapter 7.

45 This description is primarily based on the insightful account of the royals' training in Ikegame, *Princely India Re-Imagined,* Chapter 4. See also Shama Rao, *Modern Mysore*, pp. 186-7. On Mirza Ismail's background, see Mirza Ismail, *My Public Life* (London: George Allen and Unwin, 1954), Chapters I and II. On Fraser, see 'Fraser, Stuart Mitford', IOL 1905, p. 497.

46 Parsons, *Mysore City,* p. 35.

47 See Chapters 9–13 below.

48 Visvesvaraya, *Memoirs*, p. 43.

49 See [Narendar Pani], 'Introduction', in *A Bureaucrat in Princely Mysore: Selections from the Private Diary of K.R. Srinivasa Iyengar 1904–1941*, ed. Narendar Pani, typescript report, Project No. 098, IIMB (Bangalore: Indian Institute of Management Bangalore, 1982), esp. p. 6.

50 Subba Rao, *Revived Memories*, pp. 395–6; Hettne, *Political Economy of Indirect Rule,* pp. 44 and 70–1.

51 *A Bureaucrat in Princely Mysore,* pp. 73, 75, 86–7. Another Mysore bureaucrat noted that when he joined the civil service in 1918, his lack of connections meant he 'was posted to Chikmagalur in the Malnad, noted for its heavy rainfall and jungles, coffee plantations and malaria'. M.A. Sreenivasan, *The Last Mysore Pradhan* (Bangalore: Dronequill, 2005), p. 40.

52 Subba Rao, *Revived Memories*, p. 397.
53 Ibid., p. 422.
54 Pani, 'Introduction', in *A Bureaucrat in Princely Mysore*, p. 9.
55 Ibid., p. 13.
56 Ibid., esp. pp. 5 and 15–16. See also Fritz Sager and Christian Rosser, 'Weberian Bureaucracy', *Oxford Research Encyclopedia of Politics* (https://oxfordre.com/politics/view/10.1093/acrefore/9780190228637.001.0001/acrefore-9780190228637-e-166, accessed 9 January 2023).
57 M. Venkatesa Iyengar, 'A Hard Task-Master', in CENT-VOL, pp. 257–64; V.S. Narayana Rao, *Mokshagundam Visvesvaraya: His Life and Work* (Mysore: Geetha Book House, 1973), pp. 259–60.
58 Navarathna [sic] Rama Rao, 'A Prophecy Come True', in CENT-VOL, pp. 233–9. Quoted text from p. 235. For biographical details on Rama Rao, see the [translators'] Introduction to Navaratna Rama Rao, *The Vanished Raj: A Memoir of Princely India*, translated from the Kannada by Navaratna Rajaram and Rajeshwari Rao (Bengaluru: Prism Books Pvt. Ltd., 2014), [pages not numbered].
59 'Address to Mysore Engineers', 14 November 1910, MV-SPEECHES-VOL, pp. 1–14, here p. 2.
60 Ibid., p. 14.
61 Ibid., p. 12.
62 Quoted in ibid., p. 10.
63 'Reply to an Address by the Mysore Engineers' Association', 30 November 1912, MV-SPEECHES-VOL, pp. 45–50, here p. 49.
64 This is mentioned in several diary entries of K.R. Srinivasa Iyengar in *A Bureaucrat in Princely Mysore*.
65 'Address to Mysore Engineers', 22 March 1912, MV-SPEECHES-VOL, pp. 31–44, here pp. 41–2.
66 See ibid., p. 42.
67 'Address to Mysore Engineers', 15 March 1917, MV-SPEECHES VOL, pp. 406–9, here pp. 407–9.
68 [Krishnaraja Wadiyar IV], 'Speech at the Inauguration of the Mysore Economic Conference on 10th June 1911', *Speeches by His Highness Sri Krishnaraja Wadiyar Bahadur, G.C.S.I., G.B.E., Maharaja of Mysore: 1902–1933* (Mysore: Government Branch Press, 1934), pp. 87–93. Visvesvaraya also mentioned

in his memoirs that he had proposed the idea of the Economic Conference to the maharaja. Visvesvaraya, *Memoirs*, p. 44.

69 [Krishnaraja Wadiyar IV], 'Speech at the inauguration of the Mysore Economic Conference' (quoted text from p. 88–9).

70 'Address to the Mysore Economic Conference', 3 June 1914, MV-SPEECHES-VOL, pp. 142–53, here pp. 144–5.

71 'Mysore Economic Conference', TOI, 9 August 1911, p. 8.

72 Visvesvaraya, *Memoirs*, p. 44; GAZETTEER-VOL3, p. 1.

73 'The Mysore Economic Conference', TOI, 20 June 1912, p. 6.

74 See 'Mysore Economic Conference', TOI, 2 October 1911, p. 6.

75 'The Mysore Economic Conference', TOI, 20 June 1912, p. 6.

76 See Visvesvaraya, *Memoirs*, p. 45.

77 'The Mysore Economic Conference', TOI, 20 June 1912, p. 6.

78 G.O. Press No. 1928 Revenue [Madras government?], 29 June 1912, KSA-MV-VOL, pp. 4–5; No. G. 155-207—G.M. 36–11–69, 10 July 1912, Mysore Government Proceedings, General (Miscellaneous), KSA-MV-VOL, pp. 5–6. See also Visvesvaraya, *Memoirs*, p. 45.

79 *A Bureaucrat in Princely Mysore*, pp. 102 and 103.

80 Rama Rao, 'A Prophecy come True', p. 237.

81 Subba Rao, *Revived Memories*, pp. 448–9; also see *A Bureaucrat in Princely Mysore,* pp. 129 and 135.

82 'No. 1—Note, dated the 2nd October 1910, by the Secretary to Government in the Public Works Department', in 'Section I. The Cauvery Reservoir Project (Mr. M. Visvesvaraya's Scheme)', in MV-PAPERS-IEI, Vol. 11.

83 Ibid., paras 3–6.

84 Ibid., paras 16–17.

85 Ibid., paras 13–15.

86 Ibid., paras 19–20.

87 Ibid., paras 7–11.

88 Ibid., table accompanying note.

9. Reservoir of Hopes

1 A version of this chapter was published as 'Reservoir Gods', *FiftyTwo.in*, 17 September 2021 (https://fiftytwo.in/story/

reservoir-gods/, accessed 24 September 2023). I'd like to thank the editorial team at *FiftyTwo.in* for their inputs.

2 For the height of the dam (in metres), see *Operation and Maintenance Manual for Krishnarajasagara Dam: State of Karnataka* (n.p.: Chief Engineer, Irrigation South Zone, Mysore, December 2019), p. 12. Via https://waterresources.karnataka.gov.in/storage/pdf-files/O%20&%20M%20Manuals/KRS_OM_KaWRD.pdf, accessed on 27 May 2024.

3 The song as rendered by Shimoga Subbanna is available at 'Kattide Kannambadi Lyrical Video Song', YouTube Channel: Lahari Bhavageethegalu & Folk – T-Series (https://www.youtube.com/watch?v=T_2sF0JAHBc, accessed 24 September 2023).

4 I'd like to thank Geetha Chary and S.N. Chary for help with translating this verse. Any inaccuracies are my responsibility.

5 Henry C. Hart, *New India's Rivers* (Calcutta: Orient Longmans, 1956), p. 39.

6 As defined by the capacity of the reservoir.

7 M. Visvesvaraya, *Memoirs of My Working Life* (Bangalore: M. Visvesvaraya, 1951), p. 51.

8 'Cauvery Reservoir. First Stage Sanctioned', TOI, 14 October 1911, p. 9.

9 English translation quoted in A. Padmanabha Iyer, *Modern Mysore. Impressions Of A Visitor* (Trivandrum: Sridhara Printing House, 1936), pp. 26–7.

10 See 'Tippu Sultan', *Encyclopedia Britannica*, 2 February 2024 (https://www.britannica.com/biography/Tippu-Sultan, accessed 6 March 2024).

11 'Indian Irrigation: The Cauvery Reservoir', TOI, 24 October 1913, p. 9.

12 Note by Visvesvaraya, 15 October 1910, Item 1A, para 1, in 'Section III. The Cauvery Reservoir Project (Mr. M. Visvesvaraya's Scheme.) Effect of the Project on the River Supply in the Madras Presidency', MV-PAPERS-IEI, Vol. 11. The other two sections, also collected in the same volume of Visvesvaraya's papers, are titled 'Section I. The Cauvery Reservoir Project (Mr. M. Visvesvaraya's Scheme)'; 'Section II. The Cauvery Reservoir Project (Mr. M. Visvesvaraya's Scheme). Negotiations with Messrs. John Taylor

and Sons' Committee, Ooregum'. Below, I will refer to this correspondence in the following format: [Description], Item [X], Section [Y], CRP Correspondence.

13 See Chapter 8 above; see also M.G. Rangaiya, 'Versatile Engineer-Administrator', in CENT-VOL, pp. 121–33, here p. 124.

14 Rangaiya, 'Versatile Engineer-Administrator', p. 124. For the term 'conservancy measures', see note by Financial Secretary, 22 November 1910, Item 6A, Section I, CRP Correspondence.

15 See 'Irrigation in India', TOI, 31 October 1911, p. 6.

16 Note by Visvesvaraya, 15 October 1910, Item 1A, para 1, in Section III, CRP Correspondence; M.G. Rangaiya, 'Versatile Engineer-Administrator', p. 124; 'Cauvery Reservoir: First Stage Sanctioned', TOI, 14 October 1911, p. 9.

17 Rangaiya, 'Versatile Engineer-Administrator', p. 124.

18 'Cauvery Reservoir: First Stage Sanctioned', TOI, 14 October 1911, p. 9; 'Irrigation in India', TOI, 31 October 1911, p. 6. See also note by Revenue Commissioner, Mysore (A. Rangasami Iyengar), 5 January 1911, Item 28A, para 17, in Section I, CRP Correspondence.

19 MAR 1908–9, para 292.

20 Nic Dawes, 'Home is Away—India in 3 years and 3 centuries', *Hindustan Times*, 29 August 2016 (https://www.hindustantimes.com/static/home-is-away-india-in-3-years-and-3-centuries/index.html, accessed 9 March 2024); Rangaiya, 'Versatile Engineer-Administrator', p. 122; 'The Late Captain Dawes', TOI, 5 August 1909, p. 7.

21 'The Late Captain Dawes', TOI, 5 August 1909, p. 7; 'The [Dawes] Memorial', Letter to the Editor from S.M. Fraser, T. Ananda Row, S. Ismay, and C. Roe, R.E., in *The Pioneer*, 25 August 1909, p. 9; Nic Dawes, 'Home is Away'; citation for Dawes's Albert Medal, reproduced at 'Nicholas Bernard Edwin Dawes AM' (https://victoriacrossonline.co.uk/nicholas-bernard-edwin-dawes-am/, accessed 24 September 2023). The different accounts vary slightly in detail.

22 M. Visvesvaraya [to T. Ananda Row], 5 August 1909, KSA-MV-VOL, pp. 1–2. In quoting from the letter, I have corrected spelling mistakes that seem to be the result of errors in transcription.

23 Visvesvaraya, *Memoirs*, p. 46.

24 Note by Visvesvaraya, 12 December 1910, Item 3B, Section II, CRP Correspondence; H.P. Gibbs to Visvesvaraya, 12 December 1910, Item 3C, Section II, CRP Correspondence; 'Cauvery Reservoir: First Stage Sanctioned', TOI, 14 October 1911, p. 9. That the proposed site was Kannambadi is indicated in: Dewan (Ananda Row) to Visvesvaraya, 12 December 1910, Item 4, Section II, CRP Correspondence. Ananthalwar's role in the project is also mentioned in his son's memoirs: M.A. Sreenivasan, *The Last Mysore Pradhan* (Bangalore: Dronequill, 2005), p. 21.

25 See Rangaiya, 'Versatile Engineer-Administrator', pp. 124–5; Note by Visvesvaraya, 2 October 1910, Item 1, Section I, CRP Correspondence; Note by Visvesvaraya, 12 December 1910, Item 3B, Section II, CRP Correspondence; 'Irrigation in India', TOI, 31 October 1911, p. 6.

26 Note by Visvesvaraya, 12 December 1910, Item 3B, Section II, CRP Correspondence; Note by Visvesvaraya, 2 October 1910, Item 1, Section I, CRP Correspondence.

27 Note by Visvesvaraya, 2 October 1910, Item 1, para 10 (quoted text from here) and para 18, in Section I, CRP Correspondence.

28 Visvesvaraya to Dewan, 1 December 1910, Item 1, Section II, CRP Correspondence.

29 Items 2–21, Section II, CRP Correspondence.

30 John Taylor & Sons' Committee to Visvesvaraya, 29 December 1910, Item 24A; [Acting] PWD Secretary to John Taylor & Sons' Committee, 31 December 1910, Item 25; Arthur Taylor, Mysore Gold Mining Co. Ltd., to Visvesvaraya, 11 January 1911, Item 26; Visvesvaraya to Arthur Taylor, 19 January 1911, Item 27, all in Section II, CRP Correspondence.

31 Chimanlal H. Setalvad, *Recollections and Reflections: An Autobiography* (Bombay: Padma Publication Ltd, [1946]), p. 510.

32 Note by Visvesvaraya, 12 December 1910, Item 3B, Section II, CRP Correspondence; T. Ananda Row (Dewan) to Hugh Daly (Mysore Resident), 31 October 1910, Item 2, Section III, CRP Correspondence; Visvesvaraya to Ananda Row, 1 December 1910,

Items 9/9A, Section III, CRP Correspondence; Visvesvaraya, *Memoirs*, pp. 48-9.

33 Visvesvaraya to Ananda Row, 1 December 1910, Items 9/9A, Section III, CRP Correspondence.

34 Joint Secretary, Madras PWD (Irrigation), to Mysore Resident, 6 December 1910, Item 10A, Section III, CRP Correspondence; note by C.A. Smith, Chief Engineer, Irrigation, Madras, [c. 6 December 1910], Item 10B, Section III, CRP Correspondence.

35 Note by C.A. Smith, Chief Engineer, Irrigation, Madras, [c. 6 December 1910], Item 10B, Section III, CRP Correspondence.

36 Dewan to Resident (Hugh Daly), 27 March 1911, Item 26, para 8, in Government of Mysore, PWD, *Cauvery Reservoir Project (Mr. M. Visvesvaraya's Scheme). Select Papers from the Correspondence with the Government of Madras* (Bangalore: [Government Press], 1913), in MV-PAPERS-IEI, Vol. 11. Below, I refer to this compilation as [Section IV], CRP Correspondence.

37 Dewan to Resident, 1 July 1911, Item 33, [Section IV], CRP Correspondence.

38 Note by Visvesvaraya, 8 May 1911, Item 31A, [Section IV], CRP Correspondence.

39 Note by John Benton, Inspector-General of Irrigation, India, 12 May 1911, Item 34A, [Section IV], CRP Correspondence.

40 John Taylor & Sons to Chief Engineer, Mysore, 28 June 1911, Item 33A, [Section IV], CRP Correspondence; Dewan to Resident, 7 July 1911, Item 35, [Section IV], CRP Correspondence.

41 See Visvesvaraya, *Memoirs*, p. 49; Dewan to Resident, 11 September 1911, Item 41, [Section IV], CRP Correspondence.

42 Dewan (Ananda Row) to Resident (Daly), 10 September 1911, Item 40, [Section IV], CRP Correspondence.

43 [Joint Secretary], Madras PWD (Irrigation), to Mysore Resident, 22 September 1911, Item 44A, [Section IV], CRP Correspondence.

44 Dewan to Resident, 29 September 1911, Item 45, [Section IV], CRP Correspondence; Resident's First Assistant to Dewan, 8 October 1911, Item 46, [Section IV], CRP Correspondence.

45 Rangaiya, 'Versatile Engineer-Administrator', pp. 125-6; Setalvad, *Recollections and Reflections*, pp. 509-12.

46 Note by Visvesvaraya, 2 October 1910, Item 1, Section I, CRP Correspondence.

47 Among those with misgivings about his proposals was A. Rangasami Iyengar, the Revenue Commissioner. See note by Revenue Commissioner, 5 January 1911, Item 28A, Section I, CRP Correspondence.

48 M. Venkatakrishnayya and C.M. Raghavendra Rao, *At Home and Abroad: Being A Brief Sketch of the Life of Dewan Bahadur J.S. Chakravarti (Upto His Leaving Mysore in 1919)* (Calcutta: Hare Press, 1921), Chapter VII.

49 Ibid., Chapters I and VII-X.

50 Note by Financial Secretary, 22 November 1910, Item 6A, Section I, CRP Correspondence (quoted text from paras 4 and 19).

51 Visvesvaraya's 'Rejoinder . . . to the Financial Secretary's Note', n.d., Item 9, Section I, CRP Correspondence. Quoted text from paras 4, 11, 8, and 12.

52 The Revenue Commissioner, A. Rangasami Iyengar, commented thus on some of Visvesvaraya's proposals: 'There should be a clearer exposition of the ways and means of profitable employment of power before the State can undertake a costly project.' Revenue Commissioner to Dewan, 2 March 1911 (Appendix I), Item 53, Section I, CRP Correspondence.

53 See *A Bureaucrat in Princely Mysore: Selections from the Private Diary of K.R. Srinivasa Iyengar 1904–1941*, ed. Narendar Pani, typescript report, Project No. 098, IIMB (Bangalore: Indian Institute of Management Bangalore, 1982), pp. 101–3; K. Subba Rao, *Revived Memories* (Madras: Ganesh & Co., 1933), Chapter 33.

54 Dewan to Maharaja, 16 December 1910, Item 10, Section I, CRP Correspondence. Quoted text from paras 12, 10, 14 and 13.

55 Note by Visvesvaraya, 15 October 1910, Item 1A, Section III, CRP Correspondence; Dewan to Maharaja, 16 December 1910, Item 10, Section I, CRP Correspondence; Dewan to Resident, 27 March 1911, Item 26, [Section IV], CRP Correspondence.

56 See for instance Financial Secretary to Dewan, 19 December 1910, Item 16, Section I, CRP Correspondence.

57 Memorandum by Financial Secretary, presented at Dewan's Council meeting, 22 December 1910, Item 23, Section I, CRP Correspondence.
58 Note by Financial Secretary, 11 February 1911, Item 48, Section I, CRP Correspondence.
59 Financial Secretary to Dewan, 31 January 1911, Items 39/39A, Section I, CRP Correspondence.
60 Ibid.
61 Note by Visvesvaraya, 10 February 1911, Item 43A, Section I, CRP Correspondence.
62 'Cauvery Reservoir. First Stage Sanctioned', TOI, 14 October 1911, p. 9.
63 Visvesvaraya, *Memoirs*, p. 48.
64 MAR 1911–12, paras 278 and 270.
65 'Cauvery Reservoir Works', KSA-MV-VOL, pp. 14–15.
66 Ibid; MAR, 1912–13, para 254; MAR, 1911–12, para 272.
67 MAR 1912–13, para 254.
68 See for instance 'Cauvery Reservoir: Completion of the Scheme', TOI, 30 May 1913, p. 9.
69 'Indian Irrigation: The Cauvery Reservoir', TOI, 24 October 1913, p. 9. The reference to cement may be an error, as the dam used *surki*, not cement. See below.
70 MAR 1913–14, para 310; see also Rangaiya, 'Versatile Engineer-Administrator', p. 126; Setalvad, *Recollections and Reflections*, pp. 509–12.
71 MAR 1915–16, paras 338–9.
72 MAR 1917–18, para 341.
73 Henry C. Hart, *New India's Rivers* (Calcutta: Orient Longmans, 1956), pp. 34–7.
74 Hart, *New India's Rivers*, pp. 37-8; photographs and caption under the title 'The Irwin Canal: A New Tunnel in Mysore State', TOI, 23 January 1930, p. 18; 'Cauvery Works: Great Extensions', TOI, 3 November 1911, p. 9; Visvesvaraya, *Memoirs*, p. 96; M. Shama Rao, *Modern Mysore: From the Coronation of Chamaraja Wodeyar X in 1868 to the present time* (Bangalore: Higginbothams, 1936), pp. 403–4.
75 See Rangaiya, 'Versatile Engineer-Administrator', pp. 126-7.

76 Conversations with residents of various villages (B. Hattana, Maadla, Dudda, Saudenahalli) in Mandya district, 26 May 2019. I'd like to thank Mr Siddaramu, who introduced me to them and served as interpreter.

77 'Mandya pays tribute to Visvesvaraya', *The Hindu* (online), 17 September 2018 (https://www.thehindu.com/news/national/karnataka/mandya-pays-tribute-to-visvesvaraya/article24962931.ece, accessed 27 May 2024).

78 'KRS South Gate Statue Project Ruffles Feathers', *Star of Mysore* (online), 3 June 2020 (https://starofmysore.com/krs-south-gate-statue-project-ruffles-feathers/, accessed 24 September 2023); 'Sir M Visvesvaraya statue at KRS dam site! Prof Nanjaraj Urs defends his opposition with facts', *Mysooru News* (online), n.d. (https://www.mysoorunews.com/sir-m-visvesvaraya-statue-at-krs-dam-site-prof-nanjaraj-urs-defends-his-opposition-with-facts/, accessed 24 September 2023). See also P. V. Nanjaraj Urs, *Naanu . . . . Kannambadi Katte . . . .: heegondu atmakathe* (Mysore: Abhiruchi Prakashana, 2017).

79 According to a commemorative board listing the main engineers who worked on the project, the building spanned the tenures of eight chief engineers; there were many more engineers working below them. See photographs in Urs, *Naanu.... Kannambadi Katte*, p. 293.

10. At the Helm

1 MAR 1910–11, p. 49 and MAR 1909–10, p. 49.

2 M. Visvesvaraya, 'The Future of the Marikanave Reservoir Project. August 1911', esp. paras 9 and 24, in MV-PAPERS-IEI, Vol. 11.

3 MAR 1911–12, p. 2.

4 Hugh Daly, Resident, Mysore, to Col. Sir Henry McMahon, Secretary, Foreign Department, [Government of India], 27 September 1912 (typed copy), in Confidential File No. 15 of 1912, Mysore Residency, Bangalore: 'Appointment of Mr. Visvesvaraya as Dewan; formal approval of the Government of India to such appointment held unnecessary', APAC: IOR/R/2/33/316.

5 'Mysore Public Works. Great Water-Supply Scheme', TOI, 1 May 1912, p. 3.

6 *A Bureaucrat in Princely Mysore: Selections from the Private Diary of K.R. Srinivasa Iyengar 1904–1941*, ed. Narendar Pani, typescript report, Project No. 098, IIMB (Bangalore: Indian Institute of Management Bangalore, 1982), pp. 101–3 (entries dated 12 and 13 June 1911) and pp. 113–4 (entry dated 5 September 1912).

7 Ibid., pp. 113–5.

8 M. Visvesvaraya, *Memoirs of My Working Life* (Bangalore: M. Visvesvaraya, 1951), p. 55.

9 'Mysore's New Dewan', TOI, 12 October 1912, p. 8.

10 Quoted in 'Dewan of Mysore. Praise for Mr. Row', TOI, 11 November 1912, p. 8. I have corrected an error in the spelling of Visvesvaraya's name.

11 'Dewan of Mysore. Praise for Mr. Row', TOI, 11 November 1912, p. 8; 'The Dewanship of Mysore', *The Pioneer*, 13 November 1912.

12 M. Shama Rao, *Modern Mysore: From the Coronation of Chamaraja Wodeyar X in 1868 to the present time* (Bangalore: Higginbothams, 1936), pp. 247–8; 'Mysore's New Dewan', TOI, 12 October 1912, p. 8; Visvesvaraya, *Memoirs*, p. 56. See also 'Ananda Rao, Tanjore', IBD 1915, p. 11; 'Madhava Rao, Visvanath Patankar', IBD 1915, pp. 260–1.

13 Nanjundayya had been First Councillor from February 1912. See Appendix I, MAR 1914–15, p. i.

14 Meera Iyer (writer and editor), *Discovering Bengaluru. History. Neighbourhoods. Walks* (Bengaluru: INTACH Bengaluru Chapter, 2019), p. 181.

15 For instance, see Y.G. Krishnamurti, *Sir M. Visvesvaraya: A Study* (Bombay: Popular Book Depot, 1941), p. 28.

16 See Bjørn Hettne, *The Political Economy of Indirect Rule: Mysore 1881–1947* (New Delhi: Ambika Publications, 1978), Chapter 2. However, Hettne qualifies this by saying that by this time the Madras-Mysore rivalry was being replaced by a Brahmin-non-Brahmin one. Ibid. See also 'Mysore's New Dewan', TOI, 12 October 1912, p. 8.

17 Hugh Daly, Resident, Mysore, to Col. Sir Henry McMahon, Secretary, Foreign Department, [Government of India],

27 September 1912 (typed copy), Confidential File No. 15 of 1912, Mysore Residency, Bangalore: 'Appointment of Mr. Visvesvaraya as Dewan; formal approval of the Government of India to such appointment held unnecessary', APAC: IOR/R/2/33/316. This letter is also quoted in Hettne, *Political Economy of Indirect Rule*, p. 71.

18 'Mysore's New Dewan', TOI, 12 October 1912, p. 8.

19 V.S. Narayana Rao, *Mokshagundam Visvesvaraya: His Life and Work* (Mysore: Geetha Book House, 1973), p. 259.

20 'Reply to an Address by the Mysore Engineers' Association', 30 November 1912, MV-SPEECHES-VOL, pp. 45–50, here p. 47. On PWD engineers being generalists (in British India), see Aparajith Ramnath, *The Birth of an Indian Profession: Engineers, Industry, and the State, 1900–47* (Delhi: Oxford University Press, 2017), Chapter 3. PWDs in princely states were organized on broadly similar lines.

21 'Reply to an Address by the Citizens of Mysore', 7 January 1913, MV-SPEECHES-VOL, pp. 60–66 (quoted text from pp. 62 and 63).

22 See Patrick Bowe, 'Lal Bagh—The Botanical Garden of Bangalore and its Kew-Trained Gardeners', *Garden History* 40, 2 (2012): 228–38; K. Vinoda, 'The Lalbagh—A History: 1760–1932', M.Phil. thesis, Bangalore University, 1989; M.A. Siraj, 'Lalbagh's history through the ages', *Deccan Herald* (online), 27 February 2021 (https://www.deccanherald.com/india/karnataka/lalbaghs-history-through-the-ages-955724.html, accessed 8 April 2024).

23 'Reply to Bangalore Citizens' Addresses', 12 December 1912, MV-SPEECHES-VOL, pp. 50–9.

24 Ibid., p. 59.

25 'Problems in Mysore. Conditions of Progress', TOI, 14 December 1912, p. 9.

26 Hettne, *Political Economy of Indirect Rule*, Chapter 3; Shama Rao, *Modern Mysore*, Chapter XIX; Visvesvaraya, *Memoirs*, p. 63.

27 Appendix I, MAR 1914–15, p. i; *A Bureaucrat in Princely Mysore*, pp. 117–20. On Kantharaj Urs as Krishnaraja IV's uncle, see Aya Ikegame, *Princely India Re-Imagined: A Historical Anthropology of Mysore from 1799 to the Present* (Milton Park, Abingdon, Oxon;

New York: Routledge, 2013), p. 67. On Nanjundayya and Devaraj Urs as Councillors, see MAR 1911–12, pp. 2–3.

28 Appendix I, MAR 1917–18, p. i.

29 Shama Rao, *Modern Mysore*, p. 250.

30 B. Lewis Rice, *Mysore: A Gazetteer Compiled for Government, Vol. I: Mysore in General*, revised edition (Westminster: Archibald Constable and Company, 1897), pp. 763–98; and D.M. Narasinga Rao (Secretary to Government, Mysore, General Department), 'Official Memorandum', KSA-MV-VOL, pp. 150–3 (for the system c. 1916).

31 Hettne, *Political Economy of Indirect Rule*, Chapter 3.

32 Visvesvaraya, *Memoirs*, pp. 65–6; Hettne, *Political Economy of Indirect Rule*, pp. 259–62 and Chapter 2.

33 Meera Iyer, 'Air of dignified grandeur', *The Hindu* (online), 28 June 2019 (https://www.thehindu.com/life-and-style/homes-and-gardens/air-of-dignified-grandeur/article28204525.ece, accessed 28 May 2024).

34 'Dewan of Mysore. Praise for Mr. Row', TOI, 11 November 1912, p. 8.

35 See M. Venkatesa Iyengar, 'A Hard Task-Master', in CENT-VOL, pp. 257–64, here pp. 258–9.

36 Letters from the period give the Lake View address. See for example M. Visvesvaraya to Asutosh Mookerjee, 18 October 1918, in Asutosh Mookerjee Papers I, NMML. On the present name, see H.M. Aravind, 'Royal paradise', *Times of India* (online), 23 January 2011 (https://timesofindia.indiatimes.com/city/mysuru/royal-paradise/articleshow/7349197.cms?frmapp=yes&from=mdr, accessed 28 May 2024).

37 On Government House, see Constance E. Parsons, *Mysore City* (London: Oxford University Press, 1930), pp. 15–16; Ikegame, *Princely India Re-imagined,* p. 157. The Public Offices are mentioned as the venue of the Respresentative Assembly's Dasara sessions, in MV-SPEECHES-VOL, *passim*.

38 See Jamie Moreland, 'Lion hides, sacred seats and coronation rites from around the world', BBC website, 28 April 2023 (https://www.bbc.com/news/world-65258353, accessed 28 May 2024).

39 See ibid.; Sean Lang, 'How British imperial history shaped Charles III's coronation ceremony', *The Conversation*, 5 May 2023 (https://theconversation.com/how-british-imperial-history-shaped-charles-iiis-coronation-ceremony-204511, accessed 28 May 2024).

40 See the photo in H.S. Sreenath, *Bharata Ratna Sir M. Visvesvaraya: His Economic Contribution and Thought* (Bangalore: Select Book, 2013), Plate V, between pp. 32 and 33.

41 See *Mysore Administrative Papers: Karnataka Letters*, Volume III: *Dewan V.P. Madhava Rao* (Bangalore: Department of Karnataka State Archives, 1994), pp. 51–4. This correspondence is from before Visvesvaraya's time as Dewan.

42 Ikegame, *Princely India Re-imagined*, pp. 149–57.

43 See for instance Venkatesa Iyengar, 'A Hard Task-Master'.

44 See for instance the discussion of Visvesvaraya's speeches during World War I in Chapter 13 below.

45 K. Subba Rao, *Revived Memories* (Madras: Ganesh & Co., 1933), pp. 428–9; S. Hiriannaiya, 'Hard Work and Tenacity of Purpose', in CENT-VOL, pp. 224–32, here pp. 228–30.

46 Ikegame, *Princely India Re-imagined*, Chapter 8.

47 On Cobb, see Hiriannaiya, 'Hard Work and Tenacity of Purpose', pp. 230–1.

48 M. Visvesvaraya to H.V. Cobb, 11 June 1916, APAC: IOR/R/2/Temp. No. 32/332, Sheet 7.

49 H.V. Cobb to M. Visvesvaraya ('Draft'), 12 June 1916, APAC: IOR/R/2/Temp. No. 32/332, Sheet 9.

50 D.C. Subbarayappa, 'He Stood by Merit', in CENT-VOL, pp. 156–64, here p. 159.

51 '[Viceroy's] Tour. Arrival at Mysore', TOI, 7 November 1913.

52 Quoted in Shama Rao, *Modern Mysore*, p. 248. See also 'Viceroy in Mysore: The State Banquet', TOI, 8 November 1913, p. 10.

53 Visvesvaraya, *Memoirs*, p. 60. On the uses of the Khedda, see MAR 1909–10, para 261.

54 'The Viceroy's Tour: Bison and Tiger', TOI, 18 November 1913, p. 7.

55 See 'Programme for the visit of His Excellency the Viceroy to the Cauvery Reservoir Works on the 18th November 1913', KSA-MV-VOL, p. 13.
56 Shama Rao, *Modern Mysore*, p. 248.
57 'Arrival at Bangalore', *Bombay Gazette*, 20 November 1913.
58 'The Viceroy's Tour', TOI, 18 November 1913, p. 7.
59 Shama Rao, *Modern Mysore*, p. 249. On the Viceroy's tour dates, see ibid., p. 248.
60 Visvesvaraya, *Memoirs*, p. 60.
61 Ibid.
62 Shama Rao, *Modern Mysore*, pp. 249–50; Hettne, *Political Economy of Indirect Rule*, pp. 50–2 and 59; Meera Sebastian, 'The Finances of the Nineteenth Century Mysore with Special Reference to its Tribute', *Proceedings of the Indian History Congress* 53 (1992): 449–53, here p. 451.
63 Visvesvaraya, *Memoirs*, p. 62.
64 Quoted in Visvesvaraya, *Memoirs*, p. 62.
65 See the papers in 'Revision of the Instrument of Transfer; Treaty of 1913', Mysore Residency Confidential File No. 12, 1913, APAC: IOR/R/2/Temp No. 33/323. For more on Daly, see Chapter 13 below.
66 Hettne, *Political Economy of Indirect Rule*, pp. 50–2.
67 See ibid., p. 79.
68 'Address to Dasara Representative Assembly', 11 October 1913, MV-SPEECHES-VOL, pp. 95–129.
69 Ibid., p. 124.
70 Ibid., pp. 125–6.
71 'Mysore Village Schemes', TOI, 14 February 1914, p. 10.
72 MAR 1914–15, para 262.
73 MAR 1915–16, para 273.
74 MAR 1917–18, para 278.
75 N. Madhava Rao, 'He Practised what he Preached', in CENT-VOL, pp. 48–58, here pp. 50–1.
76 MAR 1915–16, para 3.
77 Madhava Rao, 'He Practised what he Preached', pp. 50–1.
78 See for instance Navaratna Rama Rao, *The Vanished Raj: A Memoir of Princely India*, translated from the Kannada by Navaratna Rajaram

and Rajeshwari Rao (Bengaluru: Prism Books Pvt. Ltd., 2014). Rama Rao's Kannada original was titled *Kelavu Nenapagalu.* See also the self-presentation of Mysore civil servant M.A. Sreenivasan in his memoirs. M.A. Sreenivasan, *The Last Mysore Pradhan* (Bangalore: Dronequill, 2005). On the bureaucratic structure of the civil service, see James Manor, 'Princely Mysore before the Storm: The State-Level Political System of India's Model State 1920-1936', *Modern Asian Studies* 9, 1 (1975): 31–58, here p. 40.

79 Subba Rao, *Revived Memories*, pp. 432–3; Hettne, *Political Economy of Indirect Rule*, pp. 259–62.

80 Subba Rao, *Revived Memories*, pp. 433–4.

81 'Speech at the Dasara Representative Assembly', 7 October 1914, MV-SPEECHES-VOL, pp. 209–15, here p. 212.

82 Analogously, R.S. Basu points out that in his irrigation works, Visvesvaraya did not see the need to consult 'peasant organisations'. However, he did learn from some local practices, as in the case of his block system. Raj Sekhar Basu, 'The World of an Engineer: M. Visvesvaraya and Irrigation Engineering in Twentieth-century India', in Arun Bandopadhyay (ed.), *Science and Society in India: 1750–2000* (New Delhi: Manohar, 2010), pp. 249–98 (quoted phrase from p. 285).

83 Visvesvaraya, *Memoirs*, pp. 62–4.

84 Ibid., p. 56.

11. From Universal Education to University

1 See Chapter 4 above. On Gokhale's presidentship of the Banaras Congress, see E.L. Turnbull and H.G.D. Turnbull, *Gopal Krishna Gokhale (A Brief Biography)* (Trichur: V. Sundra Iyer & Sons, 1934), pp. 84–5.

2 See Turnbull and Turnbull, *Gopal Krishna Gokhale*, ch. VIII; 'The Elementary Education Bill, 1911' in Shri Krishan (ed.), *Gopal Krishna Gokhale: Select Speeches and Writings* (New Delhi: National Book Trust, 2018), pp. 138–67.

3 'The Elementary Education Bill, 1911'. Quoted text from pp. 140, 141, and 151. For Gokhale's support for girls' education, see

'Female Education in India', in Shri Krishan (ed.), *Gopal Krishna Gokhale: Select Speeches and Writings*, pp. 168–82.

4 Turnbull and Turnbull, *Gopal Krishna Gokhale*, pp. 102–4; Gokhale's rebuttal speech (pp. 155–67 of 'The Elementary Education Bill, 1911').

5 Quoted in Turnbull and Turnbull, *Gopal Krishna Gokhale*, pp. 104–5.

6 GAZETTEER-VOL4, pp. 494–500. On the number of schools, see tables on pp. 499 and 500. Cubbon is quoted on p. 496. See also Parimala V. Rao, 'Elite Conflict and Women's Education in Princely Mysore, 1860–1947', in Deepak Kumar, Joseph Bara, Nandita Khadria, and Ch. Radha Gayathri (eds.), *Education in Colonial India: Historical Insights* (New Delhi: Manohar Publishers & Distributors, 2013), pp. 351–73, here pp. 353–6. For Cubbon and Bowring's tenure years, see C.E. Buckland, *Dictionary of Indian Biography* (London: Swan Sonnenschein & Co., 1906), pp. 101 and 50 respectively.

7 GAZETTEER-VOL4, pp. 500 and 502–4. On 'Sloyd training', see MAR 1910–11, para 455.

8 MAR 1910–11, pp. 71–2. The term 'private institutions' was applied to 'unaided village indigenous schools' (MAR 1911–12, para 436).

9 MAR 1910–11, pp. 71–2, and similar sections of MAR for other years in the 1910s. The reports use the terms 'depressed classes', 'depressed castes', and 'backward classes' interchangeably, but the explanations indicate these referred primarily to schools for Untouchable students.

10 MAR 1910–11, para 456.

11 See for instance 'Speech at Bangalore Central College Day Meeting', 16 March 1912, MV-SPEECHES-VOL, pp. 17–31, here p. 21; M. Visvesvaraya, *Memoirs of My Working Life* (Bangalore: M. Visvesvaraya, 1951), pp. 55–8.

12 Quoted in GAZETTEER-VOL4, p. 505.

13 Quoted in Manu Bhagavan, *Sovereign Spheres: Princes, Education and Empire in Colonial India* (New Delhi: Oxford University Press, 2003), p. 98.

14 'Compulsory Education in Mysore', TOI, 23 October 1912, p. 6.

15 Bhagavan, *Sovereign Spheres*, p. 98.

16 'Mysore Elementary Education', TOI, 19 October 1912, p. 9; 'Compulsory Education in Mysore', TOI, 23 October 1912, p. 6.

17 GAZETTEER-VOL4, p. 526.

18 'Address to the Mysore Economic Conference', 21 June 1915, MV-SPEECHES-VOL, pp. 231–41 (the term 'centres' appears on p. 233); 'Address to Dasara Representative Assembly', 19 October 1915, MV-SPEECHES-VOL, pp. 257–99 (the phrase 'a modest start' appears on p. 269); MAR 1917–18, para 542; MAR 1915–16, para 87. See also 'Mysore Council. Compulsory State Education', TOI, 6 December 1916, p. 10.

19 *Report of Dr. C.R. Reddy on Education in Mysore State, 13th May 1949* (Bangalore: Government Press, 1949), pp. 29–33.

20 James Manor, 'Princely Mysore before the Storm: The State-Level Political System of India's Model State 1920–1936', *Modern Asian Studies* 9, no. 1 (1975): 31–58. Quoted phrase occurs in several places across the article.

21 MAR 1911-12, para 425; MAR 1912-13, para 408; MAR 1913-14, para 458. On donated school buildings and private contributions towards such buildings, see MAR 1914–15, para 470.

22 Rao, 'Elite Conflict and Women's Education', esp. p. 359. See also M. Shama Rao, *Modern Mysore: From the Coronation of Chamaraja Wodeyar X in 1868 to the present time* (Bangalore: Higginbothams, 1936), p. 136.

23 Rao, 'Elite Conflict and Women's Education' (quoted text from p. 364).

24 E.g. MAR 1915-16, para 553; MAR 1917-18, para 580.

25 MAR 1917-18, para 580.

26 H.V. Nanjundayya, 'Final Note by the First Member of Council', 5 January 1915 (quoted text is from this source); Visvesvaraya to Nanjundayya, 26 March 1914 (Edu. 439–13); and other documents, all in 'Proposal for award of more Girls' Scholarships for furthering the cause of female education in the state', Education Department, Mysore, File No. 439, S. No. 4, 1913, KSA-DIGITIZED (https://archives.karnataka.gov.in/

home/viewdocument?doc_id=RGVlcGFrMTEwMDI0&doc_location=RGVlcGFrMQ==).

27 'July renewal of female education [in?] the state', Education Department, Mysore, 1913, File No. 152–13; S. No. 1–3, 7, 8, KSA-DIGITIZED (https://archives.karnataka.gov.in/home/viewdocument?doc_id=RGVlcGFrMTA5ODY0&doc_location=RGVlcGFrMQ==).

28 MAR 1911–12, para 430; MAR 1917–18, paras 547–8.

29 MAR 1917–18, para 542. There was also a boarding school for Panchamas in Mysore (ibid., para 548), but it is not clear when it was established.

30 'Reply to Dasara Addresses', 19 October 1915, MV-SPEECHES-VOL, pp. 300–2.

31 'Reply to Nanjangud Municipality', 28 February 1914, MV-SPEECHES-VOL, pp. 135–40, here pp. 138–9.

32 MAR 1912–13, para 408.

33 MAR 1910–11, para 455.

34 MAR 1912–13, para 408.

35 'Speech at the Dasara Representative Assembly', 26 October 1915, MV-SPEECHES-VOL, pp. 302–9 (quoted text from p. 304).

36 MAR 1914–15, para 470; MAR 1917–18, para 558.

37 See for instance MAR 1910-11, para 488; MAR, 1911-12, para 443; MAR 1912-13, para 425. On mandatory drill, see MAR 1912–13, para 425; for quoted phrase, see MAR 1917–18, para 569.

38 See for instance MAR 1912–13, para 426; MAR 1915–16, para 541 (quoted phrase from this source); MAR 1917–18, para 570; Shama Rao, *Modern Mysore*, p. 277.

39 'Technical education in Mysore', TOI, 13 May 1913, p. 6; GAZETTEER-VOL4, pp. 602–3.

40 Shama Rao, *Modern Mysore,* p. 276. The committee had recommended the creation of 'a College of Technology . . . in Bangalore' and 'a model school of technology in Mysore', and the upgrading of 'the existing industrial schools in the State'. 'Technical Education in Mysore', TOI, 13 May 1913, p. 6.

41 Shama Rao, *Modern Mysore,* p. 276. On the CTI building, see 'Chamarajendra Technical Institute', website of the National Mission on Monuments and Antiquities, Government of India (http://

nmma.nic.in/nmma/builtDetail.do?refId=11135&state=29, accessed 27 September 2023). On the function of the engineering school in Mysore which was absorbed into the CTI, see 'The Engineering School at Mysore', Education Department, Mysore, 1905, File No. 317–04, S. No. 4–8, KSA-DIGITIZED (https://archives.karnataka.gov.in/home/viewdocument?doc_id=RGVlcGFrMTA4ODQy&doc_location=RGVlcGFrMQ==).

42 MAR 1913–14, paras 470–1; MAR 1914–15, para 482.

43 MAR 1912–13, para 420; MAR 1913–14, para 470; MAR 1914–15, para 482; MAR 1915–16, paras 526–8; MAR 1917–18, para 557.

44 See for instance MAR 1915–16, para 528.

45 MAR 1913–14, para 472; MAR 1914–15, para 484 (quoted text from here); MAR 1915–16, para 531; MAR 1917–18, para 559.

46 See Aparajith Ramnath, 'S. Venkatasubba Setty: A Hidden Figure in English Aviation History', The Wire, 15 May 2017 (https://thewire.in/history/s-venkatasubba-setty-avro-504-kannada, accessed 15 October 2023).

47 MAR, 1915–16, para 230; 'Opening of an Agricultural School at Bangalore', Agriculture Department, Mysore, 1911–12, File No. 128, S. No. 1, KSA-DIGITIZED (https://archives.karnataka.gov.in/home/viewdocument?doc_id=RGVlcGFrMTUyMDc4&doc_location=RGVlcGFrMQ==).

48 MAR 1913–14, para 473; MAR 1914–15, para 485; MAR 1917–18, para 560.

49 MAR, various years. See for example MAR 1914–15, para 502; MAR 1915–16, paras 550–1.

50 Visvesvaraya's speech at College of Engineering, Bangalore [1954/55], in pp. 12–16 of *Avalokana: Centenary Souvenir*, brought out by VisionUVCE (an alumni association of the University Visvesvaraya College of Engineering, Bengaluru) in 2017; S.V. Setty to Karpur Shrinivasrao, Chief Engineer, Mysore, 22 June 1917, reproduced in *Avalokana*, p. 16; 'Address by VK Gokak During Golden Jubilee Celebrations', in *Avalokana*, pp. 17–19 (here p. 18).

51 As the endnotes will show, the following sections on the establishment of Mysore University rely to a large extent on

Bhagavan, *Sovereign Spheres*, Chapter 3, although I have also analysed a number of primary sources.

52 'Mysore University: A Suggestion', TOI, 20 March 1912, p. 7.

53 There had been calls for a university in Baroda from the first decade of the twentieth century, but as of 1912, nothing had come of the idea. Manu Bhagavan, 'The Rebel Academy: Modernity and the Movement for a University in Princely Baroda, 1908–49', *Journal of Asian Studies* 61, no. 3 (August 2002): 919–47.

54 Bhagavan, *Sovereign Spheres*, pp. 84–5.

55 Ibid., Chapter 3 (especially pp. 90–5).

56 Ibid., Chapter 3 (quoted phrase on p. 99).

57 In his 1912 speech, Visvesvaraya mentioned 'talk for some time past of a university for Mysore'. 'Mysore University: A Suggestion'.

58 Quoted in Bhagavan, *Sovereign Spheres,* p. 98.

59 Bhagavan, *Sovereign Spheres*, pp. 104–6.

60 'Speech at the Mysore Legislative Council', 29 June 1916, in MV-SPEECHES-VOL, pp. 339–45, here p. 340. Reddy's membership in the Nanjundayya Committee is mentioned in Bhagavan, *Sovereign Spheres*, p. 104.

61 This can be inferred from: M. Visvesvaraya (Mysore Dewan) to Hugh Daly (Mysore Resident), 12 February 1916, KSA-MV-VOL, pp. 69–73.

62 M. Visvesvaraya to Hugh Daly, 12 February 1916, KSA-MV-VOL, pp. 69–73 (the quoted text is from this source); 'Speech at the Mysore Legislative Council', 29 June 1916, in MV-SPEECHES-VOL, pp. 339–45; Bhagavan, *Sovereign Spheres*, Chapter 3.

63 Bhagavan, *Sovereign Spheres*, pp. 170–2.

64 See Chapter 13 below.

65 Speech at the Mysore Legislative Council', 29 June 1916, MV-SPEECHES-VOL, pp. 339–45, here pp. 340–1; M. Visvesvaraya to Hugh Daly, 12 February 1916, KSA-MV-VOL, pp. 69–73.

66 P.G. D'Souza (Officiating Secretary, Education/Agriculture/Industries and Commerce, Government of Mysore) to T.H. St. George Tucker (First Assistant to Resident, Mysore), June 1916 (E.D. 12 of 1916, Sl. No. 174, General and Revenue Secretariat), KSA-MV-VOL, pp. 101–4; 'Speech at the Mysore Legislative Council', 29 June 1916, MV-SPEECHES-VOL, pp. 339–45, esp. p. 341.

67 See Bhagavan, *Sovereign Spheres,* pp. 104 and 110.
68 D'Souza to St. George Tucker, June 1916 (cited above), here p. 103.
69 'Mysore University', TOI, 9 May 1916, p. 8.
70 'Speech at the Mysore Legislative Council', 29 June 1916, MV-SPEECHES-VOL, pp. 339–45; 'Speech at the Mysore Legislative Council', 17 July 1916, MV-SPEECHES-VOL, pp. 345–8.
71 'Speech at the Mysore Legislative Council', 29 June 1916, MV-SPEECHES-VOL, pp. 339-45, here pp. 343–4.
72 'Speech at the Mysore Legislative Council', 17 July 1916, MV-SPEECHES-VOL, pp. 345–8 (quoted text from pp. 346 and 348).
73 Bhagavan, *Sovereign Spheres,* p. 115.
74 Inferred from para 1 of Mysore Government Proceedings, No. 8320—EDN. 226-18-4, 6 March 1919.
75 'Opening Speech of His Highness the Chancellor at the First Meeting of the Senate', excerpted in *Report of Dr. C.R. Reddy*, pp. 149–50.
76 GAZETTEER-VOL4, pp. 512–5.
77 Para 25 of University of Mysore, 'Report on the Working of the Mysore University during the Academic Year 1917–18', enclosed with Mysore Government Proceedings, No. 8320—EDN. 22618-4, 6 March 1919. This source is hereafter cited as Mysore University Annual Report 1917–18.
78 GAZETTEER-VOL4, pp. 509–11.
79 Mysore University Annual Report 1917–18, para 17.
80 GAZETTEER-VOL4, p. 510; Mysore University Annual Report 1917–18, paras 20–1.
81 GAZETTEER-VOL4, pp. 509–11; Mysore University Annual Report 1917–18, esp. para 23.
82 GAZETTEER-VOL4, pp. 511–12; Mysore University Annual Report 1917–18, para 15.
83 Constance E. Parsons, *Mysore City* (London: Oxford University Press, 1930), pp. 111–12 (quoted text on p. 112).
84 Benjamin Zachariah, *Developing India: An Intellectual and Social History, c. 1930-50* (New Delhi: Oxford University Press, 2005), p. 244; 'Seal, Dr. Brajendranath', IBD 1915, p. 386; 'Indian philosopher dead: Sir Brajendranath Seal', TOI, 5 December

1938, p. 12; 'Prof. K. T. Shah Dead: Indian Economist', TOI, 11 March 1953, p. 5.

85 GAZETTEER-VOL4, p. 512.

86 'Speech delivered at the First Convocation of the University of Mysore on 19th October 1918 by His Highness The Maharaja of Mysore, Chancellor', in C. Hayavadana Rao (ed.), *Addresses delivered at The Mysore University Convocations 1918–1929* (Bangalore City: Bangalore Printing & Publishing Co. Ltd., 1930), pp. 1–8, here p. 7. Accessed via www.southasiaarchive.com/Content/sarf.144129/210926/002.

87 'Papers relating to the visit of Sir Asutosh Mookerji to Mysore in connection with the convocation of the Mysore university', Education Department, Mysore, 1918, File No. 419–18, KSA-DIGITIZED (https://archives.karnataka.gov.in/home/viewdocument?doc_id=RGVlcGFrMTA5MTA3&doc_location=RGVlcGFrMQ==). The quote is from the following letter in this file: Visvesvaraya to Mirza [Ismail], 16 October 1918 [copy]. See also the correspondence between Visvesvaraya and Mookerjee in Asutosh Mookerjee Papers I, NMML. On Mookerjee, see Nani A. Palkhivala, 'Sir Asutosh the greatest educationist', TOI, 16 July 1989, p. 10; 'Mukharji, Sir Ashutosh Saraswati', IBD 1915, p. 290; Satyabachi Sar, 'Asutosh Mukhopadhyay and his Mathematical Legacy', *Resonance*, July 2015, pp. 575–604.

88 'Address delivered at the First Convocation of the University of Mysore on 19th October 1918 by Sir Asutosh Mookerjee, late Vice-Chancellor of the University of Calcutta', in Rao (ed.), *Addresses delivered at The Mysore University Convocations 1918–1929*, pp. 9–30.

12. Manufactured in Mysore

1 P.G. D'Souza, 'Industries in Mysore', in *Indian Science Congress Handbook: Bangalore Meeting: January, 1924* (Mysore: Wesleyan Mission Press, 1923), pp. 80–90, here p. 80.

2 MAR 1910–11, pp. 34–6 (average number of employees per factory calculated from table on pp. 35–6).

3 MV, 'Address to the Mysore Economic Conference', 21 June 1915, MV-SPEECHES-VOL, pp. 231–41, here pp. 239–40.

4 Except where other sources are specifically cited, biographical details on Chatterton in this and the next paragraph are based on the following: 'Chatterton, Alfred', IBD 1915, p. 87; 'Obituary. Sir Alfred Chatterton', *Proceedings of the Institution of Civil Engineers* 13, no. 3 (July 1959): 440–1; 'Chatterton, Sir Alfred, C.I.E., F.C.G.I.', in J.E. Sears (ed.), *Who's Who in Engineering* (London: n.p., [1922]), entry consulted at https://www.gracesguide.co.uk/1922_Who's_Who_In_Engineering:_Name_C, accessed 5 April 2024.

5 These institutions were part of the City and Guilds of London Institute, which had been established with the backing of the London City Corporation and several of the City's livery companies (these in turn had evolved from guilds of the medieval period). See 'Administrative History', under 'City and Guilds of London Institute', online catalogue of London Metropolitan Archives (https://search.lma.gov.uk/scripts/mwimain.dll/144/LMA_OPAC/web_detail?SESSIONSEARCH&exp=refd%20CLC/211, accessed 5 April 2024); 'livery company', *Encyclopedia Britannica*, 26 February 2018 (https://www.britannica.com/topic/livery-company, accessed 5 April 2024).

6 'Aluminium Ware—A Native Industry' (Chatterton's letter to the editor), TOI, 2 January 1899, p. 3; 'Chrome Tanning in Madras', TOI, 30 March 1905, p. 4; 'Madras Industries', TOI, 16 April 1912, p. 7; Alfred Chatterton, *Industrial Evolution in India* (Madras: The 'Hindu' Office, 1912), pp. 223–44 (quoted text on pp. 225–6). On the Madras School of Arts, see Anusha Parthasarathy, 'The cradle of art', *The Hindu* (online), 19 February 2013 (https://www.thehindu.com/features/metroplus/the-cradle-of-art/article4431646.ece, accessed 28 January 2022).

7 Chatterton, *Industrial Evolution in India*, p. 49; Alfred Chatterton, 'The Indian Industrial Problem', *Science Progress in the Twentieth Century* 4, 16 (April 1910): 551–69, here p. 565; Abigail McGowan, *Crafting the Nation in Colonial India* (New York: Palgrave Macmillan, 2009), pp. 5 and 7.

8 Chatterton, 'The Indian Industrial Problem', pp. 554–5.

9 Chatterton, *Industrial Evolution in India*, p. 204.

10 Chatterton, 'The Indian Industrial Problem', pp. 563 and 561–2.

11 See for instance Bjørn Hettne, *The Political Economy of Indirect Rule: Mysore 1881–1947* (New Delhi: Ambika Publications, 1978), pp. 263–4; Dhruv Raina, *Visvesvaraya as Engineer-Sociologist and the Evolution of His Techno-Economic Vision*, NIAS Lecture L1-2001 (Bangalore: National Institute of Advanced Studies, 2001), pp. 29–30; Janaki Nair, 'Mysore's Wembley? The Dasara Exhibition's Imagined Economies', *Modern Asian Studies* 47, no. 5 (September 2013): 1549–87, here pp. 1558–9.

12 Chatterton quoted in McGowan, *Crafting the Nation*, pp. 88–9.

13 'Address to the Mysore Economic Conference', 3 June 1914, MV-SPEECHES-VOL, pp. 142–53, here p. 148.

14 A good summary of Alfred Chatterton's views is contained in Chatterton, 'The Indian Industrial Problem'.

15 Ibid., *passim*.

16 Addressing a group of private Madras citizens called the South Indian Association, Chatterton chided them for not acting on his suggestion, made in a previous lecture, to set up a company to produce chrome-tanned leather. '[Y]ou have welcomed lecturers upon various subjects connected with Indian industries and have doubtless been interested in their enthusiasm, but they have not aroused you to action, and I am not sanguine that this afternoon anything I have to say will meet with a better fate.' Chatterton, *Industrial Evolution in India*, p. 203.

17 R. Balakrishna, *Industrial Development of Mysore* (Bangalore: Bangalore Press, 1940), p. 298.

18 Hettne, *Political Economy of Indirect Rule*, p. 263; Balakrishna, *Industrial Development of Mysore*, p. 298.

19 G.O. Press No. 1928 Revenue, [Madras government], 29 June 1912, KSA-MV-VOL, pp. 4–5; Mysore government Proceedings, No. G. 155–207—G.M. 36–11–169, 10 July 1912, KSA-MV-VOL, pp. 5–6.

20 GAZETTEER-VOL4, p. 336; Hettne, *Political Economy of Indirect Rule*, pp. 262–4.

21 Hettne, *Political Economy of Indirect Rule*, pp. 262–3.

22 GAZETTEER-VOL4, pp. 336–7; Hettne, *Political Economy of Indirect Rule,* p. 262.

23 Chatterton went from being Special Adviser to the committee, to Director of the DIC. C. Ranganatha Rao Sahib (a Mysore civil servant) was secretary of the committee before becoming Assistant Director of the DIC. See C. Ranganatha Rao's 'Written Evidence' in *Minutes of Evidence taken before the Indian Industrial Commission, 1916–18: Vol. III.—Madras and Bangalore* (London: His Majesty's Stationery Office, 1919), pp. 590–6, here p. 590. This source is hereafter cited as C.R. Rao, 'Written Evidence'.

24 C.R. Rao, 'Written Evidence', pp. 590–1.

25 Ibid., p. 595; GAZETTEER-VOL4, p. 340.

26 GAZETTEER-VOL3, pp. 276–9; Balakrishna, *Industrial Development of Mysore*, pp. 79–81; Hettne, *Political Economy of Indirect Rule*, pp. 267–8; M. Shama Rao, *Modern Mysore: From the Coronation of Chamaraja Wodeyar X in 1868 to the present time* (Bangalore: Higginbothams, 1936), p. 272; Alfred Chatterton, 'The Industrial Progress of the Mysore State', *Journal of the Royal Society of Arts* 73, 3788 (26 June 1925): 714–45, esp. pp. 732–3.

27 'Administration Report for the Year 1917–18 of the Industries and Commerce Department', submitted by V. Rangaswamy Iyengar, Officiating Director of Industries and Commerce, Mysore, enclosed with Mysore government Proceedings, General and Revenue Departments, Order No. 5700–50—I. & C. 165–18–7, 21 December 1918; Balakrishna, *Industrial Development of Mysore,* pp. 81–3; Shama Rao, *Modern Mysore,* p. 272.

28 'Silk Reeling' (note by Chatterton), KSA-MV-VOL, pp. 52–4. For the context of the note, see the letter with which it is enclosed, viz. Education and Agriculture Secretary, Mysore, to First Assistant to the Resident, Mysore, n.d. [1914], KSA-MV-VOL, pp. 51–2.

29 'The Mysore Silk Industry', TOI, 1 May 1895, p. 4; 'Mysore Silk', TOI, 15 December 1897, p. 4; 'Sericulture in Mysore. Tata's Experimental Farm', TOI, 28 August 1901, p. 5; 'Sericulture in Mysore: Report on Mr. Tata's Experiments', TOI, 23 September 1901, p. 8.

30 See '[Speech at] Opening of Harihar Pumping Installation', 11 August 1913, MV-SPEECHES-VOL, pp. 86–92, here pp. 91–2; [Chatterton], 'Silk Reeling', KSA-MV-VOL, pp. 52–4.
31 [Chatterton], 'Silk Reeling', KSA-MV-VOL, pp. 52–4.
32 'Mysore Silk Industry', TOI, 7 November 1913, p. 8; MAR 1914–15, p. 2.
33 'Current Topics', TOI, 12 September 1917, p. 7; Mari's 'Oral Evidence, 14th February 1917', in *Minutes of Evidence taken before the Indian Industrial Commission, 1916–18,* Vol. III: *Madras and Bangalore* (London: His Majesty's Stationery Office, 1919), pp. 602–3; 'Address to Dasara Representative Assembly', 30 September 1914, MV-SPEECHES-VOL, pp. 165–205 (here p. 196); H. Maxwell-Lefroy and E.C. Ansorge, *Report on an Inquiry into The Silk Industry in India*, Vol. 1: *The Silk Industry* by H. Maxwell-Lefroy (Calcutta: Superintendent Government Printing, 1916), p. 33; Washington Mari's note, 'Scheme of organization', in *Minutes of Evidence taken before the Indian Industrial Commission, 1916–18: Vol. III.—Madras and Bangalore* (London: His Majesty's Stationery Office, 1919), pp. 603–6, here p. 605.
34 C.R. Rao, 'Written Evidence', pp. 592–4.
35 GAZETTEER-VOL4, pp. 336–43.
36 C. Hayavadana Rao, *Silver Jubilee Souvenir, 2nd December 1938: The Bank of Mysore Limited, Bangalore, S. India* (Bangalore: Bangalore Press, 1938), p. 1.
37 Hiralal Lallubhai Kaji, *Life and Speeches of Sir Vithaldas Thackersey* (Bombay: D.B. Taraporevala Sons & Co., 1934), ch. 1 and p. 142; 'Thackersey, Hon'ble Sir Vithaldas Damodhar [sic]', IBD 1915, p. 432; Premlila V. Thackersey, 'A Versatile Genius', in CENT-VOL, pp. 59–65, here p. 60.
38 Kaji, *Life and Speeches of Sir Vithaldas Thackersey*, pp. 136–41; Chimanlal H. Setalvad, *Recollections and Reflections: An Autobiography* (Bombay: Padma Publication Ltd, [1946]), pp. 98–9.
39 Kaji, *Life and Speeches of Sir Vithaldas Thackersey*, pp. 145–7 (the quoted text is from a letter from Vithaldas, quoted on p. 146); 'The Bank of Mysore', TOI, 27 May 1913, p. 4; Hayavadana Rao, *Silver Jubilee Souvenir*, pp. 3 and 88.

40 Balakrishna, *Industrial Development of Mysore*, p. 148; C.R. Rao, 'Written Evidence', esp. pp. 590–1; Hayavadana Rao, *Silver Jubilee Souvenir*, p. 3.

41 'Inauguration of the Mysore Chamber of Commerce', 8 May 1916, MV-SPEECHES-VOL, pp. 316–21 (quoted text from pp. 316, 317 and 319). On the perceived role of Marwari merchants, see Hettne, *Political Economy of Indirect Rule*, pp. 264–5.

42 Balakrishna, *Industrial Development of Mysore*, pp. 148–50 (quoted text on p. 149); C.R. Rao, 'Written Evidence', esp. pp. 590–1.

43 Balakrishna, *Industrial Development of Mysore*, pp. 155–8; Kaji, *Life and Speeches of Sir Vithaldas Thackersey*, p. 147; Hettne, *Political Economy of Indirect Rule*, p. 264.

44 Nair, 'Mysore's Wembley?'.

45 '[Speech at the] Mysore Dasara Exhibition', 3 October 1913, MV-SPEECHES-VOL, pp. 92–5, here p. 94. On Krumbiegel, see 'Krumbiegel, Gustav Herman', IBD 1915, p. 240.

46 Nair, 'Mysore's Wembley?', pp. 1573–4. Nair mentions that this machinery was probably made by expatriate British companies in India. Ibid., p. 1574, footnote 105.

47 Nair, 'Mysore's Wembley?', p. 1574.

48 Gilbert Slater, *Southern India: Its Political and Economic Problems* (London: George Allen and Unwin, 1936), pp. 247–8.

49 Nair, 'Mysore's Wembley?', pp. 1574–5 and 1576–85.

50 This section is based on the following sources: H. Rangachar, 'The Bhatkal Harbour Project', typed note, 4 November 1945, enclosed with: H. Rangachar (General Manager, Mysore State Railway) to O. Pulla Reddi (Minister for Revenue, Mysore), D.O. No. 211/Encs., November 1945, in 'Development of the Bhatkal Harbour and Construction of the Chamarajanagar–Mettupalaiyam Ry.', Mysore, [Railway Department], 1945–46, File No. 217/G, KSA-DIGITIZED (https://archives.karnataka.gov.in/home/viewdocument?doc_id=RGVlcGFrMzczNzQ=&doc_location=RGVlcGFrMQ==); various documents in '*Mysore:* The Bhatkal harbour project', Political Department, [Government of India], File No. P. 2309 (with File No. P. 2729/20), APAC: IOR/L/PS/11/186.

51 See Aparajith Ramnath, *The Birth of an Indian Profession: Engineers, Industry, and the State, 1900–47* (Delhi: Oxford University Press, 2017), pp. 49–50.

52 *Indian Industrial Commission 1916–18: Report* (Calcutta: Superintendent Government Printing, India, 1918), p. xv.

53 'Speech at the Mysore Economic Conference', 14 June 1916, MV-SPEECHES-VOL, pp. 332–9, here p. 334; 'Reply to Bangalore Citizens' Addresses', 12 December 1912, MV-SPEECHES-VOL, pp. 50–9, here p. 56.

54 At the end of the 1915 session of the Economic Conference, Visvesvaraya declared: 'We have learnt from Mr. Chatterton how to give and take criticism in perfect good humour.' 'Speech at the Mysore Economic Conference', 26 June 1915, MV-SPEECHES-VOL, pp. 241–50, here p. 242. In later life Chatterton recalled Visvesvaraya as 'a man of unusual energy . . . , gifted with imagination and ability to express his ideas and imbued with an ardent desire to serve his country and his native State'. Chatterton, 'The Industrial Progress', p. 729.

55 See Nair, 'Mysore's Wembley?', pp. 1558–9.

56 Quoted in Nair, 'Mysore's Wembley?', p. 1559, footnote 40.

57 Visvesvaraya, *Memoirs*, p. 45.

58 'Chatterton, Sir Alfred, C.I.E., F.C.G.I.', in J.E. Sears (ed.), *Who's Who in Engineering,* (London: [1922]), via https://www.gracesguide.co.uk/1922_Who's_Who_In_Engineering:_Name_C, accessed 8 June 2023.

59 In other words, the production of iron was 'a basic industry'. Chandan Gowda, '"Advance Mysore!": The Cultural Logic of a Developmental State', *Economic and Political Weekly* XLV, no. 29 (17 July 2010): 88–95, here p. 90. Hereafter cited as Gowda, 'Cultural Logic'.

60 See Chapter 6 above.

61 See Ramnath, *Birth of an Indian Profession*, Chapter 5.

62 Gowda, 'Cultural Logic', p. 90; GAZETTEER-VOL3, pp. 204–5.

63 W.F. Smeeth and P. Sampat Iyengar, *Mineral Resources of Mysore: A Brief Account of the More Important Economic Minerals, their Occurrence and Distribution with Notes on their Mining and*

Metallurgical Treatment and Uses (Bangalore: Government Press, 1916), pp. 72–3. On the iron-making process, see for instance 'blast furnace', *Encyclopedia Britannica,* 23 December 2023 (https://www.britannica.com/technology/blast-furnace, accessed 6 March 2024).

64 Visvesvaraya, *Memoirs*, p. 92.

65 See V.S. Narayana Rao, *Mokshagundam Visvesvaraya: His Life and Work* (Mysore: Geetha Book House, 1973), pp. 74–5.

66 Gowda, 'Cultural Logic', p. 90; Brief notice on W.F. Smeeth's *Notes on the Electric Smelting of Iron* by 'A. Mc.W.' in *Nature* 84 (1910): 103. For Smeeth's nationality, see 'Smeeth, Dr. W. F.', IBD 1915, p. 403. On Smeeth as chief of the department, see 'Re-organization of the Geological Department', No. G. 8445-93—G.M. 292-14-1, 9 February 1915, KSA-MV-VOL, pp. 58–67, here p. 63.

67 Smeeth and Sampat Iyengar, *Mineral Resources of Mysore*, pp. 75–7. This report refers to the situation in 1916, but the same would have held true in 1909.

68 Gowda, 'Cultural Logic', p. 90.

69 'Address to Dasara Representative Assembly', 19 October 1915, MV-SPEECHES-VOL, pp. 257–99, here p. 267.

70 Ibid., p. 293.

71 '[Speech at] Opening of Harihar Pumping Installation', 11 August 1913, MV-SPEECHES-VOL, pp. 86–92, here p. 87.

72 As illustrated by several speeches Visvesvaraya made during his dewan years. MV-SPEECHES-VOL, *passim.*

73 See M. Visvesvaraya, '[Speech at the] Opening of the Local Fund Dispensary at Saklespur', 15 March 1913, in MV-SPEECHES-VOL, pp. 66–73. Chandan Gowda notes that '[i]n formulating development programmes, the Mysore state elite accepted the validity of orientalist claims about Indians but believed they could be overcome'. Gowda, 'Cultural Logic', p. 90.

74 See 'Address to Dasara Representative Assembly', 30 September 1914, MV-SPEECHES-VOL, pp. 165–205, here pp. 176 and 192–3.

75 'Submitted to His Highness', note by Visvesvaraya dated 15 December 1914, KSA-MV-VOL, pp. 56–7, here p. 56.

76 'Reorganization of the Geological Department', General and Revenue Departments, Mysore, No. G. 8445–93—G.M. 292–14–1, 9 February 1915, KSA-MV-VOL, pp. 58–67 (quoted text on p. 60).
77 'Smeeth, Dr. W. F.', IBD 1915, p. 403.
78 W.F. Smeeth and P. Sampat Iyengar, *Mineral Resources of Mysore: A Brief Account of the More Important Economic Minerals, their Occurrence and Distribution with Notes on their Mining and Metallurgical Treatment and Uses* (Bangalore: Government Press, 1916).
79 Smeeth and Sampat Iyengar, *Mineral Resources of Mysore*, pp. 57–67 (quoted text from pp. 65 and 67).
80 Ibid., pp. 73–4.
81 'Address to Dasara Representative Assembly', 19 October 1915, MV-SPEECHES-VOL, pp. 257–99, here p. 293; Ramnath, *Birth of an Indian Profession*, Chapter 5 (for details on Perin and his role with TISCO).
82 Charles Page Perin, 'Report on the Development of the Timber and Iron Ore Resources of Mysore State', May 1916, p. 3. Available in 'Bhadravati Iron Works', Mysore Residency, 1891, File No. 67A, S. Nos. 2–29, APAC: IOR/R/2/Box 6/46.
83 Ibid., p. 15.
84 'Iron and Steel Scheme', Tables A, B, and C, KSA-MV-VOL, pp. 183–5; 'A Mysore Ironworks Scheme', *Pioneer*, 22 December 1916. For the names Bhadravati/Benkipur, see GAZETTEER-VOL5, p. 1284.
85 [Visvesvaraya], 'IRON SCHEME. Chronological order of events', typed note in MV-PAPERS-IEI, Vol. 15.
86 Visvesvaraya's note, 'Submitted to His Highness', 26 March 1917 (typed copy), MV-PAPERS-IEI, Vol. 15. The other firm was the Bengal Iron and Steel Company. See Rajat K. Ray, *Industrialization in India: Growth and Conflict in the Private Sector 1914–47* (Delhi: Oxford University Press, 1982 [1979]), p. 34.
87 'Select Papers regarding Iron Scheme 1916', KSA-MV-VOL, pp. 174–86, here p. 179.
88 Kaji, *Life and Speeches of Sir Vithaldas Thackersey*, p. 249.

89 'Select Papers regarding Iron Scheme 1916', pp. 174–7 (quoted text on p. 175). That the parties later settled on a twenty-five-year agreement is indicated in Gowda, 'Cultural Logic', p. 91. On Samaldas and Tata companies, see for instance: 'Tata Hydro-Electric Co.: Annual Meeting', TOI, 3 November 1911, p. 4; 'Tata Iron & Steel Co., Ld. Agents' Remuneration', TOI, 4 August 1916, p. 6; 'Tata Iron and Steel Co: Tenth Annual Meeting', TOI, 19 October 1917, p. 8.

90 'Select Papers regarding Iron Scheme 1916', pp. 177–8.

91 [Visvesvaraya], 'IRON SCHEME. Chronological order of events'; 'Select Papers regarding Iron Scheme 1916', p. 180.

92 [Visvesvaraya], 'IRON SCHEME. Chronological order of events'.

93 Ibid; Visvesvaraya's note, 'Submitted to His Highness', 26 March 1917 (typed copy), MV-PAPERS-IEI, Vol. 15. On Banerji's concerns, see also Gowda, 'Cultural Logic', p. 91.

94 Visvesvaraya's note, 'Submitted to His Highness', 26 March 1917 (typed copy), MV-PAPERS-IEI, Vol. 15.

95 R.H. Campbell to M. Visvesvaraya, 21 May 1917 (typed copy), and Visvesvaraya to Campbell, 23 May 1917 (typed copy), in MV-PAPERS-IEI, Vol. 15. Emphasis in the source.

96 Hettne, *Political Economy of Indirect Rule*, p. 79.

97 Various letters in 'Bhadravati Iron Works', Mysore Residency, 1891, File No. 67A, S. Nos. 2–29, APAC: IOR/R/2/Box 6/46.

98 Deputy Secretary, Foreign and Political Department, Government of India, to H.V. Cobb, Mysore Resident, 4 October 1917 (No. 2261–I.B.), in 'Bhadravati Iron Works', APAC: IOR/R/2/Box 6/46.

99 'Mysore Iron Works', TOI, 25 January 1919, p. 7; 'News of the Week', TOI, 25 July 1919, p. A1; 'Tata Iron and Steel: Company's Annual Report', TOI, 9 September 1919, p. 6; GAZETTEER-VOL5, p. 1286; Mysore Government, Order No. I.C. 6174–86/ I.W.136–22–1, dated 11 April 1923, MV-PAPERS-IEI, Vol. 25.

100 Perin's views are mentioned in P.G. D'Souza, Education and Agriculture Secretary, Mysore, to Major E.H.S. James, First Assistant to Mysore Resident, 16 March 1918, para 6. In 'Bhadravati Iron Works', APAC: IOR/R/2/Box 6/46.

101 Gowda, 'Cultural Logic', mentions that Mysore was well aware of the challenges, and offers a strong cultural explanation for why

they still went ahead. This is discussed further in Chapter 16 below.

13. A Dewan at Work

1 See letters from unidentified sender (13 January 1913), P.S. Govinda Rao (11 January 1913) and D.M. Narasinga Rao (9 January 1913). Facsimiles in Leela Krishnamurthy, *Bharata Ratna Sir M. Visvesvaraya—Naa Kandu Keledante* (Bangalore: Leela Krishnamurthy and Karnataka State Archives, 2010), pp. 180–2, 189–90, and 186–7.

2 The 'run-about' was sanctioned in 1914, but before it the dewan had an 8 HP DeDion, presumably for the same purpose. 'Purchase of a Motor Car (Wolseley Car) for the use of the Dewan', General Finance, Mysore, 1913, File No. 68, S.Nos. 1 and 3, KSA-DIGITIZED (https://archives.karnataka.gov.in/home/viewdocument?doc_id=RGVlcGFrMTkzOTI=&doc_location=RGVlcGFrMQ==); 'Purchase of a small run-about car at a cost Rs. 4000/- for the use of the Dewan's staff', General Miscellaneous, Mysore, 1914–15, File No. 123–14, S. No. 16, KSA-DIGITIZED (https://archives.karnataka.gov.in/home/viewdocument?doc_id=RGVlcGFrMjM4NjM=&doc_location=RGVlcGFrMQ==); 'Installation of Electric Bell Equipment for the Dewan's (Office) Room with a five-button push board', General Miscellaneous, Mysore, 1911–12, File No. 315, S.Nos. 1–2, KSA-DIGITIZED (https://archives.karnataka.gov.in/home/viewdocument?doc_id=RGVlcGFrMjM0Mjk=&doc_location=RGVlcGFrMQ==); 'Purchase of a Roneophone Dictating Machine for the Dewan's office', General Miscellaneous, Mysore, 1912–13, File No. 311, S.Nos. 1–20, KSA-DIGITIZED (https://archives.karnataka.gov.in/home/viewdocument?doc_id=RGVlcGFrMjQ5ODE=&doc_location=RGVlcGFrMQ==). Another young civil servant described the office as 'a place of great dignity and importance . . . Everyone was brisk and doing something.' M. Venkatesa Iyengar, 'A Hard Task-Master', in CENT-VOL, pp. 257–64, here p. 258.

3 Venkatesa Iyengar, 'A Hard Task Master', pp. 258–9; D.C. Subbarayappa, 'He Stood By Merit', in CENT-VOL, pp. 156–64, here p. 157. The timings as mentioned in these two reminiscences vary slightly.

4 Venkatesa Iyengar, 'A Hard Task-Master', esp. pp. 259–61; Subbarayappa, 'He Stood By Merit' (quoted text from p. 157).

5 Venkatesa Iyengar, 'A Hard Task-Master'; Subbarayappa, 'He Stood by Merit'.

6 'Continuance of Local allowance to Certain officials in the Dewan's office', General Miscelleaneous, Mysore, 1914, File No. 42, S.No. 1, KSA-DIGITIZED (https://archives.karnataka.gov.in/home/viewdocument?doc_id=RGVlcGFrMjM1MDY=&doc_location=RGVlcGFrMQ==); 'Continuance of the allowances to certain clerks of the Dewan's office till the end of June 1917', General Miscellaneous, Mysore, 1915, File No. 469, S. No. 1, KSA-DIGITIZED (https://archives.karnataka.gov.in/home/viewdocument?doc_id=RGVlcGFrMjM3Mjc=&doc_location=RGVlcGFrMQ==). The quote is from Visvesvaraya's note to the maharaja, 30 March 1916, in the latter of these files. On the salaries of clerks, an idea can be gained from the fact that an assistant commissioner on Visvesvaraya's staff as of 1917 drew a basic salary of Rs 250 per month. Table in 'Increased rate of daily allowance to Mr S. Hiriannaiya, Private Secy to the Dewan', General Miscelleaneous, Mysore, 1917, File No. 154, S.No. 1, KSA-DIGITIZED (https://archives.karnataka.gov.in/home/viewdocument?doc_id=RGVlcGFrMjQ0NzM=&doc_location=RGVlcGFrMQ==).

7 Interview with Leela Krishnamurthy and A.K.N. Prasad (daughter and grandson, respectively, of S. Hiriannaiya), Bengaluru, 25 June 2019.

8 'Increased rate of daily allowance to Mr S. Hiriyannaiya, Private Secy to the Dewan', General Miscellaneous Mysore, 1917, File No. 154–1, S. No. 1, KSA-DIGITIZED (https://archives.karnataka.gov.in/home/viewdocument?doc_id=RGVlcGFrMjQ0NzM=&doc_location=RGVlcGFrMQ==); 'Proposal to increase the local allowance of Mr. S. Hiriyannaiya, Private Secy. to the Dewan, from Rs 50/- to Rs 75/- per mensem',

General Miscellaneous, Mysore, 1917, File No. 154–17, S. Nos. 4 and 5, KSA-DIGITIZED (https://archives.karnataka.gov.in/home/viewdocument?doc_id=RGVlcGFrMjQ0NzQ=&doc_location=RGVlcGFrMQ==).

9 Interview with Leela Krishnamurthy and A.K.N. Prasad, 25 June 2019.

10 M.S. Murthy, 'A few Reminiscences of week ends with Sir M. Visvesvaraya at Muddenahalli', in *World State: Special Number on Bharatratna Dr. Sir M. Visvesvaraya,* ed. S. Visveswariah, [n.d.]. Some typographical errors (spelling, missing punctuation, etc.) have been corrected in the quoted text. On M. Ramachandra Rao, see Pandri Nath, *Mokshagundam Visvesvaraya: Life and Work* (Bombay: Bharatiya Vidya Bhavan, 1987), p. 110.

11 'Address to Dasara Representative Assembly', 11 October 1913, MV-SPEECHES-VOL, pp. 95–129, here pp. 122–3.

12 'Address to Dasara Representative Assembly', 19 October 1915, MV-SPEECHES-VOL, pp. 257–99 (quoted text from pp. 288–9); 'Address to Dasara Representative Assembly', 7 October 1916, MV-SPEECHES-VOL, pp. 366–97, here p. 392.

13 *A Bureaucrat in Princely Mysore: Selections from the Private Diary of K.R. Srinivasa Iyengar 1904–1941*, ed. Narendar Pani, typescript report, Project No. 098, IIMB (Bangalore: Indian Institute of Management Bangalore, 1982), p. 133.

14 *A Bureaucrat in Princely Mysore*, p. 126. See also Chapter 9 above on similar objections raised during Visvesvaraya's days as Chief Engineer.

15 The letter was dated 4 August 1914, and reproduced in the *Madras Mail* [28 September 1922?]. Cutting in MV-PAPERS-IEI, Vol. 14.

16 Venkatesa Iyengar, 'A Hard Task-Master', p. 262.

17 *A Bureaucrat in Princely Mysore,* ed. Narendar Pani (cited in full above). See especially Pani's Introduction.

18 *A Bureaucrat in Princely Mysore*, p. 122.

19 (Quoted in) ibid., p. 122.

20 Ibid., p. 126.

21 Ibid., p. 116.

22 Ibid., pp. 130, 128, and 136.

23 Ibid., pp. 130–1.

24 Ibid., p. 143 for an example of the latter.

25 Ibid., p. 134.

26 Ibid., pp. 133–5 and p. 127 (quoted text from here). On Iyengar seeking Visvesvaraya's trust, see also Pani's Introduction to ibid., p. 14.

27 *A Bureaucrat in Princely Mysore*, pp. 142–3 and 146–7.

28 Ibid., pp. 140–3 and 151–4; Pani's introduction to ibid., pp. 22–3.

29 Pani's Introduction to *A Bureaucrat in Princely Mysore*. On Weberian bureaucracy, see Bert Rockman, 'bureaucracy', *Encyclopedia Britannica*, 1 March 2024 (https://www.britannica.com/topic/bureaucracy, accessed 6 March 2024).

30 Visvesvaraya noted in his memoirs: 'My relations with the Government of India and their representative were generally pleasant and happy.' M. Visvesvaraya, *Memoirs of My Working Life* (Bangalore: M. Visvesvaraya, 1951), p. 88.

31 'Daly, Lt.-Col. Hugh', IBD 1915, p. 111. On the Foreign Department, see section on 'Government organization' in Stanley A. Wolpert, 'British raj', *Encyclopedia Britannica*, 1 March 2024 (https://www.britannica.com/event/British-raj, accessed 6 March 2024).

32 Hugh Daly, Resident, Mysore, to Col. Sir Henry McMahon, Secretary, Foreign Department, [Government of India], 27 September 1912 (typed copy), in 'Appointment of Mr. Visvesvaraya as Dewan; formal approval of the Government of India to such appointment held unnecessary', Mysore Residency, Bangalore, 1912, Confidential File No. 15, APAC: IOR/R/2/33/316.

33 See Chapters 9 and 11 above.

34 S. Hiriannaiya, 'Hard Work and Tenacity of Purpose', in CENT-VOL, pp. 224–32, here p. 230.

35 'Speech at St. John Ambulance Association Meeting', 19 January 1916, MV-SPEECHES-VOL, pp. 309–13, here p. 311.

36 'In memory of Mysore's friend', *Deccan Herald* (online), 23 December 2013 (https://www.deccanherald.com/spectrum/in-memory-of-mysores-friend-365946.html, accessed 18 April 2024); 'Standing tall for 100 years: Daly Memorial Hall's centenary celebration tomorrow', *Times of India* (online), 16 December 2017 (https://timesofindia.indiatimes.com/city/bengaluru/standing-

tall-for-100-yrs-daly-memorial-halls-centenary-celebration-tomorrow/articleshow/62089821.cms, accessed 18 April 2024).

37 'Confidential note by Political Secretary (Sir John Wood) on Mysore Affairs' [30 July 1917], para 7. In Foreign and Political Department [Government of India], 'Confidential—B.: Internal Branch, Section A.', No. 6 of 1918, APAC: IOR/R/1/1/1160.

38 S. Hiriannaiya, diary entry dated 3 June 1915. Facsimile in Leela Krishnamurthy, *Bharata Ratna Sir M. Visvesvaraya*, p. 194. On the name of the list, see 'King's Birthday Honours', *The Belfast News-letter*, 3 June 1915.

39 Interview with Leela Krishnamurthy and A.K.N. Prasad, 25 June 2019.

40 See IOL 1924, pp. 120, 127 and 713 (on Krishnaraja Wadiyar, Kantirava Narasimharaja Wadiyar, and Kantaraj Urs respectively); IOL 1930, pp. 158 and 160 (on Albion Banerji and Puttanna Chetty respectively); IOL 1940, p. 226 (on Mirza Ismail). On Chetty's career, see 'Puttanna Chetty, K.', IBD 1915, pp. 334–5.

41 'Indian Telegrams. Viceregal News.' *Pioneer*, 15 July 1915, p. 5.

42 Daly and the Yuvaraja were also invited to dinner that day. Ibid.

43 MAR 1915–16, para 3; M. Visvesvaraya to Hugh Daly, 12 February 1916 (E.D. 120/1916, S. No. 174), in KSA-MV-VOL, pp. 69–73, here para 2.

44 *A Dictionary of World History,* 2nd edition (Oxford: Oxford University Press, 2006), p. 697; Loring Danforth, Richard J. Crampton, and John B. Allcock, 'Balkans', *Encyclopedia Britannica*, 15 April 2024 (https://www.britannica.com/place/Balkans, accessed 23 April 2024); Dennis E. Showalter and John Graham Royde-Smith, 'World War I', *Encyclopedia Britannica*, 28 February 2024 (https://www.britannica.com/event/World-War-I, accessed 6 March 2024); Jeffrey Fear, 'German Capitalism', in Thomas K. McCraw (ed.), *Creating Modern Capitalism: How Entrepreneurs, Companies, and Countries Triumphed in Three Industrial Revolutions* (Cambridge, MA and London: Harvard University Press, 1997), pp. 133–82.

45 Barbara D. Metcalf and Thomas R. Metcalf, *A Concise History of Modern India*, 3rd edition (Cambridge: Cambridge University Press, 2012), p. 163.

46 'His Highness the Maharaja's Contribution towards the war fund', General Finance, Mysore, 1914–15, File No. 33–14, S. Nos. 3–5, KSA-DIGITIZED (https://archives.karnataka.gov.in/home/viewdocument?doc_id=RGVlcGFrMTk2NDI=&doc_location=RGVlcGFrMQ==); 'List showing the contribution to the war in the shape of men, money & material', General Miscellaneous, Mysore, 1916, File No. 233–1916, S. Nos. 1–22, KSA-DIGITIZED (https://archives.karnataka.gov.in/home/viewdocument?doc_id=RGVlcGFrMjQyODA=&doc_location=RGVlcGFrMQ==).

47 'Statement showing the contribution in men, money and material made by persons or Associations in the Mysore State in connection with the present European War', KSA-MV-VOL, p. 118; 'List showing the contributions by the Mysore Military Department to the WAR [sic]', KSA-MV-VOL, pp. 134–5.

48 'Statement showing the names of persons Societies etc., who have paid or collected Rs. 100 and above towards the Mysore Imperial Service Lancers War Fund', KSA-MV-VOL, pp. 119–22.

49 'Statement showing the [articles] of Comforts received as from Gift [sic]', KSA-MV-VOL, pp. 123–5.

50 'Kadur District: Contributions to the War', KSA-MV-VOL, pp. 128–9.

51 Visvesvaraya to Mirza M. Ismail (Officiating Private Secretary to the Maharaja), 26 April 1916, G.M. 1915, [File] 496 of 15, [S. Nos.] 1–5, 6, KSA-MV-VOL, pp. 83–4.

52 Visvesvaraya to Mirza M. Ismail, 27 June 1916, D.O. No. 4118/En. File, KSA-MV-VOL, p. 96; Lt. Col. Frank Johnson, Commanding Officer, 2/6th Batallion, Royal Sussex Regiment, to Headquarters, Territorial Infantry Brigade, Bangalore, 31 July 1916, KSA-MV-VOL, pp. 99–100.

53 'Statement showing the names of persons Societies etc., who have paid or collected Rs. 100 and above towards the Mysore Imperial Service Lancers War Fund', KSA-MV-VOL, pp. 119–22, here p. 119.

54 'His Highness the Maharaja's Contribution towards the war fund', KSA-DIGITIZED (file cited above).

55 'Speech at St. John Ambulance Association Meeting', 19 January 1916, MV-SPEECHES-VOL, pp. 309–13; 'Speech at the War

Loan Meeting', MV-SPEECHES-VOL, pp. 409–13 (quoted text from pp. 410–11).

56 Bjørn Hettne, *The Political Economy of Indirect Rule: Mysore 1881–1947* (New Delhi: Ambika Publications, 1978), p. 79; Secretary, General Department, Mysore government, to the First Assistant to the Mysore Resident, undated [1916?], KSA-MV-VOL, pp. 90–1 (quoted text from p. 90).

57 See the discussion below on the delegation of traders sent to Japan by Mysore.

58 See below.

59 'Address to the Mysore Economic Conference', 5 June 1917, MV-SPEECHES-VOL, pp. 440–52, here p. 445 (quoted text from this source); H.V. Cobb (Mysore Resident) to British Consulate, Japan (undated letter, typed copy) in 'Political activities of the first batch of the Mysore Industrial and Commercial Mission in Japan; proposal to send a second batch vetoed; discouragement of Japanese activities in Mysore State', Mysore Residency File 17 of 1917, APAC: IOR/R/2/Box 34/339.

60 Correspondence, including drafts and copies, in 'Political activities of the first batch of the Mysore Industrial and Commercial Mission in Japan; proposal to send a second batch vetoed; discouragement of Japanese activities in Mysore State', Mysore Residency File 17 of 1917, APAC: IOR/R/2/Box 34/339.

61 'Visit to Bangalore of Sasaichi Takase a Japanese suspect; growing connection between Mysore State and Japanese; employment by Sirdar Kantaraj Urs of two Japanese servants', Mysore Residency File 19 of 1917, APAC: IOR/R/2/Box 34/340.

62 D.O. No. 8-C, [H.V. Cobb, Mysore Resident] to Sir John B. Wood, Foreign and Political Department, Government of India, Delhi, 23 January 1918 (copy), in 'Visit to Bangalore . . . ', APAC: IOR/R/2/Box 34/340, Folio 29.

63 D.O. No. 171-C, unidentified sender to Sir C.R. Cleveland, Criminal Intelligence Office, Simla, 22 October 1917 (copy), in 'Visit to Bangalore . . . ', APAC: IOR/R/2/Box 34/340, Folios 26–7.

64 It is not clear whether this is supposed to have occurred during or after Visvesvaraya's tenure as dewan. D.O. No. 271-C, unidentified

sender to Lt.- Col. R.E. Holland, 28 October 1919, in 'Visit to Bangalore . . . ', APAC: IOR/R/2/Box 34/340, Folio 36.

65 C.R. Cleveland, Criminal Intelligence Office, Simla, to H.V. Cobb, 9 October 1917, in 'Visit to Bangalore . . . ', APAC: IOR/R/2/Box 34/340, Folio 10.

66 See for instance Arpita Mathur, 'India-Japan Relations: Drivers, Trends and Prospects', S. Rajaratnam School of International Studies Monograph No. 23 (2012), p. 6.

67 'Confidential note by Political Secretary (Sir John Wood) on Mysore Affairs' [30 July 1917], Foreign and Political Department [Government of India], 'Confidential—B.: Internal Branch, Section A.', No. 6 of 1918, APAC: IOR/R/1/1/1160 (quoted text from paras 1, 2, and 7).

68 Ibid., para 3.

69 Ibid., para 4.

70 Ibid., para 2.

71 Evan Maconochie, *Life in the Indian Civil Service* (London: Chapman and Hall, 1926), Chapter 13 (mention of the Maharaja's daily routine is made on p. 138).

72 Various files in KSA-DIGITIZED.

73 Quoted in K. Subba Rao, *Revived Memories*, pp. 343–4.

74 Hettne, *Political Economy of Indirect Rule*, pp. 80–1.

75 Sumit Sarkar, *Modern India: 1885–1947* (Delhi: Pearson, 2014), pp. 136–7; James Manor,'Princely Mysore before the Storm: The State-Level Political System of India's Model State 1920–1936', *Modern Asian Studies* 9, no. 1 (1975): 31–58, here pp. 38–9; 'Kantaraj Urs', IBD 1915, p. 218; Hettne, *Political Economy of Indirect Rule*, pp. 79–80 and 142–5.

76 In one case, an applicant for an engineering scholarship did not fulfil the eligibility criteria, but Visvesvaraya, noting that the student was from a disadvantaged background, endorsed the granting of a scholarship, albeit reduced in value, to the student as a special case. However, such instances only reinforced the dynamic of a hereditary elite using its discretion to bestow a favour on the disadvantaged. Proposals 'Submitted to His Highness' by M. Visvesvaraya, 9 September 1913 (and other documents) in 'Engineering Scholarships of 1913–14',

Education, Mysore, 1913–14, File No. 18–13, S. Nos. 1, 2, 4, 9–[?], KSA-DIGITIZED (https://archives.karnataka.gov.in/home/viewdocument?doc_id=RGVlcGFrMTEwMDM0&doc_location=RGVlcGFrMQ==).

77 Visvesvaraya, *Memoirs*, p. 87.

78 See Parimala V. Rao, 'Colonial State as "New Manu"? Explorations in Education Policies in Relation to Dalit and Low-Caste Education in the Nineteenth-Century India', *Contemporary Education Dialogue* 16, 1 (2019): 84–107.

79 See for instance his speech at the inaugural edition of the Mysore Civic and Social Conference, during which he said: 'The caste system, which is responsible for a great many of our disabilities, has left an appreciable portion of the population in a state of permanent degradation.''Address to the Civic and Social Conference', 3 June 1917, MV-SPEECHES-VOL, pp. 429–39, here p. 432.

80 A member of his clerical staff recalled: 'When the officials on Mr. Visvesvaraya's staff went out with him on tour either to Mysore or to any other camp, he was the first Dewan to change the habit till then prevailling of discrimination between members of one community and another in the matter of serving meals.' Subbarayappa, 'He Stood by Merit', pp. 158–9.

81 Visvesvaraya, *Memoirs*, p. 87.

82 See Aparajith Ramnath, *The Birth of an Indian Profession: Engineers, Industry, and the State, 1900–47* (Delhi: Oxford University Press, 2017), *passim*.

83 See Ajantha Subramanian, *The Caste of Merit: Engineering Education in India* (Cambridge, MA and London: Harvard University Press, 2019).

84 Hettne, *Political Economy of Indirect Rule,* p. 80; V.S. Narayana Rao, *Mokshagundam Visvesvaraya: His Life and Work* (Mysore: Geetha Book House, 1973), p. 134.

85 Quoted in Hettne, *Political Economy of Indirect Rule*, p. 80.

86 Narayana Rao, *Mokshagundam Visvesvaraya,* pp. 135–9. Mirza was Huzur Secretary from 1913–23. See Mirza Ismail, *My Public Life* (London: George Allen and Unwin, 1954), p. 19.

87 Copy of letter, Visvesvaraya to Mirza Ismail, 5 January 1917, in Visvesvaraya Papers, NMML, microfilm Reel 1. The letter is also excerpted in Sitaramiah, *M. Visvesvaraya*, Appendix II, here p. 130.
88 Narayana Rao, *Mokshagundam Visvesvaraya*, pp. 135–9.
89 M. Visvesvaraya, 'Suggested Reforms in the Mysore Administration', 11 July 1917 (Dewan's Office), KSA-MV-VOL, pp. 192–208. The memo as printed also contains the maharaja's comments as noted by Mirza Ismail, the Huzur Secretary, on 12 August 1917.
90 Ibid. Quotations from Visvesvaraya are from paras 8, 12, 5, 21, 26, and *passim* (in the case of 'efficient' and 'efficiency'). The maharaja's comments quoted here appear alongside paras 24, 26 and 27.
91 Hettne, *Political Economy of Indirect Rule*, pp. 144–5.
92 *Report of the Committee Appointed to Consider Steps Necessary for the Adequate Representation of Communities in the Public Service [1919]*, title and para 3. The version consulted is from the library (digitized) of the Institute for Social and Economic Change, Bengaluru. Hereafter cited as Miller Committee Report. On Miller's position, see MAR 1917–18, Appendix I, p. i.
93 Miller Committee Report, 'Summary of Committees [sic] Recommendations', para 1.
94 Hettne, *Political Economy of Indirect Rule*, p. 146.
95 Miller Committee Report, para 8. See also the criticism in Oliver Mendelsohn and Marika Vicziany, *The Untouchables: Subordination, poverty and the state in modern India* (Cambridge: Cambridge University Press, 1998), p. 129.
96 Miller Committee Report, para 2.
97 Ibid., para 6.
98 See Hettne, *Political Economy of Indirect Rule*, pp. 80–2.
99 Narayana Rao, *Mokshagundam Visvesvaraya*, Chapter 12. The maharaja's letter is quoted on p. 144. See also Hettne, *Political Economy of Indirect Rule*, pp. 80–2.
100 Narayana Rao, *Mokshagundam Visvesvaraya*, p. 145; Visvesvaraya, *Memoirs*, pp. 87–90.
101 Quoted in Visvesvaraya, *Memoirs*, pp. 89–90.

102 'influenza pandemic of 1918–19', *Encyclopedia Britannica*, 3 July 2023 (https://www.britannica.com/event/influenza-pandemic-of-1918-1919, accessed 1 October 2023); T.V. Sekher, 'Public health administration in princely Mysore: tackling the influenza pandemic of 1918', in Waltraud Ernst and Biswamoy Pati (eds.), *India's Princely States: People, princes and colonialism* (Delhi: Primus, 2010), pp. 194–211, here p. 199; 'Measures to be adopted for affording relief to persons suffering from Influenza in the cities of Bangalore & Mysore', Medical Department, Mysore, 1918, File No. 56, S. Nos. 127–8, KSA-DIGITIZED (https://archives.karnataka.gov.in/home/viewdocument?doc_id=RGVlcGFrMzIzNDI=&doc_location=RGVlcGFrMQ==). The quoted text is from the last of these sources.

103 This account is primarily based on Sekher, 'Public health administration', though I have also been through relevant official correspondence and government files via KSA-DIGITIZED, especially: 'Measures to be adopted for affording relief to persons suffering from Influenza in the cities of Bangalore & Mysore', Medical Department, Mysore, 1918, File No. 56, S. Nos. 127–8 (https://archives.karnataka.gov.in/home/viewdocument?doc_id=RGVlcGFrMzIzNDI=&doc_location=RGVlcGFrMQ==); 'Measures to deal with the epidemic of Influenza in the Bangalore City', Medical Department, Mysore, 1918, File No. 56–18, S. Nos. 125 and 126 (https://archives.karnataka.gov.in/home/viewdocument?doc_id=RGVlcGFrMzIzNDE=&doc_location=RGVlcGFrMQ==); 'Note on the organisation of relief measures in the Mysore City in connection with Influenza', Medical Department, Mysore, 1918–19, File No. 56–18, S. Nos. 145–6, (https://archives.karnataka.gov.in/home/viewdocument?doc_id=RGVlcGFrMzIzNTE=&doc_location=RGVlcGFrMQ==).

104 Sekher, 'Public health administration', esp. pp. 204 and 197.

105 'Advance sanctioned for Samputikarana Jvara japam and Santarpane on the Chamundi Hill at Mysore to allay the ravages of Influenza', Muzrai Department, Mysore, 1918–19, File No. 283, S. Nos. 1–8, KSA-DIGITIZED (https://archives.karnataka.gov.in/home/viewdocument?doc_id=RGVlcGFrMTM5MjQ2&doc_location=RGVlcGFrMQ==). The quoted text is from Order No.

E/Muz., Camp Mysore, 22 October 1918 ('Fair draft'), in the above file.

106 Sekher, 'Public health administration'; 'D.O. Correspondence regarding the influenza (Reports submitted to His Highness the Maharaja of Mysore)', Medical Department, Mysore, 1918, File No. 56–18, S. No. 158, KSA-DIGITIZED (https://archives.karnataka.gov.in/home/viewdocument?doc_id=RGVlcGFrMzIzNDY=&doc_location=RGVlcGFrMQ==).

107 Sekher, 'Public health administration', p. 206.

108 See preceding chapters.

14. Setting Sail

1 In his resignation letter written a year previously, he had told the maharaja that he would remain available to consult on the Krishnarajasagara project. Visvesvaraya to Krishnaraja IV, 16 November 1917, reproduced in V. Sitaramiah, *M. Visvesvaraya* (New Delhi: Ministry of Information and Broadcasting, Government of India, 1971), Appendix II, here pp. 132–3.

2 M. Visvesvaraya, *Memoirs of My Working Life* (Bangalore: M. Visvesvaraya, 1951), pp. 123–4; Hiralal Lallubhai Kaji, *Life and Speeches of Sir Vithaldas Thackersey* (Bombay: D.B. Taraporevala Sons & Co., 1934), pp. 258–9; Premlila V. Thackersey, 'A Versatile Genius', in CENT-VOL, pp. 59–65, here pp. 61–2 (quoted text from this source).

3 'The Relation Between [India] and Japan', speech by M. Visvesvaraya at Marquis Okuma's reception, in *Journal of the Indo-Japanese Association*, No. 26 (1919): 52–5, here p. 53.

4 'Emperors and Empresses Regnant of Japan', *Encyclopedia Britannica*, 1 May 2019 (https://www.britannica.com/topic/Emperors-and-Empresses-Regnant-of-Japan-1812634, accessed 6 March 2024).

5 Jeffrey P. Bayliss, review of *World War I and the Triumph of a New Japan, 1919–1930: Studies in the Social and Cultural History of Modern Warfare*, by Frederick R. Dickinson, *Pacific Affairs* 88, no. 2 (2015): 319–21. See also Jeffrey R. Bernstein, 'Japanese Capitalism', in Thomas K. McCraw (ed.), *Creating*

Modern Capitalism: How Entrepreneurs, Companies, and Countries Triumphed in Three Industrial Revolutions (Cambridge, MA and London: Harvard University Press, 1997), pp. 441–89.

6 Visvesvaraya, *Memoirs*, p. 123.

7 'The Relation Between [India] and Japan', speech by M. Visvesvaraya, p. 53. On British intelligence and Indians in Japan, see the discussion in Chapter 13 above.

8 'A Brief History of the Indo-Japanese Association', in *The Indo-Japanese Business Directory: 1938–39* (Tokyo: Indo-Japanese Association [1938?]), pp. 45–8, here p. 45. On Okuma, see 'Ōkuma Shigenobu', *Encyclopedia Britannica*, 29 March 2024 (https://www.britannica.com/biography/Okuma-Shigenobu, accessed 13 April 2024).

9 See 'A Brief History', p. 45; 'Japan and British Rule: Indo-Japanese Association', TOI, 29 November 1906, p. 9; 'The Indo-Japanese Association', TOI, 9 December 1909, p. 6; 'Indo-Japanese Society', TOI, 26 February 1914, p. 14. On Pan-Asianism, see for instance Christopher W.A. Szpilman and Sven Saaler, 'Pan-Asianism as an Ideal of Asian Identity and Solidarity, 1850-Present', *Asia-Pacific Journal: Japan Focus*, 9, 17 (25 April 2011), consulted at https://apjjf.org/2011/9/17/Christopher-W.-A.-Szpilman/3519/article.html (accessed 14 April 2024); report of lecture by Christine Shimizu on 'Artistic and cultural links between India and Japan (circa 1890–1940)', 12 December 2018, website of The Society of Friends of the Cernuschi Museum (https://amis-musee-cernuschi.org/en/les-liens-artistiques-et-culturels-entre-linde-et-le-japon-vers-1890-1940-2/, accessed 14 April 2024); Arpita Mathur, 'India-Japan Relations: Drivers, Trends and Prospects', S. Rajaratnam School of International Studies Monograph No. 23 (2012), Chapter 1.

10 M. Visvesvaraya, *Reconstructing India* (London: P.S. King & Son, Ltd., 1920), pp. 79–83, 128–33, 162–5, 173–4, 180–1, 282–3.

11 'The Relation Between [India] and Japan', speech by M. Visvesvaraya, pp. 53–4. On Takakusu, see Iwagami Kazunori and Paride Stortin, 'Takakusu Junjirō (1866–1945): Buddhist Idealist, Scholar and Educator', in H. Cortazzi (ed.), *Britain & Japan: Biographical Portraits*, Volume X (n.p.: Amsterdam University

Press, 2016), pp. 680–692 (excerpt consulted via https://www.cambridge.org/core/books/abs/britain-japan-biographical-portraits-vol-x/takakusu-junjiro-18661945-buddhist-idealist-scholar-and-educator/0E09F7BECB66AC396D76FF2667696A9E, accessed 13 April 2024).

12 Photograph in T.R. Anantharamu, *Saadhakana Hejjegalu: Bharataratna Sir M. Visvesvaraya Avara Baduku-Saadhane* (Bengaluru: Navakarnataka Publishers, 2018 [2010]), p. 28. The photograph also appears in CENT-VOL, as a plate between pp. 128 and 129.

13 'The Relation Between [India] and Japan', speech by M. Visvesvaraya.

14 Visvesvaraya, *Memoirs*, pp. 123–4; Thomas K. McCraw and Richard S. Tedlow, 'Henry Ford, Alfred Sloan, and the Three Phases of Marketing', in Thomas K. McCraw (ed.), *Creating Modern Capitalism: How Entrepreneurs, Companies, and Countries Triumphed in Three Industrial Revolutions* (Cambridge, MA and London: Harvard University Press, 1997), pp. 266–300, here pp. 273–4.

15 Visvesvaraya, *Memoirs*, pp. 124–5.

16 Pandri Nath, *Mokshagundam Visvesvaraya: Life and Work* (Bombay: Bharatiya Vidya Bhavan, 1987), p. 87.

17 Quoted in Visvesvaraya, *Memoirs*, p. 125.

18 Visvesvaraya, *Memoirs*, p. 125.

19 William E. Leuchtenberg, *Herbert Hoover*, Kindle Edition (New York: Times Books, n.d. [2009]), Chapters 1–3; 'Herbert Hoover', *Encyclopedia Britannica*, 20 February 2024 (https://www.britannica.com/biography/Herbert-Hoover, accessed 6 March 2024).

20 Visvesvaraya, *Memoirs*, p. 126 (including the quote from Hoover).

21 Barbara D. Metcalf and Thomas R. Metcalf, *A Concise History of Modern India*, 3rd edition (Cambridge: Cambridge University Press, 2012), Chapter 6 (quoted text from p. 167).

22 'Indian Reforms. Favourable British Opinion. Attitude of Political Parties', TOI, 29 November 1919, p. 11. On dyarchy, see Metcalf and Metcalf, *A Concise History of Modern India*, Chapter 6. On Visvesvaraya's view of the reforms, see also Visvesvaraya,

Reconstructing India, pp. 11–12. On Vithaldas's return to Bombay, see Kaji, *Life and Speeches of Sir Vithaldas Thackersey*, pp. 265–6.

23 Visvesvaraya, *Memoirs*, p. 60; Edwin S. Montagu, *An Indian Diary* (ed. Venetia Montagu) (London: William Heinemann Ltd., 1930), p. 124.

24 'The Future of India. Aga Khan's Tribute to Mr. Montagu. A Complimentary Dinner', *Cambridge Independent Press*, 26 December 1919, p. 10; 'Sankaran Nair, Hon'ble Justice Sir Chetur', IBD 1915, pp. 378–9; 'Aga Khan, His Highness Aga Sulthan Mohammad Shah', IBD 1915, pp. 5–6; 'Mancherjee Merwanjee Bhownaggree', 'Making Britain', website of the Open University (https://www.open.ac.uk/researchprojects/makingbritain/content/mancherjee-merwanjee-bhownaggree, accessed 16 June 2023).

25 Norman Cornthwaite Nicholson, 'H.G. Wells', *Encyclopedia Britannica*, 7 April 2024 (https://www.britannica.com/biography/H-G-Wells, accessed 14 April 2024). On Wells's interest in Indian affairs, see 'H.G. Wells', 'Making Britain', website of the Open University (https://www5.open.ac.uk/research-projects/making-britain/content/h-g-wells, accessed 14 April 2024).

26 Visvesvaraya, *Memoirs*, p. 126. On the India Office Library, see Rajeshwari Datta, 'The India Office Library: Its History, Resources, and Functions', *The Library Quarterly: Information, Community, Policy* 36, no. 2 (1966): 99–148. On the architecture of the India Office, see 'Exterior of India Office (now the Foreign and Commonwealth Office) from beside Clive Steps, Whitehall', photo and description by Jacqueline Banerjee, 2006, at *The Victorian Web* (https://victorianweb.org/art/architecture/classical/1b.html, accessed 14 April 2024).

27 Dinyar Patel, *Naoroji: Pioneer of Indian Nationalism* (Cambridge, MA: Harvard University Press, 2020), pp. 56 and 138, and *passim.*

28 Visvesvaraya's 'Form of Nomination' to the National Liberal Club, 15 September 1908; G.K. Gokhale to Secretary, National Liberal Club, 2 August 1908. Courtesy the archives of the National Liberal Club, London.

29 The India Office was located near the Clive Steps in St James' Park: see 'Exterior of India Office'.

30 M. Visvesvaraya, *Reconstructing India* (London: P.S. King & Son, Ltd., 1920).
31 Ibid., p. 2.
32 'Contents', ibid., pp. vii–viii.
33 Ibid., Chapters III and V.
34 Ibid., Chapter III (esp. p. 54).
35 Ibid., Chapters VI and VIII (quoted text from p. 141).
36 Ibid., Chapter VII (quoted text from p. 133).
37 Ibid., Chapter IX (quoted text from p. 167 and p. 161).
38 Ibid., Chapter XI (quoted text from p. 200).
39 Ibid., Chapter X.
40 Ibid., Chapter XIV, *passim.* (quoted text from pp. 266–7).
41 Ibid., Chapter XIII (quoted text from pp. 237, 239 and 243).
42 Ibid., Chapter XIII (quoted text from pp. 246 and 250).
43 Ibid., Chapter XIII (quoted text from pp. 252 and 254).
44 Ibid., pp. 280 and 284–5.
45 Ibid., pp. 288 and 297–8.
46 Ibid., p. 273.
47 Ibid., p. vi.
48 *Report of the Indian Fiscal Commission 1921–22* (Simla: Superintendent, Government Central Press, 1922); 'Brief History', page on the website of the Reserve Bank of India (https://rbi.org.in/history/Brief_History.html, accessed 8 October 2023).
49 Review in 'Books of the Moment', *Pall Mall Gazette*, 7 January 1921, p. 8; review in *The Western Mail,* 24 February 1921, p. 31.
50 Review in *The Queenslander*, 5 February 1921, p. 3.
51 'The Clubman', 'A Clubman's Notebook', *Pall Mall Gazette,* 23 October 1920, p. 3.
52 '"Reconstructing India"', TOI, 28 October 1920, p. 8.
53 K.G. Limaye, 'The New Era', *The Servant of India*, 16 December 1920, pp. 546–8. On K.G. Limaye and the *Dnyanprakash*, see J. Natarajan, *History of Indian Journalism: Part II of the Report of the Press Commission* (Publications Division, Government of India: 2017 [1955]), pp. 71 and 148.
54 V.G. Kale, 'Economic Reconstruction in India', *Servant of India*, 3 February 1921, pp. 4–5. On Kale's position at Fergusson College,

see R.P. Paranjpye, 'Fergusson College', in P.M. Limaye (author/compiler), *The History of the Deccan Education Society (1880–1935)* (Poona: A.V. Patwardhan/Aryabhushan Press, 1935), Part II, pp. 1–20.

55 Visvesvaraya, *Memoirs*, p. 126; George Buchanan, 'The Ports of India: Their Administration and Development', *Journal of the Royal Society of Arts* 68, 3522 (1920): 430–41; George Buchanan, 'The Ports of India: Their Administration and Development (Continued)', *Journal of the Royal Society of Arts* 68, 3523 (1920): 445–56.

56 'Farewell to Lord Sinha. Beginning a New Era in India', *The Times Weekly Edition*, 17 September 1920; 'Satyendra Prassano [sic] Sinha, 1st Baron Sinha of Raipur', *Encyclopedia Britannica*, 2 March 2024 (https://www.britannica.com/biography/Satyendra-Prassano-Sinha-1st-Baron-Sinha-of-Raipur, accessed 6 March 2024).

57 Visvesvaraya, *Memoirs*, p. 126.

58 In 1924, for example, only three of the nine members of the Secretary of State's Council were Indians (going by names). See IOL 1924, p. 1.

59 'After the publication of "Reconstructing India" I returned to Bombay,' writes Visvesvaraya in his *Memoirs*, p. 126. *Reconstructing India* was probably published in October/November 1920: Visvesvaraya's Preface to the book (pp. v–vi) is dated 10 October 1920.

60 Diary entry dated 27 July 1918, in extracts from Visvesvaraya's diary (photocopies) kindly shared with me by Sheshadri Mokshagundam.

61 Shakuntala Krishnamurthy, 'Sir M.—An Inside View', in CENT-VOL, pp. 280–92, here p. 284. This source indicates that Visvesvaraya had the use of this Bombay residence from around the 1890s.

62 N.N. Iengar, 'Man of Transparent Sincerety [sic]', in CENT-VOL, pp. 146–7, here p. 146. Visvesvaraya's correspondence at various points in time has his Bombay address as 3 Warden Road and 46F Warden Road. It is possible that the street numbers were changed.

63 On Visvesvaraya's pension from the Bombay government, see Chapter 6 above. On his two pensions, see for instance Pandri Nath, *Mokshagundam Visvesvaraya: Life and Work* (Bombay: Bharatiya Vidya Bhavan, 1987), p. 112.

64 Visvesvaraya, *Memoirs*, chs. XIII–XVI.

65 'Minister of Education: Hon. Mr. Paranjpye Entertained', TOI, 27 January 1921, p. 10; 'Liberals at Poona: Entertained by Students', TOI, 14 December 1920, p. 10; 'Non-Co-operation: The Liberal Campaign', TOI, 15 November 1920, p. 10; 'Bombay Council: Mr. Paranjpye's Candidature', TOI, 16 July 1920, p. 10; Limaye, *History of the Deccan Education Society*, Part I, pp. 184–5; and M.V. Bhide's recollections in Limaye, *History of the Deccan Education Society*, Part II, pp. 147–50.

66 'Bombay Council: Mr. Paranjpye's Candidature', TOI, 16 July 1920, p. 10.

67 That the committee was set up by Paranjpye is a circumstantial inference, but it is also implicitly mentioned in Visvesvaraya, *Memoirs*, p. 107. See also R.P. Paranjpye (Secretariat, Bombay government) to M. Visvesvaraya, 8 April 1921, R.P. Paranjpye Papers, NMML, suggesting the addition of a member to the committee.

68 Visvesvaraya records that he once asked Paranjpye for the use of the hall in Fergusson College for a public meeting in connection with his duties as an irrigation engineer. Visvesvaraya, *Memoirs*, p. 10.

69 E.g. the Clibborn Committee (which reported its findings in 1903), and the two-member Atkinson-Dawson Committee (1912). See 'Majority Report', in *Technical and Industrial Education in the Bombay Presidency: Final Report of the Committee appointed by Government, 1921–22* (Bombay: Government Central Press, 1923), pp. 1–72, here paras 9–10.

70 'Majority Report', para 14.

71 'Majority Report,' paras 15, 130; 'Minority Report,' in *Technical and Industrial Education in the Bombay Presidency*, pp. 73–163, here para 142.

72 Appendix L: 'Extracts from Minutes of Proceedings of the Committee', in *Technical and Industrial Education in the Bombay*

Presidency, pp. 203–48. The 'Interim Report' is reproduced as Appendix C, in ibid., pp. 164–9.

73 'Minority Report,' paras 34, 43, 52, 60, 71, and 83.

74 'Minority Report,' Introduction, para 4.

75 'Majority Report', paras 30 and 83; 'Minority Report', Introduction, para 3.

76 'Majority Report', para 130.

77 'Minority Report', Introduction, para 5.

78 Ibid., Chapter IX (quoted text from para 33).

79 Visvesvaraya had progressive, albeit paternalistic, views on gender roles by the standards of his time. He was an advocate for later marriages, widow remarriage, the use of birth control, and the creation of a public sphere that was not confined to men. Among his close associates were key figures in the promotion of university education for women. His friend Vithaldas Thackersey provided financial support to what became the S.N.D.T. Indian Women's University, promoted by the reformer D.K. Karve. Another friend, R.P. Paranjpye, became the first vice-chancellor. Visvesvaraya delivered the convocation address in 1940. See: [M. Visvesvaraya], 'Address to the Civic and Social Conference', Mysore city, 3 June 1917, MV-SPEECHES-VOL, pp. 429–39; intervention by [Anasuya] Kale in debate on birth control, *All-India Women's Conference: Tenth Session: Trivandrum: December 25, 1935 to January 4, 1936* (Trivandrum: Superintendent, Government Press, 1936), p. 90; 'The Bangalore City and its Future', Visvesvaraya's speech at the Bangalore Literary Union, 20 May 1953, reproduced in untitled souvenir on Visvesvaraya (Bengaluru: Century Club, 2017), pp. 7–25, here p. 20; Kaji, *Life and Speeches of Sir Vithaldas Thackersey*, pp. 196–9; 'Should Woman Earn and Share Financial Responsibility? Sir M. Visvesvarayya's Address At 24th Convocation of Indian Women's University', *Bombay Chronicle*, 1 July 1940.

80 'Majority Report', para 98.

81 Ibid., para 127.

82 'Minority Report', paras 46 and 136 (including quoted text).

83 'Majority Report', paras 36–39 and 126 (including quoted text).

84 See for instance Headrick, Daniel R. Headrick, *The Tentacles of Progress: Technology transfer in the age of imperialism, 1850–1940*

(New York and Oxford: Oxford University Press, 1988), Chapter 9; Aparajith Ramnath, 'Breaking Free: Technical Education Policy in India Immediately before and after Independence', MSc thesis, University of Oxford (2007); Aparajith Ramnath, *The Birth of an Indian Profession: Engineers, Industry, and the State, 1900–47* (Delhi: Oxford University Press, 2017).

85 Visvesvaraya, *Memoirs*, pp. 107–8.

86 See Visvesvaraya's Presidential Address in Indian Economic Association, *Proceedings of the Seventh Indian Economic Conference, Bombay: January 22nd, 23rd, 24th and 25th, 1924* (Bombay: H.L. Kaji, Secretary, Seventh Indian Economic Conference, 1924), pp. 1–10, here p. 4.

87 Visvesvaraya, *Memoirs*, pp. 108–9; Ministry of Education, *Scientific Institutions and Societies in India*, Publication No. 69 (Delhi: Manager of Publications, [1949]), pp. 144–7; 'Scheme for a Department of Technology in Bombay: University Committee's Report: Three Years' Course to Include Textile and Industrial Chemistry', TOI, 9 November 1931, p. 10; 'Technological Education in Bombay', TOI, 12 October 1932, p. 8; 'Chemical Technology: Bombay University's New Department: Scheme Takes Shape', TOI, 3 November 1932, p. 14; 'Bombay's New Department of Education: Governor Opens Technology Branch: Unique Event in History of University', TOI, 16 November 1933, p. 10.

88 M. Visvesvaraya, 'Scientific Institutions and Scientists', Presidential Address, Indian Science Congress, 1923, in *The Shaping of Indian Science: Indian Science Congress Association Presidential Addresses: Vol I: 1914–1947* (Hyderabad: Universities Press, 2003), pp. 121–38.

89 J.L. Simonsen, Presidential Address, Indian Science Congress, 2 January 1928, reproduced under the title 'Indian Science Congress', *Current Science* 74, 5 (10 March 1998): 480–85; David Arnold, *Science, Technology and Medicine in Colonial India* (Cambridge: Cambridge University Press, 2000), pp. 161–2.

90 Visvesvaraya, 'Scientific Institutions and Scientists', pp. 121–2.

91 Although, as David Arnold argues, the Science Congress did eventually help foster a conception of 'national science' as opposed

to 'colonial science'. Arnold, *Science, Technology and Medicine in Colonial India*, p. 162.

92 Visvesvaraya, 'Scientific Institutions and Scientists' (quoted text from p. 127).

93 Ibid. (quoted text from pp. 128 and 132).

94 Ibid., p. 129.

95 See V.V. Krishna, 'Organisation of Industrial Research: The Early History of CSIR, 1934-47', in Roy MacLeod and Deepak Kumar (eds.), *Technology and the Raj: Western Technology and Technical Transfers to India 1700–1947* (New Delhi, Thousand Oaks, and London: Sage, 1995), pp. 289–323.

96 Visvesvaraya, 'Scientific Institutions and Scientists', pp. 129–32 (quoted phrase on p. 131).

97 Ibid. (quoted text from p. 132).

15. An Engineer among the Politicians

1 John F. Riddick, *The History of British India: A Chronology* (Westport, CT: Praeger, 2006), pp. 96 and 100; Barbara D. Metcalf and Thomas R. Metcalf, *A Concise History of Modern India*, 3rd edition (Cambridge: Cambridge University Press, 2012), Chapters 5–6.

2 Peter C. Oliver, '"Dominion status": History, framework and context', *International Journal of Constitutional Law* 17, no. 4 (2019): 1173–91, here p. 1175. See also Manfred Nathan, 'Dominion Status', *Transactions of the Grotius Society* 8 (1922): 117–32, here p. 117, for a list of British dominions as of 1922.

3 Oliver, '"Dominion status"', *passim*.

4 M. Visvesvaraya, *Reconstructing India* (London: P.S. King & Son, Ltd., 1920), Chapter III, esp. p. 54.

5 'Madan Mohan Malaviya', *Encyclopedia Britannica*, 21 December 2020 (https://www.britannica.com/biography/Madan-Mohan-Malaviya, accessed 19 January 2021); 'Malavya [sic], Hon'ble Pandit Madan Mohan', IBD 1915, pp. 263–4.

6 M. Visvesvaraya, 'Pandit Madan Mohan Malaviya: Some Personal Reminiscences'. This is a printed article (no bibliographical details available) in Visvesvaraya Papers, NMML, microfilm Reel 8. That

Visvesvaraya was on leave at the time of the Congress session is confirmed by 'Note No. 1727, dated 30th December 1910, from the Dewan to His Highness the Maharaja', Item 20 in 'Section I. The Cauvery Reservoir Project (Mr. M. Visvesvaraya's Scheme)', in MV-PAPERS-IEI, Vol. 11.

7 Shiv Visvanathan, *Organizing for Science*: The Making of an Industrial Research Laboratory (Delhi: Oxford University Press, 1985), Chapter 3.

8 'Mukund Ramrao Jayakar', under 'Attendees', at the 'Conferencing the International' project website, University of Nottingham (https://www.nottingham.ac.uk/research/groups/conferencing-the-international/delegates/people.aspx?id=a6950a47-3898-46d1-bad0-8862141fc09e, accessed 3 June 2021).

9 C.P. Ramaswami Aiyer, 'Book Reviews: Jayakar's Autobiography', *The Sunday Standard*, 22 June 1958; 'Autobiography of a Moderate Nationalist', in 'Book Review Cuttings', *Hindustan Times,* 1 June 1958; and other cuttings in 'Press—opinion on M.R. Jayakar's autobiography The Story of My Life', M. R. Jayakar Papers, National Archives of India (digitized), Digital Identifier: PP_000000011045, accessed via https://indianculture.gov.in/archives/press-opinion-mr-jayakars-autobiography-story-my-life. On the Jallianwala Bagh enquiry committee, see also M.R. Jayakar, *The Story of My Life: Volume One: 1873–1922* (Bombay: Asia Publishing House, 1958), p. 277.

10 Jayakar, *The Story of My Life: Volume One*, pp. 173–4. The quoted text is from a diary entry of Jayakar's that he reproduces here. For his Thakurdwar address, see letters to M. Visvesvaraya in 'Important Correspondence – (i) With a [sic] Satyamurti, Jamnadas Mehta, Rajendra Prasad . . .', M.R. Jayakar Papers, Roll 00055, File No. 402 (Digital Identifier: PP_000000010433), NAI-DIGITIZED.

11 Jayakar, *The Story of My Life: Volume One*; M.R. Jayakar, *The Story of My Life: Volume Two: 1922–1925* (London: Asia Publishing House, 1959). See also the discussion below.

12 Sumit Sarkar, *Modern India: 1885–1947* (Delhi: Pearson, 2014), pp. 176–8; 'noncooperation movement', *Encyclopedia Britannica,* 16 November 2023 (https://www.britannica.com/event/

noncooperation-movement, accessed 6 March 2024); Metcalf and Metcalf, *A Concise History of Modern* India, Chapters 5 and 6; Ramachandra Guha, *Gandhi: the years that changed the world: 1914–1948* (Gurgaon: Allen Lane, 2018), Chapter 7; *Report of the Thirty-Sixth Indian National Congress held at Ahmedabad on the 27th and 28th December 1921* (Ahmedabad: Navjeevan press, 1922), p. 113.

13 Jayakar, *The Story of My Life: Volume One*, Chapter 8; M. Visvesvaraya, *Memoirs of My Working Life* (Bangalore: M. Visvesvaraya, 1951), p. 116.

14 *Report of the Thirty-Sixth Indian National Congress*, pp. 113–4 (including quoted text); 'civil disobedience', *Encyclopedia Britannica*, 25 February 2024 (https://www.britannica.com/topic/civil-disobedience, accessed 6 March 2024).

15 Jayakar, *The Story of My Life: Volume One*, pp. 496–503.

16 Ibid., pp. 518–25; 'Bombay Conference. An Official Report', TOI, 19 January 1922, p. 4.

17 See Chapter 3 above.

18 'Resolutions passed at the Representative Conference held in Bombay on the 14th and 15th January 1922', in 'Important Correspondence. M.R. Jayakar's Correspondence re: The Representative Conference [Malaviya Conference], 1922', M.R. Jayakar Papers, Roll 00196, File No. 1085 (Digital Identifier: PP_000000011082), NAI-DIGITIZED, Folios 2–3.

19 Ibid.; Jayakar, *The Story of My Life: Volume One*, pp. 527–8.

20 Jayakar, *The Story of My Life: Volume One*, pp. 527–8.

21 Ibid., pp. 541–600.

22 Visvesvaraya to Jayakar, 11 May 1922, in 'Important Correspondence. M.R. Jayakar's Correspondence re: The Representative Conference [Malaviya Conference], 1922', M.R. Jayakar Papers, Roll 00196, File No. 1085 (Digital Identifier: PP_000000011082), NAI-DIGITIZED, Folio 85.

23 'Our Readers' Views. A Failure' (N.V. Sarma, letter to the editor), TOI, 20 January 1922, p. 11.

24 Jayakar, *The Story of My Life: Volume Two*, p. 1.

25 'Dominion Status for India (Draft Scheme) (10-3-22)', typescript document in 'Draft scheme of Dominion status for India', M.R.

Jayakar Papers, Roll 000073, File No. 493 (Digital Identifier: PP_000000010519), NAI-DIGITIZED.

26 It bore the marks of Visvesvaraya's authorship in its general tenor and details like the frequent references to Canada and Japan. As we shall see below, the correspondence between Jayakar and Visvesvaraya also shows that it was the latter who prepared the scheme.

27 'Dominion Status for India (Draft Scheme)', para 1.

28 Ibid., para 2.

29 Ibid., *passim.* The quoted phrases are from the title of Section III (p. 24), and from para 1.

30 Ibid., para 2.

31 Ibid., para 4.

32 Ibid., para 6.

33 Ibid., para 9; see para 13 on the army.

34 Ibid., para 12.

35 Ibid., para 13.

36 Ibid., para 15.

37 Ibid., para 17.

38 Ibid., para 18.

39 Ibid., paras 19 and 20.

40 Ibid., paras 22–29.

41 Ibid., para 31.

42 Ibid., para 30.

43 Ibid., paras 35–6.

44 Visvesvaraya to Jayakar, 19 February 1924, in 'Important Correspondence . . . ', M.R. Jayakar Papers, Roll 00055, File No. 402 (Digital Identifier: PP_000000010433), NAI-DIGITIZED, Folios 344–5. See also Jayakar to Visvesvaraya, 16 February 1924, in ibid., Folio 339.

45 Jayakar, *The Story of My Life: Volume Two*, Chapter 2 and pp. 194 and 219–20.

46 Wilson to Jayakar (copy), 24 March 1924, in 'Important Correspondence . . .', M.R. Jayakar Papers, Roll 00055, File No. 402 (Digital Identifier: PP_000000010433), NAI-DIGITIZED, Folios 383–8.

47 Visvesvaraya to Jayakar, 30 March 1924, in 'Important Correspondence . . .', M.R. Jayakar Papers, Roll 00055, File No.

402 (Digital Identifier: PP_000000010433), NAI-DIGITIZED, Folios 392–3.

48 Jayakar, *The Story of My Life: Volume Two,* pp. 220 and 194.

49 Jayakar, *The Story of My Life: Volume Two*, Chapter 3; 'Ramsay MacDonald', *Encyclopedia Britannica*, n.d. (https://www.britannica.com/biography/Ramsay-MacDonald, accessed 3 June 2021). See also the copies of letters from Jayakar to Pole in 'Important Correspondence . . .', M.R. Jayakar Papers, Roll 00055, File No. 402 (Digital Identifier: PP_000000010433), NAI-DIGITIZED.

50 Metcalf and Metcalf, *A Concise History of Modern India*, Chapter 6; The Committee Appointed by The All Parties' Conference 1928, *The Nehru Report: An Anti-Separatist Manifesto* (New Delhi: Michiko & Panjathan, 1975 [1928]), Chapter I. The last of these sources is hereinafter cited as *Nehru Report.*

51 To give a few examples, the Nehru Report's aim was dominion status with a democratic government; it proposed a legislature at the centre composed of a Senate and a House of Representatives; it urged the development of an indigenously run army. *Nehru Report*, 'Introductory' chapter and Chapter VI. A significant difference was that the Nehru Report recommended universal adult franchise as opposed to one requiring literacy or the ownership of property. *Nehru Report*, p. 104; see also Maya Tudor, 'Explaining Democracy's Origins: Lessons from South Asia', *Comparative Politics* 45, 3 (2013): 253–72, here p. 267.

52 *Nehru Report*, Chapter I; ibid., p. 182 in section titled 'Supplementary Report'.

53 Balram Singh Pavadya, 'The Attitude of the Indian National Congress to Dominion Status, 1930–1947', *International Studies*, VI, 1 (1965): 285–309; Riddick, *History of British India*, pp. 109–11; Rohit De, 'Between Midnight and Republic: Theory and Practice of India's Dominion Status', *International Journal of Constitutional Law*, 17, 4 (2019): 1213–34; R.J. Moore, 'The Problem of Freedom with Unity: London's India Policy, 1917–47', in D.A. Low (ed.), *Congress and the Raj: Facets of the Indian Struggle 1917–47* (New Delhi and Oxford: Oxford University Press, 2004), pp. 375–403.

16. Critics, and Bhadravati Again

1 MAR 1917-18, Appendix I, p. i.

2 'A Mysore Letter. Finance', TOI, 4 April 1922, p. 8, cutting in MV-PAPERS-IEI, Vol. 15; Bjørn Hettne, *The Political Economy of Indirect Rule: Mysore 1881–1947* (New Delhi: Ambika Publications, 1978), pp. 280–1 and 69.

3 On Bhadravati, see for instance 'Mysore Assembly: The Dewan's Address', TOI, 7 October 1919, p. 10. On Kannambadi, see for instance 'E.D. II', 'Krishnarajasagara. A Giant Indian Reservoir', TOI, 6 Feb 1920, p. 18.

4 'A Mysore Letter. Finance', TOI, 4 April 1922, p. 8; 'Mysore Retrenchment: Committee's Recommendations', TOI, 17 August 1922, p. 8; 'Our Finances', *Mysore Chronicle*, 12 Mar 1922, cutting in MV-PAPERS-IEI, Vol. 15.

5 'A Mysore Letter. Finance', TOI, 4 April 1922.

6 D.V. Gundappa, 'Mysore Affairs. A Critical Survey. The New Regime', *The Hindu*, 15 April 1922, cutting in MV-PAPERS-IEI, Vol. 15.

7 'Special Finance Committee. A Review of the Interim Report', *Daily Post*, [22 June 1922], cutting in MV-PAPERS-IEI, Vol. 15.

8 Visvesvaraya's statement, reprinted under the title 'Mysore State Finance', *Mysore Chronicle* (Supplement), 16 July 1922, para 1. In MV-PAPERS-IEI, Vol. 15.

9 Ibid., para 2.

10 Ibid., paras 3, 7, 4.

11 Ibid., para 5.

12 Ibid., table in para 3 and *passim.*

13 Ibid., para 6.

14 Ibid., para 6.

15 'Sir M. Visveswarayya's Defence', *The Hindu*, 7 July 1922; 'Sir M. Visvesvaraya's Apologia', *Madras Mail*, 11 July 1922. Cuttings in MV-PAPERS-IEI, Vol. 15.

16 'Sir M. Visveswarayya's Defence', *The Hindu*, 7 July 1922; 'Mysore State Finances', *Daily Post*, 7 July [1922]. Cuttings in MV-PAPERS-IEI, Vol. 15.

17 'Sir M. Visvesvaraya's Statement', [header unclear], cutting in MV-PAPERS-IEI, Vol. 15.

18 'Sir M. Visveswarayya's Defence'.

19 'Mysore State Finances. Sir M. Visvesvaraya's Defence', *The Daily Express*, 19 July 1922, cutting in MV-PAPERS-IEI, Vol. 15.

20 'M.S'., 'Sir M. Visvasvaraya's [sic] Financial Statement', *Vokkaligara Patrike*, [date unclear]. Cutting in MV-PAPERS-IEI, Vol. 15.

21 For Visvesvaraya's figures, see 'Mysore State Finance', *Mysore Chronicle* (Supplement), 16 July 1922, para 3; for the government figures, see 'Statement B' in Government of Mysore, 'Financial Review and Forecast', printed report, pp. 40–41 (APAC: IOR/V/27/300/117).

22 'M.S'., 'Sir M. Visvasvaraya's Financial Statement'.

23 W.P. Barton to H. Tonkinson, Joint Secretary to Government of India, Home Department, 3 December 1924, in 'Mysore Finances, a Statement by Sir M. Visvesvaraya, K.C.I.E., late Dewan of Mysore', Mysore Residency, 1902, File No. 302, Collection No. 7, S. Nos. 57–59, Folio 208. APAC: IOR/R/2/Box14/90/Item 3.

24 Letter (dated 27 July 1922) to the editor from 'Fair Play', *The Daily Post*, date unclear [August 1922?]; 'Sir M. Visvesvaraya's Statement'. Cuttings in MV-PAPERS-IEI, Vol. 15. For Visvesvaraya's figures, see 'Mysore State Finance', *Mysore Chronicle* (Supplement), 16 July 1922, para 3.

25 'M.S', 'Sir M. Visvasvaraya's Financial Statement'; also 'Sir M. Visvesvaraya's Statement'.

26 See Chapter 9 above. See also letter from 'Fair Play', para 20.

27 The statement was marked 'Confidential', but seems to have been intended for circulation to journalists.

28 M. Visvesvaraya, 'Mysore State Finance', statement dated 8 September 1922, para 3. In MV-PAPERS-IEI, Vol. 15.

29 Quoted in ibid., para 7. Italics added by Visvesvaraya.

30 Ibid., para 11.

31 Ibid., para 10.

32 'Mysore Iron Works', TOI, 25 January 1919, p. 7; GAZETTEER-VOL5, p. 1286; para 2 of Order No. I.C. 6174-86 / I.W. 136-22-1, 11 April 1923, Mysore government's Proceedings, in MV-

PAPERS-IEI, Vol. 25; Visvesvaraya, *Memoirs*, p. 92. On the managing agency system, see for instance A.-M. Misra, '"Business Culture" and Entrepreneurship in British India, 1860–1950', *Modern Asian Studies* 34, 2 (2000): 333–48, esp. p. 336.

33 'Mysore Iron Works', TOI, 25 January 1919, p. 7; 'News of the Week', TOI, 25 July 1919, p. A1; 'Tata Iron and Steel. Company's Annual Report', TOI, 9 September 1919, p. 6; 'Mysore Assembly. The Dewan's Address', TOI, 7 October 1919, p. 10; 'Engineering in Mysore: Activities in the State. A Comprehensive Programme', TOI, 26 November 1920, p. 8; 'Indian Mining. Mysore Iron Scheme', TOI, 10 June 1921, p. A2; 'Indian Industries. Notable Schemes in Mysore. A Progressive Policy Adopted', TOI, 21 July 1922, p. 15; Visvesvaraya, *Memoirs*, p. 92.

34 'Indian Industries. Notable Schemes in Mysore. A Progressive Policy Adopted', TOI, 21 July 1922, p. 15.

35 M. Visvesvaraya, 'Bhadravati Distillation and Iron Works: Preliminary Note', 25 April 1923, para 1. In MV-PAPERS-IEI, Vol. 30.

36 Ibid., para 1 (on Perin's departure); 'Mysore News. Bhadravati Iron Works', TOI, 4 May 1923, p. A7; Hettne, *Political Economy of Indirect Rule*, pp. 272–3.

37 Hettne, *Political Economy of Indirect Rule,* pp. 272–3; Visvesvaraya, *Memoirs*, pp. 92–3.

38 Quoted in Hettne, *Political Economy of Indirect Rule*, p. 273.

39 Mysore government Proceedings, Order No. I.C. 6174-86/I.W. 136-22-1, dated Bangalore, 11 April 1923 (typescript), in MV-PAPERS-IEI, Vol. 25 (quoted text from para 6). See also 'Mysore Iron Works: Board of Management', TOI, 20 April 1923, p. A4; 'Mysore News: Bhadravati Iron Works', TOI, 4 May 1923, p. A7; GAZETTEER-VOL5, p. 1286. On Madhava Rao's equation with Visvesvaraya, see N. Madhava Rao, 'He Practised what he Preached', in CENT-VOL, pp. 48–58.

40 See for instance 'Bhadravati Iron Works: Mysore Govt. and Sir M. Visveswarayya', *The Hindu*, 30 July 1929, cutting in MV-PAPERS-IEI, Vol. 15.

41 M. Visvesvaraya, 'Bhadravati Distillation and Iron Works: Preliminary Note', 25 April 1923, in MV-PAPERS-IEI, Vol. 30.

42 Ibid.; M. Visvesvaraya, 'Bhadravati Iron Works: Second Note by the Chairman', 12 June 1923, in MV-PAPERS-IEI, Vol. 30.

43 M. Visvesvaraya, 'Mysore Iron Works: Third Note by the Chairman', 19 November 1923, para 2. In MV-PAPERS-IEI, Vol. 30.

44 Ibid., para 5; para 1 of M. Visvesvaraya, 'Present Position of the Works', note dated 2 April 1924, in MV-PAPERS-IEI, Vol. 30; Madhava Rao, 'He Practised what he Preached', p. 54.

45 M. Visvesvaraya, 'Mysore Iron Works: Third Note by the Chairman', 19 November 1923, para 3. See also Madhava Rao, 'He Practised what he Preached', p. 54.

46 See for instance the mention of a forthcoming visit by F.L. Estep, Partner in Perin and Marshall's firm, in M. Visvesvaraya, 'Bhadravati Iron Works: Second Note by the Chairman', 12 June 1923.

47 M. Visvesvaraya, 'Third Note by the Chairman. Present Position', 19 November 1923, in MV-PAPERS-IEI, Vol. 30.

48 M. Visvesvaraya, 'Present Position of the Works', note dated 2 April 1924.

49 Visvesvaraya's note to the Maharaja of Mysore, 19 January 1917, KSA-MV-VOL, pp. 179–81, here para 6.

50 Aparajith Ramnath, *The Birth of an Indian Profession: Engineers, Industry, and the State, 1900–47* (Delhi: Oxford University Press, 2017), Chapter 5.

51 See also Hettne, *Political Economy of Indirect Rule,* p. 273.

52 This description may not be a first-hand one; it comes from a politician who did not have any direct role in the Bhadravati factory. S.V. Krishnamoorthy Rao, 'Blazed India's Industrial Trail', in CENT-VOL, pp. 218–223, here p. 222. The Bhadravati Board noted internally in 1925 that as a result of cost-cutting, the employees 'are being called upon to face difficulties to which Indians [were?] hitherto unaccustomed'. 'Bhadravati Iron Works', note by C. Ranganatha Rao Sahib, Secretary, Board of Management, 20 September 1925, in MV-PAPERS-IEI, Vol. 25. On the length of Visvesvaraya's visits, see Madhava Rao, 'He Practised what he Preached', p. 54.

53 See Ramnath, *Birth of an Indian Profession*, pp. 207–8.

54 Mysore had a tradition of sending a few students abroad each year to study engineering and industrial subjects. See Chapter 11 above.

55 Para 10 of 'Bhadravati Iron Works', statement by C. Ranganatha Rao Sahib, Secretary, Board of Management, Mysore Iron Works, 20 September 1925, in MV-PAPERS-IEI, Vol. 25; M.G. Rangaiya, 'Versatile Engineer-Administrator', in CENT-VOL, pp. 121–33, here p. 128.

56 M. Visvesvaraya, 'Mysore Iron Works: Third Note by the Chairman', 19 November 1923; M. Visvesvaraya, 'Present Position of the Works', note dated 2 April 1924; Rangaiya, 'Versatile Engineer-Administrator', p. 129; R. Balakrishna, *Industrial Development of Mysore* (Bangalore: Bangalore Press, 1940), p. 67.

57 'Mysore Iron Works: Possibilities of Expansion: Proposals for the Manufacture of Steel', TOI, 30 June 1927, p. 12.

58 Visvesvaraya, *Memoirs*, p. 127.

59 GAZETTEER-VOL5, p. 1287.

60 'Mysore Iron Works: Possibilities of Expansion', TOI, 30 June 1927.

61 Ibid.; C. Ranganatha Rao Sahib (Secretary, Board of Management, Mysore Iron Works), 'Bhadravati Iron Works', note dated 20 September 1925, in MV-PAPERS-IEI, Vol. 30.

62 K.N.P. Rao, 'A brief history of the Indian iron and steel industry', pp. 1–3 (bibliographical details not available; accessed via website of the National Metallurgical Laboratory, at https://eprints.nmlindia.org/5558/1/1-7.PDF, 1 June 2024); Rajat K. Ray, *Industrialization in India: Growth and Conflict in the Private Corporate Sector, 1914–47* (Delhi: Oxford University Press, 1982 [1979]), pp. 34–5.

63 See M. Visvesvaraya, 'Mysore Iron Works: Third Note by the Chairman', 19 November 1923, para 9.

64 'Municipal Reform', letter from 'Rusty Pen' to the Editor, TOI, 23 July 1924, p. 5.

65 'Mysore Finances', Visvesvaraya's statement dated 20 November 1924, in 'Mysore Finances, a Statement by Sir M. Visvesvaraya, K.C.I.E., late Dewan of Mysore', Mysore Residency, 1902, File No. 302, Collection No. 7. APAC: IOR/R/2/Box14/90/Item 3.

66 On 'Mysore' and 'Fact' being the same person, see 'Mysore Finances. Krishnarajasagara Project. Sir M. Visweswarayya's Statement—A Reply', letter from 'Mysore', *The Hindu*, 3 December 1924, in MV-PAPERS-IEI, Vol. 15.

67 See various newspaper cuttings, and a typed compilation of extracts from critical newspaper reports ('Select Offending Passages'), in MV-PAPERS-IEI, Vol. 15.

68 See for instance letter to the editor from K.S. Ramaswami, under 'Correspondence', *Guardian*, 7 February 1925. Cutting in MV-PAPERS-IEI, Vol. 15.

69 See for instance 'Truth', 'Sir M. Visvesvarayya Committee. (Krishnaraja Sagara)', *Mysore Chronicle*, 8 August 1926, in MV-PAPERS-IEI, Vol. 15; 'Mysore', 'Mysore Engineering Schemes: A Reply to Sir M. Visvesvaraya's Letter', letter to the editor of the Engineering Supplement, TOI, 30 September 1926, p. 14.

70 Letter to the editor from 'Mysore' (Column 1), *Guardian*, 17 March 1925, in MV-PAPERS-IEI, Vol. 15.

71 'Mysore', 'Mysore Engineering Schemes: A Reply to Sir M. Visvesvaraya's Letter', letter to the editor of the Engineering Supplement, TOI, 30 September 1926, p. 14.

72 E.g. 'Mysore Finances. Krishnarajasagara Controversy. Sir M. Visvesvaraya's Reply', *The Hindu*, 29 December 1924; 'Press Communique', *The Daily* Post, 9 January 1925. (These were issued in response to earlier challenges by the same critic.) Cuttings in MV-PAPERS-IEI, Vol. 15.

73 'A Note', followed by 'Select Offending Passages', MV-PAPERS-IEI, Vol. 15. The remark in the *Madras Mail* about Visvesvaraya's salary appears in this collection of extracts.

74 'Select Offending Passages'.

75 See for instance T. Paramasiva Iyer, *Note on the Krishnaraja Sagara North Bank Canal Scheme of the Visvesvaraya Committee* (Bangalore City: Bangalore Press, 1927) collected in MV-PAPERS-IEI, Vol. 14 and Vol. 15.

76 See MAR 1917–18, Appendix I.

77 L.S. Seshagiri Rao, *T.P. Kailasam* (New Delhi: Sahitya Akademi, 1984), p. 8.

78 'Sadasiva Aiyar, Hon'ble Mr. Justice Thiagaraja Aiyar', IBD 1915, p. 373.

79 Seshagiri Rao, *T.P. Kailasam.*

80 T. Paramasiva Iyer, *The Riks: Or Primeval Gleams of Light and life* (Bangalore: Mysore Government Press, 1911), p. v. See also T. Paramasiva Iyer, *Rāmāyana and Lanka: Parts I & II* (Bangalore City: Bangalore Press, 1940), in which the author tries to identify the present-day equivalents of various locations mentioned in the Ramayana.

81 See Iyer, *The Riks*, *passim.*

82 K.R. Srinivasa Iyengar, *A Bureaucrat in Princely Mysore: Selections from the Private Diary of K.R. Srinivasa Iyengar 1904–1941*, ed. Narendar Pani, typescript report, Project No. 098, IIMB (Bangalore: Indian Institute of Management Bangalore, 1982), p. 121.

83 T. Paramasiva Iyer to M. Visvesvaraya, 27 October 1917 (including quoted text); typed extract from the *Daily Post*, 6 February 1919. In MV-PAPERS-IEI, Vol. 10.

84 'Mysore Finances, An Able Defence', *Mysore Chronicle*, 7 December 1924, MV-PAPERS-IEI, Vol. 15.

85 See Chapter 9 above.

86 Letter to the editor from K.S. Ramaswami, under 'Correspondence', *Guardian*, 7 February 1925. Cutting in MV-PAPERS-IEI, Vol. 15.

87 S. Venkatapathaiya, *Bhadravathi and Mr. T. Paramasiva Iyer: His Facts and Figures Examined [Supplement to the Mysore Patriot]*, 1928. In MV-PAPERS-IEI, Vol. 15.

88 S. Srinivasa Aiyangar, 'The Bhadravati Iron Works. An Examination of the Criticisms. Charge of Wasting Money.' *The Hindu*, 11 August 1927, in MV-PAPERS-IEI, Vol. 14.

89 Although the statement doesn't name him, it appears to be addressing criticisms made largely (or solely) by Iyer. M. Venkatanaranappa, 'Annexure II: Mysore Iron Works, Bhadravati', in 'Krishnarajasagara and Iron Works', Mysore Government (General and Revenue) G.O. No. 575.9—C.B. 36.28.1, 6 August 1928, in MV-PAPERS-IEI, Vol. 15.

90 Ibid. See also 'Bhadravati Iron Works. (A Mischievous Press Campaign)', M. Venkatanaranappa's (General Manager, Mysore Iron Works) letter to the editor, *Daily Post*, [6 July 1927], in MV-PAPERS-IEI, Vol. 15.

91 Ramachandra Guha, *Gandhi: The years that changed the world: 1914–1948* (Gurgaon: Allen Lane, 2018), p. 248; Meera Iyer, 'A house called Kumara Park', *Deccan Herald* (online), 27 June 2020 (https://www.deccanherald.com/spectrum/spectrum-top-stories/a-house-called-kumara-park-854149.html, accessed 12 June 2023).

92 M.K. Gandhi to T. Paramasiva Iyer, 29 July 1927, CWMG, Vol. 34, p. 253.

93 Venkatanaranappa reported the gist of the speech as he understood it: he tried to follow it in Hindi as the interpreter used an unfamiliar dialect of Kannada. But another, slightly different version of the speech is published in English in the *Collected Works of Mahatma Gandhi*. I have relied on the parts where both versions agree. Venkatanaranappa's typed report on Gandhi's visit, enclosed with his handwritten letter dated 19 August 1927, in MV-PAPERS-IEI, Vol. 25; 'Speech at Bhadravati', 18 August 1927, CWMG, Vol. 34, pp. 367–8.

94 Venkatanaranappa's typed report on Gandhi's visit.

95 'Speech at Citizens' Meeting, Bangalore', 28 August 1927, CWMG, Vol. 34, pp. 413–7.

96 See also Chandan Gowda, '"Advance Mysore!": The Cultural Logic of a Developmental State', *Economic and Political Weekly* XLV, no. 29 (17 July 2010): 88–95.

97 'Mysore Iron Works: Possibilities of Expansion: Proposals for the Manufacture of Steel', TOI, 30 June 1927, p. 12; 'Bhadravati Iron Works: Suggested Subsidiary Industries: Sir M. Visvesvarayya's Important Recommendations', TOI, 14 July 1927, p. 14.

98 'Mysore Iron Works: Possibilities of Expansion: Proposals for the Manufacture of Steel', TOI, 30 June 1927, p. 12.

99 'Bhadravati Iron Works: Suggested Subsidiary Industries: Sir M. Visvesvarayya's Important Recommendations', TOI, 14 July 1927, p. 14.

100 M. Viraraja Urs, Secretary, Board of Management, 'Bhadravati Iron Works: Report on Operation during the Year 1928–29', 24 September 1929, in MV-PAPERS-IEI, Vol. 15.

101 'Bhadravati Iron Works; Sir M. Visvesvarayya to Retire', *The Evening Mail*, n.d., cutting in MV-PAPERS-IEI, Vol. 15; 'Mysore Iron Works: Practical Possibilities of the Scheme', TOI, 7 November 1929, p. 18; Visvesvaraya, *Memoirs*, p. 94. Visvesvaraya claimed in his memoirs that he 'resigned . . . for reasons unconnected with the Works', which suggests his equation with Mirza might have been the stronger factor. Visvesvaraya, *Memoirs*, p. 94. On the tension between Visvesvaraya and Mirza, see V.S. Narayana Rao, *Mokshagundam Visvesvaraya: His Life and Work* (Mysore: Geetha Book House, 1973), p. 161.

102 'Mysore Iron Works. Practical Possibilities of the Scheme', TOI, 7 November 1929, p. 18.

103 Balakrishna, *Industrial Development of Mysore,* pp. 23, 67–8, and 77–8 (quoted text from pp. 77–8).

104 Ibid., pp. 68–9, 72–3, and 77 (quoted text from p. 68).

105 Gowda, '"Advance Mysore!": The Cultural Logic of a Developmental State', p. 91. Visvesvaraya, of course, was hoping that his proposed port at Bhatkal would solve this problem to an extent. See discussion in Chapter 12 above.

106 'Mysore Iron Works. Practical Possibilities of the Scheme', TOI, 7 November 1929, p. 18.

107 Rangaiya, 'Versatile Engineer-Administrator', p. 129.

108 Gowda, '"Advance Mysore!": The Cultural Logic of a Developmental State' (quoted text from p. 93).

17. Reclaiming the Metropolis

1 See Chapter 14 above.

2 See Chapter 7 above.

3 *City of Bombay: Municipal Retrenchment and Reform: Final Report by the Retrenchment Advisor* (Bombay: Indian Daily Mail Press, 1925), para 1.

4 Ibid., paras 2–3 and 7–8 (quoted text from para 2); ibid., Appendix I: 'Complete Programme of Work' (pp. 88–9).

5 See for example Appendices II–IV in ibid. (pp. 90–4).
6 Ibid., paras 5, 37, 41, 98.
7 Ibid., paras 12–13.
8 Ibid., paras 18–19 and 29–34.
9 'An Ideal Bombay. Municipal Reform. Sir M. Visvesvarayya's Report', TOI, 11 May 1925; 'Greater Bombay: Problems of Suburban Extension and City Planning', *The Indian Daily Mail*, [10 May 1925]. Cuttings in MV-PAPERS-IEI, Vol. 21.
10 'The Future of Bombay', TOI, [12?] May 1925. Cutting in in MV-PAPERS-IEI, Vol. 21.
11 [Untitled], *The Hindu*, 13 May 1925. Cutting in MV-PAPERS-IEI, Vol. 21.
12 'Karachi's Civic Needs. Sir M. Visvesvaraya's Recommendations', *Bombay Chronicle*, 20 April 1926, p. 11; 'Madras Corporation. Sir M. Visveswarayya as Retrenchment Adviser', TOI, 14 July 1926, p. 10.
13 *Report of the Committee appointed by the Government of India to enquire into the Bombay Back Bay Reclamation Scheme 1926* (Bombay: Government Central Press, 1927). Hereinafter cited as Back Bay Enquiry Report.
14 Back Bay Enquiry Report, para 5. See also Tim Riding, '"Making Bombay Island": Land Reclamation and Geographical Conceptions of Bombay, 1661–1728', *Journal of Historical Geography* 59 (2018): 27–39.
15 Gyan Prakash, *Mumbai Fables* (Noida: HarperCollins, 2010), pp. 79–82; Back Bay Enquiry Report, para 15 and para 23 (the latter paragraph quotes from George Lloyd's evidence to the committee).
16 Prakash, *Mumbai Fables*, p. 81; oral evidence of George Lloyd in *Evidence Oral and Documentary recorded by the Back Bay Enquiry Committee: 1926: Part II: Evidence Recorded in England* (London: H.M.S.O., 1927), here pp. 390–3. The latter source is hereafter cited as Back Bay Enquiry Evidence, Part II.
17 Back Bay Enquiry Report, paras 7–16; Lowther and Kidd's report of 1912, quoted in para 12 of George Buchanan's Written Statement, in Back Bay Enquiry Evidence, Part II, pp. 454–500; Prakash, *Mumbai Fables*, pp. 80–2.
18 Back Bay Enquiry Report, paras 20–3.

19 On his belief in the British Empire etc., see Jason Tomes, 'Lloyd, George Ambrose, first Baron Lloyd: (1879–1941)', *Oxford Dictionary of National Biography*, 6 January 2011 (https://doi.org/10.1093/ref:odnb/34567, accessed 2 June 2024).

20 Back Bay Enquiry Report, paras 25–6 and 32.

21 Ibid., paras 28–30, 33–9.

22 Ibid., paras 85, 61–3, 70–4.

23 Prakash, *Mumbai Fables*, pp. 81–2; oral evidence of George Lloyd, in Back Bay Enquiry Evidence Part II, here p. 421.

24 Back Bay Enquiry Report, paras 77 and 81.

25 'Back Bay Reclamation', TOI, 28 January 1921, p. 8; 'Bombay Sea Face. Hastening the Preliminaries',TOI, 10 March 1921, p. 10; 'Developing Bombay. An Ambitious Programme. What Has Already Been Accomplished', TOI, 13 May 1921, p. 11; Prakash, *Mumbai Fables*, pp. 82–6. On the starting of the wall from the two ends, see Back Bay Enquiry Report, para 98.

26 Back Bay Enquiry Report, paras 44 and 90.

27 Ibid., paras 109–10; oral evidence of George Lloyd in *Evidence Oral and Documentary recorded by the Back Bay Enquiry Committee: 1926: Part II: Evidence Recorded in England* (London: H.M.S.O., 1927), here p. 419 (on Lloyd's date of departure).

28 Prakash, *Mumbai Fables*, pp. 86–7.

29 Ibid., pp. 87–91; *Second* ad interim *Report of the Advisory Committee dealing with the Back Bay Reclamation Scheme* (Bombay: Government Central Press, [1926]); Back Bay Enquiry Report, paras 146–9.

30 Prakash, *Mumbai Fables*, p. 89.

31 'Back Bay Scheme. Progress of Inquiries. Preliminaries Nearing Completion', TOI, 17 July 1926, p. 11; 'The Back Bay Scheme. Inquiry Committee. Government of India to Appoint it. Bombay Request', TOI, 20 May 1926, p. 11.

32 Back Bay Enquiry Report, paras 2–3; 'Govt. of India Committee. Back Bay Inquiry. To Meet in Bombay on August 2', TOI, 21 July 1926, p. 10.

33 A similar irony was noted by a critic when Visvesvaraya advised the Bombay Municipality on reducing costs (discussed in Chapter 16 above).

34 Back Bay Enquiry Report, para 2; R.B. Ewbank to Secretary, Department of Industries and Labour, Government of India, 1 December 1926, in ibid., front matter.

35 *Evidence Oral and Documentary Recorded by the Back Bay Enquiry Committee. 1926. Part I. Evidence Recorded in India* (London: His Majesty's Stationery Office, 1926), 'Index' (p. ii); *Evidence Oral and Documentary Recorded by the Back Bay Enquiry Committee. 1926. Part II. Evidence Recorded in England* (London: His Majesty's Stationery Office Press, 1927), 'Index' (front matter). Hereinafter cited as Back Bay Enquiry Evidence, Part I and II respectively. On Lloyd's position in Egypt, see Tomes, 'Lloyd, George Ambrose'. On Lewis's tenure, see his testimony in Back Bay Enquiry Evidence, Part II, p. 322.

36 'Amusing Incidents During Sittings', TOI, 9 October 1926, p. 16 (on Richmond Terrace); M. Visvesvaraya to Mirza Ismail, 7 October 1926, in V.S. Narayana Rao collection (Box No. 11), Karnataka State Archives (on House of Lords); 'The Back Bay Committee. Visit to England. Sir G. Buchanan to be Examined. First Meeting', TOI, 3 August 1926, p. 9 (on venue in Bombay). On the Secretariat's architecture, see 'The Secretariat [Bombay]', Online Gallery, British Library (http://www.bl.uk/onlinegallery/onlineex/apac/photocoll/t/019pho000000937u00033000.html, accessed 20 June 2022). For examples of newspaper coverage of the sessions, see 'The Back-Bay Committee', *Bombay Chronicle*, 25 August 1926; 'Back Bay Inquiry. Evidence by Ex-Governor of Bombay', *Aberdeen Press and Journal*, 26 October 1926, p. [3?]; 'Bombay Reclamation. Meaning of Estimate', *The Scotsman*, 3 November 1926, p. 11.

37 Back Bay Enquiry Evidence, Parts I and II.

38 See for instance Back Bay Enquiry Evidence, Part II, pp. 344, 345, 430, 433.

39 For example, see his examination of K.F. Nariman in Back Bay Enquiry Evidence, Part I, pp. 400–1.

40 Back Bay Enquiry Evidence, Part II. On Cameron as Visvesvaraya's former boss, see Chapter 6 above.

41 Tomes, 'Lloyd, George Ambrose'.

42 See George Lloyd's oral evidence, in Back Bay Enquiry Evidence, Part II, pp. 390–440 (quoted text on pp. 421 and 422).

43 Ibid. (quoted text from p. 429).

44 See 'Back Bay Inquiry Committee', photograph of committee members with staff, TOI, 1 September 1926, p. 16; 'Expenses of the Back Bay Committee. A Central Government Charge. Assembly Questions Loan to a Private Club', TOI, 1 September 1926, p. 12.

45 The letters to Mirza Ismail cited below are mostly on paper with a Hotel Cecil letterhead.

46 Visvesvaraya to Mirza Ismail, letters dated 23 September 1926, 7 October 1926, 21 October 1926, 27 October 1926, 4 November 1926 [the last of these is addressed simply to 'My dear Friend', but the context indicates it is to Mirza]. Quoted text is from the letters of 7 October 1926 and 4 November 1926. V.S. Narayana Rao Collection (Box No. 11), Karnataka State Archives. On the subsidy question, see also 'Wholly Inaccurate. Rumour About Reduction of Mysore's Subsidy', TOI, 30 Sep 1926, p. 12.

47 See Chapter 16 above.

48 Back Bay Enquiry Evidence, Part II, p. 501.

49 Ibid., p. 632.

50 Ibid., *passim*.

51 George Buchanan's oral evidence, Back Bay Enquiry Evidence, Part II, esp. pp. 501–20 and pp. 620–1; Back Bay Enquiry Report, para 221.

52 George Buchanan's oral evidence, Back Bay Enquiry Evidence, Part II, p. 621.

53 Ibid., pp. 611–45.

54 'Sir George Buchanan's Defence of his Firm's Methods . . .', TOI, 3 November 1926, p. 11; George Buchanan's oral evidence, Back Bay Enquiry Evidence, Part II, esp. pp. 528–9.

55 Back Bay Enquiry Evidence, Part II, *passim* (quoted text from p. 636). See also Back Bay Enquiry Report, para 205.

56 Back Bay Enquiry Evidence, Part II, p. 640.

57 Back Bay Enquiry Report (see p. v for date of report); Back Bay Enquiry Evidence, Parts I and II.

58 Back Bay Enquiry Report, paras 200–2.

59 Ibid., paras 206–7.

60 Ibid., paras 224–5.

61 Ibid., para 226.
62 Ibid., paras 209–24. Quoted text from paras 215 and 222.
63 Ibid., para 230.
64 See Chapter 5 above.
65 Back Bay Enquiry Report, paras 167–8 and 175–6 (quoted text from para 168).
66 See Prakash, *Mumbai Fables*, pp. 75, 99, and 274–83.
67 Views reported in 'Back Bay Committee's Report. Home Opinion', TOI, 7 February 1927, p. 10. On the role of the 'expert' in this episode, see also Maansi Parpiani, 'Urban Planning in Bombay (1898–1928): Ambivalences, Inconsistencies and Struggles of the Colonial State', *Economic and Political Weekly* 47, no. 28 (14 July 2012): 64–70, here p. 69.
68 Back Bay Enquiry Report, para 203.
69 Ibid., para 227.
70 Ibid., paras 151–2.
71 '"Wishy-Washy Report." Back Bay Inquiry. Mr. H.P. Mody on Mears Committee's Work', TOI, 18 January 1927, p. 10.
72 See Prakash, *Mumbai Fables*, p. 91.
73 Ibid., pp. 92–4.

18. Constitutional Adventures

1 Bjørn Hettne, *The Political Economy of Indirect Rule: Mysore 1881–1947* (New Delhi: Ambika Publications, 1978), pp. 61–2 and 82–3; M. Visvesvaraya, *Memoirs of My Working Life* (Bangalore: M. Visvesvaraya, 1951), p. 127.
2 'Patriotism-Incarnate', *The Evening Mail,* 20 July 1927; 'The Great Speech', *The Evening Mail,* [23?] July 1927; 'Hustle', *Vokkaligara Patrike,* 27 July 1927. Cuttings in MV-PAPERS-IEI, Vol. 21.
3 See Chapter 16 above.
4 M. Shama Rao, *Modern Mysore: From the Coronation of Chamaraja Wodeyar X in 1868 to the present time* (Bangalore: Higginbothams, 1936), Chapter XLII.
5 Janaki Nair, *The Promise of the Metropolis: Bangalore's Twentieth Century* (New Delhi: Oxford University Press, 2007 [2005]), pp.

70–2; S. Chandrasekhar, *Dimensions of Socio-Political Change in Mysore 1918-40* (New Delhi: Ashish Publishing House, 1985), pp. 135–6; General and Revenue Departments, Mysore government, G.O. No. 3348–3400—C.B. 38–28, 26 January 1929, para 11. The last of these sources (available via dspace.gipe.ac.in) is hereafter cited as G.O. of 26 January 1929.

6 L.M. Crump to B.J. Clancy (copy), 3 August 1928, No. C/6141/983, in 'Fortnightly reports on the political situation in Mysore for the year 1928', Govt. of India Foreign and Political Department File No. 210-P (1928), in APAC: IOR/R/1/1/1744.

7 James Manor, *Political Change in an Indian State: Mysore 1917-1955* (Delhi: Manohar, 1977), n. 29 on p. 211; Nair, *Promise of the Metropolis,* pp. 71–2; G.O. of 26 January 1929, para 34. On the use of the term 'satyagrahis', see Manor, *Political Change*, p. 88. The term 'satyagraha' was also used in the press: see 'Counsel's Battle of Wits. Satyagraha Leaders' Case', under 'Mysore Inquiry', TOI, 13 September 1928, p. 11. On Bardoli, see Chapter XII of the report of the Visvesvaraya-led committee (more on this below) established to look into the Bangalore Disturbances (bibliographical details not available), in MV-PAPERS-IEI, Vol. 27. This source is hereafter cited as BDC [Bangalore Disturbances Committee] Report.

8 Manor, *Political Change*, p. 63; S. Chandrasekhar, *Dimensions of Socio-Political Change in Mysore 1918-40* (New Delhi: Ashish Publishing House, 1985), pp. 136–7; 'Tense Situation on Day of Bangalore Disturbances. Communal Passion Deeply Stirred. Jail Superintendent on Rowdy Behaviour of Students', TOI, 21 September 1928, p. 10; G.O. of 26 January 1929, para 15.

9 BDC Report, paras 63, 67, and 72.

10 BDC Report, paras 67, 69, and 71.

11 BDC Report, paras 76–8.

12 See Mysore government, G.O. No. 1042–1102—*C.B.* 38–28–114, 28 August 1928, in BDC Report, Appendix I (p. 91).

13 'Sir Visveswarayya', *Mysore Patriot*, [?] September 1928. Cutting in MV-PAPERS-IEI, Vol. 21.

14 BDC Report, p. 94; G.O. of 26 January 1929, para 5.

15 See newspaper reports cited in the discussion below.

16 'Mysore Disturbances. Monster Petition to Ruler', TOI, 12 September 1928, p. 10; 'Visvesvaraya Committee. Work Completed. Difference of Opinion Among Members', TOI, 24 January 1929, p. 14.
17 'Mysore Inquiry. Amazing Revelations. Abdication of Police Authority During Bangalore Disturbances. Chairman's Assurance', TOI, 13 September 1928, p. 11.
18 '"God Help the City." Visveswaraya Inquiry. Chairman's Comment on Examination of Chief Police Officer. Eye-Witness' Graphic Story', TOI, 14 September 1928, p. 9; 'Injured Boy's Statement to Visveswaraya Committee. Inspection of Mr. Abbas Khan's House. Application for Search Warrant against Magistrate', TOI, 17 September 1928, p. 11; 'Strictures on Bangalore Police Officers. "D. S. P. a Gentleman at Large." Sir M. Visveswaraya's Remarks on Deputy Commissioner's Statement', TOI, 3 October 1928, p. 12.
19 R. Chakravarti, 'Sir M.V. His fine sense of humour', in untitled souvenir on Visvesvaraya (Bengaluru: Century Club, 2017), pp. 95–6, here p. 96.
20 G.O. of 26 January 1919, para 3. See BDC Report for number of pages.
21 'Fixing Responsibility for Bangalore Disturbances. Visveswaraya Committee's Findings. Govt. Attitude Criticised: "No Steps Taken to Arrest Offenders"', TOI, 7 January 1929, p. 13.
22 BDC Report, *passim.*
23 Ibid., Chapter XI (quoted text from para 123).
24 Ibid., para 87.
25 Manor, *Political Change*, p. 63; Chandrasekhar, *Dimensions of Socio-Political Change*, p. 77.
26 BDC Report, para 87.
27 Ibid., Chapter XII.
28 See Chapter 13 above.
29 BDC Report, para 131.
30 Ibid., para 126.
31 Ibid., paras 134–9.
32 Ibid., para 128.
33 Chandrasekhar, *Dimensions of Socio-Political Change*, pp. 141–2; Manor, *Political Change*, p. 64; Hettne, *Political Economy of Indirect Rule*, p. 152.

34 Hettne, *Political Economy of Indirect Rule,* pp. 153 and 186.

35 BDC Report, para 138.

36 Hettne, *Political Economy of Indirect Rule,* pp. 50–5. While the placement of apostrophes varies in different sources, I render the relevant terms in the following discussion as *states people's conference* and *states people's movement*.

37 'History', Gazetteers Department webpage, Maharashtra government (https://gazetteers.maharashtra.gov.in/cultural.maharashtra.gov.in/english/gazetteer/SANGLI/his_modern%20period.html, accessed 25 August 2022); G.R. Abhyankar's note in P.M. Limaye (author/compiler), *The History of the Deccan Education Society (1880–1935)* (Poona: A.V. Patwardhan/Aryabhushan Press, 1935), pp. 132–7, here pp. 136–7. Abhyankar is described as a pleader on the title page of G.R. Abhyanker [sic], *Native States and Post-War Reforms* (Poona: A.V. Patwardhan/Aryabhushan Press, 1917) and as a Professor in the Poona Law College in *The Indian States' People's Conference. Report of the Bombay Session. 17th, 18th December 1927* (Bombay: G.R. Abhyankar and Manishanker S. Trivedi, Indian States' People's Conference, 1928), p. 6.

38 Abhyanker [sic], *Native States and Post-War Reforms*, p. 3. See also B.N. Sardesai, 'The Peoples' Awakening in Sangli State', *Proceedings of the Indian History Congress* 54 (1993): 433–40, here pp. 434–5.

39 Abhyanker [sic], *Native States and Post-War Reforms*, pp. 39–40.

40 Sardesai, 'The Peoples' Awakening in Sangli State', pp. 436–7.

41 Barbara Ramusack, *The Indian Princes and Their States* (New Delhi: Cambridge University Press, 2004), p. 221.

42 Hettne, *Political Economy of Indirect Rule*, pp. 173–4; Ramusack, *Indian Princes and Their States*, p. 216.

43 Hettne, *Political Economy of Indirect Rule*, p. 174.

44 Ramusack, *Indian Princes and Their States*, p. 219; *Report of the Forty-Second Indian National Congress held at Madras 1927* (n.p.: Reception Committee, Forty-Second Indian National Congress, [1928]), pp. 1 and 93; *Indian Annual Register,* 1927, Vol. 2, p. 350. On M. Ramachandra Rao, see *Indian Round Table Conference: St. James's Palace: Delegates from the Indian States and British India* [printed catalogue; no publication details], p. 56.

Accessed via https://www.nottingham.ac.uk/research/groups/conferencing-the-international/documents/india-office-guides/rtc1-delegates.pdf.

45 Quoted in Ramusack, *Indian Princes and Their States*, p. 219.

46 For the 'All-India' name, see for instance 'Representation of States Peoples: Appeal to Mr Gandhi', TOI, 23 December 1929, p. 13.

47 See 'Indian States Peoples' Conference. Committee Meeting', TOI, 5 March 1929, p. 4.

48 Sumit Sarkar, *Modern India: 1885–1947* (Delhi: Pearson, 2014), p. 313, argues that this was the case even in the late 1930s.

49 'States' Peoples' Conference. To be held in December', TOI, 22 November 1927, p. 15; 'Indian States' Welfare. Bombay Meeting', TOI, 29 November 1927, p. 4; 'Indian States' People's Conference. Preliminaries Settled', TOI, 6 December 1927, p. 4; 'Indian States and British India', TOI, 19 December 1927, p. 7. On Thakkar, see Shivprasad Rajgor, 'Thakkar, Amritlal Vithaldas', January 2014, Gujarati Vishwakosh (https://shorturl.at/TLxzM, accessed 1 June 2024).

50 'Indian States Peoples' Conference. To be held in Bombay', TOI, 30 May 1927, p. 10.

51 See for example: 'States' Peoples' Conference. To be held in December', TOI, 22 November 1927, p. 15; 'Indian States People', under 'Local Engagements', TOI, 14 December 1929, p. 19.

52 Barbara D. Metcalf and Thomas R. Metcalf, *A Concise History of Modern India*, 3rd edition (Cambridge: Cambridge University Press, 2012), pp. 189–90; 'The Constitutional Development of India 1917–1930', *Bulletin of International News* 6, 25 (19 June 1930): 3–10, here pp. 6–7; 'Butler, Sir Spencer Harcourt', IBD 1915, p. 74.

53 '"Let Not India be Split up like Ireland["]: Jamsaheb's Appeal', under 'Princes' Conference with All-Parties Representatives', TOI, 8 November 1928, p. 11.

54 *Work in England of the Deputation of the Indian States' People's Conference* (Bombay: G.R. Abhyankar, 1929), *passim*; 'Butler Inquiry. Subjects Deputation Satisfied', TOI, 30 November 1928, p. 9. On Wedgwood, see Prabha Ravi Shankar, 'Josiah Clement Wedgwood (1872–1943) and his Contribution to Indian Struggle

for Political Progress', *Proceedings of the Indian History Congress* 69 (2008): 529–35; on Pole, see 'Records of Major David Graham Pole', Archives Hub (https://archiveshub.jisc.ac.uk/search/archives/febc162c-fd5c-379e-8012-a83e9168b34f, accessed 1 June 2024).

55 'Indian Peoples and Princes: Joint Conference: Negotiations for Co-operation: Rights Demanded', TOI, 13 November 1928, p. 9.

56 P.M. Limaye (author/compiler), *The History of the Deccan Education Society*, pp. 185–6; Abhyankar's note in ibid., pp. 132–7 (here pp. 136–7).

57 Visvesvaraya to Abhyankar, 8 May 1918, in G.R. Abhyankar Papers, NMML.

58 Sardesai, 'The Peoples' Awakening in Sangli State', p. 436.

59 D.V. Gundappa, 'A Gentleman to the Press Too', in CENT-VOL, pp. 110–20.

60 Gundappa was a Mysore legislator in the 1920s and '30s. See 'Gundappa, eminent writer, dead', TOI, 8 October 1975, p. 1.

61 'Butler Committee in Mysore', TOI, 22 March 1928, p. 12; 'Indian States Enquiry Committee: Arrival in Bangalore. Three Witnesses Give Evidence', *Indian Daily Mail*, [March 1928], cutting in MV-PAPERS-IEI, Vol. 23.

62 See Chapter 16 above.

63 'S. Indian States Peoples Conference. Sir M. Visvesvaraya's Views', TOI, 29 October 1928, p. 13.

64 D.V. Gundappa, *The States & Their People in the Indian Constitution* (Bangalore: Karnataka Publishing House, 1931), p. 169.

65 'S. Indian States Peoples Conference. Sir M. Visvesvaraya's Views', TOI, 29 October 1928, p. 13.

66 'S. I. States' Peoples Conference. Opening on January [14]', TOI, 12 January 1929, p. 17.

67 Quoted in 'South Indian States Peoples Conference', TOI, 17 January 1929, p. 15.

68 'South Indian States Peoples Conference', TOI, 17 January 1929, p. 15.

69 'The S.I. States Peoples' Conference' [contains a transcript of Visvesvaraya's speech], *The Indian Quarterly Register*, January–June 1929, Vol. 1, pp. 490–502, here p. 490.

70 Ibid., p. 491.
71 Ibid., p. 494. (See also Chapter 15 above on the events leading up to the Nehru Report.)
72 Ibid., p. 492.
73 Ibid., p. 491.
74 Ibid., p. 493.
75 Ibid., p. 495.
76 Ibid., p. 496.
77 See 'States and British India', *Mysorean*, 22 January 1929 (reprints an article from the *Bengalee*). Cutting in MV-PAPERS-IEI, Vol. 23.
78 D.V. Gundappa wrote of the memorandum resulting from the conference that it was designed 'to minimise controversy and to persuade and to conciliate'. Gundappa, *The States & Their People*, p. 87.
79 'The S.I. States Peoples' Conference', p. 496.
80 'States and British India', *Mysorean*, 22 January 1929 (cited above).
81 'The S.I. States Peoples' Conference', pp. 496–7.
82 Ibid., p. 498.
83 Abhijit Dutta, 'Bengalee, The', *Banglapedia: National Encylopedia of Bangladesh* (https://en.banglapedia.org/index.php?title=Bengalee,_The, accessed 2 November 2023); 'Sir Surendranath Banerjea', *Encyclopedia Britannica*, 2 August 2023 (https://www.britannica.com/biography/Surendranath-Banerjea, accessed 2 November 2023).
84 Cutting from the *Mysorean*, 22 January 1929 (reprints an article from the *Bengalee*), in MV-PAPERS-IEI, Vol. 23.
85 Cutting titled 'States Peoples' Destiny: Sir M. Viswesvarayya's Lead' [publication unknown; date illegible], in MV-PAPERS-IEI, Vol. 23.
86 'The S.I. States Peoples' Conference', pp. 501–2.
87 Gundappa, *The States & Their People*, p. 85.
88 'Responsible Govt. in Indian States: Mr. Rao on Trivandrum Plan', TOI, 22 January 1929, p. 14.
89 'Round Table Conference: Claim of Indian States' People to Representation', TOI, 19 Nov 1929, p. 9; Gundappa, *The States & Their People*, pp. 169–70.
90 Gundappa, *The States & Their People*, p. 170.
91 Ibid.

92 I use 'Round Table Conference' to represent the actual historical event, and 'round table conference' in earlier passages to denote the kind of meeting that was being mooted.

93 'Round Table Conferences, 1930–32', 'Making Britain', website of the Open University (https://www.open.ac.uk/researchprojects/makingbritain/content/round-table-conferences-1930-1932, accessed 5 June 2024); *Indian Round Table Conference: St. James's Palace*. See also Hettne, *Political Economy of Indirect Rule,* p. 54.

94 '"From Dependency to Dominion": Visvesvaraya-Natrajan Constitution Scheme For India: Joint Responsibility of Ministers', *Bombay Chronicle*, 24 November 1930.

95 *Indian Round Table Conference: St. James's Palace*; 'People involved', under 'Round Table Conferences, 1930–32', 'Making Britain' website; photograph at the 'Conferencing the International' website (https://www.nottingham.ac.uk/research/groups/conferencing-the-international/timeline/rtc1.aspx, accessed 5 June 2024).

96 Ray T. Smith, 'The Role of India's "Liberals" in the Nationalist Movement, 1915-1947', *Asian Survey* 8, no. 7 (July 1968): 607–24; 'Round Table Conferences, 1930–32', 'Making Britain' website.

97 'Round Table Conferences, 1930–32', 'Making Britain' website; Smith, 'The Role of India's "Liberals"', p. 620; 'Papers of William Wedgwood Benn, 1st Viscount Stansgate', UK Parliament: Parliamentary Archives (https://archives.parliament.uk/collections/getrecord/GB61_ST, accessed 1 June 2024); 'Liberal Rule in India Advocated by Benn: Former British Official, Here on Visit, Would Base Policy on Gandhi's Prestige', *New York Times*, 14 February 1933, extract seen at https://www.nytimes.com/1933/02/14/archives/liberal-rule-in-india-advocated-by-benn-former-british-official.html (accessed 5 June 2024).

98 'Round Table Conferences, 1930–32', 'Making Britain' website.

99 See 'Great Hopes: The Round Table Conference Ends', TOI, 27 December 1932, p. 8.

100 'Gilder, Manchersha Dhanjibhai (1882 – 1979)', 'Plarr's Lives of the Fellows', Royal College of Surgeons of England (https://livesonline.rcseng.ac.uk/client/en_GB/lives/search/detailnonmodal/ent:$002f$002fSD_ASSET$002f0$002fSD_ASSET:378702/one?qu=%22RCS%3AE006519%22, accessed 5 June 2024); 'Sethna, Hon. Sir Phiroze', 'Who's Who 2024 & Who

Was Who', https://doi.org/10.1093/ww/9780199540884.013.U216888; Ramachandra Guha, 'The independent journal of opinion', *Seminar* 481 (September 1999), https://www.india-seminar.com/1999/481/481%20guha.htm, accessed 5 June 2024 (on K. Natarajan). The common factor was that they were all what Setalvad called 'co-operators . . . but not blind co-operators'. See 'Sir C. Setalvad's Advice: Rally the Co-operators', letter to the editor from Chimanlal H. Setalvad, TOI, 28 January 1933, p. 24.

101 See the printed statement dated 19 January 1933 issued after the conference, in MV-PAPERS-IEI, Vol. 23. Although Jayakar was by this time playing a leading role in the Bombay Hindu Mahasabha, he continued to consider himself a Liberal in political orientation. See Namrata R. Ganneri, 'The Hindu Mahasabha in Bombay (1923–1947)', *Proceedings of the Indian History Congress* 75 (2014): 771–82.

102 Statement dated 19 January 1933, cited above. On A.V. Patwardhan, see Sardesai, 'The Peoples' Awakening in Sangli State'.

103 'Public Meeting' and 'Text of the Resolution', dated 9 February 1933, in MV-PAPERS-IEI, Vol. 23.

104 'A Federal Constitution for India on the R.T.C. Model. White Paper on Reforms . . .', TOI, 18 March 1933, p. 13.

105 See typed note titled 'Article on the White Paper', in MV-PAPERS-IEI, Vol. 23.

106 'Sir M. Visvesvaraya Examines The White Paper. Economic View. No Effort to Lessen Country's Poverty', TOI, 7 April 1933, p. 11; M. Visvesvaraya, 'The White [Paper]: Examined from Viewpoint of the Country's Economic Deficiencies', typed copy, in MV-PAPERS-IEI, Vol. 23. The quoted text is from the second of these sources.

19. An Engineer among the Economists

1 Indian Economic Association, *Proceedings of the Seventh Indian Economic Conference, Bombay: January 22nd, 23rd, 24th and 25th, 1924* (Bombay: H.L. Kaji, Secretary, Seventh Indian Economic Conference, 1924), pp. xii and xiv. This source is cited below as Proceedings, Indian Economic Conference 1924.

2 'Economic Association. Conference in Bombay', TOI, 23 December 1918, p. 11. For the professors' designations, see H. Stanley Jevons, *Economics in India. Inaugural Lecture* (University of Allahabad/ Pioneer Press: Allahabad, 1915); C.J. Hamilton, *The Trade Relations between England and India (1600–1896)* (Calcutta: Thacker, Spink & Co., 1919), front matter; J.J. Thomas, 'Anstey [*née* Powell], Vera', *Oxford Dictionary of National Biography*, 23 September 2004 (https://doi.org/10.1093/ref:odnb/61350, accessed 1 June 2024). See also K.S. Aiyar's speech in Proceedings, Indian Economic Conference 1924, pp. xiv–xvii; and J. Krishnamurthy, 'Looking Back at a Hundred Years of Research in Indian Economics', The Wire, 24 February 2017 (https://thewire.in/uncategorised/hundred-years-of-research-indian-economics, accessed 1 June 2024).

3 See for instance the IEA's Executive Committee and Conference Reception Committee as listed in Proceedings, Indian Economic Conference 1924, pp. ix–x.

4 See for example 'Economic Conference. Closing Day', TOI, 2 January 1919, p. 9; 'Labour in India. Factory Act Amendment', TOI, 4 January 1921, p. 10; 'Economic Problems. Governor at Bombay Conference. Sir M. Visveswaraya's Suggested Remedies', TOI, 23 January 1924, p. 13; 'Currency Policy. Economists Differ. Plea for Gold Standard', TOI, 24 January 1924, p. 5; 'Indian Economic Structure. Need for Change. Sir M. Visveswaraiya's Speech. H.E. Governor on Human Deficits', *Bombay Chronicle*, 23 January 1924, p. 5.

5 Krishnamurthy, 'Looking Back at a Hundred Years'.

6 Proceedings, Indian Economic Conference 1924, pp. xv and xx.

7 See Chapters 4 and 8 above.

8 As Dewan of Mysore, Visvesvaraya invited Slater to help Mysore process some of the economic statistics that had been collected there. Slater was sceptical of the exercise, but did give a talk in Mysore soon after Visvesvaraya's time as dewan. Gilbert Slater, *Southern India: Its Political and Economic Problems* (London: George Allen & Unwin, 1936), pp. 247–8.

9 See Chapter 14 above.

10 For the subsequent year, 1924–25, Sydenham would supply the Secretary, Treasurer, and Auditor of the IEA's Executive

Committee. Proceedings, Indian Economic Conference 1924, pp. ix and 188.

11 'Bombay Govt. Gazette. Civil Appointments', TOI, 17 October 1913, p. 11; 'Bombay University. Appointment of Lecturers', TOI, 11 February 1914, p. 5; 'College of Commerce. Its Functions', letter from Percy Anstey to the Editor, TOI, 17 June 1915, p. 4.

12 See Chapter 11 above.

13 M.L. Tannan, 'A Man of Unique Will-Power', in CENT-VOL, pp. 134–6, here p. 134. For a mention of Tannan as Principal of Sydenham (as of 1927), see Murarji J. Vaidya, 'Sir M.V.—As I Know Him', in CENT-VOL, pp. 98–109, here p. 98.

14 See Governor Wilson's speech in Proceedings, Indian Economic Conference 1924, pp. xvii–xix, here p. xviii.

15 Proceedings, Indian Economic Conference 1924, p. xiv.

16 Visvesvaraya's Presidential Address, 22 January 1924, in Proceedings, Indian Economic Conference 1924, pp. 1–10, here p. 1.

17 Ibid., pp. 3–4.

18 Ibid., pp. 4–5.

19 Ibid., pp. 2–4.

20 Ibid., pp. 5–7.

21 Ibid., pp. 7–10.

22 Proceedings, Indian Economic Conference 1924, pp. 199–201. See also the list of papers in ibid., pp. v–vi.

23 See Nikhil Menon, *Planning Democracy: How a Professor, an Institute, and an Idea Shaped India,* Kindle Edition (n.p.: Viking, 2022), pp. 33–5.

24 *Report of the Indian Economic Enquiry Committee 1925*, Vol. I (Calcutta: Government of India Central Publication Branch, 1925), para 1; Raghabendra Chattopadhyay, 'The Idea of Planning in India, 1930–1951', PhD thesis, Australian National University (1985), p. 76 (n. 80).

25 IOL 1924, pp. 5–8. Visvesvaraya knew Samaldas from at least the time of his meeting with the Tatas in connection with the setting up of the Bhadravati plant (see Chapter 12 above). Visvesvaraya and Purshotamdas Thakurdas worked together 'on the Boards of Industrial concerns and Committees', though we do not know when these connections began. See Purshotamdas Thakurdas's

Foreword to Y.G. Krishnamurti, *Sir M. Visvesvaraya: A Study* (Bombay: Popular Book Depot, 1941), pp. ix–x. On Samaldas as IEA President, see Proceedings, Indian Economic Conference 1924, p. 188.

26 Chattopadhyay, 'The Idea of Planning in India', p. 76 (n. 80).

27 *Report of the Indian Economic Enquiry Committee*, Vol. I, p. i. On Kaul, see 'Raja Hari Kishan Kaul Dead', TOI, 27 January 1942, p. 5. Burnett-Hurst is described as 'Professor of Commerce in the University of Allahabad' on the title page of A.R. Burnett-Hurst, *Labour and Housing in Bombay: A study in the economic conditions of the wage-earning classes in Bombay* (London: P.S. King & Son, Ltd., 1925).

28 *Report of the Indian Economic Enquiry Committee*, Vol. I, paras 3–5. On the visit to the Viceregal Lodge, see cutting with the handwritten caption '28.2.25: Social & Personal', in MV-PAPERS-IEI, Vol. 21.

29 *Report of the Indian Economic Enquiry Committee*, Vol. II, Part I (printed along with Vol. I, cited above), pp. 1–7.

30 *Report of the Indian Economic Enquiry Committee*, Vol. II, *passim.*

31 *Report of the Indian Economic Enquiry Committee*, Vol. I, pp. 64–8.

32 See for instance an article appearing in *Capital*, 25 April 1929, cutting in MV-PAPERS-IEI, Vol. 13.

33 'Note of Dissent by Professor A. R. Burnett-Hurst', *Report of the Indian Economic Enquiry* Committee, Vol. I, pp. 91–111.

34 See for instance Slater, *Southern India*, pp. 248–9. See also Menon, *Planning Democracy*, pp. 34–5.

35 *Report of the Indian Economic Enquiry Committee*, Vol. I, p. 64.

36 S. Subramanian, 'A Brief History of the Organisation of Official Statistics in India during the British Period', *Sankhyā: The Indian Journal of Statistics* 22, 1/2 (1960): 85–118, here pp. 112–17.

37 It is acknowledged as such in surveys of the history of statistics in India. E.g. Subramanian, 'A Brief History'; Y.S. Naik, 'Development of Industrial Statistics in India', *Sankhyā: The Indian Journal of Statistics (Series B)* 25, 3/4 (1963): 283–322, here pp. 285–6; J.K. Ghosh, P. Maiti, T. J. Rao, and B. K. Sinha, 'Evolution of Statistics in India', *International Statistical Review* 67, 1 (1999): 13–34.

38 'Indian Statistical Institute: Proceedings of the Annual General Meeting: Dated the 16th May, 1934', *Sankhyā: The Indian Journal of Statistics* 1, 4 (October, 1934): 485–8, here p. 486; 'Proceeding [sic] of the Council of the Indian Statistical Institute. 1934–35', *Sankhyā: The Indian Journal of Statistics* 2, 2 (1936): 210–12, here p. 211.

39 *Report of the Indian Economic Enquiry Committee*, Vol. I, p. 64.

40 Raghabendra Chattopadhyay mentions that the Enquiry Committee was a kind of 'precursor of the later efforts towards planning by the [colonial] Government.' Chattopadhyay, 'The Idea of Planning in India', p. 59.

41 On Saha, see See Pratik Chakrabarti, *Western Science in Modern India: Metropolitan Methods, Colonial Practices* (Delhi: Permanent Black, 2004), p. 286; Deepak Kumar, 'Reconstructing India: Disunity in the Science and Technology for Development Discourse, 1900–1947', *Osiris*, 2nd Series, 15 (2000): 241–57, here pp. 248–50.

42 Lionel Robbins, *Economic Planning and International Order* (London: Macmillan and Co., Ltd., 1937), p. 3. Nikhil Menon also quotes Robbins's 'grand panacea' remark, adding that he was a 'free-market economist'. Menon, *Planning Democracy*, p. 12.

43 Peter Temin, 'Soviet and Nazi Economic Planning in the 1930s', *The Economic History Review* 44, 4 (1991): 573–93.

44 Daniel Ritschel, *The Politics of Planning: The Debate on Economic Planning in Britain in the 1930s* (Oxford: Clarendon Press, 1997).

45 Marcia L. Balisciano, 'Hope for America: American notions of economic planning between pluralism and neoclassicism, 1930–1950', *History of Political Economy* 30, Supplement (1998): 153–78.

46 Medha M. Kudaisya, *Tryst with Prosperity: Indian Business and the Bombay Plan of 1944* (Gurgaon: Penguin Random House India, 2018), Chapter 4.

47 Benjamin Zachariah, *Developing India: An Intellectual and Social History, c. 1930–50* (New Delhi: Oxford University Press, 2005), p. 255.

48 Francis S. Pierce, 'Thorstein Veblen', *Encyclopedia Britannica*, 30 July 2023 (https://www.britannica.com/biography/Thorstein-Veblen, accessed 19 December 2023); Edwin Layton, 'Veblen and

the Engineers', *American Quarterly* 14, 1 (1962): 64–72. Layton argues that although such engineers were seen by the sociologist Thorstein Veblen as potential social revolutionaries, they were no social radicals. They were, however, interested in applying technology to social ends.

49 Balisciano, 'Hope for America', p. 162.

50 For instance, in a speech in 1912, Visvesvaraya declared: 'As compared with Europe, our climate and traditions all predispose us to a life of inaction and ease.' 'Speech at Bangalore Central College Day Meeting', 16 March 1912, MV-SPEECHES-VOL, pp. 17–31, here p. 23.

51 Quoted in Visvesvaraya, *Memoirs*, p. 126. The meeting is also discussed in Chapter 14 above.

52 See 'At the mercy of Exploiters', *Indian National Herald,* [3?] October 1927, cutting in MV-PAPERS-IEI, Vol. 21. Also see below.

53 'Poona Industrial Exhibition: Sir M. Visveswarayya's Address', *The Hindu*, 4 October 1927, cutting in MV-PAPERS-IEI, Vol. 21.

54 Visvesvaraya's speech at Sydenham College, 17 December 1930, in MV-PAPERS-IEI, Vol. 13.

55 'A Five Year Plan for India. How to Remove Illiteracy and Unemployment. Wanted a Technological University. Sir M. Visvesvaraya's Suggestions', *Bombay Chronicle,* 2 December 1931.

56 M. Visvesvaraya, *Planned Economy for India* (Bangalore: The Bangalore Press, 1934), p. v.

57 Chattopadhyay, 'The Idea of Planning in India', pp. 29–34 and 62–3.

58 Visvesvaraya, *Planned Economy for India*, pp. 266–76 and p. 300. Quoted text from pp. 266, 268, 269 and 270.

59 Ibid., pp. 268–9.

60 Ibid., pp. 279–80.

61 Ibid., pp. 281–6.

62 Ibid., pp. 293–5.

63 Ibid., pp. 297–8.

64 Ibid., pp. 339–42.

65 M. Visvesvaraya, *Nation Building: A Five-Year Plan for the Provinces* (Bangalore City: The Bangalore Press, 1937), pp. 3–4.

66 Ibid., pp. 40–2.

67 Metcalf and Metcalf, *A Concise History of Modern India*, pp. 194–6.

68 Visvesvaraya, *Nation Building*, esp. Chapter 1 and Chapter 5.

69 Ibid., pp. 65–6.

70 Ibid., pp. 34–6.

71 See ibid., pp. 2 and 75.

72 M. Vinaik, *J.C. Kumarappa and his Quest for World Peace* (Ahmedabad: Navajivan Publishing House, 1956), p. 61.

73 M.K. Gandhi to M. Visvesvaraya, 23 November 1934, CWMG, Vol. 59, pp. 388–9.

74 M. Visvesvaraya to M.K. Gandhi, 27 November 1934. Reprinted in Shakuntala Krishnamurthy, *Sir Mokshagundam Visvesvaraya* (Bangalore: n.p., 1992 [1980]), pp. 33-4. That Visvesvaraya sent Gandhi his book is inferred from M.K. Gandhi to M. Visvesvaraya, 10 December 1934, CWMG, Vol. 59, p. 435.

75 Visvesvaraya, *Nation Building*, p. 20.

76 See the discussion of his visit to Bhadravati in 1927 (Chapter 16 above).

77 M.K. Gandhi to M. Visvesvaraya, 10 December 1934, CWMG, Vol. 59, p. 435.

78 M.K. Gandhi to M. Visvesvaraya, 24 August 1938, CWMG, Vol. 67, p. 279.

79 M.K. Gandhi to M. Visvesvaraya, 12 June 1945, CWMG, Vol. 80, pp. 301–2 ; Bjørn Hettne, *The Political Economy of Indirect Rule: Mysore* 1881–1947 (New Delhi: Ambika Publications, 1978), p. 278.

80 M.K. Gandhi to M. Visvesvaraya, 11 September 1945, CWMG, Vol. 81, pp. 249–50.

81 Chattopadhyay, 'The Idea of Planning in India', Chapter III. On the provincial Congress governments' resignation, see Metcalf and Metcalf, *A Concise History of Modern India*, p. 203.

82 'Planning Commission', *Encyclopedia Britannica*, 12 December 2023 (https://www.britannica.com/topic/Planning-Commission, accessed 23 April 2024).

83 E.g. M. Visvesvaraya, *Prosperity through Industry: Move towards Rapid Industrialization*, 3rd edition (Bombay: The All-

India Manufacturers' Organization, 1943); M. Visvesvaraya, *Reconstruction in Post-War India: A plan of development all round* (Bombay: All-India Manufacturers' Organisation, 1944).

84 See Kudaisya, *Tryst with Prosperity,* esp. Chapter 5.

85 Visvesvaraya, *Planned Economy*, p. 8. Italics in original.

86 J.R.D. Tata's Foreword to Shakuntala Krishnamurthy, *Sir Mokshagundam Visvesvaraya* (p. iii).

87 M. Visvesvaraya, *Reconstruction in Post-War India: A plan of development all round* (Bombay: All-India Manufacturers' Organisation, 1944).

88 Ibid., pp. 5 and 12–13.

89 Ibid., p. i.

90 Ibid., p. ii and p. 5.

91 Ibid., p. 49.

92 Kudaisya, *Tryst with Prosperity*, pp. 176–9.

93 See also Vinod Vyasulu, 'Nehru and the Visvesvaraya Legacy', *Economic and Political Weekly* 24, 30 (29 July 1989): 1700–1704, here p. 1700.

94 D.R. Gadgil's review, *Indian Journal of Economics*, Vol. XVII (1936–7): 109-10. On Gadgil's Cambridge background, see 'Preface to the First Edition', in D.R. Gadgil, *The Industrial Evolution of India in Recent* Times (London: Humphrey Milford, Oxford University Press, 1938 [1924]), pp. v–vii, here p. v.

95 On the debate, see Kudaisya, *Tryst with Prosperity*, Chapter 4.

96 These points are stressed by 'dependency theory', which emerged in the second half of the twentieth century. André Munro, 'dependency theory', *Encyclopedia Britannica*, 26 January 2024 (https://www.britannica.com/topic/dependency-theory, accessed 23 April 2024).

97 J.B.H. Wadia, *M.N. Roy—The Man: An Incomplete Royana* (Bombay: Popular Prakashan, 1983), p. 57.

98 See 'Manabendra Nath Roy (1887–1954)', Internet Enyclopedia of Philosophy (https://iep.utm.edu/roy_mn/, accessed 20 December 2023); Kudaisya, *Tryst with Prosperity*, pp. 90–1.

99 G.D. Parikh, 'Searchlight on the Bombay Plan: I', *Independent India* 8, no. 49 (3 December 1944): 585–6 + 588 (quoted text from p. 585).

100 Visvesvaraya, *Planned Economy*, *passim*; Visvesvaraya, *Reconstruction in Post-War India*, pp. 23–4.
101 'Sir M. Visvesvaraya's Address', in V.A. Sundaram (ed.), *Benares Hindu University: 1916–42: Silver Jubilee Edition* (place and publisher not mentioned, 1942), pp. 576–605, here pp. 596–7. No date is mentioned in this source, but the speech was given on 2 March 1937, according to a copy available in MV-PAPERS-IEI, Vol. 13.
102 Parikh, 'Searchlight on the Bombay Plan: I', p. 586.
103 G.D. Parikh, 'Searchlight on the Bombay Plan: II', *Independent India* 8, no. 50 (10 December 1944): 597–8, here p. 597.
104 Parikh, 'Searchlight on the Bombay Plan: I' (quoted phrase from p. 585).
105 'Sir M. Visvesvaraya's Address', pp. 600–1.
106 Ibid., p. 601.
107 Vyasulu, 'Nehru and the Visvesvaraya Legacy', p. 1701.
108 Parikh, 'Searchlight on the Bombay Plan: II', p. 598.
109 Vyasulu, 'Nehru and the Visvesvaraya Legacy'. See also Raina's discussion of Vyasulu's article: Dhruv Raina, *Visvesvaraya as Engineer-Sociologist and the Evolution of His Techno-Economic Vision*, NIAS Lecture L1-2001 (Bangalore: National Institute of Advanced Studies, 2001), Table 2 (p. 28).

20. Rivers Gear

1 Brochure on the opening of the Chamaraja Sagar and Water Works, Bangalore, 1933, in MV-PAPERS-IEI, Vol. 13; M. Visvesvaraya, 'Constructing a waste weir and auxiliary works for the reservoir at Thippagondanahalli Sri Chamarajendra Water Works, Bangalore', note dated 27 November 1933, in MV-PAPERS-IEI, Vol. 10.
2 See for instance Visvesvaraya's report on *Drainage and other Improvement Schemes in Hyderabad*, 1933, in MV-PAPERS-IEI, Vol. 13. See also Chapter 7 above.
3 M. Visvesvaraya, confidential note on 'Improvements to Indore City' (13 May 1935); Visvesvaraya, note on water supply works in Nagpur (1936); Visvesvaraya, confidential note on 'The Water

Supply and Drainage of Indore City'. All in MV-PAPERS-IEI, Vol. 13.

4 M. Visvesvaraya to S. Hiriannaiya, 19 February 1939, facsimile, in Leela Krishnamurthy, *Bharata Ratna Sir M. Visvesvaraya—Naa Kandu Keledante* (Bangalore: Leela Krishnamurthy and Karnataka State Archives, 2010), p. 176.

5 M.K. Gandhi to M. Visvesvaraya, c. August 1937, CWMG, Vol. 66, p. 51. See also M.K. Gandhi to the Viceroy, 16 August 1937, CWMG, Vol. 66, p. 51, which suggests Gandhi believed an engineering solution could be found.

6 M. Visvesvaraya, 'The Flood Problem in Orissa. A Preliminary Note', Bangalore, 15 November 1937. In MV-PAPERS-IEI, Vol. 16.

7 'Flood Problem in Orissa: Sir M. Visvesvarayya's Recommendations', TOI, 10 March 1938, p. 17 (including quoted text); 'Notes and Comments: Flood Control', TOI, 23 June 1938, p. 14; *Mahanadi Valley Development: Hirakud Dam Project* (Simla: Manager Government of India Press, 1947), p. 8.

8 *Second Interim Report of the Orissa Flood Advisory Committee: January 1940.* Available at https://dspace.gipe.ac.in/xmlui/handle/10973/35554. Committee members' names appear on p. 15.

9 *Second Interim Report*, pp. 1–2; 'Sir M. Visweswarayya', TOI, 12 April 1939, p. 10.

10 *Second Interim Report*, pp. 13–15; ibid., Appendix V (p. 58); *Mahanadi Valley Development*, p. 9.

11 *Mahanadi Valley Development*, pp. 9–10. On Khosla, see 'Deceased Fellow: Name: Dr AN Khosla', website of the Indian National Science Academy (https://insaindia.res.in/old_website/detail.php?id=N51-0379, accessed 23 April 2024).

12 H. Mehtab [sic], 'Resolved Orissa Flood Problem', CENT-VOL, pp. 196–8, here p. 198. On Mahatab, see 'Constituent Assembly Members: Harekrushna Mahatab: 1898–1987', ConstitutionofIndia.net (https://www.constitutionofindia.net/members/harekrushna-mahatab/, accessed 3 Nov 2023).

13 Sir M. Visvesvaraya and Nawab Ali Nawaz Jung Bahadur, *Report on the Lloyd Barrage and Canals Project in Sind* (Bombay:

Government Central Press, 1929). APAC: IOR/V/27/734/20. Hereinafter cited as *Report on the Lloyd Barrage*. On Visvesvaraya's earlier work with Ahmed Ali, see Chapter 7 above.

14 Nafis Ahmad and Deryck O. Lodrick, 'Indus River', *Encyclopedia Britannica,* 13 October 2023 (https://www.britannica.com/place/Indus-River, accessed 6 March 2024).

15 *Report on the Lloyd Barrage*, paras 10–14 and para 68 (quoted text from para 12); Daniel Haines, 'Concrete "progress": irrigation, development and modernity in mid-twentieth-century Sind', *Modern Asian Studies* 45, 1 (2011): 179–200, esp. pp. 184–5.

16 *Report on the Lloyd Barrage*, paras 1, 14–17, 86–87 (quoted text from para 86).

17 Ibid., para 6 (Barrage Administration) and para 39 (July 1923 start date).

18 Ibid., paras 2 and 87.

19 *Report on the Lloyd Barrage*, paras 3–4.

20 Quoted in *Report on the Lloyd Barrage*, para 5.

21 'To Allay Public Fear', TOI, 1 June 1929, p. 12.

22 *Report on the Lloyd Barrage*, para 6 (quoted text from here) and para 28. For a brief report on one such meeting of the committee with zamindars and bureaucrats in Mirpurkhas, see 'Lloyd Barrage Inquiry. Zemindars' Views', TOI, 3 August 1929, p. 16.

23 Date mentioned in *Report on the Lloyd Barrage*, p. 54.

24 *Report on the Lloyd Barrage*, paras 32–5.

25 Ibid., para 91.

26 Ibid., *passim.*

27 Ibid., paras 29 and 78.

28 Ibid., para 91.

29 *Report on the Lloyd Barrage*, para 90.

30 Ibid., para 21.

31 Ibid., para 19.

32 Ibid., para 90.

33 Ibid., para 86.

34 Ibid., para 21.

35 Ibid., para 92 (including quoted text) and para 67.

36 Ibid., para 92.

37 Ibid., para 66.

38 Ibid., paras 92 and 65.
39 Ibid., para 90.
40 Ibid., paras 92 and 87.
41 Frederick Sykes to M. Visvesvaraya, 24 September 1929 (typed copy), Visvesvaraya Papers, NMML, microfilm Reel 8.
42 See Chapter 5 above.
43 *Report of the Irrigation Inquiry Committee appointed by the Government of Bombay, 1938* (Bombay: Government Central Press, 1938), paras 2, 11–12, and 25. Hereinafter cited as *Report of the Irrigation Inquiry Committee*. See also Chapter 5 above.
44 *Report of the Irrigation Inquiry Committee*, para 17.
45 Sanjaya Baru, 'State and Industrialisation: Political Economy of Sugar Policy, 1932-47', *Economic and Political Weekly* 18, 5 (29 Jan 1983): PE2-PE18, *passim* and Table 2; *Report of the Irrigation Inquiry Committee*, paras 25 and 83.
46 *Report of the Irrigation Inquiry Committee,* paras 3, 11–12, 25, 127 and pp. i–ii.
47 M. Visvesvaraya, *Nation Building: A Five-Year Plan for the Provinces* (Bangalore City: The Bangalore Press, 1937), p. v.
48 Bombay PWD, Resolution No. 1985/36, 28 December 1937, in *Report of the Irrigation Inquiry Committee*, p. i.
49 *Report of the Irrigation Inquiry Committee*, paras 1–4.
50 Ibid., paras 31–2. On the block system on the Nira Canal, see Chapter 5 above.
51 *Report of the Irrigation Inquiry Committee*, paras 35–42 and Chapter IX (for the existing system).
52 Ibid., paras 70–71, 121 and 123.
53 Ibid., paras 93–7.
54 Ibid., paras 81–3.
55 Ibid., Chapter X. Quoted text from para 90.
56 Ibid., paras 72 and 85.
57 See 'Irrigation Reforms', TOI, 9 September 1938, p. 8; 'Irrigation in Bombay', *Bombay Chronicle*, 9 September 1938.
58 'Bombay Irrigation Inquiry Report: Government Order: Proposals Generally Accepted', TOI, 21 April 1939, p. 16.
59 'Minute of Dissent by Mr. J.G. More, B.A., LL.B., M.L.A.', in *Report of the Irrigation Inquiry Committee*, pp. 61–74. On More,

see for instance 'Representation in Federation: Elective Basis for the States', TOI, 17 January 1933, p. 3; 'Bombay Non-Brahmins' Plight. Need Organisation and Discipline. Poona Meeting. President Condemns Civil Disobedience', TOI, 16 January 1933, p. 10.

60 'Minute of Dissent by Mr. J.G. More' (quoted text from paras 1 and 37).

61 Ibid., paras 12–13.

62 Ibid., para 18.

63 Ibid., paras 23–26.

64 Ibid., para 30.

65 Ibid., paras 32–34.

66 'Note by the Chairman on Mr. J.G. More's Minute of Dissent', in *Report of the Irrigation Inquiry Committee*, pp. 75–6.

21. The Motor of Progress

1 M. Visvesvaraya, *Memoirs of My Working Life* (Bangalore: M. Visvesvaraya, 1951), pp. 123–4.

2 See Chapter 13 above.

3 See Y.G. Krishnamurti, *Sir M. Visvesvaraya: A Study* (Bombay: Popular Book Depot, 1941), p. 13.

4 M. Visvesvaraya, *Planned Economy for India* (Bangalore: The Bangalore Press, 1934), p. 108.

5 Visvesvaraya, *Planned Economy*, pp. 111–12.

6 'Scheme for Car Factory. Capital of Over Rs. 100 Lakhs Necessary', TOI, 20 June 1935, p. 5; G.D. Khanolkar, *Walchand Hirachand: Man, his Times and Achievements* (Bombay: Walchand & Company, 2007 [1969]), pp. 307–9; [M. Visvesvaraya], 'Proposal to Start an Automobile Industry', Bombay, 1 April 1935, typescript in 'Walchand Hirachand–552 (I)',Walchand Hirachand Papers, NMML. On Saklatvala's position at Tatas, see 'Tata Titans: Sir Nowroji Saklatvala' (https://www.tata.com/about-us/tata-group-our-heritage/tata-titans/sir-nowroji-saklatvala, accessed 9 December 2022).

7 Khanolkar, *Walchand Hirachand,* p. 309; Rajat K. Ray, *Industrialization in India: Growth and Conflict in the Private Sector*

1914-47 (Delhi: Oxford University Press, 1982 [1979]), pp. 178–9 (on the need for technical assistance).

8 V.S. Narayana Rao, *Mokshagundam Visvesvaraya* (New Delhi: National Book Trust, 1995 [1988]), p. 101.

9 Visvesvaraya, *Memoirs*, pp. 127–8; Khanolkar, *Walchand Hirachand*, pp. 309–10; entries 178–186 in 'Index' of correspondence regarding automobile project, 'Walchand Hirachand–552 (I)', Walchand Hirachand Papers, NMML. On Tookey, see obituary in *The Engineer*, 1954, reprinted at https://www.gracesguide.co.uk/William_Alfred_Tookey (accessed 23 April 2024). On Beall, see 'Has a New Car', *New York Herald*, 8 January 1922, p. 9, at https://chroniclingamerica.loc.gov/data/batches/dlc_ambrosia_ver01/data/sn83045774/0027174433A/1922010801/0336.pdf (accessed 23 April 2024).

10 Khanolkar, *Walchand Hirachand*, p. 310.

11 Manu Subedar and A.D. Shroff, 'Report of the Sub-Committee appointed by the Committee to discuss the feasibility of the manufacture of motor-cars in India', typed copy [May 1936], 'Walchand Hirachand—552 (I)', Item 33, Walchand Hirachand Papers, NMML.

12 See Khanolkar, *Walchand Hirachand*, *passim*; Ray, *Industrialization in India*, pp. 280–1.

13 M.R. Varadarajan, 'The Meticulous Engineer', in CENT-VOL, pp. 174–81, here pp. 175–6.

14 See entries 49–53 in 'Index', 'Walchand Hirachand—552 (I)', Walchand Hirachand Papers, NMML.

15 Khanolkar, *Walchand Hirachand*, p. 311. On the Congress's early interest in industrialisation, see for instance Ross Bassett, *The Technological* Indian (Cambridge, MA: Harvard University Press, 2016), p. 36.

16 Khanolkar, *Walchand Hirachand*, p. 314.

17 See entries for 1939 correspondence (esp. entries 112, 113, 119, 120) in 'Index', 'Walchand Hirachand—552 (I)', Walchand Hirachand Papers, NMML.

18 P.B. Advani, 'Father of Planning', in CENT-VOL, pp. 137–45.

19 Khanolkar, *Walchand Hirachand*, pp. 314–5; several entries for 1939 correspondence in 'Index', 'Walchand Hirachand—553', Walchand Hirachand Papers, NMML.

20 Khanolkar, *Walchand Hirachand*, pp. 315–18. See also Visvesvaraya, *Memoirs,* p. 129.

21 See telegram from Walchand and Advani (Detroit) to [Walchand's] Hindusthan Construction Company (Bombay), 18 August 1939, in 'Walchand Hirachand—553', Walchand Hirachand Papers, NMML.

22 Khanolkar, *Walchand Hirachand,* pp. 318–23 and 421–22.

23 Sumit Sarkar, *Modern India: 1885–1947* (Delhi: Pearson, 2014), p. 321.

24 Khanolkar, *Walchand Hirachand*, pp. 422–5.

25 Except where other citations are given, the following account of the aircraft venture is based on Aparajith Ramnath, 'International Networks and Aircraft Manufacture in Colonial and Postcolonial India: States, Entrepreneurs and Educational Institutions, 1940–64', *Journal of Research Institute for the History of Global Arms Transfer*, 9 (2020): 41–59.

26 Khanolkar, *Walchand Hirachand*, pp. 345–52. On Pawley, see Anthony R. Carrozza, *William D. Pawley: the extraordinary life of the adventurer, entrepreneur, and diplomat who cofounded the Flying Tigers* (Washington, D.C.: Potomac Books, 2012).

27 On Mirza and Visvesvaraya's rapprochement, see Varadarajan, 'The Meticulous Engineer', p. 181.

28 Varadarajan, 'The Meticulous Engineer', pp. 180–1.

29 V.S. Narayana Rao, *Mokshagundam Visvesvaraya* (New Delhi: National Book Trust, 1995 [1988]), p. 107.

30 See photos in 'Sir MV: The Legendary Nation Builder', brochure accompanying exhibition, Nehru Science Centre, National Council of Science Museums (n.d. [2014?]), pp. 102–3.

31 See 'D.O. Letter from Sir Charles Todhunter, Private Secretary to H.H. the Maharaja of Mysore, to Sir Mirza Ismail, Dewan of Mysore, Camp Bhopal, N.O. C. 2845, dated 20th November 1940', KSA-MIRZA-VOL, pp. 129–30.

32 Khanolkar, *Walchand Hirachand*, p. 425.

33 Ibid., pp. 425–7.

34 See below. Also see Khanolkar, *Walchand Hirachand*, p. 426.

35 'Submission Note by Sir Mirza Ismail, Dewan of Mysore, Dated 16th November 1940', KSA-MIRZA-VOL, p. 129.

36 '(c) Note on Manufacture of Automobiles', under 'Papers left with His Highness the Maharaja by Sir Mirza Ismail, Dewan of Mysore, on the 23rd March 1941', KSA-MIRZA-VOL, pp. 131–5, here pp. 133–4.

37 '(a) Note on Manufacture of Automobiles in India, by Mr. Walchand Hirachand', under 'Papers left with His Highness the Maharaja by Sir Mirza Ismail, Dewan of Mysore, on the 23rd March 1941', KSA-MIRZA-VOL, pp. 131–5, here pp. 131–2.

38 'Papers left with His Highness the Maharaja by Sir Mirza Ismail, Dewan of Mysore, on the 23rd March 1941', KSA-MIRZA-VOL, pp. 131–5.

39 Bjørn Hettne, *The Political Economy of Indirect Rule: Mysore 1881–1947* (New Delhi: Ambika Publications, 1978), p. 296. For the regnal dates of the Maharajas, see ibid., p. 69.

40 R.K. Narayan, *My Days*, Kindle Edition (n.p.: Ecco, 1999), pp. 120–1.

41 Curiously enough, the pair got on well together otherwise, Mirza having been responsible for Todhunter getting the job with the maharaja fifteen years earlier. Mirza Ismail, *My Public Life* (London: George Allen and Unwin, 1954), p. 147.

42 'D.O. Letter from Sir Charles Todhunter, Private Secretary to H.H. the Maharaja of Mysore, to Sir Mirza Ismail, Dewan of Mysore, Bangalore, dated 26th March 1941', KSA-MIRZA-VOL, p. 135.

43 'D.O. Letter from Sir Charles Todhunter, Private Secretary to H.H. the Maharaja of Mysore, to Sir Mirza Ismail, Dewan of Mysore, Bangalore, dated 27th March 1941', KSA-MIRZA-VOL, pp. 135–7. On GM's import business, see 'Cutting from "The Hindu," dated 1st April 1941, submitted by Sir Mirza Ismail to His Highness the Maharaja', KSA-MIRZA-VOL, p. 141.

44 'D.O. Letter from Sir Mirza Ismail, Dewan of Mysore, to Sir Charles Todhunter, Private Secretary to H.H. the Maharaja of Mysore, N. C. 864, dated 27th March 1941', KSA-MIRZA-VOL, pp. 137–8.

45 'Letter from Sir Mirza Ismail, Dewan of Mysore, to Sir Charles Todhunter, Private Secretary to H.H. the Maharaja of Mysore, dated 4th April 1941', KSA-MIRZA-VOL, pp. 142–9.

46 'Copy of letter from Sir M. Visvesvaraya to Sir Mirza Ismail, dated 31st March 1941, submitted in original by Sir Mirza Ismail to His Highness the Maharaja', KSA-MIRZA-VOL, p. 139.

47 'Letter from Mr. N. Salvateesvaran to Sir Mirza Ismail, Dewan of Mysore, dated 24th April 1941', KSA-MIRZA-VOL, p. 171.

48 [J.H. Gordon] to Mirza Ismail, draft letter, D.O. No. Po 16–41, 9 April 1941; Charles Todhunter to J.H. Gordon, 18 April 1941, with enclosure titled 'Automobile Factory Scheme'. In 'Correspondence . . . Motor Car Factory in Mysore State . . . Resignation of Sir Mirza M. Ismail', File No. 16, 1941, APAC: IOR/R/2/Box 42/393.

49 J.H. Gordon to Kenneth Fitze, Secretary to the Crown Representative, D.O. No. po. 16–41, 9 April 1941, in 'Correspondence', APAC: IOR/R/2/Box 42/393.

50 J.H. Gordon to Kenneth Fitze, Secretary to the Crown Representative, D.O. No. Pol. 16/1941, 23 April 1941, in 'Correspondence', APAC: IOR/R/2/Box 42/393.

51 Gordon to Fitze, D.O. No. Pol. 16/1941, 1 May 1941; 'Telegram "Q"' from Polad Simla to Mysore Resident, No. 873 P, 4 May 1941 (transcript). In 'Correspondence', APAC: IOR/R/2/Box 42/393.

52 'Note embodying (1) Questionnaire presented by His Highness the Maharaja to Mr. M. Venkatanaranappa, Chairman, Mysore Iron and Steel Works, at the latter's interview with His Highness on the 10th April 1941, (2) Answers furnished by Mr. Venkatanaranappa on the 12th April 1941, and (3) Notes prepared by Sir Charles Todhunter, Private Secretary to His Highness the Maharaja, on the basis of a discussion with Sir M. Visvesvaraya, Mr. Walchand Hirachand and others in the presence of Sir Mirza Ismail, Dewan of Mysore, on the morning of the 13th of April 1941', KSA-MIRZA-VOL, pp. 150–160.

53 Note following response to Question 23, ibid., p. 158.

54 'Submission Note by Sir Mirza Ismail, Dewan of Mysore, dated 19th April 1941', KSA-MIRZA-VOL, pp. 160–6.

55 Telegrams between Todhunter, Mirza, and Hayavadana Rao, 6–8 May 1941, KSA-MIRZA-VOL, pp. 174–5.

56 'Telegram from Rao Saheb Mr. C. Hayavadana Rao, President, Mysore Chamber of Commerce, [Bangalore], to His Highness the Maharaja of Mysore, dated, 8th May 1941', KSA-MIRZA-VOL, p. 175.

57 Charles Todhunter to J.H. Gordon, 25 April 1941, in 'Correspondence', APAC: IOR/R/2/Box 42/393.

58 J.H. Gordon to Mirza Ismail, D.O. No. Pol. 16/41, 6 May 1941, in 'Correspondence', APAC: IOR/R/2/Box 42/393.

59 'Letter from Sir Charles Todhunter, Private Secretary to H.H. the Maharaja of Mysore, to Sir Mirza Ismail, Dewan of Mysore, dated 8th May 1941', KSA-MIRZA-VOL, pp. 175–6.

60 'D.O. Letter from Sir Mirza Ismail, Dewan of Mysore, Camp: Ootacamund, to Sir Charles Todhunter, Private Secretary to H.H. the Maharaja of Mysore, No. 6940, dated 8th May 1941', KSA-MIRZA-VOL, p. 176.

61 'Telegram "Q"', Resident to 'Polad Simla', No. 85, 12 May 1941, in 'Correspondence', APAC: IOR/R/2/Box 42/393.

62 Khanolkar, *Walchand Hirachand*, pp. 435–45.

63 Ibid., pp. 453–4.

64 *A Survey of India's Industrial Production for War Purposes: Report of the American Technical Mission to India* (August 1942), p. 1. Accessed via https://indianculture.gov.in/flipbook/2845.

65 Quoted in Khanolkar, *Walchand Hirachand*, pp. 457–60.

66 Khanolkar, *Walchand Hirachand*, pp. 463–6.

67 Ramnath, 'International Networks,' pp. 49–51.

68 Khanolkar, *Walchand Hirachand*, Part 3 ('Last Period'), Chapter 6.

69 As indicated by their executive's remarks to the Mysore maharaja, discussed above. At one point the Indian GM agency considered pre-empting competition by collaborating with Walchand in some form, but this did not come to pass. See the following documents in 'Walchand Hirachand—553', Walchand Hirachand Papers, NMML: Typed note from Lalchand Hirachand to Walchand Hirachand, 14 December 1939; typed note from Lalchand Hirachand to Walchand Hirachand, 15 December 1939; H.M. Halstead (Managing Director, General Motors India Ltd.) to Lalchand Hirachand, 28 November 1939; P.B. Advani's typed

note to Walchand, Lalchand, and Visvesvaraya, titled 'Automobile Manufacture. General Motors', 20 January 1940.

70 See Gita Piramal, *Business Legends*, Kindle Edition (New Delhi: Penguin, 1999 [1998]), Introduction.

71 Ibid., section on Walchand Hirachand, Chapter 9.

72 Hettne, *Political Economy of Indirect Rule*, p. 279.

73 Khanolkar, *Walchand Hirachand*, Part 3 ('Last Period'), Chapter 9; Piramal, *Business Legends*, section on Walchand Hirachand, Chapter 10. On date of incorporation, see what appears to be the first share offering, advertised in the TOI, 4 July 1944, p. 3 under the heading 'The Premier Automobiles Ltd.' (For the situation in 1947, see PAL advertisement, TOI, 7 July 1947, p. 5.)

22. Mentor to Manufacturers

1 Y.G. Krishnamurti, *Sir M. Visvesvaraya: A Study* (Bombay: Popular Book Depot, 1941), Chapter 1. Quoted text from pp. 4, 8, and 13.

2 See preceding chapters.

3 'Need for Special Study of Reconstruction Measures', *Bombay Chronicle*, 22 September 1941.

4 N.D. Sahukar, 'Visvesvaraya—A Man of Gold', in CENT-VOL, pp. 93–7, here pp. 93–4 (including quoted text); Murarji J. Vaidya, 'Sir M.V.—As I Know Him', in CENT-VOL, pp. 98–109, here p. 98.

5 Vaidya, 'Sir M.V.—As I Know Him', pp. 99–100. On the Servants of India Society oaths, see Manorama Barnabas, 'Study in the Philosophy of Social Change: The Ideas of Some Liberal Thinkers of Nineteenth Century Maharashtra and Their Relevance to Modernization' (unpublished PhD thesis, University of Poona, 1974), pp. 331–2.

6 Membership and office address inferred from *The All-India Manufacturers' Conference Bombay: Proceedings of the first session held at Bombay on 1st & 2nd March 1941* (Bombay: [AIMO], 1941). Hereafter cited as AIMO Conference Proceedings 1941. Visvesvaraya was President of the AIMO from 1941–54: see 'Past Presidents', website of the All India Manufacturers' Organisation

(https://www.aimoindia.com/about/past-presidents/, accessed 24 April 2024).

7 On Poona, see the proceedings of the All-India Manufacturers' Conference, 21–22 March 1942, in MV-PAPERS-IEI, Vol. 16. On Baroda, Nagpur, New Delhi, see: G.V. Puranik, 'Efficiency Personified', in CENT-VOL, pp. 191–5, here p. 195; P.L. Badami, 'Lonely Seer', in CENT-VOL, pp. 199–205, here pp. 200–1.

8 Visvesvaraya's presidential address in AIMO Conference Proceedings 1941, here p. 27.

9 Visvesvaraya, 'Closing Remarks', in the proceedings of the All-India Manufacturers' Conference, Poona, 21–22 March 1942, here p. 61. In MV-PAPERS-IEI, Vol. 16.

10 Visvesvaraya quoted in *Indian Annual Register*, January–June 1943, Vol. I, p. 355.

11 *Indian Annual Register*, January–June 1944, Vol. I, p. 42.

12 'Heavy Industries on Regional Basis. Proposals Before Government', TOI, 30 November 1945, p. 4. On the Planning and Development Department, see Raghabendra Chattopadhyay, 'The Idea of Planning in India, 1930–1951', PhD thesis, Australian National University (1985), pp. 188–9.

13 Visvesvaraya's presidential address in AIMO Conference Proceedings 1941, here p. 23.

14 In 1943, the AIMO Conference passed a resolution '[expressing] grave concern over Mahatma Gandhi's fast' and petitioning the colonial government 'for his immediate and unconditional release'. *Indian Annual Register*, January–June 1943, Vol. I, p. 356. When the U.K. Cabinet Mission arrived in India in 1946 Visvesvaraya and the AIMO expressed their approval, 'since economic advancement in the country would not be possible without the support of political power which the Mission promised to transfer to Indian hands'. 'Political Power Essential. Sir M. Visvesvaraya on Industries' Position', TOI, 8 April 1946, p. 5. On the national sense of identity among Indian businesses in the colonial era more generally, see A.-M. Misra, '"Business Culture" and Entrepreneurship in British India, 1860-1950', *Modern Asian Studies* 34, 2 (2000): 333-48.

15 There were 'weekly committee meetings' (Sahukar, 'Visvesvaraya—A Man of Gold', p. 95) and 'Quarterly Meeting[s] of the Central Committee' (Vaidya, 'Sir M.V.—As I Know Him', p. 101).

16 Sahukar, 'Visvesvaraya—A Man of Gold', p. 94.

17 Vaidya, 'Sir M.V.—As I Know Him', pp. 101–2; Badami, 'Lonely Seer', pp. 201–2.

18 *Iron and Steel Industry in India, A.-I.M.O. Monograph No. 2* (1943); *Village Industrialization (A scheme for developing industries suitably grouping villages)* (1945); *Reconstruction in Post-War India: A plan of development all round* (1944). The above titles are listed in CENT-VOL, pp. 338–9.

19 M. Visvesvaraya, *Prosperity through Industry: Move towards Rapid Industrialization* (Bombay: The All-India Manufacturers' Organization, 1943 [1942]), p. 5.

20 Ibid., esp. pp. 1–10.

21 Ibid., pp. 56–62. He had used the slogan 'industrialise or perish' before. 'Sir M. Visvesvaraya's Address' [1937], in V.A. Sundaram (ed.), *Benares Hindu University: 1916–42: Silver Jubilee Edition* (place and publisher not mentioned, 1942), pp. 576–605, here p. 592.

22 H. Rangachar and P. Kodanda Rao, 'A Brief Life Sketch', in CENT-VOL, pp. 293–334, here p. 330.

23 'Indian Science Institute: Criticism of Policy', TOI, 27 March 1939, p. 6 (quoted text from this source); 'Sir M. Visvesvaraya on Applied Research in Relation to Industrial Development and Post-War Reconstruction', *Current Science* 12, 4 (1943): 101–5; S. Bhagavantam, 'Moulder of the Indian Institute of Science', in CENT-VOL, pp. 254–6, here p. 255.

24 M.S. Thacker, 'A Realist and a Man of Action', in CENT-VOL, pp. 88–92, here p. 91.

25 'Department of Metallurgical Research and Research Workshop of Mechanical Engineering, at the Indian Institute of Science', *Current Science* 11, 4 (1942): 140–1; Aparajith Ramnath, 'International Networks and Aircraft Manufacture in Colonial and Postcolonial India: States, Entrepreneurs and Educational Institutions, 1940–64', *Journal of Research Institute for the History*

of Global Arms Transfer 9 (2020): 41–59, here p. 49. See also 'Sir M. Visvesvaraya on Applied Research in Relation to Industrial Development and Post-War Reconstruction'; Rangachar and Rao, 'A Brief Life Sketch', p. 330.

26 Visvesvaraya, *Memoirs*, pp. 95–6; P.H. Krishna Rao, 'Sir M.V. and the Occupational Institute', in CENT-VOL, pp. 206–14. It is not clear why the question of Visvesvaraya's unpaid salary arose twelve or thirteen years after he stepped down from the Bhadravati board. For the start date of the Institute and a mention of Visvesvaraya's note, see P.H. Krishna Rao to heads of Mysore districts, municipalities and others, 4 December 1942, in 'Grant of Scholarships to the students studying in the Sri Jayachamarajendra Occupational Institute Bangalore', Municipal, 1942–43, File No. 10–42, S. Nos. 138–9, in KSA-DIGITIZED (https://archives.karnataka.gov.in/home/viewdocument?doc_id=RGVlcGFrMTE3OTgw&doc_location=RGVlcGFrMQ==).

27 P.H. Krishna Rao, 'Sir M.Visvesvaraya and the Occupational Institute', in CENT-VOL, pp. 206–14 (quoted text from p. 209).

28 'Granting two scholarships @ 7-8-0 pm each to two students belonging to Hassan reading at Sri Jayachamarajendra Occupational Institute for 5 months', Municipal, 1944, File No. 99–43, S. Nos. 177–8, in KSA-DIGITIZED (https://archives.karnataka.gov.in/home/viewdocument?doc_id=RGVlcGFrMTE5OTY2&doc_location=RGVlcGFrMQ==); 'Grant of Scholarships to the students studying in the Sri Jayachamarajendra Occupational Institute Bangalore', Municipal, 1942–43, File No. 10–42, S. Nos. 138–9, in KSA-DIGITIZED (https://archives.karnataka.gov.in/home/viewdocument?doc_id=RGVlcGFrMTE3OTgw&doc_location=RGVlcGFrMQ==); 'Grant of scholarship by the Davanahalli [sic] Town Ml Cl to C Vedavyasa Rao, a student of the Sri Jayachama Rajendra Occupational Institute, Bangalore, for 1944–45', Municipal, 1945, File No. 108–44, S. Nos. 5–6, in KSA-DIGITIZED (https://archives.karnataka.gov.in/home/viewdocument?doc_id=RGVlcGFrMTIwMDc3&doc_location=RGVlcGFrMQ==).

29 *The Report of the University Education Commission (December 1948–August 1949)*, Vol. I (Delhi: Manager of Publications, 1950), p. 94.

30 See 'Industrialists' Tour. Delegation Leaving Today', TOI, 21 June 1946, p. 3; 'Indian Industrial Mission to U.K.: Study Tour', TOI, 3 June 1946, p. 4.

31 'Trade Relations with Australia. Indian Member's Plea for Co-operation', TOI, 23 February 1945, p. 4.

32 'Industrialists' "Private Move". Delegation To U.K. To Get New Ideas', TOI, 11 May 1945, p. 9; 'Indian Industrial Delegation', TOI, 12 May 1945, p. 1; 'India's Industrial Delegation', TOI, 16 May 1945, p. 7.

33 'Members of the All-India Manufacturers' Organization (A.-I.M.O.) Delegation: To the U.K., the U.S.A., and Canada', typed note, enclosed with letter from P. Chaudhuri (India Supply Commission, 45/7, Mount Street, London) to H.A.F. Rumbold (India Office), 20 July 1946. In 'Industries: All-India Manufacturers' Organisation', File E. 2808 of 1946, APAC: IOR/L/E/8/4281. (This file is hereafter cited simply by the APAC catalogue number.) On Puranik, see also 'History', website of Shree Dhootapapeshwar Limited (https://sdlindia.com/history/, accessed 25 April 2024).

34 'Industrialists' Tour. Delegation Leaving Today', TOI, 21 June 1946, p. 3; 'Industrialisation of India. Aim of Mission To U.K.', TOI, 22 June 1946, p. 7; Vaidya, 'Sir M.V.—As I Know Him' (quoted text from p. 102). On the format of the final report, see K.L. Govil, Review of *Report of the Delegation Which visited the Industrially Developed Countries of the West (1946–47)*, in *Indian Journal of Economics* XXIX (1948–49): 85–6.

35 Office note, J. Thomson to H.A.F. Rumbold (both of the India Office), 29 July 1946, in APAC: IOR/L/E/8/4281; 'India Supply Commission. Procurement of Goods', TOI, 25 April 1946, p. 7. For the ISC's address, see Chaudhuri to Rumbold, 20 July 1946, cited above.

36 Office note, J. Thomson to H.A.F. Rumbold, 23 July 1946; Chaudhuri to Rumbold, 20 July 1946 (cited above). In APAC: IOR/L/E/8/4281.

37 M.J. Watt (Empire Department, Federation of British Industries) to H.A.F. Rumbold (India Office), 5 July 1946, in APAC: IOR/L/E/8/4281.

38 Handwritten note, unknown sender to J. Thomson and H.A.F. Rumbold (India Office), 8 July 1946 in APAC: IOR/L/E/8/4281.

39 J. Thomson to M.J. Watt, 11 July 1946 (copy), in APAC: IOR/L/E/8/4281.

40 Visvesvaraya, *Memoirs*, p. 130; Director, Platt Brothers and Company Limited, to Director, Indian Supply Commission, 8 August 1946 (typed copy), in APAC: IOR/L/E/8/4281.

41 'Indian Guests See What Derby Can Produce', *Derby Evening Telegraph*, 24 July 1946.

42 This statistic went into the delegation's final report. See Govil, Review of *Report of the Delegation*. Visvesvaraya carried a notebook with him everywhere, as several of his acquaintances noted in their centenary tributes in CENT-VOL.

43 'Indian Guests See What Derby Can Produce'.

44 Director, Platt Brothers and Co. Ltd., to Director, Indian Supply Commission, 8 August 1946 (copy), in APAC: IOR/L/E/8/4281.

45 'Manufacturers' Delegation. Sir M. Visvesvaraya's Tour Impressions', TOI, 19 December 1946, p. 3.

46 Various letters, but especially Chaudhuri to Rumbold, 20 July 1946, in APAC: IOR/L/E/8/4281.

47 *Indian Annual Register*, January–June 1946, Vol. I, Table of Contents (pp. v–xii) and p. 2.

48 Indian Industrial Delegation, AIMO, to Lord Pethick-Lawrence, Secretary of State for India, 13 August 1946 (copy), in APAC: IOR/L/E/8/4281.

49 Office note, [Rumbold] to Thomson, 16 August 1946, in APAC: IOR/L/E/8/4281.

50 Office note, [Rumbold] to Thomson, 16 August 1946; AIMO delegation's draft of proposed press release ('Delegation: Draft press notice'), attached with office note from [unnamed] to Secretary of State, 17 August 1946. In APAC: IOR/L/E/8/4281.

51 AIMO delegation's draft of proposed press release ('Delegation: Draft press notice'), attached with office note from [unnamed] to Secretary of State, 17 August 1946. In APAC: IOR/L/E/8/4281.

52 Red pencil noting on office note from [unnamed] to Secretary of State, 17 August 1946, in APAC: IOR/L/E/8/4281; Telegram (draft) No. 15490, from Secretary of State to Secretary, [AIMO], 23 August 1946, in APAC: IOR/L/E/8/4281.
53 G.K. Devarajulu, 'A Master Mind', in CENT-VOL, pp. 273–6, here p. 274.
54 Govil, Review of *Report of the Delegation.*
55 Ibid. On MIT and Indian students, see Ross Bassett, *The Technological* Indian (Cambridge, MA: Harvard University Press, 2016).
56 Visvesvaraya, *Memoirs*, p. 130. On the Tennessee Valley Authority, see 'Our History', website of the Tennessee Valley Authority (https://www.tva.com/about-tva/our-history, accessed 24 April 2024).
57 'Manufacturers' Delegation. Sir M. Visvesvaraya's Tour Impressions', TOI, 19 December 1946, p. 3.
58 Govil, Review of *Report of the Delegation*, p. 86.
59 'A Valuable Report', *Bombay Chronicle*, 25 November 1947, p. 6.

23. An Ageing Gadfly in the New India

1 'Indian Institute of Science: Sir A. Dalal as Chairman', TOI, 30 June 1947, p. 6.
2 Interview with Shakuntala Krishnamurthy (with inputs from Satish Mokshagundam and Lakshmi M. Satish), Bengaluru, 26 June 2019. The description of the house is based on a Films Division documentary that shows footage from around a decade later: *Dr Visvesvaraya* (c. 1961, directed by M.V. Krishnaswamy), available on the YouTube channel of the Films Division (https://www.youtube.com/watch?v=ng12ol-gvHg&t=2s). Hereafter cited as Films Division documentary, *Dr Visvesvaraya.*
3 'Industries Not Given Due Importance in National Plan—Mr. Visvesvaraya', TOI, 15 March 1953, p. 9; 'Government Aid For Steel Plants: Plea by A.-I.M.O.', TOI, 7 April 1951, p. 4; 'A.-I.M.O. Conference', TOI, 21 March 1954, p. 4.
4 'President of A.-I.M.O.: Mr. Visvesvaraya Elected', TOI, 6 July 1953, p. 5.

5 Barbara D. Metcalf and Thomas R. Metcalf, *A Concise History of Modern India*, 3rd edition (Cambridge: Cambridge University Press, 2012), Chapter 7; Rohit De, 'Between Midnight and Republic: Theory and Practice of India's Dominion Status', *International Journal of Constitutional Law* 17, no. 4 (31 December 2019): 1213–34.

6 'Move to Nationalise Air Services: Mr. Visvesvaraya Disapproves', TOI, 19 March 1953, p. 3; 'Nationalisation of Industries: Mr. Visvesvaraya's Criticism', TOI, 12 June 1950, p. 5; 'Education & Industries Make Slow Progress: Attend to Vital Problems Says Mr. Visvesvaraya', TOI, 11 January 1954, p. 3; 'A.-I.M.O. Report on Japan and S.-E. Asia: Lessons for India', TOI, 25 December 1954, p. 4 (including quoted text); 'Concessions to Foreign Interests in India: Criticism by Industrial Conference', TOI, 26 March 1952, p. 5. See also 'Raise Rs. 2,000-Crore Loan For Industrial Development: Visvesvaraya's Plea at A.I.M.O. Conference: Govt. May Nationalise Defence And Key Industries', *Bombay Chronicle*, 21 February 1949.

7 'Concessions to Foreign Interests in India: Criticism by Industrial Conference', TOI, 26 March 1952, p. 5; 'Industries Not Given Due Importance in National Plan—Mr. Visvesvaraya', TOI, 15 March 1953, p. 9. On the first Five-Year Plan, see Ramachandra Guha, *India After Gandhi: The History of the World's Largest Democracy* (London, Basingstoke and Oxford: Picador, 2007), p. 206.

8 'Move to Nationalise Air Services: Mr. Visvesvaraya Disapproves', TOI, 19 March 1953, p. 3 (including quoted text); 'Concessions to Foreign Interests in India: Criticism by Industrial Conference', TOI, 26 March 1952, p. 5; 'Nationalisation of Industries: Mr. Visvesvaraya's Criticism', TOI, 12 June 1950, p. 5. On the nationalisation of Air India, see also Team Frontline, '1953: Air India nationalised', *Frontline* (online), 11 August 2022 (https://frontline.thehindu.com/the-nation/india-at-75-epochal-moments-1953-air-india-nationalised/article65722229.ece, accessed 26 December 2022).

9 'Need for Opposition to Congress: Party Of Dissident Groups', TOI, 29 September 1950, p. 6. Visvesvaraya's concerns about the

new regime were also mentioned by Shakuntala Krishnamurthy (interview, Bengaluru, 26 June 2019, with inputs from Satish Mokshagundam and Lakshmi M. Satish).

10 'Visvesvaraya Celebrates His 90th Birthday Today', *Bombay Chronicle*, 15 September 1950.

11 'Move to Nationalise Air Services: Mr. Visvesvaraya Disapproves', TOI, 19 March 1953, p. 3.

12 See for instance 'Development on Western Lines: Mr. Visvesvaraya Lays Emphasis', TOI, 16 September 1955, p. 9.

13 M. Visvesvaraya, *Memoirs of My Working Life* (Bangalore: M. Visvesvaraya, 1951), Chapter XVII: 'Threats to National Security'.

14 'Why Not Entrust Damodar Project to Indian Engineers? Sir M. Visvesvaraya's Poser to India's Commerce Minister', *Bombay Chronicle*, 17 July 1948; 'Unjustified Slur', TOI, 2 March 1953, p. 6.

15 Quoted in 'Manufacture of Defence Armaments in India: Visvesvaraya Appeals to Governments for Satisfactory Arrangements', *Bombay Chronicle*, 26 October 1948.

16 'Raise Rs. 2,000-Crore Loan For Industrial Development: Visvesvaraya's Plea at A.I.M.O. Conference: Govt. May Nationalise Defence And Key Industries', *Bombay Chronicle*, 21 February 1949.

17 'Planned Canal Irrigation For Saurashtra: Sir M. Visvesvaraya's Suggestions Awaited', *Bombay Chronicle*, 14 October 1948.

18 'Rail Bridge Over Ganga: Mr. Visvesvaraya To Select Site'; TOI, 29 March 1952, p. 8; 'Ganga Bridge', Lok Sabha Debates, 27 June 1952, Col. 1307 (accessed via https://eparlib.nic.in/bitstream/123456789/55169/1/lsd_01_01_27-06-1952.pdf); J. Singh, 'A Note on the Selection of a Site for a Ganges Bridge in Bihar', *Sankhyā: The Indian Journal of Statistics* 8, 4 (1948): 385–88.

19 Henry Hart, *New India's Rivers* (Calcutta: Orient Longmans, 1956), pp. 45–56.

20 'Excellent Progress Under Visvesvaraya Scheme: People Support Rural Industrialisation', TOI, 1 July 1955, p. 10 (including quoted text); 'Mysore: Visvesvaraya Plan', TOI, 14 September 1954, p. 9; Mysore State Gazetteer (Kolar), 1968, p. 221 (https://gazetteer.

karnataka.gov.in/storage/pdf-files/Kolar1968Chapter5Pdf.pdf, accessed 26 December 2022); Appendix III: 'Rural Industrialisation Scheme By Dr. M. Visvesvaraya', in *Estimates Committee 1959–60: Seventy-Seventh Report (Second Lok Sabha): Ministry of Commerce and Industry: Small Scale Industries: Part I* (New Delhi: Lok Sabha Secretariat, 1960), pp. 41–3; 'Annexure B: A Scheme of Rural Industrialisation By Sir M. Visvesvaraya', in S. Kesava Iyengar, *Rural Economic Enquiries in the Hyderabad State 1949–51* (Hyderabad: Government Press, 1951), pp. 564–78.

21 M. Visvesvaraya, 'Government of Mysore Rural Industrialization Scheme', a 1956 pamphlet reprinted in untitled souvenir on Visvesvaraya (Bengaluru: Century Club, 2017), pp. 69–85.

22 'Industrialising Rural Areas: Govt. to Launch Scheme', TOI, 8 October 1955, p. 1.

23 *Estimates Committee (1965–66): Hundred and Seventh Report (Third Lok Sabha): Ministry of Industry (Organisation of the Development Commissioner, Small Scale Industries—Rural Industrialisation)* (New Delhi: Lok Sabha Secretariat, 1966), pp. 44–45; *Estimates Committee 1959–60: Seventy-Seventh Report (Second Lok Sabha): Ministry of Commerce and Industry: Small Scale Industries: Part I* (New Delhi: Lok Sabha Secretariat, 1960), pp. 14–15.

24 *Speech delivered by Sir M. Visvesvaraya, on the occasion of the Works Day Celebrations 1950 of the Mysore Iron and Steel Works, Bhadravati; Address at the College of Engineering Bangalore by Sir M. Visvesvaraya: 27th January 1955*. Printed speeches, seen courtesy of Satish Mokshagundam, Bengaluru. On the function at Central College, see Films Division documentary, *Dr Visvesvaraya*.

25 T.S. Satyan, *Alive and Clicking* (Gurgaon: Penguin, 2005), Chapter 8 (the quoted text, and the quote from Visvesvaraya, are from p. 69).

26 'Sir M. Visvesvaraya at Gopal Bagh. Coimbatore', 18 October 1952, especially pp. 8–9, 24, and 27–8. The pamphlet was consulted at the Gokhale Institute of Public Affairs (GIPA), Bengaluru, shelfmark: 926.2054 N52. On Visvesvaraya's going by plane: see photograph of his arrival, in 'Sir MV: The Legendary Nation Builder', brochure accompanying exhibition, Nehru

Science Centre, National Council of Science Museums (n.d. [2014?]), pp. 120–1.

27 'Sir M. Visvesvaraya at Gopal Bagh', pp. 33–4.

28 Quoted in '"Messiah" of Industrial Progress: Visvesvaraya Felicitated on his 90th Birthday', *Bombay Chronicle*, 16 September 1950. I have rendered the quote from Renan as it appears in his *Recollections of My Youth* (London: Chapman and Hall, 1897), p. 330.

29 'Mr. Visvesvaraya Is 92: Country-wide Tributes', TOI, 16 September 1952, p. 7. On the West End Hotel, see Bharti Nath, '125 years old, still retains grandeur of the past', *Deccan Herald*, 11 August 2012 [revised 19 November 2018] (https://www.deccanherald.com/content/270930/125-years-old-still-retains.html, accessed 23 December 2022).

30 'Mr. M. Visvesvaraya', TOI, 16 September 1955, p. 4.

31 Quoted in 'Development on Western Lines: Mr. Visvesvaraya Lays Emphasis', TOI, 16 September 1955, p. 9.

32 'Development on Western Lines: Mr. Visvesvaraya Lays Emphasis', TOI, 16 September 1955, p. 9.

33 'Mr. Nehru Receives Nation's Highest Award: Five-Word Citation at Investiture', TOI, 8 September 1955, p. 1. On Bhagwan Das, see Binay Singh, 'Dr Bhagwan Das, a freedom-fighter and scholar par excellence', *The Times of India* (online), 12 January 2022, https://timesofindia.indiatimes.com/city/varanasi/dr-bhagwan-das-a-freedom-fighter-and-scholar-par-excellence/articleshow/88843407.cms (accessed 27 December 2022). The detail about the Gandhi caps is observed from Films Division documentary, *Dr Visvesvaraya*.

34 Photograph facing p. 288 in CENT-VOL; Films Division documentary, *Dr Visvesvaraya*.

35 Shakuntala Krishnamurthy, *Sir Mokshagundam Visvesvaraya* (Bangalore: n.p., 1992 [1980]), pp. 14–15 reproduces the text of the citation.

36 'Mr. Nehru Receives Nation's Highest Award: Five-Word Citation at Investiture', TOI, 8 September 1955, p. 1.

37 'Tributes by President: Delhi Incident Recalled', TOI, 16 September 1960, p. 1.

38 Shakuntala Krishnamurthy, *Sir Mokshagundam Visvesvaraya*, p. 11.

39 E.g. see 'Development on Western Lines: Mr. Visvesvaraya Lays Emphasis', TOI, 16 September 1955, p. 9; 'Visvesvaraya Hits Preference Shown To Public Sector', *Bombay Chronicle*, 16 September 1955; 'Co-operative Farming: Dr. Visvesvaraya Advises Caution', TOI, 24 June 1956, p. 9.

40 See for instance Pandri Nath, *Mokshagundam Visvesvaraya: Life and Work* (Bombay: Bharatiya Vidya Bhavan, 1987), p. 111.

41 Mentioned in G.D. Naidu's speech, in 'Sir M. Visvesvaraya at Gopal Bagh. Coimbatore', pp. 11–12. A similar memory was related by a family friend of mine, the late Mr G.R. Vasuki of Bengaluru, who as a boy visited Visvesvaraya with his grandfather Mr Singlachar. Singlachar's father, K. Ananthacharya, had worked with Visvesvaraya on the KRS project in the 1910s. Interview with G.R. Vasuki, Bengaluru, 12 February 2018.

42 M. Visvesvaraya (5 Cubbon Road, Bangalore) to C. Rajagopalachari (Thyagarayanagar, Madras), 10 April 1954, C. Rajagopalachari papers (V Instalment), NMML.

43 See for instance Shakuntala Krishnamurthy, 'Sir M.—An Inside View', in CENT-VOL, pp. 280–92, here p. 287.

44 Interview with Shakuntala Krishnamurthy, Bengaluru, 26 June 2019 (with inputs from Satish Mokshagundam and Lakshmi M. Satish).

45 Shakuntala Krishnamurthy, 'Sir M.—An Inside View', here p. 291.

46 Interview with Shakuntala Krishnamurthy, Bengaluru, 26 June 2019 (with inputs from Satish Mokshagundam and Lakshmi M. Satish).

47 Quoted in H. Kusumakar, 'Engineer-Statesman Nears Century Mark', TOI, 13 September 1959, p. 8.

48 Pandri Nath, *Mokshagundam Visvesvaraya: Life and Work* (Bombay: Bharatiya Vidya Bhavan, 1987), p. 87 (on the story of the Chicago trader) and *passim.*

49 Visvesvaraya to Dildar Husain, 7 April 1960, facsimile in front matter of Dildar Husain, *An Engineering Wizard of India (1861–1962)* (Hyderabad: Institution of Engineers (India) Andhra Pradesh Centre, 1966).

50 Films Division documentary, *Dr Visvesvaraya.*
51 'Glowing Tributes by Prime Minister: "Life of Integrity In Cause of Nation"', TOI, 16 September 1960, pp. 1 and 7. The report is also the source for the quotations from various speakers at the event.
52 Ibid.
53 'Glowing Tributes Paid to Dr. Visvesvaraya: "Author of Planned Economy for India"', TOI, 16 September 1960, p. 5.
54 'Tributes by President: Delhi Incident Recalled', TOI, 16 September 1960, p. 1.
55 Interview with Sheshadri Mokshagundam, Bengaluru, 19 June 2019.
56 Pandri Nath, *Mokshagundam Visvesvaraya*, p. 121; 'Visvesvaraya Ill', TOI, 14 May 1961, p. 1.
57 'Visvesvaraya Feted', TOI, 16 September 1961, p. 9.
58 Pandri Nath, *Mokshagundam Visvesvaraya*, p. 121.
59 Facsimile of handwritten note by Visvesvaraya, dated 15 February 1946, in 'Sir MV: The Legendary Nation Builder', brochure accompanying exhibition, Nehru Science Centre, National Council of Science Museums (n.d. [2014?]), pp. 138–9.
60 'Government of Mysore: The Death of Bharatha Ratna Sir Mokshagundam Visvesvaraya', signed R.J. Rebello, Chief Secretary, 14 April 1962. Reproduced on p. 14 of Shakuntala Krishnamurthy, *Sir Mokshagundam Visvesvaraya.*
61 'Visvesvaraya Passes Away: Statesman-Engineer Who Placed India On Road To Planned Development', TOI, 15 April 1962, p. 1.

Epilogue: Engineering a Nation

1 Or, as one scholar from the 1960s put it, a 'century of technocracy'. William G. Carleton, 'The Century of Technocracy', *The Antioch Review* 25, 4 (Winter, 1965–66): 487–506.
2 Israel García Solares and Edward Beatty, 'A Blueprint for Modernity: Engineers and the Globalization of Expertise, 1870–1930: A Brief Project Overview', unpublished note, April 2020 (on the project, see https://kellogg.nd.edu/blueprint-modernity-engineers-and-

globalization-expertise-ca-1870-1930-virtual). On the trend in the USA, see Jeffrey K. Stine, review of *Prophets of Order: The Rise of the New Class, Technocracy and Socialism in America* by Donald Stabile, *Technology and Culture* 27, 4 (1986): 838–40.

3 See for instance Edward Beatty and Israel G. Solares's Introduction to the (as yet untitled) volume edited by them (MIT Press, forthcoming) and emerging from the 'Blueprint for Modernity' project mentioned above. See also the discussion on 'technocracy' below. On Mustafa Kemal, see Norman Itzkowitz, 'Kemal Atatürk', *Encyclopedia Britannica*, 28 May 2024 (https://www.britannica.com/biography/Kemal-Ataturk, accessed 10 June 2024). On Lenin, see Paul R. Josephson, '"Projects of the Century" in Soviet History: Large-Scale Technologies from Lenin to Gorbachev', *Technology and Culture* 36, 3 (1995): 519–59.

4 See Aparajith Ramnath, *The Birth of an Indian Profession: Engineers, Industry, and the State, 1900–47* (Delhi: Oxford University Press, 2017), Chapter 2.

5 See 'Planning Again', *Science and Culture* 15, 8 (February 1950): 292–5, here p. 293; Visvesvaraya's Bharat Ratna citation, printed in Shakuntala Krishnamurthy, *Sir Mokshagundam Visvesvaraya* (Bangalore: n.p., 1992 [1980]), pp. 15–16.

6 Chattopadhyay also sees Visvesvaraya's interventions in the 1920s as being precursors to more formal discussions of planning. Raghabendra Chattopadhyay, 'The Idea of Planning in India, 1930–1951', PhD thesis, Australian National University (1985), pp. 19 and 59.

7 See the discussion in Chapter 19 above.

8 See Nikhil Menon, *Planning Democracy: How a Professor, an Institute, and an Idea Shaped India,* Kindle Edition (n.p.: Viking, 2022), p. 263.

9 See Chapter 23 above. On Visvesvaraya taking a back seat after Independence, see also Arun Mohan Sukumar, *Midnight's Machines—A Political History of Technology in India* (Gurgaon: Viking, 2019), p. 165.

10 On Mahalanobis and the Second Plan, see Ramachandra Guha, *India After Gandhi: The History of the World's Largest Democracy* (London, Basingstoke and Oxford: Picador, 2007), pp. 206–8.

11 Medha M. Kudaisya, *Tryst with Prosperity: Indian Business and the Bombay Plan of 1944* (Gurgaon: Penguin Random House India, 2018), Chapter 7; 'Genesis', website of the Forum of Free Enterprise, https://ffeindia.com/pages/about-usmain/about-us/genesis.html (accessed 10 June 2024); 'Chakravarti Rajagopalachari', *Encyclopedia Britannica,* 3 April 2024 (https://www.britannica.com/biography/Chakravarti-Rajagopalachari, accessed 10 June 2024).

12 'Vision of a USD 5 Trillion Indian Economy', Press Information Bureau, Government of India, Ministry of Commerce & Industry, 11 October 2018 (https://pib.gov.in/Pressreleaseshare.aspx?PRID=1549454, accessed 10 June 2024); Arvind Panagariya, 'View: Niti Aayog is performing vital functions that are fundamentally different from Planning Commission', *Economic Times* (online), 2 January 2017 (https://economictimes.indiatimes.com/news/economy/policy/view-niti-aayog-is-performing-vital-functions-that-are-fundamentally-different-from-planning-commission/articleshow/56288903.cms?from=mdr, accessed 10 June 2024).

13 See N. Shankarappa, *Sir M. Visvesvaraya: Dismantling the Myths: Critical Examination of Sir M.V as a Civil Engineer,* E-book (Bengaluru: Kavya Kala Prakashana, n.d), pp. 12–13.

14 Vikas Sehra, 'Hyderabad's Musi River: Why Do Technocratic Solutions Fail in Safeguarding Urban Waterbodies?', *Economic and Political Weekly* 55, 10 (7 March 2020), 'EPW Engage' (https://www.epw.in/engage/article/hyderabads-musi-river-why-technocratic-solutions-fail-in-safeguarding-urban-waterbodies, accessed 10 June 2024); U. Sudhakar Reddy, 'Experts' thumbs down for Musi riverfront project, say not viable', *Times of India* (online), 25 April 2023 (https://timesofindia.indiatimes.com/city/hyderabad/experts-thumbs-down-for-musi-riverfront-project-say-not-viable/articleshow/99746230.cms?from=mdr, accessed 10 June 2024).

15 Thomas L. Friedman, *The World is Flat: The Globalized World in the Twenty-First Century* (London: Penguin, 2006 [2005]), p. 4.

16 'US jobs get Bangalored!', *Economic Times* (online), 24 July 2004 (https://economictimes.indiatimes.com/us-jobs-get-bangalored/articleshow/788716.cms?from=mdr, accessed 10 June 2024).

17 James Heitzman, *Network City: Planning the Information Society in Bangalore* (New Delhi: Oxford University Press, 2004), pp. 37–40; Aparajith Ramnath, 'International Networks and Aircraft Manufacture in Colonial and Postcolonial India: States, Entrepreneurs and Educational Institutions, 1940–64', *Journal of Research Institute for the History of Global Arms Transfer* 9 (2020): 41–59.

18 Vinod Vyasulu, 'Nehru and the Visvesvaraya Legacy', *Economic and Political Weekly* 24, 30 (29 July 1989): 1700–1704, here p. 1703; Ramachandra Guha, 'Standing tall . . . Lessons in leadership from Satish Dhawan', *The Telegraph* (online), 26 September 2020 (https://www.telegraphindia.com/opinion/lessons-in-leadership-from-satish-dhawan/cid/1793083, accessed 10 June 2024).

19 'The Bangalore City and its Future', Visvesvaraya's speech at the Bangalore Literary Union, 20 May 1953, reproduced in untitled souvenir on Visvesvaraya (Bengaluru: Century Club, 2017), pp. 7–25, here pp. 21 and 24. This speech is also quoted from in Janaki Nair, *The Promise of the Metropolis: Bangalore's Twentieth Century* (New Delhi: Oxford University Press, 2007 [2005]), pp. 14–15.

20 [M. Visvesvaraya], 'Note, dated the 2nd October 1910, by the Secretary to Government in the Public Works Department', in 'Section I. The Cauvery Reservoir Project (Mr. M. Visvesvaraya's Scheme)', Item 1, paras 16–17. In MV-PAPERS-IEI, Vol. 11.

21 Google Books Ngram Viewer gives an approximate sense of this: https://books.google.com/ngrams/graph?content=sustainability&year_start=1800&year_end=2010&corpus=0&smoothing=3, accessed 10 June 2024.

22 See for instance his views on the need to use river water before it reached the sea, as dicussed in Chapter 9 above.

23 Daniel Klingensmith, *'One Valley and a Thousand': Dams, Nationalism, and Development* (New Delhi: Oxford University Press, 2007).

24 Rohan D' Souza, 'Framing India's Hydraulic Crisis: The Politics of the Modern Large Dam', *Monthly Review* (1 July 2008) (https://monthlyreview.org/2008/07/01/framing-indias-hydraulic-crisis-the-politics-of-the-modern-large-dam/, accessed 10 June 2024).

25 Ibid. Emphasis in original.

26 S. Hiriannaiya, 'Hard Work and Tenacity of Purpose', in CENT-VOL, pp. 224–32, here pp. 231–2.

27 See Ray T. Smith, 'The Role of India's "Liberals" in the Nationalist Movement, 1915-1947', *Asian Survey* 8, no. 7 (July 1968): 607–24. On British Liberalism, see Terence Ball, Kenneth Minogue, Harry K. Girvetz, and Richard Dagger, 'liberalism', *Encyclopedia Britannica*, 18 December 2023 (https://www.britannica.com/topic/liberalism, accessed 26 December 2023).

28 See Shoaib Daniyal, 'Why does India, the world's largest democracy, love the idea of dictatorship?', Scroll, 18 October 2017 (https://scroll.in/article/854479/why-does-india-the-worlds-largest-democracy-love-the-idea-of-dictatorship, accessed 10 June 2024).

29 See for instance: R. Jagannathan, 'Why technocrats have no positional power in Indian politics', MoneyControl.com, 4 August 2015 (https://www.moneycontrol.com/news/politics/why-technocrats-have-no-positional-powerindian-politics-1461769.html, accessed 10 June 2024); Sam Pitroda's views as described in a review of his *Dreaming Big*: Kaveree Bamzai, 'A technocrat's total recall', *India Today* (online), 2 November 2015 (https://www.indiatoday.in/magazine/books/story/20151102-a-technocrats-total-recall-820668-2015-10-21, accessed 10 June 2024).

30 Arun Mohan Sukumar discusses Visvesvaraya, Vikram Sarabhai, and Nandan Nilekani as key technocrats in successive generations in his recent book. Sukumar, *Midnight's Machines*, chapter titled 'The Age of Rediscovery'. He also mentions P.C. Mahalanobis and Sam Pitroda: ibid., p. xxii. Nikhil Menon writes that despite the post-Independence emphasis on 'democratic planning', it remained 'a technocratic exercise in directing the economy'. Menon, *Planning Democracy*, p. 269.

31 Donald R. Stabile, 'Veblen and the Political Economy of the Engineer: The Radical Thinker and Engineering Leaders Came to Technocratic Ideas at the Same Time', *American Journal of Economics and Sociology* 45, 1 (1986): 41–52; Leroy Allen, 'Technocracy—A Popular Summary', *Social Science* 8, 2 (1933): 175–88; Francis S. Pierce, 'Thorstein Veblen', *Encyclopedia Britannica*, 12 April 2024 (https://www.britannica.com/money/Thorstein-Veblen, accessed 1 June 2024); 'technocracy', *Encyclopedia Britannica*, 23 February

2024 (https://www.britannica.com/topic/technocracy, accessed 1 June 2024). The quote from Hoover appears in Stabile, 'Veblen and the Political Economy of the Engineer', p. 43.

32 See Clive Dewey, Review of *The Political Economy of Indirect Rule: Mysore, 1881–1947* by Bjorn Hettne, *Economic History Review* 33, no. 4 (1980): 648–50. I am also grateful to Suri Venkatachalam, who made a similar observation in a conversation some years ago.

33 Vyasulu, 'Nehru and the Visvesvaraya Legacy', p. 1701. Vyasulu is referring here to Visvesvaraya in particular.

34 A.P.J. Abdul Kalam with Y.S. Rajan, *India 2020: A Vision for the New Millennium* (New Delhi: Penguin, 2002 [1998]), Figure 1.2 (p. 19).

35 Ibid., Chapter 12, epigraph (p. 268), and pp. 297–9.

36 'The Aadhaar of all things', *BLInk* (online), 15 January 2018 (https://www.thehindubusinessline.com/blink/cover/the-aadhaar-of-all-things/article64295146.ece); Varun HK and DH Web Desk, 'SC's Aadhaar verdict | Privacy vs Identity', *Deccan Herald* (online), 26 September 2018 (https://www.deccanherald.com/india/aadhaar-act-verdict-history-693614.html); BS Web Team, '7 years of demonetisation: Change in use of cash in Indian economy', *Business Standard* (online), 8 November 2023 (https://www.business-standard.com/india-news/7-years-of-demonetisation-change-in-use-of-cash-in-indian-economy-123110800689_1.html); Tikender Singh Panwar, 'An overview of the Smart Cities Mission | Explained', *The Hindu* (online), 13 May 2024 (https://www.thehindu.com/news/national/smart-cities-mission-status-an-overview/article68172436.ece); Shobhit Gupta, 'Vande Bharat Express trains now operational on over 30 routes in India: See full list', *Hindustan Times* (online), 24 September 2023 (https://www.hindustantimes.com/india-news/vande-bharat-express-trains-indian-railways-tarin-18-101684635320397.html). All links accessed 10 June 2024.

37 'Union Education Minister pays tribute to M Visvesvaraya on his birth anniversary', Yahoo! News, 15 September 2020 (https://sg.news.yahoo.com/union-education-minister-pays-tribute-042913107.html, accessed 10 June 2024); 'Engineers' Day 2023: History, significance and theme of the day', *Economic Times*

(online), 15 September 2023 (https://economictimes.indiatimes.com/news/new-updates/engineers-day-2023-celebrating-the-legacy-of-m-visvesvaraya-and-the-path-towards-a-sustainable-future/articleshow/103681063.cms?from=mdr, accessed 10 June 2024); 'PM pays tributes to Sir M Visvesvaraya during his visit to Karnataka', *Deccan Herald* (online), 25 March 2023 (https://www.deccanherald.com/india/karnataka/pm-pays-tributes-to-sir-m-visvesvaraya-during-his-visit-to-karnataka-1203416.html, accessed 10 June 2024).

38 'India's first centralised AC railway terminal in Bengaluru becomes operational', *Livemint*, 6 June 2022 (https://www.livemint.com/news/india/bengaluru-india-s-first-centralised-ac-railway-terminal-becomes-operational-read-here-11654527749920.html, accessed 10 June 2024).

39 'BJP leaders say time is right for "One Nation One Language"', *Deccan Herald* (online), 16 April 2022 (https://www.deccanherald.com/india/bjp-leaders-say-time-is-right-for-one-nation-one-language-1101272.html, accessed 10 June 2024); Sharan Poovanna, 'One Nation, One Languge: Protests across Tamil Nadu, Telangana, Andra [sic] against Amit Shah's proposal', *Mint* (online), 14 September 2019 (https://www.livemint.com/news/india/one-nation-one-language-protests-across-tamil-nadu-telangana-andra-against-amit-shah-s-proposal-1568451379436.html, accessed 10 June 2024).

40 Thanks to Rahul Sarwate for helping me think through this point.

41 On the ways in which Indian elites in the colonial era made sense of modern science, see for instance S. Irfan Habib and Dhruv Raina, 'Copernicus, Columbus, Colonialism and The Role of Science in Nineteenth Century India', *Social Scientist* 17, 3/4 (March 1989): 51–66.

Acknowledgements

Over the years I've been working on this project, an enormous number of people have helped me. Of necessity, my thanks to each will be brief, but the gratitude I feel is immense. I also fear it's inevitable that I will miss out some names, unwittingly or through lack of space: I'm really sorry, and I hope I will have the opportunity thank you in person! Needless to say, any shortcomings that remain in this book are my responsibility.

I'd like to start by thanking Manasi Subramaniam of Penguin Random House, who wrote to me in 2017 asking if I'd be interested in writing a book on Visvesvaraya. It was serendipitous: I'd long wanted to write about the legendary engineer, though I'd assumed I'd only get around to it much later in my career. I'm indebted to Manasi for the opportunity, for conversations about the project, and for her patience over the many years it took me to deliver the manuscript.

Towards the start of this project, I sought out Visvesvaraya's closest descendants in Bengaluru. Shakuntala Krishnamurthy, Satish Mokshagundam, and Lakshmi M. Satish were both gracious and helpful. They invited me home, took my wife and me out to lunch, shared reminiscences and printed materials, and answered my queries patiently, both in person and over subsequent phone calls. Sheshadri Mokshagundam also invited me home, answered questions, shared interesting primary and secondary materials, and made helpful introductions.

For sparing time to speak to me, I'm also indebted to the following individuals whose worlds intersected Visvesvaraya's to varying degrees: Leela Krishnamurthy, A.K.N. Prasad, R. Dwarkinath, and the late G.R. Vasuki. Yet others acted as local guides in various cities, and answered questions about Visvesvaraya's legacy as it impacted them. I thank Mr Siddaramu and his family in village B. Hattana, Mandya District, and the residents of nearby villages to whom he introduced me; Mr Kshirsagar of the Town Hall, Pune; Mr Vinayak of the Deccan Club, Pune; Srinivasa Bogadi and Navaratna Sudheer in Mysuru; Sushil Kumar of the National Water Academy, Pune; P.S. Rao, M.S. Raviprakash, and their colleagues at the Advanced Centre for Integrated Water Resources Management, Government of Karnataka, Bengaluru. In Mysuru, Kiran Bagade served as friend, interpreter, and guide, and ferried me to meetings with various people he thought I should speak to. He also helped me read sources in Kannada. Civil engineer N. Shankarappa, the author of a concise critical assessment of Visvesvaraya's engineering contributions, gave generously of his time. Vivek of Tata Steel Limited, Jamshedpur, kindly forwarded some information regarding Visvesvaraya and the Tatas.

This study has been made possible by the collections in a wide range of libraries and archives, and I'm grateful to the staff at each of them. In Mysuru: the Sir M.V. Study Centre at the Institution of Engineers (India), the Mysore University library, the Karnataka State Archives (Divisional Archives Office), and the Administrative Training Institute Library. In Bengaluru: the Karnataka State Archives, the Mythic Society Library, the Gokhale Institute of Public Affairs, and the Visvesvaraya Industrial and Technological Museum. Elsewhere: the Nehru Memorial Museum and Library (as it was called when I spent time there), New Delhi;

the Maharashtra State Archives, Mumbai; the Telangana State Archives, Hyderabad; the British Library, London; the Gokhale Institute of Politics and Economics, Pune; and digitised collections of the National Archives of India and the Karnataka State Archives. Thanks also to the libraries at Ahmedabad University and IIM Ahmedabad. The IIMA library provided a congenial environment for research and writing, and the staff were always welcoming, efficient, and helpful. Archivists Carol Morgan at the Institution of Civil Engineers and Charles Gillett at the National Liberal Club (both in London) kindly shared scans of Visvesvaraya-related records by email. I'm also indebted to those who contribute to and maintain various digitized databases of historical materials, some of which I have mentioned in the Introduction.

I began this project with great excitement, but also some trepidation. I had written an academic monograph before, but I was now embarking on a new (for me) genre with unknown challenges. At this stage, I was greatly helped (and becalmed) by conversations with some eminent scholars. Ramachandra Guha took time out to meet me in Bengaluru, and continued to be supportive in many ways, responding to emailed queries, giving me practical advice, and pointing me to key sources during a chance meeting in the archives. Chandan Gowda was most encouraging when I sought him out at the start of this project. He also read the manuscript carefully when it was complete and made many valuable suggestions. Maya Jasanoff provided vital encouragement, helped me think through the structure of my book, and gave helpful feedback on a draft chapter. Dinyar Patel answered queries via email, and pointed me to a very useful digitised database. Samanth Subramanian, Vinay Sitapati, and the late Patrick French shared with me their experiences of and advice on biographical projects. I wish Patrick could have witnessed this book's publication.

Along the way, I have benefited from conversations with a wide range of scholars, writers, and professionals who helped me clarify various aspects of my project, gave me valuable leads, advised me on accessing and using various archives, and/or shared important materials. They include: A.N. Manjunath, Aliyeh Rizvi, Aashique Iqbal, Arun Sukumar, C.J. Kuncheria, C.P. Ramasesh, C.S. Yogananda, Deepak Malghan, Douglas E. Haynes, G. Sreekumar, G.S. Ganesh Prasad, Gaurav Garg, Gouri Satya, John Mathew, N. Benjamin, Naveen Bharathi, Nikhil Menon, P.V. Nanjaraja Urs, Prabhash Rath, Prithvi, Pushkar Sohoni, Rajeshwari Ranganathan, Ross Bassett, U.N. Ravikumar, V.K. Natraj, V.R. Anil Kumar, Vanessa Caru, Vikhar Sayeed, Vinitha M.R., and Yashaswini Sharma. Harini Nagendra generously shared copies of some archival records and a most intriguing source that is not easily available (the diary of K.R. Srinivasa Iyengar, edited by Narendar Pani). I had many stimulating conversations with Suri Venkatachalam over the phone. Raj Sekhar Basu kindly shared with me a draft of his study on Visvesvaraya's interventions in Hyderabad. Chinmay Tumbe sent relevant literature my way, and took time out to discuss the practical aspects of the publication process. I'm particularly grateful to Karthik Rao-Cavale, who has served as a sounding board over the years. I've benefited from discussions with Karthik on many topics, ranging from the history of irrigation to the political economy of interwar India; he also read drafts of some key chapters.

At conferences and workshops in Hangzhou, Milan, Providence, and Zoom-land, where I presented parts of my work on Visvesvaraya and related topics, I had the benefit of feedback and discussions with Francesca Bray, Mikael Hård, Prakash Kumar, Renny Thomas, Madhumita Saha, Roland Wittje, Abigail McGowan, Ross Bassett, Andrew Popp, Kate Epstein, Phil Scranton, Patrick Fridenson, and many others. At the Centre for the History of Science, Technology, and Medicine, King's College London, David Edgerton hosted me for a couple of productive seminars. I'd like to thank David and the research scholars at the Centre for their deep engagement with my draft paper, and my project in general. David also read through the entire manuscript of this book. In Tokyo, Katsuhiko Yokoi and his colleagues helped me deepen my understanding (such as it was) of early twentieth-century Japan, and procured for me an important source relating to Visvesvaraya's visit to that country in 1919. Mahito Takeuchi invited me to participate in a project on the 'British World', and gave helpful feedback on my draft paper. Ted Beatty and Israel Garcia Solares invited me to be a part of the 'Blueprint for Modernity' project on the global history of engineers, based at the University of Notre Dame. I thank them and the other participants for their close reading of drafts of my paper on Visvesvaraya. Thanks also to Ted and Israel for permission to cite their unpublished drafts related to the project.

Much of the above travel was undertaken as part of international research projects or workshops, and funded by the organisers of those programmes. These include: the Society for the History of Technology, the China National Silk Museum, the Institute for the History of Natural Sciences, King's College London, Meiji University, and the 'Blueprint for Modernity' project. Travel to some conferences was sponsored by my employer, Ahmedabad University. I thank them all.

In 2020, I had the opportunity to spend a month in Bengaluru as a Sangam House fellow. It was a delightful experience, one that helped me think of myself as a writer, not just a researcher who happens to write. I learnt a great deal from conversations with the writers in my cohort (Priyanka Sarkar, Mohit Manohar, and Purva Naresh) and from the invited experts who spoke to us. Thanks to everyone who made it possible, especially Arshia Sattar, Vivek Shanbhag, Ram Guha, Jeet Thayil, Raghu Tenkayala, Trupti Prasad, Ravi Prasad, and the staff at the Jamun.

At Ahmedabad University, I've received support in various forms. I'd like to thank the leadership, especially Pankaj Chandra,

Devanath Tirupati, Patrick French, and Raghu Rangarajan, for their flexibility when I needed to take research leave. Apaar Kumar kindly took over a demanding administrative position from me at a crucial juncture. I've been fortunate to have exceptionally supportive colleagues. Aditi Deo, Amol Agrawal, Manomohini Dutta, Mary Ann Chacko, Maya Ratnam, Mona Mehta, Murari Jha, Gaurav Goswami, Ratna Ghosal, Samuel Wright, Safwan Amir, Sarthak Bagchi, Sudhir Pandey, Tejaswini Niranjana, and others—too many to name here—provided encouragement, shared sources, and/or gave me useful leads. Rahul Sarwate, Leya Mathew, and Guillaume Wadia read chapter drafts and helped me think through some important points. A.P. Ashwin Kumar helped me read Kannada sources, and gave useful suggestions.

Friends and family have supported me in myriad ways. I'm grateful to Ambrish Dongre, Mihir Balantrapu, Satwik Gade, Hrishikesh Chennakesavula, Debapratim De, and Amelia Handy. Many years ago, Jahnavi Phalkey encouraged me in my wish to write about Visvesvaraya. Anand Bhaskaran read chapter drafts and sent me his comments in his usual systematic and thoughtful way. Aditya Mohan enabled me to make contact with the Mokshagundam family, and helped me confirm the contents of some source material in Kannada. Vasanth Manickam and Swathee Vasanth helped my family find temporary accommodation in Mysuru, and made us feel at home there. Vasanth, along with Harsha Kulenur, also helped me out on an earlier visit. S.N. Chary and Geetha Chary helped translate a verse from a Kannada song, and Vinoda Ramachandra translated a newspaper clipping from Kannada. Thanks to Sathya Chary and Vikas Ramachandra for facilitating the above. Theodore Derek Cooke kindly shared photographs from his ancestor Theodore Cooke's time as principal of the College of Science, Poona (where Visvesvaraya studied civil engineering).

I also wish to thank Sharik Laliwala, Goutham Sukumaran, Meghana Choukkar, Aashna Vora, and Chinmay Khandwala, who provided crucial research assistance at various points in time. Sharik, a formidable scholar in his own right, also made useful introductions. Goutham, who tabulated digital resources, and Meghana, who collected archival information at the British Library in London, were extremely thorough and systematic. Together, all of these individuals kept me on my toes through what's been a long haul.

Versions or portions of Chapters 2 and 9 of this book were first published online, in Wire and FiftyTwo.in respectively. I thank the editorial teams at both publications for their excellent inputs.

At Penguin Random House India, many people have worked long hours to help bring out this book. In addition to being a perceptive editor, Karthik Venkatesh has been a patient and skilful coordinator. Yash Daiv has kept the production of the book on schedule despite occasional delays from my side. Thanks also to Ahlawat Gunjan for designing the cover, the copy editor and proofreader who went through the manuscript and the proofs, the indexer, the typesetters, the marketing team, and everyone else who has worked behind the scenes. They've all been exceptionally patient with my pedantic ways.

On the home front, I'd like to thank Bhavanaben Patel, Jyotiben Pandey, and Nareshbhai Prajapati for oiling the wheels of our household. I'm also indebted to the medical professionals, frontline workers, delivery personnel, and others who helped my family, and millions of others, during the Covid-19 pandemic.

I couldn't have undertaken this project without the anchor provided by my family. My parents, Ramnath and Sreemathi, and my sister, Shreya, all read chapters of the manuscript at various points. Amma's excitement, undimmed since the day I began this project, and her boundless belief in my abilities have propelled me forward. Equally important were Appa's reminders that I must let go of the book at some point. Shreya, who's a professional editor in addition to being a scholar, helped me assess if I was getting the tone right, and cast her expert eye over the proofs at short notice. My father-in-law, Mani, drew upon his experience as a groundwater engineer to answer many queries on irrigation; he also gave feedback on an important chapter. My mother-in-law, Jayashri, knew I was going to work on this book, and would have been proud to see it completed. Adarshya and Arjun have been a consistent source of support and good humour. Evie and Nino have provided a sense of perspective and countless moments of pure joy.

Akshaya Vijayalakshmi has lived with this project virtually throughout our marriage to date. She has travelled with me for conferences, planned her vacations around my fieldwork, driven me around, endured my obsessive musings over many questions, read chapters, and held the fort at home when I kept disappearing into the study (or into my thoughts). All this alongside the demands of her own flourishing career, not to mention the biggest project we've undertaken together: parenthood. In the concise language of social media: 'No words to express.'

Index

Scan QR code to access the
Penguin Random House India website